VERHANDELINGEN
VAN HET KONINKLIJK INSTITUUT
VOOR TAAL-, LAND- EN VOLKENKUNDE

186

KEES VAN DIJK

A COUNTRY IN DESPAIR

Indonesia between 1997 and 2000

Second printing

2002
KITLV Press
Leiden

Published by:

KITLV Press
Koninklijk Instituut voor Taal-, Land- en Volkenkunde
(Royal Institute of Linguistics and Anthropology)
P.O. Box 9515
2300 RA Leiden
The Netherlands

First printing 2001

Cover photo: D&R
Cover: Marque's grafische ontwerpen, Leiden

ISBN 90 6718 160 9

Printed in the Netherlands

VERHANDELINGEN
VAN HET KONINKLIJK INSTITUUT
VOOR TAAL-, LAND- EN VOLKENKUNDE

186

KEES VAN DIJK

A COUNTRY IN DESPAIR

Indonesia between 1997 and 2000

Second printing

2002
KITLV Press
Leiden

Published by:

KITLV Press
Koninklijk Instituut voor Taal-, Land- en Volkenkunde
(Royal Institute of Linguistics and Anthropology)
P.O. Box 9515
2300 RA Leiden
The Netherlands

First printing 2001

Cover photo: D&R
Cover: Marque's grafische ontwerpen, Leiden

ISBN 90 6718 160 9

Printed in the Netherlands

Contents

Appendices

Preface

It must have been in June or July of 1998 that I ran into Harry Poeze, director of KITLV Press, in the corridor and we discussed the idea of writing this book. The original intention was to concentrate on the events leading up to Soeharto's fall. What happened after May 1998, though, proved to be at least as interesting. Consequently this book describes political developments in Indonesia up to the middle of December 2000. Political realities brought to the fore the area of tension between the high hopes cherished in 1998 to transform Indonesia into a genuine democracy and the problems encountered in effectuating political and economic reforms. Within days after Soeharto's fall it also became clear that opinions differed greatly about the nature of the changes needed and that some political leaders did not hesitate to mobilize their supporters to accomplish their aims. Students, whose demonstrations had been instrumental in bringing about the downfall of Soeharto, continued to be a force to reckon with. Many of them had completely different ideas about what the 'reform era' should look like than the political inner circle, how divided the latter may have been amongst themselves. The ideal of establishing a political system different from that of Soeharto's New Order not only gave rise to a plethora of revelations about crimes committed by the Armed Forces during the New Order, implicating almost all senior army officers. The removal of tight military control also allowed for local popular movements against local authorities and local firms and estates accused of power abuses in the past, and unfortunately also for rampant violence. Separatist movements gained in strength, and radical Islamic opinions which had been silenced during the New Order could be vented freely.

The career of a number of Indonesian key politicians came to an end when Soeharto was forced to resign. Many still play a role in present-day politics. The same can be said of the leading officers of the Armed Forces. The Armed Forces, especially the army, had to relinquish much of their hold over politics. Nevertheless, retired and active army generals remain important players in Indonesian politics. In the economic sphere it also proved difficult to eradicate the influence of those who became immensely rich during the New Order. The political changes of 1998 meant that much information was disclosed about economic mismanagement and corruption and collusion committed by leading businessmen, in particular by Soeharto's children and some of the closest friends of the Soeharto family. The Asian economic crisis had brought many businessmen to the brink of economic ruin. Even before May 1998 measures had to be taken to save the banking sector from collapse and to solve the problem of enormous debts businessmen had accumulated in Indonesia and abroad. After May 1998 the restructuring of the economy was stepped up. The economic reforms gave rise to the same criticism as the steps which had been taken to accomplish political reforms. New corruption scandals erupted, and the suspicion was vented that rich businessmen still had too much influence to tackle the problems effectively, or were saved from prosecution because without their contribution and managerial skills the Indonesian economy would be in even worse shape.

Prefaces of books about Indonesia are not complete without a note on orthography. In the rare case that persons and organizations are mentioned from before 1972, they are referred to in the spelling of the period these organizations or persons were active in. Words and names derived from Arabic or Sanskrit are rendered in the way they are spelled in Indonesia. By far the greatest problems are presented by personal names. When the preference of the person in question is known, his or her name is spelled in this way. In other cases the spelling is chosen which seems to be most widespread.

Prefaces of books are also not complete without a word of thanks. So many people helped me that it is impossible to thank them all. Three exceptions have to be made: the staff of KITLV Press; the KITLV representative in Jakarta, Jaap Erkelens, who was the 'source' of much of my literature, and Rosemary Robson, who corrected my English and saw to it that I could present a presentable manuscript to KITLV Press.

CHAPTER I

Towards the election of May 1997

Pemilihan Umum telah memanggil kita
Seluruh rakyat menyambut gembira
Hak Demokrasi Pancasila
Hikmah Indonesia Merdeka[1]

The general elections of 29 May 1997 gave Golkar, the government party in Indonesia, its best election results ever. It scored 74.5 per cent, 6.5 per cent more than in the previous elections. The Islamic party, Partai Persatuan Pembangunan or PPP, received 22.4 per cent of the votes, 5.4 per cent more than in 1992. The Partai Demokrasi Indonesia or PDI came in a very poor third, receiving only 3 per cent of the votes. In 1992, when it booked its best election results ever under the then General Chairman Soerjadi, this had been 15 per cent. The outcome was that of the 425 contested seats in parliament, Golkar won 325 seats, an increase of 43. PPP got 89 seats, 27 more than it held in the previous parliament. PDI secured only 11 seats, a decline of 45. The remaining 75 seats went to appointed representatives of the Armed Forces.[2]

The Golkar victory came after a campaign period which was the bloodiest and most violent the New Order had ever seen. In the past, campaigns had also caused loss of life. The chief culprit was the motorized cavalcades, featuring cars and overcrowded trucks full of people, which were particularly attractive to young people. Such election demonstrations could reach quite a fever pitch, with participants becoming overenthusiastic, rendered all the more perilous by racing motorbikes. This time the government had taken every precaution to avoid such incidents. Parades through towns and through the countryside, which had caused the most fatalities, with people tumbling off trucks or falling victim to dangerous driving, had in fact already

---

[1]   General election marching song: The General Election has called us/ All the people greet enthusiastically/ The right accorded by Pancasila Democracy/ The blessing of an Independent Indonesia.
[2]   During the general election of 1992 only 400 seats had been contested. Twenty-five seats had been allotted to appointed members of so-called functional groups.

been banned by the authorities during the previous election campaign of 1992. The measure was not welcomed by everybody. In an editorial at that time, *Media Indonesia* described the feelings of the son of a civil servant watching a PDI parade in 1987. The boy, then sixteen years of age, was overwhelmed by the sight of the participants wearing shirts and hair-ribbons, all of them red, the colour of PDI. Most of them could still be counted among the younger generation, whose 'heroic' slogans claimed that 'the youth really had the upper hand'. Seeing all this, the boy had made up his mind then and there that at the next general election, when he was twenty-one and of voting age, he himself would take part in such a grand event. In 1992 his disappointment at the new measure, which thwarted his plan, was offset by the realization that he was allowed to cast his vote (*Media Indonesia*, 13-1-1992). The leaders of PPP and PDI had expressed their misgivings about the measure at the time. The ban did not clearly define what constituted a parade, and might be used against a group of three or four cars driving to an electoral meeting. As the campaign of 1997 was to prove again, it was virtually impossible to prevent people attending electoral meetings in great numbers and being transported there by cars and trucks, likewise forming impromptu parades afterwards as they went home. In 1992 traffic incidents related to campaign activities had still cost the lives of twenty-three people (*Rekaman* 1993:181). In 1997 the death toll was exceptionally high. At least 269 people died during the 27 days allotted to the campaign period. Some of them – about 80 – were killed in traffic accidents during rallies and parades. Riots triggered off by campaign activities and fights between supporters of rival parties took their toll as well. In Banjarmasin alone, more than one hundred people – the highest figure mentioned is 142 – lost their lives on 23 May during riots following a Golkar campaign. According to the authorities, most of the victims were plunderers caught trapped in a shopping mall – Mitra Plaza – who burned to death or were suffocated. Yet, there were reports that, in fact, some of them had been shot dead in the streets of Banjarmasin by members of the security forces. People could not help wondering why all the victims in Mitra Plaza had been found on the second floor, while there were plenty of shops to be looted on the other floors of the five-storey building. It was the most serious rioting the New Order had experienced so far. A statement issued by the local branch of the Perhimpunan Mahasiswa Katolik Republik Indonesia (PMKRI), the Roman Catholic Students Association of the Indonesian Republic, claimed that inflammatory anti-Christian pamphlets had been circulating some days before the Banjarmasin riots broke out. Others laid the blame on Golkar provocations. Golkar supporters, a PPP spokesman claimed, had wanted to match a successful massive PPP parade held the previous day. On a Friday, when life is usually quiet in Banjarmasin, they had installed sound systems all over the city. On their way to a campaign meeting, participants in a Golkar cavalcade had revved up their motorcycles loudly and had taken a route which is normally closed to traffic at the time of the Friday prayer. They passed a mosque just after the prayers had ended.

In total four shopping centres, four hotels,[3] two cinemas, five banks, four government buildings, 144 mainly Chinese-owned shops, and 130 houses went up in flames or were seriously damaged in some other way. A similar fate befell the regional Golkar office. Churches were also burnt down or damaged. More than one hundred people had to be taken to hospital.

Though serious, road accidents during the parades had not been the only problem in the past. Cavalcades could readily degenerate into violence, with people turning their anger against people and objects identified with despised political opponents. This sort of group solidarity was already manifest at the time of the founding of the first political organization with a mass following, the Sarekat Islam in the early 1910s, when non-members were boycotted, and at times, when Sarekat Islam members were involved in rows, traffic incidents, and the like or felt insulted, their putative opponents found themselves the target of mob violence. Violence has never ceased to be a factor to be reckoned with in a society in which differences in religious beliefs, social background, and political affiliation tend to coincide with social fault lines and create strong antagonisms. As an American anthropologist writing about religious differences among the Islamic population (which tended to parallel political ones) observed in Java in 1953:

> Villagers from syncretist neighbourhoods were reluctant even to pass along the roads through orthodox neighbourhoods, going well out of their way, in fact, to avoid doing so, and the villagers of orthodox communities were reciprocating (Jay 1963:76).

Outbreaks of communal violence, which continued to dog Indonesian society in the first two decades after Independence had been proclaimed, induced the new authorities who came to power at the start of the New Order to embark upon a policy of limiting the number of occasions which they believed might trigger off such incidents to a bare minimum. One of the ways to tackle this problem was to do as the Dutch colonial authorities had done before the Second World War: highlight the dangers of incitement. Four sensitive topics about which people should show restraint in whatever they wrote or said in public were identified: ethnicity, religion, race, and the very general category of inter-group relations. This concept was captured in the

---

[3]   Guests at one of these hotels included two Golkar campaigners, Saadillah Mursjid, minister and cabinet secretary, and KH Hasan Basri, chairman of the Majelis Ulama Indonesia, the Indonesian Council of Ulama, the organization created by the government as its interlocutor with the Islamic community and its different streams.

acronym SARA, standing for *Suku, Agama, Ras,* and *Antar-golongan*. Another means by which to ensure the tenor of society was not upset was to drastically reduce the freedom to hold public political meetings. Since 1965 these have only been permitted once every five years, on the eve of general elections; and when they are permitted it is only for a brief period of time, reduced from 60 days in 1971, when the first general elections of the New Order were held, to 27 days in 1997. The concept of a 'floating mass' was introduced at the same time. Under this concept, political parties should not launch membership drives. It was better if people were left in peace and simply allowed to express their choice of party at the polling station. The upshot of this was that the government allowed parties to have boards only at the national level, at that of the provinces, and at that of the regencies and larger towns; the villages or city wards are taboo. After protests lodged by PPP and PDI, a representative was allowed in village and city wards.

The ban on motorized convoys was maintained during the elections of 1997. In December 1996 the authorities announced that only public assemblies, media broadcasts, and the distribution of leaflets and other printed material were to be allowed. There were to be no parades. The previous campaigns, which such persons as the Commander of the Armed Forces, General Feisal Tanjung, observed early in 1997, had resulted in 'a lot of unnecessary deaths' (*The Jakarta Post,* 3-3-1997). As the authorities were apparently apprehensive and anxious to further limit the chances of incidents, a number of additional measures were announced. Precautions taken during the previous campaign to ensure that large public rallies of different parties in one region did not take place simultaneously in the same vicinity had proved inadequate to prevent fights breaking out between supporters of the three contestants. This time the country was divided into three zones: Sumatra, Bali, the Lesser Sunda Islands, and East Timor; Java, the Moluccas, and Irian Jaya; and Kalimantan and Sulawesi. On one particular day in each zone only one of the three parties – Golkar, PPP, and PDI – was allowed to organize campaign events. This meant that the effective campaigning time in each zone was reduced to nine days for each of the contestants. To limit the risk of confrontations even more, only the flags and symbols of the party that was to hold a large meeting could be displayed in the streets leading to the venue where the event was to be staged (to be removed when it was the turn of another party; a precaution, which, it soon emerged, only exacerbated the violence as the lowering of party flags and symbols at times sparked off the ire of bystanders). The government had made no bones about the fact that preference would be accorded to what were called 'dialogues', a construction which was a fairly exclusive indoor discussion meeting with a limited attendance. These were considered far preferable to what were dubbed 'monologues', large-scale, open-air events held at stadiums, soccer fields, public parks, and the like. Again, unpleasant past experience was the main motive behind this decision. This did not come like a bolt from the blue. As early as October 1995 Golkar had advocated an election campaign which would promote the holding of such dialogues. It did so, according to the official explanation, in view of the fact that, on earlier occasions, campaign activities had not proved very productive, and had been overshadowed by violent and unruly behaviour in various regions (*Kompas*, 16-10-1995).

Another field in which the government tried to gain the upper hand was that of what was said and written by party members working within the framework of their campaigns. There were always topics which were off-limits in campaign speeches, either because they could spark off communal violence or because they touch upon subjects the government prefers to avoid if it can or has explicitly forbidden. The latter category included remarks questioning the ideology of the state, the Pancasila, and the constitution. Anything that was considered to be tinged with a marxist or socialist viewpoint was taboo. Pleas for the establishment of an Islamic state were treated in the same fashion. The sensitive topic of religion should only be touched upon in such a way that it gives no offence. Since the early years of the New Order the Indonesian authorities always tried to play down religion in the political sphere. One of the consequences was that PPP was not allowed to present itself as a purely Islamic party. People who publicly advocated turning PPP into a real Islamic party were always castigated, but the government had never succeeded in enforcing its will completely in this respect. References to Islam and remarks about the obligation of Muslims to vote for an Islamic party had never been fully eradicated during campaigns. Nor had statements diametrically opposed to this: that it was not a sin not to vote for an Islamic party.

Besides curbing the room to manoeuvre allowed political parties, the government also punished too blunt a criticism of government policy, and verbal attacks on government officials were not allowed. Even advocating a limitation on the number of terms in office of a president raised the government's ire in the past. One of the persons to whom this was driven home was Soerjadi. In the 1992 campaign, in his capacity as general chairman of PDI, he had attacked some of the business ventures of the children of Soeharto and had proposed a limitation on the number of terms of office allowed an Indonesian president. At that time it had further appeared as if PDI would propose another candidate for the presidency. The party had conducted an election campaign with the theme 'Status Quo, No!, Changes, Yes', while various names, including that of Soerjadi, had been advanced as an alternative to Soeharto. All this cost Soerjadi the support of the government which he had enjoyed up to then. This was why he received no backing from the authorities when his leadership in PDI came under attack in the summer of 1993.

Even the conciliatory gestures he made after the campaign, speaking out, for instance, advocating the re-election of Soeharto fell on deaf ears.

In the past much of this restraint had been a matter of self-censorship. Sanctions, when they were taken, came afterwards. This time, maybe because of Soerjadi's remarks about the maximum number of terms in office of a president, the government clearly wanted to ensure that it had advance control of what was being said. When party political broadcasts on state TV channels and radio channels (also relayed by private networks – a new phenomenon intended to take the place of public rallies, and which had, as a precaution, to be pre-recorded) took the form of 'dialogue', they had to be chaired by a 'neutral' third party, appointed by the government, who could stop the session should this be deemed necessary. Seven out of the nine party political broadcasts to which a contestant was entitled had to take the form of a half-hour dialogue. During the two remaining broadcasts the general chairman of the party was allowed to deliver a fifteen-minute speech. The text of all speeches on radio and TV had to be submitted five days in advance to a special screening committee constituted for this purpose by the Minister of Internal Affairs in his capacity as chairman of Lembaga Pemilihan Umum, the National General Election Institute. This, a spokesman of the institute hastened to claim, did not imply censorship. The rules had only been made to ensure that the speeches contained nothing to undermine the Pancasila, slander government officials, or attack other political parties. Spokesmen of PPP and PDI protested, calling the procedure a new form of political censorship, and deploring the distrust to which the screening testified. In fact all printed texts, including slogans and pictures on banners and posters carried around by people on their way to or from party events or displayed at electoral meetings, had to be approved in advance by the authorities.

In yet other respects, the regulations announced before the campaign period began were more stringent than ever. People carrying or wearing 'attributes' of a party – shirts, caps, flags with the party symbol, banners with slogans, and the like – had to be a member of that party and should be able to prove this by showing their membership card when asked to do so; preventing, in theory, the very popular strategy of trying to lure voters by handing out T-shirts or caps displaying the party logo and name. Such a regulation, representatives of PPP and PDI pointed out, was in violation of the floating mass system which had been propagated by the government ever since the beginning of the New Order. It was equally frustrating that campaigners could only address a meeting after they had received permission to do so from the local police, which also was the body which had to give its consent to the distribution of leaflets and other campaign material. As a further curb on freedom, it was to be the regent/mayor working in cooperation with the police, and not the party concerned, who was to decide on the place where these electoral events were to be held. Even vehicles used to transport supporters to campaign meetings and back had to be registered with the police. This had to be done seven days in advance. The owners were provided with stickers which had to be pasted in a visible place on the car. All in all, these rules meant that when a party wanted to stage an electoral event, the local board organizing it had to submit information to the police about the form, theme, and time it was to take place, about the programme and the number of people who were to attend (a condition, representatives of PPP and PDI stressed, which was impossible to meet), and about the kind of displays and other materials to be used. Besides these conditions, the names of the people who were to address the meeting had to be provided, complete with proof that the local authorities had granted them permission to speak, and, when civil servants were concerned, a written statement from their superior giving them permission to engage in campaign activities. Yet another document which had to be handed over was the written permission of the owner of the location where the meeting was to be held. Details about the number and kind of vehicles to be used in transporting people to and from the meeting had to be supplied and information was required about the locations where the people who were to attend were to assemble before-hand.[4] All this with copies to the chairman of Panitia Pemilihan Umum Daerah, the Regional Election Committee, at the regency/town level, the chairman of the local Panitia Pengawas Pelaksaan Pemilihan Umum, Committee for the Supervision of the Elections, the head of the Office for Social and Political Affairs of the same institution, the head of the Office of Public Prosecution, the chief of police of the neighbourhood where the meeting was to be held, and the subdistrict head.

A government disquieted by the wave of violence that had swept a number of cities in previous months, ensured that special Command Posts for National Alertness were set up in all regencies, under the aegis of the Military District Command. They were expected to step in before matters got out of hand and boiled over into a disturbance. People with knowledge of activities that might create social unrest or thwart the smooth running of the elections could report there. As an additional measure to prevent violence from erupting, local authorities staged *wayang* and *ketoprak* performances to press home the message that it would be futile to incite the poor, and that people who did so would be ground under the feet of those defending just-

---

[4]   Consequently on 23 April in Surabaya when both PPP and PDI were refused permission by the police to hold a campaign meeting because not all the necessary documents and information had been submitted, the two party branches both threatened to boycott the campaign. Local authorities stated that a Golkar request had been refused for the same reason, but local Golkar leaders said they knew nothing of this.

ice and truth (Kristiadi, Legowo and Harjanto 1997:16).

These new regulations announced by the government were denounced by PPP and PDI. At the end of February 1997, a few days after the details of the rules had been announced, seven regency branches of PPP in Central Java, strengthened by the support of the provincial branch, suggested that the central board boycott the campaign, as it was almost impossible to comply with all the conditions set. Stung into an initial reaction, the general secretary of PPP, H.M. Tosari Widjaja, indicated that if local branches found it too difficult to stage an active campaign, there was no reason why they should try. Around the same time the PPP chairman, Ismail Hasan Metareum, hinted that the party would do just as well to ignore the regulations issued by the authorities and embark on campaigning methods developed by the party itself. As an example he cited a door-to-door campaign. The PDI under Soerjadi also voiced its objections. Saddled with these new rules, PDI announced that on the days it was not allowed to organize activities in a particular region of Indonesia, it would hold a 'silent campaign' in these islands. Earlier, Soerjadi himself had already suggested that holding campaign activities in the evening would provide one of the solutions to the question of how to avoid violence. He reasoned that disturbances are usually caused by youngsters who stirred matters up at the end of an electoral event just when audiences were returning home from a rally. Their motive was to attract the attention of onlookers. In the evenings, people are usually tired and sleepy and could not be bothered watching. Soerjadi was convinced that an additional advantage of such evening events was that they would add greatly to the national productivity as people would not have to leave their work.

The protests came over and above the usual ones, advanced each time general elections had taken place since 1971, that the rules governing the organization and actual execution of the general elections favoured Golkar to the detriment of PPP and PDI. Among the perennial complaints was the erection of polling booths at government offices (and closely linked to this was the request not to hold elections on a working day).[5] Another objection was to the composition of the various institutions to organize and supervise the elections. These gave Golkar every advantage. A great cause for concern was the physical and mental pressure brought to bear by the local civil service and the Armed Forces to induce the electorate to vote for Golkar. Although senior military officers always stressed their role as neutral referees, all the pressure they exerted made a mockery of the floating mass concept. To top it

---

[5]   In May the secretary-general of the Ministry of Information admitted that he had instructed the civil servants in that department to arrange for the requisite forms allowing them to vote in their offices (thus opening wide the possibility for fraud by giving them the chance to vote twice, in their home district as well at their office).

all were the irregularities which occurred during the distribution of registration forms, the actual polling, and the counting of the votes.

Another problematic issue which arose every time there was an election was that of the position taken by the Korps Pegawai Republik Indonesia (Korpri), the Corps of Indonesian Civil Servants. Were its members, virtually all Indonesian civil servants, obliged to vote for Golkar, or not? To what extent would their superiors allow them to campaign for PDI and PPP? In theory civil servants were free, as the Korpri chairman Suryatna Subrata (also secretary-general of the Ministry of Internal Affairs and of the General Election Institute) had admitted in November 1996.[6] Yet, for joining either Golkar, PDI, or PPP, and thus also for any campaigning, civil servants needed the consent of their superiors, while all the while they were also being encouraged to campaign actively in their own neighbourhoods and among their own friends and family to gain additional votes for Golkar. The idea that Korpri members had at least a moral obligation to support Golkar was confirmed as late as February 1997 by Suryatna Subrata and by his superior, Yogie SM. They were moved to do so in response to a report issued by LIPI, the Indonesian Institute of Science, which called for greater political freedom for civil servants. Only when civil servants had a free choice would 'the bureaucracy's notoriously discriminative treatment of PPP and PDI members' end (*The Jakarta Post*, 27-2-1997).

Protests voiced by politicians from PDI and PPP against the biased treatment of their parties and the various white papers published after general elections listing a great variety of instances of intimidation of the electorate and bending of the rules usually had absolutely no effect. Fed up with the situation, in March 1996 around fifty dissidents founded a Komite Independen Pemantau Pemilu (KIPP), the Independent Election Monitoring Committee, to act as an election watchdog. Among its prominent members were Permadi (a popular, critical paranormal practitioner), Ali Sadikin (a former New Order mayor of Jakarta), H. Princen (a long-standing critic of Soekarno and Soeharto), Dr Ir Sri Bintang Pamungkas (a lecturer at the Universitas Indonesia and a leading dissident within PPP, whose goal was to reform that party to make it a real Islamic one), Mulyana W. Kusumah (its secretary-general), and Nurcholish Madjid (a prominent Islamic thinker).

In early 1997 the protestations of PPP and PDI politicians inveighing against the election rules proclaimed by the government and Golkar-weighted devices caused only the barest ripple, occasioning only some minor

---

[6]   At that time Suryatna Subrata had shown himself to be in favour of treating the civil service in the same way as the Armed Forces, in the sense that civil servants would relinquish their right to vote in return for which a special number of seats would be reserved for them in the representative bodies.

adjustments. The government allowed the chairmen of the discussion programmes on state TV and state radio channels to be selected by the parties
rather than being appointed by the government, which had been the original
intention. This concession was made after PPP had indicated that it would
boycott such events if it transpired that the procedure advanced by the government undermined the party's political broadcasts. There was a formal
agreement that campaign activities would not be solely for supporters but
open to the general public as well.

All precautions to ensure a quiet campaign period unmarred by riots or
by fights between the supporters of the three parties were as chaff before the
wind. Violence had been in the air for months. On 27 July of the previous

People in Jakarta vent their anger after the attack on the PDI party office
on 27 July 1996 (photo *D&R*)

year Jakarta had experienced the worst rioting in the city since 1974. It had
cost the lives of five people, and another 149 persons had been injured.
Twenty-three persons were reported 'missing'. At least this was the final outcome of an inquiry by the Komisi Nasional Hak Asasi Manusia (Komnas
HAM, the National Committee for Human Rights), an institution established
in 1993 by presidential decree, which in spite of its origin and the doubts
originally expressed about its functioning, really acted as the independent
body it was supposed to be.[7] The material damage was also considerable,
with banks, offices, including that of the Directorate of Fisheries, and shops

---

[7]   The number of missing persons (which had initially stood at 74) was later reduced to 18.

going up in flames; according to an estimate of the Jakarta municipality damages amounted to Rp 100 billion. The riots in Jakarta, on what came to be known as Sabtu Kelabu, Grey Saturday, followed in the wake of an attack made by supporters of one faction in the PDI, headed by Soerjadi and backed by the government and the Armed Forces, on the national headquarters of the party in the Jalan Diponegoro in the centre of town. The building was occupied by supporters of the far more popular Megawati Soekarnoputri, elected as general chairwoman in 1993. His side, Soerjadi claimed, was the rightful occupier of the building, basing his assertion on the fact that a breakaway party congress in June 1996, its legality denied by his opponents but endorsed by the authorities, had re-elected him as general chairman of PDI and had proclaimed Megawati Soekarnoputri's board null and void. The attack on the building (where fierce anti-government speeches were held at a speaker's platform), which had been expected for some time, had been well prepared. The attackers, armed with clubs and stones, had been drilled beforehand and were transported to the Jalan Diponegoro in trucks.[8] In the aftermath, Megawati supporters who had defended the PDI office, 124 people in total, were tried in November. The majority of them were sen-

Policemen in Jakarta after a confrontation with protesters on 27 July 1996
(photo *D&R*)

---

[8]   For reports on the events see for instance *1996* 1997:3-34, *Peristiwa* 1997, Tim pemburu fakta 1998a, and Van Dijk 1997.

tenced to four months and three days imprisonment (the sentence demanded had been four months and ten days) for failing to obey a police order to
vacate the building issued while negotiations were going on. The sentence
meant that they could leave prison immediately. The others were given a
lighter sentence or were acquitted.

In the closing months of 1996 and at the beginning of 1997, communal violence, with young people usually playing a very conspicuous role, erupted at
various places in Java. Such outbursts had racial and religious overtones, but
they also served as an indication that institutions and persons identified with
the government were regarded as a prime target. In June 1996 a number of
churches in Surabaya were attacked by a mob and set afire or damaged in
some other way. Various versions about what had occasioned the mob violence circulated: rumours about somebody urinating against the wall of a
prayer house, a dog urinating inside a prayer house, and local Muslim children being cajoled to attend Sunday-school classes (See *1996*, 1997:76-9). In
October 1996 Situbondo in East Java was the scene of serious disturbances
specifically directed against the Christian and Chinese communities in town,
causing the death of at least five people and the destruction of churches,
Christian schools, a court building and various other premises; according to
government officials, it was an incontrovertible example of SARA-inspired
instigation. 26 December it was the turn of Tasikmalaya in West Java. This
time four people died (including one boy of six who fell from a truck transporting the mob, and was run over by the next truck), while churches,
schools, an orphanage, sixteen police stations and posts, banks, department
stores, and shops, many owned by Chinese, were destroyed by mobs on the
rampage. Damage was estimated at Rp 85 billion (see *1996*, 1997:75-90).
People venturing onto the streets wrote 'Muslim' on their cars or motorcycles,
and people who were wearing a helmet were stopped and forced to remove
their helmet to identify their race. Others (and at times of tension such signs
appeared elsewhere as well) tried to protect their property by painting on
their walls words such as *milik pribumi*, owned by autochthonous Indonesians, or *milik Muslim*, owned by a Muslim, or other texts with similar purport. Many Chinese residents had to take shelter in government offices.[9]

As was so often the case, the violence had been sparked off by a minor
incident. In Situbondo, a region where the Nahdlatul Ulama (NU), an organization uniting the 'traditional' Muslims in Indonesian Islam, is strong, rioting had started after the public prosecution had proposed a sentence of five
years' imprisonment (the maximum penalty in such a case) in the trial

---

[9]   Afterwards shopkeepers in Tasikmalaya followed the suggestion of the regent of
Tasikmalaya and painted their shop fronts white and light blue, eschewing bright colours such
as yellow (the colour of Golkar), as he had added significantly, to avoid political connotations.

against an allegedly deviant Muslim teacher, Saleh bin Abdul Kadir, who stood accused of preaching mystical, blasphemous teachings, and of defaming the memory of one of the most illustrious *ulama* of the NU, KH R. As'ad Syamsul Arifin. On hearing this decision, an angry mob made up of about three thousand people assembled outside the court. They called for the death penalty and demanded that the man be handed over to them. When this demand was ignored, the crowd literally ran riot. The security forces, present in extra numbers because a crowd had already tried to lynch the accused a few days before, stood by helplessly. The mob first set fire to the court building. When the rumour spread that the accused was hiding in a nearby church, the mob, now reinforced by people from outside the city, turned against the Christian and Chinese communities. In total eight churches were set ablaze. In one of the churches, belonging to the Pentecostal congregation, the clergyman, his wife, son, and niece, and a servant of the family were burnt alive. As unrest spread to the cities of Panarukan, Besuki, and Asembagus, even more churches were set afire or damaged (in total 16), as was one Chinese temple. Saleh bin Abdul Kadir was eventually sentenced to five years' imprisonment.[10] In Tasikmalaya, the trigger had been the beating up of a teacher (who had to be admitted to hospital) and a number of students of a *pesantren*, an Islamic boarding school, at the police station. They had been summoned after one of the *pesantren* students had complained to his father, a police officer, about the way he had been treated by a senior student who had disciplined him for stealing money from fellow students. Demonstrations, set off by the false rumour that the teacher had died from his wounds, began at the police station but fanned out after shouts had been heard urging a march on the churches to destroy them. In Tasikmalaya, as in Situbondo, people from neighbouring areas also participated in the riots.

Outside Java one of the most serious incidents took place in Ujungpandang. On 23 April 1996, a demonstration composed of about three thousand students in front of the Universitas Muslim Indonesia protesting against a rise in public transport fares spiralled out of control. When security forces tried to arrest its leaders, they were met with a hail of stones and abuse. Fights broke out during which scores of students were wounded. The next day students from other institutions of higher education in the city joined in, protesting about the brutal behaviour of the police and army troops the previous day and the arrests of their fellow-students. Again the result was harsh reprisals from the side of the security forces. Bloody April, or the Tragedy of Bloody Makassar, as the event was called, cost the lives of at least three students. The authorities claimed that they had drowned when, after trying to escape from the troops, they had jumped into a river. Not much credit was

---

[10] For the Situbondo riots see among others Hariyanto 1998.

accorded to this explanation as their wounds and bruises indicated otherwise. Some sources mention a number of victims as high as eighteen. Later,
twelve members of the Armed Forces were called to account for the brutal
way the troops had acted in suppressing the students' protest (see *1996*,
1997:41-8.).

When these cases are taken together with similar incidents in Medan, Dili,
Ujungpandang, and Irian Jaya, the total number of large-scale riots in 1996
amounted to 20 – 4 more than in 1995, and 12 more than in 1994. In view of
the many instances of communal violence that year, the Indonesian Legal
Aid Foundation gave one of its publications dealing with violations of
human rights the title '1996: the year of violence' (*1996*, 1997).

1997 started in the same mood. On 27 January angry street vendors in
Jakarta, out in the streets in greater numbers than usual as the end of the fasting month was approaching, set the office of the subdistrictdistrict of Tanah
Abang alight (incidently at a time when all available fire engines but one had
been directed to a fire raging at a shopping complex). The cause of their rage
was one òf the many individual operations within the framework of the
Gerakan Disiplin Nasional (GDN, the National Discipline Movement) to
'clean up' the city and to promote discipline among its citizens. At such times
street vendors often became the particular target of police 'razzias'. On this
occasion the raid was executed in an extraordinarily brutal manner, even by
Indonesian standards. Cars drove over their merchandise and knocked down
one of the vendors. Three days later, still during the fasting month,
Rengasdengklok was the scene of mobs looting and setting fire to churches,
Buddhist monasteries, shops, and residential houses, after a Chinese woman
(later to be arrested on the suspicion of having caused a riot) had protested
about the noisy way the young people were waking up their fellow-Muslims
for the pre-dawn meal of the fasting month. At the end of the month about
5,000 labourers (also demanding leave for pregnant women and menstruat-
ing girls) went on the rampage for five hours at an industrial complex 25 kilometres from Bandung, provoked into doing so when the company employing them failed to pay the customary fasting month allowance on time. Fear
spread to other parts of West Java when pamphlets inciting people to attack
Chinese and Christian property were found. On 18 February it was the turn
of the city of Bandung itself. Four people died. This time the violence was
sparked off by the collision between a city bus and a *becak*, in which the driver of the *becak* and his passenger were killed. Initially fighting was confined
to the bus driver and an angry crowd which had turned against him after his
bus had been involved in the traffic accident. Later, violence spread through
town. Around the same time, for more than two months Dayak and
Madurese battled each other in West Kalimantan. These clashes had started
in December 1996 and more than three hundred people were killed.

In Pekalongan on 20 March supporters of PPP attacked the house of an assistant-regent. Three days later a similar incident occurred when people protesting about the fact that they had not yet received their electoral registration forms stoned the house of a member of the local election committee. These were still only minor incidents. Pekalongan, with a longstanding reputation as a centre of devout Islam, where the PPP had scored 66 per cent of the votes, and Golkar only 21 per cent during the election of 1992, leading the Islamic journal *Panji Masyarakat* to describe it as a region of Golkarphobia, again exploded into violence on 24 March, and again on 6 and 9 April (*Panji Masyarakat*, 31-3-1997:11). The trigger this time was a public religious event in the town organized by Golkar, which was scheduled to be attended by one of Soeharto's daughters, Siti Hardijanti Rukmana, better known as Mbak Tutut, Sister Tutut. Violence started on 24 March, two days before the Golkar demonstration was due to take place, with KH Zainuddin M.Z., who had still campaigned for the PPP at the previous general elections of 1992, as one of the speakers. The event, moreover, was to be given added lustre by Rhoma Irama, 'the king of *dangdut*', a performer of a special kind of Indonesian pop music, in his case with Islamic texts, who now was being advanced as a Golkar candidate. Zainuddin and Rhoma Irama were extremely popular in devout Muslim circles, though in Pekalongan not everybody welcomed the mixing of a religious meeting with popular music. Their attendance lending cachet to a Golkar function was seen as treason; a similar explanation had been provided for the Banjarmasin violence, in that case the bone of contention being the presence of KH Hasan Basri campaigning for Golkar. Golkar seemed only to have to snap its fingers to be able to get everything it wanted, even luring much admired Islamic artists and preachers into its net. The atmosphere grew even more ominous when the rumour began to fly that on the stage, erected on the premises of a *pesantren*, the head of which hoped that the event would bring him extra funds, Tutut and her company were to stage a *dangdut* song performance. (Afterwards it was stressed that the musical performance had been planned at another location.)

Additional factors were at play as well. Local military authorities claimed that the disturbances on the 24th were triggered off by a 'verbal war' over the hoisting of the flags of political parties at gatherings, which began when those of the PPP were removed in anticipation of a Golkar public meeting. This lowering of the flags was in accordance with an agreement reached in early March that no party flags were to be raised at places where their display could trigger off unrest. Another reason for the compliance was that Pekalongan saw itself as a front-runner in the competition for the title of the cleanest town in the country. This coming on top of the deep disappointment felt that KH Zainuddin M.Z. and Rhoma Irama had switched their allegiance from PPP to Golkar, led an angry crowd to pelt the stage where they were to

A country in despair

perform with stones and Molotov cocktails, also in their rage destroying the
tents already prepared for the visitors.[11] The stage being rebuilt under the
protection of security forces and the white fence of the *pesantren* being painted yellow, the colour of Golkar, did not exactly ease the tension.[12] Next day,
just before midnight, a mob consisting of a few thousand people started to
destroy offices, among them that of the local state bank Bank Rakyat
Indonesia, and shops owned by Chinese, seizing the opportunity to replace
yellow Golkar flags and banners with green PPP counterparts.[13] In slogans
and graffiti the mass testified of its support for PPP and its hatred of Golkar
(and of Zainuddin and Rhoma Irama). On the 9th, besides shops owned by
Chinese, a housing complex for civil servants was targeted. The cry 'Hang
Soeharto' was also heard. Streets in Pekalongan were littered with slogans
castigating Zainuddin, Rhoma Irama, and Golkar, calling them dogs and
pigs, and praising PPP.[14]

Another cause contributing to the tense situation in Pekalongan was that
PPP had celebrated its founding in 1973 in early April. The way it chose to do
so was by staging meetings and street rallies. An order to postpone celebrations in Pekalongan by one day had contributed to the heating up of the
atmosphere in that city. An event had already been planned on the same day
as a Golkar meeting, but it was the latter that had been given the go-ahead.
Elsewhere in Central Java, violence triggered off by PPP supporters participating in similar anniversary celebrations, and voicing criticism of Golkar,
erupted early that month in Rembang, Temanggung, Banjarnegara, and
Wonosobo. From Rembang it was reported that rioting started after Golkar
sympathizers had burned down a stage erected by PPP members in a Golkar
stronghold on which they planned to celebrate the anniversary of their party.
In Wonosobo the main targets were village council halls. Fighting with

---

[11]   Rhoma Irama had campaigned for PPP in 1977 and 1982, and chose to remain neutral in
1987 and 1992.
[12]   The meeting took place seven kilometres from where it had originally been planned. Tutut,
it was reported, sang the song *Pertemuan*, 'Meeting'.
[13]   Central Java at that time was the scene of a colour war. Local authorities, complying with
the orders of the governor, had started in 1995 to display yellow, the colour of Golkar, as conspicuously as possible in the streets, with bridges, tree trunks, fences, pavement edges, bus
stops, and the like being painted in that colour. It was a policy described as *kuningisasi*, or the
'yellowing' of a particular region. Among the targets was the palace of the *susuhunan* in
Surakarta. After they had twice repainted the *alun-alun* white, with yellow soon reappearing on
the instruction of the major of the city, officials of the *kraton*, using such arguments as a yellow
palace was not what tourists liked to see, brought a court case against the mayor of the city. On
the order of Paku Buwono XII they withdrew their charge in 1997, but the *susuhunan* also used
this opportunity to make it clear that the colour of his palace was white. Similar incidents happened elsewhere, but in these cases those not in favour of yellow were less powerful in withstanding the pressure.
[14]   For the Pekalongan riots see among others *Panji Masyarakat*, 31-3-1997:16-21.

Golkar supporters broke out when PPP supporters who were returning home from their festive rally hauled down and destroyed Golkar flags and banners. In other cities in Central Java no incidents occurred, but shops remained closed out of fear that PPP celebrations might evoke violence.

The incidents were an indication of how strong antagonism had grown. Never under the New Order, it was observed, had communal violence been so frequent and been imbued with such a political significance as in 1996 and the beginning of 1997 (Edwin et al. 1997:113). The authorities seemed to agree with this assessment. Central Java, its military commander Major-General Soebagyo concluded in early April, was prone to riots. Commenting on what had happened in Pekalongan, the Chief of Staff for Social and Political Affairs of the Armed Forces, Lieutenant-General Syarwan Hamid, observed that the rivalry between the parties had exceeded the bounds of what was still permissible and that Central Java needed special attention if matters were not to get out of hand. Though having no proof yet, he suspected that the events had been planned by people who wanted to disrupt the elections. The repeated violence in Pekalongan was 'a mosaic of a grand pattern designed by certain parties' (*Republika*, 23-4-1997). This was an accusation frequently vented by authorities commenting on riots and violent protests, or on demonstrations by labourers and farmers, not just at that time but also in the weeks and months to come. Somebody or some group had to be behind it. This was usually as far as the statements went. In most cases no names of organizations or persons were mentioned; one exception to this rule was the Partai Rakyat Demokratik (PRD), the Democratic People's Party, a recently founded party, which was likened by the authorities to the banned Communist Party of Indonesia (PKI), one of the most serious accusations that could be made under Indonesia's New Order.[15]

With the exception of Jakarta, all the riots in Java, including the one in Surabaya, had broken out in smaller cities in regions where Islam was strong, and where the Nahdlatul Ulama had a large following. This put NU and its general chairman, Abdurrahman Wahid (also called Gus Dur, a grandson of KH Hasjim Asjari, the founder of NU), in a difficult position. Such riots, he hastened to point out, were provoked by others and intended to blacken his name and to bring the Nahdlatul Ulama into disrepute, just as the Jakarta violence had been instigated to discredit Megawati. What had happened in Tasikmalaya and Situbondo was supposed to have been provoked by an

---

[15]   The PRD had been founded in May 1994 as the Persatuan Rakyat Demokratik, chaired by Sugeng Bahagijo. The following year, after an internal split over its aims and after leadership had been taken over by Budiman Sudjatmiko, the Persatuan Rakyat Demokratik Indonesia (PADI) was founded by Sugeng Bahagijo. In April 1996 the PRD was renamed Partai Rakyat Demokratik.

Operasi Naga Hijau (ONH, Green Dragon Operation).[16] It was essential to create chaos in Nahdlatul Ulama strongholds and to prevent its members and others who might be planning to vote PPP in the coming elections from indeed doing so. Another covert reason was to convince the outside world that the Nahdlatul Ulama community could not live in harmony with other groups. Just as the Red Dragon Operation had set out to destroy Megawati as a political factor, the Green Dragon Operation was determined to do the same with the NU.[17] Abdurrahman Wahid did not specifically identify the leaders of the plot. It was speculated that the person Abdurrahman Wahid had in mind was Adi Sasono, an influential leader of ICMI (Ikatan Cendekiawan Muslim se-Indonesia, or All-Indonesia League of Muslim Intellectuals), a powerful pressure group, which had been founded in December 1990, and since its inception had been chaired by the Minister of Research and Technology, B.J. Habibie.

In view of such outbursts of popular anger and with the general awareness that mass gatherings could easily get out of hand, before the campaign period was under way, violence was already being expected. A few days before the campaigns were to start, a police spokesman, Brigadier-General Nurfaizi, warned that his officers would not hesitate to shoot on sight anybody whom they saw engineering a breakdown of law and order. To bring home the message that the government was prepared for everything and would not hesitate to act, on the eve of the campaign period a large-scale exercise in 'safeguarding the elections' was held in Jakarta. Helicopters from the army, the air force, and the civilian airline Pelita Air Service dropped troops at a number of places in the city. One of these was the parliamentary building, a prime target for demonstrators, and a likely epicentre for any unrest which might erupt.

The grim atmosphere was exacerbated by the machinations the previous year in the PDI. The government had clearly come out in support of Soerjadi. In September 1996 it had accepted the lists of candidates his party board had submitted and rejected those advanced by Megawati Soekarnoputri's board. The latter still stressed that they were the ones who legally headed PDI, and thus had the right to draw up the PDI lists of candidates. As demonstrations all over Indonesia had testified at that time, Megawati's board could count on massive support from people prepared to protest in their favour. At the height of the pro-Megawati demonstrations in June and July 1996, expecting that Soerjadi's supporters backed by the Armed Forces might attack the PDI

---

[16]   Yet another possibility advanced by the former head of the Security Force Kopkamtib, Sudomo, was that the 'DI/TII', that is people who wanted to transform Indonesia into an Islamic state, were behind the Tasikmalaya riots.

[17]   *Panji Masyarakat*, 3-2-1997:2-30, 31-3-1997:28; *Forum Keadilan Edisi Khusus Desember* 1997:28.

headquarters any moment, huge crowds had assembled in the Jalan Diponegoro to show their support for Megawati, while large demonstrations had taken place in a great many cities all over Indonesia.

Megawati's board could still mobilize mass support and this was brought home once again on 15 April 1997. On the same day that the security exercise was held, supporters of Megawati, sometimes designated *semut merah*, red ants, protested for no less than six hours at a stretch in front of the parliamentary building by their thousands, demanding that her board and not that of Soerjadi be allowed to participate in the election and the campaign leading up to it.[18]

The unsavoury happenings and tug-of-war in PDI had swelled the number of people and organizations who were disillusioned with the political system, and who were now calling for a boycott of the elections, or who were at least publicly condoning such a step. Since the first general elections of the New Order in 1971, this option has always been a way to express discontent with the existing political structure and the regulations governing it. Dubbed Golongan Putih or Golput, the White Group, a term not meant to denote a concrete organization, but used as a term of reference to indicate a specific way of protest in 1971, those refraining from voting (which is allowed on paper) or deliberately casting an invalid vote have been viewed with much suspicion by the authorities.[19] In official eyes, urging others not to go to the polls or, if they did, to cast an invalid vote (less dangerous than not voting) was a step which bordered on subversion. Apart from the unequivocal sign that by doing so a person rejected the political system of the New Order, government officials invariably stressed the moral obligation of a citizen to cast a vote. Elections, it was frequently repeated, play a vital role in Indonesian democracy. They are the expression of the sovereignty of the people, allowing Indonesians to express their political will once every five years, thus giving them a chance to determine government policy for the next five years. Financial arguments were also marshalled. Were many not to cast a valid vote, this would be a waste of the vast amount of money and energy that

---

[18] M. Yogie SM blamed Soerjadi for the demonstration because, after all, in the eyes of the government he was the general chairman of the PDI, and therefore should be capable of controlling his supporters and members of the PDI. The Soerjadi board refuted this. Its secretary-general, Buttu Hutapea, stressed that the demonstrators were not PDI members, but people who acted using the name of that party. His board was only responsible for activities organized by its own functionaries.

[19] Leading figures of the White Group from its moment of inception included Arif Budiman, Adnan Buyung Nasution (at that time already the leader of the Lembaga Bantuan Hukum, the Legal Aid Foundation), Julius Usman, Joppie Lasut, Imam Waluyo, Husin Umar, and Nurcholish Madjid (in 1971 Chairman of the Islamic Student Union HMI). Recently the abbreviation *Ortilos*, *orang tidak mencoblos* (People who do not perforate [the ballot paper]) has also come into use.

goes into organizing such a 'feast of democracy', the term which the government chose to describe the general elections. In the absence of any other indications, a high percentage of valid votes was a matter of prestige for the government, any significant drop being a blow to its public image. Nationally, the percentage of votes has never been below 90 per cent; locally, in rare cases it has even exceeded one hundred per cent.

In early 1997 leaflets with calls not to vote were secretly distributed in various provinces. Such appeals could also be read on stickers on fences, office windows, and telephone booths, and on slogans painted on walls. Trying to remove the stickers and graffiti, as the local authorities in Surabaya found, could be a hopeless task. Fresh ones appeared overnight. Not mincing his words, the mayor of the city said that the persons responsible for such acts were traitors. As at previous elections, this time the White Group seems to have been particularly strong among students and other young people. Student organizations issued statements endorsing this form of protest, while polls held at a number of universities – Universitas Indonesia in Jakarta, Universitas Gadjah Mada in Yogyakarta, and Universitas Airlangga in Surabaya – indicated that around 50 per cent of the students intended not to cast a valid vote (*Ishlah* 4-79:20). There were also demonstrations in favour of the White Group, stressing that not voting was a possibility open to anybody who wished to avail themselves of it. At the end of March, hundreds of students at Gadjah Mada University left no doubt of their opinion that people should not cast a valid vote, especially as Megawati's PDI was banned from the election. Another demonstration took place in Surabaya in early May, organized by the Aliansi Mahasiswa Untag untuk Keadilan (Seventeenth of August University Students' Alliance for Justice, or Amuk, 'Go Beserk'). Such activities were not without risk. The demonstration was a show of support for fifteen students of a group styling itself the Jember Student League, who had been arrested for advocating the same during a demonstration earlier held in front of the Regency Council building.

Oppositional groups, which at best led a semi-illegal existence, also made no secret of their stand. One of them was the PUDI, the Partai Uni Demokrasi Indonesia (Indonesian Democracy Union Party), founded in May 1996 and headed by Sri Bintang Pamungkas. For a couple of years he had been earning the displeasure of the authorities. In April 1995 a police investigation into his activities had been launched. Speeches he had given in Bandung, in which he had questioned aloud whether the Pancasila would cause a rise in the salary of teachers, and in Germany during a state visit of Soeharto that month, where he had read papers about the future challenges facing Indonesia's economy, were reason enough to start a prosecution. Even more so as Sri Bintang had enraged Soeharto. Soeharto was sure that it had been Sri Bintang's lectures that had provided the Germans who demonstrated against him during his visit with the information with which to attack Indonesia. This was treason (Santoso 1996:17). Consequently Sri Bintang was suspected of being subversive and of having insulted the good name of the president. In May the following year he had been sentenced to 34 months in prison, among other reasons for calling Soeharto a dictator when answering questions after his lecture in Berlin, an accusation which Sri Bintang Pamungkas himself denied. Outside the court building people demonstrated for and against him, while in the court itself, an angry demonstrator had hurled a shoe at the judge. Sri Bintang Pamungkas appealed to the High Court. Before a decision was taken, he and two other PUDI leaders, Julius Usman and Saleh Abdullah, were arrested in March 1997 and accused of sub-version.[20] One of the reasons for the detention of Sri Bintang Pamungkas was a fasting month/Lebaran/New Year's card he had sent members of parliament and government officials. Apart from the customary congratulations, it had contained three points, summarizing PUDI's political position: a rejection of the general elections of 1997 and of the nomination of Soeharto as presidential candidate, and a call for the setting up of a new political structure in the post-Soeharto era. On the eve of his arrest a number of members of parliament had asked the authorities to act, as they considered the texts provocative and insinuating. A second reason was that the PUDI was held responsible for the circulation of pamphlets in West Java calling for a boycott of the elections and, according to Attorney-General Singgih, the authorities also wanted to investigate the 'observation' that the PUDI had been involved in recent violence.[21] Julius Usman and Saleh Abdullah were released a month later.

Another organization that metaphorically turned its back on the elections was the PRD, which had become the victim of an intense government campaign after Grey Saturday. The authorities defamed it, alleging it was a sub-

---

[20]   Around the same time, a former leader of the Socialist Party, the Partai Sosialis Indonesia (banned since 1960), Soebadio Sastrosatomo, was investigated for the publication of *Era baru, pemimpin baru; Badio menolak rekayasa rezim Orde Baru* (A new age, new leaders; Soebadio rejects the scheming of the New Order regime), (1997). Though he had been among the members of an advisory council of the PUDI, Soebadio and the authorities both denied that his investigation had anything to do with the arrest of the three PUDI leaders.

[21]   Interrogated as witnesses in relation to the arrest of the PUDI leaders were such people as Mulyana W. Kusumah and Ridwan Saidi (a former member of parliament and chairman of MARI). MARI (Majelis Rakyat Indonesia, Indonesian People's Council), was founded on 24 June. Its members were comprised of people drawn from about 30 social organizations and NGOs, including PRD and PUDI. Muchtar Pakpahan was among its founders. At its inception the MARI formulated 'four demands of the people': 1. the dismissal of those who created discord in the nation; 2. revoking the laws which regulate the political structure; 3. raising the salary of labourers, civil servants, and soldiers; and 4. lowering prices and eradication of collusion, corruption, and monopolies.

versive organization bent on changing the constitutional principles of the state, and accused the PRD of being behind much of the current unrest. The upshot was that the members of the PRD and affiliated organizations – STN (Serikat Tani Nasional, National Farmers Union, with branches in Java, Sumatra, and Sulawesi), SMID (Solidaritas Mahasiswa Indonesia untuk Demokrasi, Indonesian Student Solidarity for Democracy), Jakker or JKR (Jaringan Kesenian Rakyat, People's Art Network), SRI (Serikat Rakyat Indonesia, Indonesian People's Union, meant for the urban poor, with two branches: one in Surakarta and one in Jakarta), and PPBI (Pusat Perjuangan Buruh Indonesia, Indonesian Centre for the Labour Struggle, with branches in some of the major industrial cities of Java, and in Medan) – were arrested or forced to go into hiding.[22] Among at least 13 PRD leaders who were arrested in the course of 1996 were Budiman Sudjatmiko (general chairman of PRD), Petrus H. Hariyanto (secretary-general of PRD), Garda Sembiring (chairperson of SMID for the Jabotabek region), and Dita Indah Sari, a member of the board of PRD and leader of PBBI. Budiman Sudjatmiko was sentenced to 13 years of imprisonment, Garda Sembiring to 12 years, and Dita Indah Sari to 6 years. In the same period Dr Muchtar Pakpahan, chairman of the independent – and in the eyes of the government illegal – labour organization Serikat Buruh Sejahtera Indonesia (SBSI, Indonesian Prosperous Workers' Union, founded in 1992) was also arrested.[23]

Abandoning their past caution and this time choosing their words carefully, a number of established organizations also indicated that they could understand should people not cast a valid vote. Among those were the Roman Catholic Church and the Protestant Persatuan Gereja-Gereja Indonesia (PGI, Indonesian Communion of Churches). Both provided guidance to their flocks, including those who, without the overhaul of the party system in 1973, would have voted for the Partai Katolik and the Parkindo (Partai Kristen Indonesia), two parties which had chosen to team up in PDI at that time rather than go under. In a pre-Easter apostolic letter, read out at the end of February in Roman Catholic churches, it was observed that people should really feel free to express their political opinions at the polling station. If people drew the conclusion that none of the three existing parties represented their choice, it was understandable that they would not bother to cast a vote. Doing so was no sin. The letter went on to state that if force were used and people were pressured to vote, they were allowed to comply instead of hav-

---

[22]   The PRD and its organizations were officially banned in September 1997.
[23]   In August 1994 Muchtar Pakpahan had been arrested and accused of having incited labour riots in Medan, considered to be the largest instance of labour unrest of the New Order era up to that moment. He was sentenced to three years' imprisonment, which was actually raised to four years after his appeal. He had to be released in May 1995 when he gave notice of cassation, and in August of that year he was acquitted.

ing to suffer the consequences of a refusal. The PGI also issued a statement underlining that people had to be able to cast their vote freely, without pressure or fear. People had to exercise their right to vote in accordance with their conscience.

Among Islamic organizations discontent was rife in the NU. Protestors claiming to represent eight of its affiliated organizations, including its youth and women's movements, issued a statement condoning a boycott of the elections on the eve of the campaign. Observing a growing dissatisfaction and, amongst other enlightenments, ascertaining that elections were only a means to legitimize the position of those already in power, as a body it underlined the fact that voting was a right and not an obligation. This incurred the ire of NU's general chairman, Abdurrahman Wahid. Its protest, Hartono Mardjono of the PPP observed, might be partly inspired by the stand taken by Abdurrahman Wahid at that particular moment. Abdurrahman Wahid had the reputation of being one of the most vocal critics in the country, and because of this had been ostracized by Soeharto. Hurt pride also played a role. Soeharto took offence at a passage in *A nation in waiting*. The author, Adam Schwarz, quotes Abdurrahman Wahid as saying that 'stupidity' was one of the reasons why Soeharto disregarded his views (Schwarz 1994:188). Among his well-known actions which had contributed to this image was the founding in April 1991 of the Forum Demokrasi to promote democracy and to combat racism and ethnic conflicts, only a few months after Habibie, with the consent of Soeharto, had established ICMI. In the months leading up to the general election, Abdurrahman Wahid was giving the impression of having withdrawn his earlier support for Megawati and entering the camp of Soeharto. He had appealed to the former to moderate her opposition, and in October 1996 for the first time for a long time had met Soeharto at a *pesantren* in Probolinggo in East Java. This meeting put an end to the impression that Abdurrahman Wahid was a person who had become *persona non grata* at the presidential palace because of his critical remarks. From the end of March Abdurrahman Wahid, whose political remarks and deeds by that time were difficult even for Indonesians to explain, accompanied Tutut on her visits in Java and Sumatra to various *istighotsah* meetings, mass prayer gatherings of the Nahdlatul Ulama, which attracted large crowds, according to some reports over 300,000 people. The meetings, which were also held in regions where PPP was strong and had been the largest party in the previous election, such as Pasuruan in East Java and Pekalongan in Central Java, took place only a few months before ballot day.[24] Such visits perfectly fitted the task Golkar had assigned to her: boost-

[24] In Jombang and Yogyakarta local NU branches forbad their supporters to attend such meetings.

ing the party's election results in the two provinces (*Golkar*, 1999:42).

For some, among them the PPP general chairman Ismail Hasan Metareum, this was a clear indication that Abdurrahman Wahid was planning to 'deflate' the PPP, an observation denied by Abdurrahman Wahid himself and a number of other NU leaders. Despite such denials, when the general elections were over and done with, one of the conclusions drawn was that Abdurrahman Wahid's actions had certainly helped Golkar to win votes in the places he and Tutut had visited, drawing rank and file members of the NU used to following the advice of their leaders to Golkar. At that time Abdurrahman Wahid, who would not meet Tutut again in 1997, admitted this had been one of his aims.[25] Afraid that the supporters of Megawati *en masse* would vote PPP, he had tried to persuade members of the NU, in particular those who supported Megawati's PDI, to vote for Golkar. It was his way of preventing Golkar from losing the absolute majority it had. Other politicians criticized Tutut and the general chairman of Golkar, Harmoko, who was also Minister of Information, for travelling the length and breadth of the country to address mass meetings. By doing so they had started campaigning for Golkar far before this was allowed according to the electoral rules, giving Golkar yet another advantage over PPP and PDI. It was one of the many ways leaders of the Golkar cadre tried to drum up advance publicity for their own party before this was formally allowed. The other side of this strategy, it was suspected, was the forging of deliberate secret conspiracies to tarnish the image of PPP and PDI, or to deprive their leaders of a chance to profile their parties. Local government officials might even, as Ismail Hasan Metareum disclosed in March 1998, ban PPP calendars in villages in Pasuruan, replacing these with calendars displaying photographs of the regent, the local military commander, and the chairman of the Golkar branch.

The authorities were also displeased with the statements about not casting a valid vote. In an initial reaction to the pre-Easter apostolic encyclical, Syarwan Hamid warned that influencing people not to vote was against the law. The calls to boycott the general elections, the eruptions of mob violence, and the demonstrations by labourers and farmers which were taking place with increasing frequency finally induced President Soeharto himself to issue

---

[25]   In November, addressing a national Nahdlatul Ulama conference in Lombok, Abdurrahman Wahid attributed part of the Golkar electoral success to his accompanying Tutut. The reasons he had done so, he disclosed, had been ideological rather than political. He had been afraid that the electorate of the PDI might turn to PPP, which could have put an end to Golkar's dominant position, and might have provided an opportunity for those wanting to establish an Islamic state to seize their chances. The latter possibility was one of Abdurrahman Wahid's nightmares, fearing that combining politics and religion would result in the disintegration of the nation.

several warnings. He did so, for instance, at the end of February 1997, during a speech in Central Java, in the small town of Donohudan in Boyolali, in which he indicated that he would not hesitate to come down on everyone who schemed to replace him in an unconstitutional way like the proverbial ton of bricks. Urging people to cast their vote, he said that he was prepared to step down, if this was what the country wanted, but that only the People's Congress could make him do so. His words were echoed by Feisal Tanjung. All groups and individuals who wanted to achieve the downfall of Soeharto in an unconstitutional way, he said, would be dealt with severely. At the beginning of April, Soeharto called upon the Armed Forces to prevent any act from whatever side and for whatever reason which might threaten the success of the general election. The heightened political awareness among the people should not be jeopardized by any irresponsible elements who led the people astray by urging them not to go to the polls. On other occasions as well he seized the chance to urge people to vote, stressing that Indonesians had grown wise enough to know how to react when the interests of the people and the state were being challenged. Not casting a vote, he had to admit, was allowed by law. But those who adopted such a position should not incite others to follow their example. If they did so they would get their just deserts. Soeharto did not hesitate to point out that people who decided not to cast a valid vote forfeited their right to work for change. Non-voters had to step onto the sidelines and stop criticizing, and they had no right to advance all kinds of demands about political or economic reform. Just prior to the start of the campaign period, for the umpteenth time Soeharto issued a warning. There might be people, he intimated, who intended to misuse the election campaigns, as they were bent on creating unrest by exploiting differences in ethnic background, religion, race, or other criteria which set groups apart. The Indonesian Council of Ulama also joined in the chorus of doom. In March it reminded Indonesian Muslims that it was the duty of a law-abiding citizen to vote. Elections, another influential Islamic leader usually known for his critical stance, KH Alawy Muhammad, also commented during a PPP electoral rally at Sampang in Madura, were one of the three festivals Indonesian Muslims could enjoy, the other two being Idul Fitri, the feast at the end of the fasting month, and Idul Adha, the sacrificial feast at the time of the hadj (*Republika*, 9-5-1997).

One big question mark hanging over the pre-election period was what the supporters of Megawati's PDI would do – not vote, or cast a vote for PPP? On 22 May, one day before the end of the campaign period and two days after President Soeharto had once again impressed on people that voting was an essential element in upholding the people's sovereignty, Megawati proclaimed that she herself would not cast a vote. She had taken this decision, she stated, to uphold the true meaning of general elections. Not explicitly asking her followers to do the same, she implored them, whatever they did, not to vote PDI. Since Soerjadi's PDI was illegal and therefore unconstitutional, voting for his PDI was likewise illegal and unconstitutional. She herself had been denied the right to stand as a candidate, depriving her of one of her civil rights. Her supporters, she stressed, should use their right to vote according to their own conscience. Her critics, though acknowledging Megawati's right not to vote, reacted by stating that as a public figure it would have been better had she kept her counsel. Her statement, especially the part in which she said that she would not use her right to vote, and the repercussions this might have, was regretted not only by the authorities, but also by KH Abdurrahman Wahid. The latter called upon PDI supporters not to follow Megawati's example, stressing that what Megawati had announced was her personal decision, and that she had not made a public appeal. Megawati's announcement was also countered by the central board of the Majelis Muslimin Indonesia (MMI or Council of Indonesian Muslims), a PDI organization of 'traditional Muslims'. It issued a statement, signed by its general secretary, H. Soegeng Sajadi, and chairman, H. Achmad Sjukry Suaidy, stressing that Muslims had the obligation to use their right to vote.[26]

Anticipating that Megawati sympathizers might be out to disturb campaign events organized by Soerjadi's boards, Syarwan Hamid had, even before the outset of the campaign, promised Soerjadi's side special protection when they staged electoral events. On 23 April, a few days before the start of the campaign, Megawati eased some of the fear that demonstrations by her supporters could create an explosive situation in Jakarta and elsewhere. Vowing that her board would stage no campaign activities in the name of PDI, she asked her supporters to do the same. PDI refrained from undertaking any campaign activities, it was explained, because its list of candidates had been rejected. Another reason cited for this decision was the fear of provocations which could discredit the party. Her supporters were urged to cooperate in an effort to make the election a democratic one. On the same day, the Coordinating Minister of Political and Security Affairs Lieutenant-General (Ret.) Soesilo Soedarman asked the parties to avoid inter-party conflicts, as these could disturb the smooth running of the elections.

[26]   Soegeng Sajadi, a businessman, was also a member of the People's Congress and secretary of the Advisory Council of Soerjadi's PDI.

CHAPTER II

Violent campaigns

Pilihlah wakilmu yang dapat dipercaya
Pengemban AMPERA yang setia
Di bawah Undang-Undang Dasar Empat Lima
Kita menuju ke Pemilihan Umum[1]

A PDI headed by Megawati might have drawn a lot of voters. Headed by Soerjadi, as predicted, it could not. Even before the campaign began, Soerjadi had complained about the lack of sufficient funds, and in October 1996 he admitted that the PDI lists of candidates did not include flamboyant personalities or public figures, as these, he argued, were often only concerned about themselves and not about the people. In public Soerjadi belittled the consequences of Megawati's popularity. After the demonstrations in front of the parliament building, he had stated that the PDI was not a tyre, and thus would not deflate. During the campaign period he kept a brave face, on a number of occasions observing that it was normal for people to change parties at elections. Similar comments were made by other leaders of his PDI. When it was predicted that the number of PDI seats in parliament would be halved, one of Soerjadi's colleagues, H.J. Soesilo, characterized this as the rambling of drunkards without a rational leg to stand on. Soerjadi was completely unable to breathe fire into the PDI campaign, and he was devoid of the magnetism to attract a large following. He even seemed hesitant to visit the strongholds of the PDI: Central and East Java, and Bali. Strangely, in view of the staunch PDI reputation of these regions, only one visit by Soerjadi had been planned in advance, to Jember in East Java. Soerjadi was also not planning to address mass meetings in Jakarta. Instead he preferred 'dialogues'. His schedule, it was stressed, was in no way affected by fear of pro-Megawati demonstrations. The only reason he had no plans to address a crowd in certain cities was that he had not received an invitation to do so.

---

[1]   General election marching song: Elect your representative who can be trusted/A faithful defender of the Message of the Suffering of the People/ Guided by the Constitution of Forty-Five/ We approach the General Election.

One of the consequences of this somewhat lacklustre performance was that the PDI campaign was the most modest of the three. It was dwarfed by that of Golkar, clearly financially the most substantial of the three, which could boast that it was capable of mobilizing 113,000 campaigners, including the members of the cabinet, and 700 artists, for whom it even arranged special training. One of the ways PDI conducted its campaign was to hand out plastic flowers and plastic bags or balloons bearing the head of a buffalo, the party's symbol, printed on them. Other activities took the form of a dialogue, the small-scale discussion meetings preferred by the government. Referring to one of the dialogue meetings organized by PDI in Jakarta, a newspaper reported that it was not a dialogue at all, as the speakers – among them Soerjadi – tended to drown in verbiage, and in response there was only one question from the audience (*Merdeka*, 29-4-1997).

Mass meetings intended to draw a large crowd were indeed organized by PDI, but not all of these were a success. Descriptions of those in Java and Bali reported that they were *sepi*, quiet, deserted, even *super-sepi*, attracting only an audience of between a few hundred and one thousand, sometimes even less in big cities like Jakarta and Surabaya. The same was reported about the indoor meetings. At some in Jakarta there were more security officials than ordinary people in the auditorium. Relatively successful, wrote *Republika* in the early days of the campaigns, was a meeting addressed by Soerjadi in Cimahi in West Java. It was attended by approximately two thousand people (some of whom afterwards, during the parade home, raided two petrol stations to fill up their cars and motorcycles for free) (*Republika*, 11-5-1997). At other places, for instance in Pontianak and Sambas, PDI meetings, with Soerjadi as one of the speakers, were attended by three thousand and seven thousand people. These went well, but elsewhere – in Jakarta, Surabaya, Jember, Manado, Ujungpandang, and Medan, to mention a few examples – Megawati supporters ruined the event. They organized 'long marches', a popular term to denote demonstrations, reminiscent of the Long March of the Siliwangi division from Central Java back to its bases in West Java after the beginning of the Second Dutch Military Action in December 1948. They would also flock to meetings organized by the Soerjadi group, making their allegiance known only after the event had started, or drowning out the campaign speeches made by Soerjadi's functionaries in an awesome rendition of pro-Megawati slogans and the revving of the engines of their motorcycles. It was a recurrent pattern during the campaign period for people protesting in favour of Megawati's PDI to leave meetings halfway through in protest, or to disrupt the occasion in other ways. At times they actually physically attacked people attending PDI electoral meetings, forcing security units to act against people shouting abuse at the PDI campaigners and yelling 'Long Live Mega, Long Live Mega'.

One particular form of protest was staged in Kediri on 19 May: just at the moment Soerjadi began to give one of his electoral addresses, snakes were set loose, causing panic among the audience. One of the more serious incidents took place in Bogor on 16 May, one of the days PDI was entitled to campaign in Java. Thousands of people, wearing white shirts displaying Megawati's portrait, and led by Ki Gendeng Pamungkas, paraded through town testifying to their support for Megawati. At first all went well. Then, when the protesters encountered PDI supporters wearing red shirts displaying the *banteng* head, the symbol of the PDI, as it once was of the PNI, the situation deteriorated. Fighting broke out and Soerjadi supporters were forced to remove their red shirts.

The upshot was that throughout the PDI campaign, driven by fear of counter-demonstrations, local PDI boards decided to cancel scheduled mass meetings. At several places, right from the start of the campaign period, local branches of the Soerjadi PDI were even reluctant to organize any activity at all, anticipating mass protests by Megawati supporters. What lay ahead was already clear as crystal at the beginning of the campaign period. On 28 April, the first day that PDI was allowed to campaign in Java, a pro-Megawati crowd of about 5,000 people stormed a PDI meeting in the Taman Bungkul in Surabaya. This happened minutes before Budi Hardjono was to address the audience, and just after a *dangdut* singer had finished the last line of her song Anggur Merah (Red Wine): 'how could you hurt me like that' (*The Jakarta Post*, 29-4-1997). One of the protesters seized the microphone and shouted pro-Megawati slogans, and part of the audience demonstratively changed allegiance. When a pro-Soerjadi PDI leader tried to retake the microphone, they started to throw stones and pieces of scrap metal at the podium.

On 1 May, the next time the PDI's turn to campaign in Java came round, fearful of a repetition of this and similar incidents the party cancelled electoral meetings in the East Javanese cities of Mojokerto, Probolinggo, Situbondo, and at Sumenep in Madura. No large public PDI meetings took place that day. In Surabaya, in view of what had happened on the 28th, local party leaders declared a campaign boycott. When at the request of the government (and with an additional assurance by the Armed Forces that they would provide security) the central board persuaded them to reconsider, they gave in, though reluctantly. They did not come right over the bridge, however, and no open-air meeting was held. Local PDI leaders pointed out that the stage and sound system had already been dismantled and that there was not enough time left to prepare for a new mass meeting. On 1 May PDI members in Surabaya confined themselves to handing out plastic roses to the public. Three days later, campaign activities were resumed in the city but on a modest scale, and these were still the target of Megawati supporters. No large-scale PDI campaign took place on 7 May, but this time heavy rainfall

PPP supporters showing their support for Megawati during as 1997 general election campaign rally (photo *D&R*)

proved a very literal wet blanket.

Though Megawati herself stayed aloof, references to her were by no means absent from the campaigns. Apart from her supporters doing their best to disturb the electoral rallies of Soerjadi's PDI, Megawati's image was very much present during PPP events. United in their opposition to the government, a process partly brought about by the revival of Islam in recent decades, their joining together blurred the distinction of previous years between PPP as a party for the devout Muslim community and PDI as one for those who were less strict in their religious outlook. There was much talk of a Mega-Bintang coalition – *bintang*, or star, being the party symbol of PPP.[2] Her name and portraits were displayed on banners and posters at PPP rallies, in cavalcades and other processions, many wore T-shirts with her picture printed on them, or had donned a headband with her name, and still others chose to dress in green (the colour of PPP) and red (the colour of PDI), wore hairbands with those colours, or had their face or parts of their bodies painted green and red. Texts like 'Mega Yes, PPP Okay' were written on placards which were paraded around, and cries such as 'Long Live Mega' were frequently raised at PPP rallies and cavalcades. The campaign was also waged in the printed media. Pamphlets circulated in support of a Megawati-PPP coalition, with texts which the authorities claimed resembled PRD propaganda. One of these, about a 'Democratic Coalition of Mega, the Star, and the People', suggested that a combination like this could succeed in replacing Soeharto as president, assuring a victory of the people. The pamphlet also listed a number of demands. Besides the toppling of Soeharto, these were: the

---

2   Some PPP leaders liked to interpret the phrase as 'a megastar', indicating the ever growing support for PPP. There were also PPP politicians who suggested that their party should nominate Megawati for the presidency.

withdrawal of the 'packet of five laws' passed in 1985 to regulate the political system, which among others stated that political parties and social organizations had to declare that the Pancasila was their *asas tunggal*, their sole base; the ending of the so-called *dwi* function of the Armed Forces, the doctrine which gave the Armed Forces a military as well as an economic and political role to play in society; the combatting of 'corruption, collusion, and conglomerazation'; and an investigation into the wealth of Soeharto's children, cabinet ministers, and senior officials. In his reaction to the pamphlet, Ismail Hasan Metareum said that any suggestion that he wanted to bring down Soeharto was downright slander, contrived to tarnish the image of PPP. The PPP aspired to 'dynamical and constitutionally democratic' changes, not revolutionary upheavals (*Media Indonesia*, 17-5-1997). The pamphlet had been distributed, he claimed, by people who had become afraid of the increasing support PPP was drumming up. Megawati reacted in a similar vein, giving equal weight to a denial that she was in cahoots with PPP to bring about the downfall of Soeharto. Anybody spreading such rumours, she added, was out to discredit her.

The references to Megawati in the PPP campaign took such a conspicuous form that the authorities felt obliged to put a stop to it. After the PPP campaign day on Sunday 11 May in Java, they made it clear that enough was enough. The following day Yogie SM, Syarwan Hamid, and representatives of the three parties met. Afterwards both Yogie SM, in his capacity as chairman of the Indonesian Election Committee, and Singgih, the attorney-general, but in this case acting as chairman of the Central Committee for the Supervision of the Elections, warned that carrying attributes which referred to Megawati or any other allusion to an alliance in PPP campaigns were in violation of the campaign rules, because such texts had not been given prior approval by the authorities. Syarwan Hamid even went as far as to announce that the security forces were to act against people shouting slogans in favour of Megawati and a Megawati-PPP coalition. As of that moment posters and banners with the words Mega-Bintang on them were sometimes confiscated, as were pictures of Megawati displayed during PPP electoral activities. This did not stop people from shouting so-called 'forbidden slogans'; in fact, it appears, it had the opposite effect, and references to a Megawati-PPP coalition only became more numerous (Kristiadi, Legowo and Budi Harjanto 1997:98, 101).

The decision was taken against the wishes of the PPP. In a statement issued on 13 May its central board protested, observing that the measure was a symptom of political jealousy because of the overwhelming support PPP was receiving. It was stressed that the Mega-Bintang appeal was a spontaneous phenomenon and as such would be difficult to suppress. The party's spokesman, deputy general chairman Tosari Widjaja, wondered why the 'creativity' of the people had to be curtailed, and why references to Megawati had to be forbidden when they caused no observable harm. PPP had had its banners and posters approved in advance by the police, but could not prevent supporters bringing their own creations along. Ismail Hasan Metareum also declared he found the ban incomprehensible. As it did not have a legal basis PPP refused to issue any instructions in relation to it.[3] In reactions from the Soerjadi PDI, its secretary-general, Buttu R. Hutapea, not surprisingly showed himself in favour of the ban. Soerjadi, who called the displaying of the disputed posters a 'campaign game', held the same view. The authorities had to act. He doubted whether many of the people demonstrating in favour of a Mega-PPP coalition were paid-up members of PDI, with a membership card to prove this. Only a very few PDI members, he was sure, had joined the PPP campaign.

At the time the furore about the Megawati pictures and slogans broke out in full force, it was plain that the campaigns, especially those involving supporters of PPP, were careering out of control. Maybe because on the first two days it had been the turn of Golkar and PDI, the campaign period in Java had started quietly, according to some even unusually subdued (Adirsyah et al. 1997:63). After two days of campaigning Yogie SM was still optimistic. He observed that matters were not yet *hangat*, 'hotting up', cautiously adding that one should not lose sight of the fact that it was only the beginning of the campaign. Soon the atmosphere changed dramatically. A vicious circle seemed to have been set in motion. At a number of places – and Jakarta was one of them – supporters, particularly those of PPP and Golkar, on the day it was their turn to campaign, were bent on avenging the insults, burning each other's flags and banners, and returning the attacks the other had committed on a previous occasion. Not a day passed without crowds somewhere running amuck and taking possession of the streets, fights erupting between groups of supporters of the different parties, and individuals being beaten up. All over Indonesia mobs turned violent. Barricades appeared in the streets where people were urged to resist the security troops or to prevent gangs supporting another party entering their own neighbourhoods, and shops remained closed. Stalls selling food or drinks were plundered, and free petrol was demanded at petrol stations. Drivers and passengers of passing cars were forced to hand over money and cigarettes, or had stones and bot-

---

3   On the same occasion PPP central board revealed that it had come into the possession of documents revealing the existence of an Operasi Fajar (Operation Dawn), showing that in regions where Golkar had suffered a defeat in the previous election it – or rather the affiliated Forum Komunikasi Ormas Islam (FKOI, Communication Forum of Islamic Mass Organizations, with as general chairman KH Chalid Mawardi, an important leader of the NU) – planned to distribute money and gifts among voters on polling day after the early morning prayer before they cast their vote.

tles hurled at their cars if they did not make the appropriate sign: one, two, or three fingers in the air, to indicate their support of, respectively, PPP, Golkar, or PDI.[4] Supporters destroyed or removed each other's banners and flags; occasionally supporters of all three parties 'competed', as *The Indonesian Times* called it, in their efforts to do so (*The Indonesia Times*, 2-5-1997). Such incidents, described as 'wars of the attributes', deteriorated into street fights and 'wars of stones'. At times they were the spark that set alight smouldering antagonism between neighbourhoods and other groups. Other clashes occurred when convoys passed by strongholds of the other party. As had been the case during pre-campaign incidents, anger was directed not only against supporters of the rival party, the authorities were also fair game. Government buildings, shops, residential houses, and police stations were prime targets of mob violence. Mosques and churches were damaged as well.

Contrary to the low-key affairs of PDI, which by choice and by discretion was forced to conduct a modest campaign, the rallies of PPP and Golkar were massive occasions, drawing at times tens of thousands of people. In anticipation of trouble, the much smaller PDI campaign events were tightly guarded by security forces – that is, by those 'directly responsible for the maintenance of order' (Pamsung, Pasukan Pengamanan Langsung, or the police, including its well-equipped Mobile Brigade) and those indirectly so (Pamtaksung, or the army, navy and air force). One of the consequences of this was that most clashes broke out around the PPP campaign, which appeared to have turned into rallying points to unleash slumbering hostility against the government and all that it represented. For ordinary citizens, PPP campaign days became days to dread.

Yet, where PDI organized meetings the crowd, in the usual pattern of mass demonstrations in Indonesia, sometimes behaved as violently as those present at meetings of the other contestants. This happened, for instance, in Sidoarjo on 1 May and again in Bandung on 4 May, where, at least according to the reports, 10,000 PDI supporters took part in motor convoys. PDI rallies in Irian Jaya got out of hand a number of times, with PDI supporters hurling stones at houses and offices. Occasionally clashes were also reported between Golkar supporters and those of the Megawati PDI, for instance in Surakarta, when Golkar supporters on motorcycles rode past a PDI office and PDI members attacked them.

It was not long before it became obvious that the ban on motorcades was worse than useless. As had been pointed out at the beginning, people had to travel to and from electoral rallies somehow, turning such occasions into pro-

---

[4]   In fact the PDI had two signs. Those in favour of Soerjadi raised their thumb, index finger, and little finger. Those supporting Megawati their middle finger, ring finger, and little finger.

cessions which to all intents and purposes were transformed into campaign cavalcades, proving as rowdy as these had been during earlier elections, if not more so. Driving in procession through the city or from one city to another was forbidden, but not when the only purpose of a cavalcade was to transport people to and from the venue of a public rally. Or, as the headlines of one newspaper, citing the words of Yogie SM, had announced at the beginning of the year, 'The Ban On Parades Does Not Mean That Parades Are Banned' (*Merdeka*, 2-1-1997). Clashes between supporters of the parties were frequent, with all sides, including those who testified to their support for Golkar, ignoring the pleas, which became increasingly insistent, not to drive around in motorized parades. It proved impossible to prevent processions of cars, buses, overcrowded trucks, and pickups, with many on motorbikes joining in, from forming up.

Minor offenses committed during such events, but nonetheless listed by the authorities, were the many violations of the rules of the road, including drivers of motorcycles not wearing a helmet, not heeding traffic lights, and using toll roads without paying. The authorities, as they had done during the pro-Megawati demonstrations of the previous year, made much of such transgressions and of the huge traffic jams such parades caused. Seemingly obsessed with keeping traffic moving and enforcing the rules, the obstruction of traffic remained one of their main arguments for prohibiting motorized cavalcades, even when the parades had degenerated into riots. Initially the police tried to enforce the rules of the road by seizing the cars and motorcycles of drivers who did not heed them, handing out fines to offenders, and issuing warnings to motorcyclists not wearing a helmet. To the young people participating, the lack of order seems to have proved an exhilarating and inspiring circumstance. They felt, it was occasionally commented, free. At last they had the opportunity to drive around on a motorcycle without having to wear a helmet, and with the engine roaring as loudly as possible.

It became abundantly clear that nobody heeded the appeals of the authorities to avoid such giant, unruly motorcades on 29 April, when PPP was allowed to campaign in Java for the first time. The day before, its supporters had already staged a large cavalcade in Banjarmasin, and on 29 April massive processions of motorcycles and motorcars characterized the PPP campaigns in Jakarta, Bandung, Yogyakarta, Semarang, Pekalongan, Surakarta, Pasuruan, and Surabaya, leading at times to equally gigantic traffic jams. Golkar leaders complained, but the next day Golkar supporters in Java followed the PPP example, behaving just as cavalierly towards the strict campaign and traffic rules proclaimed by the authorities and riding along through towns in procession.

For the military commander of Jakarta, Major-General Sutiyoso, acting in his capacity as Commander of the Operational Command to Safeguard the

PPP supporters pass a PDI election poster in May 1997 (photo *D&R*)

General Elections, it was the appropriate occasion to issue a 'final warning' to the contestants to abide by the rules and not to hold street parades. His security forces, he explained, found themselves in a very unpleasant situation. If the parades were tolerated, traffic jams and disturbances of public order would be the result. The authorities had to act, he announced, and stern measures were to be taken. Once again, Sutiyoso reiterated that cavalcades with people standing in the backs of trucks, or sitting on bonnets of cars, and motorcyclists wearing no helmets (which indeed was a reason for many of the fatalities and victims suffering serious injuries) were strictly forbidden. Golkar's chairman Harmoko, reacted by promising that Golkar would concentrate its campaign on indoor discussion meetings with a limited audience. A different reaction came from Soerjadi. Campaigning in Lombok, he stressed that street rallies stimulated the contacts between a political party and its supporters. They should be banned in the main streets and traffic arteries only, but still be allowed to take place elsewhere.

Even so, on 2 May, when it was the second turn of PPP to campaign in Java, the PPP branches of Yogyakarta and Jakarta refused to organize any activities. The same decision was taken in Irian Jaya. Incidents which had taken place earlier and conflicts with the authorities lay at the root of these decisions. The PPP in Yogyakarta announced its intention to refrain on 30 April, after people who had attended a Golkar meeting at Kotagede on that day attacked and destroyed two local PPP offices, and had beaten up a PPP party official. Speaking for Golkar, GBPH Joyokusumo, a younger brother of the sultan, tried to play down the incidents, suggesting that they had probably been caused by provocations engineered by PPP. He hazarded a guess that its supporters may have thrown stones at Golkar supporters who were passing by. He added that the Golkar branch in Yogyakarta would not discuss what had happened with representatives of the PPP. The reason was for this decision was that Golkar had been the victim of acts of destruction, but had held its peace. PPP crowds had already damaged ten houses belonging to Golkar functionaries. Yogie SM tried to give the impression that what had happened was fairly trivial. He referred to it as a minor affair caused by Golkar supporters who had not been able to control their emotions. Refusing to be assuaged, the Yogyakarta branch of PPP demanded an investigation. Its representatives explained that a major reason for not staging campaign activities was to prevent further violence. PPP supporters certainly would be out for revenge. As a token of their indignation, PPP party leaders had all the party's flags and posters displayed in Yogyakarta removed. Only posters condemning the attack on the party's offices were put up. In the *kauman*, the religious quarter of the city, a white coffin bearing the text 'Democracy is dead' was carried around. In Kotagede the protest took a more violent turn. People took to the streets, demolished street lights, and set up barricades. On 5 May campaigning was resumed.

In Jakarta the alleged reason for the local PPP to announce that it had brought its campaign to an end was that the authorities wanted to force the party to limit its electoral events to those taking the form of a dialogue. The police refused to grant permission for 'monologue' meetings scheduled in South and East Jakarta for 2 May. The reason given for the refusal to allow open-air rallies was that during its first round of campaigning in Jakarta on 29 April the PPP had violated the rules. Only small discussion meetings, organized at the level of the city ward, were to be allowed; the large outdoor events, with national party leaders featuring as speakers, had to be cancelled. As a token of protest PPP decided not to hold any electoral meeting at all in Jakarta. Ismail Hasan Metareum, it was stressed in an explanation of the decision, was none too keen on making an appearance at such a minor event. He wanted to address a larger crowd. As it turned out, on 2 May in Jakarta, in contrast to what had happened in Yogyakarta, PPP supporters still took to the streets, ignorant of the stance their leaders had adopted. Supporters drove across the city in motorcades, and in Senen PPP supporters, angry that the campaign activities had been cancelled, hurled stones at passing cars and at shops. Traffic ground to a complete standstill. Jakarta was, as it was vividly described, *macet total* (Adirsyah et al. 1997:74).

A fourth place in which a local PPP branch decided to stop campaigning in the first week of the campaign period was Medan. In this city, clashes between PPP and Golkar supporters had taken place on 27 April, after PPP members, on the day that it was their party's turn to campaign in Sumatra, spotted people hoisting Golkar flags (which according to the rules should not be there on that day) and tried to remove them. Three members of PPP were seriously injured.

Right from the start it was the PPP campaigns in particular which led to complications. With PDI discredited in the eyes of many by Soerjadi's ousting of Megawati, these formed the alternative occasion for people to testify to their anti-government feelings. In a number of places, anticipatory anti-government speeches by Islamic preachers, calling people to resist a corrupt regime, had done their work as well (Kristiadi, Legowo and Budi Harjanto 1997:104-5). Some of the early PPP electoral events had already ended in violence. Although there were minor incidents, such as pelting the houses of Golkar cadre members with stones, some matters took a serious turn. One of these took place in Ujungpandang on 1 May. When the power failed about half an hour after an open-air rally had started, an angry mob, convinced that the power had been cut on purpose, stormed the building of the state electricity company. Three days later violence re-erupted in Ujungpandang. After a PPP rally at the Karebosi soccer field, where Ismail Hasan Metareum had addressed the audience, a PPP crowd on their way home had to pass a Golkar base. After a heated exchange of slogans and abuse a fight broke out, eventually escalating into riots during which shops, houses, and cars were damaged.

On other occasions PPP participants became the victims. In autopsies of a number of such clashes, there were different versions of what had triggered them. This was the case with two incidents in Pekalongan on 2 May, which, as a report in *The Jakarta Post* put it, the police said never happened (*The Jakarta Post*, 3-5-1997). In Kajen, according to local PPP leaders, a motorcycle parade of PPP supporters returning from a campaign meeting was attacked in front of a Golkar office by people carrying iron staves and wooden clubs. Security forces stood idly by and watched what was happening. In the city of Pekalongan itself, according to PPP's version of the story, stones were thrown at PPP motorcyclists by residents who had also armed themselves with sickles and swords. The police told another story. The incident had started after PPP supporters had thrown stones at a housing complex where most of the residents were Golkar members.

Between 27 April and 4 May, according to an initial estimate by the army, as many as thirty people had died as a consequence of campaign activities. What had transpired in that first week of campaigning proved to be a persistent pattern. Motorized convoys remained the rule rather than the exception. There was mob violence in Pasuruan on 5 May during the PPP campaign, when hundreds of its supporters attacked a police station in the small city of Pohjentrek after one of their number had been arrested for jeering at the security forces. The crowd could eventually be dispersed, but formed again later in even greater numbers, this time armed with stones, sickles, and swords. Armoured cars had to be deployed. Five days later the story repeated itself. On the 10th, a PPP mob in Pohjentrek once again attacked the local police station. This time it happened after one of the participants in a parade had been arrested during a search for sharp objects by security forces.

By this time it had become clear that in Jakarta at least the parading of large masses of PPP supporters through the streets was infectious. Golkar supporters had started to follow their example. Initially they had mainly been drawn to Golkar electoral events by the artists. When they thought speeches took too long, the crowds shouted their displeasure and demanded *dangdut*, music. Gradually processions of Golkar supporters through town grew in attraction, drawing increasingly large crowds (Adirsyah et al. 1997:83-4).

The high toll in lives (at that moment the number of victims had risen to 49) and the repeated outbreaks of disturbances led Yogie SM to plead with all the parties on 14 May to put an end to the illegal parades through the cities, because, as he stated, it was especially during such events that tension heightened. Fights and mob violence were on the increase, he explained, not because the authorities tolerated such events, but because the security forces lacked sufficient troops to intervene properly. A similar appeal was issued locally around the same time by the civil and military authorities in Bogor, a city where up to that moment four people had died as a consequence of campaign activities. Political parties were asked to refrain from a 'show of force' in the form of motor convoys and parades. Observing that the campaigns deteriorated into shouting 'dirty words', into violence, and criminal acts, parents were asked to make sure that their children did not participate in electoral events. Two leading businessmen, Sofyan Wanandi and Sudwikatmono, also expressed their concern. The aggression was not only greatly frightening the general public, the entrepreneurs and 'conglomerates' were also beginning to shake in their shoes. The damage inflicted on the economy was considerable. Quite apart from the value of property that was damaged or destroyed, the indirect consequences had to be reckoned with. People were afraid to leave their homes, and shops remained closed. Hotels experienced a sharp drop in income. The violence dissuaded foreigners from visiting the country. Hotel occupancy, which was between 70 and 80 per cent in normal times, had dropped to 40 per cent. To allay the fear of the business world the government, Sudwikatmono explained, had to show that it was capable of keeping the situation under control.

President Soeharto also betrayed his apprehension. After Yogie SM and Singgih had reported to him about the increasingly violent nature of the campaigns on 13 May, Soeharto ordered them to issue a warning to the leaders of the three parties. It was they who were responsible for the brutal behaviour of their supporters. This appears to have marked the moment that, in Jakarta at least, the police and security forces tried to act with more resolution. The result was counterproductive. Earlier experiences had already shown that more violence was the likely outcome. The previous day, an angry PPP mob had attacked a police station after the identity card of a PPP supporter, who had been among a crowd which had tried to prevent the police from removing PPP signs, had been confiscated. On 14 May, during the PPP campaign in Java, supporters of the party in Jakarta threw stones at security officials who tried to bar access to one of the main streets to a procession. Others attacked a police station, after the police had arrested a man who had forced motor-car drivers to buy PPP pamphlets (which had earned the person in question Rp 20,500). Shouting 'attack', a crowd started to pelt the station with stones. Anti-riot troops had to fire warning shots to dispel them. It was also the day on which the greatest number of victims so far fell in Jakarta: six, all between 12 and 19 years of age. They had either crashed their motorcycles or had fallen off one truck to be run over by the next one. The same day serious incidents, causing damage to shops, police stations, government buildings, churches, and banks, occurred in Central Java in Kudus, Parakan, and Temanggung (where in fact it had been decided not to campaign in view of violent incidents three days earlier). What happened made various PPP branches in Central Java decide to pass up the opportunity to campaign again on 17 May. The same decision was taken in the city of Bandung. As before, in many cases such directives were ignored.

On Saturday 17 May, when the death toll had risen to at least 73, the leaders of the Jakarta branches of Golkar, PDI, and PPP agreed to hold indoor rallies only open to a limited audience. Shocked by the violence, the party leaders of the city decided to cancel all open-air rallies planned for the last five days of the campaign. Their followers were asked to be on the alert against outsiders trying to use the campaigns to stir up disorder, who were often dubbed 'anti-establishment groups'. Their decision was, as party officials already realized even as they issued it, to no avail. Next day, Sunday 18 May, Golkar street rallies in Jakarta, Yogyakarta, a number of cities in Central Java, and in Malang in East Java deteriorated into serious disturbances when Golkar and PPP crowds clashed. Most of the fights, as on earlier and later occasions, started when Golkar parades went through or passed by neighbourhoods where PPP – in Jakarta for instance around Jalan Warung Buncit Raya and Jalan Matraman – was strong, with participants in such rallies being attacked or pelted with all kinds of objects (flyovers being a convenient place for doing this). It could also happen that Golkar mobs themselves, armed with machetes, knives, sickles, clubs, and the like, took the initiative

'Mega yess' (photo *D&R*)

and attacked PPP residential areas, just waiting for onlookers to refuse to give the appropriate finger sign, or shout Mega-Bintang slogans. Three days before, some offended Golkar members had been particularly unlucky when one of them wanted to call to order a construction worker in Jalan Asia Afrika who had answered the two fingers of Golkar with the one finger of PPP. Fellow construction workers, Megawati fans who now supported PPP, took the side of their workmate, throwing stones and iron bars from their vantage point on the scaffolding down onto the Golkar parade. On the 18th they also clashed with such group as students of the Jakarta Islamic Institute of Higher Education, IAIN Syarif Hidayatullah, who also had refused to raise two fingers in the air. It was only one of many violent clashes on that day. Large-scale incidents took place in at least five places in Jakarta, with supporters on both sides pelting each other with stones, forcing the police to fire warning shots. Golkar leaders accused PPP supporters of having started it all by throwing stones at Golkar campaigners. PPP spokesmen were quick to put the blame on Golkar supporters, accusing them of destroying PPP banners.

In Yogyakarta, where Golkar supporters attacked the IAIN after rumours started that its students had thrown stones at a Golkar parade, fighting also broke out in various parts of the city. What had happened, the deputy chairman of the city's Golkar branch, Drs H. Chaeruddin, claimed, was an indication that each time Golkar campaigned, it had to contend with infiltrators set on disturbing its course. It was the second time the IAIN of Yogyakarta had been a target.

By this time the situation had become so untenable that on 19 May, four days before the official end of the campaign period, Yogie SM had to beg the parties not to pull out. Yogie SM said he understood the widespread fear of more riots, violence, and clashes, but nevertheless begged Golkar, PDI, and

PPP to continue with their campaigns.[5] Appeals to end the campaign at that time had already been voiced from various sides, including by the deputy chairman of the Muhammadiyah, Syafii Maarif, and the general chairman of the Dewan Syurah (Religious Advisory Council) of Nahdlatul Ulama, KH Ilyas Ruchiyat. Campaigning continued in most parts of Indonesia, but halted in various regions of Java. In order to protect its own people, as a local Golkar leader put it, Golkar decided to dispense with holding mass rallies in East Java (*The Indonesian Times*, 21-5-1997).

The campaign period ended in the by now familiar pattern – wrecked by violence and destruction. In Jakarta on 20 May, in spite of the decision taken by party leaders to halt campaigning, PPP supporters took to the streets. The party had lost control over its rank-and-file. In anticipation of trouble, security forces guarded the exits of the narrower streets where they joined the main roads in the city's trouble spots, where most of the rioting had taken place the previous weeks. Efforts made by the authorities to prevent people from joining motorized cavalcades only resulted in massive riots, with thousands of security troops consisting of police, soldiers, and marines, forced to use tear gas and to fire warning shots in an effort to restore order. Armoured cars appeared on the streets. Fights also broke out between groups of PPP and Golkar supporters, armed with knives and machetes. Security forces that tried to intervene were pelted by onlookers with stones and other missiles. One person was shot. This was reason enough for the military commander of Jakarta to warn that security forces, which he said had still displayed tolerance in the last few days, would act with resolution. Criminal acts would no longer be tolerated. On the same day there was violence in Bandung (where shops were pelted with stones and fights broke out between PPP and Golkar supporters), Semarang (where people returning from a rally shouted, spat, and threw stones at the police), and in Pekalongan.

On 23 May, the last day of the campaign period, in anticipation of the trouble which might be brewing, many schools, shops, and offices in Jakarta remained closed, or sent their employees home early. What transpired was a repeat of what had happened three days earlier. Though the PPP of Jakarta had decided to cancel all electoral events, including indoor meetings, announcing that it was to concentrate on a 'sympathetic' campaign, shaking hands, handing out gifts, and repairing damaged 'party attributes', violence was inevitable when the police and other security forces put up barricades in an effort to prevent PPP convoys from parading through town. Police stations were stoned, shops looted, and government offices and banks dam-

---

[5] Yogie's statement was welcomed by Mulyana W. Kusumah, secretary-general of the KIPP, who called street rallies and indoor meetings good mechanisms for the political education of the public and for attracting voters.

aged. On the same day similar incidents were reported from Tangerang, Bekasi, and Cianjur in West Java, where campaigning went on and drew PPP supporters from Jakarta, in Semarang in Central Java, and in Malang and Bangil in East Java. After the police had beaten up a PPP supporter in Bangil, an angry mob attacked banks, shops, and a police station. It was also the day of the Banjarmasin tragedy. The incidents in the vicinity of Jakarta, the military commander of that city, Major-General Sutiyoso, was to comment, had been 'small and spontaneous' (*Kompas*, 24-5-1997). One of the incidents he spoke about happened in Ciputat, where riot police had to try to control a mob of reportedly 7,000 people. In Tangerang during a PPP cavalcade of over 100,000 people, at least eight banks and a number of government offices, including the office of the regent, became the object of mob violence.

In explanation of the violence which marred the campaign period, the blame was invariably put on 'outsiders', 'troublemakers', and 'infiltrators', who as the Minister of Information, Harmoko, adding to this observation said, had displayed a 'political behaviour which was not in accordance with the Pancasila' and the 'values of the Pancasila democracy' (*Kompas*, 21-5-1997). As in observations made before the campaign period started, no names were mentioned. The one exception again was the PRD. That party was not only a convenient scapegoat, but, as future developments were to show, for one reason or another its activities greatly disquieted the authorities. On 20 May, one day before the end of the campaign period, during a press conference at the Armed Forces headquarters, Syarwan Hamid told journalists that there were enough indications to suspect that the PRD was behind some of the violence which had characterized the campaigns. President Soeharto pointed his finger at the gap between the rich and the poor. On 28 May, when he received a delegation of the Indonesian Council of Ulama, he asked reporters to show restraint and not to publish sensational reports about social disparities, because such reports could fan dissatisfaction and end up causing riots. A few days later he referred to the PRD as a small group which wanted to enforce its opinion upon the majority, and tried to make the general elections a failure, or if this proved impossible, at least put them under a cloud.

Speaking on behalf of PPP, its secretary-general, Tosari Widjaja, mentioned systematic and planned efforts to discredit his party and to create the impression among the general public that the PPP campaign was a violent one (*Republika*, 27-5-1997). The chairman of the Indonesian Council of Ulama, Hasan Basri, put the blame on 'irresponsible groups that had stirred up community jealousy to discredit the government and sow discord', stigmatizing them as those who 'have blown up the disparity between the haves and the have-nots and attacked the conglomerates' (*The Jakarta Post*, 29-5-1997).

Abdurrahman Wahid, horrified by the fact that there were people who wanted to put the blame for the rioting on the NU and himself, spoke about repeated efforts to provoke members of the NU to become involved in campaign violence. He believed this had been done to discredit the NU and to sabotage the general elections. As an example, referring to riots in Surabaya, Ujungpandang, and Banjarmasin, he mentioned the throwing of Molotov cocktails in regions where the NU was strong, simply to stir up anger. The rioting, he stressed, had nothing to do with his close relationship with Tutut. His aim in accompanying her to various meetings had not been to persuade members of the NU to vote for Golkar, but to introduce them to a future leader of the nation. Indicating that she had become the most important person in Golkar, Abdurrahman Wahid explained that what he did was a response to the fact that she and her brother, Bambang Trihatmodjo, were being given an increasingly important political role by their father. In Abdurrahman Wahid's eyes she was an extraordinary woman, combining a number of vocations. She was a businesswoman, a politician, was engaged in social work, and a whole lot more. He had invited her as early as two years before, but she had only reacted early in 1997. The majority of the other Golkar leaders, he added, left much to be desired, they were *setengah preman*, half-gangsters (*Panji Masyarakat*, 21-4-1997).

The campaign was not simply an opportunity to unleash violence. Among the themes frequently raised by PPP and PDI politicians were corruption and collusion, the naked ambition to become as rich as possible in as short as possible a time, the widening gap between the rich and the poor, the conduct of the heads of big business concerns and the adverse effects of this on small entrepreneurs, and the need for political reform, including improving the functioning of parliament. References to political injustice at a meeting in Pasuruan even cost one PPP orator a written police warning, handed over to him while he was still on the podium, as his words were considered a breach of the campaign rules, constituting an attack on the Pancasila and the Constitution, in other words an effort to incite one group against another. The PPP leader read out the warning to the crowd, who started jeering and urged him to continue. Other questions were raised on the banners displayed. In Jakarta one of these questions asked about a follow-up to the escape of Eddy Tansil,[6] the death of the labour activist Marsinah, the murder of the journalist Udin, and the demolition of houses of the poor. Similar top-

---

[6]   In 1994 it became known that Eddy Tansil or Tan Tjoe Hong, president director of the Golden Key Group, had embezzled credit of Rp 1.3 trillion or about US$ 650 million for investments in the petrochemical industry, which he had obtained in an illegal way from the state bank Bapindo (Bank Pembangunan Indonesia). To provide such a large amount of credit, four other state banks had to be involved. Eddy Tansil was sentenced to seventeen years' imprisonment, but had no difficulty in escaping from Cipinang prison in May 1996. He paid a guard Rp 3 million to take him to the Roti Holland Bakery Shop, promising him another Rp 2 million on his

ics were also inevitably raised in the Golkar campaign. At 'dialogues' Golkar politicians found themselves having to field painful questions about corruption, about the financial and tax facilities afforded the producer of Indonesia's national car, the Timor, and about the Busang gold scandal.[7] Golkar campaigners tried to convince their audience that the government was sincere in its efforts to combat poverty and corruption. They pointed out the economic accomplishments of the New Order, pledged to combat poverty, and made a host of other promises.

As had been the rule during previous elections, the campaign period was followed by a cooling-down period. It lasted five days. No demonstrations took place, but there were bomb threats by telephone in Jakarta and Medan, and elsewhere pamphlets circulated asking or warning people not to vote, or announcing the intention to set fire to polling stations. During the 'calm week', Soeharto in a televised speech once again impressed on the population how important it was for Indonesians to cast a valid vote. Polling took place on 29 May. On the days leading up to it public transport had been filled to overflowing as many people in the cities returned to their villages to cast their vote there. Many shopkeepers in Jakarta and elsewhere decided to keep their shops closed, afraid of renewed violence. People had hoarded food-stuffs and drinks to prepare for the worst. A well-known paranormal practitioner had even predicted that Jakarta would be turned into a 'flood of blood' (Adirsyah et al. 1997:136). The atmosphere, *Republika* wrote referring to Jakarta, was like that at the end of the fasting month, when many left the city to celebrate with their family (*Republika*, 30-5-1997).

At the polling stations people cast their votes for three representative bodies: the national parliament (Dewan Perwakilan Rakyat or DPR), the Provincial Councils (DPRD-I), and the Municipal and Regency Councils (DPRD-II). This time they could also do so at polling booths erected along Jakarta's main roads, which were to be used by people who wanted to cast their vote at a place near their office. Even more traffic jams were the result.

At a number of places the elections were marred by violent incidents. These were reported from Indramayu and Serang in West Java, from Situbondo, Jember, Pasuruan, and Magetan in East Java, from Madura, and from

---

return to prison. At the end of 1998 it was reported that Eddy Tansil had become the owner of a Putian Golden Key Brewery in China, a joint venture with Beck's Beer. In January 1999 Portugal was mentioned as his country of residence.

[7]	In July 1993, the Canadian-based company, Bre-X Minerals Ltd, acquired mining rights in the Busang area in Kalimantan. Initial exploration results made public by the company indicated that the region was very rich in gold. Shares in Bre-X skyrocketed. On the basis of the news the Indonesian government and Indonesian business people were also keen to participate. In the end it turned out that the field was worthless, and that probably the tests had been tampered with.

East Timor. At a polling station in Bandarlampung furious onlookers forced a re-counting of the vote, when it was announced that all but two votes had gone to Golkar. Most seriously affected was Madura. This did not come as a complete surprise. Madura had already been identified as a potential trouble spot. A few days before polling day, its chief of police had disclosed that there were twenty subdistricts in the island where disorder might erupt (Adirsyah et al. 1997:147). Extra precautions had been taken, but proved worse than useless. Polling stations went up in flames, the persons in charge, village mayors, and other civil servants had to flee angry mobs, and people tried to destroy ballot boxes which had been transported to the subdistrict offices. One schoolteacher, a member of a polling station committee, did not dare to return home for weeks after his house had been set on fire. The police had to take over his task. Somehow or other, ballot boxes got lost while being transported to subdistrict offices. The riots of 29 May were particularly fierce in five subdistricts in Sampang, especially in Kedundung, where a local police office, a post office, shops, and the offices of a village mayor and of the assistant regent were vandalized. Houses of people who had changed party became chief targets of mob violence. Next day unrest spread to the subdistrict of Pengantenan in Pamekasan and to that of Pasongsongan in Sumenep, where police headquarters and offices of government officials were attacked. The situation returned to normal only after the mediation of one of the most influential religious leaders of Madura, KH Alawy Muhammad, who convinced the chief of police on the island to release the people arrested on charges of violence and causing disorder.

The following day leaders of PPP revealed that they had already been informed about eighty-nine cases in which rules had been violated. These included the non-registration of voters in regions where PPP was strong, voting twice, the handing out of money to voters, votes being counted not at the polling station in the presence of witnesses appointed by the parties as well as the ordinary voters (sometimes urged by politicians of PPP and PDI to stay there after they had cast their votes in order to see that all proceeded according to the rules), but at government offices such as those of subdistrict heads, and the intimidation of the obligatory witnesses representing PPP and PDI at polling stations. School pupils, a representative of PPP claimed, had received forms from their teachers allowing them to vote outside their home district and had used these to vote at home as well as at school for Golkar. Pupils had been told that they would not pass their exams if they did not vote Golkar. Other complaints concerned rewards offered to village mayors if Golkar were to do well and threats of sanctions if the party did not.

Armed with many reports of examples of intimidation, vote rigging, and fraud, PPP announced that it intended to take legal action. In an initial reaction a number of branches, including those of West Sumatra and Jakarta, urged the central board not to recognize the election results for the national parliament. Such a prospect disturbed a former Minister of Religion, Alamsyah Ratu Perwiranegara, who in the past had mobilized Islamic support for the re-election of Soeharto. Beginning to fear for the resilience of the relationship between the Islamic community and the government, he tried to persuade Ismail Hasan Metareum not to overstep the mark. Leaders of PPP reacted angrily to this intervention, but could not make up their minds what to do. Consequently they left it to the provincial and regency/city branches to decide for themselves whether to recognize the results or not. Over and above this an instruction went out to the regency/city branches to report all incidents involving crimes to the police and to deal with other incidents by bringing a lawsuit against the regent/mayor as the chairperson of the Local Election Committee and thus the government representative responsible before court should the authorities not act upon the complaints. The Ikatan Advokat Indonesia (Ikadin, Indonesian League of Lawyers) and the Yayasan Lembaga Bantuan Hukum Indonesia (YLBHI, Indonesian Legal Aid Foundation) vowed to help PPP and its branches with the lawsuits they might want to bring. To cap it all, various regency branches demanded that the results had to be declared invalid and that the elections had to be held all over again; in some cases they threatened that, if their demands were not met, they would refuse to sign the official election results of their regency. PPP branches which took these steps included those of Pamekasan, Sampang, Sumenep, Bangkalan, Jember, Situbondo, and Ponorogo. Other regions where the results were contested were Jakarta, Yogyakarta, North Bengkulu, North Lampung, West Sumatra, Kampar in Riau, and Gorontalo in North Sulawesi. In South Sulawesi, West Sumatra, and Sampang in Madura a new ballot was demanded.

A few days later, after a meeting of its national and provincial boards, PDI decided to protest to the General Election Institute, the Indonesian Election Committee, and the Committee for the Supervision of the Elections about the many irregularities which had taken place right from the start of the campaign period till after the counting of the votes. According to some of its leaders, the irregularities had been more numerous and of a much more serious nature than at earlier elections.[8] Local branches should take similar steps. The party and its branches demanded new elections or a recount of the votes in various places, including West Sumatra and North Bengkulu. The PDI threatened to boycott the formal signing of the election results at all levels – regency, provincial, and national – if the government did not react appropri-

---

8   This meeting, as most meetings of the Soerjadi board, took place in the house Soerjadi was entitled to live in as one of the deputy chairmen of parliament. Since 27 July, the PDI office at Jalan Diponegoro, which had been heavily damaged on that day, had remained empty.

ately to its complaints. According to the election rules this would not make these results invalid, but if carried through to the bitter end would imply that PDI would not take up its seats, not even in the national parliament. The provincial branches of East Java and Jakarta indeed advocated that the seats in the national parliament not be taken up. The chorus of critics was joined by the National Committee for Human Rights. In a statement it drew attention to the fact that the election was legal, but that the quality of the whole operation had definitely gone downhill since the last election.

Because of the ballot boxes lost or destroyed on 29 May, the general elections had to be reheld in Sampang in Madura.[9] This, too, resulted in complications. As the government was only prepared to do this at 86 polling stations in three subdistricts and not all 1,033 polling stations throughout the whole regency, leaders of the Sampang PPP, afraid to call openly for a boycott, had let it be known beforehand that they would send no witnesses. Their protest did not dissuade the governor of East Java, Basofi Soedirman, from proceeding. He had no hesitation in claiming that new elections were legal, with or without the participation of PPP witnesses. Driving home their dissatisfaction, 45 local PPP politicians, whose names were on the lists of candidates, withdrew their candidacy for the regency council. The repeat polling, at 65 polling stations (as an investigation had shown that the results at 21 polling stations had not been lost after all; for the same reason a repeat polling at 35 polling stations in Pamekasan was cancelled), took place on 14 June. There were no witnesses from either PPP or PDI present. The PPP had refused to provide them, the PDI lacked persons capable of acting as witnesses. Security forces made their presence felt numerically. Over a thousand extra troops were sent to Madura. Three tanks were positioned at Sampang. 'It is like they are getting ready for a war rather than a festival of democracy,' an influential local *ulama* commented (*The Indonesian Times*, 4-6-1997). The military presence, it was stressed, was not intended to frighten people, but to ensure that no disturbances would take place. Yet the military commander of East Java, Major-General H. Imam Utomo, threatened that people who disturbed the re-balloting would be shot on the spot. The transportation of the ballot boxes to the regency office was also carried out under strict guard. Less than 20,000 of the roughly 32,000 people entitled to vote actually did so. At one polling station only six persons turned up. All six voted Golkar. Golkar gained 60 per cent of the votes, PPP 40 per cent, PDI 0.36 per cent. In July the local PPP decided not to fill the fourteen seats they had won in the regency council yet, but to continue to fight for the seats which had been 'stolen' from

[9]   It was hinted that government officials were responsible for the destruction of the ballot boxes, because they were anxious to hide the overwhelming victory PPP had scored. The local Golkar branch asked for the punishment of the people who had masterminded the riots.

them (*Forum Keadilan*, 28-7-1997:32).

Two weeks later violence again erupted in Jember and in Pasuruan in East Java, where on 9 June and again on 15 June two wards in a village clashed, and in Bangkalan in Madura. In Jember, where protesters against irregularities during the election carried posters around with slogans like 'Bupati, please listen to the Voice of the People' and 'Democracy, Justice, or Ruin'; firework bombs filled with nails, marbles, and glass were used as weapons during disturbances on 13 June. The office of the local administration and shops were damaged, including a showroom for the Timor car. Troops firing warning shots were powerless to control the rioters. On 14 June, in Bangkalan, thousands of people just before festivities were to start to celebrate the town's winning the Adipura Trophy, the annual prize for the cleanest city in the country, suddenly set fire to the stage. The dignitaries fled in panic. Thereupon the crowd vented its anger on banks, shops, government buildings, a church, and a Buddhist temple. Warning shots fired by the police were to no avail. Army troops had to be employed to restore order. One of the reasons for the outburst was the fact that the authorities, who had disregarded protests over election irregularities, had incited popular fury by holding a government-related celebration. Rumours were rife beforehand that the meeting had been intended as a facade to celebrate a Golkar victory. Adding insult to injury, the celebrations, at which a *dangdut* orchestra was scheduled to perform, were to be held in the square in front of the local mosque, disregarding an agreement reached three years earlier that no festivities of any kind were to be held there. Because prayer houses had also been burned down during the series of riots in East Java and Madura, Basofi Soedirman conveniently put the blame on communists. As a precaution, extra troops were stationed in other cities of Madura as well as in Jember, Pasuruan, Probolinggo, and Situbondo. Military authorities also announced that rioters were to be shot. This went too far for one local Madurese *ulama*. Calling for a more social approach, he said he believed that a shot in the leg would suffice (*Kompas*, 17-6-1997).

As could have been expected, PDI fared poorly in the elections.[10] It received only 3.5 million votes, many fewer than the Golput. The number of people who had not voted or had cast an invalid vote amounted to 13 million, or 14 per cent. In some provinces the percentage was significantly higher than the national average. In Jakarta it reached 31 per cent, in North Sumatra 27, in Lampung 20.6, in East Java 17.6, and in Yogyakarta 16 per cent (*Ishlah* 4-79:21). To mark the decline of Soerjadi's PDI, supporters of Megawati in Yogyakarta, mostly youngsters, shaved their heads.

---

[10] In Surabaya some Megawati supporters had not pierced their voting card but had pasted a sticker with pro-Megawati words over the PDI symbol.

PDI had performed so poorly that for a moment it seemed that the election results would necessitate adjustments to the established procedures in parliament. The initial provisional results gave PDI only ten seats. Such a small PDI representation, it was feared, might make it more difficult for parliament to work properly, for instance in using its right of initiative and asking information from the president, which required the participation of a quorum of members of parliament from different factions. Equally problematic, it was thought that PDI could well end up with fewer members of parliament than required for the eleven parliamentary committees. According to the prevailing rules, at least two Members of parliament of each of the factions had to sit in each committee. Before it could take decisions, a meeting of a committee had to be attended by at least half of the representatives of eac party. It was feared that the low number of PDI representatives would make the system unworkable. The poor election results also made it impossible for PDI to occupy one of the deputy chairmanships of parliament to which a party was entitled, without outside assistance. A nomination to such a post had to be supported by twenty members of parliament. To help PDI, on 1 June the chairman of Golkar announced that his party was prepared to give its surplus votes to PDI. The response to this was reserved. Buttu R. Hutapea said his party did not want sympathy from any side whatsoever, only from the people.

On 23 June Harmoko on behalf of Golkar, Ismail Hasan Metareum on behalf of PPP, and Buttu Hutapea on behalf of PDI signed the final election results. The PDI had eleven seats, and not ten, as the provisional results had intimated. According to the National Election Institute the reason for the additional seat, won in North Sumatra, was an error in counting. It secured a seat in parliament for one of Soerjadi's close associates in the PDI in the bringing down of Megawati, Fatimah Achmad. She had been number two on the North Sumatra list. Buttu R. Hutapea, number three on the list in North Sumatra, failed to gain a seat, and for a long time indeed it remained unclear whether Soerjadi, number one in Jakarta, had in fact gained a seat. He had not. The government, M. Yogie SM commented, should not be blamed for the poor election results reaped by PDI. It was the party itself, riven by internal conflicts, that had brought about its own come-uppance.

CHAPTER III

Towards an economic and political crisis 1997

> Golongan Karya pelopor pembaharuan
> Giat bekerja dalam masa pembangunan
> Golkar sadar berjuang mengemban AMPERA
> dengan semangat kekaryaan yang utama[1]

With the general elections over and done with, political attention turned to the coming session of the People's Congress in March 1998 and its task of electing a president and vice-president for the coming five years. Though it had been suggested that parties should disclose the name of their favourites for these two positions during the electoral campaign, on the whole politicians had honoured the unwritten rule of silence, highlighting, as the phrase put it, their 'programme'. Only occasionally had people indicated publicly that they no longer wanted Soeharto as president. It must have hurt him that among them were members of the Yayasan Pembela Tanah Air, Foundation of the Defenders of the Fatherland, veterans of the War of Independence (*Kabar dari Pijar*, 9-4-1997). Dissidents – even well before the campaign period had started – also made no secret of the fact that they rejected the idea of a new term in office for President Soeharto. Sri Bintang Pamungkas and Julius Usman, for instance, had done so in February 1997, advancing their own names as candidates for the presidency and vice-presidency respectively (an act which might well have contributed to the decision to arrest them early the following month).[2] In the formal campaigns the issue failed to take off, as almost all the orators took the formal, legalistic stand that the election of a president and vice-president was the prerogative of the People's

---

[1]   The functional groups as pioneers of renewal/ Working energetically in the era of development/ Consciously Golkar strives to implement the Message of the Suffering of the People/ in the highest spirit. First verse of *Mars Golkar pelopor pembaharuan*.

[2]   Wimanjaya K. Liotohe, who advanced himself as candidate for the vice-presidency, underwent a similar fate. Not much later he was arrested because he had insulted the president in his books (1993, 1997a, 1997b). A court case against him was started but it was discontinued after Soeharto's fall.

Congress and should be left to the members of that institution.

Discussions about the presidency began in earnest at the end of August 1997 when two Golkar youth organizations spoke out in favour of the renomination of Soeharto. Their words were taken up by the chairman of the Golkar faction in parliament, who was also Golkar's deputy secretary-general, Moestahid Astari. He reacted positively, stating that Golkar, as the largest party, should not wait till March 1998 (the opening of the general session of the People's Congress) to announce Soeharto as its candidate for the presidency. The party should do so no later than at a meeting of its core leaders scheduled for October. This was followed by a statement by Golkar's general chairman, Harmoko. Referring to national and local organizations which had urged Golkar to nominate Soeharto, he commented that Soeharto was the Golkar candidate and that this was to be publicly announced in October. Given the prevailing atmosphere, people were used to looking for hidden meanings behind statements, so the fact that Moestahid Astari had taken the lead was seen by some as a loss of face for Harmoko, and an indication of strong differences of opinion within Golkar itself. Within days of Moestahid Astari's remark, both the former Minister of Internal Affairs, General (Ret.) Rudini (who, since he was no longer a member of the cabinet had become a critic of the government, heading what was described as an informal military think-tank, the Lembaga Pengkajian Strategis Indonesia, Indonesian Institute for Strategic Studies) and Burhan D. Magenda hastened to explain that his suggestion of an early nomination of Soeharto should not be construed as an indication of a split within Golkar. Moestahid Astari himself refused to comment.

Following a convention seldom used in the past, Harmoko added that Golkar's formal nomination of Soeharto would only take place during the session of the People's Congress. Asked for a response from PPP, Ismail Hasan Metareum and Tosari Widjaja refused to discuss the nomination. They explained discreetly that PPP politicians were too busy preparing the party's input for the formulation of the Broad Outlines of State Policy to be followed by the government the next five years and the other decrees of the People's Congress. On behalf of the Armed Forces, Syarwan Hamid declared he himself was pleased with the mention of Soeharto's name, but hastened to stress that the Armed Forces would wait announcing the name of their candidate. This was also the line adopted by Golkar.

At the time of this discussion, the Minister of Transmigration and Settlement of Forest Dwellers, Siswono Yudohusodo, speaking in a debate on future leadership, came out with a statement which surprised many. He gave his opinion that in the post-Soeharto era which, he stressed, would hopefully only commence after 2003, the number of terms in office of an Indonesian president could best be limited to one or two. The two presidents of

Indonesia so far, he explained, had been extraordinary persons. The first, Soekarno, had led the people to Independence. The second, Soeharto, had rescued the country from communism. In acknowledgement of their merit, people had had no objections to their staying in office for a remarkably long time. Considering the atmosphere prevailing in Indonesia at that time, Siswono Yudohusodo had touched upon a controversial subject. Similar appeals had usually been viewed as veiled criticism of Soeharto. Reactions were reserved. Ismail Hasan Metareum refused to comment, but did disclose that his party had set up a committee to study the matter. He and the chairman of the PPP faction in parliament both stressed that a limit to the number of terms in office of an Indonesian president might be among the topics that could be discussed by the People's Congress. The Minister of Information, Harmoko, the Minister Coordinator of Political and Security Affairs, Soesilo Soedarman, and the Secretary of State, Moerdiono, also refused to be drawn into the discussion. All three said that the matter was the responsibility of the People's Congress. Moestahid Astari went a little further. He said the idea of limiting the number of terms in office looked like a violation of the Constitution, which left the matter open. Others rejected this suggestion, arguing as Rudini and Soesilo Soedarman did, that it was the *sikon*, the situation and condition, at the time a president had to be elected that was the decisive factor. Feisal Tanjung made it clear that though the military did not forbid a public discussion of the issue, its members would not join the debate themselves. Support for Siswono Yudohusodo's suggestion came from Sabam Sirait of Megawati's PDI and from Prof. Harun Alrasyid, a specialist in constitutional law. According to the latter, a limitation was necessary to prevent a dictatorship taking root.

There had been much talk the previous year about the *suksesi*, the succession of Soeharto, and in April when a KNPI delegation had asked him to stand again, Soeharto himself had indicated that he might be too old for the job. Nevertheless, by the middle of 1997 it was already virtually a foregone conclusion that in March 1998 the People's Congress would re-elect Soeharto for his seventh term in office.[3] This became even more obvious after 1 October, an ominous date in the history of the New Order, when the new members of People's Congress were installed. Harmoko became chairman, defeating Syarwan Hamid in the competition for that post. What followed was the familiar spectacle of people scurrying to the fore to nominate

[3]   The Komite Nasional Pemuda Indonesia (National Committee of Indonesian Youth) was founded in 1973 to serve as a national organization of Indonesian young people. At that time KNPI met with much criticism from students and a number of other youth organizations, as its foundation was clearly intended to limit the influence of the existing ideological and political youth organizations.

Soeharto; however, in contrast to five and ten years ago, there were almost no conspicuous appeals or prayer meetings from outside the major political parties and social organizations in favour of a nomination of Soeharto. On 16 October 1997, when he opened the conference of Golkar's core leaders, at which about 700 delegates were present, Harmoko once again underlined that, given the many statements and suggestions to this effect which his board had received, there was only one person whose name could be advanced as that of the next president: Soeharto. This was the wish of the mass of the people. It was a democratic must. The following day representatives of the provincial chapters followed in his footsteps. All, without exception, spoke out in favour of Soeharto. On the 17th, a deputy secretary-general of PPP, H. Muhsin Bafadal, commented that in view of the overwhelming support the nomination of Soeharto had received his party should do the same. Before the end of the month the regional faction in the People's Congress also announced its intention to nominate Soeharto. At that moment Soeharto still seemed above public criticism. Apart from the voices of long-standing dissidents seemingly still crying in the wilderness, there was nothing but praise for him.

Among the few persons who publicly called for some constraint was Soeharto himself. On the eve of the general election campaign he had already hinted that it was possible that in actual fact he was not as popular among the people as was believed. Within days of the Golkar meeting and already having stressed earlier that he did not want to be the object of a personality cult, Soeharto indicated that he might lack popular support. It was not the first time that Soeharto had hinted that his present term in office would be his last one, leading to speculations about his succession, but the emphasis on popular support was new. On 19 October, speaking on the occasion of Golkar's 33rd anniversary, he posed the question whether the people still believed in him. Though the audience cried out in chorus 'true, true', Soeharto told them that he did not want to be accused of obstructing the 'succession' and of hampering a 'regeneration'. Larding his speech with Javanese terminology, Soeharto explained that as a human being with all the shortcomings of his kind, he had the duty to indulge in introspection and to ask the question whether it was indeed true that a large portion of the population really put their trust in him. Without such support it would be difficult for him, he said, to carry the heavy burden of the presidency. Alluding to succession scenes in *wayang* stories, he explained that, as he chose to phrase it, he did not mind stepping down should the people no longer trust him. If this were the case he would *lengser keprabon madeg pandhito*, step down and become a *pandhito*, a religious person, and devote himself to religion and to the education of his children, grandchildren, and great-grandchildren. He would continue to make himself useful to the state and society in the role of advisor. With Soeharto's speech the Javanese word *lengser*, to withdraw, to step aside, had found an indelible place in the political jargon of the New Order. Soeharto also voiced explicit criticism of Golkar. What Golkar had to do, Soeharto stressed, was to abandon its paternalistic attitude and make an attempt to listen more carefully to the wishes of the people. Should Golkar have had it wrong in its assessment of his popularity, this might have negative consequences for the party. Soeharto's words put the Golkar élite in a difficult position. In the past, on more than one occasion, he had indicated that he might no longer qualify because he was growing too old – he was a TOPP, as he had described this in 1992: *tua* (old), *ompong* (toothless), *peot* (wrinkled), and *pikun* (long in the tooth) – but had never suited the action to the word. There was little chance that Soeharto would take kindly to the message that indeed he was not a popular leader. And who would convey this to him? Harmoko, at least, seems to have doubted whether Soeharto had honestly considered not seeking renomination. After Soeharto's fall Harmoko refused to be specific, but did suggest that if Soeharto had really wanted to step back, he could have done so (*Golkar* 1999:47).

Publicly there was praise all around for Soeharto's words. He had shown great statesmanship. Harmoko, for instance, called Soeharto a true democrat, a statesman who served as a model to others, a leader who set an example. Habibie reacted in a similar vein. Soeharto was a fighter who never considered his own interests, but devoted all his time, energy, and thoughts to the people whose leader he was. For students at Gadjah Mada University in Yogyakarta, Amien Rais's university, Soeharto's speech gave the green light to proceed with plans which they had been hesitant to execute. They had been planning to hold an opinion poll among the students of the university to test the popularity of Soeharto. Of the 9,587 respondents, almost one-third of all the students, 82.8 per cent rejected re-nomination of the president. It was one of a number of opinion polls held at that time, all showing the same overwhelming rejection of a new term in office for Soeharto. They indicated that Vice-President Try Sutrisno was among the persons favoured to replace him. Most of these polls were held at universities. An exception, and the most revealing opinion poll, perhaps, was organized in Surakarta by Gerakan Rakyat untuk Perubahan (GRUP, People's Movement for Change), in which religious young people and student organizations and NGOs cooperated. Seventeen thousand people, from all walks of life, responded. Only among the members of the Armed Forces who responded (58) was there a majority in favour of Soeharto staying on. Of the labourers, workers in the informal sector, farmers, civil servants, and students who had filled in the questionnaire, 80 per cent or more were against (Manggut 1998; *Forum Keadilan Edisi Khusus Desember 1997*:104, 9-2-1998:14).

There were some hints that Golkar should make a serious attempt to

sound out the population about its feelings about Soeharto and its prefer-
ences regarding the person who should be the next president. In an initial
reaction, the spokesman of the Armed Forces, Brigadier-General Abdul
Wahab Mokodongan, promised that the Armed Forces were ready to guard
public order. That would allow Golkar to investigate what the people
thought about the re-election of Soeharto. The Armed Forces would ensure
that there would be no sudden upheaval, if it suddenly turned out that
Golkar had had it wrong.

It soon turned out that Golkar leaders had absolutely no intention of starting a large-scale investigation into Soeharto's popularity. According to the
chairman of the Golkar faction in the People's Congress (concurrently
Minister of National Development Planning and Chairman of the Bappenas,
or National Planning Bureau), Ginandjar Kartasasmita, Soeharto's speech
made no difference. Golkar would not waver in its decision to nominate him.
Other Golkar leaders, most prominent among them Agung Laksono and
Akbar Tanjung, also stated that Golkar would comply with Soeharto's suggestion, but that in all probability this would make no difference to the stance
adopted by the party. The extent to which Golkar politicians intended to follow up Soeharto's suggestion was revealed by Harmoko. Golkar was planning to consult the organizations which had appealed to the party's central
board to advance Soeharto as Golkar's presidential candidate. True to these
words and not a whit taken aback, Golkar continued to press for the nomination of Soeharto, trying to convince the other factions in the Working
Committee of the People's Congress, the body that had assumed office on 1
October, charged with the task of preparing the various decisions of the
People's Congress, to do the same. Golkar, a newspaper headline read, was
engaged 'in an all-out battle for Soeharto' (*The Jakarta Post*, 25-10-1997).
Golkar leaders once more refused to reconsider their decision at the end of
December when Siti Hardijanti Rukmana, addressing students in Surakarta,
suddenly confessed that she did not want her father to be re-elected. This
would give him more time to spend with his family, something which, she
added, he had hardly been able to do during his presidency.

One of the consequences of Soeharto's statement in October was that it
gave journalists the opportunity to ask political leaders to identify the groups
opposed to the re-election of Soeharto and to report this in the newspapers.
The answers they got were vague: people who had been in prison because of
their political opposition, people who rejected the political system, or others
of that ilk, or as Rudini suggested, those who were 'too apriori', that is people who just assumed that the population no longer wanted Soeharto as their
president (*Merdeka*, 24-10-1997). It was, Mokodongan explained, not easy to
state who was against Soeharto. Such people usually did not brandish their
opinions about in public.

Among the few who dared to be explicit was Dr Muhammad Amien Rais – MAR to his friends – who mentioned students, intellectuals, and NGOs, and hinted that in business circles, in Golkar, in the Armed Forces, and in the wider society there were also people who wanted a change. These words perfectly fitted the reputation Amien Rais, a lecturer at the Faculty of Social and Political Sciences at Gadjah Mada University in Yogyakarta, had earned himself.[4] Amien Rais, general chairman of one of the two largest Islamic organizations in Indonesia, Muhammadiyah, which in contrast to its 'traditionalist' counterpart represents the 'modernist stream' in Indonesian Islam, was one of the most outspoken critics in the country at that time. In the course of 1997 he gained growing fame for his courage to identify publicly, by written or spoken word what was wrong with the New Order. The extent to which he succeeded in attracting public attention was such that, at the end of 1997, the ICMI magazine *Ummat* (of which he himself was a member of the editorial board) elected him the 'Personality of the Year'. This had been done, it was explained, partly because, aside from government officials, it had been Amien Rais who had made the most 'news' in 1997. A second reason was the contribution his statements had made to the political education of the people.[5] His blunt comments and speeches earned him a reputation as a courageous person, and also pejoratively as somebody (he was born in Surakarta) who was not 'Javanese' enough. Amien Rais spoke openly about the 'nepotism' which was invariably involved in the selection of electoral candidates,[6] the 'collusion' of high officials and civil servants with members of the business community, and the control of foreign investors over the country's natural resources, of which the position of Freeport Indonesia and Busang were glaring examples.[7] According to Amien Rais, the contracts concluded with

---

[4] Amien Rais had studied at the Faculty of Social and Political Sciences of Gadjah Mada University and at the IAIN Sunan Kalijaga in Yogyakarta. In 1968 he continued his studies in the United States, first at Notre Dame University in Indiana, and then at the University of Chicago. At the latter university he wrote his PhD thesis, *The Muslim Brotherhood in Egypt; Its rise, demise, and resurgence*, 1981.

[5] When he received the trophy at the end of December during a meeting attended by a thousand 'hysterical' (the term is from *Ummat*) people, an event which turned in an anti-government demonstration, Amien Rais introduced a new abbreviation to denote the prevailing mentality in Indonesia: *muntaber* ('cholera') or *munafik tapi beruntung* (or *berhasil*), hypocritic but profitable (or bringing results).

[6] This, of course, was a point which had not escaped others. As with many other matters, the practice soon had its own acronym AMPII (*anak, menantu, ponakan, istri, ipar*), indicating that a person had the best chance to enter a list of candidates or to become an appointed member of the People's Congress if he or she were a child, son- or daughter-in-law, nephew or niece, wife, or brother- or sister-in-law of a person who held a position of power.

[7] Freeport Indonesia is a subsidiary of Freeport McMoRan Copper and Gold, active in the mining of copper and gold in Irian Jaya since 1966. One of the points of criticism is that the share of the Indonesian state in the company is only 9.4 per cent.

such companies were in violation of the spirit of Article 33 of the Indonesian Constitution, which stated that all natural resources should be exploited in the interests of the people. Other points he touched upon included the gap between the rich and the poor, and the economic marginalization of the Islamic community, the feeling that the devout Islamic community had lost out in the competition with rich (Chinese) businessmen and foreign investments. As a consequence of his frankness, in February 1997 Amien Rais lost his position as chairman of the Council of Experts of ICMI.[8] Soeharto had ordered Habibie to take this action, but publicly the pretence was upheld that all was peace and amity (Aminudin 1999:365). After an extraordinary closed meeting of the ICMI board, the first in years, Habibie announced that Amien Rais's resignation had been accepted. As the formal reason for this step, it was stated that Amien Rais had decided to step down and concentrate on his duties as general chairman of Muhammadiyah. Amien Rais himself spoke about his feelings of guilt because his many other functions prevented him from devoting the time he should to his function as chairman of ICMI's Council of Experts, adding that he was 'too vocal' and did not want ICMI to suffer from this weakness (*Panji Masyarakat*, 3-3-1997:20). Such words did little to remove the impression that, as had indeed been the case, Amien Rais had been forced to withdraw.

Within Muhammadiyah itself, there were also some who had problems coming to terms with Amien Rais's outspoken political stance, afraid that it might involve their organization in politics or harm the way it functioned. Such persons feared that Muhammadiyah might experience the same fate as had its counterpart, the NU. Although individual *ulama* (religious leaders) had still held Soeharto's favour, NU as an organization had earned the displeasure of President Soeharto and the authorities, partly because of criticism expressed by chairman Abdurrahman Wahid. Still, shortly after his resignation as chairman of the Council of Experts, when Amien Rais went on a tour visiting major Muhammadiyah branches, the reception he was given was overwhelming. Certainly among students and younger members of Muhammadiyah his political stance was received with enthusiasm. On 11 March 1997 (Supersemar Day) Forum Kaum Muda Muhammadiyah Yogyakarta, Forum of the Muhammadiyah Youth of Yogyakarta, staged a mass demonstration in support of Amien Rais, reportedly attended by 10,000 people (*Panji Masyarakat*, 24-3-1997:17). Judging from texts of the banners carried around, such as 'Stop political intervention' and 'Amien Rais is an asset to the people, why has he been pushed aside?', those present were clearly of the

---

[8]   Amien Rais retained his seat on the Central Board, of which he had been a key member since ICMI's founding. In July 1998, after the fall of Soeharto, he was reinstated as chairman of the Council of Experts.

opinion that Amien Rais had become the victim of his opponents within ICMI. In an official declaration, protesters called for vigilance against efforts by 'certain elements' to undermine the position of Amien Rais. On a wider scale, they pressed for political and economic reforms. One of their demands was to end a political culture characterized by feudalism and attempts to silence criticism.

The government at that time let it be known that Muhammadiyah and Amien Rais had not lost its blessing completely. In Yogyakarta, Major-General Prabowo Subianto, a son-in-law of Soeharto, met a number of Muhammadiyah leaders (but not Amien Rais) and conveyed to them that there were no objections should Amien Rais continue to lead Muhammadiyah. During the conversation Prabowo put the blame for certain government decisions which had displeased the Islamic community on pressure from abroad, exerted by people who considered an Islamic Indonesia a threat to the stability of Southeast Asia. Convinced that the position of Soeharto and national integrity were at stake, it had been decided that a confrontation had to be avoided in dealing with such foreign forces (*Panji Masyarakat*, 24-3-1997:18).

Amien Rais continued along the path he had chosen, startling and delighting his audiences with the remarks he made. In doing so he contrasted sharply with the equally popular Megawati, who throughout the crisis in Indonesia preferred to keep a low public profile. In October 1997, just after the installation of the People's Congress, Amien Rais caused some commotion when, prompted by Permadi during a discussion meeting about national leadership, he professed his willingness to stand as a presidential candidate. For some time already, he had – in fact since 1993 – been agitating for a discussion about the succession, stressing that President Soeharto did not have the gift of eternal life. At the very least, Soeharto should indicate whom he was going to groom as his successor, just as Mahathir was doing with Anwar Ibrahim in Malaysia (*Forum Keadilan*, 20-10-1997:80-4). To nominate himself was seen by many as courageous. Some were afraid it might reflect negatively on Muhammadiyah, as Amien Rais had stepped into a very sensitive field by entering Soeharto's own preserve. According to Amien Rais himself, well aware that he stood no chance at all of being elected in the prevailing political climate, his willingness to be nominated was an act of political education directed to the Indonesian population, a phrase also used from time to time by others to indicate that Indonesians had for too long been subjected to a political system which required blind obedience, and that the time had come to acquaint them with the practices of a democracy. By his nomination Amien Rais wanted to make people aware that it was not correct to assume automatically that only Soeharto was entitled to became the only presidential candidate (Tim Pemburu Fakta 1998b:22-3). He was pleased with the way people had reacted. In his opinion, the positive response he had received from many quarters was an unequivocal indication that many wanted change.

A few days after Soeharto's words, Amien Rais again caused something of an uproar. He proposed that a public opinion poll be held to find out who Indonesians wanted as their next president. This was a cheap and accurate instrument to determine Soeharto's popularity, and was well suited as a task for the mass media. Soeharto's own words, Amien Rais stated, should provide Golkar leaders with the moral courage to consider the possibility of other presidential candidates. He also used the occasion to reiterate an idea he had launched the previous month: Soeharto's speech should form the starting point for a frank public discussion, a national dialogue, to get input from the society at large about the criteria a president should meet and about the most suitable candidate for the presidency, or it least who should succeed Soeharto in the future.

Others immediately blocked the suggestion by referring to the problems arising in organizing such a meeting. The People's Congress, Habibie and Siswono Yudohusodo commented, provided the place for such a dialogue, not a wider forum in which the critics of the government and representatives of NGOs could also participate. The idea won the support of Nurcholish Madjid, who urged people not to concentrate on the practical problems, but to see the suggestion as an exercise in looking for alternative leaders. Another person to take up the suggestion was Sukmawati Soekarnoputri, one of Soekarno's daughters. Early in January she formed the Komite Nasional Perjuangan Demokrat (KNPD, National Committee for the Democratic Struggle). One of its aims was to organize a national dialogue, to which critics of the government were to be invited.

In the middle of December Amien Rais went one step further, when he spoke out against the re-election of Soeharto. Were Soeharto to remain president, disaster would be the inevitable result. The People's Congress should not make the collective mistake its predecessor had made prior to 1965 when it had appointed Soekarno president for life. A seventh term in office for Soeharto would amount to the same.

With not many political leaders prepared to dispute the nomination of Soeharto publicly, partly because of the political dangers this posed, the public discussion about the vice-presidency was more lively, though often couched in veiled terms, revealing only part of what was going on behind the scenes. It was not only concerned with names. Part of the debate was about the question of whether or not the next vice-president should be somebody from the army, or whether the post could best go to a civilian. Since 1965 the vice-presidency has been held both by civilians and by people with a military background. Because Soeharto's age and for other reasons, the discussion was also about the power structure of the New Order, and the prominence of the army, its influence far outweighing that of the other branches of the Armed Forces (the navy, air force, and police). In the past few years two civilians, Habibie and Harmoko, with the backing of Soeharto, had acquired key political positions. Habibie – in 1992-1993 already mentioned as a prime rival to Try Sutrisno, then commander of the Armed Forces, in the race for the vice-presidency – was at that time a man laden with many jobs and functions – about twenty-five all told. Minister of Research and Technology since 1978 (making him the longest sitting cabinet minister), he had founded and chaired the Badan Pengkajian dan Penerapan Teknologi (BPPT, Body for the Study and Application of Technology), the Pusat Penelitian Ilmu Pengetahuan dan Teknologi (Puspitek, Centre for Scientific and Technological Research), the Badan Pengelola Industri Strategis (BPIS, Body for the Management of Strategic Industries, managing the state industrial companies), and the Dewan Riset Nasional (DRN, National Research Council). He was also the director-general of PT PAL, the state naval dockyard in Surabaya, of PT Pindad, the army industrial company for the manufacture of arms and ammunition, and of the state-owned company IPTN (Industri Pesawat Terbang Nusantara, National Aircraft Industry), founded in 1976. All three were, as was also the case with PT Krakatau Steel and a number of other 'strategic' state companies, supervised by BPIS. Further, Soeharto had entrusted him with control over the economic development of eastern Indonesia and the island Batam, and over the exploitation of the Natuna gas field in the South China Sea. Such functions, coupled with his close association with Soeharto, had not only made him a rival of army officers in the competition for important political positions, they had also opened up the possibility for him to take decisions in fields the Armed Forces considered their own preserve. It was he, for instance, who in 1992 had been instrumental in buying 39 warships from the former East German navy, which the *Far Eastern Economic Review* described as 'a navy that could barely float', involving the Indonesian navy probably only at a later stage after the decision to purchase had already been made (*Far Eastern Economic Review*, 13-5-1993:54-7, 19-2-1988:5; *Forum Keadilan*, 16-9-1993:15-6).

Harmoko, who liked to be addressed by the familiar term *bung* and not by the more formal one of *bapak*, had become general chairman of Golkar. Since the inception of the party under the umbrella of the army as an anti-communist organization in 1964, this function had always been held by retired army officers. When Harmoko became general chairman in October 1993 with the backing of Soeharto, this had been construed as a defeat for the army. It was also a clear indication that Golkar had evolved into a vehicle moving under its own power, in which leading politicians did not necessarily have the same interests as senior officers of the Armed Forces.

Now that a civilian had gained one of the most important political functions in the country (the chairman of Golkar had a great deal of influence
over who was to succeed Soeharto), losing the vice-presidency as well would
mean a further reduction in the political power of the Armed Forces, in this
case the army. Not even considering the fact that Soeharto might fall critical-
ly ill or die. There had been some reason to take such a possibility seriously.
For some months speculations about Soeharto's ill health had been rife. There
were rumours that he fell asleep while chairing cabinet meetings, or was subject to unpredictable outbursts of rage (*Kabar dari Pijar*, 9-4-1997). On 5
December 1997, on the advice of his physicians, an exhausted Soeharto took
a ten-day rest, not appearing at formal functions and cancelling a trip to
Teheran to attend the Organization of the Islamic Conference (OIC). The
president also did not go to ASEAN summit in Malaysia. Immediately
rumours began to fly that others had taken over command and that the eld-
erly president himself (he was 76 years of age) had been rushed to hospital,
even that he had died of a stroke.

In the months following the general elections, another topic of debate was
the procedure to be followed in selecting a *balon (bakal calon)*, or future candidate for the vice-presidency. Should the factions in the People's Congress –
that is, the three political parties, the Armed Forces, and the Regional
Representation – come up with one common, single candidate, as had been
the custom in the past, or could there be more candidates fielded from whom
the representatives could choose their favourite? Some politicians and officials tried to avoid making specific comments about the most suitable or likely candidate by pointing out that it was the prerogative of a newly elected
president to suggest who his deputy should be. This course should again be
pursued, it was argued, because close cooperation between the two was a
prerequisite for the smooth running of the state. A vice-president had to be
able to cooperate with the president, *ergo* had to be 'close' to him. This was,
Harmoko said in January 1998, the 'criterion plus' with which a candidate
had to be endowed. One sign of 'closeness' was to have been a witness at the
marriage of Soeharto's son Hutomo Mandala Putra (Ginandjar Kartasasmita
and Habibie). Accentuating such a factor, at times when it appeared that certain candidates were threatening to lose out in the race, one or other of his
supporters hastened to stress that the person in question, too, was close to
Soeharto.

The discussion about the appropriate moment of nomination was also not
without relevance. Past developments had shown that an early nomination
by Golkar or the Armed Forces could be decisive, as the other in this tandem
was morally obliged to keep up an outward appearance of unanimity and
virtually had no choice but to endorse the same person. In 1988 the precipitate nomination of Golkar's General Soedharmono had assured his election

as vice-president, in spite of opposition from senior army officers, the most important being General L.B. (Leonardus Benyamin, or Benny) Moerdani, then commander of the Armed Forces. At that time, one officer, Brigadier-General Ibrahim Saleh, had taken the unprecedented step, at least in the Indonesian political situation, of interrupting a plenary session of the People's Congress to protest against the choice. What happened in the general session of the People's Congress in that year had quite plainly shown that it was dangerous for a politician to advance his own name, thereby disregarding a consensus which had the blessing of the president. In 1988 H.J. Naro, then general chairman of PPP, had formally been nominated by his party as its candidate for the vice-presidency during the general session of the People's Congress. His nomination was endorsed behind the scenes by military officers who were keen to reject the candidacy of Soedharmono (see Mardjono 1997:40-1). Naro only withdrew at the last moment when, as could have been foreseen, the other factions all publicly stood by Soedharmono as the person who should become vice-president. Among the arguments Golkar put forward at that time to account for its rejection of Naro's nomination was that any uncontentious cooperation between himself and Soeharto was out of the question. The event marked the end of Naro's formal career as a politician.

The army and the powerful Benny Moerdani, appointed Minister of Defence and Security in 1988, had also learned their lesson. In 1993, when it appeared that Habibie might be the next vice-president, Lieutenant-General Harsudiono Hartas, then Chief of Staff for Social and Political Affairs, and at the same time chairman of the Armed Forces faction in the People's Congress, prematurely put Try Sutrisno's name forward as the Armed Forces candidate, pre-empting the election of Habibie.

The race for the vice-presidency for 1998-2003 promised to be as tense as on the two earlier occasions. Among the names mentioned most frequently in 1997 as suitable or likely candidates for the vice-presidency were those of General R. Hartono (Chief of Staff of the Army), Air Vice Marshall (Ret.) Ginandjar Kartasasmita (Minister of National Development Planning, Chairman of Bappenas, the National Planning Bureau), Bacharuddin Jusuf (Rudy) Habibie (Minister of Research and Technology), General (Ret.) Try Sutrisno (incumbent vice-president), and Soeharto's daughter, Siti Hardijanti Rukmana.

Of the five, General Hartono had been the political 'mentor' of Siti Hardijanti Rukmana when she had begun her political career in Golkar. Since then he had never failed to turn up each time she organized a Golkar event. The public were well aware that Hartono was the only general who had attended the Golkar conference in October wearing a yellow Golkar outfit. This close association with Mbak Tutut was enough for some to rate his chances highly. This was given an extra fillip as before the election he had also been invited by Abdurrahman Wahid to be a guest of honour at some of the meetings he and Tutut had attended. This, too, had been a bolt from the blue, as in December 1994 Abdurrahman Wahid and others had still been accusing Hartono, at that moment the Armed Forces Chief of Staff for Social and Political Affairs, of supporting Abdurrahman Wahid's main rival in the competition for leadership, Abu Hasan, during a bitter dispute within NU. A coalition seemed to be in the making, which, according to one interpretation, was to block any further advance by Habibie. Hartono was suddenly retired at the beginning of June 1997, officially to replace Harmoko as Minister of Information.[9] The cabinet reshuffle came as a shock. In view of the moment it took place, and suspecting that, as was his wont, Soeharto would select the vice-president from among people who had held a ministerial post, his appointment made Hartono a very likely candidate in the eyes of some. The following month Hartono, known to be a devout Muslim who comes from a Madurese *santri* background, announced his intention of joining ICMI, indicating that by doing so he would have a share in deciding the policy of ICMI and its newspaper *Republika*. After ICMI's general chairman, Habibie, and Hartono himself both had formally asked President Soeharto, the ICMI's patron, permission for Hartono to join the association (which was required in the case of a cabinet minister), and Moerdiono, the State Secretary, had also discussed the matter with the president, on 27 August Hartono received membership card number 060 – a singular honour, it seems, based on the statement by ICMI's general secretary Adi Sasono that card numbers below 100 were reserved for cabinet ministers and other important persons (*Merdeka*, 28-8-1997).

In Indonesian political thinking of that period, if such an important person joined such an important political organization, he must have an ulterior motive. Two theories circulated. One was that Hartono's brief was to act as a kind of watchdog to check on the political role of ICMI, and perhaps he would later become its general chairman, a theory which made some ICMI members somewhat suspicious. The other theory was that ICMI membership was a step towards strengthening Hartono's political position, possibly with the vice-presidency as his ultimate goal. Concomitant with this was the observation by some that ICMI's influence was waning, and consequently that maybe even Habibie's political career was coming to an end. A number of clues were advanced for this: Amien Rais, presented as a close associate of

---

[9]   The new Army Chief of Staff was General Wiranto, up to that moment commander of Kostrad, the Komando Cadangan Strategis Angkatan Darat, the Army Strategic Reserve Command. From 1989 to 1993 Wiranto had been Soeharto's military adjutant, and from 1993 to 1996 military commander of Jakarta. Within a month Wiranto's name was also mentioned as a possible candidate.

Habibie in this scenario, had been forced to step down as chairman of the Council of Experts. Another member, Parni Hadi, had been replaced as editor-in-chief of *Republika* in early June, allegedly because the newspaper had become too critical of the government (*Forum Keadilan: Edisi Khusus Desember 1997*:31).[10] On top of this, in August a number of prominent ICMI members – Adi Sasono (its secretary-general, and also considered too critical), Prof. Dr Muladi SH (a member of its Council of Experts), Prof. Dawam Rahardjo (a member of its Council of Chairmen), Dr Watik Pratiknya, and Dr Jimly Asshiddiqie (deputy secretary-general) – had been dropped from the list of Golkar nominees for a seat in the People's Council.[11] The following month it was rumoured that Adi Sasono was to become an ambassador, an appointment at times used to get rid of persons who found themselves out of favour. Those who followed this interpretation saw Hartono as the new star. The reason he himself gave for becoming a member was that it was something he had been wanting to do for some time, but that his active service in the army and the rule that officers should not enter social or political organizations before retirement had precluded this.

The fact that Harmoko, one of Soeharto's most trusted confidants, lost his position as Minister of Information was an equally big surprise. The more so because it was only the third time during the New Order that a minister had been replaced in between terms, and to make Harmoko's replacement less conspicuous Soeharto could have waited only a few more months, till after his re-election as president, when he would have to form a new cabinet. One of the explanations was that Harmoko, who had been Minister of Information since 1983, had displeased the president because he had failed to improve Soeharto's image in the foreign press (*Golkar* 1999:32). Another was that he had displeased Soeharto by bungling the drafting of a Broadcasting Act, though in actual fact the Act had been formulated in close cooperation with the palace.[12] The Act was endorsed by parliament in December 1996, but President Soeharto had sent it back to parliament in July for revision – a step which the speaker of parliament later described as 'unusual'. It was the first time in Indonesia's history that an Act had been returned to parliament. According to one Golkar member of parliament, Manginsara Marcos Lubis, this was a sign of Harmoko's failure to communicate 'harmoniously' with the president (*The Jakarta Post*, 8-9-1997). The changes required by the president

---

[10] Parni Hadi retained his position as editor-in-chief of the government news agency Antara.
[11] Some ICMI and Golkar leaders refused to use the term 'dropped', because of the political connotations of the word and the impression it created of a rift between ICMI and Golkar.
[12] Others were of the opinion that Harmoko had done his job as general chairman of Golkar too well, giving Golkar its large victory, which had as an undesired result that PDI had been reduced to total insignificance, upsetting the political balance which had been maintained for years.

included better conditions for private TV stations, an area in which his daughter, Siti Hardijanti Rukmana, and son, Bambang Trihatmodjo, have an important stake. Amongst other conditions, the original stipulation allowing state television to broadcast commercials was withdrawn. Then Habibie suggested publicly that Harmoko might be 'prepared' to become the new chairman of parliament and the People's Congress. This was immediately interpreted as a move by Habibie to eliminate Harmoko as a rival for the vice-presidency. Not much later, though, Harmoko supporters began to argue that two former vice-presidents had been chairmen of parliament and the People's Congress, and that this function was one of the advantages Harmoko had in his pocket in the race for the vice-presidency. Whatever the reason, intimates reported that Harmoko had been depressed and had wept after hearing of his dismissal (Golkar 1999:32).

After losing his position as Minister of Information, Harmoko was almost immediately appointed Minister without Portfolio of Special Affairs. The 'special affair' he had to see to was the 'informing' (pembekalan) of members of the new People's Congress. They were to receive information during six day-long meetings at the presidential palace in Bogor in August and September. This included special courses about the Pancasila. Harmoko stressed that the special briefings for members of the People's Congress should not be interpreted as indoctrination. The sole aim was to prepare them better for their task, at a time when the population was increasingly making its voice heard.

The third person who figured prominently in speculations about the vice-presidency, Habibie, was probably among the most controversial players at that time. He was one of the most trusted associates of Soeharto, to whom he was almost an adopted son, had ICMI as his political vehicle, and could count on a wealth of support from the Islamic organizations which form part of Golkar. In the army he had a number of Islamic-oriented officers as his supporters. Over and against his position of strength, he also had his inveterate opponents. Within the Armed Forces, widespread resentment reigned over his involvement in the purchase and production of armaments; his economic ideas came in for their fair share of criticism, while certain quarters viewed with distrust his efforts to develop ICMI. Habibie's attempt to give Indonesia her own national aircraft industry and the opinions he vented about the economic path Indonesia should follow had earned him the reputation of being a big spender. Some of his critics considered the emphasis he laid on the development of high-technology industry unsuitable to plans for the sustained development of Indonesia. In the past few years a discussion had been waged between the proponents of 'Widjojonomics', named after one of the persons who had been largely responsible for Indonesia's economic recovery at the beginning of the New Order, Widjojo Nitisastro, and those advocating a greater emphasis on the advanced technology and capital-intensive investments of 'Habibienomics', which would decrease Indonesia's dependence on the outside world in the advanced industrial sector. As early as 1993 in one of its reports the World Bank criticized the latter approach. The prevailing argument was that Indonesia should focus on labour-intensive investments, for instance, in the textile and footwear industries, so as to be able to accommodate its growing unskilled workforce. The report was critical of a 'technological leap-frogging strategy, involving the development of high-tech industries supported by direct public investment or subsidies and high levels of protection'. It judged such a policy 'ill-advised' (*The Jakarta Post*, 7-6-1993). At that time the 'Habibie' approach had gained some support from Ginandjar Kartasasmita, who, not relishing the thought of being condemned to a 'pinching sandals technology', argued that Indonesia had formed its own strategy with regard to technological development which combined both approaches (*Republika*, 7-6-1993).

Others, and Abdurrahman Wahid was one of the most outspoken in this respect, attacked both the founding and the functioning of ICMI, in which, though the political and religious orientation of its members was diverse, exponents of what is often described in Indonesia as 'radical Muslims' with a modernist background played a leading role. In their eyes, ICMI had reintroduced Islam as a factor in political strife. In view of the dangers of inviting communal disputes, they believed politics and religion should remain strictly separated. In the eyes of its critics, failure to maintain this separation made the ICMI, in Indonesian political jargon, a 'sectarian' organization. This view firmly supported the idea that religious organizations should limit their activities to the religious sphere, with outliers in the fields of welfare and education. Other organizations should take care of the interests of the whole nation, and the various groups of which it was composed. For those people who stressed the importance of Islam in all spheres of life, terms like sectarian or primordial sentiments were seen as being used to block the advance of Islam in the political sphere, and thus were an invention of the enemies of Islam (see, for instance, Mardjono 1998:27, 32).

Habibie's name had been mentioned as a strong candidate from the start. In September he was appointed deputy coordinator of the powerful Daily Presidium of the Council of Patrons of Golkar.[13] This move led to increased speculation that Habibie was being groomed for the position of vice-president. Concomitantly an influential ICMI leader, Lieutenant-General (Ret.) Achmad Tirtosudiro, from 1966 to 1972 head of Bulog, the Body for Logistic Affairs, stated that Habibie was ready for the function provided that the

---

[13]   On 31 December, Habibie was appointed coordinator of this board: Akbar Tanjung became its deputy coordinator.

people asked him to accept it. Habibie denied that he had ever discussed the topic with Tirtosudiro, adding that lengthy speculation about the names of candidates for the vice-presidency was a 'Dutch' (or Western) habit. Indonesians, irrespective of their ethnic background, should neither raise nor answer questions about such a candidacy. They should abide by the procedures laid down by Pancasila democracy.

Equally controversial was the potential candidacy of Siti Hardijanti Rukmana. When her name came up as a possible candidate for the vice-presidency, she was already a chairperson of Golkar, and a member of the ICMI Advisory Council. Many were the speculations about her rise in power in Golkar, and her being responsible for the apparent decline of Habibie's influence and Harmoko's forced resignation as Minister of Information. Some did publicly support her nomination. At one of the disputed meetings in the early months of 1997, during which Abdurrahman Wahid had introduced her as a future leader of the nation, a prayer had been said asking that Siti Hardijanti Rukmana become the next vice-president. Such a prospect seemed to recede again for a moment when the chairman of the DPA (Dewan Pertimbangan Agung, the Supreme Advisory Council), Admiral (Ret.) Sudomo, after a meeting with Soeharto, stated that it was not very likely that Tutut would be nominated as, in the past, the position had usually gone to a cabinet member or some other senior civilian or military official. Her name was mentioned again in September by KH Mustofa Bisri, a member of the Religious Advisory Council of NU, who revived Abdurrahman Wahid's qualification of her as a future leader of the nation. Mustofa Bisri claimed that one of the points in her favour was her contacts as a businesswoman with the heads of large business concerns. A second point in her favour was that she was 'close' to the president. In September such voices led briefly to a discussion about who would be a more suitable candidate – Habibie or Tutut. For others, the nomination of Tutut came too early. Suhardiman (deputy chairman of the Supreme Advisory Council, and chairman of the Presidium of SOKSI, the Sentral Organisasi Karyawan Swadiri Indonesia, one of the components of Golkar) said unequivocally that to prevent people from tossing about words such as nepotism, she should not seek the position. It would be best for her to await her election as general chairperson of Golkar, and maybe stand as a presidential candidate in the year 2003. In December her star seemed to rise again, when suddenly out of the blue Harmoko stated that there was no rule forbidding a woman from becoming vice-president. Immediately his words were seized on and construed as an indication that Siti Hardijanti Rukmana stood a good chance.

It was in the nomination of a candidate for the vice-presidency and from which group he or she was to come that the raw contest for power really revealed itself. It was a subject about which not everybody was prepared to show his cards, some preferring to wait for a clear hint from Soeharto indicating whom he preferred. Soeharto had a doubly decisive say in the matter. He was to be the new president, and as chairman of the Council of Patrons of Golkar, he had the final say in all that party did. Under the circumstances, betting on the wrong person could well have political consequences. It could, for instance, displease Soeharto. Publicly mentioning favourites meant disclosing differences of opinion and rivalries, which politicians and officers did not want to reveal to the outside world. The result was that, though names were mentioned, spokesmen of important political, social, and religious organizations and of the Armed Forces remained publicly uncommitted and refused to touch upon the subject in public. Among these was Golkar. Its official position adopted after its meeting in the middle of October was that the vice-presidency had not been discussed and that no names had been mentioned. In fact, this was not true. The provincial branch of Kalimantan Barat had put forward the names of Try Sutrisno and Harmoko as its favourites for the vice-presidency. Other Golkar leaders refused to comment when asked about this. A fortnight later the youth organization KNPI, unable to reach a consensus amongst its participants at its national working meeting, refused to touch upon the subject. Some favoured Try Sutrisno, others Hartono, while yet others did not consider the meeting the proper place to speak out.

NU was also beset by problems. Probably there was not much love for Habibie in that organization. Abdurrahman Wahid was highly critical of ICMI, and *ulama* also had some problems with ICMI's high profile, which tended to put other Islamic groups in the shade. Towards the end of October the West Java branch spoke out in support of the Minister of Defence and Security, Edi Sudradjat. He was described as a non-controversial person and not over-ambitious, who did not like to create problems, and was concerned about the poor and the ordinary people. Undeniably he had earned his spurs in serving his country. According to Abdurrahman Wahid, who responded almost immediately, such a statement contradicted NU policy. NU did not involve itself in the selection and nomination of candidates, and would not issue a statement on this matter. Abdurrahman Wahid explained this position by expressing the fear that the bandying about of names in public could well result in chaos. Advancing the names of candidates should be left to those who had the authority to do so: the members of the People's Congress and Soeharto. The rebuke did not deter the West Java branch from continuing to express its preference for Edi Sudradjat, its leaders announcing that one of the forums at which they would do so was the NU national conference to take place in the middle of November in Lombok. The branch did not stand much chance. In matters pertaining to Soeharto, vagueness seemed to be the order of the day in NU public statements. On the eve of the conference two members of its Religious Advisory Council, KH Ilyas Ruchiyat and Dr Said

Aqil Siradj, stressed that no names of candidates for the presidency or vice-presidency were to be discussed. There were plans to investigate whether the present representative system (in which, as it was argued, the representatives of the people selected by the political parties were not always known to the electorate), including the way an Indonesian president was elected, was in accordance with Islam as adhered to by NU members. NU would accept the president elected by the People's Congress. It did support Soeharto, not for re-election as president, but to execute the process of succession in a constitutional way. The national conference, Abdurrahman Wahid was to state, would not discuss the succession; that was the prerogative of the People's Congress.

CHAPTER IV

The economic crisis

Seandainya harga sembako tak tinggi
Pasti kita makan nasi bukan makan hati
Umpamanya tidak sedang krisis ekonomi kita
pasti tidak cepat darah tinggi
Mudah-mudahan kita masih dapat rejeki
Kalau saja tidak ada PHK masal
kita masih bisa bekerja dan berkhayal
siapa tahu kita jadi konglomerat.[1]

In May 1997, the exchange rate of the Thai baht came under attack. Its devaluation in early July signalled the beginning of an economic crisis in East and
Southeast Asia. Though there was some disquiet, because of the fact that by
June private foreign debts, estimated at that moment by Bank Indonesia, the
central bank, at US$ 56 billion, had begun to exceed those of the government,
the initial effects in Indonesia were still moderate, giving Indonesians reason
to hope that most of the crisis would pass the country by (*Panji Masyarakat*,
30-6-1997:83). This was a short-lived reprieve and it was not long before the
crisis hit Indonesia with full force. The country, which up to that moment had
been praised all around for its economic achievements, entered into a severe
recession, undoing the results of years of economic development. On 11 July
the exchange rate of the rupiah, which at the end of June had been Rp 2,450
to the dollar, started to slide. On 21 July, it reached Rp 2,700 to the dollar – a
sign for the general public to rush to the bank to buy dollars.

The plunge of the rupiah proved unstoppable. Bank Indonesia tried to
intervene, spending about US$ 1.5 billion between mid-July and mid-August
(Gill 1997:55). This proved ineffective. On 14 August the central bank had to

---

[1]   Fragment from 'Ngerumpi rejeki' by Erick Yusuf: If the prices of basic necessities were not
high/ We certainly would eat rice and not liver/ Were there no economic crisis we certainly
would not often suffer high blood pressure/ Hopefully we will still earn a livelihood/ if there
are no mass lay-offs we will still be able to work and perhaps dream/ who knows we will
become a conglomerate.

abandon its control over the exchange rate. On 6 October, the rupiah reached the value of Rp 3,845 to the dollar. Panic set in on the financial market. On 8 October, the Indonesian government announced that it would seek financial assistance from IMF, the World Bank, and the Asian Development Bank. On the same day, the doyen of Indonesian economists, Prof. Widjojo Nitisastro, a nationally and internationally respected Berkeley-educated expert, was assigned the task of preparing measures to tackle the problem and of liaising with IMF. In one of his very first comments Widjojo Nitisastro, recalling the opinion that in a number of countries IMF had failed to achieve results, stressed that IMF help must not fail with respect to Indonesia.

By that time the Indonesian government had already decided to postpone or put under review 76 projects planned by government ministries or state companies. Besides toll-roads, electricity projects and the like, among the investments sacrificed were a number of prestigious mega-projects. One of these blockbusters was the building of a bridge between Indonesia and Malaysia, supposed to be the world's longest bridge. Another was the construction of the world's highest tower in Jakarta, surpassing the Petronas Towers being built at that time in Kuala Lumpur, which was to hold the record. The presidential family was well represented in the mega-projects. The bridge was to be built by a consortium headed by Soeharto's daughter, Siti Hediati Harijadi Prabowo; the tower involved Soeharto's cousin, Sudwikatmono. The plan to build a bridge connecting Java and Sumatra was another victim. In November, 15 of these axed projects were revived by presidential decree. Among the projects allowed to continue were those involving the companies of Siti Hediati Harijadi Prabowo and of Soeharto's close friend and golfing partner, Bob Hasan. The decision led to a storm of accusations of nepotism. The presidential decree was revoked on 10 January.

By October it had become evident that immense problems lay ahead. Looming large among the major structural faults was the contracting in the past of huge short-term unhedged loans abroad, mostly in dollars, by Indonesian businessmen who had not expected plummeting of the rupiah, and had been attracted by the low interest rates of such loans. It became very likely that many of the roughly 2,000 companies that had foreign debts would go bankrupt in the next three months. They would be unable to pay off the short-term loans they had contracted. Their plight was exacerbated because as the rupiah continued to fall, repayment required increasingly immense amounts of rupiahs. The value of foreign debts was enormous. The general chairman of the Indonesian Chamber of Trade and Industry, Ir Aburizal Bakrie (head of the Bakrie and Brothers Concern, and informally known as Ical) estimated that the value of short-term loans in the form of commercial paper which had to be paid off before the end of the year exceeded US$ 20 billion (Jawa Pos, 12-10-1997). In January the same figure was mentioned in a joint Indonesian-IMF document as being the volume of short-term debts at the end of 1997.

The picture of corporate foreign debt, a large part of it in short-term loans, Frankenstein's monster, one magazine dubbed it, became even gloomier as the weeks passed (*Ummat*, 12-1-1998:38). In the middle of November Indonesia's Minister of Finance, Mar'ie Muhammad, mentioned a figure of US$ 65 billion in this respect. Not only did companies have difficulty honouring their financial obligations, but the redeeming of such debts put an enormous pressure on the Indonesian demand for dollars. To tackle the problem a special commission, Tim Penanggulangan Utang Luar Negeri Swasta (TPULNS, Private Foreign Debt Settlement Team), was formed at the end of December. It was headed by Radius Prawiro, who had to negotiate a rescheduling of debts with foreign creditors. He was assisted by three businessmen: Rachmat Gobel, an indigenous entrepreneur, head of the National Gobel concern, Anthony Salim, a Chinese belonging to the wealthiest business family in Indonesia, and The Ning King, a Bandung-born Chinese, heading the Agro Manunggal concern, who had grown rich from the textile industry and the production of automobile components.

At the end of January 1998 Radius Prawiro disclosed that 228 Indonesian companies had difficulty in paying off their foreign debts. The following month he was to add that an initial inventory had shown that corporate debt amounted 'only' to US$ 23 billion. The total amount of private foreign debts was US$ 74 billion. The difference of US$ 51 billion was held mostly by foreign firms and joint ventures (Mann 1998:150). The foreign debts of the Indonesian government and of state companies was US$ 63.5 billion. On the same occasion Radius Prawiro ruled out the possibility that the government would give any financial support to the companies in trouble. Judging from letters to the editor, such assistance would have been a very unpopular measure. The people's money should not be given to those who were held responsible for the monetary crisis by the general public (see for instance Ghazali 1998:49). Righteous though their anger was, without such government support and without foreign money-lenders agreeing to a rescheduling of debts, a large part of the Indonesian business world was in deep trouble.

The fall of the rupiah and all the consequences this entailed focused attention on some of the peculiar features of Indonesia's economy – features which had been the object of almost continuous criticism since the early 1970s. The rampant corruption and nepotism and the existence of trade monopolies were frequent targets for criticism. Apart from this, financial experts and others immediately began to call for the rigorous restructuring of the country's debt-ridden banking sector as a basic requirement for the restoration of domestic and international confidence in the economy. Such a suggestion directly touched the interests of the most powerful businessmen and women in

Indonesia, the so-called 'conglomerates', who headed immense business concerns, holding the majority of shares in banks and a diversity of companies,
or who had spread their capital over a great many firms. As many held shares
and board seats in the same companies, their business interests were inter-
locked, though such cross-holdings did not prevent them from fighting over
control of individual companies and new projects. In building their business
empires, these persons had made good use of preferential treatments offered
by government institutions and of their relations with holders of power, who
themselves, in turn, were rewarded with part of the gain. Sometimes, as was
the case with Soeharto's children, this was fixed by using 'empty shares',
becoming shareholders in an investment without having to provide any
money, but only, as one of them expressed it, 'good will' (Soesilo 1998:92). An
additional factor which gave some of the discussions about the position of the
conglomerates a racial undertone was that many of the business tycoons were
Chinese. Some of them came from so-called *peranakan* families, who had lived
in Indonesia for generations. Others were Chinese who had been born outside
Indonesia and had migrated to Indonesia in their youth.

Two of them in particular stood out, not least because of their close relationship with Soeharto. Most prominent among the Chinese businessmen
was Sudono Salim or Liem Sioe Liong, also referred to as Om (*oom*, or uncle)
Liem, the 'godfather' of the Indonesian Chinese business community, until
the economic crisis one of the richest men in Asia.[2] Born in China as the son
of a small farmer, he migrated to Indonesia in 1938, settling in Kudus. During
the Indonesian War of Independence he supplied the Indonesian army with
food, uniforms, and medicines. In 1951 he moved to Jakarta, where he founded the Bank Windu Kencana in 1954. This debut in the banking world failed,
but in 1957 Liem established the Central Bank Asia, which three years later
was renamed Bank Central Asia. BCA was to become Indonesia's largest and
most successful bank, with 750 branches. Liem's relationship with Soeharto
dates from the early 1950s. Later, when Soeharto had been appointed commander of Kostrad, the Strategic Reserve Command of the Army, Liem Sioe
Liong became the supplier to this command.

Among the other firms he owned or in which he had a stake were the
Bogasari Flour Mills (the largest flour producer in Indonesia, controlling
about 80 per cent of the market), Indocement Tunggal Prakarsa (producing
about half of Indonesia's cement; part of its shares are owned by the
Indonesian government, which saved the company from bankruptcy in the
1980s), Indofood Sukses Makmur (by far the largest producer in Indonesia of

---

2   For the biographies of Liem Sioe Liong and other Chinese businessmen, see Suryadinata
(1997) and Kunio (1988). For Liem Sioe Liong see also in particular *Forum Keadilan*, 15-12-
1997:87-90 and Anwari SB 1998b:24-30.

instant noodles, and products such as soya sauce and chili paste), Indomobil Sukses International, Hagemeyer, and the Hong Kong-based First Pacific Holding. The Salim Group, daily management of which is in the hands of his son Anthony Salim, consisted of over 450 companies.

Among Liem's firms which attracted a welter of public criticism was Bogasari Flour Mills, a company founded in 1969 to mill wheat given to Indonesia as food aid by the United States. It formed the basis of the present Salim imperium. Since December 1971, when its first flour mill was opened, until 1997 it held a virtual monopoly on the production of flour, which is the basic ingredient in instant noodles, of which Liem's Indofood is the major producer. The import of the wheat needed for the flour was one of the monopolies held by Bulog, the state Body for Logistic Affairs, established at the beginning of the New Order in 1966 as the government's distributor of foodstuffs. Wheat imported by Bulog went first to Bogasari to be milled, and after that it went back to Bulog to be distributed and sold. Symbolic of this flow of goods is that Ms Christine Arifin, the wife of a former head of Bulog, is a major shareholder in Bogasari. In principle she holds one-fifth of the shares to ensure that this percentage of Bogasari is used for charitable ends.

In the eyes of Liem and Soeharto there was nothing wrong with the preferential treatment of companies like Bogasari and Indocement. Their dominant position was defended to the outside world as follows: motivated by the desire to do something good for the country, Liem was the only person in Indonesia who, when the need was sorest, dared to take the risk of founding factories to produce goods the country so urgently required. Or, as Soeharto chose to put it in 1995, 'there is no collusion between me and Om Liem, it [was started] in the interest of the people and the state' (Anwari SB 1998b:25). In the summer of 1997 Liem Sioe Liong was also subject to fierce criticism when he announced the sale of 51 per cent of the shares in Indofood held by Indocement to Quality Asian Food Ltd (QAF) in Singapore, another one of his own companies. He was accused of unpatriotic behaviour and of being engaged in draining capital because he was afraid the political situation in Indonesia would deteriorate. After a visit to President Soeharto, two cabinet ministers hastened to explain that Liem had done nothing wrong. One of them, the Secretary of State, Moerdiono, commented that a sale of shares which seized the opportunities provided by the global market and enlarged Indonesia's export network was nationalism in a new guise; a description which caused Indonesians rich and poor to wonder what was meant by it. The Asian crisis spoiled Liem's plans. In January 1998 it was made known that the sale of Indofood shares had been postponed.

Of almost equal economic stature was Muhammad (Bob) Hasan, or The Kian Sing, who in contrast to Liem is referred to by his Indonesian and not his Chinese name.[3] He is a very close friend of Soeharto and because of this was supposed to wield so much political influence that Indonesians considered him to be the 'de facto vice-president' (Winarno 1997:105). Through him people, including cabinet ministers and senior civil servants, tried to get the ear of the president. As is the case with Liem, Hasan's relations with Soeharto also date back to the 1950s when Hasan, born in Semarang in 1931, was adopted as his son by General Gatot Soebroto, at that time in command of the army in Central Java and as such Soeharto's direct superior. Their cooperation had became more intense after Soeharto's appointment as commander of the Diponegoro Division in 1965. Hasan became one of Soeharto's partners in business activities, allegedly, as in the case of other officers, also involving smuggling, undertaken to supplement the division's income received from the state, which was insufficient to take care of the troops in a proper way. In this case, as Soeharto was to argue, the activities were also to help the local population. In the foundation which had been set up for this purpose, Yayasan Pembangunan Territorium Empat (Foundation for the Development of the Fourth Territorium), Hasan became, as he phrased it in 1999, Soeharto's advisor for economic and financial affairs (Dwipayana and Ramadhan 1989:90; Perspektif, 25-2-1999:25). At one point it was considered bringing charges against Soeharto, but the then Chief of Staff of the Army, Abdul Haris Nasution, decided against. Soeharto was relieved of his command to allow him to follow courses at the Staff and Command School of the Army (Nasution 1985:24-5; Kontroversi 1998:60).

Hasan heads a vast and diversified business empire, with a larger or smaller stake in about 300 companies. One of the concerns of which he is the bos, as such a position is often called in Indonesia, is the Nusamba Group (short for Nusantara Ampera Bhakti). Bob Hasan and Soeharto's son, Sigit Harjojudanto, each hold 10 per cent of the shares in Nusamba. The remaining 80 per cent is owned by three foundations founded by Soeharto, Yayasan Supersemar, Yayasan Dharmais, and Yayasan Dakab. Two other business concerns in which he figures prominently are the Kalimanis Group and the Tugu Pratama Indonesia (TPI) concern. In the latter, Nusamba owns about one-third of the shares. The TPI mainly displays itself in the fields of assurance and property, having a monopoly on insurance for export of plywood. Among TPI's clients were also Pertamina (itself holding the remaining shares, but, as one of its presidents was to complain in February 1999, the decisions were taken by Bob Hasan's Nusamba) and Garuda Indonesia Airways.

Like every respectable businessman of the New Order, Bob Hasan controlled a number of banks: Bank Umum Tugu, Bank Umum Nasional (BUN), Bank Duta (of Yayasan Supersemar, which he saved from ruin in 1995), and

3   See amongst others Ummat, 30-3-1998:29-30; Perspektif, 3-3-1999:24-5.

Bank Bukopin, partly acquired since the end of the 1980s on the instructions of Soeharto to revitalize ailing banks. He also holds the majority of shares in Indonesia's Islamic bank, Bank Muamalat, into which he injected new life in the mid-1990s. His banking and assurance activities earned him the nick-name Money King (*Perspektif*, 3-3-1999:25). Much more popular, however, is the sobriquet King of the Forest. This is because one of the core activities of Bob Hasan, at times also described as the Shadow Minister of Forestry, is in the timber industry and related fields, such as the production and import of paper, including newsprint. His being a major holder of forestry concessions made him the butt of criticism when huge forest fires afflicted Indonesia in the second half of 1997, the haze making normal life in parts of Indonesia and neighbouring countries impossible. It was one of many disasters to hit Indonesia in that year, and added more fuel to doubts about the way the country was run.[4]

His hold over the plywood trade was highly contested. Hasan was chair-man of Asosiasi Panel Kayu Indonesia (Apkindo, Indonesian Wood Panel Association), and of Masyarakat Perhutanan Indonesia (MPI, Indonesian Forestry Society), also controlling Asosiasi Mebel Kayu Indonesia (Asmindo, Indonesian Wood Furniture Association). In the course of time Apkindo had succeeded in improving Indonesia's performance in the export of plywood, but this did not save it from criticism. For years Indonesian plywood pro-ducers had been forced to sell their product via Apkindo, which set and dis-tributed export quotas, arranged sales abroad, and fixed prices.[5] Apart from the levies this Association demanded (reduced in 1997 from US$ 15 per cubic metre to US$ 10), its members were forced to ship their exports with the Karana Line and insure their cargo with Asuransi Tugu Pratama. Bob Hasan has a majority of the shares in both companies. Among his other functions was that of chairman of Asosiasi Pengusaha Hutan Indonesia (APHI, Association of Indonesian Forest Entrepreneurs). To renew their concessions, its members had to present aerial photographs. Mapindo Parama, the com-pany which held the sole right to take these photos – according to critics for too high a price, while delivery of the photos was also uncertain – was owned by Bob Hasan. He and Anthony Salim are two of the five major share-holders of Astra International, Indonesia's largest car producer, which had been founded by yet another wealthy Chinese businessman, William Soeryadjaya (Tjia Kian Liong). A third one is the lumber tycoon Prajogo

---

[4]   In December 1998 the Ministry of Forestry was to reveal that nine million hectares of for-est were owned or controlled by relatives and associates of Soeharto. The biggest concession holder (3.5 million hectares) was Prajogo Pangestu with his Barito Pacific company. Hasan ranked fourth with 1.6 million hectares. (*The Jakarta Post*, 1-12-1998)
[5]   Bob Hasan defended the Apkindo policy by maintaining that it was the Ministry of Industry and Trade which set the quotas and not his organization.

Pangestu (Phang Djun Phen). Besides its other diverse business ventures, Astra is the producer of the popular Kijang car and of Honda motorcycles.

This list would not be complete without mentioning the name of Sofyan Wanandi (Liem Bian Koen). Sofyan Wanandi, who heads the Gemala and Pakarti Yoga groups, was born in West Sumatra in 1941. In his youth he was counted among Indonesia's most prominent student leaders. In 1966 and 1967, he was chairman of the presidium of Kesatuan Aksi Mahasiswa Indonesia (KAMI, the Indonesian Students' Action Front) which spearheaded the student demonstrations against Soekarno, while for years, between 1967 and 1988, he had been a member of the People's Congress. His business career started in 1974 when Kostrad asked him to manage a number of its companies. In recent years he has acted as spokesman for the Chinese business conglomerates. Sofyan Wanandi is not liked by President Soeharto, who considers him too arrogant (*Panji Masyarakat*, 23-2-1998:18).

Equally conspicuous in the business world as some of the Chinese conglomerates, is what is referred to as the Palace or the Family, the children, grandchildren, sons- and daughters-in-law, and other relatives of Soeharto. The economic empires they were able to carve out made for much bad blood, not only among the ordinary population, but also among their business rivals who, though cooperating with them, had to contend with the economic power they could exert. Right in the forefront are the children of Soeharto, sometimes referred to by the acronym PPP, *putra putri presiden*: his daughters Siti Hardijanti Hastuti Rukmana (Tutut, Mbak Tutut, or Si Mbak, That Elder Sister), Siti Hediati Harijadi Prabowo (Titiek), and Siti Hutami Endang Adiningsih (Mamiek), and his sons Sigit Harjojudanto, Bambang Trihatmodjo (Bambang Tri or simply BT), and Hutomo Mandala Putra (Tommy).[6] His grandchildren, most prominent or notorious among them Sigit's son Ari, were also busy carving out a business empire for themselves. His notoriety was partly caused by frequent rumours that he was engaged in the smuggling of the drug ecstasy, partly also by the fact that he was engaged in the import of alcoholic drinks, succeeding for a time in getting the sole right to supply alcoholic drinks in Bali.[7]

---

[6]   In 1998 and 1999 various inventories appeared of the business interests of the Soeharto family and their close associates on internet and in bookform. See for instance *Harta Soeharto* n.d.; Anwari SB 1998a; Aditjondro 1998a 1998b, 1998c; Soesilo 1998; Sasongko 1998d. Newspapers and periodicals published such information as well.

[7]   Similar reports circulated about his uncle Tommy. In November 1998 Bob Hasan fired the editor-in-chief of *Gatra*, after the previous month this weekly had published a report on Tommy's involvement in the sale of *shabu-shabu* (crystal methamphetamine) in Australia (Loebis 1999:102). Tommy filed a lawsuit against *Gatra*, demanding compensation of 50,000 tons of rice to be distributed among the poor. His charge was rejected by the Court of Central Jakarta, as the *Gatra* article had included denials by Ari Sigit and by the Victorian police.

Tutut, Bambang, and Tommy have the highest economic profile of Soeharto's children. Siti Hardijanti Rukmana, 'the toll-road queen', heads the Grup Citra Lamtoro Gung Persada (CLG), to which firms like Citra Marga Nusaphala Persada (CMNP), participating in the building and managing of toll-roads in Indonesia, Malaysia, the Philippines, and China belong. Other firms in the Citra concern are Citra Flour Mills Nusantara, and Citra Transport Nusantara, exploiting Citra taxis and public buses. Bambang, holding 38 per cent of the shares, headed the Bimantara Citra Group, in which Indra Rukmana, the husband of Tutut, has a stake of 14 per cent.

Tommy heads the Humpuss Group, short for Hutomo Mandala Putra Soeharto Sumahardjuno, of which part of the shares are also owned by Sigit Harjojudanto. Among his many activities was that of chief director of Timor Putra Nasional (TPN). Financed at the instigation of the government by soft loans to the tune of US$ 690 million, with an exceptionally low interest rate of six per cent, furnished by a consortium of banks, among them BCA, Bank Danamon and Bank Lippo, headed by one of the state banks, Bank Dagang Negara, it was to produce what was designated as Indonesia's national car, the Timor (short for Teknologi Industri Mobil Rakyat), clearly following the example of Malaysia and her Proton national car, of which since 1994 Siti Hardijanti Rukmana had become the sole agent in Indonesia (Aditjondro 1998a:29). The stated aim was to develop Indonesia's own automotive industry. The idea was to produce a car which at the end of its first year would be made of up to 20 per cent Indonesian components, at the end of the second year 40 per cent, and at the end of the third year, when the government promised other competitors might be considered as potential producers of a national car, 60 per cent. By presidential instruction it was arranged in February 1996 that the producer of the national car was to receive exemption from import tax and luxury tax for a period of three years. In June 1996, in a special presidential decree, it was stated that the conditions also applied to completely-built-up cars produced outside Indonesia which met these criteria, and had been produced abroad with Indonesian labour. Production was started in a joint venture with the South Korean firm KIA Motors. After his fall, when he was questioned about alleged corruption, Soeharto was to defend his action by referring to the national policy of reaching economic autonomy, in particular in the field of transportation. At that time he further stressed that Tommy had been allowed to produce the national car because he was the only one who had submitted a proposal. Initially the car was entirely produced in South Korea and imported into Indonesia fully built. This gave Indonesians enough reason to change the meaning of the abbreviation *mobnas* from *mobil nasional* (national car) into *mobil buatan negara asing*, foreign-made car, while others joked that the only thing Indonesian about the car was its name (Basri 1997:56; Prasetyohadi 1998:7). The government maintained that the Timor was a national car. The reasons given were that Indonesian workers were employed in the KIA factory, while in producing the Timor KIA used parts imported from Indonesia.

From the start of the project, the special credit facilities and the exemptions on import and luxury tax were greeted with a storm of criticism. The tax department was also not overjoyed, showing this as early as September 1996, by trying to prevent the import of Timor cars before it had been ascertained that they indeed fulfilled the conditions set in the presidential instruction. Inside and outside Indonesia the Timor car was generally viewed as the outstanding example of what was wrong with the way the Indonesian economy functioned. The facilities received resulted in Japan, supported by the United States and the European Union, lodging a complaint with the World Trade Organization that Indonesia had violated the GATT (General Agreement on Tariffs and Trade). The general chairman of the Indonesian Chamber of Trade and Industry, Aburizal Bakrie, reacted furiously to the charge, threatening a boycott of Japanese products. GINSI, the Association of Indonesian Importers, made a similar threat. New problems arose in 1997 when the real producer of the car, KIA, ran into financial troubles. In June the import of the Timor, in a 'completely built up' form, was temporarily terminated, but import in 'completely knocked down' form continued. At that point, Timor sales had not yet achieved the aims set, selling approximately only two thousand cars a month, half of the target.[8]

Other Soeharto relatives were his half-brother, Probosutedjo, who is chief director of the Mercu Buana group, and Soeharto's cousin, Sudwikatmono. The latter cooperates closely with the Salim Group. Like Liem he is, for instance, a major shareholder of Indocement Tunggal Prakarsa (of which he is the president director) and Indofood Sukses Makmur. Among his other business ventures are the Golden Truly Group (supermarkets), the Subentra Group (cinemas, films, magazines), the Astenia Group (trade and real estate), and the Wijaya Kusuma Group (agriculture and mining). Bank Surya and Bank Subentra are also part of his far-flung business empire. In all he has a stake in about 300 companies. Sudwikatmono, or more familiarly Dwi, was among the first big businessmen of the New Order. His rise to economic power dates from the early years of the regime, when he joined Liem Sioe Liong and two other businessmen, Ibrahim Risjad and Djuhar Sutanto, to found Waringin Kencana. In the familiar fashion of business operations in Indonesia, Sudwikatmono's function in this 'Gang of Four' was to contact the bureaucracy and senior military officers to acquire the necessary permits and permission (*Panji Masyarakat*, 12-1-1998:36-40).

---

[8]   In November 1997, and allegedly at the instigation of IMF, Tommy resigned as president director of PT Timor Putra Nasional. He became its president commissioner.

At times Soeharto's relatives were bitter business rivals. The preferential treatment given to the Timor resulted in much bad blood between Tommy and Bambang. It adversely affected Citra Mobil Nusantara of Bambang Trihatmodjo, which produced the Bimantara cars. Rumours, only published on paper after Soeharto's fall, even had it that Mrs Tien Soeharto had not died of a heart attack in April 1996, but had been accidentally shot by a bullet fired by her son Tommy. This was supposed to have happened during a row between Tommy and Bambang over the national car facilities, both brandishing a pistol, at the Jalan Cendana, Soeharto's residence. According to this story, Mrs Soeharto had tried to calm her sons down after she heard shots fired by Tommy. Bambang, the story goes on, hid behind his mother's back, who in her turn was sheltered by a bodyguard, but a shot fired by Tommy killed his mother and the guard (*Opini*, 4/10-3-1999:3). In 1997, Bambang was one of the few who dared to protest when it was decreed that government offices and state companies had to use the Timor as their official car. Cabinet ministers were exempt from this. In March the following year, when a new cabinet was installed, the new ministers all got a Volvo as their official car.

At the end of 1996 and in early 1997, at the height of the Busang gold fever, when a fight broke out over who was to control its exploitation, and Bre-X's exploration contract was cancelled, both Sigit Harjojudanto, cooperating with Bre-X, and Siti Hardijanti Rukmana, in cooperation with the main rival of Bre-X, Barrick, wanted a share in the goldfield. In the end it was Bob Hasan who became Bre-X's local partner. In East Java Tommy, Tutut, and Bambang fought among themselves over an investment in a clean water project. In the TV world they are also each other's rivals. Bambang controls Rajawali Citra Televisi Indonesia (RCTI) TV station, Tutut Televisi Pendidikan Indonesia (TPI) station, and Sudwikatmono Surya Citra Televisi (SCTV), in which Bambang and Halimah Trihatmodjo also own shares.[9]

Besides the Family, other important concerns are owned by indigenous owners, including the family of Ibnu Sutowo, a former president of the state oil and natural gas company, Pertamina, and by the Djojohadikusumo family. The latter controls the Tirtamas Group, of which the boss is Hashim S. Djojohadikusumo. Hashim, nicknamed 'merchant' by his father, is the brother of Soeharto's son-in-law, Prabowo, and brother-in-law of the then governor of Bank Indonesia, Soedradjad Djiwandono. Among the firms belonging to the Tirtamas concern are Semen Cibinong, and Prima Comexindo, a company involved in foreign barter trade. Five banks were fully or partly owned: Bank Niaga, Bank Pelita, Bank Kredit Asia, Bank Papan Sejahtera, and Bank Arya Panduarta. A number of cabinet ministers, like Ginandjar Kartasasmita, Habibie, and Abdul Latief and their families, also owned business concerns.

[9]   Of yet another TV station, AN-TV, Bakrie Investindo is the majority shareholder.

In a sense, even the Armed Forces can be called a conglomerate, with the different armed branches and units owning their commercial companies.[10]

In spite of their interlocking interests, the relationship between the indigenous and Chinese business communities is not a smooth one. Probosutedjo is known for his penchant for occasionally striking out at Chinese conglomerates. At times he blames them, as he did during the discussion of the sale of Indofood shares by Liem, for not living up to the spirit of the Pancasila by only trying to multiple their wealth and not caring about the fate of indigenous businessmen. On the same occasion, Probosutedjo attacked the virtual monopoly Liem held in the production of instant noodles. He accused Liem of having grown rich at the expense of the poor (rich people did not eat instant noodles), and of failing to assist the government in combating poverty (*Forum Keadilan*, 25-8-1997:92-5). He is not alone in that. From time to time the conglomerates, and on such occasions the Chinese ones in particular were meant, were pressured to commit themselves to setting aside part of their wealth to assist cooperative societies or small and medium entrepreneurs, a category which invariably refers to indigenous businessmen. In March 1990, for instance, Soeharto summoned 31 conglomerate bosses to his Tapos Ranch in West Java and suggested to them that they transfer 25 per cent of the shares in their firms to cooperative societies, not specifying whether he meant selling or granting. They never did, and the rich business community continued to be urged to act more patriotically and to earmark part of their wealth for the development of the poor, indigenous sector of the economy. The last time this happened was in August 1995 when 96 of the richest Indonesians, including Bambang Trihatmodjo and Sigit Harjojudanto, met at Jimbaran in Bali to attend a Pancasila upgrading course. There, what came to be known as the Jimbaran group pledged to assist in the creation of a viable small-business sector. Sofyan Wanandi was nominated as its spokesman.

On 31 October, after what was described as a fortnight of tough negotiations, IMF, the World Bank, and ADB offered Indonesia financial assistance in the form of loans amounting to US$ 23 billion, of which IMF itself was to furnish US$ 10 billion. Bilateral donors were to furnish an additional US$ 20 billion. In return, IMF demanded a number of measures be taken aimed at the rehabilitation of the Indonesian economy and the stabilization of the rupiah. The IMF recommendations covered four basic elements: a restructuring of the banking sector; the dismantling of monopolies and cartels; the abolition of subsidies on fuels, electricity, and foodstuffs; and greater access to the Indo-

---

[10]   For the business interests of the Armed Forces see Samego et al. (1998a), Iswandi (1998) and Aditjondro (1998:53-9).

nesian market for foreign competition. Furthermore, state companies had to be privatized.

One of the major targets of the proposed reforms was the banking sector, which – as what happened a little later was to prove – was in an extremely unhealthy state. For years the banking sector and the 'cowboys' (the term is borrowed from the chief of police, Police General Dibyo Widodo) who operated in it had made it a source of countless misgivings (*Forum Keadilan*, 20-10-1997:85). This was also not the first time IMF had issued warnings (Gill 1997:24). The blame for many of the ills besetting the banking sector was laid at the door of its deregulation in October 1988. In that month the government had reopened the opportunity to establish private banks, demanding a minimum capital of only Rp 10 billion to do so. Since then the number of banks had grown tremendously. Commercial banks became a status symbol among the rich. In 1988 there were 112 banks in Indonesia. By 1996 the number had mushroomed to 239. Most of the new banks had their head office in Jakarta, with at the most a few branches in other large cities of Indonesia.

By 1997 the deregulation of 1988 had led to a number of problems. Many banks were not financially sound. They had been mismanaged, or had been considered by their owners as their private property which they could use as they pleased. They asked a higher interest rate than normal on loans, and paid a very low rate on savings accounts. Nor did they hesitate to use the banks illegally to finance new investments. Many owners and major shareholders had circumvented the ceiling which had been set on the amounts of credit to be advanced to owners and directors (10 per cent of the total volume of credit provided by a bank) and to companies belonging to the same conglomerate (20 per cent). In some cases as much as 90 per cent of the credit had gone to their own concern. Various sophisticated tricks had been devised to cover their steps, which greatly complicated the work of the public prosecutor when investigations were started in earnest after the fall of Soeharto. In September 1998 the then attorney-general had to admit that his staff was unequal to the task, not having made much headway in the last twenty years (*Jawa Pos*, 5-9-1998). One of the results of such conduct was an immense volume of so-called *kredit macet*, or uncollectable credits, which had often been used to finance large, expensive property projects run by other companies under the aegis of the bank's owners or shareholders without proper guarantees. What also happened was that the value of a project was marked up, leading to the overfinancing of an investment. Fictitious companies had even been founded to take out loans. With the steady advance of the economic crisis, the amount of such uncollectable credits, including inter-bank loans, only increased.

Bank Indonesia, the central bank, had to come to the assistance of private banks which had run into financial straits, while bankrupt banks had to be closed or sold to others. A number of financial scandals had surfaced, of which the Eddy Tansil case was the biggest to date. In 1994 when a Golkar member of parliament, Arnold Ahmad Baramuli, disclosed this scandal, other members of parliament stated that they had knowledge of at least forty similar cases, involving even more money. The Eddy Tansil affair provided a fine example of collusion. In his efforts to obtain credit Eddy Tansil had used of a letter of recommendation, signed by Sudomo, complete with the letter-head of the Minister Coordinator of Political and Security Affairs, the func-tion Sudomo held at that moment. Sudomo later claimed that he had had no intention of pressuring the state bank Bapindo into providing Eddy Tansil with the loan he demanded (Majidi 1994:48). J.B. Sumarlin, Minister of Finance at the time Eddy Tansil acquired his credit and chief commissioner of Bapindo, was implicated as well.

The problems with the banks did not leave the image of Bank Indonesia unbesmirched. It was pointed out that the central bank had failed in its task of supervising the private banking sector. Worse still, employees of Bank Indonesia were accused of corruption. In December 1997 the bank was forced to fire four of its seven directors, who were subsequently questioned by the police about their role in a series of bank scandals. Proceedings were started against three of them, but, reportedly after Soeharto had intervened, the prosecution was dropped (*Forum Keadilan*, 19-10-1998:87). If any more proof of connivance was needed, Bank Indonesia held shares in a number of banks which were being troubled by non-performing loans.

On 1 November, at a moment when President Soeharto was in Singapore, the first concrete measures were taken. In accordance with a reform package recommended by IMF, the Minister of Finance by decree closed sixteen pri-vate banks which were considered to be insolvent.[11] It was a step that Mar'ie Mohammad had already hinted at in parliament in early September. To be prepared for the worst, extra security measures were taken to be able to act if news of the decision led to public unrest.

Some of these banks were owned, or partly owned, by influential persons. 25 Per cent of the shares of one of the banks to be liquidated, Bank Andromeda, which had already been under siege for a week by clients anx-ious to withdraw their money, was held by Bambang Trihatmodjo. Probosutedjo was chief commissioner of another, Bank Jakarta. In a third, Bank Industri, Siti Hediati Prabowo held eight per cent of the shares and

---

[11]   It was reported that in 1996 Bank Indonesia had already suggested the closure of seven of these eleven banks, and that Soeharto in view of the coming general election had refused to fol-low this recommendation (*Tempo*, 2-2-2000:68-70). According to some sources, IMF had original-ly insisted on the closure of either 19 or 23 banks, including one state bank. Rumours also spoke of a score of banks in a worse state than the banks to be liquidated which had escaped that fate because of political connections.

Hashim S. Djojohadikusumo four per cent. The former head of Bakin, General (Ret.) Yoga Soegama, was the chief commissioner of Bank Dwipa Semesta; Bank Guna Internasional had Sutopo Juwono, who was also a former head of this intelligence service; and its chief commissioner, Sultan Hamengkubuwono X, was one of the shareholders of Bank Mataram Dhanarta. The owner of Bank Guna Internasional was Hendra Rahardja (Tan Tjoe Hin), who also held 38 per cent of the shares of another bank to be liquidated, Bank Harapan Sentosa (BHS). BHS had a bad reputation. It was also jokingly called *Bank Hanya Sementara* (Ephemeral Bank), *Bank Hampir Sempoyongan* (Bank on the Verge of Collapse), and *Bank Hampir Semaput* (Almost Unconscious Bank). Its 'boss', Hendra Rahardja, had run into difficulties after investing in the property business in Singapore, over-investing in the same sector in Indonesia, building bank offices and housing estates in Tangerang and Bogor.

Another victim was Bank Pacific, headed by Endang Utari Mokodompit, a daughter of Ibnu Sutowo. The bank, half of whose shares were owned by Bank Indonesia and the other half by the Ibnu Sutowo family, was already under scrutiny because of financial irregularities. Bad credit had burdened the bank with an estimated loss of Rp 3.3 trillion, a new record in the banking world, it was observed in June (*Panji Masyarakat*, 30-6-1997:81). Almost 60 per cent of its credit had gone into property and other projects (a hotel, a golf course, a parachute jump arena, for instance) of the Ibnu Sutowo family and their friends. Of the remaining credit, only about one-third was considered to be sound (*Panji Masyarakat*, 30-6-1997:74-8).

Those employees who had to be fired were promised three months' severance pay by Bank Indonesia. Perbanas (Perhimpunan Bank-Bank Nasional Swasta, or Association of Private National Banks), the Minister of Finance suggested, should step in and try to find them jobs in other banks.[12] In an initial reaction Bambang promised to do his best to place Bank Andromeda employees in his other companies. A similar promise was made to Bank Industri employees. They were to be given jobs in other Tirtamas firms. Employees of Bank Pacific, it was announced, were to be transferred to other firms in the conglomerate of which the bank was part. Probosutedjo, on the other hand, angry with the government's decision, said that the Minister of Finance had to bear the brunt when people from his bank were forcibly dismissed.

Small depositors, that is those with a maximum amount of savings of Rp 20 million, were to be reimbursed by three state banks: Bank Dagang Negara, Bank Negara Indonesia, and Bank Rakyat Indonesia. Around Rp 2 trillion

---

[12] In March the following year, the Ministry of Labour estimated 50,000 people in the banking sector had lost their jobs.

was reserved for this. People could withdraw their money on 13 November. In anticipation of unrest, special security measures had been taken to ensure order. Though there were long queues, there were no disturbances. Big depositors and creditors had to wait till the banks concerned had liquidated their assets and had paid their outstanding taxes. It was a decision which caused problems among various firms that needed cash to pay their employees. Three months later, the government promised to reimburse all the clients of the liquidated banks. Mar'ie Muhammad, who announced this in a parliamentary committee, was greeted with the cry 'Long live the Minister' by one of the bank clients who was following the session from the public gallery.

Owners and big shareholders, sixty in total, were 'dicekal' (cegah tangkal), forbidden to leave the country. Bambang Trihatmodjo and Probosutedjo were also on this list, but Bambang Tri was removed from it in January. In some instances such a measure was already too late. The owner of Bank Harapan Sentosa and of Bank Guna International, Hendra Rahardja, a brother of Eddy Tansil, the 'big corruptor', as his unofficial title described him, had already gone abroad to seek medical treatment, according to his lawyer. It was also too late for Hindoro Budiono Halim, the former owner of Elang Realty Concern and Bank Perniagaan, which had almost gone bankrupt in 1997 because of his malpractices involving between Rp 600 and 900 billion, and for Bambang Samiyono, who held 38 per cent of the shares in Bank Dwipa Semesta. Bambang Samiyono had fled the country in July, a move which had cost the bank almost all its customers.[13]

Though Bank Indonesia had indicated that there would not be a second wave of bank closures, people panicked and transferred their accounts to foreign banks en masse, forcing the government to provide several banks with liquidity credit. According to estimates, US$ 2 billion was withdrawn from private banks (Subandoro 1999:107). Problems also beset BCA, 70 per cent of which was owned by Sudono Salim and his children, with the remaining 30 per cent of the shares being in the hands of Sigit Harjojudanto and Siti Hardijanti Rukmana. It has Liem Sioe Liong as president commissioner, Sigit Harjojudanto and Anthony Salim as vice-president commissioners, and Siti Hardijanti Rukmana as one of its three commissioners. In the middle of November there was a rush on BCA offices and ATM money dispensers in Jakarta, Medan, and Surakarta occasioned by reports that Liem Sioe Liong, who was then aged 81, had died in Singapore. The rush intensified when other rumours followed hard on the heels of the first wave. People told each

---

[13]   The whole concern, including Bank Perniagaan, was taken over by the Bakrie group, which also owned Bank Nusa and Bank Nasional. Hindoro Budiono Halim died in June 1998; while being chased by the police he fell from the eighth floor of a hotel in Anyar. In May 1999 Hendra Rahardja was arrested in Sydney when he tried to enter Australia on a flight from Hong Kong.

other that BCA had been forced to close its office in Singapore and that the bank had suffered big losses on the foreign exchange market and as a consequence was to be liquidated. Security troops had to guard the bank's branches and the shopping centres where these were located. In total Rp 500 billion was withdrawn. In spite of the problems BCA experienced, it was announced a few days later that the Salim group was to acquire a significant share in Bank Danamon, one of the other large banks in Indonesia. Bank Danamon, 48 per cent of which was owned by Danamon International of the Admadjaja family, had in fact been in bad shape for years. BCA had also injected money into Bank Yama, which had, as did BCA, Siti Hardijanti Rukmana among its shareholders, taking over Bank Yama and enabling it to escape liquidation on 1 November.[14]

Two bankers refused to yield: Bambang Trihatmodjo of Bank Andromeda and Probosutedjo of Bank Jakarta. Both stressed that in view of the fact that the major shareholders headed larger business conglomerates, their banks were healthy. According to Bambang Tri, the only fault committed by Bank Andromeda was that it had violated the '3L' rule, that is the Legal Lending Limit, but this rule, he said, was transgressed by 90 per cent of Indonesian banks. Bambang Trihatmodjo argued that his credibility as a businessman was at stake. He attacked the decision to liquidate the sixteen banks for lack of 'transparency', a point others were also to make. In Bambang's opinion it was a political move. Observing that the liquidation concerned banks in which many of his relatives (he himself, Siti Hediati Prabowo, Probosutedjo, Tutut, Tommy, Sudwikatmono, and Hashim Djojohadikusomo) had a stake, Bambang suggested that among the covert objectives of this move lurked the intention to blacken his family's name, to bring his family down, and to obstruct the re-election of his father. Yet, according to the *Far Eastern Economic Review*, sources in the Ministry of Finance said that a particular reason for Bambang's anger was that his brother Tommy's Bank Utama had been dropped at the last minute from the list of banks to be liquidated (*Far Eastern Economic Review*, 20-11-1997:21).[15]

Bambang ventured to suggest that IMF might well have proposed the closure of insolvent banks, but that its negotiators would not have mentioned specific banks by name. The decision of which banks were to close must have been taken by others. Bambang was also furious about the fact that the banks themselves had not been allowed to solve their own problems. He claimed

---

[14] Bank Yama, it was reported in mid-November when the news became public, had already been in a parlous condition for a long time, and for three years in a row had not been able to produce a financial report.
[15] In fact, Bank Utama was owned by three of Soeharto's children: Tommy, Sigit Harjojudanto, and Siti Hutami Endang Adiningsih.

that on 30 October Bank Indonesia had informed him that Bank Andromeda could be saved by an injection of Rp 350 billion. When he had wanted to hand over that sum on 1 November, the money had been refused, with the excuse that it was already too late. In Bambang's view it was very likely that the Minister of Finance, Mar'ie Mohammad, had used this occasion to show the outside world that he was prepared to act, irrespective of who the shareholders were. He suggested that the president had not been informed in advance. His own assessment, Bambang stressed, should not be interpreted as a political move. It was inspired merely by business considerations and the desire to uphold the law.

That Soeharto had not been informed beforehand was very unlikely. Others, for instance Rudini, pointed out that no cabinet minister dared to take such a drastic step as to close the banks without the consent of Soeharto. To Rudini, who labelled Bambang's statement as 'emotional', the liquidation of the banks was the very best indication of the government's intention to put an end to the privileged position of members of Soeharto's family. People, Vice-President Try Sutrisno commented, should show restraint in the making of public statements which could turn a problem into a 'blunder'.

Both Bambang and Probosutedjo threatened to bring a lawsuit against the Minister of Finance, Mar'ie Mohammad, and the governor of Bank Indonesia, Soedradjad Djiwandono. As such cases concerned efforts to nullify a formal, government decision, they had to be brought before PTUN, the State Administrative Court. Their decision also placed the family factor centre stage. Were they to win or were Bank Indonesia to allow them to save their banks, this could easily create the impression that other considerations over which Bank Indonesia had no control were at work. At the height of all this, a member of the board of commissioners of Bank Andromeda defended the bank's policy on TV. Fifteen minutes for this were reserved in the newsreel *Seputar Indonesia* broadcast by RCTI, the commercial TV station owned by Bambang Trihatmodjo. The latter himself stressed that he intended to start a court case in order to restore the name of his family, claiming that it was a decision which had the support of his whole family.

Bambang's case was dealt with with amazing speed. It came before court on 5 November. Two days later, lawyers of Bank Andromeda demanded that the bank be authorized by Bank Indonesia to pay its clients out of its own money. On 12 November, Bambang Trihatmodjo dropped his case, underlining that he had not yielded to pressure from his father. The reason he had decided not to pursue his lawsuit was that the authorities allowed the shareholders of Andromeda Bank to pay its clients out of their own money without having to involve a state bank in this settlement. Consequently the shareholders prepared a Rp 60 billion fund to pay clients with a deposit of less than Rp 20 million who wanted to withdraw their money on 13 November.

As it turned out, Bank Indonesia did not place Bambang's name on the list of people banned from owning or managing a bank, which was its customary procedure with people connected with ailing banks. In December Bambang took over Bank Alfa (of which assets and obligations in turn had all been transferred to Bank Risjad Salim International, owned by Ibrahim Risjad and Liem) from Albert Halim, a son of Liem Sioe Liong, relocating all assets and obligations of Bank Andromeda to this bank.

Probosutedjo persisted. He called the closing of his bank a unilateral act, making no secret of his surprise about the fact that there had been no prior intimation of complaints about its functioning. As far as he was concerned, Bank Jakarta was suffering nothing worse than an attack of 'flu'. Angrily he refused to sign the liquidation forms and to summon a meeting of share-holders to discuss the liquidation of his bank. Probosutedjo, who had issued a demand similar to that of Bambang, hastened to give assurances that he had the interests of its clients at heart. He insisted that Bank Indonesia should publicly declare that it had never lent money to Bank Jakarta. Disregarding the liquidation order on 4 November, he had even started to pay the bank's clients (with a maximum of Rp 5 million for holders of a giro account, and Rp 2 million for holders of a savings account). Probosutedjo's action was successful to the extent that PTUN of Jakarta partly acceded to the demands of Bank Jakarta on 30 December. In the interests of the owners and customers, the liquidation order of the bank had to be postponed till the case had been decided by the appeal court. The court reached a decision that Bank Jakarta should be allowed to re-open its doors, abiding by this even should the government decide to appeal. On 2 January Bank Jakarta re-opened, not to the public (before this could be done additional consultation with Bank Indonesia was needed), but to put its internal affairs in order. On the same day the State Administrative High Court ordered the Jakarta court judgement be quashed. Administrative legislation did not provide for the postponement of a government decree till a final court verdict had been pronounced. On 6 January, Probosutedjo complained to journalists about the refusal of the Minister of Finance and of Bank Indonesia to comply with the PTUN ruling, airing his doubts about whether there was any legal security in Indonesia. Stating that it was more difficult to meet the management of Bank Indonesia than it was to meet the president, he announced that he was determined to bring the case before the court. Probosutedjo disclosed that officials from Bank Indonesia had proposed that he should start a new bank, but that he had rejected this suggestion, not wanting to create the impression that he was allowed to do so only because he was the brother of the president. On that same day the Secretary of State, Moerdiono, put an end to all doubts when he stressed that the government would not renege on its decision to close Bank Jakarta.

On 31 December, it was announced that certain state banks not in a healthy state were to merge: Bank Bumi Daya (BBD), Bank Ekspor Impor (Bank Exim), Bank Pembangunan Indonesia (Bapindo), and Bank Dagang Negara (BDN). A special company, Perusahaan Penyelesaian Kredit Bermasalah, Company to Settle Problematical Credits, was to be formed to transfer the outstanding uncollectable and dubious loans, estimated at that time at Rp 10 trillion. One of the results was that people withdrew their money from the four banks, eager to transfer it to other state and private banks. Bank Tabungan Negara was to become part of Bank Negara Indonesia.[16] In April it became known that the plan had been cancelled, and that instead BBD and Bapindo were to merge into one bank, and Bank Exim and BDN into another, but plans were to change again.

In the private sector there was talk of mergers as well. It was proposed to merge Bank Utama, owned by Tommy, with Bank Yama, owned by his sister, Siti Hardijanti Rukmana. The Association of Private National Banks formed a special committee of specialists to accelerate any such moves. Its chairman, Soebowo, feared that without strong domestic banks Indonesian bankers would once again be reduced to 'tellers'. Foreign banks would dominate the sector (*Media Indonesia*, 22-1-1998). Future mergers involving 46 private banks were announced, but never got beyond the announcement stage.

At that time it seemed as if the public had lost all faith in Indonesian banks. In the first three weeks of January, Rp 7.5 trillion was withdrawn from Indonesian banks and transferred to foreign banks. Faced with this unpleasant fact, a new body was established by the government on 26 January, Badan Penyehatan Perbankan Nasional (BPPN). Its official English name was Indonesian Bank Restructuring Agency (IBRA), and one of its tasks was a stricter auditing of the banks and the taking over and resuscitation of insolvent banks. Head of BPPN was Iwan R. Prawiranata, who had been chief director of a number of state banks. He was assisted by Rini Mariani Sumarno Suwandi, a director of the Astra concern. In February 54 banks were placed under the supervision of the agency, which had to decide which banks could still be rescued and which not. Its initial choice fell on banks which had received Bantuan Likuiditas Bank Indonesia (BLBI, a liquidity credit from Bank Indonesia) in excess of 200 per cent of their assets, or which had a capital adequacy ratio of less than 5 per cent. Amongst the BPPN 'patients' were the four state banks for which a merger had been announced, and 11 of the 27 provincial development banks, owned by the provinces. The government declared it would guarantee the deposits at about 70 medium-sized and large banks, which in their turn vowed to subscribe to the direc-

---

[16]   The operation would have left three state banks: the new one, Bank Rakyat Indonesia (BRI), and Bank Negara Indonesia (BNI).

tions laid down by Bank Indonesia. Texts announcing that the government guaranteed deposits appeared on banners outside and on notices at the counters of the banks concerned. Finally, in February, in an effort to stimulate bank mergers, Bank Indonesia announced that before the end of the year the minimum capital requirement for banks was to be Rp 1 trillion, or US$ 125 million, double that by the end of 1999, and triple that by the end of 2003. Soedradjad Djiwandono said that by taking this step the central bank hoped that by the end of 1998 the number of private banks would have been reduced from the existing 212 to 28. In February only 10 to 11 banks actually met the new capital requirement. In April, after a new round of negotiations with IMF, the minimal requirement was reduced to Rp 250 billion for 1998. In June yet another relaxation was announced. The Rp 250 billion was to apply only to new banks.

On 3 November, a second series of measures taken at the instigation of IMF was announced. These concerned a liberalization of the economy. The retail price of cement was released, while foreign companies acquired more freedom to enter the retail trade sector (which would only be opened up in 2003 with respect to manufacturing and trading companies). From 1 January Bulog was to lose its monopoly on the import (but not on the distribution) of soya beans, garlic, and wheat flour. Bulog maintained its import monopoly with respect to rice and sugar. Still not withdrawn was the much disputed monopoly of Badan Penyangga dan Pemasaran Cengkeh (BPPC, Body for the Buffer Stock and Marketing of Cloves), headed by Tommy, who himself saw as one of its accomplishments that it had succeeded in preventing a sharp fall in prices as had happened before BPPC had been founded (Soesilo 1998:194). Since the early 1990s it had held a monopoly on the cloves trade. Farmers sold their harvest to cooperatives, which were forced to sell the cloves to BPPC. In its turn it supplied the *kretek* (clove-blended) cigarette factories. Limiting the Bulog monopolies was not a sudden, unexpected decision. Such a step had been considered in the past, but had not got beyond the planning stage. Two years earlier the parliament had passed an Act on Small Businesses, aimed at ending practices such as monopolies which harmed the small business sector. Soeharto, when he received the head of the conglomerates at the presidential palace in Bogor in May, urged his guests, as was his want from time to time, to step up their assistance to small and medium firms and had spoken out in favour of the elimination of monopolies. Singling out the business ventures of the Liem concern, Soeharto had stressed that to control a commodity from the import or production of its main components to the sale of its finished product was profitable for the companies involved, but was out of the kilter with the aim of achieving a more even distribution of wealth. The plan to decrease the subsidy on wheat, and to eliminate it eventually, had already been announced in April, leading to speculations about an end to Bulog's wheat monopoly. At that time a lobby organized by Sudono Salim, springing to the defence of the profits of his Bogasari company, had still been seen as one of the factors which could prevent the realization of any such well-intentioned scheme.

By mid-December 1997, partly fuelled by rumours about Soeharto's health, the rupiah had plummeted to Rp 4,660 to the dollar, half of the value it had had in July. People began to speculate about intent. Rumours of the death of Soeharto, and also of resignation or death of Mar'ie Muhammad, which in November had also resulted in a drop in the value of the rupiah, forced Hashim Djojohadikusumo to conclude that political and economic sabotage were being given free rein. Senior officers in the army had grown equally suspicious. They launched an investigation because, as the new Chief of Staff for Social and Political Affairs, Lieutenant-General Yunus Yosfiah, explained, people who had no specific motive for doing so could not invent such wild stories (*Jawa Pos*, 13-12-1997). At the end of December President Soeharto voiced similar misgivings. He stated that stories that he was ill, or had died, were a deliberate attempt to destabilize the economy and to undermine confidence in the government. Issues raised about monopolies, corruption, and collusion were tainted by the same underhand motives. The ultimate aim was to force a *coup d'état*.[17] There were persons, Soeharto insisted, who were trying to exploit the monetary crisis for their own ends. Their sole aim in launching rumours was to cause a further depreciation of the rupiah, and they could not care less whether their actions would force companies to close and unemployment to rise. The next month, the military commander of Jakarta, Major-General Syafrie Syamsuddin, accused PRD members of spreading false reports and trying to use the economic crisis to ensure that the imminent general session of the People's Congress was a failure.

While this was going on, the authorities were growing increasingly apprehensive about the political consequences of the economic crisis. Domestic prices of foodstuffs and other daily necessities were rising, while the prices of shares were falling at an alarming rate on the stock exchange. Imports had become two to three times as expensive, affecting the labour market in industry, because many factories could no longer afford to buy the basic compo-

---

[17] The same applied equally, he said, to rumours that he had been detained and that the Armed Forces had carried out a *coup d'état* (a story which seems to have had its origin in Hong Kong). Such stories, coupled with ones that an aeroplane was standing ready at Halim airport to evacuate Soeharto and his family when trouble started and that the Armed Forces had stepped up their vigilance, continued to circulate till well into 1998. In January it was also rumoured that tanks had appeared in front of the presidential palace and that Soeharto and his children and grandchildren had fled the country expecting a *coup'détat*. By then, officers had also been upset by stories, circulating not only in Indonesia, but also abroad, for instance in the United States, Great Britain, and the Netherlands, that the Armed Forces were divided.

nents and ingredients they needed for production, and trade depended on such products from abroad. Employment was brought down still further by an acute dearth of capital and the shrinking purchasing power. As a small compensation, in the middle of January the Minister of Communications announced that people in Jakarta whose contract of employment had recently been ended because of the crisis and who wanted to celebrate the end of the fasting month in the place where their families lived were to receive a discount of 70 per cent on the outward journey by train. When the discount was announced, it was not clear how these people could be distinguished at the railway stations from the much larger number of others who had also lost their jobs or from any other poor people. In the end the government largesse became a general discount. To maintain order, the military arranged to transport people to the railway stations, which were heavily guarded. Thousands of sellers of boiled noodles from Jakarta and surrounding cities were also given the opportunity to visit their families. For this purpose Indofood Sukses Makmur hired 81 buses.

Some sectors were in a particularly bad way. Among these was the automotive industry. One of the victims here was the Timor, for which – even before the financial crisis – markets had to be sought outside Indonesia because of low domestic demand (Prasetyohadi 1998:59). Other sectors were the hotel branch and the printing industry. The last included the publishers of newspapers and magazines, which were confronted with tripling of the price of newsprint and a steep fall in advertisements. Newspapers and magazines stopped publication, decreased the number of pages, and had to raise their selling prices. What threatened the press at that moment was a 'curb new style' (*Ummat*, 2-3-1998:18). Publication had to be ceased not on government orders, but because of economic circumstances. The diminishing sales which this and the economic recession occasioned also hurt the sellers of newspapers and magazines. All, Soeharto impressed upon the owners and editors of newspapers and news magazines in February 1998, was in part their own fault. By publishing reports and rumours about the economic situation without considering the impact, they had contributed to aggravating the crisis.

Property developers, who had contracted huge loans, making this sector one of the major consumers of loans and the one with the highest amount of unrecoverable credit, also suffered heavily, dragging the cement industry along into the crisis. At the end of December, when the depreciation of the rupiah was over one hundred per cent compared with July, one of the outward signs of the crisis in which these large companies found themselves was the sale of valuable real estate. Up to November, of the 2,446 firms which were members of the industrial organization Real Estate Indonesia, 786 had closed down in 1997. Because of the weak rupiah, the 23 property companies with a quotation on the stock exchange, it was disclosed in mid-January, had an aggregate debt of Rp 28.9 trillion, far exceeding their aggregate capital, which amounted to Rp 17 trillion. They were all virtually bankrupt (*Forum Keadilan*, 15-12-1997:96, *Suara Pembaruan*, 12-1-1998). Other victims were the hotel and tourist industry and Indonesian airline companies. Increasing costs and a steep drop in the number of passengers forced the airlines to raise their tariffs for domestic flights a number of times – in January 1998 by as much as 30 to 36 per cent. The textile and garment industry also had to resort to a massive lay-off of its workforce.[18]

Rising prices and wages lagging behind had already brought rumbles of labour unrest, amongst other firms at Habibie's IPTN, where 10,000 employees went on strike in October. Two weeks later the same happened at PT PAL. Another consequence was that pawnshops found their business booming. Among the new clients were owners of small and medium business firms who had to pay the wages of their employees, or for other reasons were in dire need of cash. Some were forced to pawn their expensive cars. An additional reason for visiting a pawnshop was that banks had become hesitant to provide credit, or were no longer in a position to do so. State pawnshops were also cheaper, asking an interest rate of 1.75 per cent for fourteen days, and of 3.25 per cent for one month. The interest rate at a bank at that time could well reach 40 per cent.

At the beginning of January the spokesman of the Armed Forces, Mokodongan, estimated that over two million people (others in Indonesia spoke of 2.4 million, while later that month the *Far Eastern Economic Review* mentioned a figure of 6 million) had lost their jobs because of the crisis (*Far Eastern Economic Review*, 29-1-1998:17). He warned that the Armed Forces were ready to crack down on unrest. Mokodongan announced this when he made public a ten-point daily instruction from the Commander of the Armed Forces, General Feisal Tanjung. One of its points stressed the Armed Forces' role in maintaining stability and combatting rumours and false information. It was underlined that the Armed Forces would do their best to tackle the economic problems. Where possible, expenses were being cut. The Armed Forces were to shelve the purchase of twelve Russian fighter planes and five helicopters, reduce the number of military attachés by 70 per cent, and limit official tours in Indonesia and abroad. Other steps announced were the reduction of ceremonial and the postponement of large-scale exercises; it was explicitly stated that wedding ceremonies organized by senior officers would be reduced to modest occasions in the future. A week later, after a meeting of

---

[18]   In March the following year the Ministry of Labour estimated that one million people had lost their jobs in the construction and property industry. In the textile and garment sector the figure was 300,000.

the most senior officers of the Armed Forces, Mokodongan once again gave the assurance that the domestic situation was under control. The Armed Forces were not on full alert, he stressed, denying rumours to this effect. Yet, it would only take a few hours to step up the state of alert and take whatever measures were deemed necessary.

On that same day, 8 January, the public panicked after a new steep fall of the rupiah, which reached a value of Rp 10,100 to the US dollar (to bounce back to Rp 8,000 later the same day). One of the reasons for the exchange rate to plunge so spectacularly was the presentation of Indonesia's budget by President Soeharto on 6 January (when Rp 7,000 still bought one dollar). Though publicly Soeharto was showered with praise, the budget was in fact viewed as being unrealistic. It was based on an exchange rate of Rp 4,000 to the dollar, a four per cent growth rate of Indonesia's economy, at a point when contraction was a far more likely scenario, accompanied by an inflation of nine per cent. Disregarding one of the major demands of IMF, subsidies on fuel oils, fertilizers, and foodstuffs were maintained. Because of this it was feared that the budget could well make IMF decide to withhold its financial assistance.[19] Anxiety over this, coupled with the rising prices and reports that supplies of a variety of essential consumer goods might be limited, created a panic. Some Indonesians had already started hoarding some months previously, expecting that prices could only go up, but the announcement of the new budget alarmed the middle class. In the major cities of Indonesia in the afternoon and evening of that day, there was a rush first on supermarkets and then on ordinary markets and shops, by people intent on hoarding rice, cooking oil, sugar, instant noodles, bread, milk, soap, and other commodities. In some towns the run only started after the TV news had broadcast pictures of people in Jakarta rushing to the shops. A number of shops had to close early when their supply of basic foodstuffs ran out, while here and there fights broke out between customers at supermarkets, most of them from the middle class, some of them in their business attire. The following day, when people flocked to the stores again, they found that many were closed because they had been bought out, or only allowed their customers to buy a limited amount of certain foodstuffs, and other items such as soap and toothpaste; which, of course, people circumvented by coming back a number of times or simply going on to another shop. For the army the situation had become serious enough to have the commanders of the military districts in Jakarta report to headquarters about the situation in their district.

In an effort to put an end to the hoarding, the Minister of Information

---

[19]   *The Indonesian Observer* even reported at the end of January that in Singapore Lee Kuan Yew had commented that Soeharto had blundered by not consulting the IMF when drafting this budget. The report was immediately denied by Lee Kuan Yew's press secretary.

called together a meeting of editors-in-chief. Present were the Minister Coordinator of Production and Distribution, Hartarto, the Minister Coordinator of Industry and Trade, Tunky Ariwibowo, the Minister of Communications, Haryanto Dhanutirto, and the head of Bulog, Beddu Amang. They explained that the government had arranged for a sufficient stock of basic foodstuffs and that there was no question of shortages.[20] Other civilian and military authorities stressed that the stock of basic foodstuffs in Jakarta was large enough to last at least three months. To tackle the immediate problem, emergency droppings of food were made, an operation for which the army furnished trucks. Another reason for the droppings was to bring down prices, which had started to skyrocket. Bulog organized special sales of foodstuffs at markets, which occasionally drew such a crowd that they had to be moved to more spacious surroundings, such as the compound of a police station.[21] To stabilize domestic cooking oil prices, which had doubled in price in January compared to June 1997, the export of all commodities derived from crude palm oil (but not that of coconut oil) was forbidden, a policy immediately criticized by palm-oil producers and IMF (Mann 1998:108). The measures initially had no effect on the incipient panic. Though rushes on shops started to decrease on the 10th, they still went on for some days. Within a week, the first food riots occurred, during which shops and markets were looted and destroyed in cities and villages in Banyuwangi and Jember in East Java.

Faced with consumer panic and the approach of the end of the fasting month, the military, intimating that 'certain groups' had deliberately sown the panic, called for calm. The Chief of Staff of the Army, General Wiranto, deployed religious leaders in this exercise. Referring to the special status which such leaders enjoyed in society, he suggested that they should provide this society with 'correct' information, which would give the lie to the rumours and pamphlets which were circulating. Assuming the role with which it had been gifted, the Indonesian Council of Ulama declared hoarding, waste, corruption, and currency speculation to be sins. Changing the function of currency from a medium of exchange to a commodity with the aim of gaining a profit and hurting others was inadmissible in Islam. The MUI urged all who, in the hope of profiting from this, held American dollars to change these for rupiahs. During a national meeting of the MUI in

---

[20] Problems were aggravated by the fact that because of an exceptionally long dry season the next harvest could well be delayed by one or two months and might be much less than normal. In relation to this, at the end of December 1997 the Minister of Agriculture, Sjarifuddin Baharsjah, announced that Indonesia might be forced to import at least one million tons of rice.
[21] A little while later there were also special cheap markets for other products, such as spare parts for public transport vehicles, held at the compound of the Jakarta police headquarters. Lack of spare parts and lack of tyres was to turn into a major problem for public transport.

February which had been given the motto 'Increase Union and Unity and Social Solidarity amidst growing Concern about the Success of the General Session', the MUI called for a national holy war against speculators and hoarders. Such appeals by the MUI were merely extra proof to some Muslims that the council was nothing more than an instrument created to support government policy. The MUI was criticized for the fact that in its attempt to boost nationalism by stressing love of the fatherland it had presented something that was no more than an Arab proverb, or a false tradition at the most, as a real tradition about the life of Muhammad. Moreover, the true course of the MUI should have been to condemn conventional banking, which practised the calculation of interest, and appeal to this sector to apply the Islamic economic system. The call for a holy war did not go completely uncontested. The utmost care should be exercised in using a religious concept for political ends.

The worsening economic situation and dissatisfaction with the measures taken so far unleashed a plethora of calls from many sides for reform in the new year, for a combatting of political and economic abuses, which had been allowed to exist unmolested for too long, and for democratic freedoms, transparency of government policy. There were calls especially for measures to tackle the monetary crisis and the government's reputation. The lack of faith in the government gradually began to take a more concrete shape. One of the most illustrious persons to stress this point in January was Sumitro Djojohadikusumo. He invited journalists to his house, where he attacked 'crony capitalism' and called for an immediate replacement of the cabinet (which was to end its term in March, after the re-election of Soeharto). The equally well-known economist Mohammad Sadli urged the same, but went a step further than Sumitro, including Soeharto in his assessment.

Pressure from abroad was also being exerted. American President Bill Clinton, who sent his Deputy Minister of Finance, L.H. Summers, to Jakarta, vented his concern and underlined that Indonesia should wholeheartedly follow the IMF directives, in a telephone conversation with Soeharto on 9 January. Others who phoned Soeharto were Japanese Prime Minister Ryutaro Hashimoto, German Chancellor Helmut Kohl, and Australian Prime Minister John Howard. In the middle of January Malaysian Prime Minister Mahathir Mohamad paid a visit to Indonesia. The Prime Minister of Singapore, Goh Chok Tong, flew to Jakarta.

Stressing that the domestic and foreign business world could not operate properly in a climate of uncertainty, appeals for change also came from the business community itself. In the middle of December Sofyan Wanandi, arguing that political transparency was urgently required to overcome the financial crisis and restore the faith of the international business world in Indonesia, asked Golkar to name its candidate for the vice-presidency.

Golkar refused, saying that the party could not do so because the matter had
not yet been discussed by its central board. This was followed by an appeal
at the end of the month by Aburizal Bakrie. He urged transparency and con-
sistency in the economic and political policy of the government, including
the vexed matter of the succession. It was a burning issue on which the political élite had not yet reached agreement. In January, the Chief of Staff for
Political and Economic Affairs of the Armed Forces indicated that the army
was against any such move. Constitutional rules should be observed, Yunus
Yosfiah stated, which meant nothing could be done until the general session
of the People's Congress. Business considerations could not be the only criterion.

Even Golkar leaders began to press for economic reform. At the Golkar
meeting in October, participants were already calling for an end to all
monopolies, while at the end of December the party, though still expressing
its full confidence in government policy, again pressed for economic reforms.
Adding its voice to the growing chorus, at its meeting in Lombok in
November the NU had called for the abolition of all monopolies. More outspoken at that time was CIDES, Centre for Information and Development
Studies, the think-tank of ICMI. Linking the economic problems to the political structure, it asked for political reform, for legalization which was not
designed primarily to serve the interests of power holders, and for transparency in the matter of the succession. Around the same time, one of the
major member organizations of Golkar, Kosgoro, issued a statement, which
in those days was still considered blunt, urging for political and economic
reforms. In it the government was criticized for its interference in political
life, thereby not allowing enough room for innovative ideas to develop.
Accusing the government of aiming for a monopoly on the truth, more freedom was asked to allow people to express their opinions about fundamental
economic and political reforms required. An end had to come to the monopoly of power of what was called a group of strategic élites.

ICMI leaders joined in the calls for reform and for conceding to what were
called demands in society for democracy, transparency, and accountability.
At the end of 1997, at the closure of a national gathering and in the presence
of Habibie and the Minister of Public Housing, Akbar Tanjung, they pleaded
for more democracy and greater independence of legislative and judicial
power. Early in January its general secretary, Adi Sasono, making a plea for
national unity, suggested a 'national dialogue' between the government and
its major critics, such as Amien Rais, Abdurrahman Wahid, Megawati, and
the well-known economist and supporter of Megawati, Kwik Kian Gie. As
the devaluation of the rupiah could not be attributed solely to economic factors, it was, according to Adi Sasono, impossible for the government to solve
the financial crisis on its own. He pointed out that such a dialogue had an

additional advantage in that it lowered the chances that social violence might erupt.

Amien Rais's reaction was positive. Among the points to be discussed he listed the question of whether the present circumstances demanded a change in national leadership. He used Adi Sasono's suggestion to plead for a coalition between himself and Abdurrahman Wahid and Megawati – a cooperation which was sometimes denoted by the abbreviation AWAM (general), using their initials. Such a cooperation, he pointed out, would result in a joint effort by the leading figures of the 'nationalists', and of the traditionalist and modernist streams in Islam to try to find a way out of the economic crisis. Abdurrahman Wahid's reaction was cool. He doubted whether the government was ready for a national dialogue and pleaded for time. A meeting like that suggested by Adi Sasono needed careful preparation, as it touched upon fundamental issues. Moreover, who was the government? The dispute following the decision to liquidate Bank Jakarta had shown there was no unity within the government. The same could be said about its policy.

In government circles, it was reported, there were some who had developed an 'allergy' to the term national dialogue (*Forum Keadilan*, 19-1-1998:23). Yet officials could not but applaud when others indicated that they wanted to assist in solving the crisis. Whenever their comments went into more detail, they tended to consist mostly of objections and doubts. Akbar Tanjung underlined that a national dialogue had to be constitutional and had to be organized using existing mechanisms. General Hartono pointed out that the government had already consulted experts, including critics who had the required expertise, and that some of this could be done behind closed doors. Harmoko and Yogie SM fell back on the function of the parliament and the People's Congress. Still others expressed the fear that such a meeting would be an occasion for assigning the blame to certain individuals. Sudomo pulled absolutely no punches. He suggested that people who wanted to assist in finding an end to the crisis would do better to submit their recommendations and suggestions to the government by letter. Another helpful action would be to pray. Dialogues in which people participated who had no expert knowledge about the problem could well result in more chaos. In spite of this, CIDES decided to organize a meeting, prudently calling it a *dialog antartokoh*, a discussion between leading figures. The meeting, envisaged as a kind of talk show, about which it was later claimed Habibie had been informed in advance, was to be hosted by Dr Dewi Fortuna Anwar, a LIPI employee and one of the founders of CIDES, who after May 1998 was to become one of Habibie's closest advisors. Though it was reported that Rudini, Megawati, Amien Rais, Yunus Yosfiah, and Ginandjar Kartasasmita had promised to be present, the meeting had to be cancelled. No member of the cabinet was prepared to attend.

Indonesia Bangkit!

Memilih produk Indonesia berarti Anda membuka lowongan kerja

"Saya mengajak Saudara untuk lebih banyak menggunakan buatan bangsa kita sendiri. Sebab, semakin banyak produk Indonesia yang terjual, semakin banyak orang Indonesia yang memiliki hari esok yang lebih cerah.

Sadar atau tidak, dengan memilih produk Indonesia, Anda telah ikut membantu saudara kita. Dan Anda telah berbuat sesuatu untuk bangsa Indonesia."

"Kupilih Karya Bangsaku."

Iklan layanan masyarakat ini terselenggara atas kerjasama Departemen Perindustrian dan Perdagangan dan Majalah PANJI MASYARAKAT.

Departemen Perindustrian dan Perdagangan
http://indag.dprin.go.id

PRODINA

Indonesia Bangkit!
Peningkatan Penggunaan
Produk Indonesia

Soeharto's picture disappears from the advertising campaign of the Ministry of Industry and Trade to have Indonesians buy Indonesian products.
Panji Masyarakat, 9-2-1998 ...

Indonesia Bangkit!

Iwan Tirta,
Perancang Terkemuka

Pilihlah Produk Kelas Dunia Buatan Indonesia

"Suatu saat Anda membeli produk di luar negeri, jangan kaget jika pada labelnya tertera *Made in Indonesia.*

Memang, produk Indonesia telah dipajang dan menjadi favorit di berbagai pasar dunia. Mengapa tidak membeli di Indonesia? Lebih murah harganya dan lebih banyak pilihannya.

Bertekadlah untuk berbuat banyak bagi negeri tercinta dan berkata dengan bangga:

"Kupilih Karya Bangsaku."

Iklan layanan masyarakat ini terselenggara atas kerjasama Departemen Perindustrian dan Perdagangan dan Majalah PANJI MASYARAKAT.

PRODINA

Indonesia Bangkit!
Peningkatan Penggunaan
Produk Indonesia

Departemen Perindustrian dan Perdagangan
http://indag.dprin.go.id

... and 16-2-1998.

Others, in a spurt of nationalism and inspired by similar actions abroad tried to create a popular movement to turn the economic tide. In early January, Golkar politicians suggested that the government should declare 1998 the Year of Love for the Rupiah. On 12 January, Siti Hardijanti Rukmana started the *Aku Cinta Rupiah*, I Love the Rupiah, campaign, complete with stickers and banners along the roads. It won the support of leading businessmen, government officials, members of the People's Congress, artists, and *ulama* and other religious leaders, among them Nurcholish Madjid. Given ostentatious coverage by the press and TV, they changed dollars for rupiahs under the gaze of millions of viewers. The first of these events was interspersed with the singing of patriotic songs and the shouting of *Allahu Akbar*, God is Great. Among those who changed dollars were the Minister of Finance, Mar'ie Muhammad (US$ 1000), the Minister of Information, General Hartono (US$ 1,200), businessman Aburizal Bakrie (US$ 100,000), Tutut (US$ 50,000), her husband Indra Rukmana (US$ 50,000), and The Ning King (US$ 100,000). A prominent spiritual leader, KH Ali Yafei, changed US$ 200. Even schoolchildren, accompanied by the Minister of Education and Culture, changed their parents' dollars, while the Saudi Arabian Ambassador joined in setting a good example.[22]

In another drive, KH Zainuddin M.Z. donated 100 grams of gold in a Love Indonesia campaign he had started himself, while a businessman, Sukamdani Sahid Gitosardjono, gave a one-kilogram gold plate. Two hundred *kiai*, led by the chairman of the Religious Advisory Council of NU, KH Ilyas Ruchiyat, handed over 1.9 kg of gold when they were received by the president. They had collected this at a large prayer meeting in Jakarta in which four hundred *ulama* from all over Java and Sumatra participated. Amongst other things they had prayed for an end to the economic crisis, for greater solidarity of the rich with the poor, for people to be fans of their national products, and for a healthy President Soeharto to continue to lead the nation. KH Zainuddin was touched. The *kiai*, most of whom came from *pesantren* which themselves were severely hit by the monetary crisis, had all without hesitation donated gold when they had been asked to do so. Yet another outpouring was Gerakan Cinta Produksi Dalam Negeri, Love Domestic Products Movement. It was the framework in which the Ministry of Industry and Trade placed advertisements in journals, showing a portrait of Soeharto pleading with people to buy Indonesian products and thus create extra employment opportunities.[23] Within months the picture of Soeharto had been replaced by those of ordinary Indonesians, such as shopkeepers

---

[22] After a few days it received its official name, Gerakan Cinta Rupiah (GCR, or Getar, meaning 'shake'), the Love the Rupiah Movement.
[23] Yet another campaign was Save and Lead a Simple Life.

and construction workers.

On 19 January, Tutut launched yet another campaign, Gerakan Cinta Indonesia (Genta), Love Indonesia Movement, urging people to donate gold and jewellery to Bank Indonesia. She herself donated two kilograms of jewellery and gold. It provided a good opportunity for the MUI, by now described in a newspaper as 'a government backed Islamic group', to stress its support of this Hubbul Wathon (Love the Fatherland) a campaign promoting the idea that speculation with money amounted to gambling, and thus was not permitted in Islam (*The Indonesia Times*, 24-1-1998). Stressing the seriousness of the situation and warning that unrest might be in store, Muslims were asked to support Soeharto and the new measures that were announced. The Armed Forces started their own campaign. Their spokesman announced that, as an indication of patriotism, they would collect dollars from their officers to be donated to Bank Indonesia.

The drive to have citizens come to the financial assistance of the state was less successful than similar campaigns in South Korea and Thailand. The movement remained confined mostly to the political élite. Ordinary people rushed to banks and money changers to buy dollars and other foreign currencies, disregarding all patriotic appeals and calls not to panic. Judging from a survey by *Tempo Interaktif*, the I Love the Rupiah campaign failed to strike a responsive chord. Apart from the fact that many were convinced that the same persons who had changed their dollars would buy dollars again later to pay off their foreign debts, or to finance the education of their children abroad or an overseas jaunt for their wives, 90 per cent of the 1,170 respondents agreed to the proposition that dollars could also have been changed without such a public display and that those who had joined in the spectacle only wanted to show off their wealth. 60 per cent were of the opinion that the campaign in no way contributed to solving the monetary crisis (*Kabar dari Pijar*, 14-2-1998). The ordinary people, other reactions claimed, had always loved the rupiah. It was not they who owned dollars. The changing of the dollars only showed who had so far played false with the rupiah, and who were consequently responsible for the monetary crisis which caused so much misery (*Panji Masyarakat*, 23-3-1998:39, Ghazali 1998:187).

Publicly there were some who hastened to express their misgivings about such a welter of public display. Probosutedjo had his doubts. He himself, he stated, had, without giving this any publicity, changed US$ 15 million. Probosutedjo declared his conviction that public actions carried out in the full glare of publicity did not in any way influence the exchange rate of the rupiah. To give credence to such claims was foolish. When push came to shove, what mattered was the political will of the government to bring about reforms as soon as possible. Sofyan Wanandi, in his capacity as spokesman of the Jimbaran Group, speaking on behalf of the Chinese business magnates, also stated that the story that they were hesitant to change dollars was completely unfounded. They were reluctant to take part in what was only a 'show'. Praising the people who had handed in gold, he stated that the 'conglomerates' were not contemplating following suit. They preferred to assist in overcoming the crisis in other ways, for instance by increasing the amount of Indonesia's exports. Sofyan Wanandi indicated that the conglomerates were hard hit by the crisis. He made no bones about the fact that he thought it was unfair to ask people who had to spend enormous sums to pay off their foreign debts because of the fall of the rupiah to donate gold.

He had to walk warily, as by that time Sofyan Wanandi and his colleagues had become subject to threats by the army, an institution in which anti-Chinese feelings had been marked for many years, if not since 1945. On 14 January, the day that Sofyan Wanandi made his statement, Mokodongan disclosed that Feisal Tanjung had contacted 13 'conglomerates' asking them to change dollars or to contribute these to the government as a token of their feelings of solidarity and nationalism. To explain his request, he pointed out that people of this sort had received help at the time they had still worn a *koloran*, a cotton loincloth, but that after they had graduated to wearing a suit and tie, they had stopped caring for the fate of ordinary Indonesians. This was not as it should be. They, and he left no doubt that he meant Chinese businessmen, had enjoyed the fruits of Indonesia's burgeoning economy. A few days earlier Liem Sioe Liong had already announced that he would return the money he had moved outside the country to Indonesia. At the end of January Feisal Tanjung revealed that 13 conglomerates had reacted positively to his appeal. As an exception he mentioned Sofyan Wanandi. Others voiced similar criticism in more veiled terms. KH Zainuddin M.Z., for instance, calling for unity among all Indonesians irrespective of their ethnic background, attacked people who tried to make as much money as they could in Indonesia and then transferred their profits to banks abroad. When the country was ailing, everybody had a duty to assist in returning it to a sound state.

On 15 January, Indonesia and IMF reached a fifty-point agreement. Observing that the measures taken so far had not brought the desired results, it singled out trade monopolies, unhedged foreign loans, and the poor state of domestic banking as the major causes of the crisis. Though welcomed in certain quarters, there was ill feeling about the fact that only after pressure from IMF was the government willing to take the step which Indonesian economists had already been suggesting for such a long time.

The new agreement was signed by Soeharto, who before doing so called together his children, informing them what the implications for them would be and asking them whether they objected. According to Siti Hardijanti Rukmana, all declared themselves ready to bear the consequences of the

Camdessus looks on while Soeharto signs Indonesia's agreement with IMF
on economic reforms (photo *Kompas*)

agreement, doing so, she stressed, in the interests of the state and the country. This time President Clinton phoned President Soeharto to express his
appreciation of the result reached.

The signing, or rather its broadcast on TV and the pictures of it published,
created some indignation. The pictures showed how the managing director
of IMF, M. Camdessus, stood with his arms crossed and looked on while a
seated Soeharto put his signature to the document. One author said the scene
resembled 'an angry schoolmaster chastising a naughty pupil', a comparison
also made by others (Mann 1998:121). Later Camdessus defended himself by
explaining that to his surprise only one chair had been provided and that
when he was forced to remain standing he had remembered his mother's
advice that when he did not know what to do with his hands he should not
put them behind his back like the Duke of Edinburgh, but in front of his chest
(*Business Week*, 1-6-1998 quoted in Sinansari ecip 1998:218). Another pointed
out that such a scene caused many Indonesians sorrow, as it looked like
President Soeharto had 'lost a battle' (Kwik Kian Gie, *The Jakarta Post*, 20-1-
1998). The way Indonesia was being treated by IMF and its promise of financial aid was also compared with the inducements held out by parents to
small children to encourage them to perform a certain task (Ghazali 1998:58).
The accord called for fiscal reforms, removed restrictions on foreign banks

operating in Indonesia, opened up oil-palm production to foreign investors, abolished various monopolies, and put an end to government support for a number of projects. It also announced the intention of privatizing as many state companies as possible, including the state banks – a long-held aim cherished by advocates of the liberalization of the Indonesian economy, and consequently resisted by those having a vested interest in them, or those who viewed state companies as a counterbalance to Chinese and foreign capital (see Saidi 1998:45, 105-7). Before being privatized, the state companies had to be transferred from the various government departments of which they formed part. Consequently, within days, the state companies all fell under the authority of the Ministry of Finance.

To implement the letter of intent that had been agreed upon, Dewan Pemantapan Ketahanan Ekonomi dan Keuangan (DPKEK, Council for the Stabilization of Monetary and Economic Resilience), headed by the president himself, was constituted. Widjojo Nitisastro was appointed its secretary-general, Dr Fuad Bawazier MA, the Director-General of Taxation, its deputy secretary-general. The council held its first meeting on 21 January.

The new agreement with IMF entailed a revision of the budget President Soeharto had announced a little over a week earlier. It was presented to the parliament on 23 January. At the insistence of IMF, inflation was now estimated at twenty per cent, economic growth at zero per cent, and the exchange rate at Rp 5,000 to the dollar. Fuel and electricity subsidies, from which industry also profited, were gradually to be terminated. To protect the poor, these subsidies, except for kerosene and diesel oil, were to disappear as of April. Consequently, the amount of money earmarked for subsidies on fuel had been reduced from Rp 10 trillion to Rp 7.45 trillion.

IPTN and the Timor had been among the major targets on which IMF had set its sights, and suffered accordingly. IMF was determined that the special treatment accorded to the two projects was to stop as soon as possible. The national aircraft factory IPTN was no longer to receive money from the regular national budget or from special off-budget funds, nor was it to get special credit facilities. The agreement called for the acceleration of the intention already agreed upon in the Indonesian parliament in May 1997 that all off-budget funds gradually had to be included in the state budget. Among other sources this referred to the Reforestation Fund, managed by MPI, that is Bob Hasan, in which holders of a tree-felling concession had to pay a compensation if they themselves were unable to replant an area recently cleared. In 1996 it had led to an outcry when by presidential decree and against the wishes of Mar'ie Muhammad US$ 400 million of its money had been used for a financial injection into Habibie's IPTN. One of the reasons for turning to the Reforestation Fund for financing he IPTN had been that in return for foreign aid the World Bank had decreed that Habibie could at the most receive US$

500 million from the state budget, which covered about one-quarter of what he needed.[24] In the IMF agreement it was explicitly mentioned that the Indonesian government was no longer to use money from the fund for purposes other than those for which the fund had been established. It was the end of one of Habibie's great dreams, though both he and Soeharto vowed that IPTN would continue its projects. The only extra-budgetary source of money which remained was PT Dua Satu Tiga Puluh (DSTP, Two One Thirty), established in 1996 by Soeharto, who also became its president commissioner, to co-finance the development of the N-2130 jet by IPTN by the sale of shares. Soeharto started a campaign to have businessmen, state companies, civil servants, and others buy shares. Money from the Reforestation Fund was also used to buy shares. To have people with a low income participate, shares with a value of Rp 5,000 were issued. After Soeharto's fall, businessmen who held shares in the company, troubled by the adverse economic circumstances, would plead for its winding-up and for the return of the money to investors. One of the arguments put forward was that the buying of shares in Dua Satu Tiga Puluh had not been 'completely voluntary' (*Forum Keadilan*, 24-8-1998:73). In September even the government announced that it would sell its shares, providing that a buyer could be found. In December 1998 DSTP was liquidated. Contractual shareholders were to be repaid in full for the money they had brought in when the N-2130 project failed. This immediately led to a row about what exchange rate the shares, bought by the conglomerates in dollars, should be used for the reimbursement. The decision to do this at the exchange rate at the time the shares were bought and supplemented with interest was unacceptable to big shareholders like Arifin Panigoro, who himself had bought shares worth US$ 1 million.[25]

Tommy also felt the consequences of the IMF agreement. In October the Indonesian government had already promised IMF that it would follow the decision of the World Trade Organization with respect to the Timor car. In January it was decided that Indonesia should take this obligation seriously. The special credit facilities and tax exemptions the Timor car received were

---

[24]   Saidi 1998:111; *Tajuk*, 4-3-1999:66-70. Habibie was not the only one who had received money from this fund. Loans under favourable conditions to finance investments had gone to many others as well. Among them were Bob Hasan (to finance the building of PT Kian Kertas Lestari pulp and paper factory in East Kalimantan – with an investment of US$ 1.3 billion the largest in Southeast Asia and in which Yayasan Supersemar and Yayasan Dharmais also participated – and other projects), Probosutedjo, Siti Hardijanti Rukmana, Ari Sigit Harjojudanto (to finance a fertilizer plant), and Bambang Trihatmodjo (in his case for the Southeast Asia Games). Soeharto's fall meant that in some of these cases, such as where it concerned Bob Hasan's factory, loans had not yet become effective.

[25]   Aditjondro 1998a:28, 1998c:112-3; *Tajuk*, 6-8-1998:76-8; *Forum Keadilan*, 13-6-1999:61-2. Soedharmono became deputy president commissioner of DSTP. Chief director was Saadillah Mursjid, in the last two Soeharto cabinets secretary of the cabinet and secretary of state.

to be stopped immediately. A national car, Tommy commented during a press conference, arriving at the venue, as the magazine *D&R* noted, not in a Timor but in a Rolls Royce, had evaporated into a dream (Prasetyohadi 1998:14). He pledged he would continue with the production of the car, of which at that moment there was still an unsold stock of 15,000. Tommy denounced the agreement reached between Indonesia and IMF as a form of 'new neo-colonialism of rich countries' afraid that their markets would be flooded with products from developing countries (*Media Indonesia*, 16-1-1998). In voicing his suspicions, he was merely giving utterance to what was felt by others who could see themselves suffering from the accord that criticism abroad and the measures enforced by IMF were being propagated by those foreign business interests which had come under growing pressure from Indonesia's burgeoning economic development. Soeharto, as the Minister of Youth and Sport Hayono Isman revealed, did not agree with his son's opinion. There had been no pressure from IMF which could be interpreted as economic colonialism. Tommy proved incorrigible. Next month the Timor company asked the government for a restoration of its exemption from import and luxury taxes. The argument was that it had every right to do so, as the company had been founded at the request and with the approval of the government. His request was granted in as far as it concerned the import of completely built-up Timor cars. It was a rearguard action. The fall of his father also meant the end of the car. Production was stopped.

Tommy was also the chairman of BPPC, Body for the Buffer Stock and Marketing of Cloves. It was agreed that BPPC had to fold up at the end of June 1998 at the latest. A presidential decree to this effect was indeed issued. Tutut also suffered. She had to part with a number of toll-road projects.

The export ban on palm oil was lifted. The January agreement also called for an end to formal and informal monopolies or semi-monopolies and cartels, singling out those operating in the marketing of cement, plywood, paper, and flour. One of the consequences was that the joint-marketing association Apkindo, headed since the mid-1980s by Bob Hasan, became obsolete. Another was that Bulog lost all its monopolies, except that on rice. According to President Soeharto, the last commodity had been exempted to protect the people who were the producers and consumers of rice. Whether the formal ending of monopolies really meant a liberalization of the market in this field was difficult to determine. In February the head of Bulog, Beddu Amang, asked for the postponement of the liquidation of the monopolies Bulog held, because if this did not happen new monopolies by the private sector might be the result. The plea was ignored. At the end of January, the Minister of Cooperative Societies stated that as far as cloves were concerned, the old marketing networks were to be maintained after June 1998, not as a monopoly but on the basis of a 'partnership'. There would be no obligation to sell to a certain body. Soon, Kembang Cengkeh Nasional (KCN) owned by Hutomo Mandala Putra stepped in. In March it became clear that the Ministry of Cooperative Societies was not very eager to manage the cloves trade, and that a partnership with KCN was being considered. At the end of April cigarette manufacturers complained that they were still forced to buy their cloves from KCN. If they did not, they could not purchase excise stamps from the Directorate of Customs and Excise (*The Jakarta Post*, 24-4-1998). In early May it was made public that Apkindo would still set export quotas for the next three years and plywood producers had no choice but to obey. According to the director of Apkindo, Tjipto Wignjoprajitno, the January IMF agreement allowed for the quota arrangements agreed earlier to continue.

The market was not impressed with the new budget and the other measures announced in the IMF agreement, not least because the IMF accord offered no specific plans to solve the economic crisis or to tackle foreign debts. The exchange rate remained at Rp 13,000 to the dollar. With the end of the fasting month approaching, which itself led to a rise in price levels each year, the first reaction to the measures triggered off a new scare about rising prices.

CHAPTER V

Towards an economic and political crisis
January-March 1998

Hayo semua bersatu padu, bulatkan tekad
Kobarkan semangat, bergerak serentak maju tegap,
kerja keras sepi pamrih
Repelita, Repelita, Repelita, Repelita ambeg paramarta
Harapan bangsa dan negara Indonesia.[1]

In the memorandum of the agreement between Indonesia and IMF it had
been pointed out that since mid-July the rupiah had depreciated by 70 per
cent, and the Jakarta Stock Exchange Index had fallen by 50 per cent. In both
respects Indonesia had performed worse than other countries in the region
affected by the crisis. The memorandum observed that the main reason for
the plunge of the rupiah was 'a severe loss of confidence in the currency, the
financial sector, and the overall economy'. Banks in other countries refused
letters of credit issued by Indonesian banks. Cash was required. At home,
prices of foodstuffs like rice, instant noodles, fruits, *tempe*, *tahu*, eggs, and
milk, had soared still further, as had those of clothes. Those of rice and cooking oil had doubled or tripled. People had to economize, to *pahe* (from *paket
hemat*, 'thrifty package'). The poor formed long queues in front of improvised
selling points where Bulog, other institutions, and rich entrepreneurs distributed cheap rice and cooking oil, or, as the newspaper *Pos Kota* and the
magazine *Panji Masyarakat* did, handed them out for free. Such food queues
reminded people of the days of Soekarno. On 4 March the Indonesian government announced that it would institute price subsidies for the nine basic
commodities. By that time many had already become too poor to profit in full
from any such move. Unemployment, high food prices, and a slackening
demand for some products and services meant that in rural areas as well as

---

[1] Repelita (five-year plan) song: Let's all unite solidly, be resolute/ stir up ardour, move firmly forward in step with one another, work hard with quiet intent/ Repelita, Repelita, Repelita,
Repelita noble endeavour/ The hope of the Indonesian nation and state.

in poor urban neighbourhoods, people no longer could afford a decent meal. People started to change their diet and substituted cassava and instant noodles for rice. Forced to do so by adverse circumstances, it was reported, some even began to fast three days a week (*Panji Masyarakat*, 23-3-1998:36). Though the agricultural sector survived the crisis relatively unharmed, farmers suffered because of the rising price of fertilizers. Pesticides became three to four times as expensive. Also hurt were farmers who depended on imports from abroad. About 60 per cent of the chicken farms went bankrupt, dependent as they were on imported poultry feed (Ghazali 1998:127). The full implication of this was only felt in January of the following year when, in anticipation of the end of the fasting month, Indonesia had to import eggs for the first time. Meat production was also affected as the import of fatting-stock from Australia ground to a halt, leading to problems around Lebaran as well. In February Ginandjar Kartasasmita disclosed that per capita income might well fall from US$ 1,088 in 1997 to US$ 610 in 1998. Faisal H. Basri MA, a well-known economist from the Universitas Indonesia, even mentioned a figure as low as US$ 228 (Sasongko 1998a:9).

Health care emerged as another field of special concern, as the sector was dependent on imports for much of its equipment and medicines. Hospitals experienced additional financial problems, and people again turned to traditional healers and medicines. Many modern medicines, of which some doubled or tripled in price, had become prohibitively expensive. People had to pay enormous sums for a medicine like insulin or for treatment in hospitals, such as a dialysis for people with kidney failure. 'Two Thousand Kidney Patients Choose To Die', read a headline in a Jakarta newspaper, reporting on people who could no longer afford treatment (*Panji Masyarakat*, 2-3-1998:66). Rich people had to travel to Bali to have their blood purified (Loebis 1999:50). Early in 1998, medicines, even in hospitals and local health centres threatened to become scarce because Indonesian letters of credit were being refused abroad. People who could no longer afford treatment left hospital, while local health centres had to close down (Subandoro 1999:98). The crisis also hit the Indonesian family planning programme, for decades one of the centrepieces of New Order development policy. Contraceptives became expensive and scarce. In April the Minister of Health, Prof. H. Farid Anfasa Moeloek, suggested that women should change from the pill to the IUD. The pill had doubled in price – each pill now costing Rp 3,000 – and had become too expensive. He said that using an IUD, which had also almost doubled in price, saved money and was more effective. To soften the consequences of the plummeting exchange rate for health care, in early February the government increased the subsidy on imported medicines and medical equipment. The World Bank also promised US$ 1 billion to be used to buy medical supplies and to assist farmers hit by the drought.

At the same time the number of unemployed had risen enormously, aggravated even more by an increase in the drop-out from schools and universities of students whose parents could no longer afford the university and school fees, or who had to work to supplement the family income. Many of them returned to their village of origin, where, in regions of want, they only added to the problems already experienced by the inhabitants. According to a conservative estimate made by the Ministry of Labour at the end of 1997, one million people had already been fired as a consequence of the economic crisis. If they were so lucky as to have had an employment contract, they had received severance pay which could last them for three or four months. Other estimates at that time already spoke of about three to four million new jobless. Such figures did not include people forcibly repatriated from Malaysia and the two to three million young people who enter the labour market each year. The secretary-general of the official labour union, FBSI, Bomer Pasaribu, estimated that the unemployment rate in 1997 was 7.7 per cent out of a total labour force of 91 million. In early February he spoke of an unemployment figure for 1998 of 13.5 million (with another 48.6 million people suffering from disguised unemployment). The following month the Ministry of Labour confirmed the estimate. The number of people who were or were to become unemployed in the course of 1998 was to rise to 13.4 million. At that time the ministry estimated the number of people working less than 35 hours a week at 18.4 million, twice as many as in 1997. At the end of April the Ministry had to admit that the figure of 13.5 million unemployed had already been reached. Estimates now soared towards 20 million. The aggregate figure of disguised and undisguised unemployment was estimated at 48.6 million, or more than half of the labour force (*Republika*, 27-4-1998). Mounting unemployment, which hit all strata of society, and the threat this posed to stability, forced the government to implement special employment programmes, mainly in the field of repair and maintenance of the infrastructure, which, scarce as money was, were no more than a drop in the ocean. The Armed Forces launched their own programmes. Those who still had a job were confronted by the fact that wages had remained the same or had even fallen.[2]

To make prospects look even more gloomy, at the beginning of the year FAO predicted that because of the long drought Indonesia might well be teetering on the verge of a food crisis. Later, in April, UNDP warned that 7.5 mil-

---

[2]   In view of the economic situation, at the end of March it was decided that minimum wages were not to be raised. The Minister of Labour, who announced the decision, asked companies which were still making a profit to raise their minimum wage. He added that it would be easy to identify such firms because companies with minium assets of Rp 50 billion had to make their finances 'transparent'.

lion people in fifteen Indonesian provinces could be threatened by a shortage of food. Apart from long drought, the use of inferior seed stock and the drop in the use of fertilizers were additional reasons to expect harvests to prove disappointing. Rice imports had to be stepped up, involving among other companies firms controlled by Liem, Siti Hutami Endang Adiningsih, and Siti Hediati Prabowo (Soesilo 1998:191).

It was yet another blow for a country which had proudly declared its self-sufficiency in the rice production in the mid-1980s, but since 1991 had again started to import rice. Speaking in reaction to this news, Beddu Amang gave the assurance that though the new Bulog stock was only two hundred tons (the year before it had been 581,000 tons), Bulog could meet domestic food requirements until December at least. There was still 2.2 million tons in stock, while a number of countries had promised help. All in all, the domestic economic situation raised a storm of complaints about the many disasters which had beset Indonesia (drought, famine in Irian Jaya, extensive forest fires in Kalimantan, Sumatra, and Sulawesi, communal violence, air crashes, to name the most serious ones), while the word 'stress' gained in popularity, as did advertisements promising a cure for this now rampant complaint. The rich 'rushed' to Ki Gendeng Pamungkas, the fortune-teller, who charged Rp 15 million per hour (or Rp 80 million per hour when clients asked him to use his magic). They wanted to know what their fate was to be and what measures they should take to deal with impending disaster. Growing criminality added to the atmosphere of doom.

The economic crisis once more accentuated the position of President Soeharto, who proudly bore the title Bapak Pembangunan, Mr Development, and highlighted the question whether he was still the right person to lead the country. The *krismon* (*krisis moneter*), as the current situation was called in common parlance (the term had become so current that even babies were named after it), had not only turned to a *krisek* (*krisis ekonomi*), but had now extended its titles to a *krismor* (*krisis moral*) and a *krisper* (*krisis kepercayaaan*, crisis of confidence), with growing numbers of people losing confidence in the government and representative bodies. It was the government and the malpractices with which it was associated which emerged as the villain of the piece in the search for a source of the economic downfall. It was not long before the term *kristal* (*krisis total*) began to be bandied around. *Reformasi*, political, economic, and legal reform, became the slogan of the day. Economically it meant an end to monopolies and cartels, and to the dominant role of the big conglomerates. Politically it meant a new president, repeal of the package of the five political acts from 1985 which had become synonymous with the deficiencies of the formal political system, free general elections, and freedom to found political parties. It also included a strong legislative power, a bureaucracy and judicial power which no longer were just extensions of the power of the ruling élite, and an end to crony capitalism and KKN, *korupsi, kolusi* and *nepotisme*, or as Amien Rais on one occasion referred to it, the CCN sickness: corruption, collusion, and nepotism. Greater transparency was the order of the day; the people should know how and why decisions were taken. The way to enforce such changes was at times described as people power, massive demonstrations, taking its example from the fall of Ferdinand Marcos in the Philippines. The economic crisis became a topic of sermons in mosques, and increasingly, though initially modestly, in the press doubts were raised about whether the regime, and by analogy Soeharto, were the right persons to overcome the crisis. People began to argue that only under a new president would the much needed economic and political reforms be implemented. 'Political reformation can't be postponed' was written in bold letters on the front page of the Islamic magazine *Ummat* in the middle of January.

There were still some demonstrations in favour of Soeharto's re-election. Others, and Prof. Juwono Sudarsono, the deputy governor of the Lemhanas, a government think-tank, was one of them, were against a replacement of Soeharto for reasons of stability. Their argument was that in the critical situation in which Indonesia found herself, this would merely add to the many uncertainties, and could only aggravate the situation. There was also some trepidation about what a power struggle might unleash, the chaos and communal violence that might ride high and the old scores that might be settled when order broke down. Among the people who had testified in the past of their anxiety about what a succession could provoke were the *ulama*. In June 1994 one of them, KH Yusuf Hasyim (Pak Ud), an uncle of Abdurrahman Wahid, had even prophetically pointed out that 1997 was to be a critical year. To illustrate what he meant he recalled the political situation in the early 1960s, when he had founded Barisan Serba Guna (Banser), a grouping within NU's youth organization Pemuda Ansor, to counter the activities of the Pemuda Rakjat, People's Youth, of the PKI, alluding to the subsequent role of NU in the suppression of the PKI after September 1965. A compromise solution, suggested as early as April 1997, when Soeharto had stated that he was too old to serve once more as president, was that he should step down after one or two years. This possibility made the position of vice-president even more significant.

By now, calls for a different president had grown into a swelling chorus. Some urged for Soeharto's resignation. The sooner he resigned the better. Others suggested that the general session of the People's Congress be brought forward. Among them were fifteen NGOs from Jakarta and West Java, coordinated by the director of LBH, Legal Aid Foundation, of Jakarta, Apong Herlina SH, who presented a petition to the parliament and the People's Congress at the end of January. Urging the government to take full

responsibility for the economic and financial crisis and to take decisive action
to bring down prices, they put in a plea asking to bring forward the general
session of the People's Congress to have Soeharto account for the tottering
political and economic structure. Yet others adopted a more subtle approach.
Adi Sasono appealed to the People's Congress pointing out that in view of
Soeharto's and Tutut's appeal, it had to look for another candidate. It would
not be right to force a new term on Soeharto. A similar suggestion was made
by the board of Yayasan Kerukunan Persaudaraan Kebangsaan (YKPK), of
which the general chairman was Bambang Triantoro, who had been Armed
Forces Chief of Staff for Social and Political Affairs between 1985 and 1987.
Its secretary-general was H. Matori Abdul Djalil.[3] Stressing that, in view of
his age and health, Soeharto should not be forced to shoulder the heavy burden of a new term, YKPK advanced Try Sutrisno as candidate for the presidency, and Edi Sudradjat as his deputy. If Soeharto were re-elected, Try
Sutrisno should be elected for a second term in office as well. In the political
climate of the day, the position adopted in such a statement was immediately criticized as driving a wedge between Soeharto and Try Sutrisno, thereby
weakening Try Sutrisno's political position.

Who in actual fact was to succeed Soeharto and could muster enough
popular support was another matter. Some pinned their hopes on Megawati,
others on Amien Rais (who, some joked, even had the advantage of his name,
as *rois* is Arabic for president). Amien Rais himself suggested a praesidium
take charge. None of the people who stood any chance of succeeding
Soeharto could count on widespread, uncontested support. Were one of them
to emerge as a front runner, conflicts would certainly be the inevitable outcome. Judging from an opinion poll held by *Tempo Interaktif* prior to the general election, Try Sutrisno could count on support from society as a whole. He
got most of the votes of those who had taken the trouble to respond via the
Internet (335 persons), more than twice as much as Habibie and Megawati
(see *Pemilu* 1997:7-23).

Amien Rais had already indicated that he was prepared to be elected president, but Megawati had so far held back. On 10 January, at a meeting to commemorate the founding of PDI, Megawati, who for months had mostly
remained silent, at last announced that she was willing to be a candidate for
the presidency. It was a statement welcomed by Amien Rais as a courageous
decision, but received with stony indifference by most of the government

---

3   YKPK, stressing national unity and bringing together people of different religions, had
been founded in October 1995, ostensibly out of concern about the rise of particularistic groups,
of which ICMI was considered to be one. Among its members had been Lieutenant-General
(Ret.) Kharis Suhud, Dahlan Ranuwihardjo (a former general chairman of HMI), Frans Seda (former chairman of the Catholic Party), and politicians of the three parties.

officials asked to comment, and volubly deplored by Harmoko, who fulmi-
nated that people could not just nominate themselves.

Amien Rais and Megawati Soekarnoputri met publicly on 15 January. The
meeting, which was covered by the national and international press, took
place in the house of Mrs Supeni, the chairperson of one of the groups of dissidents that had been formed the previous year, PNI Baru, or New PNI. For
months her home had been a place where figures critical of the government
frequently gathered to discuss the political situation. In 1997 they had
formed the Group of 28 October (the Day of the Youth Pledge, when
Indonesian young people in 1928 had vowed that they had one fatherland,
Indonesia, that there was one nation, the Indonesian nation, and there was
one national language, Indonesian). Among its members were long-standing
dissidents, who right from its inception in 1980 had been members of the so-
called Group of Fifty, such as Ali Sadikin, H.M. Sanusi, and Kris Siner Key
Timu. Others who had joined were Prof. Baharuddin Lopa, secretary-general of the National Committee for Human Rights, Sabam Sirait, a PDI leader
from the Megawati camp, Usep Ranuwidjaja, and Sri Edi Swasono, a brother of Sri Bintang Pamungkas. After their meeting on 15 January they issued
a statement stressing amongst other shortcomings the lack of democracy and
the decline in the esteem and self-respect of the Indonesian nation. It was
announced that the Group of 28 October was to meet members of the
People's Congress in the hope that they would nominate Amien Rais or
Megawati for the post of president. Support for the two also emerged from
groups like SIAGA (Ready), short for Solidaritas Indonesia untuk Amien dan
Mega, Indonesian Solidarity for Amien and Mega, coordinated by Ratna
Sarumpaet, director of the Satu Merah Panggung theatre group.

Conspicuously absent at the meeting in the home of Mrs Supeni was
Abdurrahman Wahid, who had resurfaced as a critic of the government at
the end of the previous year and in a public statement had urged that social
and legal justice be upheld and that an end be made to nepotism and corruption. He blamed his absence on a misunderstanding. Reports about the
cancelling of the national dialogue prepared by Dewi Fortuna Anwar and
Adi Sasono had led him to believe that the meeting had been cancelled.
Whatever the reason for his absence may have been, Abdurrahman Wahid
kept his distance. His ostensible reason for this was that he suspected that
one of the motives of the conveners of the meeting in inviting him had been
to involve NU in a demonstration at the People's Congress. Speaking to journalists, Abdurrahman Wahid explained that it was impossible for him to
comply with any request to mobilize NU supporters. Relations between NU
members and the government were good. Even had he desired to do so, he
would not be able to persuade them to take part in anti-government demonstrations. On another occasion Abdurrahman Wahid intimated that he sup-

ported Amien Rais and Megawati, but did not intend to join them in a coalition as long as he was not sure about the objectives and methods to be employed. He clearly feared large-scale demonstrations with tens of thousands of people taking the streets for days or even weeks on end. Mass demonstrations were fraught with danger. It would be an easy task to manipulate them and escalate them into racial or religious riots. NU members should not become involved.

Before the month was out, the formal nomination of Soeharto had been decided upon. The first step was taken by Harmoko, who on 13 January made public that, as the president had asked, Golkar had conducted an investigation into the trust the people still placed in Soeharto. He had personally checked the opinion of local Golkar branches during his Ramadhan Safari (his visits all over the country which it had been his wont to undertake during the fasting month). The results had been positive. The survey had shown that the majority of the population was still in favour of Soeharto undertaking a new term in office. Nobody had opposed his nomination by Golkar. Golkar, Harmoko stressed, had to follow the wishes of the people. Formal nomination followed a week later. On 20 January, Soeharto received a delegation consisting of the leaders of the three 'components' that make up Golkar, the Keluarga Besar Golkar, 'Greater Golkar Family': Harmoko, general chairman of Golkar, General Feisal Tanjung, commander of the Armed Forces, and M. Yogie SM, Minister of Internal Affairs. Informing Soeharto of the results of the survey, they asked the president to allow Golkar to nominate him, to which he consented. On 23 January this was followed by an announcement by PPP that Soeharto was their candidate for the presidency as well. It was added that the party had already informed President Soeharto of its choice on 7 January.

Among the first to denounce Soeharto's decision were nineteen political researchers from the Indonesian Academy of Sciences. The very same day, 20 January, they issued a statement expressing their concern. In it they deplored the fact that the authorities pretended that everything was continuing as normal and closed their eyes to the fact that the pay of a day-labourer had dropped to a level that made it impossible for them to maintain their dignity and that the quality of life in many households was ebbing away fast. Another point that irritated them was that the government preferred to listen to what was said abroad and tended to view with suspicion any suggestion from outside their own circles about how to overcome the crisis. They saw proof of this in the fact that, and this argument did not escape others, that most of the recommendations now made by IMF had been put forward for years by domestic critics. The statement went on to point out that instead of taking decisive steps, the authorities procrastinated and looked for scapegoats. They stated that the crisis went deeper than economic problems alone.

As the whole sorry situation was caused by the mismanagement of the state, a change in national leadership was imperative. This was the only way the self-respect of the nation could be restored and the much needed economic and political reforms be implemented peacefully. The statement earned the nineteen a formal reprimand from Habibie, the Minister of Research. The task of LIPI scholars was to write reports for the government, not to issue statements which might only exacerbate the unrest in society. Habibie did not hesitate to accuse the researchers of engaging in 'practical politics', a term to denote activities which should be left to politicians, and frequently used since 1978 to condemn and contain student protests.

The meeting of 20 January had been important in another respect. After it Harmoko revealed that Golkar had drawn up a list of fourteen criteria the future vice-president had to meet. These included such stipulations as that the person in question had to be a far-sighted visionary and had to be a well-known figure on the international scene. The latter criterion was interpreted by some as a side-swipe at General Try Sutrisno, who was thought to lack foreign contacts. The criterion that drew the most attention was the one which stated that the vice-president had to possess a good understanding of the sciences and of technology (in Indonesian jargon *iptek*, short for *ilmu pengetahuan dan teknologi*), and to have an insight into industry and the way it could be used in the national interest. The mention of *iptek* was a strong indication that Golkar, with the blessing of Soeharto, if not indeed at his instigation, intended to put forward Habibie as the party's candidate for the vice-presidency. In early February Soeharto issued a formal denial that he was the source of the criteria promulgated by Golkar, though at that time it was already a public secret that he had mentioned some of them, including the *iptek* criterion, in earlier meetings with Feisal Tanjung and Ismail Hasan Metareum. He also indicated that he would not disclose his own favourite for the vice-presidency and that the time for the parties in the People's Congress to consult with him about their choice was after a president had been elected. Indeed, from what was disclosed, it appears that at that time Soeharto did not mention any persons by name, only reacting in a hazy, non-specific way, making vague allusions which were interpreted as being noises of approval, whenever Habibie was mentioned.

It was generally conceded that the *iptek* criterion diminished the chances of Harmoko and Hartono. From that moment on, Habibie was considered by many to be the strongest candidate. Inside and outside Indonesia there was strong criticism of this, while the rupiah plunged still further, falling to Rp 12,000 to the dollar. Among the people not pleased with the news was the first deputy managing director of IMF, Stanley Fischer. In the middle of the following month, he noted that the new fall in the rupiah had been triggered off by the fact that the new vice-president might be somebody whose devotion to new ways of doing things was limited (*The Jakarta Post*, 14-2-1998). In Singapore the former Prime Minister, Lee Kuan Yew, made a similar comment. He predicted that the economic crisis in Southeast Asia would end after Indonesia had elected a new president and vice-president, adding that the latter should have the confidence of the market. What he meant, the conclusion both in and outside Indonesia was, was that Habibie should not be elected. In Indonesia itself, people, among them Sofyan Wanandi, who made no secret of not being in favour of a nomination of Habibie, felt that if Habibie were elected the rupiah would plummet to new depths. These and other remarks, for instance about the Timor, cost Sofyan Wanandi his position as spokesman of the Jimbaran group. In January Soeharto left no doubt he thought that Sofyan Wanandi had become too critical (Wangge and Wangge 1999:156). Habibie's supporters were quick to disqualify such anti-Habibie voices as indications of discontent at home and abroad about the more prominent role Islam was assuming in Indonesian society through the efforts of the Habibie-led ICMI.

In view of the fact that the list of criteria had been compiled in consultation with Feisal Tanjung (belonging to the group of devout Islamic army officers and an associate of Habibie), another conclusion which was drawn was that Habibie was to be the nominee of the Armed Forces as well. To counter such an opinion, the assistant for social and political affairs of the Chief of Staff for Social and Political Affairs, Major-General Susilo Bambang Yudhoyono, immediately commented that the Armed Forces had not yet decided on any one name (*Panji Masyarakat*, 19-1-1998:19). It might well be that at that time within the army Habibie could count on the support of Feisal Tanjung and Prabowo, but that his nomination was opposed by such other influential officers as its Chief of Staff, Wiranto, and the Minister of Defence and Security, Edi Sudradjat.

To Habibie the list of criteria was a clear sign to begin intensifying his lobbying. From Berlin he phoned one of his confidants, Lieutenant-General (Ret.) Achmad Tirtosudiro, an ICMI chairman and former HMI leader. He asked him to contact Amien Rais to arrange a meeting. Publicly Achmad Tirtosudiro took great pains to stress that ICMI still considered Amien Rais a friend, that the position of chairman of the Council of Experts was still vacant, and that there had never been any effort to expel Amien Rais from ICMI. Achmad Tirtosudiro disclosed that there had also been contact with General Feisal Tanjung. In the eyes of the key officers of the Armed Forces, on whose behalf only a few days earlier Susilo Bambang Yudhoyono had still maintained that a decision had not yet been taken, this was reason enough to stress that they had already decided on their candidate after the general elections. The only person who could make them change their mind was President Soeharto, the person who was the choice of the people and headed the country. Even were the president to decide that he wanted Amien Rais or Megawati as his deputy, the Armed Forces would support him.

Others were quick to observe that Habibie was not the only one who met the *iptek* criterion. They pointed out that Ginandjar Kartasasmita and Try Sutrisno also met that condition. Try Sutrisno was a graduate of the Army Technical Academy and had served in the Engineering Corps. Quite apart from seeking suitable candidates with technological qualifications, a number of people played down the *iptek* factor. Rudini stressed that a vice-president had to be acceptable to all groups in society. This placed a far greater emphasis on leadership qualities. It was these qualities for which Soeharto had been accepted, and not for his insight into science and technology. These qualities had also enabled him to give leadership to experts in economics and technology who assisted him in governing the country. Yet others, among them the former vice-president, Soedharmono, the leader of the Golkar party in parliament, Theo L. Sambuaga, and Haryono Suyono, a member of the Council of Patrons of Golkar, indicated that the condition had been phrased in general terms, making it possible for a number of people to meet it, and that science and technology was not confined to the exact sciences.

Golkar came under a wave of new criticism for coming up with a list of criteria instead of a name. When the going was rough, the latter was needed to restore public faith at home and also abroad, where uncertainty about who would lead Indonesia had been adduced by the business world as one of the arguments for postponing investments in Indonesia. Ir Sarwono Kusumaatmadja, a former secretary-general of Golkar and at that time Minister without Portfolio of Environment, in an interview with *Merdeka*, suggested that in view of the political situation the sooner it became known who the next vice-president would be, the better. It was beyond belief, given the present circumstances, that people could still argue that naming the candidate before the general session of the People's Congress was against the rules. He urged that the persons who were competing for the post should meet the president as soon as possible to talk out their differences and decide on a candidate. In his eyes, *iptek* was not the most important criterion. This was trust shown by 'the market' (*Merdeka*, 24-1-1998).

As can be surmised from such statements, Habibie's nomination did not go unchallenged, not even in Golkar. Among those against were the children of Soeharto, especially Siti Hardijanti Rukmana and Bambang Trihatmodjo, building their own power base within Golkar, and his friend Bob Hasan. Reportedly, Tutut's favourite was Hartono, Bambang's Try Sutrisno.[4] By early February four major candidates still remained. Harmoko, Try Sutrisno,

---

[4]   *Far Eastern Economic Review*, 26-2-1998:15, 26-3-1998:22; *Forum Keadilan*, 6-4-1998:13; *Golkar* 1999:33-4.

Ginandjar Kartasasmita, and Habibie. Within Golkar, opposition to Habibie came from the so-called *trikarya*, Kosgoro, Musyawarah Kekeluargaan dan Gotong Royong (MKGR), and SOKSI – founding fathers, so to speak, of Golkar. In the eyes of Kosgoro leaders, the new vice-president should not be just a technical expert, he had to be a generalist. Judging from the public statements, their preference went to Try Sutrisno, Ginandjar Kartasasmita, Harmoko, or, a new name just suggested, the Minister Coordinator of Industry and Trade, Hartarto. SOKSI seems to have been in favour of Harmoko and Hartarto, MKGR of Try Sutrisno. Harmoko could also count on the support of some of the Golkar board. In early February two Golkar chairmen, Agung Laksono (also vice-chairman of the Golkar party in the People's Congress) and Pinantun Hutasoit (chairman for politics and culture of Golkar) spoke out in favour of Harmoko. Abdul Gafur did the same. General Try Sutrisno had the support of leaders of Muslimin Indonesia, one of the components of PPP, while among the persons who spoke out in favour of Try Sutrisno was Said Aqil Siradj, a secretary of the Council for Religious Advice of Nahdlatul Ulama. As the most important reasons, he mentioned that close cooperation with Soeharto was essential in such troubled times and that Try Sutrisno's religious knowledge would certainly not go amiss. A third point put forward by Said Aqil Siradj was that Try Sutrisno was a retired general. In view of the diversity of the Indonesian population, the country needed an army officer as vice-president. Ginandjar Kartasasmita (Om Jonny), well known for his efforts while he was a cabinet minister to promote the indigenous business sector, could count on the support of a number of businessmen, the so-called Ginandjar Boys, including Aburizal Bakrie, Fadel Muhammad, and Arifin Panigoro.

A suggestion by the general chairman of AMPI, Indra Bambang Utoyo, that in view of the monetary crisis Prof. Emil Salim, a former deputy chairman of the National Planning Bureau, who had held several ministerial posts since 1971, was a most suitable candidate also came in for its fair share of public attention.[5] Emil Salim, a Chairman of the Council of Experts of ICMI, who with Widjojo Nitisastro and Radius Prawiro had engineered the dawn of Indonesia's economic recovery at the beginning of the New Order, responded by stating that as a Golkar cadre member he could not but accept if this party should nominate him.

In less than a month the matter was decided. The first to withdraw was Ginandjar Kartasasmita. In a last-ditch attempt to win, Harmoko called together the chairmen of the provincial branches of Golkar to impress upon

---

5   Emil Salim had been Minister of Communications from 1973 to 1978, Minister without Portfolio of Supervision of Development and the Environment from 1978 to 1983, and after that Minister without Portfolio of Population and Environment.

them that it was only logical that the general chairman of a party which had won the general election so overwhelmingly would become vice-president. He failed. On 11 February, after a meeting of the central board of Golkar, it was announced that two candidates remained: Harmoko and Habibie. Critics of the choice were silenced. Politicians in the *trikarya* were ordered by the president to stop publicly tossing names of their favourites about. They were only allowed to discuss criteria.

The formal mention of two names was unprecedented in the history of the New Order and created the impression of deep rifts within Golkar, though this was immediately either denied or presented as an indication of nascent democracy within the party. Some bandied about the possibility that Soeharto was wavering or had not yet made up his mind. Judging from a statement made by Yogie SM, the double nomination had been made at the instigation of the 'bureaucrats' within Golkar, implying that at least some of the cadre leaders of Golkar itself and the Armed Forces were in favour of Habibie. The final choice between the 'two Hs' was to be made after consultation with the Armed Forces, the Minister of Internal Affairs, the president, and the organizations that supported Golkar.

The same day, on 11 February, the deputy secretary-general of PPP, Bachtiar Chamsyah, revealed that his party also had two candidates: Habibie and Ismail Hasan Metareum. Four days later, Ismail Hasan Metareum stated that PPP would nominate Habibie. Metareum said that the PPP board had made its decision on the basis of a set of criteria he had received from President Soeharto, which included reference to a mastery of science and technology. Habibie, Metareum explained, met these criteria better than he himself did. On 16 February, after yet another meeting of the Golkar central board during which, it was reported, discussions were heated, Harmoko stated that he wanted to concentrate on his duties as speaker of the People's Congress. It was reported that in the meeting with Soeharto the president had asked him to follow the example of Ginandjar Kartasasmita (*Panji Masyarakat*, 23-2-1998:28). The single Golkar candidate left was Habibie. Still, the same day, the general chairman of PDI, Soerjadi, declared that Habibie was the choice of his party as well. On 17 February, after a meeting with the provincial governors, the Minister of Internal Affairs, Yogie SM, announced that the faction of regional representatives in the People's Congress would nominate Habibie. On 18 February Try Sutrisno publicly declared he would not seek re-election. Finally, the members of parliament representing the Armed Forces had followed suit. Feisal Tanjung acclaimed this decision as a clear indication of their commitment to promote democracy. Nahdlatul Ulama preserved a stony silence. Many of its leaders probably preferred Try Sutrisno. After a meeting of its board, a statement was issued to the effect that the organization did not want to become entangled in the issues surrounding the forthcoming general session of the People's Congress. NU did not support any one individual. It would support the choice the People's Congress made.

In the meantime, since the middle of January, food riots and violent demonstrations had been rearing their ugly heads, occasioned by high prices of *sembako*, or *sembilan bahan pokok*, the nine basic commodities, and the absence of fresh supplies in shops. In small cities groups of youths, often drivers of motorcycle taxis, drove around on their motorcycle shouting 'Lower the prices', and other such slogans. Chinese-owned shops and warehouses were especially targeted. Food riots had spread from East Java to the rest of Indonesia. In Rembang in Central Java on 26 January, a crowd consisting mostly of fishermen damaged shops in the small town of Kragan. Two days later, similar incidents took place in Lumajang, East Java. In Tuban regency, also in East Java, riots lasted from January 28-30. On 2 February it was the turn of Ujungpandang in South Sulawesi, on 7 February Bima, on 18 February Ende in Flores, and on 9 February Sidoarjo in East Java. At Bima, where a crowd shouted 'throw, set alight', no looting took place but stocks of beer and wine were destroyed by the mob. Some owners tried to protect their shops by placing their prayer cloths and mats and the special white praying gown worn by women in front of them. The *bupati* who tried to calm down the crowd was pelted with gas lighters. Incidents continued to flare up throughout the month: in Pasuruan and Bojonegoro in East Java, in Bumiaya, Losari, Brebes, Tegal, and Cirebon in Central Java, in Kuningan, Majalengka, Jatiwangi, Pamanukan, Subang, and Pangalengan in West Java, in Buleleng in Bali, in Donggala in Central Sulawesi, in Kendari in Southeast Sulawesi, and in Praya in Lombok. Riots were also reported in Lahat and Rantau Prapat in North Sumatra. Elsewhere, shopkeepers closed their shops after rumours had started that riots were on the verge of breaking out. During '*sembako* riots', apart from damage of shops and looting, shopkeepers were sometimes forced to sell their products at a low price. It also happened that products, including foodstuffs, were assembled in the street to be set fire to. Such riots often seemed to be triggered by rumours of imminent price rises. Occasionally they were caused by unrelated events. Near Bandung, the trigger was anger about a strike of public transport drivers who protested about the rise in prices of components and lubricating oil. In Ujungpandang clashes between youths were at the root of the disturbances. Such riots, Masdar F. Mas'udi, director of the Indonesian Society for Pesantren and Community Development, suggested, might well have been occasioned by an appeal by MUI for a holy war against speculators and hoarders (*The Jakarta Post*, 20-2-1998).

Moving to stem the rising tides, the military and the police intensified operations against traders and shopkeepers suspected of hoarding, ensuring good publicity for the operations and the goods discovered. They took the opportunity to point out that under the legislation pertaining to the economic subversion, those guilty could be sentenced to twenty years or more, and could even be liable for the death penalty. All this did not blind them to the fact that there was a problem. What was the gauge of volume of stock at which hoarding began, and what should be done when stock had mounted up because of transportation problems? In March, to ensure supplies and to bring down prices, the army launched its Operasi Semar, short for *Sembilan Bahan Pokok Manunggal ABRI-Rakyat*, Nine Basic Commodities Unite the Armed Forces and the People, scheduled to last till January 1999. Targeted for *sembako* droppings, to be sold at production cost, were those regions all over Indonesia where such products were in short supply or where prices had skyrocketed. It was publicly announced that part of the funding came from voluntary contributions by businessmen in Jakarta, who up to then had felt that their hands had been tied about what to do to relieve the fate of the poor, who were hardest hit by the economic crisis, suggesting that it was the businessmen who had taken the initiative.

Since the start of the New Order in 1966, student demonstrations against rising prices and political abuses had been a recurrent phenomenon. In the closing months of 1997 and at the beginning of 1998 it took some time for these to gain momentum. In fact, so little happened that up to the end of January 1998 people were beginning to wonder about the absence of demonstrations and commented on the apolitical attitude of students, who themselves were suffering just as much as anybody else from the economic recession. It was suggested that life had become too expensive to demonstrate. Students could no longer afford to pay their tuition fees and buy books, and were, as other Indonesians, hard-hit by the rising prices of food. For some, even the buying of paper and the making of photocopies were now beyond their means. Organizing demonstrations required money for banners, food, and so forth. Another explanation was that students had been taken by surprise by the pace at which the situation had changed, and were thrown into a quandary about how to react (*Merdeka Minggu*, Minggu ke-4 Januari 1998).

There were protests, in Jakarta, Semarang, Yogyakarta, Bogor, and Bandung, for instance, but the number of students participating in them remained small. In October, during a meeting in Bandung of Ikatan Senat Mahasiswa Hukum Indonesia, the Indonesian Union of Senates of Law Students, those present spoke out against a renomination of President Soeharto. In the same month similar statements were issued at Universitas Islam Indonesia in Yogyakarta, and the universities of Muhammadiyah in Yogyakarta and Surakarta. Student groups such as Forum Komunikasi Pemuda dan Mahasiswa Jakarta, the Communication Forum of Young Persons and Students from Jakarta, Forum Komunikasi Senat Mahasiswa Jakarta (FKSMJ), the Com-

munication Forum of Jakarta Student Senates, and Forum Komunikasi
Mahasiswa Islam Jakarta, also rejected the idea of a new term for President
Soeharto, but their opinions attracted little public attention. This stood in
sharp contrast to a demonstration staged in Jakarta on 9 January by students
and young people from Pijar at the Tugu Proklamasi monument in Central
Jakarta to commemorate the Tritura, the Three Demands of the People, in
1966. They formulated a new set of demands: 1. lower prices and stabilize the
rupiah, 2. change the cabinet fundamentally, and 3. a new president.[6] On 13
January students and young people calling themselves Suara Rakyat Surabaya, the Voice of the People of Surabaya, staged a protest march. In Medan
on 11 February hundreds of students attended a 'free stage' to express concern about the rising prices. Among the posters paraded around, there were
some calling for a restriction on IMF intervention. The same day there were
protests in Palu in Central Sulawesi, where students marching to the local
representative body demanded a lowering of prices and opposed the re-election of Soeharto. Security forces reacted harshly and dozens of students were
wounded. Elsewhere, there were more student protests against rising prices.

Such manifestations still fell within the normal scenario in the months
leading to a general session of the People's Congress. Uncoordinated small-
scale protests had become the norm since the military had forcibly put an end
to large student demonstrations protesting the re-election of Soeharto in
January 1978. By banning student councils, the engine of the resistance at that
time, the authorities had deprived the student movement of its organizational network. The student senates, which were allowed, could not fill the
gap. Massive demonstrations had still coloured political life from time to
time, but only when Islamic issues were at stake. Most notable had been the
protests at the end of 1991 and the beginning of 1992 against a government-
sponsored lottery, the SDSB, organized by a foundation in which Sigit Harjojudanto and Sudwikatmono also had a stake (Sasongko 1998c:17; *Harta Soeharto* n.d.:17).

One of the few large demonstrations in the early weeks of 1998 took place
in Bandung on 16 January, when thousands of students took to the streets
after the Friday prayer to protest about the rising prices, staging a mass
demonstration in front of the Institut Teknologi Bandung (ITB). A 'free stage'
was held and a statement read out, demanding amongst other moves an end
to political rhetoric and jargon in official comments on the crisis. Student
leaders announced that they would continue to stage protests till the prices
of *sembako* fell. Another mass demonstratoin took place in Yogyakarta at the
end of January when Amien Rais and Megawati were present at a

---

6   The original Tritura formulated by students in 1966 had been 'Lower the prices, ban the
Communist party of Indonesia, and change the cabinet'.

'Ramadhan dialogue', held on the campus of Universitas Islam Indonesia. Referring to the protests the appointment of her father as president for life had drawn during the Old Order, Megawati underlined the need of protests against the fact that to all intents and purposes Soeharto was to be elected as president for life as well.

Part and parcel of Indonesian political culture is that the run-up to the general session of the People's Congress is accompanied by assessments about what is invariably called the 'heating up of the political climate' and by warnings for citizens to be on the alert for persons and groups set on creating disorder and exploiting such a situation for their own political ends. The 1998 general session formed no exception. As early as June 1997, when he became the new Chief of Staff of the Army, General Wiranto had warned that the mobilization of large crowds might be inevitable when the People's Congress met. On the same occasion, General Feisal Tanjung had spoken of groups already identified by the army who had tried to sabotage the general elections, and who would make a new attempt in March 1998. At the end of 1997 Moetojib, the head of the Intelligence Service (Bakin), observed that agitators and extremists intended to create chaos on the eve of the general session of the People's Congress. He claimed their aim was to create a state based on religion. He asked people not to believe everything reported on the Internet, where various theories about a struggle for power were circulating. For a good while Abdurrahman Wahid had been hinting at a conspiracy and possible outbreaks of violence planned by people who were set on having their own candidate elected vice-president.

President Soeharto joined in as well. On 12 February, when he received the participants at the annual meeting of the most senior officers of the Armed Forces, he instructed them to take firm measures against all persons who transgressed the law and violated the constitution, intent on bringing about national disintegration. As had become the vogue, Soeharto singled out groups that wanted to enforce their will upon others in the name of democracy and freedom. He lashed out at certain persons who wanted to exploit the financial crisis to undermine faith in the government in order to accomplish their own political aims by spreading all kinds of alarmist rumours and by playing off one group against the other. The military commander of Jakarta, Major-General Syafrie Syamsuddin, indirectly hinting at the consequences of demonstrations for the economy, put the blame on radical groups that championed basic human rights and democracy but in fact acted contrary to their ideals, as they only made the situation in which the population found itself worse. They would themselves never be among the rioters. They would 'pull the trigger' (*Republika*, 7-1-1998). He mentioned PRD by name. Such groups, he and other authorities were convinced, acted in close cooperation. Syafrie Syamsuddin said that they had met in Lampung to plan their campaign. Other reports spoke of a group styled Orde Demokrasi, held responsible for a wave of bomb threats in Jakarta, Medan, and Ujungpandang and reports of disturbances in the middle of February. According to the authorities, the group also planned the occupation of the congress building and the presidential palace.

Other people were convinced that the army was behind the unrest. On 10 February, when meeting the press during the annual meeting of senior officers, Mokodongan had to deny rumours that army officers had masterminded food riots and demonstrations, either in an attempt to achieve political gains or in an effort to divert attention from the economic situation.

By this time the situation had been complicated by the financial crisis. As had already become evident the previous year with the general public still largely puzzled about why the crisis had hit Indonesia with such a force, there was a profound suspicion that foreigners and certain Indonesians were aggravating the nation's economic downfall on purpose for their own economic and political ends. Lukman Harun, a PPP politician with roots in Muhammadiyah, pointed out for instance that Soeharto was not only the head of state, but also the leader of the Indonesian Islamic community. The Islamic community had to take a common stand. In certain Muslim quarters such ideas were coupled with the suspicion that IMF was in fact no more than an extension of the Christian West, aiming to impose Western ideas on the majority in an Islamic society. They saw the pressure exerted by IMF and the United States as part of a Christian conspiracy. In the eyes of some, the external pressure was part of an even larger plot involving Indonesian Chinese and Indonesian Christians, suffering from a 'post power syndrome', bewailing the fact that they had lost their influence in the military and in the government in the second half of the 1980s. Trying to explain what was happening, one of them, Hartono Mardjono, a member of the Indonesian Council of Ulama and of the Jakarta Council of Experts of ICMI, wrote that it was a 'politico-economic rebellion' launched by exponents of a 'domestic minority' (that is, rich Chinese businessmen and certain politicians and military officers), putting their economic power into play. At home they used groups like PRD, while internationally they were backed up by Islamophobic Western states, Western capitalists, and overseas Chinese (hence also Lee Kuan Yew's rejection of Habibie's candidacy for the vice-presidency) (Mardjono 1998:26, 30, 32, 72). He put their conspiracy on a par with the activities of PKI during the Old Order.

Tommy was not the only one to speak of neo-colonialism. The suspicion that an international neo-capitalist conspiracy was afoot was aired as well. The chairman of MUI, KH Hasan Basri, said the crisis was a new form of colonialism. Certain 'elements' had deliberately created the economic situation in which Indonesia found itself. Asked who these elements were, he replied that they were persons who no longer had faith in rupiahs and changed these for dollars. An expert from Gadjah Mada University in Yogyakarta, Dr Afan Gaffar, also spoke of a national and international market conspiracy to force Soeharto to step down (*Republika*, 23-1-1998). Yet others were convinced that the decision to try no longer to prevent the fall of the rupiah had deliberately been taken to destroy the business empires of Soeharto's family and associates (*Golkar* 1999:62). The general chairman of the Islamic organization Al-Irsyad, Geys Ammar SH, pointed to broadcastings of the BBC, the Voice of America, and Radio Nederland to demonstrate a link between forces at home and abroad. It was as clear as day that they had not hesitated to stoop to foul play. This was demonstrated by the fact that every time the Indonesian government announced measures, the rupiah sank to an even more unimaginable low.

The tone had in part been set by Premier Mahathir Mohamad of Malaysia, who put much of the blame for the monetary crisis on George Soros and suggested that the West was doing all it could to prevent viable economic rivals appearing on the scene (for Mahathir's opinions see Mahathir 1998). In Indonesia there was distrust of the ulterior motives of IMF and the United States. Many did not like the implication that Indonesia had to bow to directives from abroad, surrendering some of her rights as an independent state. Inviting IMF, Amien Rais expanded, meant that Indonesia had temporarily pawned her economic sovereignty to foreigners and been subjected to economic colonization by the West (Rais 1998:86). Consequently there were some demonstrations against IMF and its intervention in the Indonesian economy, urging the government to be cautious about accepting IMF aid and not to sell out Indonesia's honour. In the middle of January, for instance, Islamic students staged this sort of demonstration in Jakarta in front of the Ministry of Finance. Around the same time, the cover of *Ummat* carried a headline: 'Indonesia under IMF coloni[alism]' (*Ummat*, 26-1-1998). Others suggested that Indonesia should follow the example of Malaysia and reject the IMF directives. Suspicion about IMF machinations was not confined to Muslim circles. Some Indonesians, a columnist wrote shortly after 15 January, had begun to voice doubts, saying that 'IMF merely wants to take over Indonesia's sovereignty, while overcoming the economic crisis without distributing any money' (Kwik Kian Gie, *The Jakarta Post*, 20-1-1998).

Others venting their suspicions looked for scapegoats nearer home. The idea that politicians were exploiting the situation had, for instance, been suggested by the Secretary of State, Moerdiono, on 19 December. He did so after an emergency meeting had been called by President Soeharto to discuss the implications of the fall of the rupiah. On 9 February, asking members of MUI to assist in countering the many efforts being made to instigate unrest and the harmful consequences of all kinds of rumours, President Soeharto accused certain groups of exploiting a situation which had been brought about by the gambling and speculations of businesspeople for their own ends. Two days later the president was talking about the conspiracies of certain groups intent on bringing down the rupiah, destroying the economic foundations of Indonesia, and shattering Indonesia's unity through financial manipulations and the dissemination of all kinds of rumours, scaremongering, for instance, about his own ill health. He implied that they wanted to increase unemployment, which would give them a tractable labour force. Later in the month the deputy secretary-general of the new Council for the Stabilization of Monetary and Economic Resilience, Fuad Bawazier, accused persons of taking revenge because they had lost their power to exploit the crisis. By the spreading of all kinds of rumours, by using disturbances, and by sowing discord, they planned their comeback. To the amazement of many, A.H. Nasution, the critical sage of the Indonesian army and recently awarded the honorary rank of Great General, also had his say. In a special one-page press statement issued in early February, he warned of political adventurers who always appeared on the scene when a crisis was at hand.

On 22 January, when the value of the rupiah had temporarily sunk to Rp 15,000 to the dollar, Amien Rais joined those who expressed the opinion that the financial crisis had been deliberately engineered. The plunge of the rupiah, which he said could no longer be explained rationally, indicated that a 'very vulgar' game was being played with the purpose of bringing down the government. A united stand had to be taken to counteract the malicious mischief perpetrated by Indonesians and foreigners whose actions exceeded all bounds. Later, on 11 February, in an interview with *The Jakarta Post*, Amien Rais alluded to 'certain market forces and external powers' who hoped to 'precipitate political change in Indonesia through economic pressures'. By then, in the wake of Amien Rais's words in January, various people, among them Syarwan Hamid, began to speak of a conspiracy, traitors, anti-nationalists, and immoral people, who made the Indonesian people suffer in their attempts to undermine the government. According to the Minister of Religion, Tarmizi Taher, who was also an influential Golkar member, the economic crisis was being used by political adventurers. He identified them as children of communists from Madiun (the scene of a communist rebellion in 1948) and other places determined to take revenge on the Muslim community, which had joined the Armed Forces to prevent a communist *coup d'état* in 1965. Such people had infiltrated Islamic social organizations and two Islamic institutions of higher education, one in Jakarta and one in Bandung. Tarmizi Taher refused to name names, but his words were interpreted as being directed against the IAINs (an institution, which like universities and IKIPs housed many critics of the government among its students and alumni) in the two cities. Similarly, the chairman of MUI hinted at the infiltration

Prabowo Subianto (photo *D&R*)

of Islamic institutions by PRD. He asserted that their aim was to sow discord between the Islamic community and the Armed Forces (*Panji Masyarakat*, 23-2-1998:21).

Fuelled by such outspoken distrust of the purported designs of outsiders, Islamic solidarity was strongly emphasized. One of the persons to do so was Prabowo, commander of Kopassus, the Special Forces Command of the Army (formerly RPKAD). On 23 January, at a meeting of 5,000 *ulama* at the Command headquarters after sunset prayers marking the breaking of the fast, Prabowo called for the vigilance and unity of the Islamic community. It was the duty of the Islamic community to cooperate with the army in averting the threatening danger. At the end of the meeting, copies of *Lords of the Rim: The invisible empire of the overseas Chinese* by S. Seagrave were handed out – a book underlining the centuries-old economic might of overseas Chinese in Asia and the devious tricks they allegedly play (*Far Eastern Economic Review*, 12-2-1998:17). On 2 February, at the end of the fasting month, a large *halal bi-halal* meeting organized by the municipality of Jakarta and MUI was attended by hundreds of people. The highlight was the reading of the Pledge of the Indonesian Islamic Community, signed by 30 Islamic organizations. These included Nahdlatul Ulama, Muhammadiyah, Perti, Syarikat Islam, and various organizations affiliated with these. The boards of GUPPI (a Golkar organization), Dewan Dakwah Islamiyah Indonesia (DDII, an organization for former Masjumi politicians), Majelis Dakwah Islamiyah, and Al-Irsyad also chimed in with their support. Expressing concern about the economic situation, full backing was promised for measures taken by the government to overcome the crisis and all that went with it.

Deliberately or not, much of the blame was placed on the Chinese. The Chinese were identified with the rich segment of society which controlled the economy and with those who had brought about Indonesia's economic ruin. For some, it provided the opportunity to vent their anti-Chinese feelings blatantly. Others did so in more veiled terms. Calls for Muslim solidarity in the face of the attack on the Indonesian economy endorse this, as does a remark by the general chairman of Persatuan Islam (Persis), KH Shiddiq Amien, who called attention to the fact that, after Soeharto had expressed his willingness to be renominated and there were unequivocal indications that the candidate for the vice-presidency was a Muslim, the rupiah had not gained in strength, but had done just the opposite and had fallen even further. Others spoke of tens of millions of dollars 'parked' in Singapore and elsewhere outside Indonesia (a figure of Rp 85 trillion was frequently mentioned), adding that in spite of the 'I love the Rupiah campaign', none of the money had been transferred back to Indonesia.[7] Reminding people that it was the Chinese who controlled much of Indonesia's economy, in February Mokodongan stressed that the actions taken by the Armed Forces against speculators should not be interpreted as being inspired by anti-Chinese feelings. Nobody was above the law. The Armed Forces had orders to act against speculators irrespective of their race.

Anti-Chinese demonstrations took on a conspicuous form after a bomb exploded on 18 January in a slum neighbourhood, Tanah Tinggi, in Central Jakarta. The explosion occurred in a building where, so the police claimed, bombs were assembled. Later, Prabowo was to state that 40 bombs had been assembled in the house and that authorities had only been able to find eighteen of these. Where the remaining 22 bombs were was not known (*Panji Masyarakat*, 27-10-1999:22). One person, Agus Priyono, allegedly a PRD activist, was arrested. It was an event, as later developments were to show, which added greatly to the prevalent distrust in military circles of the anti-government movement in Indonesia, in particular when the eyes of the Armed Forces strayed to PRD. A week later, it was announced that police investigations had unearthed 'written indications' of a link between PRD and Sofyan Wanandi. A diskette with E-mail had been found which contained correspondence between PRD members in which Sofyan Wanandi and his brother, Yusuf Wanandi, were mentioned as persons who could be approached for a financial donation. On 26 January, Sofyan Wanandi was questioned by the intelligence service, Bakorstanas (Badan Koordinasi Bantuan Pemantapan Stabilitas Nasional, the successor of Kopkamtib), of Jakarta. Afterwards he denied ever having given money to PRD. The authorities were not satisfied. The Bakorstanas chairman of Jakarta, also military commander of the city, Syafrie Syamsuddin, claimed there was a 'psychological nuance'. Sofyan Wanandi had looked nervous when the document had

---

[7]   In the eyes of some, capital parked abroad included money invested abroad. Still others nurtured the suspicion that the foreign money was used as a leverage by the conglomerates in the succession struggle.

been shown to him.[8] Over the next few months Sofyan Wanandi was questioned again by the police as a witness in the case. The interrogation, Feisal Tanjung stressed, had nothing to do with the fact that Sofyan Wanandi was a Chinese.

The interrogation of Sofyan Wanandi was the sign for Muslim groups to take to the street. In September 1971, Sofyan Wanandi, who in his youth had been a leader of PMKRI, the Association of Roman Catholic Students, had been one of the founders of CSIS, the Centre for Strategic and International Studies, and now some of its staff had joined the chorus of government critics. The centre, of which Yusuf Wanandi was still a director, is associated with the Roman Catholic and the Chinese communities. Sofyan Wanandi's days as a student activist, moreover, were the beginning of his close relationship with two former personal assistants to President Soeharto, generals Ali Moertopo and Soedjono Hoemardani.[9] This imbued the case with highly political and religious overtones, the more so because think-tanks in Indonesia tend to be associated with political manipulation and struggles for power. In the public mind, in less time than it takes to tell, a link was made to General L.B. (Leonardus Benyamin, or Benny) Moerdani, LBM to his friends, also a Roman Catholic, and a former commander of the Armed Forces, tarred with the same brush as a patron of CSIS. Moerdani was a man whose name had become synonymous with scheming and plotting.[10] In the eyes of part of the Muslim community, among them Adi Sasono, CSIS as the think-tank of Ali Moertopo (a Muslim, and the main architect of the New Order political structure) and Moerdani is to a large extent responsible for what is perceived to have been an anti-Islam policy of the Indonesian government in the 1970s and early 1980s. Moerdani gradually lost Soeharto's ear, and was eclipsed in 1993, when he lost his position as Minister of Defence and Security, thus being punished for being considered to have been the man who had engineered Try Sutrisno's and not Habibie's election as vice president. His ousting was seen as a victory for the Islamic community, whose confidence was further strengthened by the appointment of Feisal Tanjung as Commander of

---

[8]   *The Jakarta Post*, 27-1-1998. Also interrogated was Surya Paloh, editor-in-chief of the daily *Media Indonesia*, whose name had been mentioned in one of the E-mails which discussed the support given by reports in the press to PRD.
[9]   They lost this position after the student demonstrations of 1973 and early 1974, of which they were a major target.
[10]   According to this line of reasoning, Moerdani was Ali Moertopo's protege, while Moerdani saw to it that Try Sutrisno became vice-president, defeating Habibie. Moerdani was held responsible for anti-Habibie propaganda on the eve of the general session of the People's Congress, like the YKPK proposal to elect Try Sutrisno as the next president. On the grounds of such suspicions, some suspected Sofyan Wanandi of being a major figure in the campaign to have Try Sutrisno nominated as vice-president.

the Armed Forces.[11] Coupled with the advance of Habibie and ICMI, it had resulted in a 'greening' of the Armed Forces, of the cabinet, and of parliament and the People's Congress. It was a specific form of greening, excluding for instance NU leaders, who rejected any stress on religion in politics, and whose relation with generals like Edi Sudradjat and Try Sutrisno had been cordial.

For people like Hartono Mardjono, CSIS had lurked at the centre of what they construed to be the anti-Islamic plot of the first two decades of the New Order. At the time of the interrogation of Sofyan Wanandi, CSIS was accused of having had a hand in everything which was perceived to have hurt the Islamic community in the past (and, it was sometimes added, had ensured gains for the Chinese): the Malari riots of January 1974 in Jakarta, the Komando Jihad affair of 1977, the hijacking of a Garuda airliner by a radical Islamic group in March 1981, and the bloody clash between Muslims and security forces at Tanjung Priok in September 1984. The suspected aim was the familiar one: to discredit devout Muslims in the eyes of the general public by creating the impression that a political Islam was synonymous with violence.[12] The Tanjung Priok clash was said to have been provoked by CSIS agents who incited local residents by delivering fierce speeches attacking the government's religious policy. Their sole intention was to trigger off riots, giving the military the excuse to act (see, for instance, Pusat Studi dan Pengembangan Informasi 1998:39). More generally, CSIS was accused of having formulated suggestions presented to Soeharto by his close advisors, which had been instrumental in persuading Soeharto to follow an anti-Islamic policy during much of the first two decades of the New Order. Ammunition for their attack on CSIS and Ali Moertopo was provided by a book published in January 1998 in which the commander of Kopkamtib in 1974, General Soemitro, gives his version of the Malari events, which ushered in his own downfall. Blaming Ali Moertopo for this, he suggests that CSIS – throughout the book referred to as a 'certain study institute', with one or two exceptions – and Ali Moertopo were responsible for much of government policy of those days. With respect to Malari proper, he tells about a CSIS member who is supposed to have handed out money to stir up unrest in the city, and suggests that the plans to set alight to certain buildings came from

[11]   Another reason sometimes advanced for Moerdani's fall is that he is said to have advised Soeharto to keep the business activities of his children in check.
[12]   In February 1977 the then Chief of Staff of Kopkamtib, Admiral Sudomo (a Protestant, who converted to Islam in 1997), said that there was a Holy War Command active in Java and Sumatra, which aimed at the establishment of an Islamic state. Muslims claimed that such an observation, plus similar ones made later, were invented or blown up in an effort to dissuade people from voting PPP by presenting a picture of the Islamic community as leaning towards violence.

CSIS. One of the aims of creating havoc was discredit and thus silence the protests of UI students and to make sure that Soeharto stayed in power. Elsewhere, he places the blame for the hijacking on Ali Moertopo's own intelligence service.[13]

Within five hours of Sofyan Wanandi's interrogation by Bakorstanas, about one hundred students and other young people from Jakarta, Bandung, Yogyakarta, and Lampung, styling themselves Solidaritas Mahasiswa untuk Persatuan Indonesia (Student Solidarity for Indonesian Union), staged a demonstration in front of CSIS. Shouting *Allahu Akbar*, they demanded that Sofyan Wanandi (or, as they referred to him, Liem Bian Koen) be brought before court and that CSIS be disbanded. The protest started and ended with the singing of patriotic songs, including the national anthem, *Indonesia Raya, Indonesia Merdeka*, and *Maju tak Gentar*. Next day it was the turn of Forum Pemulihan Martabat Bangsa (Forum for the Restoration of the Nation's Stature) to protest in front of the CSIS building. This time the demonstration was rounded off by a prayer. Other demonstrators, calling themselves Keluarga Besar Korban Peristiwa Tanjung Priok (Family of the Victims of the Tanjung Priok Event) and Front Pemuda Penegak Kedaulatan Rakyat (Youth Front of Upholders of People's Sovereignty), went to parliament to demand the same. Demonstrators also called for the burning down of Sofyan Wanandi's house and for hanging him.

Protests (suspected by some to have been orchestrated by the ICMI think-tank CIDES, of which Amien Rais is the deputy chairman of its Advisory Board) culminated in a mass public sermon in the Al-Azhar Mosque in Jakarta on 8 February. Its theme was *Membedah Kedok CSIS*, Dissect the Disguise of CSIS.[14] One of the speakers, Ahmad Soemargono, chairman of KISDI, gave a lecture on the political scheming of CSIS, positing that CSIS served the interests of zionism and of what he called international secularism. He was convinced that one of the major aims of CSIS in Indonesia was to incite the hostility of the Islamic community towards the government by masterminding various provocative activities, such as the issue of the Komando Jihad and the Tanjung Priok affair, and the arrest of Islamic leaders which followed in the wake of the latter affair. KH Abdul Qadir Djaelani, himself one of those former Islamic political prisoners arrested after the Tanjung Priok affair, accused CSIS and its supporters of having deliberately

---

[13]   Cahyono 1998:4, 12, 94, 183, 229. In the book Sofyan Wanandi is consistently called Liem Bian Kie.

[14]   The meeting was organized by Komite Indonesia untuk Solidaritas Dunia Islam, or KISDI (an organization founded in 1986 on the initiative of the Masjumi leader Moh. Natsir to give moral and financial support to the struggle of the Palestinians in Israel), Badan Kerja Sama Pondok Pesantren (BKSPP), the As Syafi'iyah Educational Institute, and Front Pembelaan Muslim Indonesia. Established at the meeting was Front Aksi Solidaritas Islam untuk Nasional.

planned activities which had resulted in the monetary crisis Indonesia was
experiencing. Coming down to brass tacks, he referred to a meeting between
Kristiadi of CSIS, assistants to General Moerdani, and advocates of democracy, who had studied a number of plans to make Indonesia bankrupt. What
they had discussed, he asserted, was a plunge of the rupiah, the engineering
of an economic crisis, the undermining of the trust of the people in the government, and the way in which their 'champion' could replace Soeharto in an
unconstitutional way. The audience was asked not to participate in demonstrations. On another occasion it was pointed out by Fahmi Idris, another student leader from the beginnings of the New Order, that because of his relationship with Ali Moertopo and Soedjono Hoemardani, Sofyan Wanandi had
been in the 'inner circle of power' in the 1980s (*Republika*, 27-1-1998). Fahmi
Idris also implicated other Chinese conglomerates, by pointing out that they
had never contradicted Sofyan Wanandi's statement about not being prepared to participate in the I Love Indonesia drive.

CHAPTER VI

The general session of the People's Congress

Maju terus maju terus
Pantang mundur pantang mundur
Sampai titik sampai titik
Penghabisan

Walau punya enam jam Yogyakarta lepas
  cengkraman Belanda
Tapi satu saat nanti penjajah pasti sirna di atas
bumi
Pasti lenyap dari bumi Indonesia[1]

In the second half of February, with the general session of the People's Congress only weeks away, the tempo of issuing political statements and demonstrations mounted significantly. By that time it had become a custom among some people, an idea propagated by leaflets and stickers, to wear a white ribbon tied around the wrist to indicate that one was in favour of political and economic reforms. On 10 February, alumni of the Institut Teknologi Bandung, during a demonstration in Taman Ismail Marzuki in Jakarta, rejected the prospect of a new term in office by Soeharto, holding him responsible for the economic disaster that had struck Indonesia. On 19 February, thousands of students of Universitas Indonesia (UI) organized a 'long march' around the campus, singing patriotic songs and shouting slogans in favour of democracy. Afterwards, a 'free stage' was held and five demands formulated: a decrease in prices, political reform, a change in national leadership, the restitution of student councils, and an alliance between students and society as a whole. Six days later, on 25 February, about a thousand students and former students of UI, singing the UI march and patriotic songs, again

---

[1] Ever forward ever forward/ Never retreat never retreat/ Till the till the / End/ Though for six hours only Yogyakarta was free from the Dutch grip/ There will come a time the colonizer certainly will be destroyed upon earth/ Certainly will vanish from the Indonesian soil. Verses from 'Six hours in Yogya'.

demonstrated on their campus. The protest, including the slogans to be used, had been carefully planned in advance by the chairman of the Association of Alumni of UI, Major-General (Ret.) Hariadi Darmawan, inspector-general at the Ministry of Forestry, and an in-law of Try Sutrisno (*Golkar* 1999:83). The high point of the meeting was the reading of a Statement of Concern by Hariadi Darmawan. It touched upon such issues as the growing number of unemployed, rising prices and the scarcity of basic commodities, the prospect of a poor harvest, and people who had died during famines in various parts of the country. Calling it ironic that amidst rising social and economic tension no firm, consistent, and effective measures had yet been taken, the vacillating attitude of government was identified as the culprit for the loss in confidence by the business world and society at large. The crisis, it was stressed, had its roots in the continual emphasis on economic growth, from which only a small group of big entrepreneurs profited. Adding insult to injury, it was this group which had caused a debt crisis, and then, espousing a 'New Nationalism', had 'parked' their money abroad. The highly conspicuous drive to have the people, the victims of the crisis brought about by the big concerns, part with their hard-earned dollars and jewellery came under attack, as did the abuse of power, corruption, and collusion. Public control and the sovereignty of the people, it was observed, had been eroded by unjust interventions against the press, by the symbolic way the general elections had been organized, and by the composition of the parliament and People's Congress. The dignity and morality of the nation were being eroded, and concomitantly the Armed Forces were moving steadily away from the ideals for which they had fought during the war of independence.

Afterwards, Hariadi Darmawan handed over a white cloth to the students, who covered the gigantic board on the Salemba campus with the text 'Welcome to Campus of the New Order Struggle', words which referred to the role students of the university had played in the downfall of Soekarno in 1966. They had made plans to demolish the board, but alumni had persuaded them not to do so. A second similar board was painted a symbolic black. The commander of the detective force of the police scathingly said the demonstration was futile. They would be far better employed organizing scholarly seminars which might generate some useful suggestions to aid the government. Others saw the matter differently. In view of the role played by Hariadi Darmawan, they considered the demonstration of 25 February as the starting point of the ever-swelling wave of protests, which eventually would lead to the fall of Soeharto. Next day there was a new demonstration by three to five thousand UI 'yellow jackets', this time on the Depok campus. They baptized their campus *Kampus Perjuangan Rakyat*, Campus of the People's Struggle. A new phenomenon was the presence at the demonstrations of well-known professors such as Mahar Mardjono (a former rector), Sri Edi

Swasono, Selo Soemardjan, Slamet Iman Santoso, Juwono Sudarsono, and Tuti Heraty Nurhadi. Some of them did more than just attend, and gave speeches in support of the aims of the protesting students.

Outside Jakarta there were more massive student demonstrations. These took place at Gadjah Mada University in Yogyakarta on 25 February; at the Institut Pertanian Bogor (IPB), and the Institut Teknologi Surabaya on the 27th; and Universitas Airlangga in Surabaya on the 28th. At the latter university, as at UI, the academic staff joined the protests, in this case even taking the initiative. After the general session of the People's Congress had commenced, students from a great variety of institutions of higher education joined in the protests. At some universities students distributed food for free or offered it at cut rates, even arranging transportation, as many poor people could not afford a bus ticket. In Yogyakarta, Bandung, Jember, and Surabaya students went on hunger strikes to underline their protests. In Ujungpandang, IKIP students performed the play 'The General Session for the Emperor'. NGOs and other groups such as Suara Ibu Peduli (SIP), the Voice of Concerned Mothers, headed by Dr Karlina Leksono, a staff member of Habibie's BPPT, also espoused the protests.

To prevent protesting students leaving the campus, the universities were heavily guarded by security forces. Demonstrations outside the campus were instantly squashed. Early February, 122 members of a group calling themselves Barisan Merah Putih, the Red and White Column, were arrested after they protested about high prices in front of the Department of Labour, and, participating in a demonstration at the Office of the Public Prosecution, had demanded an investigation into Soeharto's wealth. Barisan Merah Putih had also demonstrated in front of Bank Indonesia, where its members demanded the resignation of Soedradjad Djiwandono, whom they held responsible for the monetary crisis, and in front of the Bulog head office. Later the same month, the same fate befell three leaders of The Voice of Concerned Mothers. They were arrested in front of Hotel Indonesia when they read a statement of concern and sang the song *Ibu Pertiwi* (Motherland) during a demonstration against the rising prices, in particular that of powdered baby milk. Earlier the group had handed out baby milk to the poor. They were sentenced to Rp 2,250 or seven days' imprisonment, but immediately appealed. The arrests of these women elicited protests from a number of prominent people, among them Adi Sasono of ICMI. The most ludicrous action was probably the one which was staged in Jakarta at the end of the month. A pamphlet complete with the parliament letterhead was circulated widely throughout the city. It was announced that, as a token of concern of the members of the People's Congress for the effects of the economic crisis, on the morning of 23 February the nine basic commodities would be handed out for free in the People's Congress building. Free transport home was also to be arranged. The authorities were not amused. Imagining the hordes of people who might descend in response to the invitation, they saw the pamphlet as an undisguised attempt to disrupt the general session and to stir up unrest.

As had become part of the New Order political custom, the general session of the People's Congress was to open on 1 March. This was to commemorate the fact that on that day in 1949 Republican troops commanded by Soeharto had briefly occupied the Dutch-held capital of the Indonesian Republic, Yogyakarta. To honour Supersemar, the Letter of March Eleventh, the letter in which Soekarno had transferred most of his powers to Soeharto in 1966, it would be closed on 11 March. Besides its 325 members of parliament, Golkar had an additional 163 appointed members. To these 488 Golkar members have to be added the hundred so-called appointed members of groups. Among them were Yogie SM (on behalf of the bureaucracy), Achmad Tirtosudiro of ICMI, Agus Sudono of SPSI, KH Zainuddin M.Z. (religious leaders), and Anthony Salim (entrepreneurs). The PPP faction was made up of 134 (98 plus 45) members, and that of PDI of 16 (eleven plus five). The Regional Representation was made up of 149 members, that of the Armed Forces 113 (75 plus 38).

Three weeks before the scheduled opening, on 5 February, as had been the case on the eve of the general elections, the military staged a very conspicuous security exercise near the People's Congress building, complete with soldiers descending from helicopters by ropes. Repeating the 1997 scenario, spokesmen of the Armed Forces stressed that the exercise was not intended to frighten the population. Around the same time it was announced that the Armed Forces (including the police) had reserved 25,000 of its members, that is twice the force employed five years earlier, to deal with any disturbance that might take place. Special attention was paid to what were considered critical areas: Tanah Abang, Tanjung Priok, Jatinegara, and Mampang. To quell any doubts, on 18 February the military commander of Jakarta, Syafrie Syamsuddin, was adamant that his troops would not tolerate any street demonstrations. Among the alternatives for letting off steam, another senior army officer Lieutenant-General Subagyo Hadisiswoyo (a few days later to be installed as Chief of Staff of the Army) suggested that students and other malcontents could vent their complaints at the Command Posts for National Alertness, instituted prior to the general elections, or take the trouble to talk with the local military. Starting eleven days before the general session, all public meetings of a political nature, including seminars and the like, were expressly forbidden.

Many people had the feeling that something was about to happen. In February rumours had begun to circulate that active and retired officers in Jakarta, afraid that a clash within the army might erupt prior to or during the general session of the People's Congress and not trusting the military units stationed in Jakarta, had called on troops from outside the city to come to Jakarta to protect them (*Kabar dari Pijar*, 17-2-1998). The Armed Forces were not alone in their apprehension; others seriously began to contemplate the prospect of large-scale unrest. An editorial in *The Jakarta Post* had alluded to this as early as January, disappointed that during the debates in the committees of the People's Congress (which had to prepare the decrees to be accepted by the general session) the necessity for fundamental reforms had not been raised. It was pointed out that reforms could either be introduced peacefully through the People's Congress, or might be enforced from outside it, 'which could possibly be chaotic and, God forbid, violent' (*The Jakarta Post*, 8-1-1998.). In an interview with the same newspaper on 11 February, Amien Rais, too – stressing that if necessary radical change had to be brought about peacefully by 'people power' – hinted at future violence. He said such an outcome would be virtually unavoidable if the government stubbornly refused to contemplate any change: 'Unfortunately, many say bloodshed is a must and I'm afraid that it will be a self-fulfilling prophecy' (*The Jakarta Post*, 11-2-1998). With this in mind, in the middle of February, when addressing a mass Muhammadiyah meeting in Yogyakarta attended by about 40,000 people, he called for patience and the avoidance of destruction. Later in the month he disappointed some of his supporters by his refusal to lead massive street demonstrations, even avowing that for Soeharto a new term in office would be his last chance. This change in Amien Rais's attitude was linked to the meeting between Amien Rais and Habibie arranged by Achmad Tirtosudiro. Amien Rais, rumour had it, had been 'bought' by Habibie (*Panji Masyarakat*, 30-3-1998:14). Amien Rais himself explained that his cautious attitude was inspired by his desire to avoid clashes between students and security forces.

As had also become customary on the eve of a People's Congress session, changes occurred in the top echelon of the Armed Forces. In the middle of February Wiranto replaced General Feisal Tanjung, who was retired, as Commander of the Armed Forces. The new Chief of Staff of the Army was Lieutenant-General Subagyo Hadisiswoyo. In a rather unprecedented step, all regional army commanders and the commanders of Kostrad and Kopassus expressed their loyalty to Wiranto and promised to obey his orders. The following day Mokodongan hastened to caution that the pledge should not be misinterpreted or dramatized. It had been a spontaneous gesture by subordinates to welcome their new superior. Other changes announced became effective after the close of the general session. Yunus Yosfiah was replaced as Chief of Staff of Social and Political Affairs by Major-General Susilo Bambang Yudhoyono. The new commander of Kopassus, the Special Troops Command, was Major-General Muchdi Purwoprandjono, nicknamed Django. Its former commander, Prabowo Subianto, who had been responsible for a reorganization and expansion of the Special Troops

Command, took over command of Kostrad, the position his father-in-law
had held in September 1965.[2] Both Muchdi and Prabowo had earned themselves a reputation as tough commanders. Muchdi had a military intelligence
background. He had been commander of the Jayapura military district in
Irian Jaya at the end of the 1980s. At the time of the violence surrounding the
general elections of 1997, he had been military commander of East Java.

In view of the tense debates about the vice-presidency and the fact that
certainly not everybody in Golkar and the Armed Forces agreed with the
choice, great efforts were made in such bodies as Golkar to ensure that the
general session proceeded as smoothly as possible. At the time Golkar had
mentioned the names Habibie and Harmoko as its candidates, the possibility of interruptions during the plenary sessions of the People's Congress when
the final choice would be made was not excluded. To circumvent any mischief, the use of microphones during plenary sessions was arranged in such
a way that only party spokesmen could use them. With Brigadier-General
Ibrahim Saleh's step in 1988 still fresh in their memories, spokesmen for
Golkar and the Armed Forces both insisted that there were to be no undesirable interruptions. As early as April 1997, the then Chief of Staff of the Army,
General R. Hartono, had stated that the Armed Forces were not to appoint
'generals suffering from stress' as their representatives in the People's
Congress. In this way the Armed Forces hoped to prevent interruptions or
any sudden nomination by one of its representatives of a presidential and
vice-presidential candidate not advanced by the Armed Forces (*Media
Indonesia*, 8-4-1997). Speaking on behalf of Golkar, Abdul Gafur warned that
Golkar members who interrupted during the plenary session would be
recalled. To make even more sure, at the end of February Golkar members of
the People's Congress were presented with a form they had to sign, affirming they would support the nominations of Soeharto and Habibie. Harmoko
hastened to say that the forms had been distributed not out of any fear that
there might be dissenting voices, but to conform to established procedures in
electing a president and vice-president. It was confirmation that Golkar
always looked ahead. Ginandjar Kartasasmita explained that the forms were
simply a matter of efficiency and had been distributed at previous sessions of
the People's Congress as well. This was not the whole truth. The forms were
distributed at the moment when Emil Salim had made it clear that he still
considered himself a candidate for the vice-presidency. He had served the
president for 25 years, and saw no reason why he should not do so for another five years (*Forum Keadilan*, 9-3-1998:71). To baulk this, Abdul Gafur and
Kafrawi Ridwan (deputy secretary of the Golkar group in parliament) threat-

---

[2]   Later it was reported that Muchdi had been Prabowo's choice, endorsed by Soeharto but
not by the senior officers of the Armed Forces (*Panji Masyarakat*, 1-6-1998:13).

ened any Golkar member of the People's Congress who supported the nomination of Emil Salim, thereby breaking party discipline, with sanctions. Such persons were to be 'recalled', that is, dismissed. Disregarding appeals by Abdul Gafur to step down, Emil Salim retorted by stating that he would only withdraw when all parties had officially announced the name of their candidates.

Emil Salim won the support of members of various NGOs and individuals, banded together in a group styling itself Gema Madani (later called Gema Masyarakat Madani), the Echo of Civil Society, for his campaign. The group collected signatures in support of Emil Salim and handed out stickers reading *Emil Salim Pilihan Saya*, 'Emil Salim My Choice'. Among the reasons they gave for putting him forward as the most suitable candidate, they pointed out that Emil Salim was 'clean', free from the taint of collusion, corruption, and nepotism, and that he was a non-controversial figure who could work together with many of the disparate groups which were at loggerheads with each other. His economic expertise and his devotion to social causes were given their fair share of attention. To make a long story short, he met the criteria listed by Golkar. By the end of February many had signed the list drawn up by Gema Madani in favour of Emil Salim's candidature. It included many impressive names: Nurcholish Madjid, Faisal H. Basri, Prof. Sumitro Djojohadikusumo, the lawyer T. Mulya Lubis, Mrs Nelly Adam Malik and Mrs Rahmi Hatta (widows of former vice-presidents), Mrs S.W. Sjahrir (widow of one of Indonesia's most renowned politicians), Rosihan Anwar (a famous journalist), Prof. Mardjono Reksodiputro, Prof. M. Sadli (a well-known economist, and former New Order cabinet minister), Prof. Subroto (a former Minister of Mining and Energy, and secretary-general of OPEC, who was to join the demonstrating students of Universitas Pancasila, of which he was the rector, in March), and three Golkar leaders: Albert Hasibuan, Didin Sastrapradja, and Indra Bambang. Armed with the list, Gema Madani representatives, including Mrs Hatta and Mrs Adam Malik, visited parliamentary groups of Regional Representatives, PDI, and Golkar in an effort to persuade them to nominate Emil Salim.

Forwarned, the military had counted on all kinds of demonstrations in front of the congress building: mass protests by students, by supporters of Megawati, and by labourers who had recently found themselves unemployed. The army anticipated mobilization of the masses by the usually unspecified and nebulous 'enemies of the state', of whom its officers had so often warned. In the vicinity of the congress building calm reigned, and the same can be said of the atmosphere inside. Committees of the People's Congress had been preparing its decisions since October. Only seven of these were finally presented to the general session for approval. An equal number had not made it. Their content was too controversial for there to be any hope of reaching a consensus on them. Among these was a special congressional decree on human rights.[3] Right from the outset, Golkar had been against it, considering the inclusion of a section on human rights in the Broad Outlines of State Policy sufficient. PPP and PDI took a different view and supported such a decree. During its meeting in Lombok in November, NU had also pressed for it.

Another sensitive proposal came from the ranks of PPP. The party insisted on changing a phrase in a number of congressional decrees which expounded on religious practices in accordance with *agama dan kepercayaan*, religion and belief. This jeopardized the position of Javanese mystical groups, the so-called *aliran kepercayaan*. The position of these groups had been a sore point for Muslims since the session of the People's Congress of 1978, when the phrase had been included for the first time in the Broad Outlines of State Policy and in special Pancasila guidelines formulated by the government. At that time, PPP politicians and other Muslims had vehemently protested against any such step. In their eyes, mentioning religion and belief in one breath tended to set heterodox mystical groups apart from religion. It wrongly shielded such groups from Islamic missionary activities determined to convince their adherents that at least some of their religious practices were disconsonant with Islam. When the People's Congress was installed in October 1997, this phrase became the subject of Islamic demonstrations. At the end of November, representatives from *pesantren* all over Java paid a visit to the People's Congress to press for a revision of the 1978 decision. They were followed a few days later by a delegation of 50 Islamic social organizations from West Java, asking the same.[4] The old arguments were rehashed, and it was argued that the word *aliran*, literally meaning stream, should not be used to denote mystical groups. Such a usage accorded these groups a separate status. The correct, formal term was 'groups adhering to the belief in the One and Only God'. Instead of the tendency to separate mystical beliefs from religion, even running the risk of creating a new religion, the mystical groups should be returned to the fold of religion, again opening the door wide for religious instruction. At the end of the 1970s

---

3   Such a human rights decree had been included among the drafts prepared for the People's Congress by Dewan Pertahanan Keamanan Nasional (Wanhamkamnas, the National Security and Defence Council). Wanhamkamnas had involved the National Committee for Human Rights in the drafting of the proposal. Wanhamkamnas had prepared drafts for the decrees of the People's Congress since 1973.

4   The commotion was fanned by the fact that in July 1997 the Administrative Court of Jakarta had forced the Civil Registration Office to revise its decision not to register a marriage (which thus would be illegitimate) concluded according to the rules of one of such a group. The court had ruled that the marriage had been concluded according to the West Javanese adat (and not according to *kepercayaan*) and thus, according to the Marriage Act, was legal.

opposition to the Pancasila guidelines had been fortified by the suspicion that President Soeharto and his closest advisors were adherents of the Javanese mystical stream. This time Golkar supported the demand of PPP. There was no better indication of how the attitude of the government and Golkar towards Islam had changed in the last two decades. In the end, the People's Congress decided not to change the contested formula. Instead, in the Broad Outlines of State Policy, the document listing the policy principles for the coming five years, a sentence was added about guidance for adherents of the belief in the One and Only God to dissuade them from any tendency to establish a new religion and to encourage them to embrace one of the recognized religions. During the deliberations, a promise was exacted from the Armed Forces representatives that a clause stating that the people concerned had to choose one of the five religions would be included in future guidelines.

As was to be expected, the deliberations before and during the general session of the People's Congress were coloured by differences of opinion about the restrictions which characterized the Indonesian political system. PPP and PDI had a number of long-standing demands. Among these were permission to establish branches at the village level, which the 'floating mass' principle so far had blocked (a concession the Armed Forces, fearful of unrest, has always strongly resisted). PPP and PDI politicians argued that their parties only being allowed to have branches at the national, provincial, and regency levels hampered the functioning of these parties in various ways. It made it difficult for them to mobilize support at the grassroots level, which indeed had been the intention of the government when the regulation was instituted. Quite apart from this, it gave Golkar a head start, as most local military and civil officials supported that party and brought their pressure to bear on people to vote Golkar. A second long-cherished wish of PPP and PDI was to have the political parties – not the bureaucracy – organize the elections, so they would have more than a token participation. They made no secret of their detestation of the so-called monoloyalty expected of bureaucrats, in theory intended to dissuade civil servants from being politically active, in practice making it difficult for them to follow the dictates of their conscience and join PPP or PDI. During the general session of the People's Congress, PPP singled out the monoloyalty of civil servants as one of the major causes of corruption. The close link between Korpri and Golkar, and the special permission civil servants needed to campaign, was a related issue. Not discussed during the general session were a number of points which had come in for a fair share of attention in the previous months, such as a maximum age for a president and the limitation of the number of terms in office.

The first point on the agenda of the People's Congress was the speech President Soeharto gave to account for government policy over the last five years, summarizing a more than 2,000-page document. Beforehand, one of the Golkar members of parliament, Marzuki, had rightly predicted that the People's Congress would accept Soeharto's account without much ado. He said this was only logical in view of *ASOI* (fun), or *Akal Sehat Orang Indonesia*, the Sound Common Sense of Indonesians. Because they were going to re-elect him there was precious little reason to reject his account. Spokesmen of all parties, including Siti Hardijanti Rukmana, one of the six deputy chairpersons of the Golkar group, who presented Golkar's position on her father's account, used Soeharto's speech to speak out against corruption, collusion, and similar abuses, and to plead for clean government. In the People's Congress her words reaped much applause. Outside the building the reception was more sceptical. An end should come to 'thieves crying thieves', Amien Rais commented a few days later at a demonstration at UI, referring to 'Mbak', well known as a prime example of nepotism (*Ummat*, 23-3-1998:27).

Most parliamentary groups indicated that they unconditionally accepted the accountability speech. Though PDI voiced some reservations, calling the account too optimistic and pressing for political reforms to end what was called a quasi-democracy, it was PPP which broke ranks. Unlike the other groups, it postponed endorsement to later on in the session. PPP spokesmen stressed that the party was not satisfied with what Soeharto had said about the much needed political, legal, and economic reforms, citing as examples of bad government policy the withdrawal of the publication permits of a number of magazines in the past five years, which had spelled the end of such critical magazines as *Tempo*, *Editor*, and *Dëtik* in June 1994. They went on to point out that President Soeharto had remained silent about such important matters as human rights, an open political system, and justice. Yet another point of criticism was that Soeharto was not specific enough about the reasons underlying the monetary crisis. His words gave the inevitable impression that the government was bereft of any clear idea about how to tackle the economic problems. Blaming corruption, collusion, and the like for the fact that of all the countries in Asia Indonesia had been hit worst by the economic crisis, PPP indicated that in return for its consent it needed a firm commitment from the government about efforts to be made to implement a clean government. The party pleaded for a nation-wide anti-corruption campaign and, as others had already been doing for years, for a body to investigate the wealth of senior government officials. The criticism expressed by PPP was received with indignation by Golkar, the Armed Forces, and the Regional Representation, whose members at times made disapproving noises. In the end PPP, too, endorsed the decision of the People's Congress to accept Soeharto's account without any reservations or comments.

The students were also dissatisfied. On 5 March and on subsequent days they staged demonstrations at a great many universities. In Jakarta, UI students visited Armed Forces members of parliament on 5 March, presenting a 'reformation agenda', a moral message to the people's representatives, which they had called a Correction of the Result of Development, and inquired why the representatives had meekly accepted the president's account. The chairman, Yunus Yosfiah, told them that there could be no comprehensive political reformation. Reforms had to be accomplished gradually. Developments in other countries – and from earlier statements it appears that he had the Soviet Union in particular in mind – had shown that unless such a move was undertaken gradually, failure was the result. Yunus Yosfiah refuted the students' claim that there was not even talk of gradual reform. The fact that his group had received the students was proof the opposite was the case. Golkar representatives adopted the same stance. Reforms would be instituted, but only step by step. Radical, revolutionary political changes were rejected out of hand. At this juncture, Komite Indonesia untuk Pencegahan Pelanggaran Hak Asasi Manusia (KIPP HAM, the Indonesian Committee for the Prevention of Violations of Human Rights, a cooperation of a number of NGOs), issued a statement. Recalling various abuses of the past five years (27 July 1996, the curbing of the press, political violence, and fraud during the general elections) and stressing the need for a clean government, it urged members of the People's Congress to evaluate the accountability speech in earnest, and not to acquiesce in it without any real discussion.

The result of the shelving of controversial decisions which had been discussed between October and March was that the People's Congress only decided on one really new decree. This gave President Soeharto extraordinary powers to take special measures in case of an emergency. The idea had been launched in August 1997, during the *pembekalan* of the members of the People's Congress, when President Soeharto had indicated that it might be wise to revive a decree of the People's Congress from 1988 which had given him extraordinary powers to take steps required to maintain the unity of the nation and to prevent and combat social upheavals and subversion. The president had said that the decree had not been renewed in 1993 because of the positive evaluation of the stability of the domestic situation. Since then, he explained, various groups had wantonly abused the greater freedoms. Immediately, spokesmen of Golkar, PPP and PDI, and the Armed Forces sprang to his support. In the People's Congress, at a time of mounting dissension, discussion vacillated between fears that the economic troubles could trigger off widespread riots and maybe even plans for a coup and the argument that such a decree was out of kilter in an atmosphere in which many had come to demand political reform and greater democracy.

On 10 March Soeharto was elected president by acclamation. He got a standing ovation. It was Soeharto's seventh term. The following day the

People's Congress accepted Habibie's nomination as vice-president. The newspaper *Merdeka* reported that all went smoothly: there were no interruptions or protests (*Merdeka*, 11-3-1998). In his acceptance speech President Soeharto put an end to all speculations about his resigning mid-term. He was absolutely adamant that he intended to serve the full five years. Contrary to his predecessors, whose function had been mostly ceremonial, Habibie was given special responsibilities. In foreign politics he would assist the president, who had earlier cancelled a number of trips abroad in matters concerning international organizations such as the United Nations, the Islamic Conference Organization, the G-15, and ASEAN. In the area of economic policies, industrial development now fell under the competence of Habibie. His third task was to assist the president in building up the unity of the nation based on belief in and devotion to the One and Only God.

After his election Habibie received a congratulatory letter from Emil Salim, who also wrote a public letter to members of the People's Congress, expressing his great disappointment about the fact that it had been business as usual and that no special attention had been given to the social, political, and economic crisis Indonesia was suffering.

One of the tasks of a newly elected president was to form a new cabinet. Political discussions in the days prior to the announcement of the cabinet were coloured by the fact that lists about its composition, which allegedly had originated from the State's Secretariat, already circulated in society in general and on the Internet. Among the persons mentioned on them were Siti Hardijanti Indra Rukmana (as Minister of Social Affairs) and Bob Hasan (on one list as Minister of Forestry, on another as Minister of Industry). The lists inspired even more people to urge Soeharto to select his ministers with extra care. The composition of the cabinet became a major topic at student demonstrations, and was the subject of many statements and comments made by leaders of various organizations and by well-known critics of the government, all calling for an authoritative cabinet to be formed. Persis general chairman, Kyai Shiddiq Amien, stated for instance, that at a time when there was a crisis of confidence in the government the new cabinet had to mirror the demands for reformation which resounded throughout society. The new ministers had to be unimpeachable people of high moral standards, free from any taint of collusion and corruption. The chairman of the Religious Advisory Council of NU, KH Ilyas Ruchiyat, chimed in with a similar opinion. The new members of the cabinet had to be irreproachable, non-corrupt, and competent. Underlining that part of the problem was caused by lack of confidence in the government, Amien Rais also appealed to President Soeharto to look for truly competent and unimpeachable cabinet ministers. He warned that if the cabinet were to prove unable to realize any real improvements in the coming six to twelve months and if prices were to continue to rise, a political explosion could be a foregone conclusion.

The composition of the cabinet was announced with unprecedented speed. On 14 March it was made public. Among the nine posts held by army officers were those of Internal Affairs (R. Hartono), of Defence and Security (Wiranto, who combined this position with his position as Commander of the Armed Forces, the first time since 1983 that the two functions were held by one and the same person), of Minister Coordinator of Political and Security Affairs (Feisal Tanjung), and Minister Coordinator of Economic, Financial and Industrial Affairs (Ginandjar Kartasasmita). As predicted, Siti Hardijanti Rukmana became Minister of Social Affairs.[5] Her appointment was seen as leg up to an even more important post, that of general chairperson of Golkar. Her colleague for Cooperatives and Small Enterprises, Subiakto Tjakrawerdaya, asserted that people should show her more respect now that she was a member of the cabinet. Instead of calling her Mbak Tutut, they should refer to her as Ibu Tutut, Madam Tutut. Other Golkar leaders in the cabinet were Ary Mardjono (Minister of Agriculture), Theo L. Sambuaga (Minister of Labour), H.R. Agung Laksono (Minister without Portfolio of Youths and Sport), and Akbar Tanjung (Minister of Public Housing). The new Minister of Education was Prof. Ir Wiranto Arismunandar. He was well known – notorious, according to some – for the uncompromising way he had clamped down on student protests during his chancellorship at IPB in Bandung between 1989 and 1997. Probably not without reason, it was opined that these were the qualities which had prompted Soeharto to select him. Within two days of his appointment Wiranto Arismunandar had already succeeded in enraging the students. When journalists asked him to comment on their demonstrations, Wiranto Arismunandar shrugged the students off dismissively as amateur politicians. The students, seriously presenting themselves as a moral force who really cared about the fate of the ordinary people, were furious. Juwono Sudarsono was appointed Minister of the Environment. Fuad Bawazier became Minister of Finance, while Syahril Sabirin maintained his position as governor of Bank Indonesia. Bob Hasan was appointed Minister of Industry and Trade, becoming the first Chinese in the New Order to acquire a ministerial post. Tanri Abeng, who had won himself a reputation as a manager of Multi Bintang, the producer of Bintang beer, and the Bakrie Brothers concern, was given the job of revitalizing the state companies in his capacity as Minister without Portfolio of Efficiency of State Companies, a creation new to the cabinet. The task he was assigned was not an easy one. It was reported that one hundred out of the total of 164 state companies were 'unhealthy' (*Forum Keadilan*, 6-4-1998:16).

---

[5]   According to Tutut her father had already asked her in 1993 to become a cabinet minister. At that time she had refused.

The cabinet contained a number of ICMI members, among them the new Minister of Justice, Muladi, a member of the National Committee for Human Rights, and Hartono, but to the disappointment of some Muslim circles no leading members of ICMI, such as Adi Sasono and Dawam Rahardjo, had been included. The feeling was that Habibie, who – and this was also new – had explicitly been involved by Soeharto in the deliberations about who was to sit in the cabinet, had been powerless to champion ICMI interests. This was clearly seen as a setback. Five years earlier, the steady advance of ICMI in the representative bodies and the cabinet had been greeted as an indication of the 'greening' of these institutions, meaning the growing influence of Islam in them. That Habibie would fail to influence the deliberations about the composition of the cabinet had been predicted in February. It was, it was reasoned, the concession Soeharto had to make to win the support of the army for the nomination of Habibie.

The disappointment about the absence of prominent representatives of the Islamic community in the cabinet immediately drew forth comments that being a Muslim did not necessarily mean that the person exclusively championed the interests of the devout Islamic community. A month later this view was expressed in a forthright way by Nurcholish Madjid, in a discussion meeting about leadership and Islam in the Al-Azhar Mosque in Jakarta. He asked his audience not to be deceived by outward and visible signs of piety such as having performed the hajj. An Islamic image might well have to be deliberately created to gain support. As an example he mentioned leaders who prayed simply to make a political impression, but did not tell their children that what they were doing was wrong. 'People who have been unjust, despite saying their prayers and entering the Kaaba, will be destroyed', Nurcholish Madjid warned (*The Jakarta Post*, 20-4-1998). On the same occasion Amien Rais recapitulated what constituted good leadership in Islam. Evidently the Islamic image Soeharto and Siti Hardijanti Rukmana had been cultivating so carefully over the last couple of years by promoting Islamic causes and fostering ties with Islamic religious leaders was eroding.

At the first meeting of the cabinet on 17 March, in view of the economic crisis, Soeharto, himself giving the example (his pension as a general was enough to live on, he said), asked his ministers to dispense with their salaries for one year. Provincial governors and managers of state companies should do the same. Judging from the reactions of Syarwan Hamid and Ismail Hasan Metareum, Soeharto's suggestion to the ministers had filtered down as an appeal to all civil servants. Both wondered what money would be left for food or for the education of their children were civil servants on low pay to part with a portion of it. There was even some confusion about whether or not members of parliament had to follow suit. Ismail Hasan Metareum pointed out that the greatest contribution citizens, especially members of parliament, could make was their devotion to their job. In society at large, the appeal to ministers to part with their salaries was greeted with undisguised cynicism, if only because it indicated how fabulously rich some Indonesians had grown, so much so that they could part with a year's salary without blinking an eyelid. Their salary was not the major source of income for some cabinet ministers. The bulk of it came from their business interests, and for some of them the commissionerships they held in state companies which fell under the authority of their department were highly remunerative. Even greater controversy was stirred up by a second instruction given to his ministers by Soeharto on 17 March. He ordered them to provide him with a list of their assets. Though at the inception of previous cabinets ministers had been asked to do the same, this time the instruction was received like a bolt from the blue, and this did not prevent it from creating an uproar. Students and others demanded that the lists be made public. This was not done. Only to comply with a court order in a corruption trial could the information be made available. Amongst those who spoke out against publication was Siti Hardijanti Rukmana. She argued that any such publication would be a violation of the precepts of Islam about showing off wealth.

The cabinet was greeted with waves of protests. According to *The Jakarta Post*, the new cabinet was viewed in 'a pessimistic light' by the public (*The Jakarta Post*, 17-3-1998). Many qualified it as *non-reformasi* or *anti-reformasi*. The appointments which kicked up the most dust were those of Tutut and Bob Hasan. Even so, this was tempered by the observation that the president might well have had sound reasons for his decision to include them. Siti Hardijanti Rukmana faced a difficult task as Minister of Social Affairs at a time of growing unemployment and consequent impoverishment. Bob Hasan might have been selected by President Soeharto to bring the large business conglomerates into line. Being one of Indonesia's richest businessmen himself, this was a task to which Hasan might be better suited than others. Whatever Soeharto's reasons may have been, many of the protests were aimed at these two appointments. Besides the outcry about nepotism, doubts were expressed that the two, or indeed other members of the cabinet, really had the management qualities or resolution for which President Soeharto might have selected them. Managing a beer company was slightly different to managing a department.

Other ministers drew their fair share of criticism as well. The Minister of Tourism, Art and Culture, Abdul Latief, owner of the ALatief and Pasaraya concerns and Sarinah Department Store, had a record which was far from unblemished. He had created a big scandal in the summer of 1997 when he had still been Minister of Labour by using the funds of a state workers' social insurance company, PT Jamsostek, asking for Rp 7.1 billion to fête members of parliament during the discussion of a manpower bill he had introduced.

Amongst other treats, the money was used for paying a two-month-long sojourn in a luxurious hotel for these members of parliament whose responsibility it was to prepare the discussion of the bill.[6] Eyebrows were raised because the Minister of Agriculture had been replaced by his wife, and the new Minister of Mining and Energy, Kuntoro Mangkusubroto, had been fired as one of the directors-general of this ministry at the time of the Busang scandal, because he had sided with Bre-X.

Among those who did not hide their disappointment was Amien Rais. He called the new cabinet a political joke, echoing the chaotic nature of the general elections and the session of the People's Congress. Pointing out that many of the ministers were not the right person in the right place, he expressed the fear that such persons would not be able to differentiate between the interests of the state and their own private ones, or those of their family and companies. Amien Rais appealed to his followers as good citizens to support the decisions of the People's Congress and gave the government six months to prove its worth (Rais 1998:44). Speaking at a demonstration at the Depok campus of UI, as he had done before, he invited critical economists of that university such as Dr Faisal H. Basri and Dr Sri Mulyani to form a team to evaluate the performance of the new cabinet. If, after six months, the crisis not been resolved, an extraordinary session of the People's Congress should be convened to call Soeharto to account and to elect a new president. Should Soeharto refuse to acquiesce, other means had to be used to force him to resign, for instance by activating a peaceful demonstration of 'people power'. Asked about the reaction of the Armed Forces to such a course of action, Amien Rais expressed confidence that if they had to make a choice between defending a family or defending the people, they would come out in support of the latter (*Forum Keadilan*, 6-4-1998). Subroto also pleaded that the cabinet be given some time to prove itself. He ventured the suggestion that Tutut might have been included for her communicative qualities and her sensitivity to social problems (Malik 1998:56-7).

One of the first activities of the new Minister of Research and Technology, Rahardi Ramelan, after he had visited the president, was to stress that, as members of Korpri, LIPI researchers had to follow its ethical code and use proper channels for publishing the results of their research. What some of them had done in January should not be repeated. Tutut, Mohamad Hasan, and Habibie also tackled their challenges with new brooms. Tutut, described on national TV as the *melati* flower of the cabinet, took a central role in plan-

---

6   Afterwards Latief claimed to have used only Rp 2.8 billion. The State Auditor's Office mentioned a figure of Rp 2.4 billion. After Soeharto's fall, the implementation of the act was postponed. In November 1999 Latief was formally declared a subject in the investigation into misus of Jamsostek funds.

ning relief programmes for the poor, acting in actual practice as Coordinating Minister of People's Health and Combating Poverty, a function reserved in the cabinet for Haryono Suyono. Within the framework of a Program Peduli, or Programme of Concern, she selected three hundred *warung nasi Tegal* (or *warteg*, 'food stalls ') in the Jabotabek urbanized region, that is Jakarta, Bogor, Tangerang, and Bekasi, to provide free lunches worth Rp 1,500 in exchange for coupons for about 15,000 people whose contract of employment had been terminated. Tutut herself appeared at one of the *warung* in Jakarta, serving up the free meals. Money for this and other relief programmes was said to come from the salaries Soeharto and cabinet ministers had parted with and from contributions by the business community. Four months later, many of the *warteg* owners had not yet received any money at all, or when they had presented the coupons they had not been given the whole amount they were entitled to by the Ministry of Social Affairs (*Aksi*, 2-6-1998:32). On the day Hasan took over his ministry, invoking article 33 of the Constitution, he observed that as long as monopolies were in the interests of the people, they were a legal business activity and should be allowed to operate. He was adamant that the idea that monopolies were wrong was outdated. Companies which had gone public, he added, could not be called monopolies, as their shares were owned by members of the society at large. What he did object to were single companies that controlled the whole course of production and marketing of a particular product. Even here there were qualifications. If different companies acted as a group in this respect, no objections could be raised. At the end of April Bob Hasan, who himself had a big say in this industry, saw to it that for a period of three months Indonesia's two major paper producers gave regional newspapers with a circulation of less than 50,000 (which needed less than ten tons of paper a month) a discount of 30 per cent on the price of newsprint, and not 20 per cent as had originally been intended. It was a gesture that relieved the financial burden of only a limited number of newspapers. Hasan used the occasion to suggest that criticism of the plywood monopoly from abroad was inspired by selfish reasons. There had been no protests in the days when Indonesia exported only logs. It was precisely when Indonesia began to export plywood, and consequently factories abroad had run into difficulties, that criticism had started. It was a nationalist argument he was to use frequently. His entrance into the insurance world, for instance, had been a step to compete with companies abroad, which, he underlined, in contrast to his own company, did not pay corporation tax in Indonesia.

One of the points that had come up during the general session of the People's Congress was that the economic measures the Indonesian government had taken at the suggestion of IMF had evidently been ineffective, and that people had no inkling of yet how the US$ 43 billion was actually to be used to overcome the crisis. Economic conditions had degenerated even further. Economic experts in Southeast Asia, as well as elsewhere, had begun to argue that IMF had taken the wrong approach in its attempts to end Indonesia's economic crisis. President Soeharto apparently shared such feelings. In his account before the People's Congress, though pledging that Indonesia would faithfully implement the January agreement with IMF, he pointed out that there were as yet no indications that the economic situation had improved. These words strengthened the impression that President Soeharto was looking for an alternative. Clues to this had been accumulating for more than a month. On 2 February the Indonesian government had still vowed that it was going to implement the agreement with IMF. Yet a few days later Soeharto enlisted the assistance of Steve Hanke, a professor at Johns Hopkins University in Baltimore. Hanke was invited to Jakarta, where he was appointed advisor to the Council for the Stabilization of Monetary and Economic Resilience. On his advice, Soeharto indicated that the solution being considered to halt the fall of the rupiah was a currency board system (CBS) pegging the rupiah to the dollar at a fixed exchange rate, a system which had helped to solve monetary crises in a number of other countries. The rate of the rupiah immediately rose from Rp 10,900 to Rp 7,300 to the dollar. It may well have been that Soeharto had toyed with the establishment of a CBS against the wishes of the governor of Bank Indonesia, whose central bank would have to surrender many of its powers to such a board. Soedradjad Djiwandono was honourably discharged by President Soeharto on 27 February. Rumours were rife that he had in fact resigned. Others said that Soeharto had acted in anger, furious over Soedradjad's opposition to a CBS. The director of Bank Indonesia has ministerial status, and, as in the case of Harmoko, it would only have been necessary to wait until the formation of a new cabinet after the close of the session of the People's Congress. His successor, Dr Syahril Sabirin, called the CBS an attractive alternative to prevent the rupiah from plummeting still further. At the end of February, discussing the Indonesian budget, parliament had endorsed the CBS plan, asking the government to take concrete steps in that direction, but to do it tactfully, without alienating international organizations such as IMF.

IMF was dead against any such move. It considered a CBS premature. Before it could be contemplated, Indonesia first had to clean up her banking sector and solve the problem of foreign debts. Within days after it had become known that Soeharto was considering a CBS, Camdessus in a letter warned the Indonesian government of the possibility that IMF would freeze the payment of financial assistance were the CBS to be implemented. Highly sensitive to international censure, the rupiah plunged to Rp 10,000 to the dollar. Opposition groups in Indonesia came out against such a move, arguing that a CBS and its power to fix the exchange value of the rupiah at a moderate rate would only help the conglomerates, the Soeharto family, and his other associates, burdened as they were with their huge dollar debts.

Soeharto's references to a CBS ushered in a new round of phone-calls and visitors from abroad, all appealing to the government not to institute a CBS and to stick to the IMF proposals: American President Clinton, the German Minister of Finance Theo Waigel, Singapore's Prime Minister, Goh Chok Tong, a special envoy of the Japanese Prime Minister, Yoshiro Hayashi, and Derek Fatchett, British Deputy Foreign Secretary. At the end of the month, when a seemingly unbudgeable President Soeharto still persisted in his intention of introducing a CBS and it was rumoured that he was about to replace his economic advisors by close friends who supported his rejection of the IMF recommendations, Clinton sent Walter Mondale to Jakarta as his special envoy. Mondale, bearing a message from Clinton, was accompanied by the Under-Secretary of the Treasury of the United States, David Lipton, and the Assistant of the Foreign Secretary for East Asia and the Pacific, Stanley Roth. Their message was clear. The only way to restore confidence and stability was the full implementation of the IMF recommendations. A CBS was only a 'quick fix'.

Such an uncompromising attitude did not go down well in Indonesia. What the United States was trying to accomplish, an Indonesian expert in international law, Prof. Sri Soemantri, commented, amounted to interfering in the domestic affairs of Indonesia. He added that President Soeharto was not a person who let others dictate to him what to do (*Jawa Pos*, 27-2-1998). The chairman of the Chamber of Trade and Industry, Aburizal Bakrie, issued an appeal to resist foreign intervention. Reporting on the IMF threat, *Panji Masyarakat* concluded that Indonesia was an independent sovereign state, and that Indonesia alone had the right to determine what was the best for the nation (*Panji Masyarakat*, 23-2-1998:52). Mondale did not succeed in his mission. Indonesia's response was considered disappointing by Washington.

The next step came during President Soeharto's speech before the People's Congress. In this he called upon IMF and the governments which had promised financial assistance to help Indonesia in looking for a proper alternative, which he chose to baptize 'IMF-Plus'. What IMF-Plus meant, exactly, was not explained in detail. As far as the demonstrating students were concerned it meant, as one of their posters proclaimed, 'IMF plus monopolies, IMF plus nepotism, and IMF plus business for the children of Soeharto'. The only incontrovertible fact was that one of its elements was the pegging of the rupiah to the dollar, and that President Soeharto refused to abolish subsidies on rice and other basic necessities. On 8 March, when a delegation from PPP formally asked him whether he was prepared to be nominated president, Soeharto expressed strong criticism of the IMF recommendations. He did so two days after IMF had announced, as it had been threatening to do already for some time, that it was going to postpone the granting of a second instalment of US$ 3 billion to Indonesia, out of the US$ 10 billion total which it had promised and scheduled for 15 March. The first instalment of US$ 3 billion had been transferred in November. The World Bank, the Asian Development Bank, and Japan followed IMF's example, a decision which was seen as having been taken under political pressure. Soeharto fulminated that conforming to the suggestions of IMF, the 'reformation à la IMF', implied that the Indonesian economic system would be transformed into a liberal one. By choosing this term, he indicated that he believed the proposed reforms ran counter to the fundamentals of the Indonesian system. In the viewpoint of official ideology since the end of the 1950s, liberalism – whether in the economic or political field – had been almost a term of abuse, used to denote the unbridled individualism and egoism which according to this view is prevalent in Western societies. It was, as President Soeharto stated, not in accordance with the Indonesian constitution, which states in article 33 that Indonesian economic life is based upon *kekeluargaan*, 'family spirit' or togetherness, and the cooperative ideal. He stressed that to bring about economic recovery in accordance with these principles was the most difficult task he had faced. As could be expected, the statement was supported by various sides voicing concern over the possibility that IMF (and the United States) might enforce an alien economic ideology upon Indonesia. Some people, like the chairman of the Regional Representation in the People's Congress, Hasan Basri Durin, and Aburizal Bakrie, hastened to point out that some of the measures suggested by IMF, like the ending of Bulog monopolies, only added to the hardships of the ordinary people.

The only consolation at that time was the second visit to Jakarta in the middle of the month (after the session of the People's Congress had ended) of Japanese Prime Minister Ryutaro Hashimoto. He and Soeharto agreed that the reforms essential to overcoming the monetary crisis needed to be characterized by 'flexibility'. Hashimoto promised Indonesia special financial assistance, outside the framework of IMF, to cover the cost of urgently needed foodstuffs, such as milk for children, and for medicines and medical equipment. Later, Habibie was to convey to Hashimoto that President Soeharto had been very satisfied with the results of the talk. Afterwards Hashimoto contacted politicians in Australia, the United States, Great Britain, Singapore, and South Korea, trying to convince the governments of those countries to take a more lenient view in helping to overcome the monetary crisis in Indonesia. The Australian government also called for more lenience.

On 17 March Ginandjar Kartasasmita announced that Indonesia was not going to implement a CBS. It lacked the necessary currency reserves to attempt any such endeavour. The following day, negotiations with IMF were resumed. By that time representatives both of IMF and the American government had made conciliatory signs, indicating that they would take some of Indonesia's reservations into account. To some this was proof that Soeharto's tactics of taking a harsher attitude and introducing his concept of IMF-Plus had paid off. Even after he had been forced to resign, his opponents still observed that Soeharto had been a strong person who had been able to bite back at the United States and IMF. Habibie was said to lack this aggressive quality (Nadjib 1998:202).

The negotiations with IMF were still hampered by a number of sensitive points. Criticizing some of the IMF recommendations, the Indonesian government argued that they tended to go against the Indonesian constitution. One of these was the liberalization of the agricultural sector, in particular where this touched upon the trade and distribution of cloves and the Bulog monopoly on basic foodstuffs, including products other than rice. Another point on which it was difficult to reach agreement was the lowering of subsidies on fuel oils and electricity. At that time speculations were also rife that the Timor car and the postponement of some of the large projects were also on the list of points the Indonesian government wanted to renegotiate. Initially IMF resumed its unbending position. The first deputy director of IMF, Stanley Fischer, made it known in the United States that there could be no compromise with respect to the fifty points agreed upon in January. The following day, however, basing themselves on reports in the Japanese press, Indonesian newspapers reported that IMF was prepared to concede the retention of a number of subsidies. This was followed by the announcement by the Indonesian Minister of Cooperative Societies that among the subjects discussed was that of the cloves trade and that, unexpectedly, IMF had agreed to a system which was appropriate to the Indonesian situation and strengthened the role of cooperative societies in it. He added that the agreement was not reached to accommodate BPPC or Tommy Soeharto.

On 8 April, after three weeks of negotiations, again described as tough, it was announced that IMF and the Indonesian government had reached a new agreement. It had been signed behind closed doors away from the cameras by Ginandjar Kartasasmita, and not in public by President Soeharto. This time the underlying assumptions were an exchange rate of Rp 6,000 to the dollar, an economic growth of minus four per cent, and an inflation rate of 17 per cent. Commenting on the agreement signed in Kuala Lumpur, Fischer spoke sternly. He talked about special safeguards and closer monitoring to ensure that the Indonesian government was in earnest about implementing the points agreed upon before any money was to be handed over: 'What the world needs to see is not signatures but performance, and that's what we will be looking for' (*The Jakarta Post*, 8-4-1998). In the new agreement, the Supplementary Memorandum of Economic and Financial Policies, tight time schedules were laid down. By 22 April the Indonesia government was to have lifted restrictions on foreign investment in wholesale trade, by 24 April it had to announce seven state companies which were to be privatized in 1998/1999, by 30 June it should have merged two state banks, and so on. The agreement also called for a hike in fuel prices by 5 May, and Indonesia had to reconfirm her commitment to liberalize the cloves and plywood trade.

Special attention was paid to assistance to the poor. IMF had recognized the need for subsidies. Those on sugar, wheat flour, maize, soya bean flour, and fish flour were allowed to remain until 1 October. No such time limit was set for rice and soya bean subsidies. Fuel subsidies were also maintained, but coupled with a selective increase in prices. The increase for kerosene should be lowest. Electricity prices had to go up as well, but for the poor and for isolated areas subsidies should be maintained to allow for a special low tariff. Subsidies for the import of basic ingredients of generic medicines were also maintained. Ginandjar Kartasasmita maintained this was what President Soeharto had meant by IMF-Plus. There was no time for elation. The agreement made it clear that the respite was only temporary. Bulog was saved. The Indonesian government was still allowed to use it for the import of rice and distribution of food.

By this time another businessman, Arifin Panigoro, general chairman of the Indonesian Association of Engineers, 'boss' of the Medco (Meta Epsi Duta Corporation) group, among other activities engaged in oil-drilling, in which also Indra Rukmana and the Minister of Transmigration and Settlement of Forest Nomads, Siswono Yudohusodo, had a stake, had come under suspicion (Aditjondro 1998a:46). He was a Golkar member of the People's Congress, but had not attended its sessions. Illness was given by Golkar leader Abdul Gafur as the reason for his absence. Arifin Panigoro, who had supported Muhammadiyah with money in the past, and was known for the 'vocal way' in which he tried to promote the indigenous business sector, was accused of subversion. He is supposed to have tried to incite Amien Rais to use people power, the catch-word of the day. As Arifin Panigoro was a member of the People's Congress, permission to launch a police investigation had been given by President Soeharto himself before the general session had started. Some interpreted his investigation as a warning signal directed towards Amien Rais. The investigation was also used by Habibie to end the bid for the vice-presidency of Ginandjar Kartasasmita, a close associate of Arifin Panigoro.[7] Arifin Panigoro was supposed to have made his disputed remarks on 5 February, during a meeting in Hotel Radisson in Yogyakarta organized by Pusat Pengkajian Strategi dan Kebijakan (PPSK), the Strategy

---

[7]   *Panji Masyarakat*, 30-3-1998:12-4, 6-4-1998:19; *Far Eastern Economic Review*, 2-4-1998:23; *Golkar* 1999:218.

and Policy Research Centre, founded by Amien Rais in 1989. The meeting, convened to discuss political and economic reforms, had been especially called together to provide Amien Rais with information. Among those present were Prof. Ichlasul Amal, to be appointed rector of Gadjah Mada University the following month, and Dr Afan Gaffar and Dr Anggito Abimanyu, both lecturers at Gadjah Mada University. What was discussed was reported to Habibie who in turn informed Soeharto, by one of those present, Prof. Sofian Effendi, professor at Gadjah Mada University and assistant to the Minister of Research and Technology. Afterwards, Sofian Effendi, who also sent a memo to Amien Rais asking him to support the candidacy of Habibie, for the vice-presidency, was to defend what he had done by stating that he had made the report precisely to prevent those present from being accused of subversion. Intelligence agents had been present, and they might have given a distorted report of the events. Allegedly among the topics raised had been that of mobilizing one million people on 1 March to undermine the general session of the People's Congress and to bring down the government. Amien Rais admitted the so-called Sofian Memo held elements of truth, but said it was also replete with distortion and misinformation (*Republika*, 26-3-1998). After having been interrogated as a witness by the police, Dr Afan Gaffar, who had read a paper on political reform at the meeting, set the wheels in motion for a libel suit against Sofian Effendi for having written a false report about the meeting. Afan Gaffar asserted it was Sofian Effendi's personal interpretation that those present had intended to topple the government. It had been a perfectly genuine academic meeting discussing *reformasi*.

Amien Rais took full responsibility for what had been discussed, remarking that when extremely blunt remarks (*kebablasan*) had been made there was no question of discourtesy, it was simply because academics did not beat about the bush. He reiterated that nothing dangerous had been said at the meeting. Stories that, with the financial backing of Arifin Panigoro, he intended to mobilize one million people to make the general session of the People's Congress fail, he disqualified as hallucinations. Though at first the head of police, General Dibyo Widodo, stated that Amien Rais was certain to be summoned about the Radisson meeting to explain himself, in the end the police decided not to go ahead with it. After the newspapers had reported on the case for about a week, Arifin Panigoro himself asked them to call it a day.

The incident was important enough for Susilo Bambang Yudhoyono, the new Chief of Staff for Social and Political Affairs, head of the BIA Intelligence Agency of the Armed Forces, and military commander of Central Java, to schedule a meeting at the end of the month at Hotel Sheraton in Yogyakarta to bring together a number of religious leaders, the persons who had attended the Radisson meeting, and the rectors of institutions of higher education of Central Java and Yogyakarta. Afterwards Amien Rais stated that the Radisson affair was closed and that Yudhoyono had called it a misunderstanding. He also revealed that Yudhoyono had asked him to exercise his critical faculties. Yudhoyono had stressed that the leadership of the Armed Forces realized that critical intellectuals helped protect Indonesia from sliding any further towards a greater disaster. Afterwards Yudhoyono confirmed that there were no obstacles to intellectuals being critical, adding that when they felt inspired to suggest solutions they should do so in a responsible, academic way. There should be no *kebablasan*. Yudhoyono's words can be seen as an early indication that at least some senior army officers were contemplating the necessity of piecemeal political and economic reforms.

CHAPTER VII

Mounting tension

Wakil Rakyat kumpulan orang hebat
Bukan kumpulan teman-teman dekat
Apalagi sanak famili
.....
Saudara dipilih bukan dilotre
Meski kami tak kenal siapa saudara

Kami tak sudi memilih para juara
Juara diam, juara he'eh, juara ha ha ha

Wakil rakyat seharusnya merakyat
jangan tidur waktu sidang

Wakil rakyat bukan paduan suara
Hanya tahu nyanyian lagu setuju.[1]

At the close of the general session of the People's Congress, student demonstrations anticipating the announcement of the new cabinet had grown steadily in intensity of demands and in size. All over Indonesia, students staged 'long marches' on their campuses, sang patriotic songs (*lagu wajib*, 'compulsory songs', so called because they had had to sing them at school) at times adjusting the words to serve their own purposes, read poems, and recited *pantun*, quatrains, and organized free stages. They did not mince their words in criticizing the government. In speeches soon to be dubbed *orasi*, they attacked the government and all those who supported it verbally, including the police and army units complete with armoured cars which were deployed in great numbers to corral the protesting students inside the

---

[1] People's representatives are an important assembly/ Not an assembly of close friends/ Let alone of relatives/ ... You are elected, not drawn by lots/ Though we do not know who you are/ We do not want to elect champions/ Champions who remain mum, champions in sighing, champions in laughter/ People's representatives have to appeal to the people/ And not sleep during sessions/ People's representatives do not speak with one voice/ Only able to dance to the tune of yes-men. Iwan Fals, *Surat buat wakil rakyat*.

confines of the campus. Students invited well-known critics of the government and leaders of student movements of the 1960s and 1970s to address them. Once again students resorted to the tactic of a hunger strike to underline the importance of their cause and to protest about the brutality shown by the security forces during clashes that had occurred at a number of universities.[2] Members of the academic staff continued to participate in the protests. The lowering of prices, a 'return of wealth to the people', the stepping down of Soeharto, and a cabinet untainted by collusion, corruption, and nepotism, were among their main demands. Taking up the plight of the ordinary people, students at times came out in support of the poor, the workers, the recently unemployed, and farmers, as they had done before, staging joint protests with these groups. Occasionally IMF was included as a butt of their protests, although other students attacked Soeharto for not sticking to the IMF agreement. In the cities, students of different universities and other institutions of higher education had begun to coordinate their actions by establishing consultation bodies. Two rival student organizations were active in Jakarta. One was Forum Komunikasi Senat Mahasiswa Jakarta (FKSMJ), the other, uniting students from about forty institutions of higher education, was what was usually called Forum Kota (often also Forkot), City Forum, or, to give it its official name, Forum Komunitas Mahasiswa se-Jabotabek. Both groups acted without any clear leadership, presenting different *kolap* (*koordinator lapangan*, or field coordinators) at different demonstrations. Students were also putting out feelers for a nation-wide form of cooperation, contacting fellow students at other universities. E-mail and mobile phones gave the students and their supporters an additional opportunity to coordinate with each other and to make their viewpoints widely known. It also provided them with information about real or alleged examples of abuse of power by the Armed Forces, the authorities, and Soeharto and his family and friends. That the students had been able to form a network was made particularly evident when, on 15 April, students staged nation-wide coordinated protests, presenting the same demands and grievances. As a token of this cooperation, representatives of universities outside Jakarta joined the demonstration at Universitas Indonesia.

Non-student protests attracted their fair share of attention as well. On 10 March, in the period in which public political meetings were forbidden, an 'Indonesian People's Summit' or 'Indonesian Congress' at Ancol in North Jakarta organized by Ratna Sarumpaet had to be cancelled because the organizers were unable to produce a police permit which the hotel manage-

---

[2]   Hunger strikes were frequent enough to have people inquire after the religious ruling. In the question column of *Panji Masyarakat* (27-4-1998:34) it was posited that Islam did not allow self-torture and that a hunger strike was therefore forbidden.

ment demanded. It was the second time this had happened. In February, a forum at which Emil Salim and Amien Rais were to speak had to be cancelled and transformed into a lunch because the police banned it in its original form. Among the speakers scheduled at the Indonesian Congress had been Amien Rais and Megawati. Though the organizers stressed the scholarly nature of the meeting, it had been intended as a kind of alternative to the session of the People' Congress, drafting its own 'Reformation Broad Outlines of State Policy' and delegating the leadership of the state to a presidium consisting of Megawati, Amien Rais, and Emil Salim. When those present sang the national anthem and *Padamu Negeri* and joined in observing a moment's silence just before leaving, the police burst into the room ordering the meeting to disband. Police officers shouted that Ratna Sarumpaet was to be arrested. As no written warrant could be produced, a skirmish followed as those present tried to prevent the arrest. Their efforts were in vain. Ratna Sarumpaet and nine others were arrested. The police justified their action on the grounds that a permit had been given for a lunch, not for a political meeting. Ratna Sarumpaet was also accused of having defamed the president. In March, the singing of the songs and the moment of silence was reason enough for the judge to conclude that a political meeting had been planned.

The closing session of the People's Congress proved to be an occasion for a number of mass demonstrations. On 11 March thousands of students – the highest figure mentioned was 50,000 – were joined by Amien Rais and by members of the academic staff from various institutions of higher education in singing patriotic songs and the Gadjah Mada Hymn, interspersed with shouts of *merdeka* (freedom) and *Allahu akbar*, and yelling various slogans. This demonstration at Gadjah Mada University in Yogyakarta was the largest demonstration Indonesia had seen for decades. A three-metre high statue representing Soeharto was attacked by the crowd. Before setting it alight the students jeered at it, thrashing it with rattan sticks, and pelted it with sundry objects which happened to come to hand. On the same day there were fights with security forces in Surabaya when students of Institut Teknologi Sepuluh November (the Tenth of November Technological Institute) – according to some reports some 10,000 of them – tried to leave the campus to join protesting students at Universitas Airlangga. There were also skirmishes in Surakarta. Also on 11 March, one plaza at ITB was renamed *Plaza Indonesia Tenggelam*, the Plaza of Sinking Indonesia. In a statement, the students rejected the accountability speech of Soeharto because it had failed to be 'transparent' about the causes of the crisis. The following day an Action of Concern was staged at Universitas Indonesia in Jakarta. Reportedly 20,000 students came together. As in Yogyakarta, Amien Rais was present and spoke at the free stage held, presenting his demands for reformation.

The announcement of the new cabinet on 14 March triggered off a wave of demonstrations at, it would seem, almost all Indonesian universities and other institutions of higher education, throughout the length and breadth of the archipelago. Replacement of a number of cabinet ministers was added to the now familiar demands for political reform and lower prices for *sembako*.

Representatives of the government, parliament, and Golkar, PPP, and PDI usually held their peace, not reacting to the demands put forward by the students. The lead in responding to the student movement was taken by the army officers holding key positions in the Armed Forces: Wiranto, Yudhoyono, and, because of his function as Armed Forces spokesman, Mokodongan. In retrospect they were to describe it as alarming that civilian decision makers failed to respond to the increasingly strong demands for reforms (*ABRI* 1998:8). Their reaction was a finely balanced mixture of caution and appeals for dialogue. Key army officers underlined that demonstrations would be tolerated as long as they were confined to the university. In vain they tried to convince the students that the blockades set up by security forces around the universities where demonstrations occurred were not intended to suppress the protests. There was no ill will in such actions, Wiranto stated in the middle of April. Who was to protect the safety of the students should they choose to leave their campus and who was to guarantee that the students would not disturb public order? Who was to guarantee that others would not join in and provoke destruction spiralling into anarchy? It was a repeat of the same fear that had inspired the government in January 1974. Were protesting students to march through town in great numbers, agitators, thieves, and looters might see their chance to wreak havoc (Cahyono 1998:225). Around the same time Mokodongan stressed that the presence of intelligence officers on the campus should not be misunderstood. They were not there to keep a check on the students, but to prevent outsiders from exploiting the situation. On various occasions army officers seized the opportunity to assert that the Armed Forces were in favour of reformation, as long as it was pursued gradually and followed a constitutional path. Radical change would only lead to destruction and not bring about the desired improvements. Or, as Yudhoyono was to hammer home from March onwards in various statements and interviews, the Armed Forces had set their sights on 'constitutional, conceptional, gradual, well-aimed' reforms, rejecting any which were 'revolutionary, radical, and dramatic' (*Republika*, 30-3-1998). The latter could well lead to undesirable consequences, as developments in the USSR and a number of Latin American countries had shown.

On 13 March, at the request of journalists, Wiranto ventured an opinion that some protests were within bounds, but that developments at a number of universities worried him. Stating that the Armed Forces did understand why students at so many universities had staged protests, he asked the students not to confine themselves to the issuing of statements but to contribute to overcoming the crisis and helping the people who suffered from it in a concrete way. This meant that instead of squandering their energy by staging mass demonstrations, students should give priority to an exchange of views. This was even more exigent when demonstrations led to disturbances of public order. Again responding to a question posed by journalists, Wiranto stated that for their part the officers of the Armed Forces, including himself, were prepared to discuss solutions to the crisis with students and prominent critics like Amien Rais, Abdurrahman Wahid, and Megawati. Any such dialogue, which when Amien Rais and Adi Sasono had suggested it a few months before had still been taboo, Wiranto averred, was very much needed. Among those who reacted positively, responding to the idea of a dialogue with students, were Amien Rais and Ichlasul Amal. Amien Rais welcomed the idea, expressing the hope that it would remove some of the misunderstandings which spoiled relations between the two groups. All this with the proviso that there had to be a real exchange of ideas, a condition Amien Rais thought could best be met in closed meetings at which there was no need to impress the public (Rais 1998:89).

Among the first to announce his intention of visiting universities and talking to the students was the Minister of Education. Arismunandar did not suit his actions to his words of 17 March. Within days he changed his mind. In a situation bursting with what he called uncontrolled emotion, such an undertaking would only be counterproductive. General Wiranto, on the other hand, took the idea of a series of dialogues very seriously. On 20 March, airing his concern about the harmful consequences of restiveness bubbling over into society and the ever-swelling protests, he announced that the Armed Forces, in their efforts to support the government to overcome the monetary crisis in a concrete way, would engage in dialogues with students and others.[3] Officers would visit universities and invite students to Armed Forces central and local headquarters. Wiranto regretted that during the time it took to search for a solution, restive groups made their appearance on the scene. Their statements and protests, as well as the rumours they spread, interfered with the concentration so badly needed to formulate an effective policy. The chief of police, Police General Dibyo Widodo, instructed the regional chiefs of police to engage in a dialogue with students.

There were some dialogues with provincial army commanders in Central and East Java, in Ujungpandang, and in Bengkulu. In the last region, dissatisfied with the content of the discussion, students staged a 'walk out'. Yudho-

---

[3] At that time the first dialogue had already failed. In Bandarlampung four medium-ranked police officers had entered the campus of Universitas Lampung the evening of 19 March. They had been taken hostage (police headquarters refused to use these words) by students demanding the release of their comrades arrested earlier in the day.

yono spoke to students in Bandung and Surakarta. At Universitas Sebelas Maret in Surakarta, the meeting ended in violence when security forces and students came to blows. Fifty students and six policemen had to be treated in hospital. Rated more successful were the visits senior officers such as Yudhoyono paid to Yogyakarta and Bandung to speak to religious leaders, university staff, representatives of NGOs, and others at the end of March. Their mission was to explain the position of the Armed Forces and to find out what motivated the students and what changes people in society at large most looked for. During such discussions a great variety of subjects were touched upon: the position and immense wealth of President Soeharto, the composition of the new cabinet, trade monopolies, the defects of the political system, the five political acts, and so forth. Not everybody was pleased with the direction these meetings took. Some of those attending the one held in Yogyakarta complained afterwards that it had been more of a monologue by Yudhoyono than a dialogue (Malik 1998:98).

Having coordinated their response at meetings in Jakarta and Bandung, the majority of students repudiated the idea of a dialogue. 'UI rejects symbolic dialogue', one of the posters in Jakarta read. They saw this sort of event as no more than a ploy to perpetuate existing power relations, and could not rid themselves of the feeling that the suggestion had only been made to silence them. They argued that in the past there had been many such meetings in which they had presented their demands to the authorities and politicians. The result had always been zero. Only when there was a real prospect of any concrete results were they prepared to talk. The students had often brought their complaints and suggestions to the attention of parliament. Its members always said that they would act upon these, but had never actually done anything. An additional reason to refuse such overtures was the fact that the Armed Forces were seen as an ineluctable part of the establishment and as such equally culpable for the crisis. Armed Forces representatives in parliament and the People's Congress had done nothing in the past to correct the abuses of the New Order.

In Jakarta, as an opportunity to express their refusal to conform, a protest meeting attended by thousands of students was organized on the campus of IAIN. During the free stage students demanded that the Armed Forces account for the harsh, repressive way in which they had curtailed students' freedom of expression at a number of universities. It almost turned into an ugly incident when security forces tried to prevent students handing out white roses to passing car drivers. At other universities in Jakarta and in other cities the rejection was also seized upon as a valid reason to stage large demonstrations. Among students' demands was the stipulation that before a dialogue could take place the Anti-Subversion Act (UU 11/PNPS/1963) and the articles of the penal code referring to defaming the president be withdrawn first. The former was a condition, it seems, the government could live with. At the end of April the Minister of Justice announced that the government was prepared to repeal the Anti-Subversion Act.

Others wanted to speak only with Soeharto and nobody else. They argued he held the ultimate power and he was the person who ultimately would decide whether or not any change were to take place. Some were very keen that such a meeting should not take place in his palace or in his office, as only a small number of students would be able to attend. This, Giri Ayu, chairman of Lembaga Mahasiswa Front Indonesia Muda Bandung, the Bandung Young Indonesia Front Student Foundation, feared might lead to discord among the students themselves, as they would then have to select representatives. Had such a meeting between Soeharto and students taken place, it may well have been a bizarre confrontation, as one of the major demands insisted upon by the students was that Soeharto resign. Others were prepared to settle for a discussion with Harmoko in his capacity as chairman of the People's Congress, should a meeting with Soeharto prove impossible.

The suggestion of a meeting of Soeharto and the protesting students was rejected out of hand by the Minister Coordinator of Political and Security Affairs. There were rules for such an occasion. When journalists reminded Feisal Tanjung that, as every television viewer could bear witness, President Soeharto often chatted directly with farmers, fishermen, and other groups, Feisal Tanjung retorted that when students took up farming, they might meet the president. He stressed that, as the future leaders of the nation, students had to follow the proper hierarchical channels and observe the rules of etiquette. They could present their wishes in the national and regional representative bodies. Other key army officers were opposed, too. Mokodongan was quick to label the students who wanted to have a dialogue with Soeharto and refused to settle for cabinet ministers arrogant. His colleague Yudhoyono rejected a student meeting with Soeharto on the grounds that it would be improper. Hartono was far from happy with the idea. Castigating journalists for their coverage of the student protests, he made much of the fact that the students did not represent the whole population. Only parliament could do this. Students had set their sights too high.

Perhaps Soeharto had an inkling that Feisal Tanjung and the other officers had been too blunt. Within days, Minister Agung Laksono indicated that the president was prepared to talk to students, but that such a meeting would not be of much use if most of the points to be raised could have been discussed just as well with cabinet ministers. Some interpreted it as a positive sign, as Agung Laksono's words had not been a downright rejection. Only, as he had indicated, a meeting between the president and the students had to be prepared very well, and had to be preceded by a meeting already planned between representatives of the universities and a number of cabinet ministers. In an interview in the newspaper *Republika*, Agung Laksono even hinted that, once such discussion meetings had been held, a dialogue with the president might be unnecessary. In the same interview, he made no bones about his opinion that the students' demands for reforms were nonsense. The government was already implementing economic, political, and legal reforms (*Republika*, 6-4-1998). Even Yudhoyono now stated that all strata of society could speak to the president. It depended upon the urgency, the topics, and the atmosphere in which the dialogue was to take place. The students had to present their ideas armed with clear concepts. Yet he believed it could not be other than incorrect when students obstreperously demanded that they wanted to speak to the president and nobody else. The president was not the only person who made decisions or formulated policy. Army officers and cabinet ministers had their own spheres of action.

The army did not give up its plan to hold dialogues. Wiranto claimed that these were very much needed to prevent mutual misunderstandings. They were a must. For their part, students continued to refuse to attend such meetings, in particular when they involved only the Armed Forces. They did not want to discuss political matters with army officers. Nor were they prepared to discuss the economic crisis with them, pointing out that economics was hardly a speciality of army officers. The only subject they were prepared to talk about with them was the security measures the Armed Forces had taken to fence off the universities.

With army officers underlining the usefulness of such a step, it came as no surprise that various dialogues were eventually held. The first, lasting for three and a half hours, took place on 11 April, at the Ministry for Youth and Sport. It was attended by 79 people representing 32 youth organizations. The Armed Forces were represented by Wiranto, Yudhoyono, Mokodongan, and Lieutenant-General Fachrul Razi (Chief of Staff for General Affairs of the Armed Forces). Wishing to make a protest and to show their solidarity with the students, a number of youth leaders who had been invited, among them Riza Primahendra, chairperson of the Roman Catholic student movement PMKRI, came to the building but refused to enter the meeting room. On finding out which youth groups were present, representatives of Gerakan Mahasiswa Nasional Indonesia (GMNI), Indonesian National Student Movement (associated with the former PNI), and Gerakan Mahasiswa Kristen Indonesia (GMKI), Protestant Indonesian Christian Student Movement, left before the meeting had begun. After Agung Laksono had opened the meeting Wiranto explained that the Armed Forces were in favour of gradual reform but totally against revolutionary change. The fate which had befallen Yugoslavia had to be avoided at all costs. He used the occasion to underline for the umpteenth time that protests should be confined to the campus. Violent and unethical outcries for reforms would be acted upon swiftly and without compunction, whether or not they took place on campus. He himself, for instance, was planning to sue students who had burned his pictures. Once again Wiranto repeated that the security forces assembled in the vicinity of the campus were there to prevent students being 'contaminated', adding that he knew of 'a third party' involved in the demonstrations (*The Jakarta Post*, 13-4-1998). Several of those present criticized the Armed Forces for not siding with the people. Wiranto was also asked why his wife and daughter were members of the People's Congress. Afterwards Wiranto announced similar meetings with *ulama* and students.

On 18 April Wiranto, accompanied by more than ten other ministers, including Ginandjar Kartasasmita, Hartono, Bob Hasan, and Siti Hardijanti Rukmana, and a number of senior officers, came to a meeting called 'Through a Dialogue We Shall Develop a Vision, Perceptions and Various Thoughts about National Problems', attended by 250 people. To highlight its democratic nature, before it began it was heavily emphasized that it was to be a 'round table' dialogue to which scholars like Didik J. Rachbini and Sjahrir, and retired officers, among them Rudini, were also invited. The meeting, intended for students and other young people, was organized by the Armed Forces. Among the leaders of the 25 youth organizations who attended were those of GMNI and HMI. Universities were represented as well. Absent were delegations of student senates from universities which were at the heart of the student protests, such as UI, ITB, IPB, the IAINs, Universitas Padjadjaran, and Gadjah Mada University. They held their own meeting at IPB in Bogor on the same day. The discussion in Jakarta, during which each participant was allowed to speak for five minutes only, concentrated on political issues, the five political acts, and the widespread corruption and nepotism. It failed to convince those present not to demand Soeharto's resignation. One of the questions posed was how to deal with the fact that, according to the rebellious students, the re-election of Soeharto as president was contrary to the wishes of the people. Wiranto, who once again vowed the support of the Armed Forces for gradual reforms, refused to go into the matter. The decision of the People's Congress was final. A few days later, HMI also organized a meeting in Jakarta with the Minister of Internal Affairs, Hartono, not a figure known for his sympathy for the student movement. Its theme was 'The urgency of political reformation for the development of a dignified nation'. Among the topics discussed was a proposal formulated by HMI to change the package of five laws – a topic which at that time the government and Golkar still categorically refused to discuss. Some students were far from happy with the fact that Hartono took the HMI concept as the point of departure. His explanation that there were mechanisms in place for the formal revision of laws also made the students angry, as did his answers regarding the general elections. It was a meeting beset by interruptions. To the loud applause of the others, some students walked out.

By that time students at various universities had clashed with the police and other security troops. Incidents in which students were being beaten up and arrested – and sometimes with security forces and students assailing each other with stones and other objects – had already occurred in Surabaya, Surakarta, Bandarlampung, and Denpasar. The frequency of such incidents had stepped up after demonstrating students had started to venture off campus around the beginning of April. Such instances showed that the authorities' fear of wider unrest were not without ground. Passers-by cheered the protesting students and joined them in their marches through the streets. In some cases the students reacted to Feisal Tanjung's appeal to talk to members of national and local representative bodies, though not in a way he would have wanted. On 2 April students tried to do so in Bandung, Semarang, Yogyakarta, Purwokerto, Surabaya, Ambon, and Pontianak. In Yogyakarta on that day, the most serious clash since the protests had started took place, when security forces tried to prevent participants in a student demonstration at Gadjah Mada University, organized by a Komite Perjuangan Rakyat untuk Perubahan, Committee of the People's Struggle for Change, and reinforced by street singers, organized in the Serikat Pengamen Indonesia (SPI), whose members also joined student protests elsewhere, vendors, high school pupils and others, marching to the provincial parliament. There were also skirmishes at IAIN Sunan Kalidjaga, where students, having lost faith in the provincial parliament, stated their intention of marching to the *kraton* to meet Sultan Hamengkubuwono. Students claimed that between eighty and ninety students were injured. About thirty had to be taken to hospital. The army put the figure at thirty wounded, three of them seriously.

The next day these scenes were repeated at Gadjah Mada University and at IKIP of Yogyakarta, when demonstrators tried to join their fellow students at Gadjah Mada University, where students of other universities had also assembled. Armoured police cars fired tear-gas canisters and riot troops entered the campus of Gadjah Mada University, which was seen by students and staff as a blatant violation of campus sanctuary. In protest, thousands of students and school pupils, united in Gabungan Pelajar Cinta Indonesia, Union of Pupils Loving Indonesia, demonstrated against the brutality of the security forces. On 4 April two police officers in civilian clothes were attacked and mishandled by students on the campus of Gadjah Mada. This incident, a student leader explained afterwards, had to be seen as a spontaneous reaction by a demonstrating crowd. It was indissolubly linked to the psychological state of the students, who had clashed with security forces on the two previous days (*Kompas*, 15-4-1998). In an initial comment, Mokodongan blamed outsiders for the violence. He found all the proof he wanted in the slogans shouted, some of which called for independence for East Timor. A

Fretilin flag had been carried by the demonstrators. Referring to these events a few days later, Abdurrahman Wahid, recovering from a stroke and still weak as well as virtually blind, in a statement read by the deputy secretary-general of Nahdlatul Ulama, Arifin Junaidi, asked the students to take another tack and to moderate their actions. He urged them to be on the alert against agitators. The security forces should keep cool and do their best to act and to deal with the student protests persuasively and in a way which should instruct the students. Abdurrahman Wahid made his statement after reports that paid agitators, who had every intention of inciting clashes between students and the units guarding the university, had arrested. As on other occasions when he suggested that violence had intentionally been provoked, Abdurrahman Wahid refused to be more specific.

After the clashes in Yogyakarta fifteen persons were reported missing. A week later seven people, two students and five street singers, were still unaccounted for. The National Committee for Human Rights, which sent a delegation to Yogyakarta to investigate, declared that what had transpired amounted to a serious incident. This evaluation was not based solely on the fact that persons were still missing but also on the knowledge that students and security forces had both been guilty of brutality. The committee also guaranteed the safety of students who had been detained by the police and wanted to make statements about how they had been treated. The committee was acting on claims by students that while they were being detained they had been manhandled and forced to strip. These accusations were strongly denied by the police.

Elsewhere political activists and students had also begun to disappear mysteriously. Some had gone into hiding fearing reprisals by the army, only to turn up again later. Others had been abducted before as well as after the session of the People's Congress. This was 'the second wave' of disappearances since July 1996. The first had been during the campaign period leading up to the general election. To avoid any chance of abduction, student leaders began to change their place of domicile frequently. Among the first to disappear was Pius Lustrilanang, secretary-general of Aliansi Demokrasi Rakyat (Aldera), People's Democracy Alliance, and secretary of SIAGA. Later it turned out that he had been abducted on 4 February in front of Cipto Mangunkusomo Hospital in Jakarta by men with close-cropped hair (see Suhartono and Situmorang 1999:vii-xvii). Around the same time Desmond Junaedi Mahesa, director of the Jakarta branch of Lembaga Bantuan Hukum Nusantara (LBHN, Nusantara Legal Aid Foundation,) went missing. He had been one of the founders of Forum Kebangsaan Pemuda Indonesia (FKPI, National Forum of Young People of Indonesia). Another victim was Andi Arief, chairman of SMID, who like other members of PRD and SMID had been wanted by the security forces since 1996. Andi Arief had been seized in

Bandarlampung on 28 March by armed men, again described as having close-cropped hair and with pistols strapped to their waists. Since then his family had been terrorized by threatening telephone calls.

In the middle of April a number of people were still unaccounted for. Among them were Andi Arief, Haryanto Taslam (deputy secretary-general of Megawati's PDI), Pius Lustrilanang, Desmond Mahesa, Herman Hendrawan (a student at Universitas Airlangga), Faisol Reza and Rahardjo Walujo Djati (both students at Gadjah Mada University). The latter three were members of SMID and founders of a Komite Nasional Pro Demokrasi (KNPD), which had rejected Soeharto's accountability speech. Also the general secretary of SMID, Nezar Patria, and another one of its members Aan Rusdianto, a student at Diponegoro University in Semarang, had been abducted. Later in the month Pius Lustrilanang, who had been released as early as 3 April, resurfaced. To explain his absence his kidnappers had instructed him to say that he had gone into hiding after being accused of being a member of PRD (Pandjaitan and Tanuredjo 1998:27). Haryanto Taslam and Desmond Mahesa were also set free. Initially they refused to disclose anything about their ordeal. The military police announced its intention to interview them to find out what had happened. Its commander, Major-General Syamsu, said that this was in part to silence efforts to discredit the Armed Forces by linking them with the mysterious abductions. Andi Arief was 'found' at Jakarta police headquarters on 24 April. He had already been held there for a couple of days on suspicion of having been involved in the explosion at Tanah Tinggi earlier in the year, admitting that he had been there when the bomb went off. Andi Arief, who had been kept blindfolded for almost three weeks, had been handed over to the police by his abductors on 17 April. Despite the stage management, there had clearly been a cover-up. On 22 April the chief of police was still declaring he had no knowledge of the whereabouts of Andi Arief. The following day, on 23 April, his family received a warrant for his arrest dated 29 March, and Widodo now maintained that Andi Arief had been in police detention since 28 March.[4] Faisol Reza, Nezar Patria, and Aan Rusdianto also now resurfaced. Being members of a forbidden organization and also suspected of involvement in the Tanah Tinggi explosion, they, too, had been handed over to the Jakarta police by their kidnappers. They were only to be released on 7 June.

The National Committee for Human Rights left no stone unturned in its efforts to locate the missing persons and to protect those who had been freed. The other organizations which were most active in this respect were Tim

---

[4] Andi Arief was released on 14 July after a campaign of Kontras, which considered his detention illegal as it took place after his abduction.

Relawan untuk Kemanusiaan, Humanitarian Team of Volunteers,[5] representing 16 organizations, among them women's and legal aid organizations, and
Kontras, Komisi untuk Orang Hilang dan Korban Kekerasan, Committee for
People who Disappeared and for Victims of Violence. Kontras was coordinated by Munir SH, and worked from the office of the Indonesian Legal Aid
Foundation. It had Mulyana W. Kusumah as coordinator of its advisory
council. These groups expressed their worry about the lack of freedom from
fear prevailing in Indonesia, pointing out that the people who had surfaced
refused to speak about their experiences. Outside Indonesia the kidnappings
and the fears they occasioned caused a great deal of concern. Human rights
groups abroad protested, and on 29 April the ambassadors of Austria, Great
Britain, the Netherlands, the United States, and the European Union issued a
joint protest and visited the Indonesian Minister of Justice to discuss the disappearances. In Washington, the United States government issued a statement urging a thorough investigation into the matter. Relatives of victims
also reported the disappearances to the International Committee of the Red
Cross. This sort of international attention was a source of embarrassment,
and became the catalyst for additional pleas for light to be shed on the matter. This accelerated when a rumour circulated that at a meeting in Geneva at
the end of April the Commission for Human Rights of the United Nations
was to condemn Indonesia.

The first to speak in public about his ordeal was Pius Lustrilanang. To the
National Committee for Human Rights he revealed on 27 April that during
his two-month ordeal he had been kept blindfolded and handcuffed, had
been kicked and beaten, had been pushed under in an open water tank, and
had been subjected to electric shocks. His interrogators had worn masks. He
disclosed this, Pius Lustrilanang said, 'at the risk of death' (*The Jakarta Post*,
29-4-1998). His capturers had released him, as they were also to tell others
they set free, threatening to kill him should he speak in public about what he
had gone through while in captivity. Others, who according to him were held
in the same location as he, were Rahardjo Walujo Djati, Faisol Reza, and
Herman Hendrawan. The three had gone missing in Jakarta in March and
were released on 26 April. Pius Lustrilanang also asserted that Sonny and
Yani Afri (both drivers and Megawati supporters, missing since May 1997,
and suspected by the authorities of being involved in a bombing attempt in
a shopping mall prior to the general election), Desmond Mahesa, and
Haryanto Taslam were also being held there.

At the end of the month the whereabouts of Yani Afri and Sonny were still

---

[5]   Among the members of the Team were Abdurrahman Wahid in his capacity as representative of Forum Demokrasi, Karlina Leksono Supeli of The Voice of Concerned Mothers, and
Sandyawan Sumardi.

unknown, as were those of students and PRD members Bimo Petrus Anugerah and Suyat. Deddy Hamdun, a supporter of PPP, his friend Noval Alkatiri, and the latter's chauffeur, Ismail, who had disappeared in May 1997, were also still missing. Determined to resolve the matter, the National Committee for Human Rights contacted Yudhoyono, who gave them the assurance, that the Armed Forces had issued an order to try to locate those still missing and that those who had surfaced and talked publicly about their fate were to be protected. In spite of this assurance, the same day he had talked to the commission Pius Lustrilanang fled to the Netherlands. In the Netherlands, Germany, and the United States he tried to drum up international attention for the fate of those who had disappeared in Indonesia.

For some time Pius Lustrilanang was to remain the only one who dared to speak out in public. Haryanto Taslam, who had not been physically tortured during his forty-day captivity, would do no more than to disclose that his abduction had something to do with his political activities as a member of the Megawati PDI board. It was 12 May before a second victim, Desmond Mahesa, broke his silence. He, too, had been beaten up, had been tortured with electric shocks, and had been immersed in water. Faisol Reza and Rahardjo Walujo Djati had a similar story to tell. Other victims, it emerged later, had been tortured as well. Some had been forced to lie down on blocks of ice.

The disappearances put the army command in a precarious position. As the National Committee for Human Rights also acknowledged at the end of April, there was a strong suspicion that army officers were involved, reinforced by the frequent observation that the abductors were strongly built persons with close-cropped hair. At the end of the month Mokodongan threatened that the army would press charges against any of the mass media that reported that the Armed Forces were behind the abductions. He stated that a list of those who made this claim had already been compiled. Throughout the uproar, officers at army headquarters steadfastly denied any involvement. On several occasions Wiranto and other officers promised to press on with the search for the missing persons. In a press statement it was stressed that Wiranto had ordered the chief of police to conduct a full investigation into the disappearances. *The Jakarta Post* reported that Mokodongan even indicated it was no secret which 'parties' were responsible and that the police had been informed of this (*The Jakarta Post*, 30-4-1998). When he received the five ambassadors, Muladi seemed unaware of this and stated that the perpetrators had not yet been identified. Syarwan Hamid, speaking in his capacity as one of the deputy chairmen of parliament, also urged for an investigation which left no stone unturned. Some of the senior officers, among them Wiranto and Mokodongan, even went as far as to voice their concern about the disappearances. They hinted at efforts to discredit the Armed Forces. Such strenuous denials did nothing to banish the growing distrust. In view of the continuing expression of national and international indignation, at the end of April the Armed Forces formed a special Fact Finding Team to investigate whether military men had indeed been involved in the kidnappings. On 8 May the team visited the National Committee for Human Rights for an exchange of information.

In the meantime the government had tried in vain to put a halt to the student demonstrations. On 5 April, the Minister of Education, Wiranto Arismunandar, forbade students and staff to engage in 'practical politics' on campus. Initially he refused to give a clear definition of what this phrase meant, merely giving demands that 'a functionary' had to resign as an example of practical politics (*Panji Masyarakat*, 13-4-1998:12). A few days later, after he had had some time to reflect or to consult, he defined practical politics as activities which directly or indirectly influenced the making of political decisions. Vowing that he did not want the campus to be transformed into a political arena, he threatened harsh sanctions would be taken against students who did not heed the ban. They faced suspension or expulsion. Students had to apply themselves to their studies again. Arismunandar's step elicited a fresh wave of protests, joined by university authorities. The latter sprang to the defence of the students and refuted the claim that student demonstrations could be classified as practical politics. They argued that the student demonstrations should not be construed as a political action, but should be interpreted as an expression of the students' concern. The students merely acted as messengers who presented the wishes of the people to the government. According to one of them, Prof. Soleh Solahuddin, rector of ITB, practical politics had to do with the acquisition of power, while the students were engaged in moral and intellectual activities. Bambang Triantoro also dismissed the announcement as very confusing. He found it difficult to understand what was meant by 'practical politics'. He argued that, if it was what he thought it was, it should be clearly differentiated from moral politics, which strove to improve any given situation. Amien Rais, who feared that the ban might have the undesirable effect of forcing students to look for other ways to protest outside campus, introduced yet another term: high politics.

Arismunandar singularly failed to reach his aim. The students ignored the ban. They recalled his harsh attitude when he had still been rector of ITB, and reiterated that there was nothing wrong in what the students were doing. Ten student senates in Jakarta issued a joint statement in which they dismissed Arismunandar's attitude as arrogant, and pointed out that it was the duty of a Minister of Education to protect students. He was there to act as an intermediary through whom they could channel their objectives. In less time than it takes to tell, posters appeared demanding his resignation. Appeals by Soeharto equally fell upon deaf ears. In the middle of April, on three successive occasions President Soeharto took it upon himself to comment on the student unrest. First, on 15 April, through his Minister of Education, he let it be known that students should return to their studies and that universities should resume their original function. Otherwise, education would suffer. On that occasion, when questioned by journalists, Arismunandar denied that he had ever said that student demonstrations were an example of practical politics. The students, he said, were a moral force. He went on to complain about media coverage of the demonstrations. Were the media to stop reporting on 'oddities', the protests would dry up. Press coverage must have been a point that also greatly bothered Soeharto. Next day, after a meeting with the president, the Minister of Information, Muhammad Alwi Dahlan, conveyed the fact that Soeharto had expressed his concern about reports in the media, which could stand in the way of the restoration of the Indonesian economy. Even here there were ifs and buts. Not all blame could be laid at the door of the media. Alwi Dahlan admitted that cabinet ministers did not always provide the best information, and suggested that when they felt themselves ignorant of all the ins and outs, it would be better if they refrained from commenting at all. Alwi Dahlan's words allow the conclusion that Soeharto was angry with his cabinet ministers as well. He instructed them to speak only about matters which directly concerned their own ministry. Alwi Dahlan was assigned the task of coordinating government information. Still that same day, 16 April, in a written address to Kopassus, on the occasion of its 46th anniversary, Soeharto stressed that only under very pressing circumstances, and then still within the limits of the law, were the Armed Forces allowed to resort to repressive measures. Even so, Soeharto's message held a veiled threat. In his statement the hope was expressed that society and the police could maintain security and public order and that Kopassus would not have to be called in. On 17 April, and this time using the new commander of the Central Java-based Diponegoro Division as his mouthpiece, Soeharto once again underlined that life at universities should return to normal. Universities were meant to educate and prepare future leaders. They should continue to function in this way.

The admonishments were in vain. *Reformasi total, reformasi menyeluruh,* or *reformasi paripurna* (complete reformation) had irrevocably entered the jargon. Inside and outside the universities demonstrations continued. Among the groups that came to prominence was Kesatuan Aksi Mahasiswa Muslim Indonesia (KAMMI), Action Front of Indonesian Muslim Students, founded on 29 March at Universitas Muhammadiyah of Malang by 63 religious propaganda groups (Lembaga Dakwah Kampus) active in universities all over Indonesia, with Fahri Hamzah as its general chairman.[6] KAMMI students,

---

6   Its emergence, according to some as a rival to the existing student senates at the univer-

staunch supporters of Amien Rais, were conspicuously present at demonstrations throughout the length and breadth of Indonesia. In Jakarta, on 10 April, KAMMI members and others assembled at Al-Azhar Mosque after the Friday prayer. A crowd of 10,000 people listened to speeches by student leaders. Labourers who had been fired, petty traders, and primary school teachers also took the stage to describe how difficult life had become for them. Al-Azhar was transformed into a sea of *jilbab* (veils), read one newspaper headline (*Jawa Pos*, 11-4-1998). In Yogyakarta there was a large prayer meeting organized by Muhammadiyah, at which Amien Rais was one of the speakers.

A new demand by the students, given utterance in the middle of April, was to convene an extraordinary session of the People's Congress. On such an occasion President Soeharto had at the very least to account for the crisis, calls for an extraordinary session might set in motion the procedure to force him to resign. The last was the aim with which demands for an extraordinary session had always been associated during the New Order, the government invariably coming down harshly on anybody who made such a suggestion. An extraordinary session was immediately rejected by members of parliament such as Ny. Aisyah Amini. Achmad Tirtosudiro, though stressing that reform was inevitable, also pointed out the complicated procedures which had to precede the summoning of an extraordinary session. Yet, he said, in his opinion students' demand for such a session had somehow to be acted upon. ICMI, he announced, was to hold a special seminar in May, organized by CIDES, to formulate a specific and detailed reformation programme, in order to establish quite unequivocally what exactly was meant by the word reform. Another new demand was that not only the government, but also Golkar, which till the monetary troubles began had always claimed the credit for Indonesia's development successes, had to account for its part in the economic crisis.

At the universities protests continued unabated. Students demonstrated in the thousands, joined by members of the academic staff, and as happened on 21 April, Kartini Day, in Yogyakarta by the wife of the rector of Gadjah Mada University, Mrs Ichlasul Amal, and other women of the Dharma Wanita (the compulsory civil servants' wives organization) unit at that university. Street vendors, taxi drivers, workers, housewives, and other ordinary citizens also joined the protesting students.

Over and above these grassroots stirrings, various organizations including NU, Muhammadyah, PPP, and PDI clearly spoke out in favour of *refor-*

---

sities, led to all kind of speculations about its link with Prabowo, ICMI, and CIDES. Leaders of KAMMI also expressed their distrust of officers like Wiranto, suspecting that Benny Moerdani had their ear.

masi. (One of the members of the NU Religious Advisory Council, KH Said Aqil Siradj, called attention in early May to the fact that reform was mentioned 41 times in the Koran.) On 15 April, the NU central board urged the Armed Forces to protect and support those who demanded reform, or *ishlah*, the Arabic word which Muslims preferred to use. The Armed Forces should not suppress them. Change, it was stressed, was *sunnah*, to be recommended. Students were asked to control their emotions and to beware of being duped by provocation. Mokodongan reacted at once, stating to the press that from the start the Armed Forces had supported and even initiated reformation. He claimed that military officers had been calling for change even before the session of the People's Congress. Mokodongan added that since Yunus Yosfiah had become Chief of Staff for Social and Political Affairs in September 1997, the latter had expressed the support of the Armed Forces for gradual political reform. However, reformation was a gradual process, and could never be 'total'.

The NU statement was followed on 19 April by one from Muhammadiyah, criticizing the government for its 'cosmetic and symptomatic' approach to the crisis. More concrete and fundamental measures were essential. Muhammadiyah let it be known in no uncertain terms that it was in favour of striving for political, economic, and legal reforms in a constitutional, gradual, and peaceful way. The Indonesian population was asked to have the moral courage to put an end to the 'chronic diseases of nepotism, corruption, and collusion' in order to create a clean government which would have unimpeachable authority. It was up to the Armed Forces to take a positive and creative attitude in coping with the various crises the nation was facing and in dealing with the reform movement. They should give proof of their often repeated slogan that 'what is good for the people is good for the Armed Forces' (*Republika*, 20-4-1998).

In parliament, PPP and PDI representatives proposed changing the much contested acts on the political parties and Golkar (including its name[7]), the mass organizations, the representative bodies, and the general election. On 23 April PPP issued another statement expressing its concern about the lack of response from the government towards the demands made by society.

Sharpened by the clashes between security forces and students and the disappearance of students and other activists, the atmosphere grew increasingly ferocious. Soldiers and police officers took offence at the abuse they received from students, who called them dogs and other insulting names, and the attacks on the Armed Forces which were prominently displayed on posters and banners. At times there were exchanges of insults and reciprocal

---

[7]   Formally Golkar at that time was not a political party, but (together with PPP and PDI) an organization partaking in the general election.

pelting with stones lasting for hours between students and the troops guarding the campus. Physical clashes took place when demonstrating students wanted to leave the campus, costing victims on both sides. Students, soldiers, and policemen all had to be taken to hospital for treatment. In spite of this, the comments made by the military authorities continued to be moderate. At the beginning of April, for instance, the military commander of Jakarta, Syafrie Syamsuddin, refuted the suggestion that the student movement was a radical one. It was a moral and intellectual force contributing to the development of the nation. As long as the students were productive and ethical and did not denigrate people, everything was still all right. At the end of the month, the Minister of Internal Affairs, Hartono, stated that demonstrators were allowed to shout to their hearts' content as long as they did not violate the rules and the law.

In early May student protests escalated. There were two immediate reasons for this. The first was what was disclosed after a meeting on 1 May between the president and senior politicians and military officers to discuss the swelling wave of student demonstrations all over the country. It had been attended by Habibie, leaders of Golkar, PPP, and PDI, leaders of the various groups in parliament, the chairman and deputy chairmen of parliament, cabinet ministers, and the top brass of the Armed Forces. In itself, the meeting, which lasted for 80 minutes, was already extraordinary. Never before had Soeharto been forced to hold such an emergency consultation. Still, the meeting was more of a monologue by Soeharto. Who would dare to interrupt the president, Budi Hardjono of PDI stated after the meeting (Basyaib 1998:132). Afterwards the Minister of Information, Alwi Dahlan, and the Minister of Internal Affairs, Hartono, recapitulated what Soeharto had said. Hartono recalled that the president had stressed that he was not against change, providing that it took a constructive form and did not derail stability. The president was prepared to consider reforms and to make concessions. So far so good, but it was the timetable put forward which enraged the students. Soeharto had underlined his opinion that in view of the economic crisis, the country needed stability for the coming five years. People were of course free to express their opinions about the changes they wanted in the political system, including the election system. All the ideas would be taken into consideration by the members of People's Congress who were to formulate the next Broad Outlines of State Policy in 2003. This formalistic view insisted on sticking to the Broad Outlines of State Policy accepted in March, which would have to be unswervingly followed. At the earliest, reforms could be implemented in 2003. Hartono was most explicit: the president and his assistants were not against reformation, but stability during the next five years was paramount, the sobriquet by which cabinet ministers were often alluded to in order to denote that the president was the head of the government and the

person who ultimately determined the policy and also the fate of his ministers. Action had to be taken against any threats which might undermine stability. Hartono said that Soeharto had explained that reform had been an
ongoing process ever since before the Indonesian Republic had been proclaimed. One example of past reforms Hartono mentioned was the decision
taken in August 1945 not to include a phrase in the constitution obliging
Muslims to follow Islamic law. Instead, the Pancasila, which did not have this
obligation, had been included. Hartono added that changing the five controversial political laws could be considered. He explained that the president
had touched in particular upon replacing that the proportional electoral system by a district one. Critics of the regime had hailed this as a great improvement. There was the feeling the proportional system, coupled with the fact
that votes were for lists and not for persons, had contributed greatly to the
distance between electorate and people's representatives. A district system
would change this. During the meeting Soeharto had recollected that at the
inception of the New Order, the army had been in favour of a district system.
Soeharto claimed that at that time the political parties had rejected this on the
grounds that they did not have a sufficient number of well-qualified party
cadres in the regions. In 1998, after more than 30 years of the New Order, he
pointed out there were now graduates even in the remotest corners of the
country. Alwi Dahlan confirmed that when people wanted reforms which
were contrary to the Broad Outlines of State Policy, they would have to wait
till 2003, and that if they refused to do so they could expect reprisals.

Ismail Hasan Metareum recalled the meeting somewhat differently. He
claimed that Soeharto had stated that reforms were possible right away.
Alterations to the existing legislation could be implemented at the 2002 elections and during the session of the People's Congress in 2003. His words
received scant attention. The general impression was that Soeharto had
refused to consider any changes before 2003. The outcry was such that within one day Soeharto summoned Alwi Dahlan and Hartono and instructed
them to explain that it was untrue that he would only allow changes after
2003. Only decrees of the People's Congress had to remain unamended till
2003. Acts of parliament could be changed when parliament and government
agreed this should be done. Work on that could start immediately.

The rectification came too late to prevent an avalanche of demonstrations
on 2 May, National Education Day (renamed National Stupidity Day), by
students determined to take to the streets, demanding 'reformation now, not
in 2003'. At some universities they had now also resorted to Molotov cocktails to supplement stones in their battles with security forces. The cities
where the most violent clashes occurred were Jakarta and Medan. In Jakarta
at least 33 students were seriously wounded. Afterwards students and student movements, among them HMI, demanded a public apology from

Wiranto for the way his troops had acted. In protest two students began a hunger strike at the office of the Indonesian Legal Aid Foundation.

The situation raged out of control in Medan. After students broke through the security cordon, riots erupted, leading to the usual damage to shops. The events in Medan and Jakarta were serious enough for Wiranto to warn after he had visited the president on 4 May that the Armed Forces would act firmly to put down demonstrations which threatened to deteriorate into anarchy and destruction outside campus. Provincial commanders and heads of police had already been instructed to act accordingly. As he had done in months preceding, Wiranto once again tried to convince the general public that his soldiers and police officers kept the demonstrating students on campus not to curtail their right to speak out, but to prevent the student movement being unscrupulously infiltrated and manipulated so that the image of the students was stained. Referring to the demands for an apology, he stressed that it was not he but the students who should apologize. Many members of the Armed Forces had been injured. He claimed it was incorrect to assume that this policy made the student actions less effective. The protests on campus could still be covered by the press and the TV. As they had done on other occasions, students reacted by complaining to the National Committee for Human Rights about the brutality of the security forces. The members of this body in their turn called for reformation within the Armed Forces and an end to the violent way in which student demonstrations were being tackled (Lampito et al. 1998:10).

Medan exploded for the second time on the evening of 4 May. After a crowd which had assembled outside the local IKIP had attacked security forces guarding the campus, students once more succeeded in breaking through the cordon and, joined by school pupils and others, started demonstrating in the city itself. This was the beginning of three days of rioting and plundering, of which the Chinese community was the main victim. Unrest spread to various neighbouring cities in Deli Serdang such as Tanjungmorawa, Lubukpakam, Galang, Delitua, and Tebingtinggi, finally even to Pematangsiantar, 135 km away. Kostrad troops had to be called in from Jakarta to restore order. Shops selling food and clothing were the special target of the mobs. As had happened elsewhere people tried to prevent the looting of their shops by placing their prayer mats in front of them or painting signs on the shutters and walls that the owners were Muslims and indigenous Indonesians. At least six people died. Hundreds of Chinese fled to Singapore, Malaysia, Australia, and Hong Kong, all places for Chinese Indonesians to take refuge since the election campaign of 1977. Others took refuge in the luxury hotels in the city.

The second grudge which gave the students reason to protest was the announcement on 4 May by the Minister of Mining and Energy, Kuntoro

Mangkusubroto, that by presidential decree fuel and electricity prices were to rise, the new prices to come into effect on the following day. The announcement took everybody by surprise. Three days earlier, after a meeting with PPP members of parliament, Kuntoro had still denied that any hike was imminent. The price rise was only made public after Kuntoro had visited Soeharto. Premium petrol rose by more than 70 per cent, from Rp 700 to Rp 1200 per litre. The price of diesel oil went up almost 60 per cent, from Rp 380 to Rp 600 per litre, and that of petroleum, used by ordinary people and street vendors for cooking and for lighting, rose from Rp 280 to Rp 350 per litre. The prices mentioned were those charged by the distributors; retail prices were higher. The immediate result was that drivers all over Indonesia flocked to petrol pumps, jamming up ordinary traffic. Electricity prices increased by 20 per cent, to increase again by another 20 per cent in August and again in November.

The measure, to which the Indonesian government had committed itself in its agreement with IMF, met with widespread opposition. Unhappily it came precisely at a time when an increasing number of people found themselves destitute or had lost some of their purchasing power, and the consequence would be an almost universal rise in prices of goods and public transport. Parliament decided to call Kuntoro to account. Its members, indignant that they had not been consulted before the announcement, and now in the changing political climate not afraid to testify to their feelings, gave Kuntoro a difficult time. One Golkar member went so far as to state that it would be best for Kuntoro Mangkusubroto to step down if he failed to revoke the presidential decree. If he did not, members of parliament would resign. Parliament, with the full support of Golkar, spoke out in favour of rescinding the rise in fuel and electricity prices.

For the first time in weeks, Megawati let her voice be heard. In a special press release, her PDI urged the government to cancel its decision. A better solution for coping with the financial problems of the day would be for the government to ask the persons who had built up the largest foreign debts and those who had profited most from monopolies to sell off their wealth to settle their debts. The IMF agreement was no excuse for the government to abandon its responsibilities. During the negotiations with IMF the Indonesian government had not tried its hardest to defend the interests of the little people, the man-in-the-street. Others pointed at the fact that the rise in fuel prices was yet another indication that the government was more concerned with a small group of businessmen than with the fate of the people. The money saved on subsidies was dwarfed in comparison to the financial injection given to ailing banks.[8]

---

8   Syamsuddin Haris, 'Kenaikan BBM dan radikalisasi aksi' (Malik 1998:282-4).

Protests also poured in from public transport drivers. Some went on strike, others demonstrated in front of the parliament building. Another demonstration against the rise in fuel prices which attracted widespread public attention was the one staged by doctors, nurses, and medical students, who marched trough the city of Surabaya on 8 March in their uniforms, singing patriotic and religious songs. They participated, *The Jakarta Post* reported, 'happily' (*The Jakarta Post*, 9-5-1998). Onlookers honked their horns in approval, applauded from the sidelines, or joined the march. On the same day *becak* drivers also demonstrated in Surabaya.

The hike became a major topic at student protests all over Indonesia, and this occurred just at a time people had begun to express the fear that the conflict over the presidency might result in civil strife. On 5 May, clashes occurred in Jakarta at Universitas Nasional, in Ujungpandang at Universitas Muslim Indonesia, and in Yogyakarta at IKIP. In Yogyakarta on the evening of 5 May, shops in the vicinity of the IKIP campus were looted and destroyed. After their path had been blocked, the students, who had intended to march to the provincial parliament, took the chairman and a member of that body, both representing of the military, hostage. They forced them to shout reformation slogans and to hold up protest posters. The chairman was released after an hour, but his colleague, who had volunteered to take his place, was held for six hours. In Ujungpandang two civil servants were stripped of their uniforms. In a later demonstration in the same city, a member of the security forces was stripped naked. Between 4 and 8 May there were fights between students and security troops in Bandung, Bogor, Jember, Samarinda, and Surakarta as well. In some of these places demonstrations spilled over into riots. In Surakarta 120 people, having been hit by rubber bullets and stones or simply beaten up, had to be admitted to hospital after clashes between demonstrators and security forces. More than 30 policemen also had to be hospitalized. In Samarinda 18 students and 32 members of the security forces were wounded. In Yogyakarta violence erupted at Gadjah Mada University and other places in the city on 8 May. One person, Mozes Gatutkaca, died. Later, the street where he was killed was named after him.[9] The military commander of Central Java, Major-General Tyasno Sudarto, blamed 'recidivists' for the riots. A day later, 9 May, demonstrating students at Universitas Juanda in Bogor suddenly attacked two police officers in civilian dress who had just left a mosque near the campus. One died (as an autopsy revealed, from a coronary), the other was seriously injured.

---

[9]   In October 1999 the High Court of Yogyakarta ruled that the chief of police of Yogyakarta, responsible for the behaviour of the policemen under his command, had to pay compensation of Rp 2.2 million to the brother of Mozes Gatutkaca.

CHAPTER VIII

Soeharto's resignation

Betapa hatiku takkan rindu
telah gugur Pahlawanku.
Betapa hatiku tak akan sedih
hamba ditinggal sendiri.[1]

By the beginning of May increasing numbers of organizations were beginning to speak out in favour of the students' demands. Among them was the Indonesian Communion of Churches and INFID, International Forum on Indonesian Development, uniting 120 Indonesian and foreign NGOs. The staff and senates of institutions of higher education, among them those of Trisakti University, Universitas Indonesia, Gadjah Mada University, Institut Pertanian Bogor, Universitas Airlangga, and Institut Teknologi Bandung, also joined in, some stating outright that Soeharto had to step down. Another group which expressed its support was Komite Nasional Indonesia (KNI), which brought together various public figures of the so-called Generation of 45. On 11 May KNI representatives read a statement to this effect in Mrs Supeni's house. Present that day were retired officers of the Armed Forces well known for their critical attitude: Ali Sadikin, Solichin Gautama Purwanegara (former governor of West Java and a former member of the Supreme Advisory Council), and Hoegeng Imam Santoso (a former chief of police), former Minister of Education and of Information, Mashuri SH, and senior leaders of PNI and PDI such as Abdul Madjid, Sabam Sirait, Prof. Usep Ranuwidjaja, and Manai Sophiaan.

The students and their radical demands for reform also received support from unexpected sides. On 29 April, the chairmen of parliament visited Soeharto, informing him that for the first time in its existence parliament was going to use its right to introduce new bills, one on monopolies, one on the protection of consumers, and one on the hajj (*DPR* 1998:1-7). Publicly, though

---

[1]   How can my heart not yearn for my fallen Hero/ How can my heart not be sad now that I am left on my own. From *Gugur Bunga* by Ismail Marzuki.

still rejecting the idea of an extraordinary session of the People's Congress, Harmoko urged the government to respond positively to the protests. He announced that parliament was going to revise the five political acts and the Subversion Act. It was a show of independence and initiative parliament (under attack on all sides for its weakness) had never before displayed under the New Order. On 6 May, after a meeting of members of the central board with those of provincial and regency branches, ICMI leaders also declared themselves in favour of total reformation and attacked the 'show of charity, which would not solve the problem at all and would even sow greater public cynicism' (The Jakarta Post, 7-5-1998). Qualifying the latest government statements about reforms as 'vague, too little and too late', ICMI deplored the kidnappings and the 'violence, especially if carried out by the state whose task was to protect and serve the public already feeling restless by the crisis' (The Jakarta Post, 7-5-1998). When they handed out the statement to the press, Achmad Tirtosudiro and Adi Sasono proposed calling for an extraordinary session of the People's Congress and a reshuffle of the cabinet. In their view, reforms could not be carried out by a government of which the members were contaminated by corruption, collusion, and nepotism. Only 'pro-reform' figures would be able to achieve this. In his capacity as general chairman of ICMI, Habibie hastened to explain that their words did not reflect the official ICMI position. He stressed that the remarks about an extraordinary session of the People's Congress and about changes in the cabinet had been the personal opinions of Achmad Tirtosudiro and Adi Sasono, expressed in response to questions put to them by the press. In Habibie's eyes, both points were equally impossible to implement. An extraordinary session of the People's Congress, only two months after the general one, was 'an insult to democracy and an insult to the people' (Media Indonesia, 10-5-1998). Changing the cabinet was the prerogative of the president delegated to him by the People's Congress. Formulating a similar demand on behalf of Badan Koordinasi Umat Islam (BKUI), Coordination Body of the Islamic Community, in which organizations like ICMI, Dewan Dakwah Islamiyah Indonesia, Persis, Al-Irsyad, and KISDI cooperated, Achmad Tirtosudiro did not agree. Driving home the point that since Habibie had been elected vice-president it was he, Achmad Tirtosudiro, who called the shots in ICMI, he denied that his earlier statement had been inspired by frustration arising from the fact that a number of ICMI leaders had not been included in the cabinet, and he stood by his words. The people had more authority than the People's Congress. If they wanted an extraordinary session, so be it.

The Armed Forces appeared to give way as well. The previous month Syarwan Hamid had already indicated that the Armed Forces were prepared to reconsider the five contested political acts. On 7 May Wiranto followed suit. Stating that the government understood the student demands but that it would take time to come up with concrete proposals, he announced the establishment by the Armed Forces of a special team headed by Yudhoyono to draw up a list of reforms required in the eyes of the Armed Forces. In the weeks to come, this team was to consult a variety of social and political leaders, including Nurcholish Madjid and Faisal Basri. In view of the response to their demands, he asked students to end their protests and devote their time and energy to helping people survive the economic crisis. On one point, key military officers adamantly refused to yield. They rejected an extraordinary session of the People's Congress. Mokodongan thought that such a session was superfluous, seeing that other ways to settle the crisis were still open. The Armed Forces, he explained, would investigate which reforms could be implemented immediately, which ones needed time to be realized, and which ones had to be rejected.

On 9 May, amidst mounting student protests, Soeharto left Indonesia to attend the G-15 summit in Cairo. Before boarding the plane, he called for calm and asked for understanding for the rise in fuel prices. Without political stability and security it would be all the more difficult to overcome the economic crisis. Soeharto defended the rise in fuel prices by explaining that such a step had already been contemplated for months and that the timing was now right. The abolition of fuel subsidies came during harvest time, when life was 'not so difficult' for the people. While he was in Egypt, Jakarta was transformed into the scene of unprecedented communal violence. A wave of protests and accompanying unrest had been expected, but not until later, on 20 May, the Day of National Awakening, renamed by some students National Reformation Day, on which it was planned to commemorate the founding of the first indigenous nationalist organization in 1908.

The explosion in fact came earlier. On 12 May, during yet another series of demonstrations, live ammunition was fired at students of Trisakti University in Grogol, allegedly by units of the Mobile Brigade of the police force. Four students and two other people died. Twenty students were wounded. The shootings took place after security troops had prevented Trisakti students from marching to the parliament building. After staging an hour-long protest instead at the town hall of West Jakarta, a few hundred metres from their university, the students agreed to return to their campus on the condition that the soldiers and police withdrew as well. All appeared to go well, but tension mounted after a former student, who had studied at the university in the 1970s and was acting suspiciously, was identified by the students as an *intel* (a secret agent) and to escape them fled to the security forces. It was then, between 6 and 7 pm, that the shots were fired. Afterwards, the campus radio and other private stations played *Gugur Bunga*, 'A flower has fallen'.

The following day a multitude of public figures visited Trisakti University to express their condolences. Among them were Emil Salim, Ali Sadikin,

Megawati, Amien Rais, Mrs Karlina Leksono Supeli, Mrs Ernalia Sri Bintang Pamungkas, Mrs Supeni, Kwik Kian Gie, Adnan Buyung Nasution, Arifin Panigoro, and representatives of Kontras. Soerjadi and Sofyan Wanandi, who also came to the university, were pelted with anything hard which came to hand. At many places the flag was flown at half-mast. The dead students were declared Heroes of Reformation.

The incident worked as a catalyst. Demonstrations to protest the shooting and to mourn the victims were held all over Indonesia. Students joined by others took the streets *en masse*, overwhelming local authorities. On 13 May there were clashes with security forces in Yogyakarta, while in Semarang students forced the mayor and the local Golkar chairman to join their ranks. In Bandung Gedung Sate, the seat of the governor of West Java and of the provincial parliament, was occupied. The following day Semarang students occupied the office of the governor of Central Java and the local RRI radio station, which started to broadcast calls for Soeharto's resignation and for an extraordinary session of the People's Congress. On these and following days, regional parliaments elsewhere were occupied. In Surabaya and Padang, students succeeded in taking over the RRI station.

Hardest hit were Jakarta and Surakarta, on 13 May. In Jakarta unrest started around midday after a crowd of people on their way to Trisakti University, shouting anti-Soeharto slogans and screaming that the members of the Armed Forces were murderers, clashed with security forces. They tried to incite the students to join in, but the latter refused and stayed within the confines of their campus, a scene which would unroll the following day at UI as well. The rioting continued on the 14th. Violence spread to Tangerang, Bekasi, and Depok. In Tangerang two churches and a maternity hospital were ransacked. In Bekasi, rioting was sparked off by angry commuters who could not travel to Jakarta. As in Medan luxury hotels became a place of refuge, while an exodus of Chinese and foreign residents got under way. Some obviously not expecting to return soon and in desperate need of ready cash, sold their cars cheap at the airport (*The Jakarta Post*, 15-5-1998).[2] The Japanese government sent two military planes to Singapore to prepare for an evacuation of its citizens. The American government also made preparations.

Normal life ground to a standstill. Shops and markets closed, as did most government and private offices. Tanks and armoured cars guarded the presidential palace and the RRI station on Merdeka Square. *The Jakarta Post* reported that the city 'looked like a war zone' (*The Jakarta Post*, 15-5-1998). *Media Indonesia* described Jakarta and Tangerang as 'dead cities' (*Media Indo-*

---

2   In the middle of July the chairperson of Badan Komunikasi Penghayatan Kesatuan Bangsa (Bakom PKB), Communication Forum for the Belief in the Unity of the Nation, Rosita S. Noer, estimated that 40,000 Chinese had fled the country.

Jakarta, May 1998 (photo Mariëtte van Selm)

nesia, 15-5-1998). Another description was that of a hell, the air thick with black haze from fires (Lampito et al. 1998:19).

Crowds of thousands of people went on the rampage. Mob anger was directed against the Chinese community, although autochthonous Indonesians were among the victims as well. Chinese were dragged from cars and buses and beaten up and knifed. Some burnt to death while cooped up in their cars or in their shops, which were set alight (Kwik Kian Gie and Nurcholish Madjid 1998: 14). Chinese girls and women were undressed in public, assaulted, and reportedly gang-raped on the streets or in their homes, and, according to some reports, even burnt to death afterwards. Because Chinese property was specifically targeted, people tried to protect their shops and houses by putting up signs that the owner was a *pribumi*, an indigenous Indonesian, a Betawi (original inhabitant of Jakarta), a Muslim, a haji and so on. Citations from the Koran and texts like Alumni Trisakti, Supporter of Reformation, *maaf milik pribumi* (Sorry, owned by a *pribumi*) could also be seen on walls and on banners. People even tried to divert the masses from destroying their property with phrases like 'indigenously owned, without special facilities' and 'it is true that the bank is Chinese-owned, but the manager of this branch is a *pribumi*' (Sembiring 1998: 101).

Among the regions where violence was particularly brutal was Glodok, the Chinese quarter of Jakarta, where many buildings went up in flames. At Jalan Hayam Wuruk a crowd shouting 'Burn! Burn!' and 'Immoral! Immoral' set fire to a discotheque. In the same street bank employees prevented the destruction of ATMs by throwing bank notes into the crowd (*The Jakarta Post*, 15-5-1998). Looting took place on a massive scale. It was reported that looters repeatedly yelled 'Long Live Economic Reforms' (*The Jakarta Post*, 15-5-

1998). It was a 'party for the people', one of the looters commented (*Forum Keadilan*, 1-6-1998:15). Loot consisting of refrigerators, washing machines, and mattresses was even transported back home on the roof of a train (Pour 1998:68). Others sold the products they had taken to onlookers. People justified their taking part in this by referring to the economic crisis and stating that the looted goods were the property of the people. But there were mobs which set fire to the goods taken from the shops, stressing, as it was reported of one person, that they were no thieves.

People from all walks of life, it appears, seized their chance: not only the urban poor but also housewives, schoolchildren, and executives joined in the looting. *Orang berdasi*, men wearing ties (executives), were seen taking books from a bookshop, afterwards driving off with them in their cars (Krishna 1998:5). At one place cash from a BCA bank was burnt in the street. Houses were also subject to looting. In some cases everything that was moveable, including doors, was taken away, in other instances in a frenzy of rage furniture was smashed to smithereens and clothes were torn to shreds. In North Jakarta, where police guarded the roads to a residential quarter in which many Chinese were living, plunderers entered from the sea side by proa (Anwari SB 1998b:4).

On 14 and 15 May, Surakarta was also the scene of extremely violent riots, in which again the local Chinese community was the main target. The trou-

Surakarta, May 1998 (photo H. de Jonge)

ble erupted after townspeople had joined in a battle between students and security forces at Universitas Muhammadiyah. Shopping centres and shops went up in flames. An appeal for restraint by an army officer was met by the retort 'Long Live the Armed Forces', but failed to cut any ice. Rioting spread to the élite neighbourhood, Solo Baru, where the house of Harmoko was ransacked, and spilled out to neighbouring cities. Rioting also occurred in Palembang. Yogyakarta narrowly escaped a similar fate. In the early morning of 15 May the situation in the city looked threatening, but Sultan Hamengkubuwono succeeded in calming the crowd down.

In the aftermath the National Committee for Human Rights blamed the Armed Forces for the absence of 'serious efforts by the security forces to prevent the spread of the rioting' (*The Jakarta Post*, 5-6-1998). In Jakarta the Armed Forces did indeed appear helpless. Syafrie Syamsuddin had stationed sixteen armoured cars in front of the Ministry of Defence and the Headquarters of the Armed Forces in Jalan Medan Merdeka Barat. Only after Prabowo had suggested so did he have a number of them patrol Jalan Thamrin and Jalan Sudirman. The whole situation had been exacerbated, as was revealed later on, by a lack of communication between the police and the army. Though as early as the evening of 12 May the Armed Forces in Jakarta were put on full alert and on the 13th units were ordered to the city from elsewhere, it seems that the army was unable to cope. Policemen were hesitant to appear in the streets in their uniforms, afraid of being attacked by people who held them responsible for the shooting of the Trisakti students (Sinansari ecip 1998:66). In some places soldiers and policemen confined themselves to preventing shops being burnt, standing idly by and allowing the looting. At times they even encouraged people to take goods and participate in the destruction (Djajadi 1999:36). Elsewhere they, as did ordinary citizens, came to the assistance of Chinese who were threatened with becoming the victims of mob violence. In yet other instances there was no policeman or soldier in sight. Except for some élite neighbourhoods, able to pay for the protection, this seems to have been the rule rather than the exception. It was up to the people themselves to protect their property by organizing neighbourhood patrols (Djajadi 1999:36). Prabowo, one of the officers who should have acted, seems to have been short of ideas about how to tackle the situation. In the early morning of 15 May, when passing Abdurrahman Wahid's house, Prabowo, accompanied by Kivlan Zein, decided to visit him. He knew Abdurrahman Wahid well and visited him regularly to give him a massage. Abdurrahman Wahid was still sleeping, so, while waiting for him to wake up, Prabowo meditated as a way of helping to improve Abdurrahman Wahid's poor health. Prabowo asked Abdurrahman Wahid, once he had woken up, for advice on how to overcome the rioting. Abdurrahman replied that as military men they should know the answer themselves and that if people had listened to him no riots would have occurred (*Media Indonesia*, 6-11-1998).

Afterwards Wiranto, who himself had travelled to Malang on the morning of the 14th to act as inspector of a Kostrad military ceremony, tried to explain why the Armed Forces had failed to prevent the rioting.[3] There were so many economic centres and everything happened so fast, he said. The Armed Forces were also perplexed. They were trained to protect the people, not to be confronted by them (*Forum Keadilan*, 1-6-1998:16). He asked for forgiveness for the victims who had fallen at Trisakti University. In Solo, the military had a similar excuse: not enough troops had been on hand, partly because units had been ordered to Jakarta (Pour 1998:82).

On 15 May, tension subsided a little. In Jakarta soldiers were very visibly present in the streets. In an effort to calm down the population a TV pool was instituted. The six TV channels were to broadcast the same news about the rioting and its aftermath. No independent reporting by the commercial stations, which had broadcast thrilling pictures of the rioting, was allowed. Sporadic rioting continued on 16 May. It was the 17th before normal life hesitantly began to resume. Material damage was enormous. In Jakarta and neighbouring cities two hospitals, two subdistrict offices, 13 markets, 40 shopping malls, 11 police stations, over 65 bank offices (of which many were BCA offices), 383 private offices, 24 restaurants, 12 hotels, over one thousand private homes, and thousands of shops had gone up in flames or had been seriously damaged. Material damage was estimated at US$ 250 million by the municipality of Jakarta; insurance experts spoke of four times this amount. Among the houses plundered and burned was that of Liem Sioe Liong. Liem himself was in Los Angeles. The police put the death toll in Jakarta at 451 people. The figure given for Jakarta by the army was 463, that by the municipality of Jakarta 288. In early June the National Committee for Human Rights mentioned a death toll of 1,188. The Humanitarian Team of Volunteers spoke of 1,218 killed in Jakarta, of whom 1,193 had died in fires, and 33 elsewhere. As had happened in Banjarmasin during the election campaign, most of the victims had been looters trapped in department stores which had caught fire. They either burnt to death, suffocated, or died after jumping out of windows in their desperation to escape. Many of the victims had been burnt beyond recognition.

---

3 Prabowo had been one of the senior officers who accompanied Wiranto to Malang. On 13 May, according to his own account, Prabowo had tried to convince Wiranto to postpone the event in Malang, and had also asked whether it would not be better were either he himself or Wiranto to stay in Jakarta. The commanders of the navy and of the marines also left Jakarta to attend a naval ceremony in Jonggol. When Prabowo and Wiranto returned at eleven o'clock in the morning the city was already ablaze (*Tempo*, 16-11-1998:29; *Forum Keadilan*, 30-11-1998:87; *Panji Masyarakat*, 27-10-1999:23).

Shocked by what had happened *reformasi damai*, peaceful reformation, was the catchcry bandied around. People could buy head bands, which were also worn by prominent critics of the government, bearing this text. During a brief speech at the Salemba campus of UI, Yudhoyono expressed his support for peaceful reforms, reiterating the Armed Forces standpoint that change had to be gradual. The violence caused Amien Rais to abandon a plan he had developed in collaboration with others to establish a kind of cabinet watchdog organization to judge the behaviour of this body. Instead, on 14 May and earlier than he had intended to announce the watchdog organization, he founded Majelis Amanat Rakyat (MAR or MARA), or Council of the Message of the People. In founding it, great care had been taken to avoid any suspicion of sectarianism and therefore it included representatives from the various religious communities. Among its 56 members were Amien Rais, Emil Salim, Frans Seda, Adi Sasono, Nurcholish Madjid, Emha Ainun Nadjib (a well-known Muslim intellectual and author), Ichlasul Amal, Siswono Yudohusodo, Arifin Panigoro, Goenawan Mohammad (editor of the banned weekly *Tempo*), Adnan Buyung Nasution, Ali Sadikin, Faisal Basri, and Ratna Sarumpaet. Convinced that domestic political and economic developments had made it futile to evaluate the performance of the cabinet, MAR members called for Soeharto to step down. They also called upon the Armed Forces and students to avoid violence. The founding of MAR and the persons it united within it made a great impression. The rumour immediately spread that Amien Rais was going to be arrested, while Prabowo, suspecting it to be a counter-government, qualified MAR as an unconstitutional organization. Prabowo took great pains to deny, as had been mentioned, that his father, Sumitro Djojohadikusumo, was a member of MAR.[4]

After the riots the rupiah dived from Rp 7,000 to Rp 14,000 to the dollar; in Singapore it even plunged to Rp 17,000. Another consequence of the disturbances in May was that investors from Hong Kong, Singapore and Taiwan, obviously shaken by the anti-Chinese riots, postponed investments. Conversely, in Indonesia itself much was made of the money which had fled the country together with its Chinese owners, fuelling resentment against the Chinese community.

BCA also suffered. A rush started on its offices and ATMs, as had happened in November when it was again rumoured that Liem Sioe Liong had died and that the bank was to be liquidated. As so often when unpleasant developments take place in Indonesia, a conspiracy theory surfaced. It was

---

[4]   After Soeharto's fall it was reported that, during a meeting of the cabinet, Soeharto had ordered Amien Rais's arrest. The then attorney-general, Soedjono Chanafiah Atmonegoro, is said to have refused to do this, stating that the case of the people who had disappeared should be solved first.

alleged that some unnamed persons had deliberately aimed to sabotage the bank. Mochtar Riady, himself a wealthy businessman and head of the Lippo group, reckoned that the rumours had been spread on purpose by people who wanted to see the Indonesian economy bite the dust. He said that the first queues at BCA banks had been formed by people who withdrew only small amounts of money. Seeing the queues, others had panicked. In popular parlance the bank came to be known as *Bank Capek Antre*, or Tired of Queuing Bank. Other banks built up an extra stock of cash in case the rush proved contagious.

On 28 May, when the rush had lasted for a fortnight and customers had withdrawn between Rp 15 and 20 trillion, BCA had to be put under the tutelage of the Indonesian Bank Restructuring Agency, because, the financial assistance by Bank Indonesia had by far exceeded BCA's own capital. It was reported that in its efforts to help BCA Bank Indonesia had been forced to print extra banknotes. In total Rp 35 trillion (approximately US$ 3.5 billion) had to be lent to BCA to enable it to survive. The take-over by BPPN did not at first put an end to the panic. Even more people wanted to withdraw their money. To restore faith in BCA, Mar'ie Muhammad and others suggested it be nationalized, or at least that Siti Hardijanti Rukmana and Sigit Harjojudanto should hand over their shares to the state.

In the meantime, during a meeting with the Indonesian community in Cairo on 13 May, President Soeharto had stated that if the people no longer wanted him, so be it. He would not defend his position by force of arms. The following day, after these words had reached Indonesia, Harmoko, in his capacity as general chairman of parliament, announced that the chairmen of the People's Congress would meet to discuss what to do next. It just happened that when Harmoko said this to the press, Adnan Buyung Nasution, the poet W.S. Rendra, and a number of lawyers who had just visited one of the parliamentary committees overheard his words. A tense discussion followed. Adnan Buyung Nasution castigated Harmoko for his slow response to Soeharto's apparent willingness to resign. With fires burning all over the city, decisive action not words was required. It was Harmoko's duty to leave for Cairo to present Soeharto with the 'aspirations of the people'. Harmoko refused. Soeharto was to return to Jakarta earlier than planned and were he, Harmoko, to travel to Cairo the two might miss one another. Before all else, the constitutional rules had to be observed. Such an attitude was unacceptable to Adnan Buyung Nasution. Following procedures and convening an extraordinary session of the People's Congress to effectuate Soeharto's resignation would take too long.

Soeharto returned from Cairo in the early morning of 15 May, well ahead of schedule. A few hours after his return, after having consulted his children and his son-in-law, Prabowo, Soeharto made it known through the Minister of Information, Alwi Dahlan, that in Egypt he had not said that he would resign, but had only ruminated out loud about what he might do if the time came that the people no longer had any faith in him. True to the ideal he cherished about the way a ruler should step down, taking his example from the Javanese *wayang* tradition, he indicated, as he had done in November, that in that case he would devote himself to religion, counsel his children and grandchildren to behave well, and would remain prepared to give advice when necessary. The only condition he posed was that whatever the decision taken, his replacement had to proceed in accordance with the constitution.

Alwi Dahlan added that the president welcomed political and economic reforms. Another development on 15 May was that after Ginandjar Kartasasmita had consulted Michel Camdessus of the IMF by phone, the price increases on fuels were partly revised. The price of premium petrol was fixed at Rp 1000 per litre, that of automotive diesel at Rp 550. The price of kerosene regained its original level of Rp 250 per litre.

More concessions were to follow. The next day Harmoko and the other chairmen of parliament visited Soeharto to present a 'reformation agenda', including the revision of the political acts, and to inform him, as the press so carefully put it, of the aspirations society had presented to them and other members of parliament, meaning that they had told Soeharto that it would be best if he were to retire gracefully. They had informed Soeharto that the people wanted 'total reform', desired him to resign, and demanded an extraordinary session of the People's Congress (*DPR* 1998:20). In response Soeharto promised a cabinet reshuffle. Referring to his possible resignation, Soeharto stated that if parliament wanted him to go, he would, leaving no doubt that the opinion of parliament would suffice and that there was no question of convening an extraordinary session of the People's Congress. He made it known that in order to protect 'the people, the citizens, the assets of the state, and to safeguard Pancasila and the Constitution of 1945', he intended to use the special powers the People's Congress had given him and form a kind of Kopkamtib (*DPR* 1998:20-1). The public was informed of Soeharto's words, with the exception of his opinion about his resignation and his reference to Kopkamtib. Rumours flew that 15 ministers, including Siti Hardijanti Rukmana, Wiranto Arismunandar, and Bob Hasan, were to be replaced. According to these reports Hartono, who had been most cynical about the calls for reformation, pretending not to understand what the students wanted with their demands for reforms and democratization, was to keep his position.

Earlier in the morning Soeharto had already received a delegation of the academic staff of UI, headed by its rector, Prof. Asman Boedisantoso, who came to present the results of a symposium on Indonesia's future structure. They had pleaded with Soeharto that he should resign, probably the first instance in which Soeharto was told so straight to his face and without beating around the bush. On this occasion Soeharto had once again repeated that stepping down was no problem for him.

The moment of decision had come for the persons in the inner circle around Soeharto, who up to that moment had only contested each other's secondary positions of power. The prospect of Soeharto's replacement meant that behind the scenes an acute struggle for power gained momentum. The main players were Wiranto, Prabowo, and Habibie. In the army there were tensions between those who were dubbed the green generals, officers who had close contacts with Islamic organizations, advocates of a greater role for Islam and the Muslim community in politics, including Prabowo, Hartono, Feisal Tanjung, and Syarwan Hamid, and the red and white or 'nationalist' officers, stressing a nation-wide loyalty, with Wiranto, Edi Sudradjat, and Yudhoyono as some of the principal representatives. It was well known that Wiranto and Prabowo disliked one another, and that the quick rise of the relatively young Prabowo – he was 47 – to such an important command post as that of Kostrad, without ever having had to serve as a commander of a territorial unit, had rankled with fellow officers. The pros and cons Habibie evoked in the Armed Forces and in Golkar were yet another contributing factor. A sudden resignation of Soeharto would elevate him to the position of president, an outcome some of the officer corps and some Golkar leaders wanted to avoid. Habibie himself was preparing for it, perhaps right from the moment Soeharto had left for Egypt (*Golkar* 1999:66). One of the ways to block such an eventuality was to delay the succession question and press for an extraordinary session of People's Congress which would have to accept Soeharto's resignation and elect a successor. Yet another position at stake was that of commander of the Armed Forces. Prabowo, who if the rumours are to be believed let no opportunity pass to denigrate Wiranto in the eyes of Soeharto, might have urged Soeharto to replace Wiranto and Yudhoyono at least as early as 17 May. On that same day he is said to have presented Soeharto with a copy of a press release – Mokodongan claimed it was distributed by unknown persons – that the Armed Forces wanted Soeharto to resign (*Tajuk*, 4-3-1999:82).

Pressure was added by the unremitting student demonstrations and the constant stream of delegations visiting parliament. Critics finally made Harmoko and the other chairmen of parliament and the People's Congress suddenly realize that the institutions they headed represented the people and that the time for foot-dragging was past; now they had to do something. It was they who had to set in motion the procedure for an extraordinary session of the People's Congress. Besides the clamouring students, they also had to cope with the many delegations and statements by much respected people calling for an end to the Soeharto era, sometimes softening their message by expressing support for Soeharto's own assertion that he was willing to resign. Conspicuous among those urging for the Soeharto era to be brought to an end were politicians and officers of Soeharto's own generation, the so-called Generation of 45. They included prominent retired military officers, all with an impressive military career, of whom most had fallen out with Soeharto in the course of the New Order. Many of them, who had turned from being key figures in the New Order's military and civil administration into proponents of democracy after the end of their career, had been scorned by those still in power as Barisan Sakit Hati, the Column of the Offended, though this derogatory term, as so often is the case, was also transformed into a nick-name proudly borne. On the 15th, in a statement about a dozen of them had spoken out in support of the student protests and demanded an extraordinary session of the People's Congress. The initiative had been taken by Achmad Kemal Idris, a former Kostrad commander. Co-signers were Ali Sadikin, Muh. Kharis Suhud (a former chairman of the People's Congress), Bambang Triantoro, Hoegeng Imam Santoso, Rudini, Wahono (a former general chairman of parliament and People's Congress and former general chairman of Golkar), Lieutenant-General (Ret.) Hasnan Habib (a former ambassador to the United States), and Solichin GP.[5] This was followed by a statement in support of complete reformation and the resignation of Soeharto issued by KNI, now calling itself Komite Nasional Indonesia untuk Perubahan dan Penyaluran Aspirasi Rakyat (KNIPP), Indonesian National Committee for Change and Conveying of the Aspirations of the People. Among the signatories were Mrs Supeni, Ali Sadikin, Roeslan Abdulgani, Sabam Sirait, Hoegeng Imam Santoso, Manai Sophiaan, Prof. Deliar Noer, and Solichin GP. Many others also signed. On behalf of ICMI, Adi Sasono and the head of the editorial staff of *Republika*, Parni Hadi, stressed that a mere cabinet reshuffle was not enough. The people demanded a change in national leadership; in other words Soeharto had to go.

In the constantly swelling movement to make Soeharto resign, the much talked about people power seemed to materialize. The parliament compound became the focus of political attention. It was the place where students, academic staff, public figures (Amien Rais, Andi Mappetahang Fatwa, Sukmawati Soekarnoputri, Guntur Soekarnoputra, Deliar Noer, Goenawan Mohammad, Adnan Buyung Nasution, and many others), former cabinet ministers, artists such as Rendra, and retired officers flocked to to voice their

---

[5]   Others who endorsed the statement were Vice-Admiral D. Pardjaman, Lieutenant-General Sayidiman Suryohadiprodjo, Lieutenant-General Himawan Soetanto, Prof. Dr Harun Zein, Marshal Ashadi Tjahjadi, Major-General Koesparmono Irsan, Lieutenant-General Wiyogo Atmodarminto, Marshal Sukardi, Marshal Saleh Baserah, Vice-Admiral Edy Soeprapto, and Police General Awaluddin Djamin.

Students occupy the People's Congress (photo *Tempo*)

demands and suggestions. In most cases they pressed for the resignation of Soeharto, an extraordinary session of the People's Congress, and total reform. Among them were members from Komite Nasional Indonesia untuk Reformasi (KNI-Reformasi), Indonesian National Committee for Reformation. Chairman of KNI-Reformasi was Prof. Subroto, a former New Order Minister of Mining and Energy and a former secretary-general of OPEC.[6] Other delegations represented SOKSI (which in January had still been suggesting that Soeharto should be honoured with the title of *Bapak Pembaruan*, Mister Reform, and now only asked for an unimpeachable cabinet), Kosgoro (pressing for the resignation of Habibie as well), KNPI (usually not the greatest example of a critical youth organization), and Keluarga Alumni Himpunan Mahasiswa Islam (KAHMI) of Jakarta.

Amien Rais also left no doubt about what he wanted, though he called for Soeharto's resignation in a courteous, Malay manner (Lampito et al. 1998:46). Similarly, Achmad Tirtosudiro called upon Soeharto to step down. Abdurrahman Wahid was among the few who were more reticent. He pointed out the fact that in spite of what the demonstrators wanted, Soeharto had been elected by the People's Congress. Shocked by the violence in the middle of

---

6   Deputy chairman was Prof. Kusnadi, while Dimyati Hartono, a law professor and a politician in the Megawati PDI, was chairman of its executive body.

May, Abdurrahman Wahid also criticized the student movement. He blamed its change from a moral to a political force for the riots. Because their demands for reformation had turned into a political movement, they would never achieve what they had hoped for. Replacing Soeharto was a difficult, time-consuming process because he had a legal mandate, conferred by his election by the People's Congress. Citing the example of the life of Joseph, who had needed seven years to accomplish his aim, Abdurrahman Wahid stressed that religion taught gradual change.

The majority of those coming to the parliament building were students. Efforts were no longer made by Wiranto's security forces to contain the demonstrations to campus. Although on his return Soeharto had held out for tough measures, none were taken. On 17 May students decided to occupy the parliament building. The following day, a Monday, students from the Jabotabek area and Bandung demanding Soeharto's resignation followed by his trial came to parliament in the thousands, where another group had assembled in the early morning displaying a banner stating that they were prepared to die for Soeharto. Significantly the Armed Forces made no effort to prevent the anti-Soeharto students from entering. The protesting students remained on the premises after failing to meet Harmoko. Speeches were held at a free stage, posters and banners displayed, among them one expressing the resolve of the students, *Reformasi atau mati*, Reformation or death, slogans were shouted, and patriotic songs sung. They also sang *Surat buat wakil rakyat*, Letter for the representatives of the people, a song by the popular protest-singer Iwan Fals. A puppet representing Soeharto was trampled on.

In the afternoon of 18 May, after having had to deal with protesting students and numerous delegations for eight hours, the five chairmen of parliament – Harmoko, Abdul Gafur, Syarwan Hamid (who gave the impression of being one of the staunchest supporters of the demands of the students), Ismail Hasan Metareum, and Mrs Fatimah Achmad; all people, as Amien Rais later was to comment, who were usually so afraid of Soeharto (*Merdeka*, 11-6-1998) – made up their minds: the president had to be asked to resign. They announced a meeting with the leaders of the parties in parliament to discuss the convening of an extraordinary session of the People's Congress. When Harmoko made the decision public, his words were greeted with applause by the journalists present. Some wept. Soeharto was sent a letter in which the leadership of parliament asked for an audience after midday on the 19th, a bold step, as it was usually left to Soeharto to determine date and time.

Satisfied, most of the students left the parliament building. About one hundred stayed behind, disgruntled that Harmoko had not been specific about a date for the extraordinary session. They received permission from Syarwan Hamid to do so. They could bring their guitars, he stated, adding that their safety was guaranteed (Lampito et al. 1998:46). A few hours later, after consulting the leaders of the Armed Forces and then meeting President Soeharto, Wiranto, who himself was not keen on seeing Habibie replace Soeharto, responded by pointing out that what had been issued was a private statement which was therefore not legally binding; only a decision by a plenary session of parliament would be properly valid. Wiranto said that what was needed was the replacement of a number of cabinet ministers and total reformation (which must have meant something different to him to what it meant to the protesting students). As an alternative, Wiranto suggested the formation of a Dewan Reformasi, a Reform Council, made up of representatives of the government, academics, and prominent critics. The conflicting positions taken by Wiranto and Syarwan Hamid prompted a worried reader of *Panji Masyarakat* to phone the magazine to inquire whether a civil war was on the cards (*Panji Masyarakat*, 1-6-1998:48). A reaction similar to that of Wiranto came from the secretary-general of Golkar, Ary Mardjono, a 'Tutut man'. That evening, after a meeting at party headquarters at which Harmoko and Abdul Gafur were also present, he underlined that Harmoko had not spoken officially in his capacity as general chairman of Golkar.

The likelihood of an extraordinary session being summoned meant that people began to ponder the composition of the People's Congress; especially that part reserved for Golkar and for the Regional Representations, the guaranteed preserve for government officials, Golkar leaders, and regional military commanders. Students demanded its dissolution (and that of parliament), while others argued more moderately that at least those members of the People's Congress who were guilty of nepotism, collusion, and corruption had to be replaced. Their places had to be taken by persons like Amien Rais, Abdurrahman Wahid, Megawati, Emil Salim, and other critics. This was the only way the People's Congress would really reflect the wishes of the people.

The political strife that was rife in Jakarta, riven by conflicting opinions on whether Soeharto should resign, and if so when, and whether Habibie was the right person to replace him, inspired the Faculty of Geography of Gadjah Mada University to suggest in a letter to Sultan Hamengkubuwono that Yogyakarta should once again become the capital of Indonesia, as the city had been during most of the War of Independence when the country had found itself embroiled in a somewhat similar crisis. Infected by its 'moral pollution' and contaminated by personal ambition, Jakarta was not the most conducive place for leaders to act in a wise and proper fashion.

On the morning of 19 May, a meeting of the chairmen of parliament and the leaders of the parties in parliament spoke out in favour of Soeharto's resignation. No agreement was reached about the timing. The Armed Forces leader opposed the words 'as soon as possible', which would have paved the way for Habibie. At that same moment yet another emergency meeting was taking place at the presidential palace, this time with nine people present: an expert on constitutional law from UI and one of Soeharto's speech writers, Prof. Yusril Ihza Mahendra, and eight prominent religious figures. Among the latter were Malik Fadjar of Muhammadiyah (not Amien Rais – Soeharto had ignored a hint by Nurcholish Madjid that he had a college friend from Chicago), KH Ali Yafei of MUI, and Abdurrahman Wahid, Ahmad Bagdja, and Ma'aruf Amin of Nahdlatul Ulama. KH Cholil Baidowi of Muslimin Indonesia, Nurcholish Madjid, and Emha Ainun Nadjib were also present. The meeting had originated from an idea put forward by Nurcholish Madjid. Two days earlier he, in the presence of Emha Ainun Nadjib, had offered a way out for the crisis, to which the leading army officers found they could agree, and which in all probability had persuaded Soeharto to convene the meeting. The leading army officers, Nurcholish Madjid was to reveal later, had turned to him for advice on how to proceed (*Forum Keadilan*, 15-6-1998:79). The idea was that Soeharto should announce that he was to resign in a peaceful and constitutional way as soon as possible and that in the meantime he would replace those cabinet ministers who were opposed to reforms. Soeharto should apologize for the economic crisis and promise to take the lead in carrying through reforms and setting right the wrongs of the past. As an initial step, Soeharto and his family should hand over their wealth to the

Nurcholish Madjid and Abdurrahman Wahid (photo *D&R*)

nation. After this the political legislation had to be revised to allow a general election, which would be different to those held since 1971, to take place in January 2000 at the latest. In March (Nurcholish Madjid was well aware of the importance attached by Soeharto to that month) of that year the People's Congress should convene to elect a new president. Nurcholish Madjid averred that this was the best course to pursue. Were Soeharto to step down at once and a successor be appointed, the harvest might only be new waves of protests and strife. On 18 May, at the instigation of Yudhoyono, he had given the text of his proposal to the Secretary of State, Saadillah Mursjid, who in turn presented it to Soeharto. On the evening of that same day, Nurcholish Madjid was invited to Soeharto's residence at Jalan Cendana. On this occasion Soeharto confided to him that he had enough of being president and was prepared to resign at any moment.

Afterwards Amien Rais attacked the meeting of the 19th for its 'sectarian' nature. To his disappointment, only Muslims had been invited. No persons representing the other religions were given a chance to say what they thought. The reason Emha Ainun Nadjib gave for this seeming oversight was that at that moment Soeharto was resolved to resign and wanted to find spiritual peace (Nadjib 1998:57). Soeharto's resignation indeed was the main topic of the meeting, which lasted for two-and-a-half hours. Hence the invitation to Yusril Ihza Mahendra. Wiranto was also briefly present to explain his reaction to Harmoko's statement. Afterwards Nurcholish Madjid described the atmosphere as frank. Among the topics discussed was how Soeharto's replacement by Habibie would be received, and whether there was in fact anybody who would be acceptable to the majority as the new president. Soeharto was made to understand that the demands for reforms meant that people wanted him to resign immediately. Asked by Ali Yafei whether he found this a bitter pill to swallow, Soeharto had replied that this was not so and that he was *kapok*, he had had it. He would not seek re-election, but refused to step down immediately, because he was convinced that if Habibie, whom he realized was not popular, succeeded him this would not put an end to the waves of protests and mounting disorder. Soeharto feared that if he was to be succeeded by his vice-president, the domestic situation might deteriorate even further into the abyss. He does not seem to have looked forward to an extraordinary session of the People's Congress either, venturing to expostulate that should it fail to reach a quorum he might find himself president again for yet another term (Nadjib 1998:77). In November in an interview with *Tempo*, Yusril Ihza Mahendra disclosed that it had been agreed that Soeharto would resign within six months (*Tempo*, 9-11-1998:32).

After the meeting, around noon, in a televised press conference, recalling his speech on the Golkar anniversary of 19 October, at which he had asked for assurance that he indeed still had the support of the nation, Soeharto explained that resigning presented no problem to him. He had not sought the presidency because of the prestige attached to it, but because he felt responsible for the future of Indonesia. Another reason he gave for any reluctance he might show was that he did not want to be accused of abandoning the country while it was mired in a crisis. Once more, Soeharto stressed that after his resignation he would *ngamandhito*, assume the role of a *pandhito*, and concentrate on spiritual affairs. He would do his best to see to it that his children were good citizens, and would give his all to assist the country. Bluntly Soeharto stated that if he stepped down immediately the constitution required him to hand over power to Habibie at that moment, and that such a step would probably only result in more misery. Habibie might well be forced to resign as well, his successor idem ditto, and that chaos, maybe even bloodshed and civil war, would be the outcome. Calling for calm and stressing that he would not seek re-election, Soeharto announced a number of measures. To speed up his resignation, a general election based on a new General Elections Act was to be held as soon as possible. He also offered a revision of the Act on the Composition of Parliament and People's Congress, and the drafting of new acts on the combatting of corruption and monopolies. To accomplish all this, a Reformation Committee, headed by himself (and not, as the Armed Forces had wanted, by Try Sutrisno) was to be called into being. It was to be composed according to Wiranto's suggestion. A Reform Cabinet was to be formed. The composition of both these institutions was to be announced on 21 May.

Emha Ainun Nadjib claimed the text read out by President Soeharto had been dictated to him by Yusril Ihza Mahendra: 'like one teaches a primary school boy to write' (Nadjib 1998:75). In fact, Soeharto himself had prepared an advance draft which had been corrected by the others. It had already mentioned the Reformation Committee (Pour 1998:131). Emha stressed that the outcome of the meeting had prevented Indonesia from falling easy prey to intervention by capitalist countries (Nadjib 1998:77). Yusril Ihza Mahendra said he thought that what had been agreed upon was the maximum that could be accomplished to avoid the danger of a national disaster, meaning that he and the others who had attended the meeting only expected more trouble were Habibie to succeed Soeharto.

The outcome was a blow to Habibie, who, as he was to tell Soeharto, had been angered by the way Soeharto had cast doubts on his ability to succeed him. Soeharto had denounced him in public and had refused to resign immediately. The latter was what Habibie had counted on happening. His staff had actively been drumming up support for this scenario and for him becoming president. Among the persons they had approached was Harmoko, who, in spite of their rivalry over the vice-presidency, now appeared to act in concert with Habibie. Rumour had it they were counting on Prabowo's support (Bhakti et al. 1999:105).

Soeharto's decision and the role the nine had played in bringing it about was not well received. Some branded the nine 'traitors to the reformation' who had hastened to the rescue of Soeharto. Amien Rais was also disappointed. He had been informed in advance about the meeting in the presidential palace. In his opinion (and in that of people like Emil Salim) Soeharto should have announced his resignation, or at least should have presented a clear timetable for this. Speaking of elections as soon as possible was too vague. Amien Rais dismissed as a 'political joke' the idea that Soeharto himself wanted to head the Reformation Committee. Among the many voices rejecting Soeharto's announcement was not that of Abdurrahman Wahid. He pleaded with the students to end their actions and to accept the compromise. Their goal had been reached. Soeharto was going to resign. In retrospect, one of Abdurrahman Wahid's personal assistants was to defend the appeal by pointing out that Abdurrahman Wahid feared that Soeharto might resort to violence were the students to continue with their protests (Al-Zastrouw Ng 1999:82).

The students thought differently. Soeharto's speech spurred them on to demand his resignation with even more resolve. Still on the 19th, students from universities all over Indonesia flocked to the parliament building, where they discovered that its car-call system carried much farther than a megaphone. Their numbers, according to some estimates, reached 30,000. The demonstrating students won widespread popular support. A public kitchen was organized by The Voice of the Concerned Mothers. Academic staff, Arifin Panigoro, Kosgoro, NGOs, and members of the public saw to it that the students were provided with food and drink. The support was overwhelmingly. More food was supplied than the students could eat. Others provided swimming goggles and handkerchiefs to be used by the students should security forces open fire with tear gas. Students and staff of the UI medical faculty arranged a medical team, complete with ambulances. New groups arriving enthusiastically shouted *Hidup Reformasi*, Long Live the Reformation, a cry which was echoed by those already on the premises. Non-students, initially not allowed in by the students, demonstrated outside the complex. This time the students really occupied the parliament building. They climbed its dome, and prevented members of parliament from leaving, hoping that in this way they could speed up a decision about the convening of an extraordinary session of the People's Congress. Some members of parliament succeeded in escaping by donning a sarong, pretending that they had just gone to the mosque in the parliamentary complex to pray (Sinansari ecip 1998:91).

There were some tense moments. One of these occurred on 19 May, when, clad in their battledress-like uniforms, members of Pemuda Pancasila, Panca-

sila Youth, an organization headed by Yapto Suryosumarno and Yorrys Raweyai, usually considered to be a strong arm of the government, arrived.
They shouted pro-Soeharto and anti-Harmoko slogans. One of their shouts
was 'Hang Harmoko'. Banners stating that they supported reform with
Soeharto as president were brandished. The arrival at the same time of members of Forum Komunikasi Putra Putri Purnawirawan ABRI (FKPPI), Communication Forum of Sons and Daughters of Retired Armed Forces Officers
(an organization chaired by Bambang Trihatmodjo), of Pemuda Panca
Marga, and of a *pencak silat* (martial arts) group calling itself Persatuan
Pendekar Persilatan Seni Budaya Banten, Banten Union of Silat Fighters,
added to the anxiety.

The tension that was building up in the country was augmented by the
fact that the following day it would be 20 May, National Awakening Day, a
flashpoint on which demonstrations and protests had peaked in the past. In
many cities students planned demonstrations, which in view of the recent
statement by Soeharto that he was not to resign, could only become more
massive and determined. Amien Rais, who had indicated by the middle of
March that he was prepared to head 'people power' providing that, as in the
Philippines and Iran, no blood was shed, called for mass demonstrations all
over the country. In Jakarta itself he invited the people to come to a massive
prayer meeting at the National Monument, dubbed Aksi Hari Kemenangan
Reformasi, Action of the Day of the Victory of Reform, organized by KAMMI.
On 19 May the retired military officers of the Generation of 45 who had
issued a statement on the 15th joined in. In a blaze of publicity they visited
parliament and vowed that they were prepared to share the lead in a long
march. Demonstrations by hundreds of thousands of people had also been
announced in Bandung and Yogyakarta. In anticipation of mounting unrest,
Chinese Indonesians and foreigners fled the country, taking refuge in
Australia, Singapore, Hong Kong, and other Asian countries.

On 20 May shops and offices remained closed in Jakarta. To be prepared
for the worst, the army had detailed still more troops to the city. Judging
from information provided by Syafrie Syamsuddin, the number of soldiers in
Jakarta had tripled since 12 May (*Tajuk*, 15-10-1998:19). Roads were deserted;
those leading to the National Monument, located close to the presidential
palace, had been blocked by soldiers, tanks, and armoured cars. Major shopping centres and office buildings were equally heavily guarded. Marines (formerly the KKO) and Kostrad soldiers were stationed at the parliamentary
complex. It was claimed that one of the reasons for this was to protect the students against violence from outsiders (*Panji Masyarakat*, 1-6-1998:49).
Another, more likely motive was to prevent the students leaving and marching to the National Monument. Nothing happened. In view of the overwhelming presence of troops, Amien Rais, by some called Bapak Reformasi

Nasional, Mister National Reformation, by now had called off the prayer meeting at three o'clock in the morning in a speech broadcast on TV and radio. Amien Rais described the vicinity of the National Monument as looking as if preparations were under way for World War Three (*Forum Keadilan*, 15-6-1998:82). He feared bloodshed. The more so as an army officer stated that he could not care less if a Tiananmen-like incident were to take place. If Amien Rais did not believe him, he had said, he should just take a look at the roads leading to the National Monument. Amien Rais did not disclose who this officer was. Later it leaked out that Amien Rais had come to his decision after meeting Prabowo in the Regent Hotel.[7]

In other cities mass demonstrations and marches did take place. In Bandung the Senate of ITB issued a statement, read in the presence of thousands of students, urging for a change to be made in the presidency as soon as possible. In Lampung students occupied the provincial parliament and forced the governor of the province to sign a statement in support of reforms and the resignation of Soeharto. Most impressive of all was what happened in Yogyakarta. Hundreds of thousands of people, according to some reports one million, took to the streets to demand Soeharto's resignation. Out of sympathy and some with the ulterior motive of protecting their shops, residents provided those marching through the city with snacks and drinks. At Gadjah Mada University people who wanted Soeharto to resign could add their signature to a 400-metre long banner. Sultan Hamengkubuwono joined the protests as an alumnius of the university. He had emerged an undisputed reformation figure. Four days earlier, in no uncertain terms, he had supported the student protests, attacking the widespread corruption and dismissing the majority of the Indonesian leaders as conceited and arrogant individuals who did not give tuppence for the opinions of intellectuals. This time, addressing the crowd, he rejected the compromise reached the past few days in Jakarta and stated he was prepared to lead the reform movement. In his speech he pointed out that food, clothing, and housing were not the only things that mattered. The people had been robbed of their rights. These must revert to them. Indonesians had to be freed of tyranny and injustice. Later in the day the *kraton* became the focus of protests. In the presence of Paku Alam VIII, who had signed a joint statement in favour of reform with the sultan, and religious leaders he once again expressed his willingness to be in the vanguard of the struggle for total reformation.

---

7   Newspaper reports do indicate that it was indeed the officer whom Amien Rais met, who made the Tiananmen remark. Still, not everybody is convinced that Prabowo is the person implied. According to *Golkar* (1999:88) it was Wiranto who took the uncompromising position, while Prabowo had been in favour of allowing the demonstration to take place. According to this version Prabowo had informed Amien Rais about the precautions taken on the orders of Wiranto.

On National Awakening Day an isolated Soeharto found himself virtually without support. Members of a student delegation who had visited Harmoko and left him in no doubt that they themselves were planning to summon an extraordinary session of a people's congress which would be composed of public figures and pro-reformation people, disclosed that Harmoko gave Soeharto two days (till 22 May) to consult with the chairmen of parliament about his resignation. Should he fail to do so, Harmoko would set in motion the procedure for convening an extraordinary session of the People's Congress. Harmoko himself refused to explain to the press what had been decided, leaving this to the students. Harmoko seemed to have discovered the courage of his convictions, the *Jawa Pos* commented (*Jawa Pos*, 21-5-1998). Other Golkar politicians deserted Soeharto as well. Still on 20 May the Golkar representatives in parliament convened to discuss four alternatives: Soeharto and Habibie both had to resign and temporarily hand over leadership of the nation to a triumvirate made up of the Ministers of Defence, of Internal Affairs, and of Foreign Affairs (an option initially supported by Ginandjar Kartasasmita and Siswono Yudohusodo (*Golkar* 1999:72; *Merdeka*, 20-5-1998)); Soeharto had to take the lead in carrying through reforms in all fields; Soeharto had to resign, with Habibie being promoted to acting president; and parliament had to ask the People's Congress to hold an extraordinary session. A clear majority of those present spoke out in favour of an extraordinary session of the People's Congress. Soeharto should tender his resignation at such a session, but having done so he should not be forced to account for his policy. Golkar was divided on the question of whether Habibie had to resign as well though a majority appears to have been in favour of such a step. The result was somewhat blemished by the fact that staunch supporters of Soeharto had not been informed that the meeting was to be held (*Golkar* 1999:72). The PDI and PPP groups in parliament spoke out in favour of Soeharto's resignation.

Worst of all, Wiranto had withdrawn his support. The previous day, on the basis of the extraordinary powers the People's Congress had bestowed on him a few weeks earlier, Soeharto had given Wiranto the authority to act, but Wiranto had refused to use it. Some reports speculated that Wiranto, not looking forward to a confrontation between the Armed Forces and the ever mounting wave of anti-Soeharto demonstrations, had even indicated that were Soeharto not to resign the Armed Forces no longer could or even would want to protect him. Almost all the people Soeharto consulted on the 20th, including Soedharmono and Try Sutrisno, advised him to resign. Those who were still prepared to cooperate with him were very few. Of the 45 persons he had invited to his residence at Jalan Cendana to discuss their inclusion in the Reformation Committee, 42 refused. Nor could he find politicians prepared to join his new cabinet. Among the members of the old cabinet, Abdul

Latief was the first to desert him. On 17 May he had tendered his resignation. On the evening of the 20th, during a meeting chaired by Ginandjar Kartasasmita, with whom Soeharto had discussed the composition of the Reform Cabinet the previous day, 14 ministers in the economic, financial, and industrial fields – among them Ginandjar Kartasasmita, Akbar Tanjung, and Tanri Abeng – decided to inform Soeharto that they would refuse a seat in the Reform Cabinet. Bob Hasan (who had not been invited) and Fuad Bawazier were not present. Ary Mardjono, Minister without Portfolio of Agrarian Affairs, also attended. He refused to sign.

It was the final blow. Unable to compose a cabinet, Soeharto surrendered. By now convinced that were an extraordinary session of the People's Congress to be held, a military *coup d'état* could not be ruled out should it fail to reach an agreement on his succession, Soeharto decided to step down the following morning (Sinansari ecip 1998:131; Lampito et al. 1998:49). Soeharto's resignation may have been brought forward by only a few days. Habibie said that Soeharto had made up his mind in the early evening of 20 May to hand over the presidency to him on 23 May, one day after the Reform Cabinet had been installed.

On the morning of 21 May, Ascension Day, a public holiday, the chairmen of parliament were finally received by Soeharto in the presidential palace for the 'consultation' for which they had been asking. They had been invited late in the evening of the previous day after Soeharto had made up his mind, but had not been informed of this, only having heard of Soeharto's imminent resignation from other sources. Fifteen minutes later, at nine o'clock in the morning, Soeharto resigned. Harmoko and the other chairmen were not allowed to attend the ceremony. Soeharto had ordered them to wait in another room. Before the chairman, deputy chairman, and junior chairmen of the Supreme Court, Habibie was sworn in as Soeharto's successor. Suddenly Indonesia had a civilian and a non-Javanese as its president, and over and above a person with an Islamic image. His becoming president was the surprise outcome of the succession struggle. Later in the day in a speech to the nation, Habibie promised gradual, constitutional reform in all fields.

Wiranto also issued a statement. In it the Armed Forces expressed their support for Habibie and their resolve to continue to guard the honour and safety of Soeharto and his family. It was a speech of great significance. In the months to come, this protection offered Soeharto by Wiranto was to cast considerable doubt on his personal commitment and that of the Armed Forces to the new Reformation Order and their dedication to the fundamental political and economic changes many wanted.

The *Era Reformasi*, or, as Habibie called it expectantly in August during his Independence Day Speech, *Era Kebangkitan Demokrasi*, Era of the Rise of Democracy, had commenced. Reformation carried the day. There was hardly a group formed but it had the word blazoned in its name. The magazine D&R changed its name from *Detektif dan Romantika* to *untuk Demokrasi dan Reformasi*, while the newspaper *Merdeka*, later renamed *Rakyat Merdeka*, adopted the slogan *reformasi total untuk rakyat*, total reform for the people, as its motto. The popularity of the word *reformasi* spread to advertisements. Special offers for office space were announced as a Reformation Packet, Australian universities tried to lure Indonesian students with reform facilities, and religious journeys to Mecca were advertised as *umroh reformasi* (*The Jakarta Post*, 21-6-1998). There were also reformation apartments for sale, and in September the Minister of Education and Culture promised that government financing of the supply of books to secondary schools, up to then characterized by KKN, would be reformed.

Among the victims of the transfer of power was Prabowo. An acute struggle for power sealed his fate. Soeharto's fall offered a good opportunity to try to curtail Wiranto's power by separating the function of Minister of Defence and Security and that of Commander of the Armed Forces. The former post, the less important of the two, those in favour had decided, had to go to Wiranto, the latter to somebody else. Prabowo might have considered himself a strong candidate. He claimed that more than three times Habibie, who, he added, considered him to be his son, had promised him the post were he to become president (*Panji Masyarakat*, 27-10-1999:24). What is certain is that Prabowo expected some reward, even considering himself a kingmaker who should have a major say in determining Indonesia's new power structure.

In reality Habibie decided that it was not opportune to relieve Wiranto of his function as Commander of the Armed Forces, and, to make matters worse, completely ignored Prabowo. Prabowo felt betrayed (*Panji Masyarakat*, 27-10-1999:24). It was reported that on 22 May he mobilized units of Kostrad, Kopassus, and the Jakarta Military Command to force his hand, though afterwards he was to deny that this had been his intention. The idea of staging a *coup d'état* also had not entered his mind. To underline his innocence, Prabowo pointed out that in a tense situation troop movements to guard the president and vital objects were standard procedure. In a countermove, Wiranto brought units of the marines into action. In this tense situation, feeling insecure in his own house, Habibie moved his family to the presidential palace. He did so after reports had reached him that Kostrad units had been sighted near his house. In February the following year, in an impromptu speech Habibie revealed that he had received the information about the Kostrad troops from Wiranto, and that Prabowo had planned the troop movements. Habibie seems to have made the same mistake as his predecessor who, from time to time, had created an uproar by ill-advised impromptu speeches. A political row broke loose. Prabowo denied the allegation, stressing in a letter to Habibie that he had only wanted to protect him.

A number of his friends, Janus Hutapea, Fadli Zon, and Ahmad Soemargono, sprang to his aid. They stated on TV that Prabowo had had no intention at all of threatening Habibie in any way. Wiranto also stressed that nothing out of the ordinary had happened. What had taken place was a consolidation of troops, not a concentration. Reacting to these denials, Habibie immediately let it be known that he had made his statement only to convince people that in times of crisis one could count on the Armed Forces. When Habibie went on to state that Prabowo had merely intended to consolidate his troops and that he had not wanted to encircle Habibie's house, Habibie's story fuelled the fires of Wiranto's enemies. In May Wiranto had incorrectly informed the new president, and certainly had had his reasons for doing so.[8]

Whatever may have been the real course of events, Prabowo was relieved as Kostrad commander on the morning of 22 May. A strong-willed and ambitious man (his final goal, it was said was to become president), he did not give in gracefully and decided to protest. Around two o'clock in the afternoon, dressed in his military uniform with a pistol on his hip, his car guarded by two landrovers laden with troops, Prabowo went to the presidential palace to demand a meeting with Habibie.[9] It was to no avail. Prabowo found himself on a slippery slope, distrusted by many who suspected him of being one of the main players behind the unrest and the political manoeuvring in the last days of Soeharto's reign. Soeharto and his children regarded him as a traitor. Soeharto refused to receive him. His children also distanced themselves from Prabowo. One reason might well be that Prabowo was among those who had advised Soeharto to resign, but probably not to do so immediately. He had, as Fadli Zon was to describe this advice in March 1999, proposed a 'soft landing' for Soeharto, and in the days leading to Soeharto's resignation had conferred with people like Amien Rais, Achmad Tirtosudiro, Adi Sasono, and Habibie. Soeharto even suspected Prabowo of being one of Habibie's accomplices in the latter's effort to engineer Soeharto's downfall (see interview with Prabowo in *Panji Masyarakat*, 27-10-1999:20-4). In May 1998 there were even reports, and Prabowo had come to the same conclusion,

---

8   In June Habibie was to state that the first to alert him to the Kostrad troops was a member of his staff at that moment, Honorary Lieutenant-General Sintong Panjaitan, who was to become Secretary of the Management of Development Operations, a functionary of the State Secretariat. He was a former commander of the troops in East Timor and had joined Habibie's staff in 1994 after Soeharto had discharged him from the army because of his responsibility for the Santa Cruz incident in Dili in November 1991.

9   Later Prabowo denied that he had been armed when he wanted to meet Habibie. As a well-behaved guest, he had left his pistol at the door. The troops accompanying him had been his usual escort as commander of Kostrad. His only reason for visiting Habibie, he said, had been because in the past Habibie had said to him not to hesitate to call upon him when he had something on his mind (Far Eastern Economic Review, 4-6-1998:18; Panji Masyarakat, 27-10-1999:24; Suara Pembaruan, 18-10-1999).

that his transfer had been suggested by Soeharto himself. Prabowo may have lost Habibie's trust as well in the last days of Soeharto's reign. One reason mentioned for this is that Prabowo vacillated about whom he should support after Habibie and Soeharto had fallen out over Soeharto's TV speech on 19 May. Habibie had tried to reach Prabowo by phone, but Prabowo had not responded (*Merdeka*, 30-3-1999; see also *Tajuk*, 4-3-1999:79-4). After Soeharto had made up his mind to resign on 21 May, Prabowo decided to back Habibie, but not to abandon his conflict with Wiranto. Prabowo remained a popular figure in certain Muslim circles, but his fall from grace had immediately led to his debunking by others. Stories began to circulate averring that when he wanted to enter the Military Academy at Magelang he had failed his physical test, and that the psychological test had indicated that he was power hungry.

Prabowo was posted to the Staff and Command School of the Armed Forces in Bandung as commander. He was replaced as commander of Kostrad by Major-General Johny Lumintang. The change in the Kostrad command was effectuated in the early evening of 22 May, without anybody from the press being present and without the customary pomp. In vain, Wiranto tried to pretend that nothing out of the ordinary had taken place, arguing that the move had been made so that Prabowo would gain experience in the field of military education, a career step he had not yet taken. Major-General Muchdi, Commander of Kopassus, was also relieved of his command. His successor was Major-General Sjahrir M.S. Lumintang became the shortest-serving Commander of Kostrad. After just sixteen hours he was replaced by the military commander of West Java, Major-General Djamari Chaniago, and had to return to his old post at Armed Forces headquarters. The official explanation was that Lumintang had only been the caretaker used to fill the gap after Prabowo had been relieved of his command and Djamari Chaniago had been able to travel from Bandung to Jakarta to take over. Someone had to keep the Kostrad units in check. The real reason Lumintang had to leave was because he was a Christian and that the replacement of Prabowo, so thoroughly identified with his Islamic image, by a Christian had met with a hostile reception from some of Habibie's closest Islamic advisors. Some officers who considered Lumintang 'close' to Moerdani were also opposed to his appointment (Urbaningrum 1999:145). The following week it was the turn of the chief of police of Jakarta, Police Major-General Drs Hamami Nata, who was succeeded by Police Major-General Drs Nugroho Djajusman.

More changes were to follow. The replacement of Syafrie Syamsuddin, considered a 'Prabowo man', by Major-General Djaja Suparman as military commander of Jakarta was announced at the end of June. Syafrie Syamsuddin became Assistant for Territorial Affairs to the Chief of Staff for General Affairs of the Armed Forces.[10] By the time the Chief of Staff of

Kostrad, Major-General Kivlan Zein, a friend of Prabowo, who had held this function since the middle of April, was replaced, Jakarta was abuzz with talk about a de-Prabowo-ization of the army. The replacements were all part of a major reorganization. Major-General Roesmanhadi succeeded Dibyo Widodo as chief of police, while new chiefs of staff were also appointed for the air force and navy. At the end of August Lieutenant-General (Retired) Zaini Azhar Maulani, one of the 'Islamic officers' and a close associate of Habibie, became head of the intelligence service, Bakin.

The students were jubilant about Soeharto's resignation. They were already planning large-scale demonstrations for 17 August (Independence Day) and 10 November (Hero's Day) in which they had laid plans to forge even closer links with other groups in society (Adnan and Pradiansyah 1999:171-2). Habibie's being sworn in as president divided them. Some had already left the parliamentary complex before Soeharto's resignation was announced; others did so afterwards. Some were satisfied with Soeharto's stepping down, others wanted to avoid a conflict over the question of whether or not Habibie was acceptable. Most of the students who decided to leave belonged to FKSMJ. The remaining students, including those from Forum Kota, turned their resentment against Habibie. Speeches rejecting his appointment were given, and posters were displayed with texts like *Turunkan Habibie* (Down with Habibie), *Tolak Habibie* (Reject Habibie), and *Habibie nepotis asli, apakah pantas jadi presiden* (Habibie a nepotist *pur sang*, is it right and proper that he becomes president?).

With Habibie as president the situation was somewhat reversed. Up to the 21st people had feared that his appointment would divide the nation and would lead to further bloodshed and chaos, now people were beset by worries that efforts to bring Habibie down might very well have this result, as a number of Muslim groups might take offence. That the latter possibility could not be dismissed out of hand was immediately evident. On 22 May, a fight was narrowly averted at the parliament building when a group of youths entered the premises. Transported to parliament on trucks, they had donned white *jubbah* and wore headbands with the text *Reformasi Konstitutional*, in this way testifying that Habibie's appointment had not, as some argued, been in violation of the law. Professing to belong to 44 Islamic organizations, including Ansor, HMI, and Umat Islam Banten (Islamic Community from Banten), they called themselves Komite Umat Islam untuk Reformasi Konstitutional (KUIRK), Committee of the Islamic Community for

[10]   In August 1999 Syafrie Syamsuddin would be in the limelight again when he was spotted in Aceh, and later in the month (together with Zacky Anwar Makarim) was sent to East Timor. His presence in Aceh and East Timor gave rise to the suspicion that he was on a secret intelligence mission to the two troublesome regions.

Constitutional Reform. Greeted by slogans from the car-call system like 'Hang Habibie', they themselves shouted *Allahu Akbar*, bellowed support of Habibie, and started to harass the students. Some suspected the action to have been planned by Eggi Sudjana and Fadli Zon. Eggi Sudjana, a former general chairman of HMI, was chairman of Persaudaraan Pekerja Muslim Indonesia, Indonesian Brotherhood of Muslim Workers, a member of ICMI and of CIDES, and in the 1980s leader of the faction in HMI which opposed the *asas tunggal*. He also is a close friend of Adi Sasono. Fadli Zon was a member of the People's Congress and director of the Institute for Policy Studies (IPS), an institute sponsored by Prabowo and chaired by Prof. Dr Jimly Asshiddiqie, and a deputy chairman of ICMI (Aditjondro 1998a:42). Other names mentioned of those allegedly involved were Toto Tasmara (a former executive of Bimantara) and Ahmad Soemargono, a friend of Prabowo and KISDI leader. According to yet another story, on the evening of 20 May, just before Soeharto informed others of his intention to resign, an IPS meeting had taken place, at which instructions from Prabowo (at that moment still in favour of Soeharto staying on, for the time being at least) to mobilize tens of thousands of Muslims to expel the students from the parliamentary complex were discussed (Sinansari ecip 1998:150-2; *Tajuk*, 4-3-1999:83).

The situation grew tense when after a 'war of slogans' – KUIRK members yelling 'Long live Habibie' and students raising the cry 'Long live the people' – KUIRK members began to destroy anti-Habibie posters, replacing these with ones in his favour, saying for instance that people who rejected Habibie would have the Islamic community to deal with. After a while Kostrad soldiers and marines intervened to keep the two sides apart. Still on 22 May, around midnight, after most students had left peacefully amidst rumours that a strong-arm squad was to arrive to eject them, the remaining students left and were transported by bus to nearby Atma Jaya University. They were only prepared to acquiesce in this plan if they were accompanied by marines, the only force they trusted. Onlookers yelled *Tolak Habibie* and 'Long Live the Marines'.

Habibie announced the composition of a 'Development Reformation Cabinet' on 22 May, about one hour later than had been intended because he and Wiranto first had to discuss how to react to Prabowo's moves. The announcement occasioned some demands that its members had to disclose their assets and other sources of income, but as other political matters preponderated, these demands were more subdued than they had been in March. The programme of the new cabinet, Habibie explained a few days later, was total reform. Wiranto, Feisal Tanjung, and Ginandjar Kartasasmita maintained their positions, as did ministers like Muladi and Tanri Abeng. Juwono Sudarsono was the new Minister of Education and Culture, Adi Sasono (a grandson of Moh. Roem) that of Cooperative Societies and the

Development of Small Entrepreneurs. Yunus Yosfiah, considered a 'green' officer, became Minister of Information. Akbar Tanjung held the post of State Secretary. Bambang Subianto, who not so long before had resigned as chairman of the Indonesian Bank Restructuring Agency, became Minister of Finance. To improve the independence of the central bank, the governor of Bank Indonesia was no longer an *ex officio* cabinet member, a step probably already contemplated by Soeharto at the instigation of IMF.

Among the most striking appointments was that of Syarwan Hamid as Minister of Internal Affairs. Within a matter of days he was attacked by supporters of Megawati, who said that in the past, when he had still been Chief of Staff for Social and Political Affairs, he had always come down hard on movements for greater democracy. His appointment continued the New Order tradition that this post had to go to an army officer. For the first time since 1965, the cabinet contained non-Golkar politicians: Hamzah Haz (Minister without Portfolio of Mobilization of Investment Capital and head of the Coordination Body for Capital Investments) of PPP; Dr Ir Ahmad Muflih Saefuddin (Minister of Food and Horticulture), a member of the Council of Experts of ICMI, was also of PPP; and Dr Panangian Siregar (Minister without Portfolio of Environment) of the Soerjadi PDI. Their names had been suggested by PPP and PDI groups in parliament. Within PPP, Saefuddin was supposed to represent Muslimin Indonesia, and Hamzah Haz Nahdlatul Ulama, although some of its supporters considered him to be a 'politician without *ulama* status', which undermined his claim to represent Nahdlatul Ulama. As Panangian Siregar was from the Soerjadi PDI, his assumption of office created a storm of protests. Not included in the cabinet was Ichlasul Amal, who as rector of Gadjah Mada University had become a kind of role model of how such a functionary had to behave because of his support of the protesting students of his university. He had declined the invitation, being of the opinion that Habibie should seek the assistance of a presidium made up of critics of the Soeharto government, to form his cabinet. Kwik Kian Gie of the Megawati PDI also declined a ministerial post.

On 25 May, during the first meeting of his cabinet, Habibie in a 24-page paper, presented outline of his policy. Besides a commitment to root out nepotism, corruption, and collusion, it called for revision of the five political acts and a general election to be held as soon as possible. The legislation on subversion was to be revised, and Habibie suggested the number of terms in office for a president should be limited to two. Identifying the securing of a sufficient supply of foodstuffs and other basic necessities and the rebuilding of economic life as the most pressing tasks of his government, he committed himself to the agreement concluded with IMF. True to this last statement, Habibie confessed on various occasions in the following weeks that in the past he had been too obsessed with high technology, but that as president he had to give priority to the welfare of the people.

Among the first concrete steps taken by Habibie was the granting of amnesty to political prisoners, beginning with Muchtar Pakpahan and Sri Bintang Pamungkas. Hundreds of people went to Cipinang prison, where the two had been detained, to cheer them. The event turned into a 'reformation party', with political prisoners addressing the crowd. Warders and other prison officials looked on. At first Bintang and Pakpahan refused to leave prison. As they had done nothing wrong, they declined amnesty. They insisted on being freed without any such ado. This the Minister of Justice refused to do, asserting that there were no legal grounds for such an unprecedented step. Muladi's argument was accepted by Bintang and Pakpahan. More prisoners were released in the following weeks, including people from East Timor and some of the PRD leaders. The decision about who was to be set free, it turned out, was not taken by either Muladi or Habibie, but by the army. To qualify for release, a political prisoner should not have been a member of the Indonesian Communist Party, should not have committed a serious crime, and should not have aspired to replace the Pancasila as the ideology of the Indonesian state.

The second criterion meant that within a matter of weeks problems arose over Islamic political prisoners, including members of the Free Aceh Movement, some of whom were released in August. They had been accused of championing an Islamic state or an independent Acehnese state, and in a number of cases had used violence to attain their ideal, and thus in principle were not eligible for amnesty. Muslim groups, sensitive because of past experiences of the way the government had treated them, considered this an example of downright discrimination. They claimed that most of the prisoners who were released were well known abroad and had the good fortune that American senators had written to the Indonesian government on their behalf asking that they be set free. Or, as one of them stated, in the past Indonesia had been colonized by Soeharto, and at present by the United States (*Panji Masyarakat*, 17-6-1998:16). Some interpreted it as an indication that the army still considered such Muslims a danger (Basyaib 1998:237). The upshot was that a variety of groups staged protests calling for the release of Islamic political prisoners, who, it was argued, had been treated more cruelly after their arrest than Pius Lustrilanang had been (*Panji Masyarakat*, 17-6-1998:17). Among these action groups was Kesatuan Aksi Penyandang Cacat Indonesia, Action Front of Indonesian Handicapped. They demonstrated in favour of Husein al-Habsy, a blind man, convicted for a bombing attempt at the Borobudur in the wake of the Tanjung Priok affair. Another organization which actively called attention to the fate of Islamic political prisoners was Komite Penyelidik Kejahatan Politik Soeharto (KPTAPOS), Committee of Investigators of the Political Crimes of Soeharto.

Habibie's coming to power also signalled liberalization in a number of other fields. As the protesting students had demanded, Habibie agreed to the so-called Normalization of Campus Life being abolished, and stressed the principle of freedom of association, extended to include trade unions. In June the authority of the Minister of Information to withdraw permission to publish newspapers and news periodicals was revoked. The conditions for acquiring a permit were made easier. In spite of the problems of the day, in the relaxation of the law the printing industry really found its feet and this was marked by a blossoming of periodicals. In five months 350 new permits were issued, many of these for the publication of so-called tabloids. Dailies and periodicals for which permission had been revoked in the past could apply for a new one. Consequently *Tempo* appeared again at the end of September. Journalists were allowed to establish their own organizations and abandon Persatuan Wartawan Indonesia (PWI), Indonesian Union of Journalists, which in the Soeharto years was the only organization of journalists allowed. Private radio stations, also swelling in numbers, were allowed to broadcast their own news services. They were no longer forced to relay the news of the state radio. During the following months the Minister of Information, Yunus Yosfiah, even speculated about the abolition of his ministry. Still in June, a National Plan of Action for Human Rights of Indonesians was announced. In its framework Indonesia was to sign various international human rights and labour conventions.

A new agreement with IMF, the fourth one, was concluded on 25 June. The premises behind the Second Supplementary Memorandum of Economic and Financial Policies were an inflation rate of 80 per cent, economic growth of minus ten per cent, and an exchange rate of Rp 10,000 to the dollar. The actual rate at that moment was around Rp 14,500. IMF agreed to allow continuation of subsidies on food, fuel, and electricity. The Indonesian government committed itself to the liberalization of the import and distribution of wheat, soya beans, and sugar. To help the swelling numbers of poor, stress was laid on the building up of a sound 'social safety net'. Labour-intensive public works were to be expanded, and a food-for-work programme in regions suffering from drought was announced. Another point in the new agreement was that the auditing procedure used by Pertamina and Bulog had to be reformed to meet international standards.

CHAPTER IX

Skeletons in the cupboard

Datang bergandengan tangan
Datang dengan helikopter
Datang dengan truk
Datang dengan senjata model baru
Datang untuk membunuh kami
Datang untuk makan kami.[1]

An inevitable consequence of the frankness which characterized the atmosphere in Indonesia after the fall of Soeharto was that investigations were demanded for a number of scandals and acts of repression that had marred his regime. The calls were not new. Similar ones had appeared in the press and in statements of protest in earlier years, but usually were expressed with caution and circumspection. After the events of May 1998 had paved the way, much more information about what had actually happened, or was supposed to have happened, could be published. Violations of human rights on a massive and brutal scale emerged as a topic of everyday conversation. The government also joined in the fray. On 15 August, in his Independence Day speech, Habibie begged the nation's forgiveness for what had happened in the past.

Some of the stories which broke went back almost to the beginning of the New Order regime. One of these concerned the events in Bogor on 11 March 1966. On that day, amidst massive students demonstrations, Soekarno had hurriedly left a cabinet meeting in the presidential palace in Jakarta after he had been told that unidentified troops – in fact troops commanded by Kemal Idris – were approaching. He had been flown by helicopter to the other presidential palace in Bogor, where later that same day he was visited by a delegation of army generals. Informing him that without a special mandate Soeharto would no longer take responsibility for maintaining law and order,

---

[1]   They come hand in hand/ They come by helicopter/ They come by truck/ They come with the latest weapons/ They come to kill us/ They come to eat us. Fragment from an Indonesian translation of a song of the Amungme of Irian Jaya (*Tajuk*, 20-8-1998:27).

they forced Soekarno to sign away most of his powers to Soeharto in the so-called Order of 11 March, or Supersemar. In August 1998, a former member of the Bogor palace guard, Sukardjo Wilardjito, visited the Legal Aid Institute in Yogyakarta. He told a different tale, claiming that Basuki Rachmat, M. Jusuf, and Amir Machmud, as had gone down in history, were not the only ones to have come to Bogor. There had also been a fourth man, Maraden Panggabean. This would not be very significant had Sukardjo not alleged that in their efforts to compel Soekarno to sign the Order of 11 March, Basuki and Panggabean had drawn their pistols, a detail that had never before been mentioned. From his story it could also be construed that Soekarno may only have considered granting Soeharto the special powers on a temporary basis. Sukardjo said that after he had signed the order, which was to be used by Soeharto to establish his grip uncompromisingly over Indonesia, Soekarno said that the mandate had to be returned to him as soon as order was restored, a matter which Soeharto failed to remember. Sukardjo also claimed that the generals had presented Soekarno with a pre-written order. The official version still current up to that moment was that the order had been drafted in Bogor after consultation between Soeharto and the generals.[2] Jusuf and Panggabean, the only two of the officers still alive, both denied that the story was true, Jusuf averring fervently that he and his two companions had not carried any arms when they visited Soekarno. Sukardjo Wilardjito was undeterred. To prove that he spoke the truth he said he was prepared to swear a *sumpah pocong*, an oath involving sleeping a night in a mosque, dressed in a shroud. Sukardjo's statement attracted a huge wave of media attention. As was to become habitual after May in such politically sensitive cases, an investigation was launched by the Jakarta police, but no concrete results have ever been made public.

For the first time, people publicly dared to refer to what had happened in March 1966 as a *coup d'état*, which indeed it had been. Because of revelations like that made by Sukardjo Wilardjito, doubts began to creep in, if they had not been there already, about Indonesia's recent history as it had been written down and taught during the New Order. There were calls for reform in this field as well. For the first time in twelve years, the film *Pengkhianatan G30S/PKI*, Treason of the Thirty September Movement/PKI, was not shown on TV on the evening of 30 September. Disparaged now as an example of a personality cult, the film was deemed by the Ministry of Information as out of kilter with the spirit of the times. Later, in March 1999, when ten political prisoners, jailed because of their alleged part in 1965, were released, children of the generals who had been killed in September 1965 expressed the hope

---

[2]   In two books written by staunch Soekarno supporters it is mentioned that Soekarno was presented with a draft. See Hanafi (1998:266) and Sophiaan (1994:229).

that those set free would talk of their experiences and that the truth of what had happened in those days of tribulation would finally emerge. Two months later the Association of Retired Air Force Officers announced the publication of a white paper spelling out the role of the air force at that time and the actions of then Chief of Staff Omar Dhani, tried for his involvement in the *coup d'état* of 1965. The book, *Menyingkap kabut Halim 1965*, Clearing the mists from Halim in 1965, was published in November 1999 (Katoppo et al. 1999).

Of particular interest to the public at large were a number of murder cases which had caught the imagination of Indonesians and had become examples *par excellence* of suppression and the miscarriage of justice during Soeharto's New Order.

One such notorious case was the murder of Marsinah, a young female employee at a watch factory, whose mutilated body had been discovered at the edge of a wood in Nganjuk in East Java in May 1993. She had led a strike demanding that minimum wages be paid and that women should no longer have to work after dark. These demands were met, but the leaders of the strike were forced by the local military to sign a letter of resignation. Marsinah had refused to capitulate. She had threatened that if more workers were fired in this underhand manner, she would reveal the illegal activities in which the factory was engaged. This signed her death warrant, and she was abducted and killed. Initially the police refused to link Marsinah's death with the labour conflict, mentioning as possible motives for the murder a dispute over inheritance and a love affair. Students and NGOs who thought otherwise started a campaign to have her murderers stand trial (See Marsinah 1994). Marsinah became a symbol of the fight of the workers. Sympathy, also in the army, was on her side. In February 2000 the officer who had forced the leaders of the strike to resign complained that already for seven years his family had a hard time. Everyone called him Mayor Marsinah, his wife had been refused membership of the association of army wives, and his children did not dare to go to school (*Kompas*, 25-2-2000). Ratna Sarumpaet wrote a stage play about the case in 1994, *Marsinah; Nyanyian dari bawah tanah* (Marsinah; A song from the world of the dead), which in spite of various difficulties was performed a number of times (Sarumpaet 1997). In 1997 she also composed a monologue about her, *Marsinah Menggugat* (Marsinah Accuses), which the Soeharto government banned her from performing. The owner, members of the staff, and a local army captain were tried for Marsinah's murder. The convicted civilians appealed and were exonerated and freed. From the moment of the first trial there was a lingering suspicion that those convicted had been tortured into confessing to hide the more important role the local military had played in her killing. This suspicion was one of the reasons why the Marsinah case became a symbol of the miscarriage of injustice under the New Order and the collusion of the army and the business world. In June PPP suggested that Marsinah should be declared a heroine of the labourers' struggle.

A second long-standing case which attracted widespread public attention involved the *bupati* of Bantul in Yogyakarta, Colonel Sri Roso Sudarmo, who had shown himself to be a staunch Golkar activist and proponent of the *kuningisasi* of his region in the past.[3] In early June, during a special session in the presence of a large audience, the Representative Body of Bantul demanded his resignation. Among the charges brought against him was that in 1996, when he had been left in no doubt that after he had completed his term in office as *bupati* his military superiors had another position in mind for him, he signed a statement that he was planning to donate Rp 1 billion to one of the foundations set up by Soeharto, Yayasan Dharmais, should he be reappointed. What had given the matter a particularly sensitive twist was that the person acting as mediator was a local village mayor, Noto Suwito, one of Soeharto's stepbrothers. A second accusation brought against him was that he was implicated in the beating to death in August 1996 of a journalist from the Yogyakarta daily *Bernas*, Fuad Muhammad Syafruddin or Udin, who had revealed embezzlement and misconduct perpetrated by local administrators, citing as one example the *bupati's* promise to donate Rp 1 billion.[4] The Yogyakarta police blamed Udin's death on the revenge of a jealous husband and arrested a suspect in October. He initially confessed, but retracted his confession within a day. He claimed that he had been plied with drink and made drunk, had been drugged, and had been promised a financial reward for his confession. The arrest was highly disputed for other reasons as well, with the police being accused of fabricating a sexual affair in its eagerness not to have to start an investigation of the people who were really responsible. Public opinion was convinced that Udin's death had been the result of an effort to teach him a lesson and dissuade him from publishing any further derogatory reports. During the May 'spring cleaning' Sri Roso Sudarmo, who had received no more than an official reprimand from the Minister of Internal Affairs for promising a donation to the Yayasan Dharmais, was dismissed, and later sentenced to nine months' imprisonment for corruption. Like Marsinah, Udin became a symbol of courageous behaviour shown in the repressive climate under the New Order. In June PPP suggested Udin should be declared a hero of the struggle for the freedom of the press.

---

3   Preferring yellow, he had argued, had nothing to do with a particular party. One had to think rationally: Green was less flattering for people with a dark skin, making them still darker, while red could hurt the eyes (Hendratmoko 1997:42).
4   Udin's articles are reprinted in Massardi 1997. Probably Sri Roso Sudarmo would have remained bupati anyhow. In order to ensure a Golkar victory in the general elections it seems to have been government policy to avoid replacing sitting bupati (Hendratmoko 1997:158).

Another old case which refused to lie down and be buried was that of Pak De, a *dukun* who catered for the élite. He had been convicted for the murder of a fashion model, Dice Budimulyono. For years it had been rumoured that in fact Pak De was innocent, and that the 'Palace' was behind the murder. After the fall of Soeharto in May it was freely written that the murder may have been committed by a female police officer acting on the orders of Tutut, who had become enraged over the fact that her husband, Indra Rukmana, had made Dice Budimulyono pregnant (see for instance *Adil*, 26-8-1998:20).

The success of the reformation movement meant that demands to investigate specific cases of the violation of human rights rose to a crescendo. Part of the attention focused on the recent disappearances of students and other political activists, but these were just the tip of the iceberg. In the course of the New Order many more people had vanished without a trace. Such offences had been a regular occurrence during army operations in Aceh, Irian Jaya, and East Timor. Other disappearances had occurred in the 1980s and 1990s in Lampung, in Tanjung Priok, and in relation to the attack on the PDI office in Jakarta. In contrast to the attention paid to these cases, what had transpired in 1965 and 1966 and the routing of PKI and other leftist organizations barely rated a mention in the public debate. Almost no questions were asked in public about the mass killings which had marked this two-year period. Among those who did speak out was Sri Bintang Pamungkas, because he did not have much faith in the resolve of the Habibie government to try Soeharto. He seized this past violence as one of the reasons for suggesting that Soeharto should be tried by the International Court of Justice (Wangge and Wangge 1999:16). In spite of the change in the political atmosphere, for many, and in particular for the leaders of the Muslim community, communists remained the arch enemy. The goal on which they set their sights was to draw attention to the discrimination and oppression suffered by sections of the Islamic community during most of the New Order – period which they claimed had endured at least till the mid-1980s, when the government had begun to take a number of initiatives to comply with Islamic demands, and there was a visible 'greening' of the military and of Golkar, in other words an increase in the share of devout Muslims in the distribution of key military and civilian positions and a concomitant decrease in the influence of Protestants and Roman Catholics.

The raking up of instances of army brutality touched powerful persons. In the last resort Soeharto was responsible, and indeed, in December 1998, lawyers in Portugal preparing a trial against him for the murder of 200,000 people in East Timor asked for Soeharto's extradition. The persons on whom attention centred in Indonesia, where calls to account for army brutality in East Timor were rare, and when they were made usually concentrated on Soeharto, were the top brass of the army: Try Sutrisno, Commander of the

Armed Forces when some of the operations in Aceh, East Timor, and Irian
Jaya had taken place, Syarwan Hamid, Feisal Tanjung, and last but not least
Prabowo. At the time of the Tanjung Priok affair in September 1984, Try
Sutrisno had been military commander of Jakarta. Finding out what had really happened might not only incriminate him, but also besmirch Benny
Moerdani, who at that moment had been Commander of the Armed Forces
and Commander of Kopkamtib, and ultimately Soeharto. That these three
powerful persons were involved was reason enough to explain to Muslims
why a thorough and independent investigation had never been conducted
into the Tanjung Priok affair. As the incumbent Chief of Staff of the Armed
Forces for Social and Political Affairs, Syarwan Hamid was responsible not
only for government policy towards PDI and the attack on its headquarters
in Jalan Diponegoro. His culpability stretched far further. From 1990 to 1993
he had served as Commander of the Liliwangsa Military Resort, with its
headquarters in Lhokseumawe, in charge of military operations in Pidie,
North Aceh, and East Aceh, at a time when the military actions in the
province had been particularly brutal. Prabowo was considered a very likely
candidate to have been the mastermind behind the disappearances and the
riots in Jakarta in 1998. His military exploits in East Timor and Irian Jaya also
provided an ample amount of fuel for debate. Around 1976, in an effort to
counter the reconciliation approach promoted by the then commander of the
Indonesian troops in East Timor, Brigadier-General R. Warouw, working
hand in glove with Syafrie Syamsuddin, at that time commander of intelligence operations in East Timor, he is said to have set up a special intelligence
force of civilians to intimidate the population. Its members, who were paid
by Prabowo himself, dressed in black for their operations. This custom gave
rise to their nickname: 'ninja' (*Panji Masyarakat*, 1-6-1998:15). Among other
persons implicated in abuses in Lampung were Hendropriyono, Minister of
Transmigration in the Habibie government, and Sudomo, the then head of
Kopkamtib.

What really had happened at Tanjung Priok was among the first cases into
which an investigation was demanded. In September 1984 Muslims in
Tanjung Priok, one of the poorest areas in Jakarta and well known for the
Islamic fervour of its citizens, had spoken out in their opposition to the five
political acts, particularly incensed by the fact that two of these required all
political, social, and religious organizations to mention in their statutes that
their basic principle was the Pancasila, and not, for instance, Islam. The second major point which had incurred their ire had been the ban on the wearing of veils and long skirts by girls attending public schools, because this sort
of outfit did not comply with school uniform regulations which left the head
and part of the legs uncovered.

Muslims were sure that the Tanjung Priok incident had been provoked. In their eyes, what happened at Tanjung Priok was one in a long line of other dubious events which had marred the first two decades of the New Order, including reports in 1977 of the existence of a Jihad Command determined to create an Islamic state, and the Imran case (which among other outrages had led to the hijacking of a Garuda plane in March 1981). All these, it was believed, had been manipulated to bring the Islamic community into discredit. They put the blame fairly and squarely on Benny Moerdani and Ali Moertopo as the main plotters. The two were thought to have hired agitators who magnified insignificant, spontaneous protest movements into large-scale violent incidents. Their reason for doing so was supposed to be to drag the name of Islam through the mud, making it synonymous with violence, in an effort to dissuade the population from voting for PPP in general elections and to persuade Soeharto to sanction policies hostile to Islam.

These Muslims had had their suspicions aroused by the fact that while elsewhere in Indonesia at that moment Islamic sermons and public speeches had been closely monitored by the authorities, there had been no such restraints visible in Tanjung Priok. Fiery preachers like H. Amir Biki, and Abdul Qadir Djaelani (who from the start, in 1978, had shown himself to be radically opposed to the government's Pancasila policy and was arrested after the Tanjung Priok affair) had been free to speak out to their hearts' content. They had attacked the eviction of people from their land, the growing gap between the rich and the poor, the government's family planning programme, and at that time especially the political laws which forced Islamic organizations to acknowledge the primacy of the Pancasila. In their eyes government policy was fraught with undisguised hypocrisy wherever it was called upon to express its attitude towards Islam. Ostensibly government officials stressed the importance of religion as one of the fundamental characteristics of Indonesian society, but in actual fact did all in their power to obstruct efforts to promote an Islamic way of life. These Islamic critics argued that the financial and organizational assistance which the government provided for religious activities paled into insignificance in comparison to the steps it had taken to prevent Islam from becoming a dominant force in society.

Muslims fielded the argument that such speeches could only have been permitted in an effort to ripen the atmosphere for a clamp-down. At the time, the extraordinary leniency had already raised suspicions. Fearful of falling victim to provocations, well-known Islamic political leaders, highly distrusted by the government, such as Sjafroedin Prawiranegara and Moh. Natsir, both former leaders of Masjumi, had refused invitations to speak in Tanjung Priok, or had suggested to others that it would be better not to do so.

The situation had finally exploded after a soldier had used gutter water to try to soak off posters which had been pasted on the wall of a prayer house.

These posters called for such things as the wearing of an Indonesian-style veil by women. Adding insult to injury, the rumour had spread that he had entered the prayer house without removing his boots, a fact which the soldier himself denied, but which came to figure prominently in the stories about what had provoked the anger of the crowd. Indignant Muslims wanted him to apologize. When he refused to do so, he was threatened and his motorcycle was set alight. Four people suspected of having played a part in this were arrested. On 12 September, around 11:00 o'clock at night, a larger demonstration, consisting of between 1,200 and 1,500 people, many of them (according to the official version of the story) armed with crowbars, knives, and sickles, marched to the local police station and local army headquarters to demand the release of the four.[5] They were led by a local leader, Amir Biki, who had succeeded in getting arrested persons released in the past, but this time was the exception which proved the rule. When the assembled crowd refused to disperse, shots were fired. Muslim sources claim a massacre then ensued. According to some accounts, people who had survived the shooting were kicked and beaten to death. Others had been killed when they had been run over by the heavy trucks (see Pusat Studi dan Pengembangan Informasi 1998). Fire engines were used to clean the blood from the street. During the incident a number of shops went up in flames, causing the death of eight members of a Chinese family and their domestic servant.

Initially, during a press conference called after radio stations abroad had reported on what had happened in Tanjung Priok, Moerdani spoke of nine people killed. Later he mentioned a figure of forty. The actual number of deaths was believed to be much higher than the official tally mentioned. People claimed to have seen large military trucks (as many as ten), and some even said garbage trucks, transporting away the bodies of those who had been killed. There were persistent rumours about at least one mass grave in a village in North Jakarta, since covered by a toll-road, but it was intimated there were probably more. Even of the nine persons who had died according to the initial official account, the grave of only one of them, Amir Biki, is known. In June 1998, during a mass meeting at Al-Husna Mosque in Tanjung Priok, demonstrators from 1984 and relatives of those who had been killed or had subsequently vanished established an organization called Solidaritas Nasional Peristiwa Tanjung Priok (Sontak), National Solidarity for the Tanjung Priok Event. Its general chairman, Mochammad Syarifien Maloko, himself one of the fiery Muslims orators in Tanjung Priok in 1984, and afterwards sentenced to ten years' imprisonment for his pains, spoke of 421 families who had reported that relatives were missing, hazarding a guess that the actual

---

5   According to some Muslims the crowd was not armed, as before starting their protest march they had attended a religious gathering.

number of persons who had vanished might reach one thousand. They were said to have been buried in twelve mass graves. H. Lukman Hakim, secretary of a PPP fact-finding team, spoke of at least five hundred victims (*Tajuk*, 17-9-1998:72). Even before the fall of Soeharto there had been calls for an investigation, among them one in 1996 issued by relatives of the victims, and the matter had surfaced again at the time of the investigation of Sofyan Wanandi. Once the barriers went down in May, it was pursued with even greater intensity. Yusril Ihza Mahendra and others argued that the government's continuing to shrug off requests for an investigation and refusing to bring those responsible to trial was proof the government and the Armed Forces had colluded to discriminate against the Muslim community, or as some others chose to express it, were still allergic to Islamic activities (Pusat Studi dan Pengembangan Informasi 1998:12; *Sabili*, 16-9-1998:17). In June the Petition of the Group of Fifty also demanded a new investigation into the incident and information about where the victims were buried. It was not a new request. In 1984 the Group of Fifty had earned the extreme displeasure of the government by casting doubt upon the official explanation of what had happened and urging that an independent fact-finding commission be instituted to go into the matter. The request had been one of the factors which eventually led to the prosecution and imprisonment of two of the Group's members: Hartono Rekso Dharsono (between 1966 and 1969 commander of the West Javanese Siliwangi Division) and Andi Mappetahang Fatwa (one of the most outspoken and most popular Islamic critics of the government in the 1970s and 1980s), discharged from the Group in September 1996, after he and Anwar Harjono had disagreed with the demand of the Group that Hartono be discharged as Chief of Staff of the Army.[6] Both were accused by the authorities of having incited students to bomb BCA offices in October of that year.[7]

Shortly after the new appeal launched by the Group of Fifty, relatives of the victims formed Front Keadilan Peristiwa Berdarah Tanjung Priok (FKPBT) 1984, Front for Justice for the 1984 Bloody Event of Tanjung Priok. Their demand that the case be reopened was supported by a variety of organizations. At a mass meeting in Al-Azhar Mosque in Jakarta, KISDI affirmed its support for an investigation. It declared that it was crucial to obtain some clarity about the number of victims and to find out where they had been buried. To leave no doubt about what they wanted, demonstrators on this and other occasions carried around posters and banners demanding the trial

---

[6] In 1996 Fatwa had commented that from several statements by the Group of Fifty, including one about the attack on the PDI office, it could be concluded that the Group tended to engage in practical politics and no longer was a strict moral force, as it tended to support the Megawati PDI and disregard the radical leftist position of groups such as PRD.

[7] In October 1993 the Group of Fifty had brought up the matter again in a letter to the Armed Forces faction in parliament, but had received no satisfactory reply.

of Soeharto, Moerdani, and Try Sutrisno. Rudini, in 1984 Chief of Staff of the Army, who at the time had blamed all on communists posing as *ulama* and using religion to foster their cause, kept out of harm's way (Pusat Studi dan Pengembangan Informasi 1998:141). In June, during a national party conference, PPP joined the ranks of those demanding an investigation into the Tanjung Priok affair and the bringing to trial of its '*dalang*'. Muhammadiyah made a similar decision in July. In September Amien Rais joined those calling for a an investigation by an independent committee to find out what had really happened and who had been responsible.

An additional weapon in the armoury of these protesters in their demands for a trial was that there was a precedent: the shooting at Santa Cruz in East Timor in November 1991. It had been followed by the establishment of a fact-finding team by the army and the trial of those officers thought to be guilty of the massacre by a Military Honour Council. Refusing to set up an investigation and even going to the extent of prosecuting people, such as Fatwa, who had called for an investigation, was one of the many indications perceived as the discrimination by the government experienced by the Muslim community during the New Order regime.

Army officers remained dead set against reopening the case. Wiranto dismissed this and other requests for an investigation into alleged past military brutalities as efforts to discredit the Armed Forces. In September, he explained to parliament that in any effort to evaluate such affairs, the circumstances of the time had to be taken into account. The Armed Forces were not the only ones who should be in the firing line. Wiranto spoke about collective responsibility. Try Sutrisno asked that old wounds not be reopened. Yet, as he had stated on earlier occasions during the New Order, Try Sutrisno did not object to an investigation. He denied that what had happened was an example of army brutality. He said Tanjung Priok had been an accident nobody had wanted. In an explanation of why shots had been fired, he recalled that at the police station ten to fifteen soldiers and policemen had been confronted by a crowd of about 1,500 people armed with sickles and crowbars – an argument that had also been trotted out in 1984. Try Sutrisno was scornful of the opinion that the incident had been engineered and that it formed part of a scheme to discredit the Muslim community. He himself was a Muslim, after all. The Muslim community, as the majority of the Indonesian population, could not be cornered (*Suara Pembaruan*, 13-9-1998).

Those demanding an investigation into the Tanjung Priok affair often extended their demands to other incidents during Soeharto's New Order, about which it was rumoured that many Muslims had fallen victim to army operations or had disappeared. One such case was what had happened in Lampung in early 1989. At that time an Islamic community in the province, headed by Warsidi, began to arouse the suspicions of the local population, among other reasons because many newcomers were arriving there from Jakarta and other cities in Java. The group lived an isolated life on a small plot of land in Cihideung, a hamlet in Central Lampung. They were determined to lead a life guided by the Koran and the example of Muhammad, and they branded the Indonesian government a government of infidels. Warsidi and his followers, who were bound to him by an oath of loyalty, seemed to be preparing themselves for violent action. They trained in the art of self-defence, and armed themselves with poisonous arrows made from spokes of umbrellas and motorcycle wheels, catapults, Molotov cocktails, and machetes. Summons issued to them by the local civilian and military authorities to report and explain their activities were ignored. Warsidi claimed that Islam taught that temporal leaders should come to religious leaders, not the other way around (Siswoyo 1989:19). On 6 February 1989, when there could no longer be any doubt that Warsidi was not going to heed their calls, a delegation of civilian and military officials, accompanied by a small detachment of soldiers, drove to Cihideung to investigate what was going on. According to one account, one of them, the commander of the local military rayon, Captain Sutiman, had a heated discussion with Warsidi. Sutiman became angry, fired his gun, and missed. It was he who was killed by Warsidi. Another version said that Sutiman was harassed by poisoned arrows shot by two guards shouting *Allahu Akbar*, before he had the chance to get off his motorbike. Though he succeeded in firing some shots, he was hit by a hail of arrows fired from the bamboo houses, and was subsequently stabbed to death (Siswoyo 1989:20-1). Sutiman's party retreated.

Next day government troops and police led by the then Colonel Hendropriyono, commander of the military district, attacked Cihideung. Bamboo huts and sheds went up in flames. According to official figures 27 members of Warsidi's community, defending themselves with arrows and Molotov cocktails, were killed in the attack. Among them was Warsidi himself. Others, even at the time, were already mentioning a figure of one hundred, and in August 1998 a recently founded committee by local NGOs and other organizations, Komite Solidaritas Mahasiswa Lampung (Smalam), Lampung Students Solidarity Committee, spoke of 246 victims. They alleged that many of the victims had had nothing to do with the Warsidi group (*Tempo*, 30-9-1989:22; *Republika*, 29-8-1998). Muslims accused the Indonesian army of having resorted to extreme violence, wondering why heavily armed troops had been brought in to stage a ferocious attack on a small group of people armed only with arrows. They claimed that dozens of women and small children had been burnt to death during the assault. At the time of Soeharto's fall, thirteen people were still in jail because of the Lampung affair.

Aceh was another hot topic in the hunt to root out perpetrators of military brutality. During the campaigns to suppress the Free Aceh Movement, which

had been active since 1976, many Acehnese had been killed or had disappeared. In 1989 Aceh had been designated one of the DOM (Daerah Operasi
Militer, Military Operation Areas) regions in Indonesia.[8] Under the New
Order, Indonesian and foreign human rights organizations had called attention to what was happening in Aceh, but it was only after May 1998 that victims and relatives of victims found the courage to report in any great numbers about people who had disappeared, about killings and mass graves,
people being buried alive, torture, and rape. The atrocities were particularly
concentrated in Pidie, North Aceh, and East Aceh, where the military operations had been most intense. Genocide was a word that occasionally cropped
up to describe the way Indonesian troops had operated. Testimonies indicated a huge number of persons had been killed or had disappeared. For the
period of the most intense struggle, between 1989 and 1993, a figure as high
as 39,000 was mentioned (*Forum Keadilan*, 29-6-1998:25). Others just spoke of
hundreds for the *kabupaten* and thousands for the province as a whole. A fact-
finding team of the regency of North Aceh reported that it had information
about 760 people who had been killed or had disappeared during operations
carried out by government troops and the Free Aceh Movement. The representative body of the *kabupaten* of Pidie had records of 597 persons who had
disappeared, a Komite Aksi Reformasi Mahasiswa Aceh (KARMA) of about
700. The Legal Aid Institute of Lhokseumawe spoke of 292 cases, that of
Banda Aceh of 208 cases, and so on. A report compiled by Amnesty International, which could only be published in Indonesia after Soeharto's fall,
speaks of 2000 persons who were killed, had disappeared, or had been
unlawfully been detained during that period (DOM 1998:vi). One member of
parliament, Ghazali Abbas Adan, recalled how, almost every night in 1991,
bodies were to be found along the sides of the road (*DëTAK*, 17-8-1998:19).

    In June, the National Committee for Human Rights was visited by vari-
ous action groups from Aceh and by Acehnese widows whose husbands had
been killed by the Indonesian army or had disappeared. It then launched an
investigation. The commander of the military police, Syamsu Djalal, took the
same step. Parliament itself also constituted a special fact-finding team,
chaired by Hari Sabarno, which visited Aceh at the end of July. The conclusion of the National Committee for Human Rights, made public in May 1999,
was that the violations of human rights in Aceh during the DOM periodhad
been grave. The committee called for bringing to trial those presumed guilty
and for a change in the training of the Armed Forces to eradicate the incul-
cation of a militaristic culture which had made the crimes committed in Aceh
and elsewhere possible.

---

[8]   DOM was not part of official Armed Forces terminology. The term was invented by the
press.

The DOM status was lifted on 7 August 1998, during a visit to Aceh by Wiranto. While in Lhokseumawe, he apologized for the military excesses and promised that the safety of the province would be guarded by the people of Aceh themselves. The implication was that combat troops which had been sent to Aceh in the past, such as Kopassus, were to be withdrawn. Security would become the sole responsibility of the provincial army division and the police. At the end of the month, after a ceremony to see off troops, among them some Kopassus soldiers, as they boarded the trucks which were to transport them back to their barracks, the vehicles were pelted with stones by an angry mob in Lhokseumawe, demanding that an informant be handed over to them. It was the beginning of a two-day rioting and looting spree in the city, the first large-scale outbreak of public resentment in years. Two people died. About two hundred buildings and shops were damaged. As elsewhere, government and Golkar offices as well as banks were the prime targets. The unrest spread to neighbouring cities, even reaching as far away as Idi in East Aceh. In a reaction Jakarta ordered the withdrawal of army troops to be postponed. Extra troops even needed to be detailed to Lhokseumawe to guard the nearby oil and natural gas installations. Immediate speculations were made – for instance people by Ismail Hasan Metareum, himself from Aceh, and by Munir of Kontras – that the army had engineered the riots to have an excuse to cancel the troop withdrawal. It was also pointed out that informants, who with the lifting of the DOM and the withdrawal of troops had been left out in the cold, might have had a hand in the rioting. Proof of these theories was seen in the fact that it had been observed that secondary school pupils and young people had been transported by truck to Lhokseumawe and other cities where rioting took place. Later, in August 1999, when the situation in Aceh had deteriorated considerably, Ghazali Abbas Adan stated that he was prepared to file a case at the International Court against all the commanders of the Armed Forces under whose command operations had been launched in Aceh – Moerdani, Try Sutrisno, Edi Sudradjat, Feisal Tanjung and Wiranto – and Soeharto.

Syarwan Hamid was also in for a difficult time because of the coup within PDI and the events surrounding the attack on PDI headquarters on 27 July 1996. As Chief of Staff for Political and Social Affairs of the Armed Forces, he was held directly responsible. Among the persons who pointed this out was the director of PBHI, Hendardi, who disclosed that the command post for the assault had been set up at Syarwan Hamid's office. Syarwan Hamid was not the only one implicated. Feisal Tanjung, in 1996 commander of the Armed Forces, and Yogie SM were equally accused of having had a hand in the actions to destroy the Megawati-led PDI.

As she had already indicated before the start of the Medan PDI congress in 1996, Megawati had brought civil action against those PDI politicians she held responsible for this equivocal congress and the subsequent election of a rival board. She was also determined to sue the Minister of Internal Affairs, the commander of the Armed Forces, and the chief of police. The last three – Yogie SM, Feisal Tanjung, and Dibyo Widodo – were subpoenaed for having given permission to hold the disputed congress, and for the later support they gave to Soerjadi's board. A team of lawyers, Tim Pembela Demokrasi Indonesia (TPDI), Team of Defenders of Indonesian Democracy, was formed under the leadership of R.O. Tambunan to prepare the charges, which were entitled 'Indonesian democracy accuses'. The team also had provincial wings to deal with the charges to be brought against those who had attended the Medan congress in the name of their branch allegedly without a mandate.[9]

On 1 August 1996 the hearing began at the Central Jakarta court but was immediately adjourned because the chairman of the court was suffering from toothache. Three weeks later the hearing was resumed. In October the judge ruled against the charge, because in his opinion the legality of the PDI leadership was an internal affair of that party. Appeals were filed.

The first victory the Megawati supporters scored came almost one year after Grey Saturday, after the so-called Group of 124, the defenders of the PDI office who had been convicted for their refusal to evacuate the building, had started legal proceedings against Soerjadi and the chief of police of Central Jakarta. To the surprise of many, the court decided that it had the authority to judge the case, because it considered what had happened on 27 July a criminal matter. Around the same time it became known that the High Court of Jakarta had ruled that the Central Jakarta court had been wrong in ruling that it had no authority to judge Megawati's case against Soerjadi and Fatimah Achmad in October. The High Court agreed with the assessment that it was beyond the jurisdiction of the Central Jakarta court to deal with the charges brought against Yogie SM, Feisal Tanjung, and Dibyo Widodo, as their actions concerned matters of national security. In August 1998 the Supreme Court confirmed the ruling.

The fall of Soeharto provided a good opportunity to start the ball rolling again. Before the end of the month, Tambunan and other TPDI members visited Syarwan Hamid and urged him to resign because of the role he had played in the disputed Medan congress and in the attack on Megawati's headquarters in July 1996. Politicians of what was by now called PDI Perjuangan, Struggle PDI, also emphasized that Buttu Hutapea, who had been identified as one of the people who had organized the attack, would never have dared to act in July 1996 without the permission of Feisal Tanjung and Syarwan Hamid. They also saw more proof of army implication in the

[9]   In August 1998, Kwik Kian Gie revealed that representatives of the Megawati PDI had brought two hundred court cases all over Indonesia.

fact that, when TPDI had demanded his resignation as Minister of Internal Affairs because of his involvement in the affair, Syarwan Hamid had reacted by stating that as an officer he had simply followed orders. Soeharto did not escape scot-free. It was reasoned that as president and as supreme commander of the Armed Forces he must have been informed about the steps to be taken prior to the assault. Somewhat later, in a number of cities, Megawati supporters occupied PDI offices then in the hands of Soerjadi supporters. In Medan this attempt to take over degenerated into a brawl between the Megawati and Soerjadi camps. Twenty-four Soerjadi supporters, beaten up and pelted with stones, were wounded.

The army officers charged denied any responsibility, stating that what had happened was an internal PDI affair. Feisal Tanjung put the blame for the attack on Buttu Hutapea. He announced his intention to haul anybody who accused him of complicity up before the court. Yogie SM, appointed as a member of the Supreme Advisory Council by Habibie, was equally adamant in refuting that the government or the army had engineered the internal strife in PDI. When he alleged that one of the persons who had accused him of responsibility, Soetardjo Soerjoguritno, was 'mad', the latter brought an action for slander. Syarwan Hamid threatened to take the newspapers and individuals who had publicly 'sentenced' him to court, demanding an investigation of the periodical *DëTAK* and of the newspaper *Merdeka*. The affair also brought Syarwan Hamid into conflict with the secretary-general of the Department of Defence, Lieutenant-General Soeyono, Chief of Staff for General Affairs of the Armed Forces in July 1996. Syarwan Hamid took offence at the latter's assessment that the attack on PDI headquarters had been a 'socio-political' operation and not a military one, which implied that Syarwan Hamid was responsible. This, too, was possibly another consequence of *reformasi*. It was the first time in decades that military officers had fought out their differences of opinion in public (Basyaib 1998:242).

The discussion about what had happened in 1996 which was dragged up again exactly two years after the attack on PDI headquarters was in part instigated by Soerjadi. At the end of July, Soerjadi, who had also been appointed as a member of the Supreme Advisory Council by Habibie, suddenly let fly with the opinion that the government should be summoned to account for what had transpired. Placing the events in a broader perspective, he argued that throughout the New Order, political parties had never been free from government interference. Soerjadi, who clearly did not want to bear the full blame alone, implied the government had indeed been involved in the shunting out of Megawati and the attack on the PDI office. Leaders of local PDI boards also found the courage to reveal publicly what had already been rumoured in 1996, namely that local military commanders had offered them money and air tickets for the trip to Medan to attend the PDI congress

A country in despair

which elected Soerjadi instead of Megawati as PDI general chairperson. Syarwan Hamid was not at all shocked by these revelations. He admitted that money had been provided to organize the Medan congress. There was nothing wrong with this. It was normal practice for the government to provide financial support to political parties for such an event.

No serious official investigation had ever been ordered. There had been the court cases brought by Megawati, her supporters had been sentenced for refusing police orders to leave the premises when the attack on the PDI office took place, Soerjadi had been questioned, but there had been no follow-up. Those who attacked the PDI building had never been tried, and it had never been unequivocally clear who they actually had been and what role the military had played in planning and executing the assault. In July 1996 some information had come to light. At that time Pakpahan had drawn attention to the fact that hundreds of criminals and workers, all of whom had been promised Rp 15,000 each, had been recruited by the Soerjadi faction to attack PDI headquarters. The following year, in May 1997, 51 people, all members of a foundation for the rehabilitation of delinquent youths, filed a lawsuit against Soerjadi and his associates because they had not yet received the amount of Rp 200 million in cash promised to them for their participation in the assault. They claimed that Soerjadi's people had tricked them into believing that they had been hired to reinforce the ranks of defenders of PDI headquarters. They said that they had been part of a group of 400 people, who had assembled at the police headquarters of Jakarta prior to the attack. The plaintiffs claimed that after realizing that they had not been hired to defend Megawati's office but on the contrary to attack it, some of them had taken off, while the others had consented to take part in the attack under psychological pressure. Around the same time it was reported that valium had been put in the bottles of water delivered to the people defending the PDI office (*Panji Masyarakat*, 9-6-1997:81). In 1998 other stories told of the recruitment of local criminals by the military, ostensibly to guard disputed land, only at the last moment discovering that the real target was the PDI office (*Tajuk*, 23-7-1998:79-81).

In early August 1998, on behalf of the Megawati PDI, TPDI members visited the headquarters of the military police. They asked its commander, Major-General Syamsu Djalal, to launch an investigation into the alleged actions of Buttu Hutapea and eight officers: Feisal Tanjung, Syarwan Hamid, Yogie SM, Dibyo Widodo, Major-General Hamami Nata (the head of Jakarta police), Major-General Sutiyoso (the then military commander of Jakarta, at present its governor), Lieutenant-Colonel Abubakar Nataprawira (the then chief of police of Central Jakarta), Major R. Sunaryo (a commander of the Jakarta Mobile Brigade), and Lieutenant-Colonel Moeldoko (in 1996 military district commander of Central Jakarta). The step was taken after Syamsu

Djalal had declared that he was prepared to investigate the case. When TPDI visited him, Syamsu Djalal did not hesitate to reiterate his commitment. Indonesia was a constitutional state. Whenever Wiranto ordered him to do so, he could launch an investigation against anybody at all (*Media Indonesia*, 1-8-1998). The following month, on the orders of Wiranto, Syamsu did begin an investigation into the 27 July events. Nothing was ever heard of it again.

Megawati Soekarnoputri (photo *D&R*)

CHAPTER X

Investigating recent sins

> Kepulan asap hitam menari di udara
> Gemuruh suara yang mencekam jiwa
> Tertegun kumelihat kekalutan manusia
> Kobaran api di mana-mana
> Derita seorang gadis hilang harga dirinya
> Mahkotanya yang suci dijarah orang
> Hancur luluh hatinya
> Putus asa jadinya
> Ke mana lagi harus mengadu?[1]

Even more attention was paid to what had happened in May and who was to blame. An additional reason for doing this was that on a number of occasions in the past, unrest and chaos had been instrumental in bringing about the downfall of rivals competing for supreme power. Supersemar was only one example. Later in the New Order, an upswing of demonstrations in 1974, spilling over into riots in Jakarta, had marked a power struggle at the top. One of the strongmen of that period, General Soemitro, commander of Kopkamtib and deputy commander of the Armed Forces, had been forced to resign after the riots, which came to be known in Indonesian as Malari, or Malapetaka Januari, the January Disaster. His lenient attitude towards student protests in the months preceding the upheavals and his initial refusal to act with the requisite resolution to suppress mass demonstrations on 15 January, raised suspicions that he had acted like this intentionally in order to erode the position of rival officers. Soemitro himself, who went into retirement soon after, maintained his innocence in two autobiographies written some twenty years later. It had been his enemies, he suggested, who had plotted against him and had prevented him from acting instantly to regain

---

[1]   Dense black smoke dances in the air/ An eerie thundering sound of voices/ Bewildered I watch the chaos/ Fires rage everywhere/ The grief of a girl who lost her self-esteem/ Robbed of her purest crown/ Shattered/ Desperate/ Where does she have to turn to? *Trauma 14 Mei*, sung and composed by Deddy Dores.

control of the situation in Jakarta (Ramadhan K.H. 1994:311-33; Cahyono 1998).

Knowledge of such past experiences coloured the interpretation of what had happened at Trisakti University and of the rioting following it. The suspicion was that chaos had been deliberately created by someone to strengthen their own position and to weaken that of rivals. Almost every scenario, likely and unlikely, was advanced. Some were convinced that the riots had been planned to show that Wiranto was not capable of keeping law and order, paving the way, it was speculated, for his replacement by Prabowo, just as the Malari riots had been used to achieve the downfall of Soemitro. Others ventured that it all might have been part of a scheme to show Soeharto that it was no longer any use clinging to his throne, or conversely to have Soeharto entrust one of his confidents with the execution of the extraordinary powers the People's Congress had granted him. There were others who considered the Trisakti shooting a failed warning to the students to end their anti-Soeharto protests.

Reports and rumours began to circulate immediately after the May riots. They were replete with agitators who had incited people to riot and had directed them against the Chinese community. The same was the case with stories about organized mob rape of Chinese women in public, often also in front of their own family. Some such incidents were said to have taken place in apartment buildings where many of the residents were Chinese, and to which gangs had forced entry.

In a preliminary report, I. Sandyawan Sumardi SJ of the Humanitarian Team of Volunteers drew attention to the fact that the rioting had broken out at several places at the same time, which indicated to him that there was a well-organized plan behind it all.[2] Sandyawan also drew attention to individuals directing people to certain sections of the city, and to the role played in inciting mobs by people with tattoos, by athletically built individuals, wearing boots and with close-cropped hair, and by adults in secondary school uniforms who had reportedly been sighted (*Kabar dari Pijar*, 19-5-1998). Others alleged that certain individuals had moved from one spot to the other by car. By instigating anti-Chinese or anti-government slogans, they had done their best to stir up people in city kampongs and any onlookers and passers-by to fever pitch. On other occasions they had started destroying property and then melted away after a crowd joined in (Sinansari ecip 1998:66; *Forum Keadilan*, 29-6-1998:68). Yet other accounts told stories of riot-

---

2   Sandyawan was well known for his work among street children and the poor in Jakarta. In 1996 he had been the centre of attention as the founder of the Team of Volunteers to Help the Victims of the Jakarta 27 July 1996 Incident, and as a person who for humanitarian reasons had given shelter to some PRD members wanted by the authorities.

ers who had been brought in by open truck and bus, in one instance carrying jerrycans, shouting 'burn, burn' (*Forum Keadilan*, 1-6-1998:16, 15-6-1998:12; Djajadi 1999:44). One fact which emerged was that people spoke of outsiders to their neighbourhood, unknown to them, who had tried to encourage them to join in the destruction and to kill Chinese (*Panji Masyarakat*, 25-5-1998:19-20). Among the many speculations and stories circulating, there was also talk of persons who had been given advance warning by people from the military, and about BIA intelligence members urging a mob to set fire to a Bimantara showroom (*Tajuk*, 3-9-1998:13-14, 19; Djajadi 1999:45). In post-mortems of the riots in Medan and Surakarta, events were cited which also indicated that there had been advance planning and which implicated the army (*Tajuk*, 15-10-1998:12-5).

Inside the army itself, there were officers who readily gave the opinion that the riots must have been provoked, at the very least by people who had incited the mobs on the spot. In an initial reaction, Wiranto even stated that it was known who were behind the rioting, but that names could not be made public yet. Speaking about what had happened in Surakarta and the surrounding areas, the commander of the Central Javanese Diponegoro Division said that the disturbances must have been organized and that the targets which were to be set alight had been selected in advance (Lampito et al. 1998:22). This fact, which in this case meant that among the special targets were businesses associated with the palace, such as the BCA bank and the Timor car, caused others to speculate that there had been at least some level of organization. Such critics underestimated the fact that at least some of the crowd's wrath had been directed against symbols of the government.

Syafrie, who was occasionally mentioned as one of those who had played a role in organizing the May riots, was more hesitant. At the most he was prepared to admit that 'some of the riots were sporadically organized by small groups in certain areas in Greater Jakarta' (*The Jakarta Post*, 15-6-1998). He observed that people from outside Jakarta, from Lampung, and from Central and East Java had been among the rioters, even going as far as to suggest that primary school children had been brought in from Central Java by truck (*Tajuk*, 15-10-1998:19). Syafrie disclosed that one instigator had been arrested. He was suspected of having incited a mob in the vicinity of Liem Sioe Liong's house. Syafrie described him as a former convict-turned-Muslim-preacher. His name was Anton Medan, a Sumatran-born Chinese. In jail he had repented and had embraced Islam. After his release he had become the head of a *pesantren* in Bogor. Anton Medan denied all accusations. He stated that he had been trying to prevent looting, and afterwards had visited the National Committee for Human Rights to condemn the riots.

Anton Medan was small fry. The figure most frequently mentioned as having been responsible not only for organizing the riots, but also for having

ordered the shooting of the students at Trisakti University and the kidnap-
ping of students and other activists, was Prabowo. Ironically, it was Prabowo
himself who was one of the first to point out the possibility that the riots in
Jakarta had been deliberately instigated to destabilize the government. He
did so after he had toured the riot-ravaged town in his capacity as commander of Kostrad. His conclusion was that the pattern of destruction justified such an observation. A counter theory was put forward by people like
Ahmad Soemargono. Such strict Muslims and friends of Prabowo did not
preclude the possibility that Moerdani was the mastermind behind the riots
and some of the abductions, pointing out a secret meeting he had allegedly
held prior to the rioting (*Tajuk*, 15-10-1998:14, 36, 6-1-1999:16).

Such theories warranted a thorough investigation. Habibie instructed the
Armed Forces to investigate whether the rioting had indeed been fomented
on 11 June. He did so during a ceremony in which Wiranto presented him
with the views of the Armed Forces about the essential political and economic changes which should be carried out; this was the result of the work
of the committee Wiranto had installed in early May. Though it had not yet
been released for publication, Wiranto stressed that some of the reforms suggested were to achieve urgent short-term objectives, of which some should
be implemented before the end of the year. Among the 150-some officers
present was Prabowo, albeit seated in the back row. The following month,
again on the instructions of Habibie, a Team of Five was formed, made up of
Wiranto, Muladi, the attorney-general, Syarwan Hamid, and Ali Alatas
(Minister of Foreign Affairs) to investigate the May riots. Muladi said its
composition indicated that what had happened in May was considered a
matter of collective responsibility, and not only the Armed Forces could be
blamed for the course of events. On 23 July the five, now joined by the
Minister without Portfolio of Women's Role in Society, Mrs H. Tutty
Alawiyah, set up a Joint Fact-Finding Team, Tim Gabungan Pencari Fakta
(TGPF), to investigate the riots in Jakarta, Surakarta, and Medan. The team
was chaired by Marzuki Darusman, a deputy chairman of the National
Committee for Human Rights. Consisting of 19 members, it was composed
of military officers, among them Major-General Syamsu, senior civil servants
of the departments involved, members of the National Committee for
Human Rights, and representatives of NGOs, including Sandyawan. The
team heard the evidence of various officers, including the military commander, the governor, and the head of police of Jakarta. During one of its sessions, the head of BIA, Major-General Zacky Anwar Makarim, admitted that
since April there had been indications that something on the order of the May
riots was brewing, and that BIA had warned the military authorities, including those in Jakarta, of the possibility of large-scale unrest. BIA had expected
the eruption to come on 20 May, so events had been precipitated. Makarim

deduced that, sensing an escalation, on 11 May BIA had warned that whatever happened there should be no martyrs. This would only result in a rapid
deterioration of the situation (*Forum Keadilan*, 30-11-1998:86). Makarim also
disclosed that the army and police had been weakened by the physical and
psychological burden of being held responsible for controlling the riots during the election campaign, safeguarding the general session of the People's
Congress, and keeping student demonstrations in check (*Republika*, 3-9-1998).

The discussions centred on the rape of Chinese women. Discontent was
fuelled by the fact that military officers, certain Muslims, and also the government using H. Tutty Alawiyah as its mouthpiece, reiterated the lack of
concrete evidence to prove such accusations. Therefore they could not accept
the contention that there had been mass organized rapes. There was also confusion and debate about what constituted rape (*pemerkosaan*), whether it
included stripping and feeling up (*Tempo*, 12-10-1998:59). Disgusted by this
pettifogging various groups started their own investigation. Among them
were Mitra Perempuan, Female Partners, and the National Committee for
Human Rights. To counter any suggestion that no abuses had occurred,
members of the National Committee for Human Rights revealed that they
had talked to women who had been victims of rape. They and other sources
also disclosed that the rapes had continued at least till the beginning of July.
In July the Humanitarian Team of Volunteers let it be known that it had solid
evidence of at least 168 rapes of women and children, all of them Chinese
(152 in Jakarta and the others in Surakarta, Medan, Palembang, and
Surabaya). Twenty women and children had died as a consequence of their
experience. They had either been murdered by their assailants, had been
burned to death after they had been raped, had died from their injuries, or
had committed suicide. One of the cases revealed by members of the team
was that of a nine-year-old girl who had been gang raped and then had had
her genitals mutilated. The girl died in hospital.

Progress in investigating what had happened was slow. On 7 July, to
protest this dilatoriness, a delegation of 75 women, all dressed in white, of
Koalisi Perempuan Indonesia untuk Keadilan dan Demokrasi (KPKD),
Coalition of Indonesian Women for Justice and Democracy, paid a visit to the
National Committee for Human Rights. Among them were Mrs Nuriyah
Abdurrahman Wahid, Ratna Sarumpaet, and Maria Pakpahan. They accused
the committee of not acting energetically enough. In a statement, the committee itself blamed the government for allowing a security vacuum to form
and a breakdown of protection of its citizens which had created a climate in
which the rapes were possible. Criticizing the government's insensitive attitude towards the victims, it asked the government at least to admit that the
rapes had taken place and to issue a public apology.

Confronted by such implacable criticism, during a meeting some days later with the National Committee for Human Rights, Tutty Alawiyah, on behalf of the government, condemned the rapes. She stated that during a cabinet meeting, Habibie, who had copied Soeharto's habit of having others convey his messages, had expressed his regret and had said he was convinced that such rapes had indeed taken place. As yet she refused to offer an official apology on behalf of the government. Before such a decision was taken, an investigation had to be conducted into who the perpetrators were and what their background was. On 15 July, and within days after Tutty Alawiyah's statement, when he received a delegation of women from various organizations, Habibie also expressed his regret about what had happened in May. By this time, Indonesian sensational newspapers had begun to print gory stories about what had happened to victims of rape and gang rape (see for instance *Pos Kota*, 12-7-1998, 13-7-1998).

Muslim organizations and individuals reacted with indignation to the amount of attention the rapes received and the protest demonstrations staged by Chinese communities abroad. Defensively, they pointed out that no concrete evidence had been presented, and no rape cases had been reported to the police, which employed a special team of female policewomen to facilitate the investigation. A special phone line at the Ministry of Women's Role also failed to produce much evidence. Letters to the editor expressed the sentiment that it was not right that NGOs and others should pay so much attention to the issue, when they had remained silent about what had happened to Muslims in Aceh and other regions of Indonesia. In one such letter, reacting to a statement by Arief Budiman that the rapes were not racially motivated because many indigenous Indonesians had expressed their concern or had offered help, the writer wondered whether the Chinese would be willing to act in a similar way if the victims had been indigenous Indonesians. The Chinese, the writer maintained, had never expressed their sympathy for the victims who had fallen in Tanjung Priok, Lampung, and Aceh (*Forum Keadilan*, 7-9-1998:8).

The accusation that the rapists had been religiously inspired caused enormous offence. KISDI pressed charges against the periodical *Jakarta Jakarta*, published by the Roman Catholic *Kompas* concern, because it had published one of the stories circulating on Internet and widely copied in the foreign press. It was the story of Vivian, who lived in an apartment building with her family. It claimed that before committing their act the rapists had shouted *Allahu Akbar*. Another organization, Badan Koordinasi Mubaligh se-Indonesia, All Indonesia Coordinatory Body of Islamic Missionaries, demanded a thorough investigation. It was moved to this step because it genuinely suspected that the affair had been used to discredit the Islamic community. To substantiate this, its general chairman, KH Drs Toto Tasmara, pointed to reports in the foreign press, for instance like that in the *The New*

York Times, which contained sentences like 'Some of the rapers said: "You must be raped because you are Chinese and non-Muslim".' (*Republika,* 23-7-1998.) Doubts were also expressed by *Republika.* This ICMI newspaper said it suspected that reports in the national and international press, and protest demonstrations abroad formed part of a campaign to blacken the name of Indonesia. It also spoke of the libelling of Islam on Internet. *Republika* accused the press of uncritically swallowing information originating from NGOs which had not provided any concrete proof to substantiate their claims (*Republika,* 2-8-1998). To underline the truth of such suppositions it could be pointed out that pictures shown on Internet of a woman who had had a knife thrust into her vagina proved to be unrelated to the May riots.[3] The Vivian story, which had captured so much attention, was also palpably untrue. The head of the intelligence service Bakin, Lieutenant-General (Ret.) Moetojib, had personally visited the apartment building where the crime was supposed to have been committed and had found no proof. He called a special press conference, dismissing the many stories about mass rape as a campaign to vilify Indonesia and to topple the government. Emha Ainun Nadjib also ventured that the stories circulating about the rapes formed part of efforts to bring down Habibie (*Sabili,* 16-9-1998:51).

In the middle of August, and much to the surprise and disappointment of TGPF, government officials again voiced their doubts. The chief of police, Roesmanhadi, warned those who were calling attention to the mass rapes that they could be prosecuted for spreading unsubstantiated rumours. At the end of the month, adding his voice to a swelling chorus, the Minister of Information, Yunus, said he believed that the whole issue was nonsense. To give credence to his news, he pointed out that, as a spokesman for the Jakarta police had also stated on TV, the police had investigated 103 reports of rapes, none of which could be proven. Megawati was also among those who expressed their doubts. An acquaintance of hers, a police officer, had checked on the condition of a woman said to have been raped and had discovered that the story was untrue (*Republika,* 2-8-1998).

Others continued to stress that mass rape had indeed taken place and that they knew victims of rape. They explained that the victims did not dare come forward to testify because they, their families, witnesses, and people helping them such as hospital staff and members of the Humanitarian Team of Volunteers had received threatening anonymous letters and phone calls or were terrorized in other ways by persons again described as heavy-built with close-cropped hair, aimed to prevent them from making public what they

---

[3]   According to some, the photos had been copied from porno sites on the Internet and the book *Free East Timor* edited by Jim Aubrey (1998) (*Adil,* 26-8-1998:4-5; *Forum Keadilan,* 7-9-1998:18-20; *Sabili,* 16-9-1998:50-1; *Tempo,* 12-10-1998:56-61).

knew. The psychological difficulty rape victims found in testifying was emphasized, especially when they had to report their ordeal to the police, considering that those who had violated them were members either of the army or the police. The discussion was complicated by the fact that the figures mentioned later on were much lower than those which first had been announced. A representative of the Team in Surakarta even went as far as to deny that Chinese women had been raped in this city (*Adil*, 26-8-1998:4).

At the end of September the government backtracked once more. After receiving the provisional recommendations of TGPF, the Minister of Justice affirmed that organized rape on a massive scale had taken place. Muladi stated that though victims had not yet come forward, other testimonies pointed inexorably in the direction of planned destruction and rape. Legally this could not be proven, but sociologically it could, and this sufficed. Asked about the statements of cabinet ministers who had expressed their doubts about the validity of the accusations, Muladi explained that these had been individual statements made when they had felt cornered by pressure from abroad, exerted by people who depicted Indonesia as a country of barbarians. They had been looking for normative legal proof, which for various reasons was difficult to provide in the case of rapes. Doubts continued to be expressed by such people as members of parliament, while in October, Wiranto once again stressed that the investigation launched by the Armed Forces had yielded no concrete proof. He revealed that the police had checked twenty hospitals in Jakarta, and had extended its investigation to several hospitals in Singapore and Perth, where it had been reported that victims had been treated. No proof had been found.

A second controversial point was who was responsible for the deadly shots fired at Trisakti University. Five fact-finding teams were active in the investigation of the Trisakti killings: from Trisakti University, the Armed Forces, the police, parliament, and the National Committee for Human Rights. In June 1998 the first members of the Mobile Brigade had to stand trial. The trial satisfied nobody. Friends and relatives of the students who had been shot were disappointed, considering it a mockery, a view shared by members of the Mobile Brigade and other units of the police force. The former were dissatisfied with the fact that the accused were small fry, two platoon commanders accused of not having prevented their subordinates from beating up and shooting Trisakti students, disregarding orders from their superiors to retreat. Senior officers of the Armed Forces seemed to be getting off scot-free. A proper, thorough-going investigation should reveal the 'dalang'. Members of the Mobile Brigade thought much the same way. They, too, protested in the courtroom that the trial was a cover-up and that those who had really fired the shots should be tried. There were even some who thought that it was a plot cooked up to drag the name of the police through the mud. The two were sentenced to ten and four months' imprisonment and appealed. Their sentencing led to new student protests, as students were convinced that the real offender had not been tried.

A year after the shooting, there was still no certainty about whether the fatal shots had been fired by members of the Mobile Brigade or by other units. When four hundred Trisakti students protested about the lack of progress in the investigation in front of the Ministry of Defence and Security on 31 March 1999, having duly informed the police in advance as the law now required, the demonstration was brutally dispersed by riot troops. Three students were seriously wounded.

The Trisakti killings and the trial of the two platoon commanders had not improved relations between the police and the army. Initial ballistic investigation by the police forensic laboratory showed that the shots could have been fired by a type of weapon which was different to those used by the police. The military police refused to accept these results and demanded an independent investigation. New tests were conducted at the ITB, which some said confirmed the earlier findings, but others were of the opinion that the results indicated weapons used by the Mobile Brigade and Kopassus. In May 1999, a few days before the first commemoration of the killings, when the official investigation into who had fired the bullets had not yet yielded results, a member of the fact-finding team of Trisakti University suggested turning to the FBI for a more up-to-date ballistics investigation of the bullets fired than any which could be conducted in Indonesia. In the end the bullets were investigated at Forensic Technology Inc. in Montreal, where research identified the type of weapons as those used by the Mobile Brigade and Kopassus.

Senior army officers put full blame for the killings fairly and squarely on the police. Dibyo Widodo, on the other hand – and the National Committee for Human Rights tended to support his view – denied the accusation, pointing out, as the chief of police of Jakarta had also done immediately after the shooting, that police procedure forbade the use of live bullets in a confrontation with crowds. The police were equipped only with rubber bullets. Another source of conflict was the fact that the two police officers were defended by a team of lawyers from the police force supplemented with well-known civilian lawyers headed by Adnan Buyung Nasution, who by undertaking the case incurred the wrath of Trisakti students. Reportedly, the hiring of these civilian lawyers was also against the wishes of Wiranto, who was quite satisfied with the competence of military lawyers. Dibyo Widodo's persistence in what he himself stressed was the defence of his subordinates may well have contributed to his replacement as chief of police on 24 June 1998.

Such acrimonious conflict came on top of already strained relations between the army and the police. Police officers were convinced their force was a Cinderella compared to the army, which respect to pay and the distribution of civilian jobs. The events of May had increased frustrations in the police force. There was a strong feeling that the army had sacrificed them on the altar of necessity (*Tajuk*, 1-10-1998:79). The head of police in Jakarta, Hamami, shocked by the many police stations which had fallen victim to mob wrath and by the hatred shown his corps, wondered what the reason behind this was, and why soldiers had not acted to stop such attacks, at times not even coming to the assistance of beleaguered policemen (*Tajuk*, 15-10-1998:20). What happened in Pontianak at the end of September 1998 was an extreme example of bad blood between the two. A brawl between members of the Mobile Brigade and a cavalry unit of the army turned into a full-scale battle lasting half an hour. This flared up spontaneously when the two units met by chance and exchanged insults. Incensed, the cavalry drove their armoured cars to the Mobile Brigade's headquarters and fired at it. Equally furious Mobile Brigade members shot back. Four people were killed, two on each side.

With respect to the third recent case, the search for who was responsible for the abduction of the activists and students in 1997 and 1998 was continued. The turbulence in the weeks leading up to Soeharto's resignation had been the cause of new disappearances, and at least one suspicious death, that of the Surakarta street-singer Gilang, who had disappeared on May 21 and whose body was found two days later. Of those whose disappearances had been reported by their relatives to Kontras and the National Committee for Human Rights, nine had been set free by their captors. At least twelve persons were still missing. Posters bearing their portraits were distributed, but this step failed to garner any additional information. It was feared that they had been killed outright or tortured to death. The kidnappers had announced to their victims that some would leave captivity alive and some not, and that they were 'very selective' in deciding whom to execute (Suhartono and Situmorang 1999:x, 70).

Information provided by those who had been abducted pointed primarily in the direction of Kopassus. From the talks Andi Arief had had with his captors, it had emerged that some had served in East Timor. One had spoken about a course in Great Britain, meaning an MA course in Security Studies said to be taken by Kopassus officers at the University of Hull. Suspicion also fell on the Office of the Military District of East Jakarta. Some prisoners had been taken there before being moved to an unknown location for interrogation. Among the officers implicated was Syafrie. Some of those who had been kidnapped thought that they had recognized his voice (*Siar*, 13-5-1998). The testimonies unequivocally revealed that the captors had been particularly interested in the activities of PRD, KNPD, and other opposition groups, and in the support, financial and otherwise, which might have been provided by Moerdani and Sofyan Wanandi. Another topic the interrogators had wanted to know more about was the relations of the activists with Megawati, Amien Rais, and other vocal critics of the regime. Some captives had also been questioned about the whereabouts of Andi Arief, at that time still a fugitive.

The results of the investigation by the Armed Forces' own fact-finding team, which critics accused of working far too slowly, were made public in the middle of July 1998. Earlier, at the end of June, Wiranto had admitted that military men were involved. The investigation had revealed that the people abducted had been held at Kopassus Group IV and V Army Post in Cijantung in East Jakarta. They had been kidnapped by a *Tim Mawar* or Rose Team, formed in July 1997 and made up of eleven of the best Kopassus soldiers, which had targeted activists suspected of trying to thwart the general session of the People's Congress. The team was headed by Major Bambang Kristiono. There was no trace of those still missing in Cijantung.

Attention focused on Prabowo. On 3 August 1998 Wiranto established a Dewan Kehormatan Perwiraan, Officers' Honour Council, to try Prabowo and two other officers implicated. First to be summoned were Muchdi and Colonel Chairawan, commander of Kopassus Group IV. On 10 August it was Prabowo's turn. He admitted that he had made a mistake. He had misunderstood instructions to monitor the activities of students and other activists in view of the coming session of the People's Congress. Prabowo admitted having been involved in the kidnappings (some of which had taken place after the session had ended), though the order only spoke of gathering information, but he hastened to add all persons had subsequently been set free. Stressing that his aim had been to prevent activists from disturbing the People's Congress and that it was his subordinates who had held the victims in captivity for a longer time, he himself did not want to speak of kidnapping (see interview with Prabowo in *Panji Masyarakat*, 27-10-1999:20-4). On the recommendation of the Officers' Honour Council, Prabowo was honourably discharged from the army on 24 August by Wiranto, who could not but be pleased that the military career of one of his main rivals was in tatters. Prabowo had heard the news about the Officer's Honour Council's decision from the radio. Again Johny Lumintang followed in his footsteps, being posted to the Staff and Command School of the Armed Forces in Bandung as commander. Muchdi and Chairawan were relieved of active duty. Nothing was put in Prabowo's way to prevent him from leaving the country. After the trial he ended up in Jordan, where he knew the crown-prince well. Prabowo claimed he had gone to this country to begin a new career as businessman working for the business empire of his brother, Hashim Djojohadikusomo. His friend, Fadli Zon, added he also went there to perfect his Arabic. His stay in Jordan turned out to be a kind of exile, and may indeed have been intended so. In March his brother, Hashim Djojohadikusumo, stated that Prabowo wanted to return home to defend himself against the accusations being made against him, but that the time was not yet ripe. In July 1999 Fadli Zon repeated this, adding that his friends, among them Abdurrahman Wahid and Yusuf Hasyim, had advised him not to return for the time being.

The procedure followed did nothing to alleviate any misgivings people may have been nurturing. The Officers' Honour Council was not a court martial that could pass a prison sentence. It met behind closed doors and could only decide whether an officer could stay in the Armed Forces or not. A public trial before a court martial was called for. Military officers responded by pointing out that convening a court martial after the Officers' Honour Council had pronounced its verdict could still be done any time. They did not even rule out a trial before an Extraordinary Military Court, as had been the fate of those suspected of having had a leading role in the *coup d'état* of 1965. When Wiranto announced Prabowo's discharge from the army, he promised that the latter and the two other officers would be court-martialled, should any further investigation uncover criminal acts. It was assumed, and probably feared by some, that if Prabowo were tried by a military court, he might reveal who had actually given the orders. In recapitulating one of his conversations with him, Abdurrahman Wahid indicated that Prabowo himself did not want to appear before such a court, because under such circumstances he would be obliged to speak (*Merdeka*, 2-9-1998). Yet another interpretation was that Prabowo was prepared to stand trial, and was even eager to do so to clear his name, but that this would only be fair if those responsible for the other atrocities of the New Order, Tanjung Priok, Lampung, and so on, were brought before court to answer for their misdeeds, a move the Armed Forces was not prepared to make (*Tajuk*, 6-1-1999:13; *Panji Masyarakat*, 6-1-1999:25). For Habibie, in view of his connections in certain Muslim circles, Prabowo remained a factor in internal politics. Via Prabowo's relatives and friends, he let it be known a number of times that Prabowo should patiently endure his fate, awaiting the moment he, Habibie, would again call upon his services (*Tajuk*, 4-3-1999:80).

It was not disclosed who had given Prabowo the order to monitor the opposition. In spite of Prabowo's statement, people remained convinced that the same person was also guilty of ordering the kidnappings. Because Kopassus fell directly under the command of the Commander of the Armed Forces, the number of persons who had the authority to give such orders was limited: Feisal Tanjung and Wiranto, though the name of the former Chief of Staff of the Army, Hartono, was also mentioned. It was reasoned that Hartono, because of his close relationship with Tutut, had every reason to protect the palace. Attention centred on Feisal Tanjung, as he had been Commander of the Armed Forces right up to the end of February 1998. There were indeed rumours that Feisal Tanjung had known about the abductions. Prabowo even stated that he had reported his actions to him. Feisal Tanjung categorically denied having given any orders to abduct people.

Another person who could have given the order was Soeharto, in his capacity as Supreme Commander of the Armed Forces. It would have been very easy for him to discuss military and security matters with his son-in-law, Prabowo, without involving the hierarchy of the Armed Forces. People still had vivid memories of Soeharto giving orders for extraordinary campaigns in the past. In his autobiography, the former president had disclosed that it was he who had secretly ordered what at the time, in 1983 and 1984, had been called, *petrus, penembakan misterius*, the 'mysterious shootings' of criminals, leaving the bodies lying in the street as a warning, or as Soeharto himself called it, 'shock therapy' (Dwipayana and Ramadhan 1989:390). Pius Lustrilanang was convinced that the order had come from Soeharto. Otherwise such a senior officer as Widodo would never have stated that Andi Arief had been in police custody since his disappearance (Suhartono and Situmorang 1999:x). In October 1999 Prabowo admitted that Soeharto had given him a list, found in the building, containing the names of 28 persons whose activities had to be investigated a few days after the bomb explosion in Tanah Tinggi. He said that Soeharto had asked him to look into the matter, not to abduct anyone. Prabowo did not remember exactly, but was almost sure, that names of PRD members were not on that list. They were on a list of people wanted by the police. Prabowo revealed that almost every day Armed Forces headquarters had inquired whether these people had already been apprehended. He called what he had done an intelligence operation – during which, he stressed, it was usual to arrest and interrogate people, and if possible make them work for the force – and claimed that Wiranto and various cabinet ministers knew that such an operation was going on. The abduction of Pius Lustrilanang, Desmond Mahesa, and Haryanto Taslam he called a mistake. He had never ordered their arrests (see interview with Prabowo in *Panji Masyarakat*, 27-10-1999:20-4).

In December 1998 the trial against the eleven members of the Rose Team of Kopassus began. They had been in jail since 14 July. All had served in Aceh, East Timor, and Irian Jaya. They were tried only for the abduction of the nine activists who had been released.[4] As had been the case with the trial

---

[4]   Pius Lustrilanang, Desmond Mahesa, Haryanto Taslam, Andi Arief, Faisol Reza, Rahardjo Walujo Djati, Nezar Patria, Aan Rusdiyanto, and Mugiyanto. Among the imputations put forward about the fact that Kopassus only took responsibility for the abduction of these nine, was that there might well have been yet another intelligence operation active at the same time, one which was really responsible for other disappearances. In relation to this, the names of Moerdani, and of Sofyan Wanandi (as financier) were mentioned.

of the members of the Mobile Brigade accused of having fired live bullets at the Trisakti students, the fact that the investigation had turned up only one unit of the Armed Forces that was to blame and that senior officers were apparently being protected and did not have to stand trial, was fiercely criticized by human rights activists and others. A new word was added to the Indonesian language: *di-Trisakti-kan*. Munir of Kontras was by no means a voice crying in the wilderness when he called the trial a 'farce' (*The Jakarta Post*, 24-12-1998). Marzuki Darusman was quick to point out that the trial did not mirror the sense of justice which had taken hold in society. He said this in January when, in its annual report, the National Committee for Human Rights asked that the court case be declared null and void and thrown out of court. One of the reasons for this demand was the chance the impression could very easily be created that an attempt was being made to hush the matter up and to protect those who were responsible for the abductions. The trial itself was interspersed with protests. Some of the victims refused to testify. They demanded an explanation of the relationship between the eleven accused and Prabowo and the other two officers tried before the Officers' Honour Council. Two other objections of critics were that the charge did not include torture and that it did not mention those persons who were still missing. Commenting on such criticism, the Minister of Justice admitted that it would be fairer for strategic witnesses (as he called them) to be heard. In this context Muladi mentioned the name of Hartono, who, he suggested, knew about the case. In court, the leader of the Rose Team, Bambang Kristiono, stated he had acted on his own initiative. He had not followed orders, but had been driven by his 'conscience'. He claimed that he himself had taken the decision to abduct activists, considering them a real threat to national stability, interpreting this as the best way to implement the order to gather information. Prabowo did not know anything about it. His confession raised some eyebrows, not least because Prabowo had already admitted that the kidnappings had been the outcome of his misinterpretation of an order. There were some who wondered what the Indonesian army was coming to when underlings did not await orders from their superiors but acted as they thought best, however laudable their concern for the safety of the state. In April 1999 the eleven were sentenced to between 12 and 22 months' imprisonment, less the time they had already spent in custody. The maximum penalty for their crime was seven years. Five of them were discharged from the army. The alleged torture of their prisoners was not discussed in court. The military prosecutor explained he had not raised the issue because no reports about torture had been found in the defendants' dossiers. Nor had it been satisfactorily explained whether other units – those mentioned in the press were the Military Command of Jakarta, the Military Command of East Jakarta, BIA, its head Makarim, the police, and the military police – had been involved.

On 3 November TGPF announced its much awaited report. It was not undisputed. People wondered why such key persons as Moerdani and Wiranto had not been heard by the team. Within the team itself, where two of the major bones of contention had been the number of rapes and the complicity of the Armed Forces in the riots, there was much uproar. Some members could not bring themselves to agree with the conclusions, while government officials were clearly piqued. Only nine of the nineteen members had signed the report. Among those who had not done so were its chairman, Marzuki Darusman, and its secretary, Rosita Noer. None of the ministers who had instituted the team was present at the press conference at the Ministry of Justice, when the 28-page report was presented, and the attorney-general was conspicuously absent. Afterwards Wiranto blamed TGPF for having overstepped its brief. Its task had been to find facts, not to draw conclusions or make recommendations. Still, he was prepared, if necessary, to act on the findings of the report. TGPF called for the prosecution of two army officers. One was Syafrie Syamsuddin, the person responsible for the safety of Jakarta. The report accused him of having failed to take sufficient action to prevent and contain the rioting, which could have been anticipated. The other was Prabowo. The report stated that the riots had been caused by the fortuitous interlocking of two processes. The first was the strife within the political élite arising from the equivocal position of Soeharto, and the second was the deteriorating economic situation. Among the most important conclusions was that the rioting had been intentionally organized, a strategy adopted to create an emergency situation in which the special powers the People's Congress had granted to Soeharto could be invoked. The report, linking the shooting at Trisakti University and the May riots, stressed that the highest-level decision makers could not wash their hands. It spoke of the complicity of various parties, including criminals, political parties, mass organizations (Sandyawan mentioned the name of Pemuda Pancasila[5]), and the military in the riots. TGPF confirmed the role of agitators, establishing enough evidence to identify a recurrent pattern throughout the rioting. In various places well-built people with close-cropped hair, usually outsiders, had incited the people to violence and destruction. According to the report they appeared well-trained, highly mobile, and were equipped with ample fuel and Molotov cocktails.

One of the greatest stumbling blocks within TGPF had been the number of rape victims. The conclusion reached on this point represented a compromise, which apparently did not satisfy anybody. The report stated that the team had directly or indirectly verified 76 cases of sexual abuse of women,

[5]   The chairman of the presidium of Pemuda Pancasila denied this, pointing out that in the days leading up to the riots people had been buying UI and Pemuda Pancasila uniforms.

most of them Chinese: 52 rapes, 14 sexual assaults, and 10 cases of sexual harassment. Most rapes had been gang rapes and had been committed before the eyes of onlookers. Some of the victims had been raped before or after the May riots: five in Medan between 4 and 8 May, two in Jakarta on 2 July, and two in Surakarta on 8 July. After the publication of the report, the spokesman for the Armed Forces, by now Major-General Syamsul Ma'arif, once again hammered home that no mass rapes had taken place in May. Others had their reservations as well. *Ummat*, basing itself on a source within TGPF, wrote that of the 52 rapes only 13 (other reports spoke of 16 and 18) had been medically verified (*Ummat*, 23-11-1998:32). The then Minister without Portfolio for Human Rights Affairs, Hasballah M. Saad, disclosed in August 2000 that up to that moment no witnesses or victims of the rape of Chinese women in May in Jakarta had dared to come forward. They were afraid to testify. He said that the same problem was encountered in the prosecution of grave violations of human rights in Aceh, Irian Jaya, and the Moluccas. Witnesses were terrorized and disappeared (*Kompas*, 8-8-2000).

A second point which caused immediate controversy was the recommendation made by the team that an investigation be launched into a meeting of between 20 and 30 people which had taken place on the evening of 14 May at Kostrad headquarters.[6] Among those present had been Prabowo, Kivlan Zein, Muchdi, Fahmi Idris (Minister of Labour in the Habibie government), Hashim S. Djojohadikusumo, Fadli Zon, Farid Prawiranegara (a businessman and friend of Prabowo), Adnan Buyung Nasution, Rendra, Setiawan Djody (a businessman), and Bambang Widjojanto (director of the Indonesian Legal Aid Foundation and a member of TGPF). The meeting became the object of an acrimonious dispute. Wiranto said the Armed Forces had already investigated the matter and had come to the conclusion that the meeting had nothing to do with planning any subversive or criminal acts. It had been an ordinary meeting of people looking for information, as was perfectly normal for leaders to do in times of tension. This was also the position taken by most of those who had been present. It had just been a meeting of friends concerned about the situation, at which information had been asked about the situation in Jakarta, and Prabowo and the other officers present had been fervently urged to step up efforts to put an end to the rioting and to alleviate the fear that had gripped the inhabitants of the city. Others, Rendra and Setiawan Djody, had come anxious to hear from Prabowo himself whether the rumour that he was involved in the Trisakti killings was true. To some it appeared

---

[6]   Among the other recommendations was the suggestion that *premanisme* be rooted out, the recruitment of street gangs and criminals, forbidding civil organizations to use military-like uniforms, and introducing legislation on the tasks, rights, and supervision of intelligence organizations.

somewhat strange that TGPF had questioned a meeting at which one of its own members had been present. The explanation came from Bambang Widjojanto himself. He had the impression that there had been other meetings before and after the one he had attended.

Prabowo denied the TGPF conclusions, vehemently reiterating that he had done all he could in May to get the situation in Jakarta under control. In a brief statement issued at the end of December, he explained that he had not made any statements, because he wanted to contribute to a climate in which democracy could take root and develop. When necessary and when the time was right, he would give a detailed account. His friends dismissed the TGPF report as libel. Ahmad Soemargono condemned it, calling it a big lie (*Forum Keadilan*, 30-11-1998:82). Among those who questioned the conclusions of the TGPF report was Ali Yafei, chairman of the Indonesian Council of Ulama. He greatly regretted the fact that no admissible proof had been presented in the report and asked that a new fact-finding team be set up. As a follow-up, Habibie formed a committee to study the TGPF report. On 21 December, after Habibie had received the members of the fact-finding team, Akbar Tanjung announced that the government was going to invite those who had been present at the meeting at Kostrad headquarters explain what had transpired there. On this occasion Akbar Tanjung mentioned that 52 women had been raped, that 24 had fallen victim to sexual attacks and cruelty, and that four had been indecently assaulted. He added that Chinese women were not the only victims. Akbar Tanjung denied that there had been any systematic mass rape. In March Hashim Djojohadikusumo announced that Wiranto had ordered his brother to return to Indonesia to explain about the 14 May meeting, and that Prabowo was going to comply. The following month Fadli Zon stated that Prabowo had changed his mind, considering the mood in Indonesia still too hostile. As was usually the case with investigations started or promised, the matter simply seemed to fade away, with no concrete follow-up and no court cases ever brought against those alleged to have really been behind the violence. It took till 13 September 1999 before Muladi sent a letter to the National Committee for Human Rights, stating that an investigation into the Kostrad meeting had unearthed no evidence of Prabowo's involvement in the riots. The letter offered a good opportunity for Prabowo's family and friends to come to his defence. During a press conference in early October Hashim Djojohadikusumo in the presence of Fadli Zon and Farid Prawiranegara, stressed that Prabowo's dismissal from the army had been unfair and that Prabowo had been the victim of 'slander, political conspiracy, and character murder' (*Kompas*, 8-10-1999). Hashim added that Muladi's letter indicated that the conclusions of TGPF were wrong. Muladi's letter also goaded him into an attack on Wiranto. It mentioned Prabowo's failure to maintain order as the reason for his dismissal. Countering this view, he pointed out that the person responsible for maintaining order was Wiranto, not Prabowo. A fax by Prabowo read by Hashim also stressed this point. Hashim disclosed that a court case against Habibie or Wiranto contesting Prabowo's dismissal from the army was being prepared.

The way the civilian and military authorities dealt with the 'Old Order sins' only added to mounting indignation in Islamic circles. Discontent ran high in spite of a number of reconciliatory gestures by the government. As early as August 1998 Dharsono (who had died in 1996) and Fatwa had been rehabilitated, while political prisoners from Aceh and Lampung were among those who were released in the course of time. Though the disquiet was not primarily directed against Habibie, who in the circles from which the protest came was still considered an asset to Islam, it did cause ripples in their relationship with him. Habibie thought such criticism unfair and an attempt to undermine his position by dragging up old matters, which were not his doing (*Panji Masyarakat*, 10-3-1999:74). Apart from their indignation about the amount of attention received by the calls for an investigation into the reports of mass rapes, they could also point out the fact that within weeks after Soeharto's fall an Officers' Honour Council had been formed to try Prabowo and his associates, and that in the past a similar institution had been established in the case of East Timor, which had been chaired by Feisal Tanjung. In stark contrast, in cases of cruel oppression against Muslims, a crime to which many had fallen victim, there had never been a concrete follow-up. This claim was not entirely justified, as the National Committee for Human Rights did establish a special team, chaired by Baharuddin Lopa, to investigate the Tanjung Priok case, but it was accused of working much too slowly in comparison with the other investigations started by the Committee. Baharuddin Lopa countered the criticism by pointing out that investigating the Tanjung Priok affair was much more difficult than trying to find out what had happened in Aceh. He claimed that witnesses who had seen that dozens of people had been killed with their own eyes in 1984 had not come forward to testify while, in Aceh the team had been visited by hundreds of witnesses. On 9 March 1999 the National Committee for Human Rights presented Habibie with three recommendations. The first was that the government should explain what had happened in Tanjung Priok and should reveal the location of the mass graves. The second was that the government should provide assistance to the victims and surviving relatives. Thirdly it was recommended that those responsible should be tried.

Another point which cropped up with some frequency was that rapes of Muslim women by the military in Aceh had not led to a public outcry anything like the uproar caused by the rapes in Jakarta. To add insult to injury, groups asking for the investigation of cases like the Tanjung Priok incident had been received not by ministers or the head of the military police, but by their assistants. The alleged disregard for Muslim victims of the New Order was also linked to the fact that, in contrast to the rapes in Jakarta and the abductions, such cases had not aroused emotions in the West, where the donor countries of Indonesia were to be found. It was pointed out that what had happened to Muslimsin Tanjung Priok, Lampung, and Aceh was a more serious violation of human rights than the attack on the PDI office, and that people in Aceh had been treated much more cruelly than the persons who had been abducted. These critcs blamed NGOs, not failing to mention financial support from the West to such institutions, for a tendency to stress cases in which Muslims did not feature as victims. They even went as far as to suggest that cases which put the Muslim community in a bad light were deliberately selected.

To elaborate on the theme that devout Muslims with political aspirations were the underdogs in Indonesian society, from time to time it was argued that NGOs received so much publicity because very few devout Muslims were employed by the mass media, while many members of NGOs were journalists (see, for instance, *Sabili*, 16-9-1998:10-3, 15-9, and Basyaib 1998:234-49). On 12 October 1998 such sentiments led to an incident in which members of a Komite Suara Rakyat (KSR), Committee of the Voice of the People, of a Front Penyelamat Bangsa (FPB), Front of Saviours of the Nation, and of a Komite Aksi Dai Pro-Reformasi 2000, Action Committee of Islamic Missionaries pro Reformation 2000, damaged the office of the Indonesian Legal Aid Foundation in Jakarta. They were protesting about the tendency they had observed of the Legal Aid Foundation jumping on the bandwagon and only taking on cases that would increase its popularity and status abroad.

CHAPTER XI

KKN

Reformasi
Jadi kata trendi
Untuk akrobat selamatkan diri

Banyak orang kaya takut
Karena kekayaannya
Dan banyak pejabat takut
Karena jabatannya[1]

Within days of Habibie being sworn in, Golkar warned its politicians that sanctions would be taken against anyone who had gained his or her position in parliament and the People's Congress through nepotism and yet had no intention of resigning before the coming extraordinary session. So that there would be no doubt as to whom this accusation applied, lists of people's representatives who met this criterion appeared in the newspapers. Consequently, to avoid the stigma of nepotism, many relatives of power holders with Golkar seats resigned. The wife and daughter of Wiranto, the wives of Harmoko, Syarwan Hamid, Yogie SM, Feisal Tanjung, and Hartono, as well as the brother and son of Ginandjar Kartasasmita, all resigned as members of parliament or of the People's Congress within weeks of Soeharto's fall. The daughter of the chairman of the Central Java branch of Golkar, and the wives of the governors of North Sulawesi, Southeast Sulawesi, and West Sumatra did the same. By the middle of June over twenty members had resigned. Also among them were KH Zainuddin MZ, Syarwan Hamid, and Yogie SM. Elsewhere in the country, members of the local representative bodies stepped down. Siti Hardijanti Rukmana, Bambang Trihatmodjo, Hutomo Mandala Putra, and Siti Hediati Prabowo, and Bambang's wife, Halimah, stayed on. Their refusal to give up their seats only fuelled resentment against Soeharto's

---

[1]   Reformasi/ has become a trendy word/ to denote acrobatics to save oneself/ Many rich people are afraid/ for their wealth. /And many office holders are afraid /for their office. Fragment from *Kita dan Reformasi* by Jaka & Acil BIMBO.

children. Hutomo Mandala Putra said it was up to the people of South Sumatra who had elected him as a member of the People's Congress. It was their wishes he would follow; he would not bow to the suggestions of others. No sooner had he made this statement than a delegation from South Sumatra visited the Golkar group in the People's Congress to urge it to make Tommy Soeharto stand down.

At the end of May and early June, various sides were demanding an investigation into the wealth of state officials and businessmen in an effort to determine whether this was the fruit of corruption, defined in a corruption act of 1971 as illegal activities and misuse of position to enrich oneself or others to the detriment of the national economy and the finances of the state. Money acquired through corruption or special facilities had to be returned to the people. On 29 May, to assist such an investigation, a number of public figures formed Gerakan Masyarakat Peduli Harta Negara (Gempita or roaring), Movement of the People Concerned about the State's Finances.[2] Others established similar groups, such as Komite Independen Peneliti dan Pengusut Aset Para Mantan Pejabat, Independent Committee for the Investigation and Prosecution of Assets of Former Officials. Other groups active in this field were the Indonesian Corruption Watch (ICW), with Teten Masduki, who was also head of the Labour Division of YLBHI, as coordinator, and Masyarakat Transparansi Indonesia, Indonesian Transparency Society, headed by Mar'ie Muhammad, sometimes referred to as Mr Clean.

The prime target was Soeharto, his children, grandchildren, and other members of the family, by now collectively referred to as *Keluarga Cendana* (KC), or the Cendana Family, and their close associates who had built themselves business empires, aided in this undertaking by the special facilities they had enjoyed, ranging from support for Tommy's Timor car, and the right to collect the TV licence fee by a company owned by Sudwikatmono, Sigit Harjojudanto, and Henry Pribadi, to Bambang Trihatmodjo's monopoly on the sale of stickers for the 1997 Southeast Asia Games. At the base of such preferential treatments almost invariably lay a special decision or instruction assigning such persons immensely profitable projects, issued for these purposes by Soeharto and cabinet ministers.

As it was assumed that the Soeharto family had acquired most of its wealth illegally, voices calling for an investigation into how they had come by it were now joined by yet more, demanding that the 'Cendana wealth' should devolve to the state to assist in its efforts to overcome the economic crisis, for instance, by being used to pay off the gigantic amount of foreign debt and to finance indispensable imports. Amien Rais advanced such a step

---

2　　Among them were Dr Albert Hasibuan, Prof. Baharuddin Lopa, Goenawan Mohammad, and Faisal Basri.

as a condition for Soeharto to be able to enjoy, as he phrased it, his old age in peace. The slogan that the '$oeharto fortune' was the property of the state or the people also became a favourite text on posters borne by demonstrating students. The most radical demands called for the confiscation or nationalization of all their companies and property. ICW went as far as to propose a special decree of the People's Congress for the sequestration of all the wealth acquired illegally by Soeharto, his family, and his cronies. Confiscation of Soeharto's wealth, Mohammad Sadli argued when he met the Indonesian community in New York, was an essential move because if legal procedures were to be followed this would be a complicated and time-consuming process. Action against the Marcos family in the Philippines had proved this. The country urgently needed capital, citizens were crying out for their basic commodities. At that moment, because it was still uncertain if and when IMF, which after the May riots had postponed remitting its aid, would pay up, the best course of action was to concentrate on the question how the assets of the Soeharto family could be returned to the state as quickly as possible. A more moderate suggestion was that, pending an investigation, Soeharto and his children should hand over a portion of their wealth, for instance half of it, to the state, to enable to country to overcome the economic crisis and to buy food for the poor.

Others, including Gempita members, refused to consider such a course of action. The law was the law and ineluctable. Yet, at the end of May, Christianto Wibisono, a Gempita member and director of Pusat Data Bisnis Indonesia (PDBI), suggested a general amnesty for people guilty of KKN, including the Soeharto family, in return for the transfer to the state of 55 per cent of their fortunes (25 per cent as a penalty and 30 per cent in tax). This would lay a good foundation for the restoration of the health of the Indonesian economy. Christianto Wibisono, whose family was to suffer from threatening phone calls and anonymous letters, estimated the wealth of the Soeharto family at Rp 200 trillion. One magazine, *Prospek*, claimed that the family, 'Soeharto Inc.', owned a total of 1,247 companies (*Prospek*, 6-6-1998:16-9, 30-3).

In describing Soeharto's past sins, people often did not mince their words. All this Soeharto bashing became too much for Megawati. In early June she said she felt hurt by the storm of written and verbal statements defaming and insulting Soeharto. This should stop. After all, Soeharto had been Indonesia's second president. Wiranto, true to his promise to protect Soeharto, similarly appealed to people to stop the vilification of Soeharto. He did so, Yudhoyono quickly explained to remove the impression that Wiranto was on Soeharto's side, to remind the Indonesian people that it was not part of their culture to scorn and slander their former leaders (*Tajuk*, 25-6-1998:14). Sultan Hameng-kubuwono, though not mentioning Soeharto, also expressed his shock at the bluntness of expression which seemed to have become the vogue.

The Soeharto family also let it be known they were offended. On Sudwikatmono's SCTV television station one of Soeharto's lawyers, Dr Yohannes Yacob PhD, asked the Indonesian government to take action against those who slandered and libelled Soeharto.[3] He used the occasion to indicate that Soeharto might have the law on the Indonesian government, should it violate the rules in any attempt to investigate his wealth. Stressing that the attacks on Soeharto had transgressed the boundaries of moral and humanitarian values, he appealed to Habibie, Wiranto, and the National Committee for Human Rights to see to it that Soeharto's legal rights were respected and that a halt was called to the inhumane attacks on the former president. He said that extra security measures had to be taken at Jalan Cendana to protect Soeharto. This was indeed done. The street was closed off, extra uniformed troops plus some in plain clothes guarded its entrances and those to nearby streets, barbed wire appeared, and armoured cars were stationed on the premises of a neighbouring house.

Considering the climate engendered by the speculations about Soeharto's fortune, it takes no great strength of the imagination to guess that the announcement in July that the government was to pay Soeharto Rp 26 billion for a house, constructed by Yayasan Purna Bhakti Pertiwi (a foundation established by his wife) and located near the Taman Mini Indonesia Indah complex, created a furore, in parliament as well. The government's argument that the house was a present to Soeharto, and that according to an act of 1978 all former presidents and vice-presidents were entitled to a house like this, failed to cut any ice. On 6 September, apparently heeding the uproar, Soeharto declined the gift. He announced his decision in a TV speech broadcast by the TPI station owned by his daughter Siti Hardijanti Rukmana. In the same speech Soeharto – and he was to do so a number of times in the months to come – denied that he had any foreign bank accounts or shares. He claimed it was untrue that (as many people believed) he was the richest man in the world after Queen Elizabeth, King Fahd of Saudi Arabia, and Sultan Hasanal Bolkiah of Brunei. Soeharto challenged his TV audience to prove that he had any bank accounts abroad. He indicated he was disposed to be very helpful. Anybody who thought they might have proof to the contrary should report this to the Indonesian embassy in the country concerned to enable a speedy transfer of the money to Indonesia. If they needed a signed document in order to get access to bank accounts, he would provide this within 24 hours. The following day the new attorney-general, Andi Muhammad Ghalib, asked his fellow countrymen not to doubt Soeharto's word.

---

3   Yacob, a lawyer employed by the Humpuss Concern, was a relatively unknown lawyer who, observing the many public attacks on Soeharto, had offered Soeharto his help on his own initiative.

Soeharto was a former president, a person who deserved trust. In the eyes of Amien Rais, however, Soeharto's statement was an indication that, having learned his lesson from the efforts in the Philippines to recover Marcos' wealth, he had had the time to launder his money abroad and that he was confident that nobody could now trace it. He believed Soeharto had been smarter than Marcos, Mobutu, and the shah of Iran (Anwari SB 1998b:93).

The demands for an end to corruption and nepotism focused primarily on Soeharto's family and their business associates. Soeharto's fall from power had devastating consequences for their business endeavours. Not only did the shares of the companies they controlled take a desperate plunge, but the firms associated with them became the object of attacks, threats, and demonstrations. People even stole concrete and asphalt from their toll-roads. They also lost commissionerships, board functions, and contracts. New projects they had looked into were shelved. Business links with the Soeharto family began to be seen as a liability. Companies which had sought their cooperation in the past because it had won them contracts now tried to dissociate themselves from them, for instance by taking over their shares. Symbolic of the rush to distance themselves from the Soeharto family was that the name of the building holding the headquarters of the Bimantara Citra concern was changed from Bimantara Building to Kebun Sirih Building (*Far Eastern Economic Review*, 13-5-1999:12). Tommy decided to sell his Lamborghini shares to Audi. Another of his hobbies which went sour was the Sentul motor racetrack in Bogor. It was heavily in debt and almost no car or motorcycle races were still being held there. Those who profited were the local population. Part of the terrain was planted with rice and cassava.

Soeharto's downfall also meant that forest concessions and plantation licences held by firms in which shares were held by members of his family or by business tycoons like Bob Hasan to turn forest land into plantations were withdrawn or not renewed because they reeked of KKN, and that the contracts concluded with state companies, ministries, and local administrations were called in for review or cancelled. Although some of these decisions were taken on the spur of the moment in May and June, other contracts were cancelled only months later, after the government had completed KKN investigations in the departments and state companies.[4] Various reasons were given by the new government to explain the need for these measures. One was the unfavourable terms which had been imposed by Soeharto's children and oth-

---

[4] In July 1999, when eight such concessions were revoked, the Minister of Forestry and Plantations, Muslimin Nasution, had to admit that on paper and according to the regulations of the New Order, the concessions had been obtained in a legal way. Consequently there would be no legal follow-up. At the same time four timber estates, with Bob Hasan, Siti Hediati Prabowo, and Bambang Trihatmodjo among their owners, had to return Rp 50 billion to the state, reforestation money received because of a mark-up of the costs of the projects.

ers who had used their relationship with Soeharto as leverage. Two other reasons were that even though the companies concerned had failed to meet their obligations, they had still received the money for the contracts, or that they had marked up the value of the projects they had embarked upon considerably. In many cases, the chief accusation was that there had been no proper tender or even no tender at all. Even the organization of the hajj by the Ministry of Religion came under investigation. The money pilgrims had to pay far exceeded the costs. Garuda charged much more than was necessary, in turn blaming the costs of aeroplanes they had to hire from firms owned by Ponco Sutowo, Siti Hardijanti Rukmana, and Hutomo Mandala Putra for this. The money paid by the pilgrims which for one or another reason was not spent by the Ministry of Religion was not returned to the pilgrims but ended up in a special foundation set up by Soeharto (*Tempo*, 8-3-1999:40-7). The result of the review was that the cost of the pilgrimage was reduced from US$ 2,730 to US$ 1,200.

The first to feel the chill winds of change was Sigit Harjojudanto. On 23 May, two days after Soeharto's fall from power, the director of PAM (Perusahaan Air Minum) Drinking Water Company of Jakarta, announced that he had cancelled the contracts concluded some months earlier with two private clean-water companies owned by Sigit Harjojudanto and Anthony Salim, which had Lyonnaise des Eaux and Thames Water International as their respective foreign partners. They were accused of having neglected their contractual obligations. Later, after pressure exerted by London and Paris, the cooperation was picked up again but with Sigit Harjojudanto and Anthony Salim banned from the equation. Lyonnaise des Eaux and Thames Water had bought out their shares (Soesilo 1998:128; Wangge and Wangge 1999:158). Still in May, the contracts concluded by Citra Marga Nusaphala Persada (CMNP) belonging to Siti Hardijanti Rukmana, and Jasa Marga, the state company responsible for the construction and management of toll-roads, also came under review. Jasa Marga's bad financial shape was attributed to the unfair contracts it had been forced into. A few days later the chief of police announced that he intended to cancel the contract with Citra Permatasakti Persada, another one of Tutut's firms. This had to do with the computerization and management of the issuing of driving licences. She also lost her investment in the construction of a new airport in Medan. Ostensibly because of the adverse economic climate, the project was postponed. In East Java the governor, Basofi Soedirman, announced that all contracts in his province which had been awarded to the children of Soeharto were to be reviewed.[5] Basofi's colleague in Jakarta, Sutiyoso, called for a review of the

---

5   About a month later Basofi Soedirman changed his mind. In view of the growing unemployment, he called for the continuation of labour intensive projects, even if they were in the hands of the Soeharto family.

contracts concluded by his municipality.

Other drinking water companies, the State Electricity Company PLN (Perusahaan Listrik Negara), and other state companies such as Pertamina and Garuda soon followed suit. As did the board of Jasa Marga, the PLN board blamed the Soeharto family for its grave financial problems. The private power plants in which they had a share (which had also run into financial difficulties) had overcharged for the electricity they supplied. These plants financed by foreign capital had entered the market in 1990, when the demand for power had been greater than the supply, but had stayed put after PLN had increased its own production. On the basis of a take-or-pay clause, PLN had been forced to pay for a fixed amount of electricity whether it needed it or not, at a price which, according to its management, was higher than its own production costs and higher than what PLN charged the public (Soesilo 1998:172). To make the financial burden even higher, all contracts with private power plants stated prices in US dollars. Seizing the advantage of the reform climate, PLN prepared the renegotiation of the power purchase agreements with private power plants in which such figures as Sudwikatmono, Siti Hardijanti Rukmana, and Hashim Djojohadikusumo had a stake. It was the start of a long legal fight in which Jakarta had to bear the pressure of foreign governments coming to the assistance of the foreign investors who had financed the power plants. So desperate was the company's financial plight that Bank Indonesia refused to provide it with credit any longer without the security of stand-by letters of credit (*The Jakarta Post*, 12-6-1998; *Republika,* 24-6-1998).

In an initial statement, the state oil and natural gas company Pertamina, the greatest money-spinner of all, and a company in which (as the Minister of Mining was to describe this a year later) many matters had been 'untouchable', announced that it would reconsider its contracts with no less than 149 companies, blaming these for huge additional and unnecessary costs (*Republika,* 15-7-1999). Among these companies were those controlled by Bambang, Tommy, Tutut, Mamiek, Bob Hasan, and Sudwikatmono (see for instance Soesilo 1998:96-116 and *Tempo,* 16-11-1998, pp. 39-51). They embraced a wide range of activities, from shipping and the provision of chemicals to oil exploration and the building of private refineries. Among the contracts to be terminated by the Ministry of Mining were those involving mediation in the export and import of crude oil and the transport of liquified natural gas, with firms in which Bambang Trihatmodjo, Hutomo Mandala Putra, and Sudwikatmono had a stake. In September, Hartarto, Coordinating Minister of the Supervision of Development and the Reform of State Institutions, whose own family was active in the Garama group, revealed that if these and other contracts with the Soeharto family and Bob Hasan were cancelled it would save Pertamina US$ 82.8 million per year (*Republika,*

2-9-1998). In the next few months a figure of 159 contracts leading to a savings of around US$ 100 million was bandied about (*The Jakarta Post*, 10-10-1998). In December Kuntoro Mangkusubroto stated figures of US$ 64.7 million and Rp 313.3 billion (*Media Indonesia*, 19-12-1998).

Garuda was yet another state company which seized the opportunity to complain about the strangling contracts it had been forced to sign with companies linked to the Soeharto family. Their activities ranged from the renting out of aircraft and insurance to the cutting of grass at airports. In April of the following year, one of its directors revealed that Garuda's foreign debts amounted to US$ 1.08 billion. It was calculated that it would take 35 years to fully repay these debts (*The Jakarta Post*, 8-4-1999, 18-2-2000). Employees blamed mismanagement and demanded the sacking of the management, including its president, Soepandi, a former adjutant to Soeharto. They insisted the management was riddled with collusion and nepotism.

Following the initial post-May rounds, in October 1998 the government revoked three presidential decrees concerning large projects. One involved the development of the Jonggol region in the vicinity of Bogor into a new city, a plan to be carried out by a consortium headed by Bambang Trihatmodjo, who dreamt that he could build Indonesia's new capital there. As in the case of the Timor national car, the example had been provided by Malaysia, a country to which Indonesia did not want to consider itself inferior. Bambang immediately got rid of his shares, and also sold off the land on which the new city was to be located.[6] The other two were projects to turn coastal areas of Jakarta into luxurious housing complexes, complete with tourist resorts. One had been undertaken by the Salim concern, the other by Soeharto's daughter, Siti Hutami Endang Adiningsih. Apart from the fact that only three projects were cancelled, the decision came under vehement attack because it did not venture upon what was really needed, the prosecution of those profiteering from such dealings. The annulment of presidential decrees did not go nearly far enough.

Besides losing contracts, the children of Soeharto and their business associates were confronted with the fact that tax holidays, soft loans, access to extra budgetary funds, and other special facilities which had been provided in the past on the argument that their investments pioneered the development of specific industries or regions, came under scrutiny. One of the side-effects was that Timor car owners began to fear that, when they needed to renew their driving licences, they would be assessed for the taxes from which the car's producer had been exempted. Persistent rumours to this effect forced the management of Timor Distributor Nasional to state that Timor

---

6   The following year it was reported that 3,200 ha of land at Jonggol had been sold to Tommy Winata, head of the Artha Graha concern (*Tempo*, 6-6-1999:42).

owners had nothing to fear. When it came to payment of back taxes, it was the company, not they, which would have to pay. The Ministries of Industry and of Finance also left no shadow of a doubt that it was Tommy who had to pay.

Before the year was out, the Ministry of Finance demanded Rp 3.5 trillion in retroactive tax and import duty on sold and unsold cars, arguing that local components made up less than nine per cent of the car and that the Timor producer had thus failed to fulfil the condition that after one year this should be twenty per cent. The dire financial straits in which Tommy found himself (he also had a huge number of loans to pay off) made the Timor car a much-sought-after object. The Ministry of Finance, looking for a way to collect the retroactive taxes and duties; BPPN, in an effort to find a way to cover the debts the car factory had incurred at banks and private creditors all wanted to seize the cars. The strongest claim came from BPPN, which had been given the right to foreclose on debtors' assets, stealing a march on the other creditors. In vain Tommy tried to fight the claim of the tax department in court. In July 1999 the Director-general of Taxes announced that the government was indeed to confiscate 14,000 Timors and would not hesitate to seize Tommy's private assets were the value of these cars insufficient to pay off the taxes and import duties owed by the Timor company.

Unpaid taxes were not the only worry besetting Timor owners. As the riots in 1997 and 1998 had shown, Timor showrooms and cars were among the prime targets as objects associated with a hated regime. For safety reasons, Timor owners started to drive a car of another manufacturer, if they could afford to do so. Drivers of Bimantara cars did the same. As with all objects associated with the Soeharto family, Timor and Bimantara cars had become the things of acts of destruction by angry individuals or by mobs.[7]

The review of facilities provided in the past also took a fine-tooth comb to projects by other conglomerates, such as that of Kiani Kertas, one of Bob Hasan's companies, which had been granted a ten-year income-tax exemption because it was argued that the investment formed a valuable contribution to the economic development of Kalimantan, and PT Trans-Pacific Petrochemical Indotama of Hashim Djojohadikusumo. In the middle of June, the Minister of Investments temporarily halted the granting of special tax facilities to both Indonesian and foreign firms, purportedly awaiting the drafting of new criteria. Existing facilities were not terminated, but funding promised to the conglomerates but not yet paid was withheld.

Another consequence of the deluge of demands for the prosecution of

---

[7] The Timor case put no definite end to plans to produce an Indonesian national car. Discussions resumed in January 1999 after it had become known that the Minister of Industry and Trade was considering the prospect of stimulating the development of an Indonesian-made car.

those guilty of KKN, Soeharto first and foremost, was that individuals and the public prosecution dared to bring to court or to subpoena as witnesses individuals who before May had been immune to such treatment. In Jakarta, first on the list were relatives of Soeharto, their business associates, and former cabinet ministers. Newspapers and periodicals published repeated pictures of Soeharto's children and Bob Hasan entering or leaving police stations and the office of the attorney-general. With satisfaction it was reported that they did not look very happy on such occasions, and that they did not have as much to say for themselves as they had had before May. Outside the capital, legal proceedings were begun against local civil servants who had been powerful enough to escape prosecution or had enjoyed strong backing in the past.

Of all Soeharto's children and associates, it was Hutomo Mandala Putra on whom the prosecution came down hardest. As early as the end of June, Hutomo Mandala Putra had been forced to discuss with the governor of Jakarta the matter of the vacating of a new office building owned by the Humpuss Concern at Jalan Medan Merdeka Timur, located on a site where urban planning rules forbade company offices. Tommy had tried to circumvent this rule by persuading the municipality to give the part of the street where the office of his Timor car and Humpuss Concern had been built another name, but in the wake of May such a stratagem had become unacceptable. He had to vacate the building. The building was sealed up in March 1999, but this had to be reversed again after Humpuss took the matter before the Administrative Court. In July the building was seized by the tax department in an effort to recover the taxes Tommy owed.

Opinion sas to why he was singled out differed. Some saw Tommy as the sacrificial lamb immolated to divert attention from the investigation of Soeharto. Others said he was Soeharto's Achilles' heel. Most attention was inevitably attracted by his Timor car, which had become a symbol of the financial abuses of the New Order, and which was to figure prominently in the investigation into KKN practices of his father. Hutomo Mandala Putra also had the honour of being the first of the Soeharto family to stand trial as a suspect, a status conferred upon him in early December 1998. The matter at stake was a *ruilslag*, a practice quite common in the New Order, in which government institutions and private firms swopped land. In this case it concerned a 50-hectare tract of land and warehouses owned by Bulog in Kelapa Gading in North Jakarta acquired by Hutomo Mandala Putra (as president commissioner of PT Goro Batara Sakti), who in return should have provided Bulog with a 70-hectare piece of land in Marunda, where it could build a more modern facility nearer the port of Tanjung Priok.[8] Tommy, who was

---

8   One of the witnesses interrogated by the office of the attorney-general was Moerdiono, who stated that Soeharto (who as president had to agree to trades involving land with a value

also involved in a *ruilslag* with premises on which the headquarters of the Jakarta police and those of the Indonesian air force are located, using a cash guarantee from Bulog, borrowed Rp 23 billion from Bank Bukopin to pay for some of the land and the building of new warehouses promised in the deal. His company was unable to repay, forcing the bank to claim the Bulog guarantee. The head of Bulog, Beddu Amang, also provided Rp 32.5 billion to Goro Batara Sakti (which in the meantime had started to renovate warehouses on the former Bulog land, an activity which according to the public prosecution cost the state another Rp 10 billion) to enable it to buy the Marunda plot. According to the public prosecutor the total damages to the state had been Rp 95 billion.

While this case was sub judice, as early as 20 November 20, Tommy had been forbidden to leave the country. He and Bambang Trihatmodjo, upon whom this measure was imposed seven days later, were the only two of Soeharto's children against whom this sanction was taken. In April 1999 a court case was brought against Hutomo Mandala Putra and Beddu. The indictment against Beddu was dropped. In his charge the public prosecutor had failed a number of times to specify which part of the law Beddu had allegedly violated. Apart from this legal lapse, the permission to launch an investigation into Beddu submitted by the office of the attorney-general had been signed by the State Secretary and not by Habibie. Providing such permission was a requisite step because Beddu was a member of the People's Congress, but the rules were not clear about whether the president personally had to sign it or not. In the past a case had been brought against Sri Bintang Pamungkas on the basis of permission signed by the State Secretary. Nevertheless, the judge in Beddu's case took the position that the president had to sign. The public prosecution announced that it would prepare a fresh court case against Beddu.[9] The case against Hutomo Mandala Putra was continued. At the first session Hutomo Mandala Putra, arriving in a Timor jeep, was surrounded by supporters chanting 'Long live Tommy'. On his way out they sang patriotic songs. Such protests in support of himself and of his father were also staged on other occasions when Tommy went to court or was heard by the public prosecution. At the end of August 1999 the public prosecution demanded two years imprisonment for Tommy. The public prosecutor explained that only two years was demanded because Tommy was still young and had never before been convicted of a crime.

As many of the posters carried around by demonstrating students testi-

---

of Rp 10 billion or more) had approved of the *ruilslag* because the rice warehouses were located in what was designated as a residential area.

[9] Beddu Amang was arrested on 28 November 2000. The reason given for the arrest was that he might try to leave the country and destroy evidence.

fied, Habibie himself was not free of the smear of KKN.[10] In the Soeharto era he had received reforestation money to finance his aircraft factory. As a consequence of his control over BPIS and over the development of eastern Indonesia, Batam, and the Natuna oil and gas field, his economic power had been great. Since 1978, when Soeharto had appointed him head of Batam Industrial Development Authority, the development of Batam (an island south of Singapore) as an industrial and holiday resort had practically become the reserve of the Habibie family. In this, as in their other ventures, they cooperated closely with members of the Soeharto family and other conglomerates. His brother, Suyatim Abdurrachman (Timmy), headed the Timsco Indonesia concern, his son, Thariq Kemal Habibie, the Repindo Panca group. Timsco Indonesia consisted of about a hundred companies. In it Timmy Habibie held 55 per cent of the shares; the remainder was owned by Habibie's mother and the wife of Habibie's brother Junus Effendi (Fanny) Habibie. This construction allowed Habibie to declare at the end of May that he did not own the Timsco Concern and its companies. Apart from this, relatives of Habibie had indubitably profited from the special business opportunities the New Order had offered its élite, and from contracts concluded with the government bodies Habibie had headed. Some had found employment in the state companies and institutions Habibie controlled.

Consequently, almost immediately after his swearing in, Habibie's relatives resigned from jobs. Fanny Habibie stepped down as chairman of Batam Industrial Development Authority. His son, Dr Ilham Akbar Habibie, resigned as special assistant to the head of BPPT, but retained his function as project head of the N-2130 jet. The impression this was supposed to make was more than offset in August 1998 when Habibie's wife and his brother, Fanny, were awarded a decoration during the annual deluge of honours on Independence Day. People were quick to point out that it had been Habibie's brother who had been responsible for the purchase of a ten-year-old passenger ship, which had subsequently sunk in 1981, costing the lives of 775 persons. In the months to come, appointments made to high positions led to accusations about nepotism perpetrated by Habibie, who himself had been born at Parepare (South Sulawesi), which were captured in acronyms like SDM (*Semua dari Makassar*, All from Makassar) and SOS (*Semua Orang Sulawesi*, All People from Sulawesi). In the cabinet Yunus Yosfiah and Tanri Abeng came from South Sulawesi, the new attorney-general Ghalib was from the same region, while yet another person from South Sulawesi, Baramuli, was appointed chairman of the Supreme Advisory Council.

---

10   Also with respect to Habibie, various books and articles gave information about the companies and projects which Habibie and his family control or have shares in. See for instance *Panji Masyarakat*, 10-6-1998:68-70, Aditjondro 1998a, 1998c, and *Harta Soeharto* n.d.

Painful for Habibie was the fact that the demonstrations against corruption did not leave members of his cabinet who carried the whiff of KKN unscathed, one reason for Amien Rais to call in June for the sacking of such people in one 'big bang' of a number of bold measures. His Minister without Portfolio of Agrarian Affairs, Hasan Basri Durin, found himself the target of student protests in Padang. The demonstrators claimed that during his two terms in office as governor of West Sumatra, Hasan Basri Durin had been guilty of four cases of corruption, ten of collusion, and seven of nepotism (*Panji Masyarakat*, 10-6-1998:16). In Bali students demonstrated against the appointment of the former governor Ida Bagus Oka as Minister of Demographic Affairs. Other cabinet ministers, and in fact many of the persons who held senior positions during Soeharto's New Order, might well be tainted. One of them was Ginandjar Kartasasmita, who became the centre of a KKN scandal in the middle of October. An American, Jeffrey A. Winters, professor at Northwestern University in Illinois, accused him of having assisted Aburizal Bakrie to lay his hands on 9.4 per cent of the Freeport Indonesia shares for Indocopper Investama of the Bakrie Brothers concern (a company which was taken over by Bob Hasan, using a foreign loan for which Freeport stood security, and by Freeport McMoRan in early 1997). He was supposed to have managed this during the renewal of the contract between the Indonesian government and PT Freeport Indonesia in 1991 when he was Minister of Mining and Energy. The police launched an investigation, not into Ginandjar but into Winters for libelling a member of the cabinet. In March 1999, when Winters visited Indonesia to be heard as a suspect, the American embassy in Jakarta received anonymous phone calls claiming that a team of 20 snipers was ready to assassinate him.

The actions against the corruption committed by power holders in Jakarta were part of a larger movement in which all over Indonesia crowds of people rebelled against authority in the name of the battle against corruption, collusion, and nepotism. Or, as Wiranto summed up the situation: those who did not like the *bupati* staged a demonstration, those who did not like the head of their office staged a demonstration (*Merdeka*, Minggu ke-I Juli 1998). Outside Jakarta an offensive was launched against companies held by the families of local civil servants and administrators, in the wake of which contracts were also cancelled or reviewed. This went hand in hand with a great many demonstrations against those office holders suspected of providing their relatives with profitable business opportunities, of having gained their positions through bribery and corruption, and in some instances of having used the services of persons reputedly endowed with magical powers to obtain or protect their post. Some found themselves the object of demonstrations, accused of the 'arrogance' they had exhibited in the past. KKN was the major issue, but at times the demonstrations, in particular when these touched upon governors, were as much a manifestation of frustrations about the high-handed way in which Jakarta had appointed such office holders in the past, blossoming into demonstrations in favour of greater regional auton-omy and a fairer distribution of the money generated in the provinces between the region and the centre.

After the fall of Soeharto, scenes unfolded outside Jakarta which were reminiscent of what had happened in many regions in Indonesia after the Proclamation of Independence. At times the situation led to incidents which resembled what Anderson, writing about the months following the Japanese occupation, has dubbed *daulat* actions – 'the deposition, humiliation, kidnap-ping, or murder of hated officials or other representatives of authority' – except for the fact that no officials were killed (Anderson 1972:334). A typical example was the fate that befell the Minister without Portfolio of Agrarian Affairs, Hasan Basri Durin, in September. His inclusion in the cabinet had already led to protests by students, giving vent to their displeasure by occu-pying the provincial parliament of West Sumatra. When he visited the province of which he had been governor for a decade, IKIP students stopped the bus in which he was travelling. Hasan Basri Durin was forced to get off and to account for the cases of corruption and nepotism of which the stu-dents considered him guilty. After four hours the students let him go, snarling at him that there was no need for him to return to West Sumatra.

Demonstrations demanding that governors, mayors of cities, *bupati*, *camat*, and other senior regional civil servants right down to the mayors of villages and their staff be sacked unfolded all over Indonesia. The mayor of a village in Jombang was even forced to contract debts to repay his villagers the money he was said to have earned from corruption. How frightened local administrators had become is illustrated by the fact that in July village may-ors and other village officials, demanding protection from the many protests, staged a demonstration at the office of the *bupati* of Kebumen. Village admin-istrators suffered, but so did more senior local civil servants. In North Sumatra, where the mayor of Medan was one of the targets, the demonstra-tions and threats emanating from the protests pushed the local administra-tion to decide in September to arm half of the civil servants of the provincial office with clubs.

In East Java the governor, Basofi Soedirman, and his deputy were both accused of KKN, as were most, if not all, of the *bupati* and mayors. Among them were the *bupati* and village mayors of Banyuwangi, a region which was soon to require a gruesome reputation for the lynching of people suspected of sorcery. In Central Java, among those falling foul of the people's wrath were the *bupati* of Kudus and Batang, and the mayor and *bupati* of Tegal, against all of whom demonstrations were staged. In the same province, in Lamongan, angry fishermen burnt the house of the chairman of the local cooperative society, a body seen in many places in Indonesia as an extension of the government. In West Java students and others demonstrated against the *bupati* of Cianjur and Bogor, and against the installation of the provincial governor for his second term. What had enraged them in the last instance was not simply his alleged involvement in corruption, but reports of an excessive item in the budget to pay for his uniforms. Later, in September, students in Indramayu demonstrated in Jakarta demanding the resignation of its *bupati* because he had failed to develop the *kabupaten*.

In West Sumatra the *bupati* of Sawahluntu and the mayor of Padang became the targets of demonstrations. In Palembang the governor of South Sumatra was held for hours by a crowd wanting him to proceed with the installation of the new mayor of Palembang, something about which the governor had procrastinated because he considered the situation too dangerous. In Pekanbaru the building of the Provincial Representative Body of Riau was ransacked in early June after students, calling themselves the Forum Mahasiswa Riau untuk Reformasi (Formasi), Riau Student Forum for Reformation, had staged demonstrations against corruption, collusion, and nepotism in the province for over a week. One of their demands was the resignation of the governor of Riau. They threatened to occupy the building till the governor was prepared to speak to them. When he did, they criticized him fiercely, demanding that he explain how he had acquired his wealth. Other targets of the student protests in Pekanbaru were the mayor of the town and the head of the provincial Directorate for Social and Political Affairs. The latter was accused of being behind some of the gambling and prostitution in the province.

In South Sulawesi students accused the governor, the mayors of Ujungpandang and Parepare, and various *bupati*, among them those of Gowa, Bone, Pinrang, and Maros, of KKN, or, as another abbreviation put it, KKNF, the F standing for feudalism. In September, when a new governor was to be inaugurated, they demanded that the ceremony be postponed till it had been unequivocally established whether the new governor had bought votes in the provincial parliament or not. The governor of Southeast Sulawesi did not escape attack. It was reported that he had appointed 29 members of his family to the civil service of the province (*Panji Masyarakat*, 17-6-1998:26). In North Sulawesi the *bupati* and mayor of Gorontalo and the *bupati* of Bitung were the targets of frequent protests. Amongst other charges, the *bupati* of Gorontalo was accused of having embezzled religious tax money. In Samarinda in East Kalimantan it was the new governor who was the target of student protests even before his official installation, while in Mataram there were demonstrations against the re-election of the governor of the Western Lesser Sunda Islands. By July 1999, the government had dismissed various regents, including Sudarmo of Bantul. At that time an investigation into twenty governors was promised.

A new phenomenon in this upsurge of people power was the frequent occupation of land. Part of the problem in these cases was dissatisfaction with the compensation villagers and the urban poor had been forced to accept in the past when being evicted from land on which they had toiled or built their dwellings. They had been forced to make room for roads, real estate projects, large-scale agricultural, forestry, and mining enterprises, golf links, and other endeavours by which the conglomerates thought they could make a profit. In many cases it concerned land held in long lease since colonial days by Dutch estate companies, which had been nationalized by the Indonesian government in 1957. At that moment the land had become national domain (*D&R*, 31-5-1999:29). Some of these lands of former Dutch plantations had lain waste for years after World War Two, giving the local population the idea that they had a right to till the soil, when suddenly during the New Order state, provincial, and private companies had began to work them. In many instances, force had been used to evict people from such land. People had been too scared to resist or report rough handling, and if they had protested they had had little or no chance of success. In other instances land was expropriated which, according to tradition, the local population considered communal or ancestral land. Even the palace of the Sunan of Surakarta prepared a court case in which it protested against the purchase of land from its domain by Soeharto's wife in 1970 (Ismawan 1998:29).

With people imbued with new hope that change could be accomplished, demands to redress such wrongs, which were already being voiced before May, grew more vocal. In September 1998, for instance, nine hundred villagers from Sukabumi protested in front of the Provincial Parliament of West Java. They insisted that 2,000 ha of land be returned to them. This had been expropriated by Tutut, under the pretext that the land was being taken over in the interests of the state. They claimed that those among them who had refused to sell had been intimidated with the threat of arrest on the trumped-up charges that they were PKI members or had obstructed national development. Nobody had ever been allowed to harvest their crop. Those who tried to do so were chased away and accused of theft. The villagers had not yet reoccupied the land, but threatened to do so if hunger drove them to this pass and they were still forbidden to cultivate the soil. Other victims brought lawsuits against the companies which had ordered evictions. Soeharto himself became directly involved when legal proceedings were brought against a company once owned by his wife over a tract of land in Southeast Sulawesi.

In other instances the local population took the law into their own hands by efforts to reoccupy and divide amongst themselves land they had once owned or of which they were convinced that they had the right to till the soil. Suddenly parts of estates and golf courses were planted with cassava, peanuts, maize, and other crops. When authorities or owners tried to undo the occupations, this almost invariably stirred up fights between villagers and the mobile police, and other characters who tried to evict the former again. The clashes also involved students and members of NGOs who came to the assistance of the farmers in their struggle. Such clashes, with the mobile police using brute force, in some instances firing live bullets at protesters, went on well into 1999. Elsewhere, authorities, owners, and concession holders had to look on or were confronted with what in their eyes were excessive demands for compensation by the local population. Especially hurt were timber companies operating in Irian Jaya, Kalimantan, Sumatra, and Sulawesi. In March 2000 the chairman of APHI, Association of Indonesian Forest Entrepreneurs, revealed that at least fifty timber companies which controlled about ten million hectares of forests had been forced to stop their logging operations because of actions by local residents. He also said that conflicts between timber companies and the local population had made a number of foreign firms decide to postpone new investments, while others had threatened to pull out of existing contracts because the local partner could not deliver.

Among the first targets after May 1998 were plots of land and estates believed to be owned or controlled by members of the Soeharto family, including the site of the Jonggol project, were immediately homed in on as prime targets for occupation. Reports claimed that the determined efforts made by farmers to retake their land forced the Soeharto family to hire extra guards to protect what it considered their property all over Indonesia (*The Jakarta Post*, 18-7-1998). The most spectacular example was what happened to the Tri S (Start-Sari-Silang) cattle ranch, better known as Tapos, at Ciawi, near Bogor. The ranch (encompassing an area of 750 ha, about half of which was fenced in, the rest of the area was just lying waste) had been a favourite retreat of Soeharto, a place to entertain, and to invite groups to mark the beginning of social and economic campaigns which were close to his heart. The land was owned by the state and was located on what had been a former quinine estate, which had lain derelict since World War Two. After 1945 the local population had gradually began to cultivate the soil, claiming their rights from this. Between 1972 and 1974 they had been progressively evicted from the land in what they described as an illegal and brutal way by PT Rejo Sari Bumi, the company to which the government had given the right to use the land till the year 2000, and in which the shares were owned by Soeharto's children. Villagers related how their crops had been destroyed by bulldozers and by cattle which had suddenly been allowed to roam free. When the villagers protested and asked to be given a month's grace until after harvest time, the answer had been that the evictors were acting on instructions from Soeharto. Villagers, who up to then had made a decent living, were forced to seek employment as agricultural workers or had to move to Jakarta to find work (Ismawan 1998:35). In July 1998, about three hundred of them, men, women, and children, assisted by student and legal right activists, once again began to cultivate the soil within the enclosure, demarcating sections of it, clearing plots and planting them with cassava, maize, and other crops. They had to stand up to strong-armed tactics by thugs, who were specially brought in on trucks to scare them off the land. An all-out fight was prevented, but seedlings and markers were removed. Next day the farmers returned. They persisted, planting part of the land.

How Soeharto had obtained the Tapos ranch was a public secret. In May 1980 a retired general, M. Jasin, had protested about the way Soeharto had acquired and fitted out the ranch (see Jenkins 1984:164-7 and Jasin 1998). He had disclosed how Solichin GP, at that time governor of West Java, had been instructed by Soeharto to acquire a suitable piece of land for a retreat near Bogor, and how the first cattle for the ranch had been imported from Australia on a naval vessel which had been especially equipped with air conditioning to allow the animals to adjust to the temperature during the voyage, accustoming them to the differences in climate between Australia and Indonesia. The Minister of Public Works had been instructed to take care of the infrastructure of the ranch. In 1998, Jasin brought the same information up again and suggested a court case be launched. He claimed the way in which the Habibie government tackled the Tapos affair would form a good test case to see whether it was indeed a reform government. Solichin reacted furiously. He denied he had ever given any land to Soeharto, maintaining that there had been a proper tender and that the new use to which the neglected estate was put had been nothing but beneficial. Refuting any accusation that he had been involved in any kind of KKN activity, he suggested that Jasin should not act as if he was the only person in the country who opposed the way Soeharto had acquired his wealth.

CHAPTER XII

Soeharto's wealth

Aku ingin beli TV color, rumah mewah, istri cantik
Sendyakalaning Indonesia
Romo, romo, romo, romo ono maling, tapi pake dasi
Maling! Maling! Bapak maling, anak maling
Semua maling!
Sendyakalaning Indonesia.[1]

Understandably, the person who attracted most attention was Soeharto. His prosecution was, without a doubt, one of the principal goals of students and others. It was felt that the time had come for Soeharto to account for his political and economic crimes, for the cruelty shown by the Armed Forces in Aceh, East Timor, Irian Jaya, and Tanjung Priok, and for the presidential decrees from which his family and business friends had profited so royally. Occasionally his *coup d'état* against Soekarno was included in the misdeeds for which Soeharto should be called to account. Initially not many persons hazarded a prediction about the outcome and consequences of Soeharto's prosecution. One of the few to do so was Amien Rais. Calling to mind what had happened in South Korea, he suggested that after his conviction, since he was an old man, Soeharto should be pardoned. Amien Rais mentioned two conditions for this. Soeharto's fortune had to be returned to the people, and he should beg forgiveness for his crimes. One of the reasons which led Amien Rais to propose a pardon was that he believed that all Indonesians shared in the burden of guilt, having treated Soeharto like a god for more than thirty years (*Perspektif*, 25-2-1999:7).

Initially the government acted speedily and with some decision. On 1 June, the then attorney-general, Soedjono Chanafiah Atmonegoro, announced the launching of an investigation into the wealth of state officials, includ-

---

[1]   I want to buy a colour TV, live in a luxurious house, have a beautiful wife/ The sunset of Indonesia/ My betters, my betters, my betters, my betters are thieves, but wear ties/ Thieves! Thieves! The father is a thief, his sons and daughters are thieves/ Everybody is a thief!/ The sunset of Indonesia. Song by a street singer cited in *Gatra*, 9-5-1998:86.

ing Soeharto and his family. A team of 35 members was formed. To enlist the support of the public, it was pointed out that it would be possible to send information about corruption and collusion committed by the Soeharto family and others to a special post office box number at the attorney-general's office. In the middle of the month Soedjono, who had held the function for only three months, was replaced by Major-General (two days later promoted to Lieutenant-General) Andi Muhammad Ghalib, head of the legal department of the Armed Forces. Ghalib, whom Soeharto had refused to consider as a candidate for the attorney-generalship in 1993 and 1998, was considered to be close to Habibie. The irony of Ghalib's appointment was that, just before his promotion, he had selected a team to defend Soeharto in legal proceedings instituted against him over the transfer of power to Habibie. As a retired officer, Soeharto had turned to the legal department of the Armed Forces, which has a section providing free legal aid to active and retired military men. When the transfer was effected, civil servants were not pleased that an outsider was appointed and protested, carrying posters with texts like 'We love Soedjono', 'Don't leave us', and 'Soedjono Yes, Ghalib No'. Soedjono, who publicly expressed his surprise about his sacking, stated that he could not imagine why he had been removed from his post. His forced resignation was surrounded by conflicting interpretations. One was that the reason for his replacement was that he was prepared to act too resolutely in the fight against KKN. Those who held this view pointed to a meeting Soedjono had had with Habibie on the morning of 15 June. On that occasion he is said to have presented proof of the illegal practices perpetrated by Soeharto's foundations, in his opinion enough to allow Soeharto to be heard as a suspect, and of KKN crimes committed by Ginandjar Kartasasmita, Feisal Tanjung, and relatives of Habibie. Soedjono was told that he had been replaced by Ghalib as attorney-general when he visited Habibie for a second time during the afternoon of the same day. Others suggested a conflicting scenario in which Soedjono had been replaced because he was hesitant about beginning an investigation into Soeharto's wealth, failing to act on the evidence which had already been unearthed. This view saw Soedjono as being too close to 'Cendana', as having been appointed attorney-general under the auspices of Siti Hardijanti Rukmana, and as having himself grown rich through corruption.

Suspicion about the resolve of the government to bring Soeharto to court was augmented by a seemingly widely shared feeling that Habibie and Wiranto, of their own accord or at the instigation of Soeharto, were trying to shield the former president from a thorough investigation, an impression not alleviated by a clumsy remark by Habibie to the effect that Soeharto was 'poor' (Sasongko 1998b:10). Consequently, an investigation set up by Soedjono and Ghalib did not seem to be enough, not least because there were indications that the companies and persons involved were busy cleaning up their business affairs. Soeharto was also suspected of taking measures to render an investigation futile. A public prosecution headed by a direct underling of Wiranto or by a special team instituted by Habibie, therefore, did not seem to guarantee a truly independent investigation. Those holding such views called for a national committee with the same independent status as the National Committee for Human Rights, or, even better, a committee which derived its authority from a special decree of the People's Congress.

When it came down to the financial brass tacks, the money amassed by Soeharto's children was the most clear-cut. Everybody knew that they headed vast business empires, though the exact magnitude of what they owned was difficult to put a finger on. Assessing Soeharto's own personal wealth was a more difficult exercise. He and those speaking on his behalf, including Soedharmono and Probosutedjo, categorically denied that he had garnered a huge personal fortune, let alone that he was as immensely rich as the outside world claimed. Before his TPI speech in September, Soeharto had already indicated that no case could be made against him. In the middle of June, through his lawyer Yacob, he had let it be known that he did not fear the insistent calls that his fortune should devolve to the state. As he did not own anything, he had nothing to fear. Around the same time, large banners had suddenly appeared in the streets of Jakarta with texts asserting that to avoid bloodshed there had to be an end to the defamation and investigation of former President Soeharto, fuelling the suspicion that Soeharto was fighting back. Before the month was over Soeharto once again, this time through another lawyer, Abdul Aziz Muhammad Balhmar, gave people to understand that he did not fear an investigation, challenging them to come up with proof of the fortune he allegedly possessed. The following month Soeharto issued a press release stating that he did not have any bank accounts abroad.

At the root of the problem lay the charitable foundations Soeharto had founded and personally chaired, and which were managed by his confidants and relatives.[2] In their statutes, care had been taken to mention that the funds pertaining to these foundations did not form part of the personal wealth of its founder. Soeharto himself declared there was nothing amiss with the foundations. They were not owned by himself, his family, or the members of the board, and their one and only aim was to finance charitable activities. Soeharto indicated he was confident that any investigation into the foundations would unearth nothing that could incriminate him. Soeharto went as far as to offer a room in his house to be used as a study for those who wanted to check the books of the foundations. Such an arrangement would be

---

[2]   Lists of such foundations can be found in publications about Soeharto's wealth, and in Sasongko (1998c) and Ismawan (1998).

very convenient: when they had questions they could just knock on his door. The offer was ignored (*Forum Keadilan*, 14-12-1998:84). Those defending him stressed with a vigour equal to his own that the foundations were used only to raise money for the needy. Soeharto's critics did not believe a word of this. As far as they were concerned, the social aims mentioned in the statues were only a blind.

Like banks, charitable foundations appear to have evolved into a status symbol. Similar institutions had also been established by relatives of Soeharto and other rich Indonesians. Soeharto and his family between them chaired about 95 such foundations. The most wealthy ones had grown rich by investing money in companies and banks, many of these controlled by relatives and associates of Soeharto. At that time they were still considered healthy, but later many of them had fallen victim to the financial and economic crisis. They held shares in banks such as Bank Duta, BUN, Bank Andromeda, Bank Bukopin, and Bank Muamalat, and in commercial companies such as Indocement, Bogasari, Sempati Air, and Citra Marga Nusaphala Persada. Stakes in companies were also held indirectly through Bob Hasan's Nusamba. Another major source of income for the Soeharto foundations was the 'voluntary' contributions expected to be made by a great variety of groups of people who had been asked or ordered to contribute.

Five of the Soeharto foundations stood out in the glare of publicity now turned upon them:
- Yayasan Dharmais, or Yayasan Dharma Bhakti Sosial, Social Voluntary Work Foundation. Founded in 1975, its stated aim was to provide assistance to orphans and to homeless and disabled people, and to supply health services to the poor. Initially, on the basis of a presidential regulation of 1976 and later, after 1978, on one issued by the Ministry of Finance, all state-owned banks were obliged to contribute 2.5 percent of their net profits.
- Yayasan Dakab, or Yayasan Dana Karya Abadi, Eternal Work Fund Foundation. Dakab's pockets were lined by compulsory contributions made by civil servants, with a minimum of Rp 5,000 a year for the lower echelon, and Golkar members of representative bodies. Golkar members of parliament, for instance, had to pay Rp 750,000 a year. Founded in 1985, its purpose was to support the activities of the 'greater Golkar family'. Soeharto was to defend the founding of the Dakab Foundation by pointing out that he had felt sorry when he learned that people were collecting money for Golkar illegally and were being punished for this. To prevent such malpractices he had come up with the idea of establishing a special fund-raising foundation for Golkar (*D&R*, 31-5-1999:23). Yayasan Dakab provided the money to conduct election campaigns for Golkar. Each time elections were in the offing, Soeharto contacted Liem to arrange for the conglomerates to make a special contribution. According to Sofyan Wanandi, who himself usually con-

tributed Rp 1 billion, Liem would give Rp 20 billion (Anwari SB 1998b:2). Some money also went to organizations like Muhammadiyah and HMI. In July, in an interview with the magazine *Dharmais*, Soeharto made it clear that Golkar had no say at all in the way its money was spent (*DëTAK*, 17-8-1998:4-5). As an indication of this, and to show his disagreement with developments in Golkar after his fall, Soeharto tried to bypass its central board, contacting the provincial boards directly to arrange to distribute Dakab money.
– Yayasan Supersemar, established in 1974 to provide scholarships for school pupils and university students. State banks were obliged to contribute over 2.5 per cent of their profits to this foundation.
– Yayasan AMP or Yayasan Amalbhakti Muslim Pancasila, Pancasila Muslim Charity Foundation. Founded in February 1982, one of its major aims was to finance the building of mosques, all in a similar, traditional Southeast Asian style, and other religious activities. Since November of that year, Muslim civil servants and soldiers had been required to give a monthly contribution to the foundation. The lowest ranks contributed Rp 50.
– Yayasan Dana Sejahtera Mandiri (DSM or Damandiri), or Autonomous Welfare Fund Foundation. Meant to provide financial assistance to the poor, it had been founded in January 1996 as one outcome of the Jimbaran meeting and was especially intended for contributions made by conglomerates. Companies with an annual profit of Rp 100 million or more had to donate two per cent of their profits. Originally, a presidential decree of 1995 had only spoken of a voluntary contribution, but a new presidential decree of 1996 made the donation compulsory.

In June 1998, the first information about the assets of these foundations was provided by Soedharmono. Speaking about the Dharmais, AMP, Supersemar, and Dakab foundations, Soedharmono tried to explain that at first glance their aggregate capital (according to him, Rp 2 trillion) sounded impressive, but that compared to the state budget the sum did not amount to much. Transfer of the money would be no more than a symbolic gesture. Soedharmono made his statement in an effort to convince the general public that nothing was amiss with the foundations. He failed. His statement that the foundations owned only Rp 2 trillion met with a surge of indignation. Transfer of the capital to the state and an independent investigation were demanded.

In July, in an initial step to curtail the foundations, Habibie revoked all presidential decrees and instructions which provided for the foundations and directed the way they acquired their money. He instructed governors, *bupati*, and state companies to do the same with stipulations made by themselves or their predecessors regulating the acquisition of funds for the disputed foundations. Furthermore, their exemption from taxes on interest on deposits was revoked and a legal and financial audit of the foundations was launched by the attorney-general. The first results were made public on 1 September. Ghalib claimed that there were strong indications, as almost everybody already knew or suspected, that some of the money of the foundations had not been used in accordance with the aims listed in their statutes. Ghalib refused to be specific. He only disclosed that money had been lent to a businessman, identifying the person with his initials 'BH'.

In the middle of July, when he vowed he had no foreign bank accounts, Soeharto explained the background of the establishment of such foundations. He recalled how, during the military actions to take Irian Jaya which he had led in 1962, many under his command had died. The following year, feeling responsible for their relatives, he had founded Yayasan Trikora to pay for the education of those children whose fathers had died in the campaign. Soeharto, who did not recall the history of the foundation he had founded when he was commander of the Diponegoro Division in 1956, claimed that in later years the venture had inspired him to establish foundations to care for children and the poor. It was a practice which had been spearheaded by his wife, with her involvement in Yayasan Harapan Kita, Our Hope Foundation, in the early 1970s. To illustrate the good work the foundations had done, Soeharto recalled that Yayasan Harapan Kita and Yayasan Dharmais had financed the building of a heart hospital and a cancer hospital, and had helped regional state hospitals in various ways, for instance, by paying the electricity bills. Defiantly he announced that Yayasan Dharmais and Yayasan Supersemar would step up their financial assistance to social institutions and to school pupils and university students. It was one of the ways he could underscore his intention to become a *pandhito* after stepping down.

Still in July, to show his goodwill, Soeharto handed over to the state three hospitals belonging to Yayasan Harapan Kita and Yayasan Dharmais. At the end of November, he transferred seven foundations – the five mentioned above plus Trikora Foundation and Yayasan Dana Gotong Royong Kemanusiaan, Humanitarian Mutual Aid Fund, a foundation for aid to victims of natural disasters – to the state.[3] The transfer was made at the request of Habibie, but as a matter of fact Soeharto had already decided to take this step. At that moment the seven foundations had an aggregate worth of Rp 5.7 trillion. In the letter in which he handed over the foundations, Soeharto advised Habibie to use the money to alleviate the sufferings of the poor. A few months later, Soeharto expressed his doubts about the transfer. By handing over the foundations to the state, they had come under the control of the

---

[3]   This was the story presented in 1998. In November 1999 it was explained by the Indonesian government that the foundations had not been transferred to the state and that the Indonesian government had only had a say in the way the foundations' money was spent. The final decision still rested with the foundations, that is Soeharto.

parliament, which, according to him, could well mean that the foundations could no longer function efficiently, and that many of the institutions which in the past had been supported would no longer receive money (D&R, 31-5-1999:23).

Soeharto's TPI speech on 6 September and the calls by his lawyers for the protection of his legal rights only swelled the number of voices insisting on an investigation and the confiscation of his wealth. It helped Habibie to make up his mind. In the middle of the month he announced the setting up of a Team to Investigate Former President Soeharto. The team was headed by Ghalib, and had representatives from the police and the State Auditor's Office among its members. Their brief was to concentrate exclusively on Soeharto's wealth. This, as explained by Ghalib, who took the action of sealing the State Secretariat to prevent official documents from disappearing, was what people wanted first and foremost. The other crimes of which Soeharto was accused could be investigated at a later stage. Within two days Habibie modified his announcement. The name of the team was changed to Clarification/Confirmation Team (meaning confirmation of the words of Soeharto), while Habibie joined those who proposed that Indonesia's cultural values should be honoured and that the slandering of Soeharto had to stop.

The TPI speech goaded Ghalib into action. On 21 September, he and Hartarto visited Soeharto at Jalan Cendana to inquire about what he had said on TV and to inform him that a summons for an interrogation was to follow. Soeharto used the opportunity to strike back at his critics once more. He made it clear that he might well launch a court case himself against persons who spread unsubstantiated stories about his fortune.[4] Even so, Ghalib said afterwards, the meeting had been a pleasant one. Soeharto had been most cooperative and had promised to hand over a list of his possessions to Habibie. Two days later, in response to calls to set up an independent committee to investigate Soeharto and to stem the growing tide of criticism about the way in which he conducted the investigation, Ghalib announced that he was to be assisted in unearthing how rich Soeharto really was by a special team of 'experts', chaired by Adnan Buyung Nasution, in which Amien Rais and Christianto Wibisono were also invited to participate. As with all other schemes to give the investigation more credibility, it came to nought. Ghalib

4   In October Soeharto's lawyer Yacob mentioned the names of people who could be charged: Amien Rais, Christianto Wibisono, and George Junus Aditjondro. The threat was repeated in February. In the same month Probosutedjo brought charges against Aditjondro for stating that Probosutedjo's house in London was the fruit of KKN. Probosutedjo, denying that his import of cloves constituted a monopoly, made it known that he had offered Rp 100 billion to someone who claimed to have proof that he had been guilty of KKN should that person really be able to substantiate the charge.

was only prepared to tolerate an advisory team, not one with the same powers the public prosecution had. This was not what others had in mind. Adnan Buyung Nasution wanted to play an active role in the investigation into Soeharto's wealth (interview with Ghalib *Forum Keadilan*, 19-10-1998:78-9). Amien Rais refused because he doubted the sincerity of the Habibie government in combatting KKN. Two days later, Soeharto, waving to reporters, went to the attorney-general's office for the first time to submit two letters: one allowing the investigators to open bank accounts anywhere in the world that bore his name, the other to transfer funds abroad – if he had any – to the state.

The investigation of Soeharto's wealth was one of the controversial points in the preparations for the extraordinary session of the People's Congress in November. PPP and PDI demanded a special congressional decree, hoping that, empowered with the authority of the highest legislative institution, real progress could be made. The Armed Forces, Golkar, and Regional Representation were against. Their standpoint was that an investigation was the responsibility of the attorney-general. Spokesmen of the Armed Forces did not seem to have much to say about the matter. It reminded people once again of Wiranto's pledge in May to protect Soeharto. As a compromise, it was agreed during the extraordinary session of the People's Congress to mention Soeharto's name in a decree about a clean government free of corruption, collusion, and nepotism. The decree called for firm action to be taken in the fight against these three evils wherever they had been committed by present and former officials, their families, and cronies, and against private individuals and conglomerates, including former President Soeharto. The Golkar group, acting in this way, it was suspected, at the instigation of Habibie, initially had not wanted to name any names, arguing that by having elected Soeharto in the past, former People's Congresses shared the blame. It was an argument that made sense. Almost no Indonesian politician was innocent.

By this time many who were disappointed in the slow progress the investigation was making had become convinced that Ghalib had to go. Suspicion of Ghalib's intentions was fuelled by remarks like those he had made in reaction to Soeharto's TV speech in September, and again in early November in which he ventured that Soeharto had issued the much disputed presidential decrees to promote the welfare of the people, and that matters had only gone wrong in the implementation (*Ummat*, 9-11-1998:6). Many failed to understand why it was so difficult to declare Soeharto a suspect. Some paperwork was all that was needed. In November, such remarks spurred Amien Rais to remark that Ghalib had been more of a public relations officer to Soeharto than an attorney-general (*Jawa Pos*, 20-11-1998). On another occasion he called Ghalib Mister Nanti, Mister Marking Time, because of his continuous promises that he was soon going to act against Soeharto (*Adil*, 16-6-1999).

Students showed they felt the same. On 24 November, they presented Ghalib, whom they considered too afraid of Soeharto to act, a hen, a bra, and a pair of ladies' knickers. Ghalib, who, it turned out shortly, could be extremely touchy in his reaction to criticism, did not show any emotion. Later the students made him a five-star general, reasoning that as a three-star general he would never find the courage to confront Soeharto, a five-star general. As an equal he would. Later still, students of Universitas Indonesia presented Ghalib with the 'Soeharto Award', an award intended for a public champion of the status quo and anti-reformasi interests.

Disappointed with the outcome of the extraordinary session of the People's Congress, students had turned their attention to Soeharto's residence as the target of their demonstrations. One of the results was that even tighter security measures were taken in Jalan Cendana and neighbouring streets. On 16 November, about fifty students united in Komite Penyelamat Ekonomi dan Hak Rakyat (KPEHR), Committee of Saviours of the Economy and the Rights of the People, tried to force their way into Soeharto's house. They were stopped by marines. This marked the beginning of a new trend. Three days later, five thousand students from Jakarta and other Javanese cities made a second attempt, tactically approaching Jalan Cendana from various directions. On 2 December, after a similar attempt, Trisakti students marched on to the presidential palace, breaking the security cordon. It provided an example of how desperate the ordinary soldier had become. *The Jakarta Post* quoted one of them: 'This is nuts. We did not expect the crowd to be this huge' (*The Jakarta Post*, 3-12-1998). Soeharto's house in Surakarta, which he had inherited from his wife, also was not safe from protesters. On 20 November, KAMMI students staged a demonstration in front of it.

Commenting on these events, Hutomo Mandala Putra, stressing Soeharto's innocence and conveying the message that the protests only made the life of ordinary citizens more miserable, asserted that demonstrations were not necessary. His father was ready to stand trial providing that strong evidence had been found. Tommy challenged the students to come up with proof and not just to make a song and dance about his father's alleged crimes. Soeharto seems to have changed tactics. At the end of December Soeharto was quoted as having stated that he had initially decided to lie doggo, like a guerilla fighter who was fired on from every direction, and that he would continue to do so (*Merdeka*, 24-12-1998). His actions belied these words. After the extraordinary session of the People's Congress, he chose to go on the offensive. On 28 November, a few days after Tommy's statement, Yacob had an even stronger message. Any trial of Soeharto could reveal information about money and property acquired through KKN practices by incumbent and former office holders and their 'cronies'. It could drag down the government. Yacob warned that a trial would be both fatiguing and time-consuming, something Indonesia could ill afford in a time of economic crisis.

The investigation of Soeharto devolved into a tragi-comedy. A week earlier, on 21 November, as a follow-up to the extraordinary session, Akbar Tanjung had announced that an independent committee would be formed to investigate before the end of the month. This, as it was pointed out from various sides, a competent police force and the attorney-general's office could do just as well, though of course there were others who seriously doubted their competence. But in the latter case, it was pointed out by such persons as Amien Rais, the best course of action was to fire Ghalib. The conflict surrounding the team Ghalib had announced in September reared its head again. The authorities were not at all eager to see an independent, active team. Lists of possible members which circulated in society created an uproar, as many on these lists were considered to be guilty of KKN themselves. This was one of the reasons why the plan failed. It prompted some of those invited to sit on it to refuse the honour. Among them were Adnan Buyung Nasution, Mar'ie Muhammad, and Nurcholish Madjid. This forced Habibie to adjust his plans and follow the suggestion of Adnan Buyung Nasution and invite public figures, such as Todung Mulya Lubis, Hoegeng, Ichlasul Amal, and Frans Seda to sit on a really independent committee with full powers to investigate, to summon people to give evidence, to punish them should they refuse to present the information asked, and to seize assets. To speed up the procedure, a Government Regulation in Lieu of an Act was drafted to set up such a commission. The form chosen was extraordinary and testified to the importance attached to the committee. The constitution (Article 22) allowed this sort of sublet to promulgate an act without prior consultation with parliament only in a dire emergency. Muladi was also able to agree. When the plan was being worked out in secret, Akbar Tanjung suddenly divulged that the task of the committee was limited to an investigation and an evaluation of the facts thereby obtained. Akbar Tanjung said it was to be instituted by a presidential decree, which, if this was indeed the intention, would have limited the committee's freedom to act. In the end Habibie backed down. No committee was formed. Wiranto would only consent if the Armed Forces were represented, Ghalib would not agree to a committee which had the same powers as his own office, and Habibie's Islamic advisors also wanted a finger in the pie. On 2 December, the members of the team to be formed assembled at Muladi's house and in vain awaited the announcement of the committee. After a meeting of the cabinet it was announced that the plan was postponed. Adnan Buyung Nasution inferred that it was incorrectly feared the committee would expand its work to officials still in office.[5]

5   Mangoenprawiro 1999:137; *Tajuk*, 10-12-1998:18; interview with Adnan Buyung Nasution in *Forum Keadilan*, 28-12-1998:76-80.

The following day Habibie ordered Ghalib to take 'proactive, effective, and efficient' action immediately in the fight against KKN, without any exceptions, not even the investigation into Soeharto. Later, at the end of the month, Habibie gave Ghalib till the general elections to complete his investigation. Ghalib, using equally brave language, like preventing Soeharto from leaving the country or the city, summoned Soeharto to his office on 4 December. Five days later Soeharto was interrogated for the first time in earnest about his foundations, about Tapos, about Taman Mini, about the Timor car, and about his bank accounts. At one point Soeharto referred to Habibie as the Wapres, the vice president.[6] During his interrogation Soeharto was addressed as *saudara* (brother) and not as *pak* (Sir), which, according to one of the prosecutors, was in accordance with the penal code. During the press conference afterwards, Soeharto was referred to as 'he' or HMS.

By now some of the results of the investigations had been made public. Immediately after the session of the People's Congress it was divulged that after a search at seventy domestic banks it had been discovered that Soeharto held bank accounts to a total value of Rp 21 billion. Soeharto did not deny this. To the editors of *Dharmais* he explained that the money formed his savings from the salaries and retirement pay he had received during his lifetime and from the income of two houses in Jakarta he had rented out to foreigners. Apart from this, the public prosecution had got wind of land owned by Soeharto in Jakarta and Yogyakarta. At the end of the year the Minister of Agriculture, Hasan Basri Durin, disclosed that the Soeharto family controlled 204,983 ha of land, of which only 82 hectares was individually owned; the rest was the property of the firms and corporations of which they sat on the board or held at least 80 per cent of the shares. The figure did not include forest land.

One of the aims of the investigation into Soeharto was to reveal how much of the money of the foundations had been inappropriately used to buy shares and land or to provide cheap loans to companies owned by Soeharto's family and friends. That percentage could be quite high. According to information provided by *Forum Keadilan*, for instance, auditing had shown that only 16 per cent of the money of Yayasan Supersemar had been spent in accordance with the foundation's statutes, of YDSM a little over 18 per cent (*Forum Keadilan*, 14-12-1998:83). In determined efforts to draw the net closer, others were also interrogated. Among them were the treasurers of the Soeharto foundations (including Bambang Trihatmodjo and Siti Hardijanti Rukmana, Bob Hasan (also questioned about the Nusamba concern, the use

---

[6] *Forum Keadilan*, 14-12-1998:84. A transcript of the interrogation was published by the Surabaya daily *Surya*, which also put it on the Internet. From it the weekly *D&R* concluded that the session had been much like a lecture by Soeharto about the Pancasila (*D&R*, 14-6-1999:4).

of reforestation funds, and the use of foundations' funds for Sempati Air[7]),
Moerdiono, and Tunky Ariwibowo (Minister of Industry at the time the idea
of a national car was broached, who had done all he could to convince foreign governments and WTO to accept the preferential treatment given to the
Timor car)). Tunky put the full blame for the Timor car fiasco on Soeharto. He
was the one who had come up with the idea. Hasan mentioned Soeharto as
the *pembina*, the councillor or patron, that is the real boss, of the Nusamba
concern.

In early February, in the midst of all this, a scandal broke loose when *Panji
Masyarakat* published the text of a recording of a mobile telephone conversation between Ghalib and Habibie (*Panji Masyarakat*, 24-2-1999:76). It quoted
Ghalib as saying that Soeharto (referred to as Bapak) had been questioned for
three hours, because had the interrogation been any shorter people might
start to wonder what kind of comedy was being played out. Three hours was
a little on the brief side. Other interrogations lasted much longer. Tommy was
once questioned for twelve hours. Habibie replied that three hours was
indeed enough. People close to Habibie admitted that he thought it possible
that it was his voice on the tape. Ghalib resolutely denied it. It took till May
before he indirectly admitted that the recording might be real (*Panji
Masyarakat*, 26-5-1999:29). The tape undermined the credibility of the government. It casted even more doubts on Habibie's intentions and those of
Ghalib. The feeling was that the investigation was no more than a 'political
play', a subterfuge to lull the student demonstrators persistently demanding
the prosecution of Soeharto. For a moment it appeared that the tape would
put Habibie in a difficult position and that the scandal might be used by his
rivals in Golkar not so much to bring him down, as to prevent the party nominating him as their presidential candidate. This seemed even more likely as
the affair came on top of the negative reaction in Islamic circles towards his
revelation about the troop movements by Prabowo on 22 May the previous
year. Another question in people's minds was the person or persons behind
the making and leaking of the tape which had landed Habibie and Ghalib in
such an awkward position. Baramuli, deputy chairman of the advisory council of Golkar, accused the intelligence community, which could be construed
to include the intelligence section of the office of the attorney-general. They
were the only ones who had technology advanced enough to record such a
conversation. The person who was ultimately to suffer was Syamsu Djalal,

---

7   Bob Hasan, and via him some of Soeharto's foundations, and Hutomo Mandala Putra both
owned one-fifth of the shares of Sempati Air. According to *Tajuk* (19-9-1998:84) the two had
entered Sempati in 1990, after, according to a former president director, the year before Soeharto
had ordered the holding company of Sempati Air, PT Tri Husada Bhakti, that is the army, to sell
some of the shares to them. In the same article Edi Sudradjat (at that time Chief of Staff of the
Army) denies that Soeharto gave such an order.

the former commander of the military police, who had not long before been appointed deputy attorney-general for 'intelligence'. He lost this position after having served in his new post for only five months.

In the middle of April Soeharto once again chose to go on the offensive. A few days after the trial against his son Tommy had started, and one day after Soeharto himself had denied all charges against him in an interview with a Japanese newspaper, one of his lawyers warned that Soeharto had proof of corruption by Habibie and other members of the cabinet. His side would not hesitate to hand over such information were Soeharto to be declared a suspect. People were also quick to assume that the book written by one Servas Mario Patty, and launched at the end of April, about Soeharto's services to the nation fitted neatly into this offensive (Patty 1999). It was followed in May by a second volume, in which his leadership qualities were evaluated very positively. The front cover featured a large portrait of Soeharto. The blurb on the back cover stressed that 11 March 1966 was not a *coup d'état*, and that constitutionally Soeharto could not be tried. In between its two covers the book sings the praise of Soeharto's policy and his clear-sighted ideas about reform. The promise of a third volume, about Soeharto's management qualities, was dangled before the public.

The scandal about the tape was a storm in a teacup compared to the one which was to erupt in June, shortly after Ghalib, who in February had still maintained that an investigation abroad had not revealed any foreign bank account held by Soeharto, and Muladi, on the instructions of Habibie, had visited Austria and Switzerland in search of alleged bank accounts in the name of Soeharto. The journey to Europe by the two had been a consequence of a report in the Asia edition of *Time* magazine of 24 May that, shortly after 21 May the previous year, the Soeharto family had transferred US$ 9 billion from Switzerland to a bank in Austria, a country where bank secrecy was stricter. The *Time* story, which gave details about the property owned by the Soeharto family, caused a great commotion in Indonesia. On 2 June, Soeharto himself went in person to the headquarters of the police to lodge a complaint against *Time*, and once again appeared on TV to deny the allegations. Three days later, when formally filing the lawsuit, his lawyers demanded US$ 27 billion and US$ 40 million as compensation for immaterial and material damages respectively.[8] The news also goaded the public prosecution into action. Not only did Ghalib and Muladi make their European trip, at the end of May and the beginning of June all Soeharto's children were summoned for questioning. Tommy arrived in a Timor. They all denied that there was a grain of truth in the *Time* article.

---

[8]   The court rejected the defamation claim because of lack of evidence in June 2000.

The trip was an example of a spur-of-the-moment decision and bore all the hallmarks of overhasty reaction. As such, it was doomed to fail. The Indonesian government had failed to take the necessary steps to open doors to banks in Switzerland and Austria. It had not brought any formal charges against Soeharto, a prerequisite which had to be observed before Swiss banks reveal information about their clients, and had not asked the Ministry of Domestic Affairs in Vienna for legal assistance, which was an equally indispensable prior step. Ghalib and Muladi did take along a new letter from Soeharto allowing them to open any bank accounts he might have abroad, but this did not carry much legal weight.

On 3 June, while in Austria, Ghalib celebrated his 53rd birthday. Had he stayed in Indonesia, one of his birthday presents would have been the presentation of a book singing his praises. In Jakarta, another less welcome birthday surprise had also been prepared. On 3 June, Teten Masduki of ICW, who on one occasion was to speak of the *kleptokrasi* in Indonesia, called a press conference to disclose that a number of persons had transferred a total amount of Rp 1.8 billion to accounts at Lippo Bank in the name of Ghalib and his wife. ICW had reported this to the military police. Two names were disclosed: that of The Ning King and that of Prajogo Pangestu. At that time both were being questioned for banking fraud. The Ning King had even been forbidden to leave the country, but shortly after he had transferred the money to Ghalib's account, Teten Masduki pointed out later, his request to have the ban lifted was granted.[9] Surely, one of the conclusions the public was bound to draw was that if Ghalib could be bought by businessmen, he certainly could be bought by Soeharto. Ghalib maintained that he was innocent of any corruption. He claimed that the money was intended for the Indonesian Wrestling Association, of which he had become general chairman on 22 March. ICW pointed out that the first payment had been made on 12 February.

Soon reports were rife saying that Ghalib was greedy, and that his wife was a spendthrift. The latter accusation Ghalib refuted out of hand, praising his wife for her fashionable taste and attractive appearance. Ghalib, who had to suffer jokes made by fellow ministers during a cabinet meeting, was furious. He called Teten a coward because he had not come to him first to ask for clarification. Beast was another epithet used by Ghalib to describe Teten, whom he threatened to hound all the way to his grave. Ghalib filed complaint against ICW alleging slander, and threatened to sue Lippo Bank for

---

[9]   A few days after Teten's press conference, the office of the law firm of Todung Mulya Lubis, the legal representative of *Time*, was broken into. The only files to be stolen were related to the Ghalib case, that of *Time*, and that of Arifin Panigoro, an avowed opponent of Habibie who had been accused by the authorities of corruption.

violating bank secrecy. Ghalib pointed out that he had been made to feel
ashamed, referring to *sirik*, a Buginese concept involving hurt feelings and
revenge. This inaugurated a brief discussion of what *sirik* exactly was and
whether Ghalib had been right to use it in this context. People from South
Sulawesi were thrown into a maelstrom of agitation. They visited the residence of both Habibie and Ghalib, some coming out in defence of Ghalib,
some denouncing him for what he had done. Habibie had to send Muladi to
Ghalib's house to calm some of them down.

Initially Ghalib only resigned as chairman of the wrestling association.
Habibie refused point-blank to accept his resignation as attorney-general.
The reaction was widespread condemnation, though, as had become normal
in such circumstances, there were also demonstrations in support of Ghalib.
Habibie gave in on 14 June, when he suspended Ghalib temporarily, replacing him with Feisal Tanjung. A fresh hail of cries of indignation broke over
his head. Habibie was forced to appoint Ismudjoko caretaker attorney-general. An investigation was launched by the military police. Ghalib retaliated
by having his lawyers hand over information to parliament about bank
accounts of five ministers. The balances were said to have been received from
the public, just as ICW had received information about Ghalib's accounts
from the public. Names were not disclosed. On 29 July, it was announced that
the investigation into Ghalib had been stopped, or suspended as it was later
to be called, because of lack of evidence. Ghalib's acquittal, one newspaper
concluded, choosing the heading The Ghalib Case *Aneh* (strange) *bin Ajaib*
(miraculous), was a bad precedent, showing how difficult it still was to bring
members of the élite before court (*Media Indonesia*, 2-8-1999). The police
investigation into the complaint lodged by Ghalib against Teten Masduki
was continued.

A week earlier, on 20 July, Soeharto had suffered a slight stroke and had
been admitted to hospital. Soeharto and his children refused to allow
Habibie to visit him. It was reported that Siti Hardijanti Rukmana invited
five *dukun* to her father's sickbed. The five had indeed been there and had
presented their business cards to the assembled journalists, but Tutut denied
that she or any other of Soeharto's children had asked any such persons to
come. Two days after Soeharto was admitted to hospital, Ismudjoko
announced that on humanitarian grounds the investigation of Soeharto was
to be temporarily suspended. Initially, care was taken to stress that the investigation had not been stopped, but at the end of the month Muladi seemingly went yet further than Ismudjoko. Because of Soeharto's debilitated physical condition, the government would not seek any legal winding up of
Soeharto's case. A political solution was to be sought. Among the persons
firmly opposed to this suggestion was Ismudjoko. He announced that his
office would go on with the investigation. Reacting to the protests the deci-

sion had provoked, Muladi specified that many had misunderstood his words. A political winding-up was not a 'purely political winding-up', but was also based on a legal winding-up, acting upon the results of the investigation so far. This statement was followed by a new one by Muladi on 17 August, in which he said that within seven to ten days a decision would be taken about whether Soeharto was to be prosecuted or not. A week later the final decision was announced for 26 August. On this day the government remained silent.

CHAPTER XIII

Searching for a new political system

Di mana-mana rakyat menjerit
Di mana-mana rakyat menangis
Harga-harga melambung tinggi,
tetapi banyak yang ngomong soal politik
Kami tak butuh partai baru
karena rakyat kecil tak tahu politik
Yang kami tuntut harga sembako turun.[1]

The economic situation Habibie inherited had only grown worse since the onset of the monetary crisis. According to the agreement with IMF of 25 June, 'a very serious crisis' lay in store because of the social and political upheavals in May. The distribution network had been 'badly damaged, economic activity, including exports, generally disrupted, and business confidence severely shaken'. Some forecasts were even more pessimistic than that of IMF. The Indonesian Central Bureau for Statistics predicted that Indonesia's economy would contract by ten per cent in 1998, an economist at the World Bank mentioned a figure of fifteen per cent. Gloomier projections spoke of thirty per cent (*Forum Keadilan*, 24-8-1998:82; Basri 1999:8). It was expected that per capita income would drop from US$ 1,000 before the crisis to US$ 300 by the end of the year (Arryman 1998:117). Foreign investors stayed away, and would continue to do so for a considerable time. The flight of capital was considerable, according to figures from Bank Indonesia between October 1997 and September 1998 amounting to US$ 20.4 billion.[2] Overseas banks continued to refuse to accept Indonesian letters of credit (which many troubled banks no longer could provide even had they wanted to). The refusal hurt the Indonesian industry, as well as those producing for foreign markets

---

[1]   Everywhere the people yell/Everywhere the people cry/Prices skyrocket, but many discuss political problems/ We do not need new political parties because the ordinary people do not give a damn about politics/ What we demand is lower *sembako* prices. Song by a street singer in Jakarta (*Forum Keadilan*, 10-8-1998:92).

[2]   In September 1999 an economic observer at Gadjah Mada University, Tony Prasetiantono, estimated that since 1997 US$ 80 billion had fled Indonesia (*Kompas*, 30-9-1999).

but needing components from abroad. It also made it more difficult for the Indonesian government to import rice.

Domestic trade and industry were fighting for survival. Many companies had stopped paying their domestic and foreign debts. Most of the conglomerates found themselves in dire financial straits. The periodical *Tajuk* spoke sarcastically of *konglomelarat*, impoverished conglomerates, wondering whether there were still even any conglomerates at all (*Tajuk*, 25-6-1998:75). The title of an article in another magazine joked that 'the conglomerates are rich in debts' (*Panji Masyarakat*, 25/4-6-1998:68). The flagships of their concerns were consistently losing money and had run up huge debts: Indofood, Indocement, Astra International, PT Semen Cibinong, the Timor car, and the many banks which come to depend on financial injections by the government were floundering.[3] Many public companies were threatened with delisting. In June and July 1999 a total of 85 companies were put on a watch list by the Jakarta Stock Exchange. This meant that they had been operating at a loss for the last three years and had a net equity of less than Rp 3 billion. Among them were Bank Negara Indonesia and a score of private banks, including Bank Bali, a number of Lippo companies, Bakrie and Brothers, Astra International, Indomobil Sukses International, Citra Marga Nusaphala, and Semen Cibinong.

Speculations about immense domestic and foreign debts were rife. Various lists circulated. According to one of these, published in *Panji Masyarakat* in June, fifty conglomerates had foreign debts exceeding US$ 50 million, five of them more than US$ 1 billion. The champion was Eka Tjipta Widjaja (or Oei Ek Tjong, supposed to be the richest Indonesian after Liem Sioe Liong), whose Sinar Mas concern was said to have a foreign debt of over US$ 4.6 billion. Liem's Salim group was supposed to owe its creditors abroad US$ 3.2 billion, Astra US$ 2.5 billion, Bakrie Brothers US$ 2.3 billion. The list also included the concerns headed by Hashim Djojohadikusumo (US$ 1.8 billion), Bambang Trihatmodjo (US$ 839 million), Bob Hasan (US$ 704 million), Siti Hardijanti Rukmana (US$ 491 million), Arifin Panigoro (US$ 413 million), The Ning King (US$ 351 million), Abdul Latief (US$ US$ 257 million), Timmy Habibie (US$ 220 million), and Hutomo Mandala Putra (US$ 162 million) (*Panji Masyarakat*, 24-6-1998:69).

Between July 1997 and June 1998 in Jakarta alone twelve thousand com-

---

[3]   Astra, which had debts amounting to US$ 1 billion and Rp 1 trillion, had fallen victim to the national car scheme. Not only had the value of its shares plummeted as a consequence of the preferential treatment given the Timor car, allowing Nusamba to acquire one-fifth of the shares (and have Bob Hasan become president commissioner), it had also taken up the challenge that all models of cars with 60 percent domestic components after three years could acquire the appellation national car, borrowing heavily to finance the required investments. See *Far Eastern Economic Review*, 17-12-1998:51-2.

panies had gone bankrupt, about 40 per cent of the total number registered (*Republika*, 15-7-1998). The Indonesian airlines, including the national carrier Garuda, were faced with bankruptcy. Garuda had to abandon six of its ten routes to Europe and return six leased aircraft. Sempati Air had stopped flying at all since 5 June. Reportedly it had run up a debt of US$ 200 million (*The Jakarta Post*, 11-6-1998). Mandala Airlines, jointly controlled by Bob Hasan, Sigit Harjojudanto, and Kostrad, had also gone bankrupt. The same fate threatened state-owned Merpati Nusantara Airlines. A former director of Merpati put part of the blame on the fact that in the past his company had been forced to buy airplanes produced by IPTN (*Tajuk*, 23-12-1998:80-3). Among those who suffered from the economic crisis were also the owners and staff of food stalls (*warteg*). In August almost one-third of the seven thousand *warteg* in Jakarta had already been forced to close down.

Supplies of rice, cooking oil, sugar, and wheat were still a cause of great concern, sharpened by the additional fear that a shortage might manifest itself in November, when the extraordinary session of the People's Congress was to take place; in December, with its festive days; and in January, when the fasting month was to end, a period when prices would invariably rise. In July, in view of the dire food situation, Habibie asked his fellow countrymen to fast on Mondays and Thursdays. He himself had been doing so for years. Habibie praised this as a healthy habit because it encouraged a better blood circulation through the brain. The practice enabled people to accomplish great deeds. What was more, were 150 million Indonesians to fast twice a week, Indonesia would no longer have to import rice. Habibie's suggestion was jeered out of court. People were quick to point out that many Indonesians already had no choice. They were fasting out of sheer economic necessity.

Rice imports had to be stepped up. Because of the prolonged drought, Bulog had only been able to procure 96,500 tons of rice. The supply of rice stocked by Bulog for the whole of the year was estimated at no more than a mere 250,000 tons, at the most 500,000. In the fiscal year 1998/1999 Bulog intended to import 4.1 instead of the originally projected 3.1 million tons of rice.

The atmosphere was not helped by the widely held suspicion that there was something amiss. The government assured the public that there was still enough rice to go around, and produced statistical data to substantiate this claim. Yet supply shortages and high food prices contradicted this assurance. As had been the case in January, the accusation was heard that stocks were being kept back for economic and political reasons. Alluding to such practices, Muladi warned that legislation allowed a death penalty for economic crimes. At the end of September the chief of police was to disclose that his force had confiscated some two million tons of rice in Jakarta and two million tons elsewhere, in its war against hoarders. On top of this, stocks of rice rotting away were discovered in warehouses. Such facts cost the head of Bulog in Jakarta his job. Earlier, on 26 August, his chief, Beddu Amang (also treasurer of ICMI), had been formally sacked on the suspicion of embezzlement; though his downfall might well have been speeded up by a conflict of opinion about who should be Bulog's partners on the supply and distribution side. This controversy, like so many others, had political as well as economic ramifications. In the background loomed the long-standing strife between Ginandjar Kartasasmita and Habibie, but the immediate issue at stake was the redistribution of economic power. For reasons of efficiency, Beddu seems to have been in favour of maintaining old partnerships. The Minister of Cooperative Societies, Adi Sasono, the Minister of Trade and Industry, Rahardi Ramelan, and the Coordinating Minister in this field, Ginandjar Kartasasmita, preferred to replace these contacts (who were often Chinese) by indigenous ones and cooperative societies. As an additional condition, they wanted to ensure that free tenders for the import of, for instance, rice would not result in Cendana-related firms winning the contracts. They were firmly convinced that certain companies had to be excluded from putting in a tender. These tenders turned highly controversial, with contracts for rice imports being won by Hartarto's son-in-law and by a Bakrie company (*Tempo*, 3-10-1998:72; *Far Eastern Economic Review*, 13-5-199:15). For the time being, Bulog was to be managed directly by Rahardi Ramelan. Beddu's sacking immediately made him the target of demonstrations. Amongst the groups out for his blood were HMI students who, to the chagrin of members of the association of HMI alumni, demanded that the association dismiss Beddu Amang, who was chairman of its presidium, and other members guilty of KKN from their ranks.

Because of the rise in food and fuel prices, inflation had reached a level of 40 per cent between January and May 1998. In the same period of the previous year, it had been less than three per cent. At the end of August the inflation rate reached 69 per cent, five percent more than the interest on bank deposits. To lessen the impact on real wages, minimum wages were increased by an average of 15 per cent in August. Unemployment was still growing. The International Labour Organization foresaw that the number of unemployed might increase by another ten million people in 1999 (*Perspektif*, 25-2-1999:11). According to the Central Bureau of Statistics, the number of Indonesians living below the poverty line by September 1998 had reached 79.4 million, or 39 per cent of the total population.[4] It set the country back more than twenty years, to 1976. Were the economic situation not to improve

4   *Tempo*, 12-10-1998. In his accountability speech before the People's Congress in October 1999, Habibie stated that the number of poor people in December 1998 had been 49 million.

it, ILO predicted that in 1999 the figure could well rise to 66 per cent (*Kompas*, 1-9-1998).

Research conducted by the National Family Planning Board established that half of these people, or 40 million Indonesians, were too poor to afford sufficient food of good quality. The Ministry of Labour spoke of 50 million (Subandoro 1999:95). Worrying was the rise in infant mortality and the increase in the number of malnourished babies and children, the victims of the high price of milk. In March 1999 the Minister of Health, Prof. Farid A. Moeloek, disclosed that since the onset of the economic crisis the percentage of children under five years of age suffering from a severe protein deficiency had increased from five to nine percent. Approximately two million children were affected. At that time children had begun to die from malnourishment. Other estimates were much higher. In October 1999 the UNICEF representative for Malaysia and Indonesia, S.J. Woodhouse, said eight million Indonesian children under the age of five were suffering from nutrient deficiency. Farid A. Moeloek and others expressed the fear that a lost generation was being created, people who would suffer for the rest of their lives from the physical and mental consequences of inadequate nourishment in their infancy (*The Jakarta Post*, 6-10-1999). What was feared was, as one Indonesian put it, 'a boom in the stupid generation' (*Republika*, 15-6-1999). Such a prospect had not yet taken into account the many schoolchildren from poor families who without additional financial support were forced to leave school. In June the Coordinating Minister of Public Health estimated their number at between five and six million. He appealed to society at large to donate money to help such children, and announced that the government itself had reserved Rp 2 trillion for this purpose (*Media Indonesia*, 15-6-1999).

Alerted by such warnings, and as a follow-up to the special attention Jakarta and IMF had agreed to pay to the setting up of a Social Safety Net, in July 1998, to help 'people threatened by a food crisis', the government initiated a special programme allowing family heads to buy ten kilos of medium-quality rice per month at the special price of Rp 1,000 per kilo, about one-third of what they would have to pay at the market. In September, it was realized that the sights had to be re-adjusted. Originally intended to help 2 million poor families, the programme was extended to serve 7.5 million families. This was still a moderate target. Within days after the news had been made public, the Minister of Food and Horticulture predicted that 17 million families in Indonesia would face 'food shortages' (*The Jakarta Post*, 14-9-1998). The programme, which was commenced in Jakarta, had to cover the whole of Indonesia by October. In that month the Indonesian government had to launch yet another relief programme to help combat malnourishment of children below the age of two and to provide medical care financed by a loan from the Asian Development Bank. Poor families with children younger than two years of age were given Rp 750 per day to buy food. Pregnant women received Rp 1,000 per day (*Kompas*, 25-10-1998). On top of this came still other programmes to help the poor. Some offered employment, or credit to start a small business. Others handed out additional food to primary schoolchildren and provided grants to schoolchildren who would otherwise have been forced to leave school. As at the outbreak of the crisis, private individuals and domestic and foreign companies arranged for food stalls, where the poor, including students, could buy a cheap meal, or found other ways of distributing cheap food. Among the Indonesian firms was Indofood, which set up a Noodle Concern Programme selling cheap noodles. In Riau food aid was provided by the Singapore Armed Forces.

Such programmes could not prevent impoverished, hungry people looting stores for foodstuffs. What seemed to alarm the authorities in particular was a steep rise in the theft of agricultural produce, such as cacao and coffee in Java, Sumatra, and Sulawesi. In West and East Java the plundering of shrimp ponds occurred with some frequency. Another popular target for plunder was wood. In Blora, teak trees were cut down by a group of about 60 people. Three of them were shot by security forces. In retaliation, houses of forestry personnel were set on fire. A similar incident happened in Jepara. Later it turned out that, at least in Blora and Ngawi, local policemen and soldiers were involved in the theft of teak wood.

Within weeks of Soeharto's resignation, the looting of produce had became so frequent that Wiranto issued a special warning stating that he had instructed local army commanders to take firm action and prosecute the guilty. The new chief of police, Police Lieutenant-General Roesmanhadi, announced that when necessary the police would fire on looters using live ammunition. Initially a more lenient attitude was taken by the Minister of Food and Horticulture, Saefuddin. On 20 July, he stated that he would condone such actions as long as they did not occur on too large a scale, as the people involved in them were driven not by the prospect of financial gain, but by hunger. Instead of adopting a harsh approach, Saefuddin called for 'persuasion', and the involvement of local religious leaders and civil servants in a campaign to prevent a repeat – at least for cases where hunger could be proved to have been the prime motivation. The following day he had to retract his statement. At the end of the month, the first looter of a shrimp pond was shot dead by police in a village in Tangerang. In early September a three-day special police operation against looters of teak wood in Central Java was conducted with such ferocity that people fled from their villages in panic.

Try as they might, army and police could not put an end to the looting or to protests. In the following months the theft of agricultural produce continued, and among the targets were also rice mills and chicken farms. In some instances the crowds completely ignored the warnings of local security troops. They challenged them, jeering at them, disregarding warning shots, even singing and dancing to the tune of the shooting, inviting the troops to continue to fire shots to liven up the atmosphere (*The Jakarta Post*, 18-7-1998; *Tajuk*, 23-7-1998:41). On other occasions people marched en masse to police stations to demand the release of comrades who had been arrested in looting incidents, or threatened to do so if arrests were made. In one case – in Serang on 1 December – it came to an actual exchange between people arrested on the suspicion of having stolen wood and forest policemen held by villagers. These were by no means the only violent confrontations. In February a crowd demanding the release of three people arrested for the theft of latex from a rubber plantation destroyed the main police station in the subdistrict of Tanjungbintang in South Lampung. The following month villagers in Lampung took three policemen and three marines hostage after the rumour spread that during their raid to arrest people suspected of stealing cassava from an estate they had stolen money.

Theft from plantations, or, more radically, occupation of their land and destruction of their products and facilities, assumed such proportions that in June 1999 the Association of Plantation Companies of West Java announced that its members would not pay their taxes and levies as the Armed Forces had failed to protect them. At that time the Director-General of Plantations estimated the damage done in 1998 at Rp 2.6 trillion (*The Jakarta Post*, 15-6-1999).

Coupled with the '*daulat* actions' and with a sharp rise in crime, the looting of produce gave an early indication that the domestic situation was spinning out of control, and that the Armed Forces were no longer capable of maintaining law and order. This came on top of widespread feelings of insecurity, particularly rampant among the Chinese community, brought about by the events leading up to the May riots and the rioting itself. Fearing new disturbances, many women and children remained abroad after May or moved out of Jakarta. Bali became a favourite place of refuge. The island was considered a haven of peace. It continued to hold this reputation in spite of the fact that Bali had its own anti-KKN demonstrations and the occasional public brawl. In August 2000 one estimate had it that since 1997 the population of Bali had increased with fifty per cent because of immigration. After some time, new tensions developed. Local residents began to protest the competition for jobs, especially less affluent Chinese who had recently taken up residence. One of the complaints was that Chinese tourists preferred these new arrivals as guides, because they spoke Mandarin. Elsewhere, ordinary citizens bought firearms and trained themselves to use guns. In the cities, more women saw to it that they had a defensive weapon or gun at hand when they drove through town. Truck drivers, alarmed by the frequent holdups of trucks, also armed themselves. With the riots and demonstrations, and fear of more of the same in the offing, insurance became an expensive item. How afraid people were, or how insecure Indonesia had become, was clearly apparent in January 1999 during the fasting month, when many people visiting their family, in contrast to their wont in previous years, only travelled by car in daylight and avoided secondary roads. Some went by train, afraid of being robbed should they use a private car or take the bus.

Problems for the government were aggravated by the fact that, as a consequence of the high dollar rate, fuel and food subsidies turned out to be far more expensive than had been calculated. Coupled with plummeting tax revenues, the upshot was that Indonesia grew increasingly dependent on foreign loans and aid, now no longer as in the past used for economic development projects, but for routine expenditure. In June the Minister of Mining and Industry, Kuntoro Mangkusubroto, estimated that in the fiscal year 1998/1999 Rp 35 trillion might have to be spent on fuel subsidies, instead of the Rp 9.5 trillion estimated on the basis of an exchange rate of Rp 6,000 to the dollar. At that time, expenditure on rice subsidies had already reached Rp 5.6 trillion, more than the limit of Rp 5.3 trillion the Indonesian government and IMF had agreed upon as the maximum amount of subsidies for the import of basic commodities. Initially subsidies had to be maintained on soya beans and wheat flour as well. These were terminated on 2 September, just before a new IMF agreement was signed on 11 September. As of 1 December, the government annulled the subsidy on fertilizers. Prices doubled, and angry farmers demanded the sale of fertilizers at the old price. After this had led to disturbances in Blora, the provincial military commander urged the government to yield to the farmers' demands. The price rise also sparked off a brief dispute between the ministers of agriculture and trade, the first holding the second responsible for the inexplicable shortage of fertilizers on the market. The only option was to find a way of coping, and so farmers began to use cheaper fertilizers that were slightly less efficacious.

IMF was hesitant about honouring its financial commitment. At the beginning of May it had decided that Indonesia was to receive the second tranche of aid worth US$ 3 billion in three monthly instalments. After the riots later in the month, IMF decided to postpone the transfer of US$ 1 billion scheduled for June. The World Bank and the Asian Development Bank followed suit, delaying the granting of loans to Indonesia. Stunned by this reluctance, 163 members of parliament urged IMF to release the money. When a statement to that effect was presented to the IMF director for Asia and the Pacific, Hubert Neiss, one of those present in the parliament building expressed the hope that IMF would be no NATO, or No Action Talking Only (*Jawa Pos*, 16-6-1998). Amien Rais was equally offended. On 26 June, he refused to receive Hubert Neiss, pointing out that South Korea and Thailand were receiving tens of billions of dollars, while Indonesia had to be content with a mere US$ 1 billion a month. Linking IMF's behaviour to a request by American senators for a referendum in Irian Jaya, Amien Rais voiced the suspicion that IMF was being used by an outside force to stimulate the disintegration of Indonesia. It was only in the middle of July that another US$ 1 million was disbursed. At the end of the month the Consultive Group on Indonesia (CGI), the consortium of donor countries, committed themselves to loans worth a total of US$ 7.9 billion, US$ 2.6 billion more than the previous year. To keep the production of books going, the Ford Foundation allocated US$ 400,000.

A small ray of relief had appeared a little earlier on 4 June in Frankfurt when an agreement was reached with the thirteen major foreign creditor banks about the rescheduling of Indonesia's private foreign debts which would fall due in 1998.[5] At that moment the amount was estimated at between US$ 29.2 and US$ 34 billion. One of the aims of the accord was to relieve pressure on the rupiah by facilitating a rescheduling of debts. Corporate debts were given a roll-over of up to eight years, with a period of grace of three years for the repayment of the principal, provided that the Indonesian companies concerned resumed loan payments. The instalments could be paid monthly in rupiahs through the mediation of an Indonesian Debt Restructuring Agency (INDRA), which would pay the creditors in dollars. In October, foreign debts which had to be repaid before the end of 1998 were estimated by INDRA to amount to US$ 20 billion. At that moment, foreign exchange reserves had shrunk to US$ 14 billion. INDRA, established to cater for those companies which were still viable and had reached an agreement with their creditors about the redemption of their debts, proved a failure. None of the roughly two thousand companies with foreign debts turned to it for mediation. In November, after it had become clear that INDRA had failed, the 'Jakarta Initiative' was organized. This was a conference to bring together Indonesian companies and their foreign debtors. The outcome was the setting up of a special task force to facilitate out-of-court corporate debt settlement. The Jakarta Initiative was better received than INDRA. Before the end of the month, 52 companies had joined the new scheme for the restructuring of their debt obligations. In June 1999 the chairman of the Jakarta Initiative, Jusuf Anwar, revealed that it was involved in the restructuring of 28 per cent of private foreign debts, the total of which was now estimated to be US$ 65 billion.[6] In that same month, in an attempt to facilitate debt-to-

---

[5]   In March 1999 an agreement was reached between the Indonesian government and thirteen foreign banks on the restructuring of the debts of Indonesian banks.
[6]   *Forum Keadilan*, 20-6-1999:17. In October new figures were provided. 284 companies had sought the help of the Jakarta Initiative. Their total debt was US$ 23.2 billion and Rp 15.6 trillion. 27 firms had concluded a debt restructuring agreement by that time (*The Jakarta Post*, 9-10-1999).

equity swaps, the Indonesian government allowed foreign companies to establish holding companies or to acquire a hundred per cent stake in domestic ones.

There was also a reprieve for government debts. At the end of September, at Jakarta's request, Indonesia's major creditor nations, united in the Paris Club, allowed a rescheduling of the US$ 4.2 billion Indonesia was due to pay on its government debt between August 1998 and March 2000. The only fly in the ointment was Japan, a country in principle against giving fresh loans to countries receiving debt relief from it. Tokyo refused a roll-over, but promised Indonesia a new loan to be able to meet its financial obligations.

In this picture of unremitting gloom, it was easy to overlook that there was another side to the coin. The crisis also generated unexpected wealth. Though non-oil and gas exports experienced a drop due to the crisis, those who could still cater for the foreign market, including small and large producers of export crops such as rubber, wood, and pepper, experienced golden times because of the fall of the rupiah. The weakness of the rupiah meant that when they had a choice between selling on the domestic or the foreign market, their preference went to the latter, leading to a greater scarcity at home, a notable instance being palm oil, the basic ingredient of cooking oil.

Politically, Habibie's position was not easy either. His taking over the presidency had not halted the demonstrations and protests. The 'Reformation Order' which had come into being was not much more than the New Order minus the Soeharto family. By and large, the old political and bureaucratic structures had survived. The other leaders were still in place, while Habibie himself was too much a representative of the old regime to be trusted to carry through the 'total reform' people were talking about. For years he had been the *anak mas*, the protegé of Soeharto, his closest associate, and would never have become president had not Soeharto selected him as his deputy. One of his critics, Soebadio Sastrosatomo, formulated this metaphorically by saying Habibie was 'the little dictator rocked by his father, the great dictator'. He was the 'most loyal and perfect product and epigone of Soeharto' (Sastrosatomo 1998:7, 26).

As the developments surrounding the investigation into Soeharto's wealth showed, Habibie's past made him vulnerable to attacks, not least by the Soeharto camp. In September, Probosutedjo, for instance, tried to argue that it was not Soeharto who had Habibie eating out of his hand, but the reverse. What country, he asked, would start an aircraft factory before it was capable of doing so (*Media Indonesia*, 5-9-1998)? Apart from disliking Habibie and ICMI, others considered him nothing but a marionette in Soeharto's hand, and a tried and tested exponent of corruption, collusion, and nepotism, through whom Soeharto continued to pull the strings.

The same feelings were fostered with respect to Wiranto and his fellow officers. Though the Armed Forces had not cracked down on the student movement, as they finally had done in 1974 and 1978 after months of massive student protest, and through his calls in April and early May for a dialogue and for gradual reforms, Wiranto had taken an accommodating attitude towards the protests, he, too, was seen as a person through whom Soeharto might continue to rule from behind the scenes, and might even try to plan a comeback. People could not forget that Wiranto had been one of Soeharto's adjutants, who had reached the position he held thanks to the former president. Wiranto headed an officers' corps which not so long before had been regarded as loyal to Soeharto.

Compounding such misgivings was the knowledge that the top army brass had remained on a cordial footing with Soeharto. Some generals visited him regularly, and on 8 June were present at a small, exclusive party to celebrate Soeharto's birthday. Habibie was not welcome, according to Probosutedjo because Soeharto did not want to put Habibie in a compromising situation. The actual reason went deeper. Soeharto believed that Habibie, who himself never grew tired of expressing his admiration for Soeharto, had betrayed him. These cordial relations with the Armed Forces were made all the more conspicuous at the end of the month when Soeharto performed Friday prayers at the headquarters of the Military Command of Jakarta, the army, and the Armed Forces. Army officers were quick to stress that there was nothing behind such contacts. All was simply an indication of the respect officers still felt for a former superior.

Among the accusations Wiranto found himself having to deny was that the Armed Forces had allowed the student demonstrations to continue after Soeharto's fall in order to benefit from the resulting chaos and then take the opportunity to seize the upper hand, or to use them as a warning to Habibie that he was dependent on the Armed Forces for his protection. By the middle of June, these sorts of speculations had reached such proportions that Wiranto was forced to ask the Indonesian press to publish his denial prominently on the front page. Wiranto also had to underline on no less than three occasions – on 21 May, 3 June, and 11 June – that the Armed Forces supported Habibie's government and its reformation agenda. The last occasion was probably the most important one. On that day Wiranto presented Habibie with the Armed Forces' view of the reforms they considered necessary, the conclusions reached by the Yudhoyono team that had been formed in early May. It was a grand event, attended by more than 150 senior officers. Among them was Prabowo, who was allocated a seat in the back row. In its evaluation of the domestic situation, the leadership of the Armed Forces had come to the conclusion that the main reason underlying the crisis was that too much attention had been paid to the economic development of Indonesia and too little to political and legal reforms (see *ABRI* 1998). Among the evils blamed for the wrongs of the day were the lack of transparency in the decision-making process, the absolute dominance of Golkar and the concomitant unwillingness to comply to popular demands for greater political participation, and an electoral system that produced weak representative bodies which were no match for the strong executive. A similar imbalance was observed in the relationship between Jakarta and the regions. The latter had suffered under what was castigated as a 'neo-feudalistic centralistic' relationship (*ABRI* 1998:7). Consequently, part of the 'total reform' proposed by the Armed Forces consisted of measures to curb the powers of the president, and to set in motion the amendment to the five political acts. Other suggestions were to change the legislation on subversion, the press act, the land reform act, and the legislation covering the relationship between the centre and the regions. The Armed Forces also expressed support for new acts on the freedom of association and expression, on human rights, and on monopolies and cartels. The report also spoke out in favour of the ratification of the international human rights conventions. Finally, it was suggested that steps be taken to bring about a change in mentality by intensifying the National Discipline Movement, which was close to Wiranto's heart. This could be strengthened by the establishment of a National Efficiency Movement and a revival of the Live Simply Movement. Love of the rupiah and of domestic products should be promoted as well.

Had Habibie hoped, on 21 May, that he could stay in office for five years (minus the two-and-a-half months Soeharto had served as president), such hopes were immediately dashed. Those not pleased with him but still not rejecting his presidency outright were inexorable that in their view Habibie's government was only transitional and that it would be inconceivable for him to remain in office for a longer period. An early general election was to be the touchstone to bring someone to the fore whom the majority of Indonesians could accept as their president. In the eyes of many who threw themselves wholeheartedly behind this, that person was not Habibie. Consequently, in the days following the resignation of Soeharto, 'general elections as soon as possible' remained the slogan on everybody's lips. On 27 May, bowing to such ineluctable pressure, Habibie and Harmoko agreed on a general election in 1999. A few days later, Habibie presented a timetable. Before the end of the year it would be necessary for an extraordinary session of the People's Congress to convene, after which general elections could be held in May 1999. The People's Congress had to meet not to call Soeharto to account for what had happened between March and the end of May, as some wanted, or to elect a new president, as was high on the agenda of others, but simply to revise its regulations related to the general election.

Those who opposed Habibie as the successor to Soeharto made an extraordinary session of the People's Congress at an even earlier date their principal demand. During such a session, they argued, the People's Congress should revoke its decision to elect Soeharto and Habibie formally, and thus also replace Habibie as president, for instance by setting up a presidium. Among the persons who put forward this sort of argument were Rudini, the retired officers who had joined forces in May, Hariadi Darmawan of Iluni UI, and Subroto, in his capacity as chairman of a (Forum) Gerakan Reformasi Nasional (GRN), or (Forum of) the National Reformation Movement.[7]

To substantiate their rejection of Habibie, such people generally pointed out that the resignation of Soeharto and the swearing in of Habibie had not followed the letter of the law. Their main argument was based upon two decrees ratified by the People's Congress in 1973. One mentioned that the People's Congress could discharge a president in three situations: at his own request, if he was permanently unable to perform his duties, or if he had acted in contravention of the Broad Outlines of State Policy. The other decree stipulated that before automatically becoming president a vice-president should have been sworn in before parliament. The relevant article in the constitution to which Soeharto had referred in his resignation speech stated that when a president resigned he would be succeeded by the vice-president for the rest of his term. It did not go into detail about how the transfer should take place.[8] One additional argument fielded was that a president who had received his mandate from the People's Congress had to return it to this institution, or have it withdrawn by it.[9] Some wanted to move fast. On 1 June,

---

[7]   The Presidium of this National Reformation Movement included Mrs Supeni, Ali Sadikin, Frans Seda, Kemal Idris, Bambang Triantoro, Awaluddin Djamin, Hasnan Habib, Sri Edi Swasono, Kharis Suhud, Dimyati Hartono, Ir Sanusi, Jacob Tobing, Sabam Sirait, Matori Abdul Djalil, and Julius Usman.

[8]   Soeharto and his legal advisors had realized the legal problems. It was one reason for Soeharto to take, as it was formulated, a 'unilateral decision' and to state that he had decided to resign. Had he asked to be relieved of his office or been asked by others to go, this would have required a follow-up. They also argued that the swearing in of Habibie before parliament was impossible because of the occupation of the parliament building by the students and the fact that 21 May was a holiday. According to the decree of the People's Congress, under such circumstances the swearing in had to take place in front of the Supreme Court. The chairmen of parliament had proposed a swearing in of Habibie on 22 May, and in fact had already begun to prepare for this, but that alternative was turned down in order to avoid the creation of a power vacuum. Everything indicates that Soeharto chose 21 May to avoid any turmoil in the People's Congress or parliament. See for instance Mahendra (1999) and *DPR* (1998:36, 95-101).

[9]   At the end of May, more than fifty lawyers from the Team to Defend Indonesian Democracy began a court case against the chairmen of the People's Congress, its five party groups, Soeharto and Habibie, disputing the legality of the general session of the People's Congress. They argued that because of the fact that most of its members had been appointed, its composition was therefore in violation of the constitutional stipulation that sovereignty was in the hands of the people. Consequently all its decisions were invalid. A compensation of Rp 15 trillion was demanded to be spent for the promotion of democracy and human rights. Around the same time 51 lawyers united in Persatuan Pengacara Reformasi Indonesia (PPRI), Union of

Forum Pemurnian Kedaulatan Rakyat (FPKR), Forum for Full People's Sovereignty, which featured among its leaders Deliar Noer and Abdul Madjid (a former rival of Ismail Hasan Metareum in the contest for leadership of PPP), urged for the calling of an extraordinary session in July at the latest. Three days later a delegation from Gerakan Reformasi Nasional (Subroto, Dimyati Hartono, and Selo Soemardjan) asked for an extraordinary session in June.

Others gave Habibie the benefit of the doubt. Amien Rais, who rejected an invitation from Habibie to become chairman of the Supreme Advisory Council, appealed to all sides, including those who disputed Habibie's swearing in, to exercise restraint and allow Habibie to concentrate on improving the economic situation. He and Emil Salim initially gave Habibie's cabinet six months to prove itself. Amien Rais – and he was not the only one – opposed a session of People's Congress called for the specific purpose of replacing Habibie, not because Habibie had his unreserved support, but because he feared that since the People's Congress was composed as it was, such an event might be used to pave the way for another unacceptable person, maybe even an associate of Soeharto, to become president. Those mentioned most often in this respect were Edi Sudradjat, Try Sutrisno, and Soedharmono. For a similar reason, Amien Rais rejected the option of a presidium. Trying to compose such an institution would only lead to new conflicts and demonstrations.

The most vocal and most radical group in expressing its opposition to Habibie was the students. As events at the end of the occupation of the parliament building had indicated, they disagreed among themselves about the strategy to be followed and the attitude to be adopted towards the new government. KAMMI was prepared to give Habibie a chance, but FKSMJ and Forum Kota would not have him and continued to protest. Before the end of May, FKSMJ issued a statement in which it called for an extraordinary session of the People's Congress, cleansed of KKN elements, to discharge Soeharto and Habibie and to call Soeharto to account. Outside Jakarta, students showed that they were of like mind. They marched to the representative bodies to demand the resignation of Habibie and an extraordinary session of the People's Congress. At such a session either a new transitional president with limited tenure or a presidium had to be elected; in both cases the main task of whoever was chosen would be to prepare a general election.

Forum Kota was even more radical. It demanded a Komite Rakyat Indonesia (KRI), Indonesian People's Committee. Two reasons were ad-

---

Indonesian Reformation Lawyers, began a court case against Soeharto and the chairpersons of the People's Congress for having transferred the presidency to Habibie unlawfully. They demanded a compensation of seven rupiah.

vanced to justify this demand. The first was that the sitting People's Congress did not reflect the aspirations of the people, as it was composed of appointed members and members who had been elected on the basis of a 'deformed general election'. The second was that the transfer of the presidency to Habibie had been unconstitutional, and that Habibie himself was a prime example of all that had been wrong in Soeharto's New Order. The job of the committee would be to act as a provisional government and take the place of the People's Congress till a new one had been elected in a truly democratic way. It would have to revise or abolish the disputed political legislation, and prepare for the holding of a general election. In the opinion of the Forum Kota students, an Indonesian People's Committee was the only way to assure a total departure from Soeharto's New Order. They argued that they had learned their lesson from the student movement in 1966, when the students had been satisfied with the fall of President Soekarno. They had given no thought, or not enough thought, to the question of how to prevent economic and political abuses in future (Abdullah 1998:51). The Forum Kota students remained vague about how an Indonesian People's Committee should be elected. As a moral force it was not their task to ponder the nitty-gritty of this.

Almost from the day Habibie had been sworn in, the ongoing student protests worried the new government. On 4 June, at a meeting of rectors of institutions of higher education, Habibie asked the participants to remind their students that they should end their political activities. Students should return to the campus, as their protests were threatening the livelihood of the rest of the population. A week later, on 11 June, Wiranto appealed to them to end political activities and to support the government in its efforts to overcome the economic crisis. He announced that he had instructed regional commanders to take action against groups which, sheltering under the guise of reformation, acted unconstitutionally. There was no absolute freedom. Referring to excessive demonstrations outside Jakarta, farmers occupying land, the looting of crops, and demands for the resignation and trial of local officials guilty of KKN, Wiranto pointed out that these incidents would endanger stability and the legitimation of the government were they to continue.

Student demonstrations were tolerated. Less lenience was shown by the Armed Forces towards agitation among the labour force. The number of strikes by labourers demanding better working conditions and a pay rise to compensate for the increasingly high cost of living swelled immediately after May. According to the Ministry of Labour, there had been 83 strikes in June alone (*Far Eastern Economic Review*, 17-6-1999:22). Such strikes were still quickly stifled, at times harshly so. The Armed Forces reacted equally uncompromisingly towards plans drawn up by Pakpahan and SBSI to organize a mass labour demonstration in Jakarta on 24 June. After originally announcing a demonstration of one hundred thousand, Pakpahan had offered a peaceful demonstration in which ten thousand people would participate to underline his demand that the People's Congress should convene as soon as possible to replace Habibie and constitute a provisional government. In early July such activities earned Pakpahan a warning from the Minister of Justice, Muladi, who unhesitatingly ventured to suggest the possibility of a new arrest if Pakpahan violated the law.

On 1 July, in an effort to control the domestic situation and to curb the rash of demonstrations, Wiranto presented Habibie with a draft of a Freedom of Expression Bill, defining the limits within which street protests could be staged. On 24 July, at a moment when parliament was in recess, a Government Regulation in Lieu of a Law was issued. Signed by Habibie, it was based on Wiranto's draft. It became effective as of that day. The regulation required that a permit be obtained for demonstrations in which more than fifty people participated. If this number was not exceeded, notification of the police sufficed. In practice it might be thought it would be difficult to keep the number of demonstrators within this limit, but Muladi did not foresee any problems, or pretended not to. When others wanted to join a small demonstration, its organizers could simply ask them not to do so (*The Jakarta Post*, 25-7-1998).

To justify the issuing of the Government Regulation in Lieu of a Law, government officials reiterated what had been stated in the preamble of the regulation about the wave of seemingly uncontrollable demonstrations taking place that minute all over Indonesia, right down to the village level. These, it was posited, formed a threat to national unity, and often led to senseless destruction, arson, and looting, causing material and immaterial damage and generating a feeling of insecurity. In all probability, though both Syarwan Hamid and Muladi denied this, the speed with which the government acted was inspired by the desire to prevent plans being forged by Megawati's PDI to commemorate the attack on their headquarters on 27 July 1996 by holding a mass meeting in Senayan Stadium. When permission was refused, a surrogate ceremony at Megawati's house was held instead. Except for Yogyakarta, where supporters of PDI and PPP clashed, it remained quiet on 27 July.

Immediately dubbed 'controversial' and linked to the practices of the Soeharto regime, the new regulation elicited a storm of opposition from demonstrating students, the National Committee for Human Rights, and others, all of whom were not so convinced that, as the government argued, it was an emergency situation justifying the issuing of a Government Regulation in Lieu of a Law. Among the articles most disputed was one which included dissemination through print and electronic mass media among the forms of public expressions of opinion, which therefore had to be reported to the police three days in advance. The inclusion would have given the police the authority to act on such manifestations, thereby opening the door wide for press censorship. Muladi and Habibie both admitted they did not know how this stipulation had found its way into the regulation. The blame fell on the Ministry of Defence, from which the first draft had come, but it turned out that haste was the real culprit. The disputed text had been inserted by Bambang Kesowo, deputy secretary to the cabinet, in an effort not only to cover demonstrations, but also to be able to deal with incitement by pamphlets and documents circulated on the Internet. Bambang Kesowo had only received the draft around midnight of the day before Habibie had to sign the regulation, and his mind was distracted by preparations for the marriage of one of his children. This 'fatal mistake' cost him his job. As usual in such cases, any causal link was denied. Government spokesmen presented his dismissal as having been planned some time earlier.[10] In a climate in which distrust ruled the roost, Bambang Kesowo was even questioned by Bakin on the suspicion that he might have inserted the phrase on purpose in an effort to discredit Habibie (Tanuredjo 1999:25-8).

After a shaky start, the regulation seemed doomed to failure and indeed did not make it. The constitution stipulates that such a regulation needs the approval of parliament in the body's next session. Even before the parliamentary debate had been begun, the regulation was put on ice. On 13 August, due note having been taken of the many protests, it was decided to postpone implementation until parliament had pronounced its opinion. This happened after the Supreme Advisory Council had met with representatives of the National Committee for Human Rights, at which Muladi and Roesmanhadi were also present. At the end of the following month, when it looked like parliament would reject the regulation, Wiranto announced that the government would withdraw it. His statement was greeted with loud applause. When some adjustments had been made, the regulation was immediately reintroduced as an ordinary bill. The disputed censorship clause had been dropped, while the minimum number of people participating in a demonstration requiring permission was put at one hundred. Sanctions were added against those who, by force or threat of force, tried to prevent demonstrations which met the conditions of the act. Again haste was made, cutting short the procedure of parliamentary debate. At the end of October the bill was accepted. Permits were no longer needed. Notification of the police in writing three days in advance was all that was required. No notification was required for scholarly meetings at universities or for religious gatherings. Wiranto was pleased, praising the members of parliament for their positive and constructive contribution and for having put national interests above their own personal or group interests. The government considered the act

---

[10]   Muladi to Kesowo 16-9-1998 (Tanuredjo 1999:49).

important enough to have its major points disseminated through advertisement in newspapers and displayed on banners in the streets. The act was issued just in time for the extraordinary session of the People's Congress. Students made its repeal one of their demands. Though the act proved ineffective – almost nobody took the trouble to notify the police in advance of a demonstration, or if they did made a mockery of such a condition – it did give the authorities the legal means to act against some of their fiercest critics.

All this happened at a moment when the political landscape was changing fast. The new freedoms to organize meant that old mass organizations, which had been forced to disband or had been unable to function under the New Order, reemerged. One of these was Himpunan Kerukunan Tani Indonesia (HKTI), Indonesian Farmers' Association, which was revived by Soekarno's daughter, Rachmawati. Developments in the political field were even more lively, with a multitude of new parties being established.

One of the parties to suffer most from the new circumstances was Golkar. In the days immediately before and after Soeharto's fall, some Golkar members had started to defect. One of them was Mien Sugandhi, who at the end of May announced that MKGR, which she claimed had 25 million members, as it was indeed to do, would transform itself into a political party. The image of Golkar was bad. As a member of a Team of Golkar's Saviours, Iskandar Mandji, vividly expressed the situation, it was well known that the Golkar representations in parliament and the People's Congress were 'a viper's nest of collusion and nepotism' (*The Jakarta Post*, 3-6-1998). Having provided its government with political legitimation, Golkar was now blamed for the wrongs of the New Order. Demonstrators demanded Golkar's dissolution and carried around posters bearing texts like 'The present national disaster is the responsibility of Golkar'. In the eyes of its critics it did not help that Golkar, disregarding the pleas of Marzuki Darusman and some others of its leading politicians to do otherwise, refused to issue an official apology for the role Golkar had played in the New Order and for the responsibility it shared for the economic crisis, preferring to put the blame on an all-powerful Soeharto, and to regard the economic crisis as having been brought on by external factors beyond the control of the Indonesian government. It was also argued that an apology would not solve any problems. It was more important that past mistakes were corrected. Another blow was that *reformasi* meant that Golkar, in theory at least, could no longer count on the backing of regional military and civil servants, whose support and mental and physical force had been instrumental in achieving Golkar's earlier election results.

Soerjadi's PDI had survived reformation, leading to the joke that when the crunch came, Soerjadi was more powerful than Soeharto. Soeharto had been forced out of office, Soerjadi had escaped this fate. With Syarwan Hamid as

Minister of Internal Affairs, his group was still recognized by the government as the legal PDI. The only concession made was to acknowledge that the two PDIs each had a right to exist, a policy initially rejected by Megawati and other members of her board. They continued to stress that hers was the only true PDI. To underline this stance, since May Megawati avoided meeting Habibie. Megawati declined a number of invitations by Habibie. Among these was an invitation to attend the official Independence Day celebration. Haryanto Taslam stated that Megawati wanted to meet Habibie only in her capacity as chairwoman of PDI. At the end of June 1999 the two still had not met.

At the end of August 1998, with the consent of the government, Soerjadi held a PDI congress in Palu in Central Sulawesi. Though Palu was far away from Java, it did not save Soerjadi and his associates from harassment by Megawati supporters. The latter travelled to Sulawesi intent on making the congress a failure, or, by guarding seaports and airports, tried to prevent Soerjadi supporters from leaving Java and entering Sulawesi. Those politicians of the Soerjadi PDI who made it to Sulawesi were greeted with threatening texts, such as 'Welcome to Palu, a mass grave has been prepared for you' (Adil, 26-8-1998:14). Many regions sent no delegates to Palu. In most of these, the branches had joined the Megawati camp. Other delegates were hesitant to attend, fearing for their safety. As expected, the atmosphere in Palu was tense. The congress, which was opened by Syarwan Hamid who read a message from Habibie, was overshadowed by an atmosphere of violence. Fighting erupted between guards of Soerjadi's PDI, Megawati supporters, and security forces.

Before it was held, there were some who hoped that the congress would end the conflict within PDI. One option was that Soerjadi's PDI could change its name to PNI. Another option was the election of Megawati as general chairwoman. The latter possibility presented itself because Soerjadi had decided not to run for the general chairmanship. Directly after the general election, which had been so disastrous for his PDI, various of its leaders had already called for his resignation. At that time Soerjadi had refused, but he had announced he would not seek re-election. In Palu there were delegates who put forward Megawati as the new party leader. For technical reasons (she was not present and had not signed a form stating her willingness to be elected) their suggestion was ignored. Disappointed delegates 'walked out'. The new general chairman was Budi Hardjono, Megawati's main rival for this post when she was elected general chairwoman of PDI in 1993. Symptomatic of the fate of Budi Hardjono's PDI was what happened when he wanted to fly back to Java. After having taken their seats, he and other PDI politicians had to leave the plane again, to make room for a group accompanying the director-general for social and political affairs of the Ministry of

Internal Affairs. A booking error was blamed for this misfortune.

Budi Hardjono refused to disband his PDI, withstanding pressure from Megawati supporters who pelted his house with stones and threatened to wield 'terror' tactics by visiting members of the new PDI board to force them to sign a statement saying that they resigned from their position (*Kompas*, 1-9-1998). For his part, and in accordance with one of the decisions agreed upon at Palu which had called for a reconciliation, Budi Hardjono turned to Abdurrahman Wahid seeking his mediation. After consulting Megawati, the latter refused.

Megawati's PDI fared much better. Partly because she was a daughter of her father, and partly because she had been an unquestionable victim of New Order machinations, she could count on wide popular support. Her many followers were extremely loyal to her. The word *fanatik* was used to describe this. The massive support she could muster in many places was very visible, initially through the many Posko PDI Perjuangan – leaving it to people to guess whether the abbreviation meant command (*pos komando*) or coordination post (*pos koordinasi*) – advertising their existence with banners, and later through the great many PDI flags hoisted. After May her party was given an additional boost. Many people wanted to join her ranks. Retired officers of the army and of the marines became members as well. Most conspicuous among them were a number of retired army generals, including Major-

A Posko PDI (photo *Tempo*)

General (Ret.) Theo Syafei (a former Golkar member, who during his military career had served as commander for operations in East Timor) and Major-General (Ret.) Raja Kami Sembiring Meliala (a former military commander of Irian Jaya). Jacob Tobing, a former chairman of Golkar, Julius Usman of PUDI, and Hasyim Wahid, a brother of Abdurrahman Wahid, also joined up.

The influx of such members at the end of September and the beginning of October, some of whom were presented during special ceremonies with a red vest bearing Megawati's portrait, formed welcome publicity at a moment when the authorities made no secret of the fact that they still recognized the rival camp as the legal PDI. Not only had the government not objected to the Palu congress, initially it refused to grant permission for Megawati's PDI to hold a congress of its own in Bali planned for 8-10 October. Roesmanhadi was prepared to allow this to go ahead only if Megawati's PDI changed its name. The response was to point out that only a national congress could decide to do so. What was more, as Kwik Kian Gie stated, the party did not need recognition by the government. What counted was the support of the people. Megawati's PDI was backed in this by the retired officers, who had united in their opposition against Soeharto in May, and by Budi Hardjono, who stated he did not mind that there were two parties with the same name. Budi Hardjono also asked his own supporters not to interrupt the Bali congress. At last, a week before the opening of the congress, Wiranto gave his permission. The condition was that the party had to ensure the smooth running of the congress.

Beforehand Megawati had appealed to her followers not to travel to Bali en masse. Her plea was ignored. People flocked to Bali by the tens of thousands, many travelling in motorized convoys of cars, buses, trucks, and motorcycles. Megawati's open-air address, with which she opened the congress, one of her few public appearances, was attended by approximately 50,000 people. Conspicuously present were Kemal Idris, Sarwono Kusumaatmadja, Ali Sadikin, Edi Sudradjat, Hariadi Darmawan, Frans Seda, and Arifin Panigoro. In her speech Megawati paved the way for a change of name, calling the congress a gathering of the Partai Demokrasi Indonesia Perjuangan (PDI-P). Though not everybody wholeheartedly supported the proposal, as it implied a recognition of Budi Hardjono's PDI, the legality of which had been denied right from the start and had been contested in so many court cases, the congress accepted the new name. Megawati and Alex Litaay (originating from the Protestant Parkindo) were re-elected as general chairwoman and secretary-general. Theo Syafei and Dimyati Hartono became two of its chairmen. All had gone peacefully, giving a lie to rumours that the congress would end in violence because of plans being concocted by outsiders to 'criminalize' PDI-P. The only ripple was caused by representatives from East Timor and the Eastern Sunda Islands who had threatened that, if the congress did not confer the status of presidential candidate on Megawati, and also if she failed to become president, the two provinces would declare themselves independent. The statement caused some shockwaves. Members of Megawati's board hastened to explain that such statements had been 'emotional'. Afterwards Syarwan Hamid tried to get his own back by warning that a leader should be more than a charismatic figure, alleging that such persons often tended to act in an authoritarian way – an assessment other political enemies of hers were to repeat as her chances of becoming the next president grew.

When it was first announced that people would be free to found political parties warnings were sounded from various sides, pointing out that the establishment of a great many political parties could endanger national unity and could well lead to an upswing of particularistic sentiments and the revival of Old Order political practices. Indonesia should not repeat the mistake of the 1950s when scores of political parties had been founded. The appeals fell on deaf ears. Parties which had announced their existence in the Soeharto era, though at that time they were still considered illegal, including PUDI of Sri Bintang Pamungkas and Masyumi Baru (Masyumi in this case standing for Masyarakat Umat Muslimin Indonesia) of Drs H. Ridwan Saidi, strove for formal recognition. A plethora of new parties was announced, while PDI and PPP did not succeed in keeping together the various elements of which they were comprised.[11] Former parties which had been forced to delegate their political activities to these two at the beginning of the New Order re-emerged: IPKI, Murba (now standing for Musyawarah Rakyat Banyak or People's Conference, with Mrs Nelly Adam Malik as chairwoman of the Advisory Council), and PSII. Of the latter, there were even two off-shoots: the PSII chaired by H. Taufik R. Tjokroaminoto (which had registered first) and the PSII 1905 chaired by Drs KH Ohan Sudjana.

The larger components of PDI and PPP had the same amount of trouble in trying to maintain unity. Though PDI drew much of its following from the electorate of the former PNI, new PNIs were founded. At one point there were even four of this name, chaired respectively by Ms Supeni (hence called PNI-Supeni, founded on 20 May 1998, and supported among other persons by Prof. Usep Ranuwidjaja and Sukmawati Soekarnoputri as chairpersons); by Bachtiar Oscha Chalik (later called the PNI-Massa Marhaen, founded on 22 May); by Irawan Sunaryo (founded on 4 August); and by Probosutedjo (who succeeded in defeating Rachmawati Soekarnoputeri in the contest for the general chairmanship of the PNI-Front Marhaenis, founded in February 1999). Besides these four, Partai Nasional Demokrat (which was to present

11   See for the programs and leadership of the parties Mustaib and Basumin (1999), *Profil* (1999), Suryakusuma et al. (1999), and Wangge (1999).

Guntur Soekarnoputra as its presidential candidate), Partai Rakyat Marhaen (which had Soenardi as general chairman and Mrs Rahmi Hatta as one of its chairpersons), and Partai Mega Bintang (of which the founders intended to nominate Megawati's brother, Guntur Soekarnoputra, as presidential candidate) were founded, all catering for the groups from which PNI had drawn its strength in the past. Not all were to participate in the elections, but of the 48 parties which did, six displayed the head of the wild bull as their party symbol.

Within the ranks of the Islamic community, traditionalists as well as modernists established their parties. Nahdlatul Ulama and Muhammadiyah did not transform into political parties, but, in spite of calls from various sides not to weaken the Islamic community by the establishment of too many parties, Islamic leaders could not resist the temptation to found a variety of parties. Among NU circles, by far the most important initiative was the establishment of Partai Kebangkitan Bangsa (PKB), Party of the Awakening of the Nation, proclaimed in the house of Abdurrahman Wahid on 23 July. Very conspicuously present at the meeting to which many Chinese Indonesians had also been invited were Try Sutrisno and Edi Sudradjat, praised on this occasion by Abdurrahman Wahid as leaders who truly thought 'nationally' (Muhammad 1998:9). Pictures in Indonesian newspapers showed them flanking Abdurrahman Wahid.

Matori Abdul Djalil was appointed general chairman of PKB. He was secretary-general of YKPK and a former secretary-general of PPP from the ranks of NU. In 1994 he had tried in vain to take over the leadership of PPP from Ismail Hasan Metareum. His appointment did not go uncontested in NU circles. Abdurrahman Wahid had to defend his choice by pointing at Matori's excellent political track-record. PKB, which could count Rhoma Irama among its supporters, had Drs A. Muhaimin Iskandar, a nephew of Abdurrahman Wahid, as its secretary and H. Imam Churmain, a former Golkar leader, as its treasurer. Abdurrahman Wahid held no formal position. He was 'declarator', the founding father (there were in actual fact five of them), or as Amien Rais was to phrase this its 'godfather'. PKB was presented as a party sensitive to the interests of all Indonesians, hence the use of the word 'nation' and not, for instance, 'ummat'. True to this ecumenical position, a Chinese dance was performed, which had as its high point a PKB flag emerging from the mouth of the dragon, during a mass rally in December in Surabaya. To prevent any mishap, members of Banser guarded churches in Surabaya which PKB supporters attending the event had to pass. As another indication of the openness of PKB, the party was to involve not only *ulama* but also people like Hadi Soesastro and J. Kristiadi of CSIS, Dr Martin Wanandi (a brother of Sofyan Wanandi), and leaders of the Christian community, such as Frans Magnis Suseno in the election campaign of 1999. PKB aimed, in fashionable

political jargon, at being an inclusive party, not an exclusive one. It was a
'nationalist', a 'red and white' party, not a 'green' Islamic one. When PKB was
founded, its leaders did not preclude a coalition with Megawati's PDI. As one
of the members of the religious council, Dr Said Aqil Siradj, chose to put this
delicately: PDI was nationalist religious, the PKB was religious nationalist
(*Jawa Pos*, 29-7-1998). In spite of all this, its link with NU was undisputable.

PKB was not the only NU-affiliated party. At least seven could be count-
ed. The most important ones were Partai Kebangkitan Umat (PKU), Party of
the Awakening of the Religious Community, launched at the end of
September, with KH Yusuf Hasyim as its general chairman and Ir H.
Salahuddin Wahid, a brother of Abdurrahman Wahid, as first chairman;
Partai Nahdlatul Ummat (PNU), established in the middle of August, with
KH Syukron Makmun and KH Dr Idham Chalid among its leaders; and
Partai Solidaritas Uni Nasional Indonesia (Partai Suni), with H. Abu Hasan
MA, a Jambi-born businessman, who had fought a bitter battle with
Abdurrahman Wahid over control over NU in December 1994 as general
chairman.

The birth of these parties to some extent reflected past conflicts within NU
and anger about the fact that Abdurrahman Wahid, who was accused of
wanting to have it all his own way, presented PKB as the party which had the
support of the NU board. In part their founding had been inspired by disagreement with Abdurrahman Wahid's stress on nationalism, vaunting it
above Islam. For adopting this stance he laid himself open to charges of being
an enemy of Islam, an apostate, a supporter of Christian groups who, in his
aversion to the enforcement of Islamic law in Indonesia went further than the
colonial government had ever gone to stand in the way of this. PKB was dis-
paragingly referred to as Perkumpulan Kiyai Bingung, a Bevy of Bewildered
Kiai (Jaiz 1999:9, 52). A crucial factor at that time was the support
Abdurrahman Wahid gave Megawati and the possibility of a coalition
between PKB and PDI-P.[12] The boot was also on the other foot. Abdurrahman
joined the choir of NU leaders who began to rail at colleagues who had made
a different political choice. He was not exactly complimentary about his
rivals. In May 1999 he compared NU to a hen, and the parties with what
came out of her. PKB was her egg and others her incredibly stinking shit.
Relations with members of his own NU board had even deteriorated by that
time. When board members protested some of his moves and comments or
said they did not understand why Abdurrahman Wahid acted the way he

---

[12]   In February 1999 Abdurrahman was to explain his renewed support for Megawati by
pointing out that many PDI-P supporters behaved in a reckless and dangerous manner, especially when PDI-P held open-air meetings. They needed a lesson in correct behaviour,
Abdurrahman said.

did, he was to state that there were a great many differences of opinions between himself and the NU board. He claimed the latter failed to comprehend the power constellation of that moment, and, more often than not, acted stupidly (*Tajuk*, 23-12-1998:31).

The establishment of PKB formed a serious setback for PPP. Following Soeharto's fall, PPP had experienced a similar fate to Golkar. On 8 June hundreds of its supporters had held a day-long demonstration at the PPP office in Jalan Diponegoro, demanding the disbanding of the party and the resignation of Ismail Hasan Metareum. They berated Ismail Hasan Metareum, branding him a product of the Soeharto era, contaminated by KKN, and therefore co-responsible for the dire situation Indonesia was in. As was the case with Golkar, PPP was deserted by some of its members. Nahdlatul Ulama leaders in particular had been dissatisfied with their position in PPP for a long time. They had felt outmanoeuvred by politicians from their modernist counterpart, Muslimin Indonesia, who had effectively succeeded in putting their stamp on PPP. In an effort to rescue the party's appeal, PPP politicians toyed briefly with the idea of inviting Amien Rais and his supporters to join its ranks. Amien Rais was not attracted by the idea. He was busy pondering the opposite scenario: PPP becoming part of the party he himself intended to found; at the end of July he even suggested that this was the outcome of meetings between him and PPP politicians. In August PPP made a new attempt to woo him to its ranks. The party offered him the chairmanship of its newly founded Council of Experts. Initially Amien Rais agreed, and signed a letter to this effect. Shortly afterwards he refused, blaming opposition against him by PPP members from Muslimin Indonesia and possibly also from Nahdlatul Ulama objecting to him acquiring a prominent position in that party.

In spite of all the fuss, PPP could continue to count on the support of influential *ulama*, one of the most conspicuous being KH Alawy Muhammad from Madura. One of the reasons for him not to leave was that he did not consider PKB an Islamic party. Other NU leaders and members who stayed in PPP seem to have had similar reservations. It appears that they belonged to the uncompromising segment of the NU community. Some were soon to brand PKB a party of *kafir*, infidels. Besides this, the PPP organizational structure had remained intact, allowing for a smooth mobilization of its followers. An indication of this was evident during the national congress the party held at the end of November. *Republika* reported that the occasion had turned Jakarta green (*Republika*, 30-11-1998). In cavalcades, over a hundred thousand supporters descended on Senayan Stadium, beating *bedug*, mosque drums, chanting prayers, making Islamic-style music, and tooting car horns. One of the most important results of the congress was the decision to highlight PPP's Islamic character. One expression of this intention was to reinstate the displaying of a depiction of the Ka'bah, which the New Order government had forced it to abandon and to replace with a star. Hamzah Haz took over the leadership from Ismail Hasan Metareum, defeating Saefuddin, his main rival. It was the first time a NU leader headed PPP. Metareum became chairman of the Advisory Council.

The modernist community, with Muhammadiyah, and in the past Masjumi, as its main vehicles, was just as unsuccessful in maintaining a united front. Yusril Ihza Mahendra travelled the country to prepare the way for the establishment of a new party, Partai Bulan Bintang (PBB), Crescent and Star Party. For a while he and others hoped that Amien Rais would join, or even be one of its founders, but this he declined to do. One of the reasons he gave for doing so was that he could not agree with the name, which was too closely associated with Masjumi and the group from which it drew its support. PBB did not suit the plans of Amien Rais. He did not want to lead an 'exclusive' party, but fostered the goals of establishing a party which would transcend dividing lines and appeal to all segments of society, irrespective of religion, race, or ethnic group. PBB was founded on 17 July, and was formally constituted at a mass meeting in Al-Azhar Mosque on 26 July. Yusril became its chairman. Among its leading politicians were Abdul Qadir Djaelani, Farid Prawiranegara (a son of the former Masjumi leader Sjafroedin Prawiranegara), Ahmad Soemargono, Fadli Zon, KH Kholil Ridwan, and Anwar Sanusi. As these names indicate, PBB draws part of its support from those Islamic organizations which had sought a confrontation with the students who occupied the parliamentary complex in May. Citing the example of the political behaviour of Masjumi in the 1950s, its politicians could argue that PBB, though an Islamic party, did not exclude political cooperation with other groups.

On 27 July, Amien Rais finally announced the establishment of Partai Amanat Bangsa (PAB), Party of the Message of the Nation, or Partai Amanat Nasional (PAN), Party of the National Message, as its name was to be was proclaimed during a mass meeting at the Senayan Stadium on 23 August. Faisal Basri became secretary-general. As with MAR, Amien Rais took great pains to stress that PAN was a national organization, and did not cater exclusively to Muhammadiyah and Masjumi circles or to the wider Islamic community. Consequently there were at least two mainstreams within PAN: one with its base firmly set in Muhammadiyah, HMI, and kindred organizations; the other composed of people attracted by MAR, which also stayed in the running. Amien Rais described PAN as a 'miniature Indonesia', aiming at as many segments of Indonesian society as possible (*Forum Keadilan*, 7-9-1998:23). Its board reflected this stance and included people from different religions. Among its leading members were people like Fatwa, Dawam Rahardjo, Christianto Wibisono, H.M. Sanusi, Goenawan Mohammad, and

Pius Lustrilanang (to be put on the sidelines within months when he spoke out in favour of Megawati as a presidential candidate). The tactic of including persons from diverse backgrounds did not prevent people from continuing to consider PAN a Muhammadiyah-related party. It also could not free PAN from an association with educated city-dwellers, and maybe even strengthened this impression. Others drew the opposite conclusion and feared that as PAN did not champion the interests of their Islamic community exclusively, it was not worthy of their support.

PBB and PAN found themselves surrounded by other kindred parties. Among them were Partai Ummat Muslimin Indonesia (PUMI), headed by H. Anwar Yunus SH, and Partai Ummat Islam (PUI), launched at the end of June during a meeting at Al-Azhar Mosque, and headed by Deliar Noer and H.M. Sanusi. Masjumi was revived. On 28 August, at Al-Azhar Mosque in Jakarta, Partai Politik Islam Indonesia Masyumi was founded by Mawardi Noor. Naro also resumed his political role, now advertising his bid for the vice-presidency in 1988 as a heroic deed. He became chairman of Partai Persatuan, Unity Party, taking the former PPP star as its symbol.

New in the Islamic political constellation was Partai Keadilan (PK), Justice Party, founded on 20 July by a group sometimes described as Muslim or *dakwah* activists. The party was officially launched during a mass meeting at Al-Azhar Mosque on 9 August. Partai Keadilan, with Dr Ir M. Nur Mahmudi Ismail as president, drew its support from the same group as KAMMI (whose chairman Fahri Hamzah opted for PPP): young Islamic preachers, campus mosques, and Lembaga Dakwah Kampus. Its members are fairly strict, symbolized by the fact that the party head office has separate waiting rooms for men and women. Female supporters scrupulously follow Islamic dress codes, turning, as was the case with KAMMI, party meetings into 'a sea of white jilbabs'. A handshake between a man and a woman is taboo. Despite this display of piety, its leaders take care to stress that Partai Keadilan does not want to impose Islamic law, at least not before society is ready for this (*The Jakarta Post*, 3-5-1999).

Though more than 150 political parties were founded, attention focused on Golkar and the parties of the three most respected opposition figures of the day: Abdurrahman Wahid, Amien Rais, and Megawati; ostensibly receiving more public acclaim than Habibie. The three represented respectively the 'traditional' Muslims with their bulwarks in Central and East Java; the 'modernist' Muslims, many living in non-Javanese regions and in urban centres; and what in the past used to be called 'syncretist' Javanese Muslims and the 'nationalists' in and outside Java. Bali was also Megawati territory.

It took months, and deterioration on the domestic political front, before Abdurrahman Wahid, Amien Rais, and Megawati were to act in concert. The riots of May had briefly brought them together. Joining in the Advisory Body of a Forum Kerja Indonesia, an Indonesian Work Forum, founded on 15 May, they had appealed to students and others to channel their demands in a peaceful way by presenting them to representative bodies all over Indonesia. The cooperation did not last long. As in the 1950s, when because of a shared cultural background it was easier for leaders of the Nahdlatul Ulama community to cooperate with politicians of a Javanese-based party like PNI, this time PKB and PDI seemed closer than PKB and PAN. Another fault line was the structure of the Indonesian state. Though on numerous occasions Amien Rais had made it clear that he had not committed himself on this point, his reluctance to reject the possibility of a federal state outright set him apart from Megawati and Abdurrahman Wahid. It was one of the few political issues on which Megawati expressed strong views. As far as she was concerned, the unitary state was not open to debate. Abdurrahman Wahid took the same uncompromising position. Those aiming to establish a federal state he dubbed 'civilian Masyumi' supporters or 'Muslims with a Masyumi background', breathing new life into the antagonism which had dogged the NU and the Masjumi of the 1950s and 1960s. Likewise, Abdurrahman Wahid noted the existence of an 'Armed Forces Masyumi', which strove to emphasize Islam in political life (*Republika*, 22-9-1998; *Visi*, 1998 no. 5:15).

Abdurrahman Wahid had resumed his political support for Megawati, speaking out a number of times in her favour even after PKB had been founded. Amien Rais seemed to be excluded from this block. Considered to be too blunt, even by Muhammadiyah members, in NU circles he was an even more controversial figure. An early example of this mistrust manifested itself in the middle of June when Amien Rais went on a tour in East Java, a bulwark of Nahdlatul Ulama. People opposed to his visit in East Java said they were afraid it might stir up tensions and conflicts in the Muslim community, referring to unrest that had erupted in Lamongan a few weeks after Amien Rais had been there. After arriving by plane in Surabaya from Jakarta in the early morning of 14 June, Amien Rais cancelled his trip to Bangil and Pasuruan. He decided to do so at the last moment when he was already on his way to Pasuruan by car. Amien Rais was advised to do so by the military commander of the province, who had already been against the visit, and had only agreed after local Muhammadiyah leaders had threatened to arrange for Amien Rais's safety during his stay in East Java themselves. The decision not to proceed was taken to avoid protests and possible disturbances on the part of a group styling itself Gabungan Reformasi Damai Arek-Arek Pasuruan, Peaceful Reformation Federation of People hailing from Pasuruan. Armed with stones and patrolling the road leading into the city from Surabaya in their hundreds, they stopped every car to see whether Amien Rais was in it. Days before, banners had already been on display in Pasuruan, stating that 'Amien Rais is not a Reformation Figure'. On other banners he was stigmatized as a political broker, a traitor to the nation, and a snake-in-the-grass. Amien Rais then travelled on to Pamekasan in Madura. This trip was also not without its problems. Informed that demonstrations were to be staged in the port of Kamal, a plan was developed to smuggle Amien Rais out of Surabaya, keeping his departure secret even from the police and secret agents watching him, who clearly were not trusted by Amien Rais and his company. Wearing a helmet and a black jacket, Amien Rais sneaked out of the house where he was staying. He left Surabaya at one o'clock in the morning, hours earlier than planned. In this way he avoided a demonstration in Kamal, where one of the banners carried read that 'Amien Rais is not the property of the Islamic community. He is the property of Muhammadiyah'. In Pamekasan all went well. A large crowd came to listen to Amien Rais. His journey back to Surabaya was surrounded by the same scenes as those during his leaving that city. In order to hide the fact that he left earlier than scheduled, Amien Rais changed cars to lead astray the authorities, who were told that he still wanted to visit a number of *pesantren*. The reason for all this cloak-and-dagger stuff was a plot to have Amien Rais murdered by criminals, who had been indoctrinated to believe that Amien Rais was an enemy of NU (for a detailed account of the trip, see Najib 1998:67-95).

Mistrust of Amien Rais's intent within the Nahdlatul Ulama community played an unquestionable role in this brittle reception. In August the rumour spread among NU supporters that were Amien Rais to become president, one of his aims as a 'modernist' Muslim would be to stamp out religious customs practised by the 'traditionalist' NU community, trespassing on the core of their religious beliefs, such as specific funeral rites, the celebration of the birthday of the Prophet, and visits to sacred graves. Another reason why Amien Rais could not count on the sympathy of NU supporters was that they had become annoyed by the attention Amien Rais, Mister Reformation, received as one of the major figures of the reform movement and the acclaim he had attained in this role, in particular in student circles, overshadowing the achievements of their own leader, Abdurrahman Wahid.

All the new political parties could only be officially recognized as such after the legislation had been adjusted. Within days of Habibie having assumed the presidency, a committee headed by Prof. Dr Ryaas Rasyid was formed to prepare three new acts: on the general election, on political parties, and on the composition of the representative bodies. In the middle of September the three bills were submitted to parliament.[13] Were a general election indeed to be held in May, discussion about it had to be rounded off by the end of January. It was proposed that political parties that wished to be

---

[13]   LIPI published draft bills also, together with one about the presidency and its powers. See Samego et al. 1998b.

allowed to participate in the general election had to have boards in more than half of Indonesia's 27 provinces (with respect to the election of 1999 this was reduced to one-third), and in these provinces in half of the *kabupaten* and cities. Besides limiting the number of parties participating in the election, the condition was also intended to discourage the emergence of particularistic, regional parties. To prevent workplace pressure being exerted on voters, election day was to be held on a holiday. Another substantial new proposal, and one of the suggestions the Armed Forces had made in June, was that party boards would no longer have the right to recall representatives, a mechanism used in the past to remove vocal and controversial members of parliament and the People's Congress.

The discussion of the acts in parliament was a somewhat odd affair. It involved only the Armed Forces, Budi Hardjono's PDI, PPP, and Golkar. It left out PDI-P, PAN, PKB, and all the other political parties which had been formed. A main bone of contention was the statutory presence of the Armed Forces in the legislative bodies. The senior officers of the army were prepared to adjust the number of seats reserved for the Armed Forces to the 'way matters developed', but refused to give up their presence in parliament and the People's Congress completely (*ABRI* 1998:15). In an attempt to justify their position spokesmen of the Armed Forces asked rhetorically who would bother to voice their aspirations if they had no seats. The military had no right to vote. Did they have to yell outside the building as well (*Republika*, 10-11-1998)? The members of parliament could do little else than comply. The Working Body of the People's Congress, which had started its discussions on 10 September and which was responsible for preparing the decrees to be accepted during the extraordinary session, had already agreed that the Armed Forces would maintain their presence in the representative bodies. The general assembly of the People's Congress, the institution which was to decide on the principles of politics, would follow suit in its November session. The only concession made was that the number of seats reserved for the Armed Forces was to be reduced gradually over a period of time. How many seats were to be allocated to the military had to be decided by parliament.

This was one of the three subjects on which a deadlock threatened in parliament. Agreement would only be reached at the last moment, after intense lobbying. The government and the Armed Forces aimed at ten per cent of the seats for the Armed Forces in the national and regional representative bodies. The most staunch opponent of Armed Forces representation was PPP, its politicians arguing that they had to honour the decrees of the People's Congress and would not go any further than two per cent. In the end it was agreed to allocate the Armed Forces 38 of the 500 seats in parliament. Immediately these were dubbed gratis seats. In the regional representative bodies 10 per cent of the seats were reserved for the military. The former quota had been 20 per cent. The People's Congress was to have 700 members. Of the additional seats, 135 (five for each province) were reserved for regional representatives, the remaining 65 were for representatives of social groups. Political parties would no longer have appointed members in the People's Congress.

Accepting the compromise on the Armed Forces seats was part of the give and take which characterized the final deliberations in parliament in January. Another controversial point in the bargaining was the position of civil servants. In view of the support civil servants had given Golkar in the past, their political role was a very sensitive subject rivalling the tricky topic of the military. It was proposed that civil servants would not be allowed to become members of a political party. They would have to remain neutral during general elections. Were they to continue to be party members, they had to resign from the civil service. Understandably, most of the opposition to this provision came from Golkar, in which civil servants (and cabinet ministers) had a lion's share on the various boards.[14] Its politicians, stressing that the issue was a matter of principle, not of politics, argued that the proposal was in violation of human rights and was tantamount to a limitation of the political rights of civil servants. PPP was its fiercest advocate. The subject was also taken up by demonstrating students. To support such protests, and probably also as a token of their aversion to Korpri, UI staff ceremonially stripped themselves of their Korpri uniforms and handed them over to students to be distributed among the poor.[15]

Akbar Tanjung and other Golkar politicians persisted, going against the wishes of Syarwan Hamid and Habibie. The deadlock lasted till the last moment when, as had already been suggested for some weeks, as a compromise and to avoid a vote, the subject was not mentioned in the general election act but in a separate government regulation issued at the end of January – a face-saving device often used during Soeharto's New Order. According to the regulation, civil servants who joined a political party had to leave the civil service. They were to be compensated for this by retaining their pay for a maximum of five years.

The third crucial question to be solved was whether the division of seats in parliament was to be determined by the election results in the provinces as a whole, as PPP and PDI wanted, or by that in the separate *kabupaten* and larger cities, from which Golkar might profit and which certainly would be

---

[14]   Another party to suffer was PAN, which had many university teachers, including Amien Rais and Faisal Basri, among its politicians. Others affected by the regulation were Yusril Ihza Mahendra, the general chairman of PBB, and Dimyati Hartono of PDI-P.
[15]   Many Korpri members had become afraid to venture out of doors dressed in a Korpri uniform, putting their uniform on only after they had arrived at their office.

to the detriment of the smaller parties. Also on this point Golkar had to bow its head.[16] On 28 January, exactly according to schedule, parliament endorsed the three laws. Among the other points agreed upon was the establishment of the independent Komisi Pemilihan Umum (KPU), General Election Commission, replacing the government-controlled General Election Institute of the past as organizer of the general elections. KPU would also decide how the 65 seats reserved for representatives of social groups were to be allotted. Political parties were allowed to have boards down to the village and city ward level. Those who, as the phrase went, were involved in the *coup d'état* of 1965 and PKI, were still banned from standing for representative bodies.

One important matter remained to be settled, brewing up an immense row between Habibie and the fledgling KPU, which was headed by Rudini. At the end of March, KPU decided that all civil servants and members of the Armed Forces would not be allowed to campaign, holding out the sanction of disqualification of the party concerned were the ban to be disregarded. The conflict that emerged focused on the cabinet ministers, figures who had always been among the main Golkar campaigners in the past. Rudini claimed that, by deciding in this way, KPU had followed the people's aspira= tions. Habibie was furious. Not only was he of the opinion that he alone could decide whether or not cabinet ministers were allowed to campaign (they were after all his 'assistants'), the decision also robbed Golkar of some of its potential vote-winners. The party, which had already threatened to leave KPU were it to take this decision, had assigned Akbar Tanjung, Agung Laksono, and Theo L. Sambuaga to be important campaigners. The government itself had decided that only Hartarto, Muladi, Syarwan Hamid, Wiranto, and Ghalib would not be allowed to campaign, but that the other ministers were free to do so. Within days Syarwan Hamid asked the Supreme Court for a ruling. The Supreme Court decided in favour of Habibie, that is it issued a legal opinion stating that the president was in charge of the general elections, but did not issue an edict to this effect. It argued that KPU had no authority to take decisions affecting the position of cabinet ministers or for that matter any other civil servant. KPU members did realize that such persons fell outside its jurisdiction, but made the point that it had the right to issue regulations with respect to the political parties which had to field such persons as campaigners. The Supreme Court also ruled that KPU members, the majority made up of representatives of the political parties, were not allowed to campaign or to stand as parliamentary candidates. This suggestion, too, flatly contravened the decision KPU itself had taken. KPU persist-

---

[16]   In this combination of a district and a proportional system it was seen to that the number of parliamentary seats contested in Java was about half of the total number of seats to be won at the general election (234 of the 462 seats).

ed and won. From 10 May Akbar Tanjung and Hamzah Haz withdrew from
the cabinet. The position of Secretary of State went to Muladi, who continued
to be Minister of Justice.

Defences against demonstrations (photo's C. van Dijk)

CHAPTER XIV

Political strife

Hai Anto
Apakah kau dengar jerit mahasiswa
Apakah kau bangga di atas tumpukan mayat mahasiswa
Yang merupakan anakmu juga.
Hai Anto
Katanya kau jendral yang bijaksana
Tapi kenapa kau tembak mahasiswa
yang jelas tidak pakai senjata.[1]

The first major test for Habibie had been whether he could gain control over Golkar. Golkar was still an important asset, a significant institution in the political configuration. It had a major say in parliament and the People's Congress and, in a general election, might well retain some of its support in the countryside, where military officers, government officials, and social and religious leaders still largely determined how people would vote. In Java and the regions to which Javanese had migrated, Megawati and Abdurrahman Wahid would reap much of their support. There Golkar mostly met with hostility. Elsewhere the situation might be different, and Golkar might hold on to some of its support. From a sheerly practical point of view, Golkar was thought to have much more money to spend than other parties.

The first to go was Harmoko. At the meeting at party headquarters on the evening of 18 May, he and Abdul Gafur had been criticized – put on trial, was the term at times chosen to describe what had transpired – by fellow Golkar leaders for the U-turn the two had made by first urging Soeharto to accept his nomination as presidential candidate and then, within a matter of months, assisting in bringing about his downfall. Soeharto, as he had confided to Nurcholish Madjid, had felt betrayed by Harmoko (*Jawa Pos*, 6-6-1998).

---

[1]   Hi! [Wir]anto/ Do you hear the students' scream/ Are you proud of the pile of corpses of students/ Who are also your children/ Hi! Anto/ They call you a prudent general;/ But why did you shoot students/ who clearly used no weapons. Fragment from the song Kutukan Mu (Lagu untuk Wiranto), Cursed Are You (A song for Wiranto), *Kabar dari Pijar*, 20-11-1998.

On 18 May, Abdul Gafur and Harmoko had been berated so severely that both had burst into tears. The criticism did not stop with Soeharto's fall. On 3 June, after eight provincial branches had urged him to step down, Harmoko declared that he would not seek re-election as general chairman at an extraordinary national congress of Golkar which was scheduled for the following month.

The contest over the succession to Harmoko was the first instance of a return to old-fashioned political manoeuvring. There was much at stake, first and foremost Habibie's presidency. The new general chairman of Golkar had the power to replace rival Golkar members of the People's Congress by introducing his own supporters, and to put the election of a new president on the agenda of the extraordinary session of the People's Congress. Habibie's 'green side' might lose out to those who detested the advance of Islam in politics, and consequently at times were dubbed the secular nationalists. Conversely, if Habibie's side won at the extraordinary session, this could give his presidency a greater aura of legitimacy.

There was yet a third possibility. The struggle for power in the Habibie era was fraught from the very outset with an even more sensitive dimension as Soeharto loomed in the background. Soeharto was still chairman of what on paper was the all-powerful Council of Patrons, and was perhaps capable of mobilizing enough support to have one of his own favourites take over Golkar leadership to protect his interests and to take revenge on Harmoko and Habibie. One outcome could be a 'Soeharto-friendly' People's Congress, using its power to replace Habibie as president, perhaps by either Try Sutrisno or Soedharmono. A People's Congress composed in such a way could also ensure that during its extraordinary session, proposals which demanded that Soeharto was to account for his policy, or spoke out in favour of the confiscation of his wealth and that of his family, would not be accepted. Others, largely retired generals and students, just dreamt of a Habibie-hostile People's Congress, eventually speeding up the latter's resignation.

The events leading up to the extraordinary Golkar congress indicated that Soeharto still could flex some muscle. On the initiative of Habibie, who acted in his capacity as coordinator of the Daily Presidium of the Council of Patrons, Akbar Tanjung, Wiranto, and Syarwan Hamid, representing Golkar, the Armed Forces, and the bureaucracy respectively, met on 21 June to discuss preparations for the extraordinary congress. Habibie's next step was to call a second enlarged meeting of the three groups, to which their representatives on the provincial level were also invited. To the chagrin of Habibie the meeting, scheduled for 29 June at the headquarters of the Armed Forces in Cilangkap in East Jakarta, never took place. Soeharto forestalled Habibie and instructed Try Sutrisno, deputy chairman of the Council of Patrons, to convene a plenary session of the Council of Patrons one day earlier, on 28 June.

Although it meant that Habibie was outmanoeuvred, this meeting did not materialize. Instead, in an effort to talk out the differences, Try Sutrisno and Habibie agreed to call a meeting of the Daily Presidium of the Council of Patrons on 3 July. As Try Sutrisno was later to explain during a press conference – leaving no doubt that his words had the blessing of Soeharto – Habibie had to follow the rules and should not try to bypass other members of the Council of Patrons, in particular not its chairman, Soeharto, when he convened a meeting. The newspaper *Merdeka* removed any shadow of a doubt about Soeharto being behind Try Sutrisno's action by publishing pictures of Try Sutrisno with a portrait of Soeharto in the background.

On the instructions of Soeharto, Try Sutrisno changed the nature of the meeting of the 3 July, making it into a plenary session. He invited the other members of the Council of Patrons by phone. At the meeting Try Sutrisno read a 13-page message by Soeharto, replete with criticism of the conduct of the Golkar Central Board under the leadership of Harmoko. Soeharto (as he had done at the last Golkar national congress in 1993, when he had tongue-lashed Harmoko's predecessor, Wahono) blamed the group for not responding adequately to changes in society and the calls for reform, and for failing to take steps to restore a sense of calm and to reassure those who had fallen victim to the violence, many of them Golkar members, after the May riots.

Sutrisno's action and the banners which had appeared in the streets of Jakarta bearing the message that the Soeharto bashing had to stop and praising the latter for the suppression of communism in 1965 fuelled rumours that Soeharto, or at least his supporters, and the people who had lost out after 21 May planned a comeback. In Medan people had also begun to demonstrate in Soeharto's favour, demanding his return to power, and showing their displeasure by burning an effigy of Amien Rais. Suspicion about the manoeuvring of the 'Cendana camp' was strong enough to have Yudhoyono state publicly once again on 19 June that the Armed Forces were firmly behind the Habibie government and would thwart all attempts by 'old forces' to scheme for a comeback.

The three-day-long extraordinary congress, which took place at Hotel Indonesia, began on 9 July. Its motto expressed Golkar 's commitment to reform. Outside, alongside protesters demanding the disbanding of Golkar, Lasykar Pembela Pancasila, Defenders of the Pancasila, carried around pictures of Soeharto. Their banners stated that it was better to start a hunger strike to remove Habibie than to die of hunger under a Habibie government, and that, when Soeharto headed the country, national stability was secure. Inside the hotel, exponents of Soeharto's New Order, ministers of his cabinets, who at such occasions had been very popular figures in the past, surrounded by a crowd of admirers, were shunned. Nobody wanted to be seen speaking to Hartono or to Moerdiono, the once powerful and lionized

Secretary of State, and their like.

During the congress Soeharto tried to make his influence felt. This manifested itself right from the outset when a decision had to be taken who the seven chairmen of the congress were to be. The selection of six of them passed off smoothly enough. Problems arose over the question of who was to be the chairman representing the Council of Patrons; the board, as the developments surrounding the cancelled meeting planned by Habibie at the Armed Forces headquarters in Cilangkap had shown, was split into two camps. Try Sutrisno asserted that he carried a mandate from the Council of Patrons and handed over a letter to the chairman of the meeting, Harmoko. It mentioned his own name, with the provision that he delegated the task to Siswono Yudohusodo. Harmoko, on this occasion again siding with Habibie, refused to acquiesce in the suggestion. He stressed that the note carried only the signature of Try Sutrisno, whereas the Council of Patrons consisted of many more members, not all of whom could agree with Sutrisno's choice of himself being their representative. The sight of leading Golkar politicians publicly at loggerheads with one another made an impression. It was the first time Golkar politicking was fought out in the open and not behind closed doors (*Golkar* 1999:140). At the suggestion of Akbar Tanjung, the matter was referred back to the Council of Patrons. It took some time before a decision was taken. When the members of the council, including Habibie, could not reach an agreement, Soeharto was consulted. He confirmed his approval of Try Sutrisno's suggestion. Later during the congress, Try Sutrisno (and not Habibie) read a statement from Soeharto. In it Soeharto once again reminded the audience that he himself had been hesitant to take on yet another term as president and that he had asked Golkar to check whether the people really still wanted him. He went on to urge Golkar to become a pioneer of reform.

The congress was attended by about one thousand Golkar leaders. Only 27 of them, the provincial chairmen, had the authority to elect the next general chairman. There were two main candidates. The first was Edi Sudradjat, a long-time critic of Habibie and his ICMI, who had, for instance, opposed the buying of East German warships. He could count on the backing of Try Sutrisno, who had recently become general chairman of the Union of Retired Armed Forces Officers. He was thus in a key position to influence the choice of retired officers, whose role was crucial, as they chaired 21 provincial boards, and consequently they had a major say in determining who was to become Golkar's next general chairman. Their overwhelming presence in the provincial and sub-provincial boards had been a consequence of an earlier contest of power in Golkar in 1993. In that year, unable to block the election of Soeharto's favourite Harmoko as general chairman, the first civilian to hold this post, the army had launched a deliberate drive to gain control of as many branches as possible. In this way, senior military officers hoped to maintain a say in Golkar by dominating the deliberations at its national congresses. A victory for Edi Sudradjat would return Golkar to the retired officers. Because of the support Edi Sudradjat received from Try Sutrisno, he was also considered to be the candidate favoured by Soeharto. This was a stigma everybody wanted to avoid. Edi Sudradjat tried to remove the impression that 'Cendana' was scheming for his election by underlining that, when he had been a cabinet minister, he had been among the people to whom Soeharto had taken a dislike. Among those who spoke out in his favour were Rudini, Kemal Idris, Ali Sadikin, Abdurrahman Wahid, Sri Edi Swasono, and Arifin Panigoro. A similar position was adopted by Kosgoro leaders, and the members of a Reformation SOKSI borne of the disappointment with the position taken by the chairman of SOKSI, who had vacillated about withdrawing his support for Soeharto, in May. Outside the hotel, Lasykar Pembela Pancasila demonstrated in Edi Sudradjat's favour, but this enthusiasm was more or less offset by other demonstrators who linked him to Try Sutrisno and the Tanjung Priok massacre.

Edi Sudradjat's rival in the contest for Golkar leadership, a struggle in which the opposition between 'red and white' and 'green' and between Javanese and non-Javanese regions played a role, was Ir Akbar Tanjung, a former chairman of HMI and KNPI. Akbar Tanjung, born in Sibolga in Sumatra, was Secretary of the Council of Patrons, and held the strategic post of Secretary of State in the Development Reformation Cabinet. Akbar Tanjung was 'Habibie's man', and could count on the support of ICMI, the members of the cabinet, and of Wiranto. His opponents argued that in contrast to Edi Sudradjat, he would be no match for Habibie. Arifin Panigoro said that Akbar Tanjung had always been close to people in power, first Ali Moertopo, and thereafter Soedharmono, Soeharto, and Habibie. It was an assessment probably as lethal as the claim that Edi Sudradjat was a Soeharto candidate.

The efforts made by Try Sutrisno to ensure a sufficient number of provincial chairmen from the Armed Forces voted for Edi Sudradjat failed. Akbar Tanjung received 17 of the 27 votes. The Edi Sudradjat side put the blame on pressure exerted on the chairmen of provincial branches by the regional military commanders and governors on the orders of Wiranto and Syarwan Hamid at the request of Habibie.

Another important decision taken at the Golkar congress was to do away with the Council of Patrons and similar institutions at the provincial and sub-provincial levels. Not only did this signify the end of the all-powerful position Soeharto in theory still had in Golkar, but on paper at least also freed the branches from the influence of governors, *bupati*, and mayors, as well as from the requests of local army commanders. The Council of Patrons was replaced by an Advisory Council, headed by Harmoko, who was maintained as chair-

man of parliament and the People's Congress out of appreciation for the role
he had played in May and during the extraordinary Golkar congress.

Intense disappointment about Edi Sudradjat's defeat was felt among
retired officers, such as Kemal Idris, Solichin GP, Kharis Suhud, Harsudiono
Hartas, and Bambang Triantoro, who clearly did not share Wiranto's view
about deference to former superiors. On 17 July, they joined forces with others disillusioned by the outcome of the Golkar congress. A coalition was born
among these aged dissidents, most of them in their sixties and seventies,
joined by some of their younger retired colleagues, including Edi Sudradjat
and Major-General (Ret.) Syamsir Siregar (a former head of the Armed Forces
Intelligence Body), and dissatisfied civilian Golkar leaders of MKGR,
Kosgoro, and SOKSI. Among the latter were Mrs Mien Sugandhi, Rachmat
Witoelar (a former secretary-general of Golkar, who had been appointed
ambassador in Moscow when he fell from grace with the advance of
Harmoko in Golkar in 1993), and Sarwono Kusumaatmadja (also a former
secretary-general of Golkar, and a member of the Council of Patrons),
Bambang W. Soeharto (a chairman of Kosgoro), and Indra Bambang Utoyo
(secretary-general of the Communication Forum of Sons and Daughters of
Retired Armed Forces Officers). Others who joined this camp were Dimyati
Hartono, Subroto, Theo Syafei, and Sembiring Meliala.

The retired officers and their civilian counterparts united in what was initially called Eksponen Barisan Nasional, soon shortened to Barisan Nasional
(Barnas) or National Front. It came complete with its own think-tank. Barnas
was proclaimed during a meeting on 6 August, at which Megawati was also
present. Kemal Idris, who had fallen out with Soeharto at the beginning of
the New Order, partly because he had demanded the prosecution of
Soekarno, which Soeharto had refused, was elected chairman. Subroto was
deputy chairman, Rachmat Witoelar general secretary. The Barnas members
were to become major players in the conflicts among the political élite in
Jakarta. They made no secret of the fact that their aim was to weaken Golkar
and have Habibie, whose assumption of the presidency they considered illegal, replaced by a presidium. This goal would have been achieved, Kemal
Idris was to state in November, had Edi Sudradjat become general chairman
of Golkar. Another consequence would have been the summoning of
Soeharto to account for his policy (*Golkar* 1999:213). Earlier, Kemal Idris had
already indicated that, if Habibie was not prepared to step down at the session of the People's Congress in November, people power, a united front
composed of students and the people, would have to force him out of office
(interview with Kemal Idris, *Tajuk*, 6-8-1998:28-33). One of the logical consequences of this attitude was that Barisan Nasional members expressed their
support for a Megawati-Abdurrahman Wahid coalition. In fact, they seemed
prepared to back anybody as long as that person opposed Golkar (*Jawa Pos*,

25-7-1998).

A few days after the establishment of Barnas, Gerakan Keadilan dan Persatuan Bangsa (GKPB), Movement for Justice and Union of the Nation, was founded under the leadership of Siswono Yudohusodo (a Kosgoro leader). Among its initiators were Kemal Idris, Ali Sadikin, Edi Sudradjat, Rudini, David Napitupulu, Hariadi Darmawan, Sarwono Kusumaatmadja, Ary Mardjono, Subroto, Sofyan Wanandi, and Said Aqil Siradj. In September, there was an additional indication of discontent with developments within Golkar, when the Union of Retired Armed Forces Officers, chaired by Try Sutrisno, and the Communication Forum of Sons and Daughters of Retired Armed Forces Officers, chaired by Bambang Trihatmodjo, ruled that there was no longer any obligation for wives and children of members of the Armed Forces or for retired officers to vote Golkar.

Despite all these moves, it was 15 January 1999 before such Golkar dissidents launched their own party, which had been founded one month earlier. It was built on the national network established by GKPB: Partai Keadilan dan Persatuan (Justice and Union Party). Edi Sudradjat became chairman of PKP, and Hayono Isman, a Kosgoro leader and former Minister of Youth and Sport, its secretary-general. Among its founders were Said Aqil Siradj and Sri Edi Swasono.[2] The PKP founders did all they could to stress that, contrary to what was being rumoured, PKP was not a Cendana party, let alone that it was being financed by Soeharto. They apologized for Golkar policy during the New Order. A few days later Akbar Tanjung, at a moment which bristled with significance in Indonesian culture, just before the end of the fasting month when people are accustomed to ask forgiveness for whatever wrong they may have done, would finally do the same on behalf of Golkar. His gesture came too late and did not make a great impression.

Among those not impressed were the students. Their demonstrations, which had continued, although perhaps a little less vociferously after Soeharto's fall, had regained momentum once lectures had resumed in September 1998, at times leading to the familiar pattern of an exchange of insults between students and the security forces, and a mutual pelting of stones. At times the situation heated up, escalating into clashes. On 7 September students, many of them belonging to Forum Kota, made their first attempt since early June to force their way into the parliamentary premises. To prevent a repeat performance, extensive security measures were taken the

---

[2] Not all the disgruntled generals joined PKP. Apart from those who had joined the PDI-P, others, for instance Solichin GP, became members of Partai Kebangsaan Merdeka, Free Nationalist Party. Rudini was even mentioned as leader of two parties: Partai Kebangsaan Merdeka and Partai MKGR. Kemal Idris and Ali Sadikin were fielded as candidates during the general election by PUDI.

following day. All roads around the parliament building were blocked by security troops, spawning, as could have been expected, gigantic traffic chaos in Jakarta. On 10 September, FKSMJ organized a mass demonstration near the presidential palace. On the day in between, 9 September, Habibie had a difficult time when he visited Surabaya. Thousands of students, labourers, and Megawati supporters thronged the streets. They forced Habibie to take another route, and later in the day besieged his car. Habibie shrugged it off, saying that nothing serious had happened. Those who had surrounded his car had not been angry demonstrators, but enthusiastic students who had wanted to shake his hand. Later in the month, when Habibie visited Manado, there could be no such interpretation. There were out-and-out demonstrations and clashes between students and security forces.

The students' demands remained unaltered: Soeharto had to be hauled up before the courts (if he were not hanged first), hence texts like 'Soeharto, don't die before you are tried' were paraded around. Prices of the basic commodities had to come down, hence the texts 'The people do not need political parties, they need *sembako*' and 'Remember: the people don't need statements, they need food'. Of course Habibie had to go, hence the text 'Down with prices, down with Habibie'. In a sense, the demands that Habibie had to resign and that Soeharto had to get his just deserts were interlinked. Because Habibie was supposed to be a protector of Soeharto, a prosecution of the former president would only stand a good chance of a fair hearing after Habibie had been replaced. Demonstrating students also repudiated the extraordinary session of the Peoples' Congress scheduled for November. Forum Kota students demanded an Indonesian People's Committee to replace it. Others simply insisted on an earlier date for the purpose of electing a provisional government as soon as possible. Because of the clashes that had taken place between students and security forces during the previous months and the growing body of evidence of army brutality in the past in Aceh, East Timor, and other places, the dual function accorded the Armed Forces, one of the basic elements of the political structure of the New Order, became one of the major targets of student demonstrations as well. It was not just that the army had to return to its barracks and leave politics completely. Feelings of hatred had entered as well. Hence the banner 'Go to hell with ABRI' which was displayed in early September at Gadjah Mada University (Bhakti et al. 1999:119).

The new wave of massive protests fuelled speculations about plots to topple Habibie. Suspicion was rife about the intentions of Barisan Nasional, and students, particularly those of Forum Kota, were accused of deliberately wanting to create chaos simply to bring Habibie down. Nurcholish Madjid, for one, argued that the frequent demonstrations organized in Jakarta in September were engineered to ensure that the economic situation of the common people deteriorated in order to fan up their anger. The whole situation

was a ploy to create an explosive situation in November, when the extraordinary session of the People's Congress was scheduled to convene. In addition, accusations, such as those expressed by the military commander of East
Java, were flung around asserting that in the months leading to the extraordinary session certain groups aimed to set off a 'social revolution' by fanning
up social unrest. Syarwan Hamid also suspected ulterior motives. He was
convinced that the demonstrations were masterminded by people who were
not prepared to wait for the general election, or who were only too well
aware that they would not receive as many votes as they would have wished.

From various sides Forum Kota, the most radical of all the student groups
in voicing its demands, found itself accused of all kinds of ideological and
political sins. It was said to have become an instrument of an unholy alliance
between Christians and communists. Strange bedfellows though these two
groups may appear, some Muslims had become convinced that the United
States and 'Christian forces', unhappy with the fact that a devout Muslim was
Indonesia's president, were plotting to use Christians and communists to
'destroy Islam' in Indonesia (see, for instance, *Ummat*, 30-11-1998:64). Others
voiced the suspicion that the Forum Kota students were being paid by
Barisan Nasional or alternatively by Arifin Panigoro, who indeed had continued to support protesting students, in an attempt to thwart the success of
the extraordinary session of the People's Congress.

The allegation that Forum Kota, which included in its ranks students from
Christian universities such as Universitas Kristen Indonesia and Atma Jaya
University besides Islamic students, for instance from IAIN, played a prominent role could already be heard before 21 May. Fuelled by the idea of
'Christianization' of Indonesian society, it was repeated with growing tenac-
ity when domestic political strife intensified. After 17 September pamphlets
began to circulate which suggested that the students of Forum Kota – a name
which was said by their enemies to stand for Forum Komunis Total – were
taking their lessons from communist strategies. Students were also criticized
for the fact that their actions were said to impede economic recovery and
weaken the rupiah. Forum Kota students reacted furiously to the accusation
that their actions were a threat to political and economic stability, stressing,
as they always did, that they formed a moral and not a political force. Not all
the complaints were on the level of political mud-slinging. There were everyday frustrations too. People began to whine about the traffic jams which were
the inevitable consequence of the demonstrations. This, as well as the material damage caused, became a major cause of complaint. Even demonstrations against demonstrations made their appearance.

Some of the 'communist' commotion was brought about by the stress
Forum Kota and other groups laid on the need for people's committees. In
Amien Rais's eyes, a people's committee mirrored what Lenin had propagat-

ed (Abdullah 1998:49-50). Suspicion was perhaps augmented by the cry 'Revolution', which could be heard at times during demonstrations, not to mention the threats uttered by students and by others who declared that if the malpractices of the New Order were not stamped out, revolution would follow. In many places, too, students had reached out to workers and farmers, and had established a great variety of organizations to assist them and other poor people in their plight. Students had clearly taken the side of evicted farmers. One of the occasions on which this was brought home nationwide was on 23 September, the day when the Agricultural Act had been enacted in 1960. This was the law which had banned large private landownership in Indonesia. To commemorate this, students at Universitas Indonesia organized a discussion meeting with hundreds of farmers, members of Federasi Serikat Petani Indonesia (FSPI), Federation of Indonesian Farmers' Unions, whom they welcomed to their campus. Among the demands formulated on this occasion was the restoration of the rights of farmers who had been evicted from their land, sacrificed to the economic and business interests of a small group of people. To make the spectre of a social revolution the more daunting, some were quick to liken the occupation of land by villagers to the unilateral actions propagated by PKI and its farmers' union in the early 1960s.

Links with the labour movement had been established as well. PRD activities had been the most obvious manifestation of this, but PRD activists were not the only students who forged links with workers. Any students who supported labour activism continued to run the risk of being arrested for inciting workers. Most of the resulting tension was confined to the local level, but there were national ramifications as well. In Jakarta, police and army prevented a mass demonstration advocating the doubling of wages from taking place at the Salemba campus of UI on 21 June. It had been organized by Komite Buruh untuk Aksi Reformasi (Kobar, Flare Up), Workers' Committee for Reformation Action. Workers from Jakarta, Tangerang, Bekasi, and Bogor were prevented from entering and those who were already on the campus were removed from it. Another example attracting wide public attention occurred in Medan, where the authorities were especially concerned about a group styling itself Aliansi Gerakan Reformasi Sumatera Utara, Alliance of the North Sumatra Reform Movements. During protests staged by public transport drivers at the beginning of September, the governor of North Sumatra was forced to agree to the establishment of a People's Collective Council, encompassing farmers, fishermen, drivers, and workers. This was to advise the province on how to improve living conditions.

Supporters of Habibie, mobilized by various Islamic organizations, came out in force as well. On 14 September, protestors from Banten, among them *silat* practioners, demonstrated against Forum Kota in front of the parliament building. A few days later banners appeared at strategic crossroads in Jakarta, placed there by PPP, KISDI and other organizations, such as Kelompok Mahasiswa Pendukung Reformasi Konstitusional (KMPRK), Students Supporting Constitutional Reform, and Badan Kontak Pemuda Remaja Masjid Indonesia, Indonesian Contact Body of Young Mosque-goers, inveighing against the communist danger and Forum Kota (Forkot). One of these stated: 'State was on the threshold of danger. The third PKI uprising in September 1998'. Another stated that 'Communists, Nasakom, PRD, Forkot ... always used the people'. Yet others blamed communists, PRD, and Forum Kota for the rioting and the plunder of agricultural produce (*Tajuk*, 1-10-1998:74-5; *Tempo*, 12-10-1998:20). Similar warnings reverberated in mosques. KISDI leaders like Ahmad Soemargono could be seen wearing headbands bearing the text *Reformasi Konstitusional*. Apart from Soemargono, Fadli Zon and CIDES members were accused of organizing the anti-student campaign (*Siar*, 16-11-1998). Similar warnings reverberated in mosques.

One of the victims of such an action was Arifin Panigoro. On 2 October, his house became the object of a demonstration by a group called Front from the Saviours of the Nation. They suspected Arifin Panigoro of having financed anti-Habibie pamphlets distributed by students. Stones were thrown. Ten days later, the same front was among the demonstrators at the Indonesian Legal Aid Foundation. This time they demanded a halt to the bashing of Soeharto.

As September drew to a close, warnings against subversion proliferated. On 24 September, addressing a 'Commanders Call' of the Armed Forces, Habibie called attention to the fact that demonstrations had overstepped the bounds of propriety, and that outside Jakarta the looting and destruction had to stop. He instructed the military to take firm action against any group which had set its sights on obstructing political reform by destabilizing the country. Wiranto joined in the fray. Alerting his audience of the most senior military officers in the country to the communist danger, he called for vigilance against groups which he claimed intended to topple Habibie and form a transitional government. The way Wiranto phrased his warning left no doubt that, at that moment, he had in mind the group styling itself Koalisi Nasional untuk Demokrasi. A great many groups from all over Indonesia participated in this National Coalition for Democracy, headed by Ratna Sarumpaet. On 15 and 16 August, it had formulated its programme during a meeting at Hotel Indonesia. The programme called for the dissolution of parliament and the People's Congress, the formation of a transitional government, the constitution of regional people's councils, and an end to the dual function of the Armed Forces. In the middle of September, after the National Coalition had drawn up a plan of action at a meeting in Ciawi, Ratna Sarumpaet was summoned by the police for questioning as a 'witness' in relation to the Hotel Indonesia meeting. The charges were insulting the president and having staged a public event without police permission. Ratna Sarumpaet ignored the summons. She and other members of the group were careful to point out that they wanted to achieve their aims through a session of the People's Congress. Fired with this purpose, they actively tried to enlist the support of its members. When it transpired that the latter were not much inclined to follow their suggestions, this did not go down well. In November, when visiting the Armed Forces group in Congress, Ratna Sarumpaet and other activists, among them H.J.C. Princen and Pius Lustrilanang, walked out angrily when they got the impression that they were not being taken seriously.

The Commanders Call let loose a host of warnings about the communist danger, a subject prone to strike a favourable chord with many in the Muslim community. Reporting on the Commanders Call, *Republika*, which alleged that Forum Kota aimed to set up a National People's Committee and Regional People's Committees on 30 September, sported bold front-page headlines stating that the Armed Forces would be on their guard against the '30-S Forkot Movement' (*Republika*, 29-9-1998). A clearer link with the '30 September Movement', held responsible for the coup d'état in 1965, could not be made. For the students it was reason enough to stage a demonstration at the newspaper's office. On 30 September, Muladi joined the chorus of government officials warning of attempts to unseat Habibie. He reminded Indonesians of the severe penalties such efforts entailed. He still stopped short of condemning Forum Kota. These students did no more than talk. They were not planning a plot. Though he had to admit that they had every right to try to win support in the People's Congress for their ideas, Muladi could not conceal his suspicions about the intentions of the National Coalition.

Intentionally or not, the atmosphere was heated up a few degrees by rumours about scenarios being planned to bring Habibie down by a new nation-wide wave of demonstrations. There was talk of plans to stage massive protests in a number of cities between 22 September and the beginning of October, and of a 'Ciawi document' which was purported to outline the strategy to be followed. Among the alleged aims were the occupation of the provincial parliament of East Java in Surabaya and of the municipal councils of Surabaya and Jakarta. According to the published version of the Ciawi document, having been taken hostage, members of these bodies and others would be forced to sit on a people's committee, whose task was to elect a presidium. The protests were to culminate at the end of September – 30 September was sometimes mentioned – in demonstrations and looting in Surabaya on a scale larger than what had taken place in May in Jakarta. Others expected a climax on 10 November, Heroes' Day, and the first day the

People's Congress was scheduled to convene.

The authorities took the reports seriously. On 22 September, policemen, soldiers, and marines were posted all over Surabaya to guard government offices, shopping centres, and the like. In Jakarta, where on that day Forum Kota did stage a demonstration, special security precautions were also taken.

By now the time had come for supporters of Habibie to show their strength. On 30 September, the Indonesian Council of Ulama staged an anti-communist mass rally at Istiqlal Mosque in Jakarta. Some 20,000 people attended. Among them were Zainuddin M.Z. and Emha Ainun Nadjib. Established under the auspices of the Council was Forum Umat Islam Penegak Keadilan dan Konstitusi (Furkon, the difference between right and wrong), Muslim Forum of the Upholders of Justice and the Constitution. Its office was in Istiqlal Mosque, for which one of Furkon's leaders, Rear Admiral (Ret.) Adang Safaad, was the executive secretary. Another Furkon leader was Faisal Biki, a brother of Amir Biki and a close associate of Adi Sasono. He claimed that 100,000 Muslims were ready to defend the general session of the People's Congress. A special commission for mass mobilization was constituted to muster support. In its first statement, Furkon declared the transfer of the presidency to Habibie legal, warned against the danger of communism, and denied that any mass rapes had taken place in Jakarta in May. Furkon was also responsible for the banners which appeared in the streets of Jakarta in favour of the session of People's Congress.

Tension continued to mount. Barisan Nasional came under increased suspicion after Kemal Idris, Subroto, Ali Sadikin, and Dimyati Hartono attended a student meeting on 1 October in Bandung, coordinated by Koen Soekarno. The organizers, calling themselves Potensi Gerakan Reformasi se-Jawa, Potency of the All-Java Reform Movement, were aspiring to organize student protests in Java and Bali. At the meeting a proposal calling for mass demonstrations over a period of 40 days, starting 5 October, Armed Forces Day, had been accepted. The objective of the exercise was to replace Habibie with a presidium or a people's committee. Barisan Nasional members present had expressed their support for the students' intentions.

The words *makar* (subversion) and anarchy fell. Leaders of Barisan Nasional and Edi Sudradjat were indignant. Barnas was a moral force. What it wanted was a government expunged of any slightest remnant of the Soeharto period. Espousing this goal, they supported the students who had a similar aim. Kemal Idris commented that Barisan Nasional had explained its programme only to the students, distancing himself from the plans put forward at the meeting in Bandung. In their own group, Rudini spoke out against any such objectives, deploring the support expressed for any actions intended to bring down the government in an undemocratic way.

On Armed Forces Day, this time a rather modest affair because of the economic problems, Habibie, carrying out an official inspection for the first time, underlined the danger. He noted the 'emergence in a small group in society of the seeds of a radical and revolutionary movement acting in the name of the reform movement' (*Republika*, 6-10-1998). He claimed such people wanted to enforce their ideas by inciting violence in Jakarta and elsewhere. The Armed Forces had to take 'proactive' action.

Protests culminated on 28 October, the Day of the Youth Pledge, when the largest demonstrations since May were staged in a number of cities. In Jakarta on that day, students and members of NGOs demonstrated for hours in the vicinity of the parliamentary complex, where the People's Congress was to convene. The demonstration, called a *latihan menggoyang*, an exercise to cause [the People's Congress] to waver, had been organized by Aksi Rakyat Bersatu, United People's Action, or AKRAB (Close Friends). AKRAB brought together various groups. Among them were the National Coalition for Democracy, Forum Kota, and FKSMJ, which was by now aware that the People's Council would never comply with the students' demands, and had decided to reject the holding of the extraordinary session. Kobar and Front Aksi Mahasiswa untuk Reformasi dan Demokrasi (Famred), or Student Action Front for Reform and Democracy, which had been split off from Forum Kota, also joined in. Other student groups, among them the Islamic HMI, KAMMI, and Hammas, and the Christian student organizations PMKRI and GMKI, explicitly endorsed the session, but were vocal in voicing their demands about the decisions the People's Congress should take.[3]

On the same day in Jakarta, a separate demonstration rejecting a 'Habibie People's Congress' took place on the UI campus, organized by Iluni UI. Among its participants were Ali Sadikin, Kemal Idris, Usep Ranuwidjaja, Sri Edi Swasono, Sri Bintang Pamungkas, Subroto, and Hariadi Darmawan. PDI-P supporters had been drawn en masse to the campus by the rumour that Hariadi Darmawan had also invited Megawati. Students and staff of Universitas Indonesia reacted with indignation. In their eyes the PDI presence was an infringement of the principle that the campus was not to be used for 'practical politics'. Matters almost deteriorated into a brawl when students tried to prevent Megawati supporters from entering. The students demanded a formal apology from Hariadi Darmawan, not to mention a *reformasi total* of the Iluni board.

Lines had been drawn. On the one side rallied radical students who could count on at least the moral support of Barisan Nasional, whose members

---

[3]   Hammas or Himpunan Mahasiswa Muslim Antarkampus, Inter Campus Association of Muslim Students, was founded in October by students belonging to HMI, the student association of Muhammadiyah, and Pelajar Islam Indonesia (PII), the Organization of Indonesian Islamic Pupils.

likewise called for a transitional government, and gave the impression that they were not averse to using 'people power' to reach this aim. From the outset, Barisan Nasional members had testified to their aversion to Islamic parties. In their view nationalism should come first. The primacy of Islam could only lead to the disintegration of Indonesia, with provinces in which non-Muslims formed a majority breaking away (interview with Kemal Idris, *Tajuk*, 6-8-1988:28-33). On the other side were ranged the 'greens'. They considered Habibie's coming to power a victory for their side, one which now threatened to be undone if the uncompromising critics of the government had their way. The cabinet, Ahmad Soemargono was to state in January, was *ijo royo-royo*, really truly green (*Tragedi* 1999:104). For them a defeat of Habibie was a defeat of Islam. These Habibie supporters were able to draw and then mobilize support from the more uncompromising segments of what is often designated the modernist Islamic community. Among them were past and present members of organizations like HMI, especially the HMI-MPO (Majelis Penyelamat Organisasi or Council of Saviours of the Organization), the HMI faction which had refused to yield to the New Order's *asas Pancasila* policy, and Pelajar Islam Indonesia (PII), the organization of Indonesian Islamic Pupils, and Gerakan Pemuda Islam (GPI), Islamic Youth Movement, two organizations which had taken a similar stand and having done so had been forced underground during the New Order. Among the people who shared this background were Abdul Qadir Djaelani, Z.A. Maulani, Muchdi, and Kivlan Zein.

The leaders of the 'green side' were not afraid to use Islam as a symbol of mobilization, and frowned upon the efforts made by Islamic politicians like Abdurrahman Wahid and Amien Rais to stress the 'national' aspect of PKB and PAN, to underplay their religious background. By the beginning of November accusations were flying thick and fast, with each side accusing the other of paying demonstrators. Had the more radical opponents of Habibie accused his government of being unconstitutional from the start, now it was the turn of those backing Habibie to state that trying to obstruct the extraordinary session of the People's Congress was unconstitutional. Habibie supporters denounced those who opposed the session of being against *reformasi*; not to be outdone, the latter blamed the former of rejecting reforms. Both camps had become deeply suspicious of the other, suspecting all kinds of tricks on the part of the adversary to prevent the other from gaining ascendancy.

This time the political atmosphere had really heated up in the run-up to the session of the People's Congress which was scheduled to convene from 10-13 November. The People's Congress of November was no longer the same body which had convened in March. The members who had relinquished their 'nepotism' seats immediately after 21 May had disappeared, while after the Golkar national congress Soeharto's relatives, including Sudwikatmono and Probosutedjo, had been replaced. In between these resignations, Habibie had recalled almost half of the one hundred members appointed by his predecessor as representatives of social groups. The Golkar representation had also not escaped changes. Among the victims were Sarwono Kusumaatmadja, Siswono Yudohusodo, Hayono Isman, and Indra Bambang Oetojo of Barisan Nasional and GKPB. Edi Sudradjat was not recalled, but he resigned five days before the commencement of the extraordinary session. In an effort to separate the executive from the legislative power, cabinet ministers had to relinquish their seats as well.

In the eyes of Habibie's critics, these changes were mere window-dressing. The cleansing from the People's Congress of members stained by KKN, and those who were considered to be *antireformasi* or *Soehartois* continued to be insisted upon among the demands voiced during demonstrations of students, who did not reject an extraordinary session outright, which had initially been the case with FKSMJ. They were convinced the changes did not go far enough, or, worse still, had only been made to strengthen the position of Habibie. As far as they were concerned, the session of the People's Congress, dominated as this institution still was by representatives of Golkar and the Armed Forces, was no more than an effort to legitimize his position, and to safeguard the interests of the Armed Forces and Golkar, and in extension also those of Soeharto, by its decrees. As grounds for their suspicion they could point to the fact that many of the new members appointed were, for instance, close to Habibie and had links with ICMI and BPPT. The changes had been presented as a genuine attempt to give substance to the reform climate, but Habibie's critics spoke of a new-style nepotism. Sceptics saw proof in the refusal of the Working Body of the People's Congress to issue separate decrees demanding an investigation into Soeharto's wealth and one to end the routine presence of the Armed Forces in representative bodies.

Armed Forces representation raised the spectre of the wider issue of the dual function of the Armed Forces. Senior army officers promised change. As early as 25 May, Yudhoyono had given public assurance that the military were keeping track of the aspirations in society. The military was prepared to relinquish some of the Armed Forces' political and social influence, but the army top brass refused to go all the way. On 5 October, to show his good will, Wiranto said that he and the other leading officers were aware of the need for introspection. He promised that the one-sided 'security approach', which had characterized the Armed Forces up to then, would be a thing of the past. As an indication of his intention to return the military to its original function, he revealed that the Armed Forces were to be renamed Tentara Nasional Indonesia (TNI). The change in name was a conscious attempt to dissociate the Armed Forces of the reformation era from the abuses which had been committed under the New Order and to recall the image of the positive role the Armed Forces had played during the War of Independence. A second measure Wiranto announced on that day in the effort to diminish the socio-political role of the military was the severing of the police from the Armed Forces. In theory the latter step meant that the police would become responsible for maintaining domestic order, while the Armed Forces would concentrate on their defence tasks.[4]

As a next step, on the eve of the extraordinary session the central and regional offices for social and political affairs of the army which in the past had been responsible for the planning of Armed Forces interference in national and regional politics were abolished. In future, Yudhoyono was to be Chief of the Territorial Staff, no longer Chief of Staff for Social and Political Affairs. Simultaneously it was announced that officers with a civilian function, with the exception of those who held seats in representative bodies, had to resign from the Armed Forces or take early retirement, neatly making them independent of the military command structure. The approximately 6,000 officers concerned were given till April 1999 to choose between active service in the Armed Forces and a civilian career. It was said that ninety per cent opted for the second alternative and chose retirement. Those who wanted to return to active service were made to understand that they should not count on preferential treatment to gain a proper position in accordance with their rank. One of the consequences of this new policy was a sudden re-influx of generals, an 'inflation of generals' one magazine called it, many on the eve of their retirement, who had held a civilian post, for whom it was almost impossible to find a suitable function in the Armed Forces (*Siar*, 7-6-1999:19).

Wiranto's concessions did not impress the critics of the regime. His gesture could not prevent another wave of student protests all over Indonesia denouncing Habibie and other 'defenders of the status quo', another term which had become all the rage to denote persons and groups rejecting radical reforms. From time to time brave words were bandied about. Protesters vowed that they were prepared to die in their struggle to bring Habibie down. Others ominously foretold that blood would flow, or talked about 'people power' and the occupation of the People's Congress, should, as they chose to put it, the aspirations of the people be disregarded.

In reaction to this barrage, the 'green side' came out in support of Habibie and of the Armed Forces. They felt challenged by the students and Barisan Nasional. They saw the massive student demonstrations as an unjustified and inappropriate show of force. Equally bellicose statements were made on

---

[4]   Both measures became effective as of 1 April 1999. The police remained part of the Ministry of Defence and Security.

their side to underline their resolve not to shrink from a confrontation with the demonstrating students. At a press conference on 27 October Achmad Tirtosudiro of ICMI stated he was not afraid of a confrontation with Barisan Nasional and Forum Kota during the coming session of the People's Congress. His side was prepared. People who wanted to thwart the 'constitutional effort' had to be confronted (Hamzah et al. 1998:136-7). In a similar vein, Faisal Biki indicated that a bloody confrontation might lie in store (Hamzah et al. 1998:137). Later, on 11 November, when the extraordinary session had already begun, KH Ali Yafei, chairman of the Indonesian Council of Ulama (KH Hasan Basri had died on 8 November), uttered similarly pugnacious words. Convinced that the anti-Habibie demonstrations were incubated and hatched at Universitas Kristen Indonesia, he wondered why the people who supported the session – rather than those who tried to thwart it – were put in an unfavourable light. If the latter did not moderate their words and their actions, he said, the former would be ready for a confrontation. The atmosphere had grown so heated that student senates of Roman Catholic universities expressed their regrets about the impression that those who were against the extraordinary session of the People's Congress, were automatically against Habibie and against Islam (*Kabar dari Pijar*, 11-11-1998).

As the extraordinary session drew closer, Muslims held their own manifestations. In various cities in Indonesia demonstrations in support of the session were organized. In Jakarta this at times took the form of a show of force. On 1 November, a Forum Ummat Pendukung Konstitusi (Fungsi), Forum of the Islamic Community Supporting the Constitution, in cooperation with the Golkar-affiliated Forum Komunikasi Ormas Islam (FKOI), Communication Forum of Islamic Mass Organizations, staged a large meeting in the parking area of Senayan Stadium. To show that they were ready to 'protect' the extraordinary session, this was followed between 3 and 7 November by *apel siaga*, roll-calls, in fifty subdistricts in the Jabotabek region.

One climax of Muslim support was a mass meeting of reportedly one hundred thousand Muslims who came to pray for the success of the session at Senayan Stadium on 5 November. Many were dressed in white, the women donning a head-shawl, the men wearing a white cap and jubbah. The event was organized by Forum Silaturahmi Ulama-Habaib dan Tokoh Masyarakat Islam, Friendship Forum of Ulama, Descendants of Muhammad and Islamic Public Figures. Muslims left no room for doubt that they were ready for a physical confrontation, if needed, to prevent the occupation of the parliamentary complex. Ismail Hasan Metareum, Ahmad Soemargono, Eggi Sudjana, H. M. Cholil Badawi, Fadel Muhammad (a businessman, and treasurer of Golkar), and leaders of PBB, and Partai Keadilan all made an appearance at the meeting. Endorsement of the extraordinary session also came from a Kongres Umat Islam Indonesia (KUII), Congress of the Indonesian

Islamic Community, the first time since 1945 that the major Islamic organizations, including NU and Muhammadiyah, held a joint public congress. Held between 3 and 7 November, it attracted two thousand participants.[5]

In the days leading up to the extraordinary session, Jakarta was transformed into a military bastion. Even the navy had warships on stand-by ready to be brought into action if necessary. Soldiers and policemen were deployed in great numbers to be able to cope with mass demonstrations and to prevent protesters from entering the congress building. It was even contemplated shielding the congress premises with a wall of barbed wire which could be electrically charged. Over and above this, Wiranto decided to recruit civilians from a variety of youth organizations to assist the Armed Forces in maintaining peace in Jakarta. Those involved, in theory under the command of the head of the Jakarta police, were named Pasukan Pengamanan Swakarsa, Voluntary Security Guards, or Pam Swakarsa, a term usually used to denote of citizens' groups given the task of guarding their own village or neighbourhood. According to the head of police of Jakarta, the plan was to involve 125,000 civilians to reinforce the 118,000 policemen and 50,000 soldiers who were to be deployed in the capital. In the original plan, members of groups like Pemuda Pancasila, Pemuda Panca Marga, Ansor,[6] and the Boy Scouts had been counted on. It turned out that the bulk of Pam Swakarsa was made up of members of militant Islamic groups, some of them just as great fans of Iwan Fals as many of the students were, and which in actual fact fell outside the competence of the supervision of the police. Organizations like KISDI and Gerakan Pemuda Islam (GPI), Islamic Youth Movement, provided Pam Swakarsa contingents. A major component was supplied by Furkon. Furkon leaders claimed it was 31,000 men strong. Its members wore green and white caps and had donned headbands with the text 'There is no God but God' written on them. Some of them camped in the East Senayan carpark, arriving there days in advance of the extraordinary session, anticipating that if they did not do so, protesting students might already have occupied the parking area before they arrived. Others were lodged at Istiqlal Mosque. Upon arrival they were whipped into a bellicose mood by being

---

[5] Among other points it considered significant the congress stressed the importance of Article 33 of the Constitution and announced its intention to establish an Economic Council for the Islamic Community. It also spoke out in favour of an investigation into the violation of human rights, including those alleged to have taken place in East Timor and Irian Jaya.

[6] The intention to involve Pemuda Pancasila caused speculations that part of the money to finance Pam Swakarsa came from Soeharto and his inner circle. The pay-off was that it should be seen to that the People's Congress took decisions which were not too unfavourable for him. Pemuda Panca Marga is a rival youth organization of Pemuda Pancasila, with links with Golkar and the army. For Pemuda Pancasila and Pemuda Panca Marga, see Barker (1998) and Ryter (1998). Ansor withdrew, it was explained, because its members were needed to protect *pesantren* and *ulama* in Jakarta. They also provided guards for Abdurrahman Wahid's house.

Members of Pam Swakarsa (photo *Tempo*)

told that they had been called on to defend Islam, and by appeals to wage a holy war to defend religion and the state, implying that they were to be involved in a fight against infidels. There were references to conspiracies to weaken the Islamic community and deny them their political role. A propaganda campaign had done its work. Pam Swakarsa members confided to *Tempo* journalists that they 'were ready for a holy war against the communist students who were supported by non-Islamic groups like CSIS, Benny Moerdani and Sofyan Wanandi' (*Tempo*, 30-11-1998:43). Others, the unemployed and drop-outs from schools, had been lured by the promise of free meals and money. Some of these Pam Swakarsa, most of them paid up to Rp 10,000 a day, came from neighbouring areas in West Java, but some were recruited as far away as Madura. Among them were the *silat* fighters from Banten, a group of persons from which members of Golkar's Satgas were also recruited again featured prominently.[7] According to those opposing the

---

7   Satgas comes from Satuan Tugas, Task Force. Each party of any importance had such army-style uniformed guards at the various administrative levels. Such organizations were in addition to existing ones with similar functions. Nahdlatul Ulama had its Banser. Muhammadiyah could fall back on its Komando Kesiapsiagaan Angkatan Muda Muhammadiyah (Kokam), Vigilance Command of Muhammadiyah Youths; it was founded in 1965, when, similar to Banser, it had played an active role in the purge of PKI members. Often such units received a para-military training. At times they appeared in the streets armed with clubs and knives, and occasionally

deployment of Pam Swakarsa, many of them were farmers, the unemployed and local toughs.

As customary at moments of intense political tension in Indonesia, a plethora of names was mentioned in any discussion of those instrumental in recruiting Pam Swakarsa: Adi Sasono (Farid Rasyid, a former student activist from the 1970s, even went so far as to call Pam Swakarsa Sasono's troops (*Republika*, 12-11-1998)), Achmad Tirtosudiro, Eggi Sudjana, Moh. Jumhur Hidayat, H. Amidhan (of the Indonesian Council of Ulama), Faisal Biki, Abdul Qadir Djaelani, and Kivlan Zein, to mention the best known. Those connected with CIDES, like Adi Sasono and Jumhur Hidayat, denied any involvement, dismissing such reports as a plot to blacken the name of CIDES.

The presence of Pam Swakarsa, some of whom had received training from soldiers, and the resolve of students to stage a mass protest only made the chance of a violent confrontation all the more likely. Rudini and others had predicted a spilling of blood, and a break-down of the whole system, should the People's Congress disregard the demands being voiced by society (*Merdeka*, 2-11-1998). Remembering what had happened in May, many people, particularly Chinese and foreigners, fled the city to take refuge abroad. Others who did not have plans to go were hesitant to leave the safety of their houses, and groups of people stepped up patrols to guard their own neighbourhoods.

In the days leading up to the extraordinary session, demonstrations in favour as well as those against the extraordinary session were held all over Indonesia, with Jakarta becoming the focus of such manifestations. The groups protesting the extraordinary session were of manifold origin. Some were from individual universities, from Forum Kota and FKSMJ, from Famred, Kobar, Aliansi Demokrasi Rakyat (Aldera) or People's Democratic Alliance, Komando Barisan Rakyat (People's Front Commando), and Aksi Rakyat Bersatu (People Unite Action). Others were members of Forum Bersama (Forbes) or Joint Forum, Komite Mahasiswa dan Rakyat untuk Demokrasi (Komrad) or Students' and People's Committee for Democracy. Yet others protested in the name of Parlemen Mahasiswa Indonesia (Parmi) or Parliament of Indonesian Students, Keluarga Besar Universitas Indonesia (KBUI) or the Greater Universitas Indonesia Community, or Koalisi Nasional untuk Demokrasi (KNUD). Ikatan Mahasiswa dan Pemuda Timor Timur (IMPETTU) or League of Students and Youths from East Timor, waving the East Timorese flag, and Komite Pendukung Mega (KPM) or Committee of

---

also with swords. PDI-P Satgas members dressed in a black uniform and wore a red beret. Other Satgas preferred army camouflage battledress. Boots and often dark sunglasses completed the uniform. Some Muslim groups, such as Jundullah (Army of God) of KISDI, stressed their Islamic background in their choice of dress.

Mega Supporters were also present.

Students had prepared well. They had arranged for medical and logistic teams to be on stand-by, and as had happened in May were to be given cash, food, and drinks by the academic staff, NGOs, and members of the public. In addition to this, on 7 November the rectors of 159 institutions of higher education issued a statement in support of the students. They asked the Armed Forces to protect the students who, they hastened to emphasize, acted as a moral and intellectual force in striving for reforms. The Minister of Education, Juwono Sudarsono, endorsed the statement. GRN of Subroto and his friend even went further, appealing to graduates to join the student demonstrations to be staged at the parliamentary complex (Habeahan et al. 1999:39; *Tempo*, 16-11-1998). Sounding an equally bellicose note was Kemal Idris, who threateningly predicted that if Habibie had not stepped down before 7 November, mass protests would be staged at the parliamentary complex (Habeahan et al. 1999:2; *Tempo*, 9-11-1998).

Shouting *Allahu Akbar*, Pam Swakarsa were out on the streets of Jakarta in full force as well, their activities coordinated by 'handy-talkies'. They were directed to places where protesting students might assemble: the streets surrounding the parliamentary complex; nearby Senayan Stadium and the Semanggi cloverleaf, with the Jakarta police headquarters and Atma Jaya University on opposite sides; Proclamation Monument and Taman Ismail Marzuki. Having been strategically deployed, Pam Swakarsa had prevented the staging of a People's Extraordinary Session at Proclamation Monument on 9 November. On that same day it became clear that some of the problems were being caused by Pam Swakarsa, who had armed themselves with *bambu runcing*, bamboo spears, clubs, sickles, and rocks, some even carrying *kelewang*, sabres, and swords. Their provocative behaviour led to fights and near-fights with students and residents. Pam Swakarsa members driving around the centre of Jakarta in trucks and buses provoked students of the Roman Catholic Atma Jaya University. When onlookers threw plastic bottles at Pam Swakarsa, they reacted by pelting the students with stones. To prevent worse from happening, policemen and soldiers had to order Pam Swakarsa to make themselves scarce. In the ruckus in which Pam Swakarsa were involved at Proclamation Monument, the authorities even needed to ask for the mediation of Munir to arrange their safe retreat in the midst of an angry crowd. The incidents were ominously symptomatic of what was going to happen. Ordinary citizens, in particular school pupils and other young people, taking offence at the overwhelming and provocative presence of Pam Swakarsa in the streets of Jakarta and in their own neighbourhoods, gave vent to this indignation by chasing and beating up Pam Swakarsa members, hurling stones at them. They turned against the security forces as well. Embarrassed by the actions of Pam Swakarsa and the criticism to which this gave rise, army and police started to disarm some of the Pam Swakarsa units, denying that it had ever been their intention to employ groups armed the way they were. Critics remained unconvinced by such acts.

In a last bid to have their ideals realized, students of FKSMJ, ITB, and Universitas Siliwangi tried to bring Abdurrahman Wahid, Amien Rais, Megawati, and Sultan Hamengkubuwono together. On 8 November, they marched to the houses of both Abdurrahman Wahid and Megawati to convince them to come out in support of *reformasi*. Both refused to receive them. The following day the students 'kidnapped' Amien Rais at Jakarta airport on his return from Surabaya, accompanying him to Abdurrahman Wahid's house and then to that of Megawati. Neither was at home. Yet the students succeeded in arranging a meeting of the four on the afternoon of 10 November in the house of Abdurrahman Wahid in Ciganjur in South Jakarta. Others – Kemal Idris, Ali Sadikin, Rachmat Witoelar, Sarwono Kusumaat-madja, Setiawan Djody (a businessman who had been close to Cendana and of whom it was also said that he had a good relationship with Abdurrahman Wahid and Wiranto), Arifin Panigoro, Matori Abdul Djalil, and Said Aqil Siradj – had hastened to assemble there as well. The students prevented them from participating in the meeting. They were not allowed to enter the house, and had to wait outside. Wiranto was not present. Later, Setiawan Djody was to state that he had offered Wiranto a helicopter to fly to Abdurrahman Wahid's house. Setiawan Djody said that Wiranto had refused the offer. Assuming that the main point on the agenda would be to discuss an appeal to Habibie to resign, Wiranto had declined because he did not want to become involved in an unconstitutional act.[8]

What came to be known as the Ciganjur Agreement was not what many students had wanted to hear. Some of them saw the four as the most likely candidates to sit on a presidium. The Ciganjur Agreement dashed any such hopes. It was an unequivocal endorsement of the extraordinary session of the People's Congress, which the four saw as a prerequisite for democratic elections as the first step towards a truly legitimate government. The four also called for the disbanding of Pam Swakarsa in order to prevent any escalation. The agreement did not demand an end to the dual function, only for its gradual reduction within a time period of six years. In a statement read by Amien Rais, the person who, Abdurrahman Wahid said, had also drafted it, the four also spoke out in favour of a unitary state, decentralization, and a general election organized by an independent body followed within three months by a session of the People's Congress to elect a new president. Real efforts to end

[8]   Setiawan Djody revealed this information in an interview with *Forum Keadilan* (27-2-2000:23), significantly at a moment when Wiranto found himself in big trouble, being held responsible for the bloodshed in East Timor following the referendum.

corruption, collusion, and nepotism were welcomed. Broaching the topic of the dual function, Abdurrahman Wahid explained that people had to be realistic. Military officers who were governors or *bupati* and the hundreds of others who held civilian posts could not all be replaced in the blink of an eye. From statements made on other occasions by PDI-P politicians and by Megawati herself, it could be construed that the PDI-P top was not greatly inclined to dissolve the dual function. Amien Rais indicated that he – and this was also the formal position of PAN – preferred to see an immediate end to the dual function, but that the other three had talked him around. Asked by journalists for a reaction, Wiranto refused to discuss a timetable for the abolition of the dual function. The 'redefining, repositioning and reactualization' of the Armed Forces' socio-political role, as the jargon went, would proceed in 'accordance with the maturity of society' (*Media Indonesia*, 15-11-1998).

The Ciganjur meeting failed to clear the air. In fact, the reverse was true. The atmosphere grew increasingly grim, though there were also ludicrous moments, for instance on 12 November, when students of Trisakti University presented ear swabs to members of congress in an effort to impress upon the latter that they had to listen to the people (Sonata 1998:22). Offices, shops, and schools remained closed, while, as one Indonesian author describes this, on 11 November, soldiers and police began to become 'emotional' (Loebis 1999:30). On that day, students staged a People's Extraordinary Session at Proclamation Monument, withstanding attempts by security forces to prevent this from taking place. Among the speakers were Andi Arief and Matori Abdul Djalil, which was to provide the latter's political opponents in later days with the opportunity to argue that he had sided with the left. Initially the students had hoped that Amien Rais, Megawati, and Abdurrahman Wahid would address the crowd as well, but the Ciganjur Agreement of the previous afternoon had dashed any such hopes. Afterwards thousands of students marched towards the congress building to continue their extraordinary session there. Ordinary residents, many of them probably belonging to the city poor, joined in, seeking a confrontation with security troops who blocked the way. The boiling point was reached when an UI student, according to fellow students after panicking during an attack by security forces, drove a car into a blockade at Jalan Imam Bonjol. Seven soldiers were seriously injured. Among the wounded in the ensuing skirmish, in which security forces 'in blind rage beat everyone within reach', were a number of photojournalists (Loebis 1999:31). The unexpected result was that the only demonstration inside the parliamentary complex during the extraordinary session of the People's Congress was staged the following morning by journalists.

The events of 12 November were not over. Tens of thousands of people – newspaper reports spoke of about 100,000, while an E-mail report even mentioned a figure of one million – singing, holding impromptu speeches along the way, and shouting slogans against the extraordinary session and against the dual function of the Armed Forces, advanced towards the heavily guarded parliamentary complex from various directions and tried to break through the barricades erected around it (*Kabar dari Pijar*, 12-11-1998). In the skirmishes which followed, one police officer and a high school student were killed. More confrontations seemed inevitable. Accusing the students of trying to overthrow the government, Abdul Rasyid Abdullah Syafi'ei of Ulama Friendship Forum called upon the Islamic community to be ready for a confrontation with the students. Meanwhile, the students had become upset by rumours that Pam Swakarsa were holding 'student razzias', beating up any individual students they chanced to come upon.

In the early evening Amien Rais spoke on TV about the possibility of a small civil war. Abdurrahman Wahid called for calm. In the morning of the following day, 13 November, Wiranto seemed to be ready to give reassurances. He pledged that Jakarta was safe and that the Armed Forces had the situation under control. What really happened was very different indeed. During mass demonstrations – people power was once again the term used to describe the immensity of the protests (*Golkar* 1999:216) – matters spiralled completely out of hand.

During the afternoon and in the evening, parts of Jakarta were to turn into what *The Jakarta Post* described as 'a virtual battlefield [...], pitting students, supported by the masses, against heavily armed police and soldiers' (*The Jakarta Post*, 14-11-1998). Another journalist wrote that watching TV was like watching a war movie (Loebis 1999:36). Security units employed light tanks, armoured cars, and water cannons. Soldiers could be seen taking up firing positions. Protesters fought back with stones, Molotov cocktails, and any other missiles which came to hand.

The worst carnage occurred in the Semanggi region, in front of Atma Jaya University, about one kilometre from the parliamentary complex, where thousands had assembled, shouting their disgust and disgruntlement with the extraordinary session and the dual function, listening to speeches, and singing nationalist songs (*Kabar dari Pijar*, 14-11-1998). All was relatively orderly until Pam Swakarsa provocations provided the trigger, after which chaos ensued. Officers no longer had their troops under control. Orders not to fire were ignored. Soldiers and policemen challenged the students, jeering at the demonstrators and working themselves up by singing their own war songs. Crowds of angry citizens, banging roadside railings as a token of support for the students, tried in their turn to attack the troops, calling them communists, murderers, and criminals. Cries of 'Hang Wiranto' and 'Hang Habibie' were raised. The police and the army were pushed onto the defensive, barely able to hold their ground, and sometime before midnight, conveniently after the session of the People's Congress had been closed, had to ask the students for an 'armistice'.

The scenes which ensued were worse than during the Trisakti shooting. Radio stations once again had to play *Gugur Bunga*. Elsewhere in the city a number of Pam Swakarsa were lynched by an angry mob. Their eyes were gouged out, their faces were smashed, while one victim was found with a piece of wood fifty centimetres long protruding from his mouth. The death of the Pam Swakarsa member, Faisal Biki commented, was one of the risks which had to be taken in the struggle (*Tempo*, 30-11-1998:42).

Different sources put the death toll at between 15 and 19. The official figure presented by Roesmanhadi in a televised speech on 18 November was that 13 people had died, of whom 4 had been students (other reports spoke of 6, 7, or 8 students killed) and one had been a member of the Armed Forces. More than 500 persons had been injured, 89 of them (29 students, 20 soldiers and policemen, and 38 others) had needed hospitalization. Material damage was estimated at Rp 16.5 billion.

The shooting again brought Jakarta on the brink of a maelstrom of riots. Policemen and soldiers found themselves the target of popular anger, the people holding them responsible for the violence perpetrated the previous day. On the day following Semanggi, people in Jakarta held what was described as a *razzia militer*, checking cars and public transport in search of soldiers and policemen, beating up such persons when they could lay their hands on them. Even a military housing complex almost fell victim to mob wrath. One of the lasting consequences of the hatred the military had evoked was shown in Jakarta, where such feelings were especially strong. The anti-riot troops, present in streets all over the city in an effort to give the citizens a feeling of security, took to dressing in plastic rain coats which hid the insignia of the army units to which they belonged. It was an attempt to prevent citizens taking revenge on soldiers of those units which had had a lion's share in the ferocious battles with the demonstrators. To keep the situation under control, the military commander of Jakarta and the city governor asked residents not to leave their homes after ten o'clock in the evening.

Sporadic looting took place in various parts of the city, carried out by people shouting that they were hungry and yelling 'Long live the students'. No traffic was possible between the airport and town. This time the security forces succeeded in preventing the unrest from spreading. Marines, assisted by students, took a lion's share in this. During the May riots in Jakarta, it had already become evident that the marines were the only military body able to control the crowds by persuasion, approaching them in a friendly way, mixing with protesters, joining in their songs, and praying together with them. The same phenomenon was repeated in November. On 14 November, marines had to warn members of the army that it was dangerous to drive alone in the streets, and that their military vehicles might be set on fire by enraged citizens (*Kabar dari Pijar*, 16-11-1998; *Suara Pembaruan*, 15-11-1998). At a number of places in town, marines, unarmed and not carrying shields like the other security forces deployed to suppress riots, positioned themselves between demonstrators and soldiers or asked army units to withdraw to avoid a confrontation. They also accompanied students and others who joined them in their tens of thousands to march to parliament. On their arrival there, the students sang *Gugur Bunga* and prayed. Thereupon speeches were delivered by Sri Bintang Pamungkas, the well-known critical economist Sjahrir, and others. All went well, not least because the marines succeeded in preventing a confrontation with a particular group, also marching to parliament giving voice to their pro-Habibie sentiments.

The other security forces were not at all happy with the behaviour of the marines. They began to consider them the enemy. This became blatantly apparent in October the following year during the ordinary session of the People's Congress when a fight between marines and other units could barely be prevented. It began when members of the Mobile Brigade, of the anti-riot troops of the military command of Jakarta and Kostrad insulted the marines and called them cowards and traitors. Marines answered in kind. A fight erupted. Guns were even pointed at the marines. Members of the Mobile Brigade also turned upon the military police, who tried to separate the two sides. Officers had to intervene to prevent worse from happening.

Later that month, Wiranto admitted that members of the Armed Forces had reacted 'overdefensively', and, disregarding procedure, had shot at and beaten up students. He announced disciplinary measures would be taken against those involved in the beating up of journalists on 12 November, and the shooting at Semanggi on 13 November. Disciplinary measures were to be taken against those who had fired what were stated to be rubber bullets and against officers who had been unable to control their troops. Wiranto steadfastly claimed no orders to fire had been issued. In a repetition of the aftermath of the Trisakti killings, mystery enshrouded the shooting. There was talk of outsiders firing the fatal shots, and newspaper reports added to the confusion by talking about troops firing at the students and the masses from the roofs of nearby skyscrapers (*The Jakarta Post*, 14-11-1998). Equally mysterious was the fact that some of the victims had been hit by so-called 'quick-shot' bullets, which exploded into pieces after entering the body. The spokesman of the Armed Forces, Syamsul Ma'arif, was baffled by this. Such bullets were not standard-issued ammunition to the Armed Forces.

Indignation over the way the Armed Forces had behaved during the days the People's Congress was in session was enormous. Equally great was anger about the fact that Harmoko and the other members of the People's Congress had closed the extraordinary session in a festive mood, at the same moment

that students and others lay dying nearby. Everybody had been able to witness what had happened in Jakarta on the commercial TV stations. Sarwono
Kusumaatmadja was in tears. Abdurrahman Wahid put the blame fairly and
squarely on the security forces, which, he noted, at the time of the War of
Independence had defended the people, but now had turned against them
(Al-Zastrouw Ng 1999:153). He observed that the students had been forced
to use Molotov cocktails as they had nothing else to fight back with when
they were shot at. He pledged that he and the NU would continue the students' struggle. The rectors again came out in full support of the students.
Those of Islamic institutions of higher education deplored the use of Islamic
symbols to gain political ends. They were especially offended because some
of the youths who had been employed had reeked of alcohol (*Media Indonesia*, 20-11-1998). Soeharto joined in the chorus of condemnation. Probosutedjo quoted him as saying that he did not understand why the Habibie
government had caused so much bloodshed. He himself had resigned to
avoid this sort of incident from happening. Habibie, Soeharto's message was,
should have listened to the students (Habeahan et al. 1999:10).

Many, among them advisors of Habibie, demanded Wiranto's resignation.
Others vociferously demanded that Habibie and Feisal Tanjung had to go as
well. Some stressed that at the very least the three had to be held to account
for what had happened. Still others wanted to bring Wiranto before a military court. Hatred of the Armed Forces had mounted. Bashing the Armed
Forces by the general public and in the press became almost as popular as
bashing Soeharto. Pamphlets started to appear urging soldiers and non-com-
missioned officers to disobey their superiors and to join in the struggle
against Habibie.

Students were joined by other citizens all over Indonesia in staging
protests and long marches, often with the local military headquarters or the
regional parliament as the destination, berating and pouring scorn on the
Armed Forces, demanding an end to the dual function and the resignation of
Wiranto, and mourning the dead who had fallen. In a number of cities, local
and national radio and TV stations were forced to broadcast statements of
protest and grief. Airports in Ujungpandang, Bali, Padang, and Medan were
occupied. In Medan, students at Santo Thomas University read a 'Second
Proclamation of Independence Statement': 'We students of St. Thomas
Medan herewith declare the independence of the people of Indonesia.
Matters concerning the trial of Soeharto and his cronies, the abolition of the
dual function of the Armed Forces and the resignation of Wiranto have to be
settled in the shortest possible time.' (*Siar*, 16-11-1998.) In spite of all the criticism, Wiranto himself was proud of what he had accomplished. He
remained convinced that by preventing the occupation of the congress building by the students and other protestors he had frustrated efforts to commit

a coup d'état (see for instance *The Straits Times*, 8-2-2000).

The huge question mark that remained was whether there were any particular people behind the unrest. On 12 November, Amien Rais had already warned students to be aware of the possibility that their demonstrations might be used by people who wanted to take over power. The following morning he had repeated his warning, blaming a small, vocal, and aggressive group which he saw as set to disrupt the extraordinary session and to topple Habibie. Afterwards, Achmad Tirtosudiro blamed Barisan Nasional for having exacerbated the situation by its campaign against the extraordinary session. He left it to the authorities to decide whether or not arrests were called for. A week later, Baramuli did not scruple to denounce Kemal Idris, Ali Sadikin, and their associates as *pengkhianat besar*, super traitors, who should be banished to the prison island of Nusa Kambangan. Almost everybody took great care not to accuse students of being the principal instigators of the disorder, putting the blame on 'provocateurs', in some instances merely referring to people who had shouted inflammatory slogans or who had been the first to throw stones, but in other instances were thought to be pawns in a deliberate plot to create chaos.

The government also had its suspects, putting the blame on 'provocateurs' wearing student jackets. On the 14th, in a televised speech, Habibie announced that he had instructed Wiranto to take the necessary measures against what he described as acts of rebellion of which the object was to topple the government. Two days later Juwono Sudarsono explained that groups composed of radical young people strategically positioned in the front rows of the demonstrating crowd had pelted security forces with stones, which had made the latter lose their temper. Once they had succeeded in this objective they had withdrawn, leaving the brunt of the fight to the students. He had personally witnessed such radical groups gathering in front of buildings close to where the fighting erupted. From there they had organized their actions. He said that the 'provocateurs' had chosen to be active in the afternoon and evening, because at that time it was very difficult to differentiate between 'genuine students' and radical groups (*Republika*, 18-11-1998; *Kompas*, 19-11-1998; *Forum Keadilan*, 14-12-1998:17). Juwono Sudarsono, who also expressed the suspicion that snipers had been at work, refused to reveal who these radical groups were. This, he said, would be explained by Wiranto. Two days later, it was Roesmanhadi's turn to blame the troubles on infiltrators and 'provocateurs'. At the end of the month Wiranto lashed out against a small radical group, hungry for power, but with so little support it stood no chance of realizing its ambitions through a general election. It looked as though a new Soeharto era had dawned. Nobody could or would be specific, and only spoke about 'groups' but never got down to brass tacks.

Not all the blame was heaped on the heads of the anti-Habibie die-hards.

Another interpretation was that the incident had been deliberately provoked by a faction in the Armed Forces which wanted to get rid of Wiranto. One of the persons who advanced this theory was Juwono Sudarsono. Munir of Kontras also spoke about the infiltration of soldiers and others, disguised by wearing student jackets, with the sole aim of provoking the students to violence. They had been the ones who had thrown stones and Molotov cocktails and had shouted inflammatory slogans, giving the soldiers and policemen an excuse to act. He claimed that some had been caught and had confessed to Kontras and to the students who had captured them. On 21 November, one of them told his story to the National Committee for Human Rights, claiming to have been recruited by a member of the military police who guarded the office of the vice-president. He revealed that several hours before the Semanggi shooting he had been warned on his pager to leave the Atma Jaya campus. He also confessed to having enlisted civilian guards in a number of cities in Java, who on their arrival in Jakarta had been taken to the Kopassus barracks in Cijantung, making the journey in army trucks.

Just who the government had in mind burst in the full light of day immediately after the Semanggi incident, when at least seventeen persons were interrogated by the police. Among them were Kemal Idris, Ali Sadikin, Hariadi Darmawan, and Sri Edi Swasono. Others were Sukmawati Soekarnoputri, Sri Bintang Pamungkas, Meliono Suwondo (a deputy treasurer of PDI-P), and Permadi (as a member of the UI alumni association).[9] They were accused of *makar*, of planning a conspiracy with the aim of toppling the government. Once again people suspected a diversionary manoeuvre: to distract people's thoughts from Semanggi, from the investigation of Soeharto's wealth, and so on. Those interrogated were furious, again reiterating that they only formed a 'moral' movement. Some threatened that they would sue the government. Sri Bintang Pamungkas was questioned because of his participation in the student demonstrations. The others found themselves interrogated about a meeting at Hotel Sahid Jaya on 12 November. The authorities took pains to stress that what had transpired there was not the only indication that Barisan Nasional members and others were guilty of subversion, tracing their suspect activities back to the Bandung meeting of 1 October. No prosecution was launched against Barisan Nasional members.

A Joint Communique National Declaration had been issued after the Sahid Jaya meeting. Observing that the people did not recognize parliament and the People's Congress, the declaration urged that the extraordinary session be closed for the sake of national unity, as there was a general conviction

---

[9]   Sjahrir was also interrogated. The authorities were eager to know more about his relations with Barisan Nasional members. An additional reason to hear him was the speech he had held on 14 November in front of the parliamentary complex.

that it would not issue decrees which mirrored the aspirations of the people. If this goal were to be achieved, a Reformation People's Congress should be formed to elect a presidium, which in its turn should form a Provisional Reformation Cabinet. The presidium should consist of leading figures in society, and representatives of the student movement, social organizations, and the new political parties which had recently been founded. The National Declaration also called for an investigation into abuse of power by all former government officials who were guilty of political, economic, and socio-cultural crimes, with Soeharto and Habibie at the top of the list. According to Sri Edi Swasono, the only aim of the meeting had been to provide 'an alternative' thought out by people who had observed the massive student protests and were concerned about the violent clashes which had occurred. Government officials thought differently. In their eyes the meeting constituted a clear act of subversion. The statement was seen as an endorsement of the students in their attempts to occupy the People's Congress.

One of the Barnas members interrogated, Roch Basoeki Mangoenpoerojo, deputy secretary of GRN, was also linked to a meeting which had been planned for early November. Acting in the name of a Forum Revolusi Sekarang Juga, Revolution Now! Forum, he had invited Theo Syafei, Arifin Panigoro, Ratna Sarumpaet, and a number of other vocal critics of the government to participate. The three did not show up. Nor did another 11 of the 17 people Roch Basoeki had invited. It was alleged that at the meeting, which had to be cancelled, Roch Basoeki had wanted to discuss how to derail the extraordinary session of the People's Congress, and how to constitute a People's Committee. To facilitate the discussion he had compiled a 'Terms of Reference for the setting-up of a revolutionary infrastructure' which could then be discussed.

There were rumours that Abdurrahman Wahid was to be interrogated as well. Some reports had it that he had already been arrested because of his blatant support for the students. On 12 November Abdurrahman Wahid had been joined by Megawati in calling upon students to resist the temptation to be provoked and not to be deflected from their purpose. After Semanggi, Abdurrahman Wahid said that NU was ready to continue the students' struggle. He attacked the Armed Forces for their inhumane behaviour. Reacting furiously to rumours of Abdurrahman Wahid's arrest, the Bandung and Semarang branches of NU declared their resolve to wage a holy war if it turned out he had really been taken into custody. To calm down the NU members, Abdurrahman Wahid arranged a press conference to announce that Wiranto, Yudhoyono, and the military commander of Jakarta, Major-General Djaja Suparman, had all guaranteed his safety and had assured him that he was not on the list of people to be interrogated.

On 20 November, called on the initiative of Wiranto, probably to clear the

air, the top brass of the Armed Forces held a two-hour meeting at the
Ministry of Defence with retired officers who sympathized with Barnas or
had joined it. Wiranto explained that the interrogations were not aimed at
Barisan Nasional as an institution. He took the opportunity to draw their
attention to the activities of Ratna Sarumpaet and her National Coalition for
Democracy. Speaking out on his side's behalf, one of the retired officers was
reported to have asked for action to be taken against Kivlan Zein and two
other senior officers (*Tajuk*, 26-11-1998:14). Though presented as a routine
meeting, one in a regular series, this was not how the public perceived it,
especially because Moerdani, a person whose influence, despite his fall from
grace, was still thought to be substantial among retired officers, had been
present.

Some people declared themselves satisfied with the results of the extraordinary session. Members of the People's Congress had been free to speak out,
not afraid of how an all-powerful government would react. Contrary to the
way proceedings were carried out in the Soeharto era, this time special
preparations had been made to allow for interruptions and voting. Moreover,
though originally only intended to pave the way for a general election, the
extraordinary session had discussed a much wider agenda. The Ciganjur
agreement had also not failed to leave its mark. Therefore, Golkar politicians
and Habibie claimed that the decrees of the People's Congress mirrored the
aspirations of society. Spokesmen for the new political parties, such as PKB,
PBB, Partai Keadilan, and PAN, were also moderately positive in their evaluation, pointing out that some, but not all, of their wishes had been met.

Indeed, the decrees agreed upon had wrought some changes in the formal
political structure. The 1998 decree on the special powers of the president
had been repealed. The same fate had befallen the 1983 decree on the conditions for a referendum. This paved the way for the withdrawal of the
Referendum Act, one of the five disputed acts, which had made it almost
impossible to change the constitution. It had stipulated that this could only
take place after a referendum in which 90 per cent of those entitled to vote
had participated and 90 per cent had spoken out in favour. Also revoked was
the 1978 decree about special guidelines for the interpretation of the
Pancasila, which at that time had been accepted by the People's Congress
amidst a chorus of opposition from Muslim circles. It heralded the end of the
special government body instituted to promote these guidelines and to
supervise Pancasila indoctrination. The March 1998 decree on the Broad
Outlines of State Policy had been superseded by a much shorter version,
identifying the improprieties in the political system of the past, stressing,
among other points, Article 33 of the Constitution, and urging for a more balanced relationship between the central government and the provinces. Yet
another decree limited the terms of office of a president to two. Real innova-

tions were decrees on regional autonomy and on human rights. The latter guaranteed freedom of religion according to a person's religion and beliefs. In an indirect way the *asas Pancasila* stipulation had a painless demise. In the act on political parties, all that was mentioned was that political parties had to mention in their regulations that the Pancasila formed the ideological basis of the Indonesian state. Separatist parties continued to be banned, as was the propagation of communism or any other ideology considered to be in contradiction to the Pancasila.

Among the suggestions on the agenda which had not made it was one tabelled by PPP demanding a reversal of the burden of proof in cases against high officials accused of KKN. PPP also had to swallow the disappointment of not being able to carry through its original intention of having a special decree abrogate Soeharto's title of Mister Development. The way in which Habibie had become president was passed over in silence. Probably also with the intention of not eliciting any debate about his presidency, the congressional decrees of March appointing Soeharto and Habibie were not abrogated, which some said implied that Soeharto was still *de jure* Indonesia's president (Pandjaitan and Tanuredjo 1998:87).

Examined in the cold light of day, the extraordinary session had solved nothing. If anything, it had made matters worse. Students and unbending critics of the government refused to recognize the decrees it had issued. They continued to demand the establishment of a presidium or, as Forum Kota continued to stress, an Indonesian People's Committee. Others wanted the People's Congress to be replaced by a new provisional body. Because of what came to be dubbed Grey or Black Friday, or *Semanggi berdarah*, Semanggi bloodbath, they were even more intent on continuing their protests. Their opposition seemed to harden and to become more unyielding. In the middle of December, protesting students started to arm themselves with *bambu runcing*, iron bars, wooden clubs, catapults, and Molotov cocktails. The first time this happened was on 17 December when a crowd of thousands of demonstrators clashed with security troops near the parliament building. They also burnt and looted army tents. The Jakarta army command spoke of a brutal criminal action.

Semanggi had occasioned some rethinking about crowd control. Shortly afterwards the chief of police of Central Java ordered ordinary police to dispense with the use of combat shields, clubs, and firearms when confronted with demonstrators. A 'sympathic approach' was what was in order. Smiling, friendly policewomen should form the front row and persuade protesters that the police were there to see to it that all went well and to accompany them to their destination. Should looting and violence break out, other units of the police and of the Armed Forces should be called in.

In Jakarta sterner measures were worked out. On 4 December, Akbar

Tanjung disclosed the establishment of a special security body, for which in fact a presidential decree had already been issued on 9 November. Four days later, Dewan Penegakan Keamanan dan Sistem Hukum (DPKSH), Council for Maintaining Security and the Legal System, was announced. The council, which was intended to act as a kind of crisis team in times of large-scale unrest, was made up of the attorney-general, other cabinet ministers, the chief of police, the head of Bakin, the secretary of the management of development operations, representatives of the five religious communities, and the National Committee for Human Rights; in total 32 persons.[10] It was chaired by Habibie himself. The secretary was Habibie's advisor and ICMI deputy secretary-general, Jimly Asshiddiqie. Wiranto was chairman of the board's daily executive, Muladi deputy chairman. Critics likened DPKSH to the feared army security body, the Kopkamtib of the past, a comparison refuted by Wiranto on the grounds that DPKSH had no command structure reaching down to the regions. Others just wondered out loud why such a new body was needed anyway.

On 9 December, undeterred by what had happened a month before, Feisal Tanjung, troubled by a shortage of policemen and by the fact that in view of the political unrest in Jakarta units of the Armed Forces had to be sent to that city from elsewhere, announced the establishment of a new civilian security guard made up of youths who had become unemployed as a result of the economic crisis: Pasukan Rakyat Terlatih, Trained People's Troops, Ratih for short, each member to be equipped with a shield, a club, handcuffs, and, most importantly, a whistle.[11] They were to receive a little bit more than regional minimum wage. Employing them instead of recruiting new policemen would save money. Another consideration was that if they were to be given a full police training they would not be ready by the time the elections were held (interview with Roesmanhadi in *Ummat*, 28-12-1998:26). Though presented by some members of the cabinet as a body to assist the police in regions where the crime rate was high, Ratih was as much a precaution against anticipated political unrest during the months to come. Forty thousand were to be trained before the general election, another thirty thousand before the general session of the People's Congress scheduled for November 1999.

It was a controversial step. Persons like Amien Rais, A.H. Nasution, Edi Sudradjat, Said Aqil Siradj, and Munir were against. Apart from calling to

---

10   The National Committee for Human Rights and the Indonesian Bishops' Conference refused to take the seat reserved for them. The Indonesian Council of Ulama, PGI, and the organizations representing the Buddhist and Hindu communities acquiesced in their nomination.
11   One of the arguments used by him and others to defend Ratih was that the police-population ratio in Indonesia was much lower that in many other countries in the world.

mind what had happened in November, those opposing the plan expressed their doubts that the Armed Forces, which themselves had not exactly given an example of restrained crowd control, could train Ratih in such a way that excesses would be avoided. Abdurrahman Wahid and H.A. Najri Adlani, general secretary of the Indonesian Council of Ulama and general chairman of Furkon, were in favour. Hamzah Haz also raised no objection, providing that Ratih members were properly trained, and Akbar Tanjung expressed the hope that Golkar youths would join up.

Muladi put on the brakes, agreeing with those who argued that the new force had to be established by an act of parliament.[12] At the end of January Ghalib took his own personal precautions, distributing one-metre-long and five-centimetre-thick rattan clubs among his employees.

An example of slogans displayed in the streets to evoke good citizenship. The text reads: Inspired by feelings of solidarity and unity we carry out reforms to overcome challenges in political and national life. (photo C. van Dijk.)

---

[12] Instead the Ministry of Defence hired about 40,000 'assistant policemen', also called civilian policemen, or Kamra (short for Keamanan Rakyat or People's Security) at the beginning of 1999. They got a two-year contract.

CHAPTER XV

Mysterious killings

Persoalan demi persoalan
Kerusuhan demi kerusuhan
Dari kasus korupsi
Sampai kasus kolusi
Dari Pulau Sumatera sampai Irian Jaya
Semua hanya membawa bencana.[1]

What is wrong with the nation? This is the question Habibie posed in his speech to mark the end of 1998. Why had Indonesia become so fraught with violence? The riots in Medan, Jakarta, and Surakarta in May had shocked many, as had what had happened in November. Nor were these the only instances of bloodshed. Communal violence took an increasing toll of victims. Reform had not spelled an end to the endemic fights between pupils from different schools, causing a number of fatalities each year. A sad record still to come was the death of 15 schoolboys from Jakarta in March 1999, who jumped into a river in panic and drowned when they were chased by a crowd after a brawl with Bogor pupils.

After the May riots there had been various calls for moderation and tolerance. Abdurrahman Wahid, who had made no secret of his fear of where mass mobilization might lead in the months leading to May 1998, did his best to calm emotions down. His pleas to people to abandon their feelings of hatred made him a figure to whom people of the Christian and Chinese minorities turned as a person committed to the prevention of communal violence. Amien Rais also pleaded for religious, ethnic, and racial tolerance. Though this had previously received less public attention, he had been doing this for years. Chinese, he stated on one occasion, were also descended from Adam and had to be protected (Rais 1998:75, 96-7; Trimansyah 1998:15).

---

[1]   Problem after problem/Riot after riot/ From corruption/To collusion/From Sumatra to Irian Jaya/Nothing but disaster. From *Janganlah mentang-mentang*, 'Don't think you can do everything you want' by GPK Grup, Gerakan Penentang Ketidakadilan Grup or Anti-Injustice Movement Group.

Habibie made his contribution as well, stressing that an indigenous Indonesian was a person who had the nation's interests at heart, and issuing a presidential decree banning the use of the words *pribumi* and *non pribumi* from official correspondence and parlance.

Whether such efforts made much difference is questionable. In an interview, Amien Rais related how people accused him of being used by Christians after he had met representatives of the Christian community. After he talked to Chinese, others had asked him since when had he been coddled by the Chinese (*Forum Keadilan*, 15-6-1998:85). When Abdurrahman Wahid held 'open house' in the fasting month and people visited his home in great numbers to complain or offer advice, one of the questions often asked was why he protected the non-Muslim community and by his actions hurt the interests of the Islamic majority (Al-Zastrouw Ng 1999:224). As these examples indicate, virulent anti-Chinese sentiments and religious animosity continued unabated. Anti-Chinese slogans were still visible on walls, and leaders like Probosutedjo kept up the attack on Chinese businessmen, castigating their alleged lack of nationalism. Probosutedjo went as far as to state that the looters in May had done nothing more than claim their rights (Kwik Kian Gie and Nurcholish Madjid 1998:71; *Tajuk*, 17-9-1998:28-33). Others poured scorn on Chinese for fleeing the country in May and again in November, denouncing such behaviour as unpatriotic. Calling their nationalism into question, a member of the provincial parliament of North Sumatra even asked for an investigation of those Chinese who had since returned from abroad after fleeing the country in May (Aditjondro 1998c:73). In Bogor, Ki Gendeng Pamungkas continued to advertise the Anti-Chinese Movement he had founded. In September 1998 a police investigation was started against him for inciting racial animosity. When Gendeng was questioned, there was a three-hour-long power failure at police headquarters, which was presented as proof of his supernatural powers. Also, during the extraordinary session of the People's Congress, and much to the dismay of James T. Riady, head of the Lippo Concern, and others, PPP delegates wanted to include the word *pribumi* in the decree on economic democracy. The solution was an Old Order one. The final text spoke of small- and medium-scale entrepreneurs, which in actual fact referred to the indigenous sector.

Soeharto's resignation had not stopped the frequent rioting. Between May and August 1998 69 such incidents were counted, one-third of them triggered off by SARA issues. The remainder had an economic and political background (*The Jakarta Post*, 26-9-1998). Roesmanhadi, who revealed these figures, stated that the provinces particularly prone to such violence were North Sumatra, and Central and East Java. In the months which followed, many more riots and clashes between groups were to occur. In some the number of deaths and injuries and the extent of the destruction made for extensive front-page coverage in the press.

One such incident erupted in the city of Kebumen on 7 and 8 September 1998. After a row between a Chinese shopowner and her Javanese assistant who had spilled a can of oil, more than 70 Chinese shops were looted and torched. The first shop to go was that of the angry shopowner, located on the opposite side of the street from a police station. From there a policeman phoned her to say that he was unable to do anything to contain the crowd. Elsewhere in the city four soldiers also refused to act against the angry crowd. Their excuse was that they had not received orders from their superiors to interfere.[2] On 14 September, it was of Medan's turn. Hundreds of 'pro-reformation' drivers and owners of public transport vehicles, shouting 'We are hungry' and 'We don't want promises but rice', demanded cheaper basic commodities. The prices of spare parts, which had risen by 400 per cent, while public transport fares had only been allowed to be raised by 40 per cent, had to come down. While the drivers, pupils, and students were staging their protest in front of the office of the provincial governor, others who were waiting in vain for transportation showed their impatience by destroying Chinese-owned shops. Before the end of September, houses belonging to Chinese, shops, places of worship, and government offices were destroyed in Bagansiapi-api in Riau. Rioting had started after rumours had spread that an indigenous Indonesian injured in a traffic accident, in which a Chinese had also been involved, had been beaten to death. The stories failed to agree on whether the culprit was a Chinese or a policeman.

By September mob violence had become such a repetitive pattern that suspicions that there was a *dalang*, a person or group deliberately engineering chaos, hatred, and fear, grew rapidly. Such voices gained additional force after a series of mysterious killings upset East Java, and later spread to the rest of the island. Among the first indications of what was happening was a report at the end of September by the chief of police of Jember that his men had arrested five hired killers, paid between Rp 200,000 and Rp 1 million each, who had murdered five villagers in the previous month. The victims were all between 50 and 60 years of age. Those arrested had incited other villagers to join in the murder spree by accusing their victims of being *dukun santet*, practioners of black magic.

It was the tip of the iceberg. Usually persons suspected of practising black magic were made to swear a *sumpah pocong* (a strong oath, which, when the murders intensified, no longer saved them from being killed), or were expelled from the village. Occasionally in the past *dukun santet*, targets of pop-

---

[2]   *Forum Keadilan*, 2-11-1998:52-3. It was further observed that people from outside the city had entered town by the truckload, and that a person had been sighted carrying a map of the town on which the building to be set afire had been indicated.

ular fear and anger, had been lynched, causing a number of casualties each year. Suddenly, since the fall of Soeharto, the assaults had become more frequent. A new aspect was the calculated brutality with which the murders were committed. In August, September, and October scores of people suspected of being practitioners of black magic were gruesomely slaughtered in the cities and countryside of East Java. The victims were beaten and stabbed to death or burnt alive. In early October it was reported that there had been over one hundred casualties. Before the end of the month, the chief of police of East Java stated that 170 persons had been killed since January.

The reports published in the mass media were slanted in such a way that the murders appeared to form part of a well-organized campaign, involving *provokator*, agitators who had come in from elsewhere, incited a crowd, and started the lynching. Initially the campaign seemed to be aimed at sorcerers accused of having caused the death of people and, in exceptional cases, of cattle. After a while it emerged that another category of people actually formed the main target, beginning with local religious teachers and soon after this more influential *ulama*, *kiai*, heads of *pesantren*, and other Islamic religious leaders. In some cases this distinction was a very thin line. By virtue of their position, ordinary *kiai* and *ulama* carried with them an aura of supernatural power. Many of the victims were affiliated with NU, but members of Muhammadiyah, PAN, and Partai Keadilan were also murdered. Other religious leaders received threatening phone calls, accusing them of being sorcerers, and pamphlets began to circulate specifically targeting religious figures. These were signed by groups styling themselves Gerakan Anti Tenung, Anti-Sorcery Movement, Gantung ('hang') for short, or Gerakan Anti Kiai, Anti-Kiai Movement, Ganti ('replace') for short.

Most of the victims had been beaten up and stabbed to death by angry mobs or, as was widely reported, by groups of 'ninjas', persons dressed in black with a black mask covering their faces. It was occasionally reported as an additional gratuitous piece of information that such persons were very skilled in walking on roofs.[3] Often the killers operated at night, power cuts preceding their actions and reinforcing the atmosphere of fear, but murders were also committed in broad daylight. The wave of killings had started in Banyuwangi, a region notorious for its reputed sorcerers, spreading from there to other parts of the province where NU influence was strong. Within weeks the murders and the stories about people being killed by masked men had reached Central and West Java. At the end of October it was reported that popular religious figures in Jakarta, among them KH Zainuddin M.Z., had also become the target of a hate campaign.

---

[3]   In November even a 'white ninja', a person in a white *jubbah* and hiding a sickle, was apprehended.

The killings assumed such proportions that in Banyuwangi and Besuki people who were known to be sorcerers, in Banyuwangi about 250 in total, were evacuated to police stations, army barracks, and government buildings for their protection. To carry this out, in the middle of September the *bupati* of Banyuwangi, H. Turyono Purnomo Sidik, ordered mayors to draw up a list of black magicians in their villages.[4] His instructions had unfortunate consequences. The lists leaked out, identifying potential victims to the public. For some this was reason enough to conclude that Purnomo Sidik was one of the persons behind the killings. Leading local *ulama* and prominent figures in the region did not go that far, but still demanded his resignation, holding him morally responsible. In an untenable position, Purnomo Sidik resigned in March 1999.

Whole regions in Java were gripped by fear. People compared the atmosphere to that which reigned during the time leading up to the coup d'état of 1965. Villagers and city residents intensified their night watches, equipping themselves with a variety of arms, distrusting and suspecting all strangers and all unknown vehicles which happened to pass by. Entrances to villages and city wards were closed off with oil drums and barbed wire at night. Some people, fearing that they might be the next victims, did not dare to sleep in their own homes. Others stayed at home after dark. The times of religious gatherings, like Koran recitation sessions, were moved from the evening to the afternoon, or were stopped for the time being if they were led by *kiai* who had only a small following. The University of Jember cancelled its evening classes. It was even reported that people were afraid to go to the mosque or to prayer houses, to have the call to prayer resound loud and clear over their neighbourhoods, or – in South Blitar – to wear the black cap or hajji cap, which identified them as devout Muslims (Rahim 1998:4-5; Loebis 1999:8). In a few instances people, hounded by fear after they or relatives had been accused of being *dukun santet*, hanged themselves. Local *kiai* and *ulama* took refuge in police stations, armed themselves with machetes and sickles when they left their houses, and turned to their own community for physical and spiritual protection. In some places Banser members who had armed themselves with sickles and swords compounded fear by threatening to take

---

4   Earlier in the year a similar list had been compiled, in some villages complete with photos taken of alleged *dukun santet*. The reason given was that if the nation had to be defended, people with magical powers were much needed (*Tajuk*, 15-10-1998). With respect to this registration, it was also claimed that the information it provided had made it easier for the killers to select their victims. An NU fact-finding team mentions that Turyono Purnomo Sidik had ordered the first registration to be prepared should something undesirable happen (Al-Zastrouw Ng 1999:98). One of the local chiefs of police presented as an explanation to justify the registration of *dukun santet* in his area that it was done so that at a certain moment in the future they might assist security forces. (*Tempo*, 19-10-1998:27).

revenge on any village in which an NU member was killed. Members of NU, Banser, and *pencak silat* groups arranged special guards for their *kiai* and *ulama*, and *kiai* arranged for special martial arts training for their pupils. Members of the KOKAM of Muhammadiyah were also asked to assist in protecting their leaders. In Jakarta one *pesantren* invited an *ulama* from East Java to instruct local *ulama*, religious teachers, members of Banser, and even journalists in *ilmu kebal*, invulnerability magic, which would make them immune to bullets and sharp weapons. Some persons also began to boast that that their own magical powers were stronger than those of a ninja.

In some instances villagers assumed collective guilt. This happened in a village in Demak where a *kiai* was dragged from within a prayer house in which he was saying his evening prayer with a rope around his neck and beaten to death. After four suspects had been arrested, angry villagers marched to the police station demanding that every single one of them had to be put in jail. Not just those arrested, but the whole village had killed the *kiai*, who had been a sorcerer and, the villagers claimed, had often boasted that he had caused the death of people by supernatural means. After one of their fellows had suddenly died, the villagers had decided that the *kiai* was responsible and had to be killed. On other occasions police stations were attacked in attempts alternately to free or lynch those arrested for having had a hand in the killings. In early November, in the city of Pemalang in Pekalongan, such an incident turned into a full-fledged riot complete with the destruction of shops. It began when police arrested two members of a mob – some of whom reportedly had been drunk – who had killed three persons. These three had left their car in a nearby village to buy cigarettes, and they had been taken for ninjas. One of the victims had been stripped, sprinkled with petroleum, and set on fire. After the arrests, about 2,000 people marched to the police station, creating havoc in the town. A few days earlier, mob anger had erupted in Pasuruan after a mentally ill person, who had been acting strangely, had been apprehended and the rumour spread that he was a ninja and that Christians and Chinese had financed the killings.

The latter incident was one indication that by October the situation had taken an even more sinister turn. Many of the persons killed or hounded by mobs because they were suspected of being ninjas were retarded or mentally ill persons, unable to give a precise answer when asked where they came from. Apart from an influx of such people being admitted to asylums, where they would be safe, the observation led to speculations that somebody or some group deliberately set on creating unrest had dropped mentally ill people at places where they would arouse suspicion. Another theory which was bandied around was that in order to conceal the involvement of members of the Armed Forces in such killings, ninjas handed over to the authorities had been substituted at police stations by mentally ill persons. Munir of Kontras and local NU leaders said they had proof of this. This was why some of the latter suggested that people take a photograph of a suspect before handing him over to the authorities (Rahim 1998:24, 37, 47-9). Outward appearances also became a point in question. There was considerable doubt about the claims of some of those arrested that they were farmers, because they sported tattoos and wore rings in their ears and noses (Rahim 1998:25).

By this time the situation had spun completely out of control. It seemed, as Amien Rais was to comment, as if a section of the Indonesian population had gone crazy (*Kompas*, 5-11-1998). Mobs and night patrols set upon innocent strangers they suspected of being ninjas, beating and stabbing them to death, hanging them, or setting them ablaze after pouring petrol over them. Others were lynched when an angry mob had attacked policemen trying to protect a potential victim or when frightened policemen had handed over suspected killers to crowds besieging local police stations. It was estimated that up to the end of October at least 35 persons had been slaughtered simply on the suspicion that they were ninjas.

Victims, alleged sorcerers as well as suspected ninjas, were killed in a particularly gruesome way. In Malang the stomach of one person, suspected of being a ninja because he wore boots and was dressed in black, was slit open and a stone the size of a fist was thrust into the cavity. He was a retarded person, who had not been able to give an answer to where he came from. In a village in the same region an alleged ninja, who was also reported to be mentally ill, was decapitated. His blood was drunk. His head was triumphantly speared on a sword and carried around as a trophy in a motorcycle parade. His body was also tied to a motorcycle and subsequently dragged around behind it. In the middle of October, in the whole of Malang regency, in the space of two days, more than ten persons suspected of being ninjas were slaughtered. In West Serang in West Java, where such sorcerers are called *dukun teluh*, a suspect was submitted to a trial by ordeal. First he was called to the mosque, where he was questioned about his role in the deaths of four villagers. When he denied any guilt, he was thrown into a pond in front of the mosque with his hands and feet tied. If he survived, he was not a sorcerer, if he drowned he was. Each time he surfaced and tried to breathe he was beaten and stabbed by some of the one hundred onlookers.

Speculations abounded about the motives behind the killings. Wiranto, the chief of police of East Java, Major-General M. Dayat, and Roesmanhadi tried to calm down public opinion, which had become overheated by all kinds of accusations. They maintained they were dealing with what they called ordinary crimes without a political motive, occasioned by a cocktail of personal feuds, feelings of revenge, mutual hatred, and financial rewards. It was denied that ninjas were active. This was a fantasy. Others advanced religious motives to explain the turmoil. They saw the whole affair as a campaign which was being waged against the form of Islam practised by the NU community.[5]

History also played a role in the interpretations. Under the Old Order Banyuwangi had been a bulwark of PKI. In 1965 the area had been one of the regions were killings had taken place on a large scale. Revenge for this and the crucial role the NU youth organization, Banser, had played in the slaughter, was therefore adduced as one of the explanations. Influenced by such theories of revenge, on the eve of 30 September rumours were rife that a new massacre was about to take place. Some relatives of communists, it seems, indeed took their chance to exact their pound of flesh, admittedly only by distributing leaflets, but none the less adding to the feelings of fear. Among those who put the blame on communists was Roesmanhadi. He drew attention to the fact that in the recent past South Banyuwangi and South Malang had both been PKI regions. Others did not choose to become so specific, and, as the military commander of East Java, Major-General Djoko Subroto opted to do, simply pointed out the similarities between what they described as communist tactics before September 1965, and what was happening in 1998. He said the aim was to ripen the climate for a social revolution by destroying the trust of the population in the government and Armed Forces, and by creating an atmosphere of terror. Rudini went back even further, recalling the slaughter associated with the Madiun rebellion of 1948. Yusuf Hasyim disclosed that he had been threatened that he had better not repeat his mistakes of 1965, and of 1948, when he had captured the city of Bondowoso from leftist troops with a battalion commanded by Kemal Idris (*Forum Keadilan*, 2-11-1998:34).

The accusation that communists, out avenge the killing of relatives by Banser and other NU members in 1965, were behind the murders was a possibility strongly contested by local and national leaders of NU, though individual *ulama* thought otherwise. One of the arguments they adduced to back this up was that the killers usually arrived by car, which relatives of former PKI members were too poor to own, and, as the NU secretary of East Java stated, the perpetrators would not dare to act as they did without backing (Basyaib 1998:302). The background of the people eventually arrested did not confirm the theory that PKI members or their relatives were involved in any significant numbers.

A more frequently advanced suggestion was that what was happening reflected strife among the political élite in Jakarta and was part of a larger plan to create unrest all over Indonesia. A great variety of possibilities were speculated on. An early one was that the unrest in East Java was an elaborate

---

5   Yet another explanation put forward was that part of the killings were the work of members of a heterodox Islamic sect out to avenge the killing of their leader (*Tajuk*, 15-10-1998:86).

ploy created to thwart the PDI congress in Bali by preventing Megawati supporters travelling to Denpasar via East Java. A suggestion which cropped up
more often was that the plotters aimed to have the general election postponed. Some offered the opinion that Habibie supporters wanted to accomplish this consummation, or at least desired to create a situation in which
upset voters would flock to the security of Golkar. Others were sure that
Cendana was behind a plan to create chaos in order to put off, for the time
being at least, the possibility that Habibie would be replaced by somebody
who would make a serious attempt to haul Soeharto up before court.
Rumours were rife that the killings had been ordered by supporters of
Soeharto and Prabowo whose career, political power, or economic position
had declined after May. One of their alleged aims was to make people realize that they could not count on the Armed Forces commanded by Wiranto
to guarantee their safety. Yet other theories were that the killings were an
effort to split the Islamic community, or to abort an Armed Forces-PKB-PDI-
P coalition, intended to drive a wedge between Wiranto and NU, or alternatively between NU and PDI-P.

Among those who subscribed to the interpretation that the killings had
been planned in an effort to create an atmosphere in which a general election
was impossible was Abdurrahman Wahid. He also claimed to know who was
behind it all. In October he ventured to say that among those masterminding
the killings was a member of the cabinet. He refused to name names because
he did not have the proof required to substantiate his charge in a court of law.
Members of the cabinet asked Abdurrahman Wahid to report to the police
the moment he had concrete evidence. Among them was Adi Sasono, the person many, including he himself, were sure Abdurrahman had in mind. This
had been the case in early 1997 when Abdurrahman Wahid had aired his suspicions about a Green Dragon Operation. Another name that came up in
speculations about the 'dalang' was Eggi Sudjana, a person whose name was
mentioned with some frequency in relation to schemes to hit out at opponents of the green faction. This was after Abdurrahman Wahid had stated
that one of the persons involved had the initials ES, in which some found the
meaning Eyang Soeharto, Grandfather Soeharto.

The killings became a highly embarrassing affair for the government.
Though the army and the National Committee for Human Rights formally
started an inquiry, the dukun santet murders added to the list of violent events
into which Muslims were demanding a thorough investigation. They were
fed up with the way such cases were being tackled by the government and
the NGOs, both of which they suspected of dancing to the West's piping. The
lack of response to their demands fortified their conviction that these NGOs
and well-known human rights activists did not turn a hair when it was
Muslims who fell victim to violence. The PKB secretary of East Java, for

instance, complained that there was always an outcry when one or two Chinese were murdered, but that when numerous indigenous Indonesians were killed the same people who had demanded justice in the first instance remained silent (Basyaib 1998:303).

The Armed Forces were put in a particularly difficult position by the *dukun santet* affair. Their image was damaged by the failure to call a halt to the killings and the threats. In October extra army and police troops were dispatched to East Java, but this did not have much impact on public opinion. Religious circles in East Java indignantly asserted that this performance contrasted sharply with the way the army and police had reacted to the looting of shops and agricultural produce. It made one of them wonder whether the life of a Muslim was worth less than *sembako* (Rahim 1998:7). Army and police spokesmen refuted such fears. The security forces had a great deal of trouble on their hands – it was the time of the widespread looting of agricultural produce – and Banyuwangi, it was pointed out, was a vast area, inhabited by people who were inherently hesitant to turn to the authorities to solve their problems.

Adding to the Armed Forces' predicament were the persistent rumours that military men had had an active part in the planning and the execution of the lynchings and about alleged links between criminals thought to be behind some of the killings and the police. The names of Kopassus and of Prabowo were mentioned, as were those of Djoko Subroto and of the Intelligence Service of the Armed Forces. Another story published in the magazine *DëTAK* claimed that Siti Hardijanti Rukmana and Hartono (usually mentioned as a pair in theories about Cendana involvement in unrest) had hired Kopassus deserters in an effort to turn attention away from the investigation into Soeharto's wealth (*Tajuk*, 12-11-1998:81). Echoing the abductions and the May riots, physical appearance was presented as proof that soldiers were behind the killings. The perpetrators were said to be well-trained and to have acted in a military fashion, but this, and their ability to disappear quickly after they had committed their deed, the authorities argued, were not characteristics only of soldiers. Another argument that the Armed Forces were involved was the observation that, when the local population had arrested someone they suspected of being one of the murderers, policemen were on the spot within minutes, and this without anybody having reported the incident to them. When it came to ordinary crimes and traffic accidents, it was observed, it took much longer for the police to arrive.[6]

Dukun santet killings did abate at the end of the year, but continued well into 1999. A region which was particularly hit at the end of 1998 and at the

---

6   Conclusion of the Fact Finding Team of Partai Keadilan of East Java (*Kabar dari Pijar*, 23-10-1998; Rahim 1998:27).

A demonstration by Papuans in downtown Jakarta in August 2000
(photo C. van Dijk)

beginning of 1999 was Ciamis in West Java. The army was forced to send a
battalion to the region, but this only seems to have increased the fear among
the population. Villagers refused to cooperate in the investigation. Munir,
who saw in this reluctance an indication that members of the Armed Forces
were involved, said that between November and May 57 people might have
been killed in Ciamis. An exact figure was difficult to give, as people were
afraid to report such murders to the authorities. The police put the death toll
at 24. Munir also disclosed that the first victims had been people suspected
of sorcery, but that later on the scope had widened to traditional healers,
dukun who assisted in abortions, arrogant rich villagers, and people who had
defamed Soeharto. He was sure the killings were organized.

   One of the other big problems with which Jakarta was confronted was
that of separatism. May 1998 had also been the time that people who wanted
independence for their region seized their chance to air their demands. In
Irian Jaya or West Papua, where Freeport was seen as a prime example of
economic exploitation backed up by the military power of Jakarta, supporters of the Organisasi Papua Merdeka (OPM) movement took to the streets in
early July 1998. They raised the 'Morning Star' flag of an independent West
Papua, a gesture which constituted an unequivocal act of subversion which
should be suppressed at all costs in the eyes of Wiranto and other army offi-

cers. In actual practice the military lacked the power to undertake any immediate action. In the initial stage Indonesian troops were put on the defensive.
During a demonstration at Universitas Cenderawasih south of Jayapura, an
Indonesian police officer observing the protest was attacked by a mob. He
died because lack of blood to give him a transfusion. At least one person died
on the side of the demonstrators. On the island of Biak, a crowd armed with
machetes, arrows, and Molotov cocktails, yelling the battle cry 'attack',
assaulted Indonesian troops. For days the protesters held their ground. The
flag of Free Papua which had been hoisted could only be removed by shooting at it from a distance. Harsh military intervention finally broke resistance.
According to the *Far Eastern Economic Review* at least 11 people were killed.
13 people had gone missing.[7] In Sorong pro-Free Papua demonstrations led
to the destruction of houses, offices, and shops. Troops had to be flown in
from Ambon to regain control of the city. Manokwari also saw its fair share
of disturbances. After these incidents unrest continued in Irian Jaya, but not
much of this reached the Indonesian press.

For East Timor, Timor Timur for the Indonesian government and Timor
Leste for those who opposed Indonesian rule, the new Habibie government
had held out wide-ranging autonomy as early as June 1998. When Portugal
refused to consider this possibility as more than just an intermediate stage on
the way to full independence, the Indonesian government came up with a
new proposal on 27 January. On that day, after a cabinet meeting attended by
ministers whose competence covered the political and security field, the
Minister of Foreign Affairs, Ali Alatas, announced that should the population
of East Timor reject the option of wide-ranging autonomy offered them,
Jakarta was prepared to accept the independence of the province. The
People's Congress would be asked to revoke its decree on the integration of
East Timor. By the end of the year, Habibie himself stated a few days later, the
East Timor question would hopefully have been resolved, allowing the Indonesian government to concentrate its attention on the remaining 26
provinces, where there was also a fair amount of trouble. The possibility of
granting independence to East Timor was immediately rejected by Abdurrahman Wahid and Megawati. They saw East Timor as an integral, insepara-
ble part of Indonesia. Megawati pointed out that the Habibie government
was only a transitional one and as such did not have the right to decide on
such a fundamental issue. Her followers hammered home that Habibie
should have left the decision of what to do with East Timor to the next president. By acting as he had, he had saddled his successor with a time bomb.

---

7   *Far Eastern Economic Review*, 29-4-1999:22; *Forum Keadilan*, 5-10-1998:23. Not long afterwards, 31 bodies were washed ashore in Biak. According to the authorities they had been victims of a tidal wave in Papua New Guinea. Local people doubted the explanation.

Later, before the People's Congress, Habibie would defend the decision by pointing out that autonomy as an intermediate stage would only have result-ed in more unrest in East Timor, and that before announcing the new option he had conferred with the leaders of parliament and the various parties.

Opponents of independence for East Timor not only deplored the seces-sion of part of Indonesia's territory, they were extremely uneasy as they con-sidered the promise made by the Indonesian government highly dangerous. It would only intensify the fighting in East Timor, and by creating a prece-dent it might strengthen demands for independence elsewhere. Usually Aceh and Irian Jaya were mentioned in this respect, but in Riau regional senti-ments were also strong. One of the consequences was indeed a campaign of violence by pro-integration militias, armed with homemade guns, occasion-ally supplemented by firearms of a more sophisticated make in East Timor. These militias, it was widely thought, were backed and armed by army offi-cers, who found it absolutely impossible to stomach the idea of independ-ence for East Timor.[8] The circumstances created by the promise could only lead, as it did in Aceh, to feelings of fear among local informers and collabo-rators of the Indonesian army. It also generated feelings of unease among Indonesian civilians, teachers, and traders, most of them from Java and South Sulawesi, who had migrated to East Timor in great numbers. Their exodus, which had already started in July, now began to step up.

In another trouble spot, Aceh, the situation escalated at the end of December and early January. Fighters of Gerakan Aceh Merdeka (GAM), Free Aceh Movement, who succeeded in procuring fresh weapons from abroad, and the Indonesian security forces were embroiled in a mutual spi-ral of violence. Both sides intensified their actions. The major theatre of war, as it were, was still the north coast, but other parts of the province did not escape the violence. The immediate cause of the upsurge of hostilities had been the kidnapping and killing of a number of soldiers on leave. They were on their way from Lhokseumawe to Medan by public bus at the end of December 1998. In a sense the fear evoked by the *dukun santet* killings lay at the root of the escalation of violence in Aceh. In December the abduction and killing of the soldiers on their way to Medan, which had formed the turning point in the escalation of violence, was actually inspired by it. At an inter-section the bus in which they were travelling had been stopped by a crowd of hundreds of people checking the occupants of passing vehicles near a

---

[8]   As early as the end of January the spokesman of the Armed Forces Major-General Syamsul Ma'arif admitted that part of the local Wanra (Perlawanan Rakyat, People's Resistance), a civil-ian militia, had been equipped with firearms. This had been done, he stated, to allow them to protect themselves against attacks by armed groups striving for independence. The activities of the latter were also the stated reason why the army refused to disarm them.

small city in East Aceh. The core of them may have been GAM fighters, but local residents had joined in to prevent ninjas from reaching a nearby *pesantren* (*Tajuk*, 6-1-1999:74). Operasi Wibawa, Operation Authority, was launched by the army in retaliation for the attack on 11 January. During the military operation the feelings of revenge among the members of the Armed Forces involved to avenge their fallen comrades ran high.

In an effort to regain the faith of the Acehnese, Habibie, accompanied by Wiranto and Feisal Tanjung, paid a one-day visit to Banda Aceh on 26 March. The visit was marred by mass demonstrations and clashes with security troops which began when students, who had been demonstrating for days, tried to join in a dialogue with Habibie in Baiturrachman Mosque. Security forces had to fire tear gas and warning shots to disperse the crowd. Inside the mosque Habibie was shouted at and confronted with all kinds of awkward questions. On behalf of the government and the military he apologized for excesses which had been committed during military operations in the past and promised that such acts of brutality would never happen again. He pledged to prosecute soldiers and policemen who were guilty of human rights violations. The government would pay for the reburial of victims of army brutality, who had been hurriedly buried in mass graves, in accordance with the prescripts of Islam. Other promises held out by Habibie were the release of political prisoners, extra money for the economic development of the region, and financial aid to victims of military operations.

Habibie's visit could do nothing to prevent civil war in Aceh intensifying. The conduct of the army was such that as early as January, Amien Rais did not hesitate to speak of genocide, a term at times also used for what had happened during the period Aceh was declared a Military Operation Area (*Kompas*, 13-1-1999). In a number of incidents, well-covered in the Indonesian press, dozens of people were killed during army operations or when troops fired shots into crowds of protestors. One estimate of an incident which occurred near Lhokseumawe on 3 May mentioned a death toll of 110, whereas the authorities spoke of 38. Another massacre took place on 23 July when a *pesantren* in Beutong Ateuh in West Aceh was attacked. Afterwards an official investigation alleged that 65 people who were attending a Koran recitation had been killed. One of the consequences of the continuing unrest was that the number of refugees swelled. In the middle of July, according to figures provided by the provincial government, 80,000 people, not only Acehnese but also frightened Javanese migrants, had fled their homes. By August their number had risen to around 150,000. Conditions in the refugee camps were appalling. Many refugees suffered from diarrhoea, cholera, and malnutrition. Some fled to the camps afraid of being branded GAM sympathizers by the Indonesian Armed Forces. Others did so out of fear of GAM. A third category probably consisted of those who had been urged by GAM activists to flee their village and, once in the camps, to stay there. There are indications that GAM used large refugee numbers as a means to attract international attention and to paint the image of Jakarta's repression all the more brutally. Acehnese became caught in between the government, which wanted to reduce the number of refugees and rebels, and *pesantren* students, some united in an organization called Thaliban, who wanted to swell this number (see *Far Eastern Economic Review*, 2-9-1999:16-8).

The refugee camps also began to serve as schools after over a hundred schools in the Pidie, and North and East Aceh went up in flames. Contractors were afraid to rebuild them. The authorities blamed GAM for this. Others speculated that army instigators were at work. They also saw the hand of such people in other violent incidents. The question who was responsible was complicated by captured GAM members whom the army had turned into informers, and of whom it was not sure whether they acted on the orders of the Free Aceh Movement or on those of the army.

The deteriorating situation elicited urgent pleas to seek a political solution and to withdraw the troops brought in from outside the province. Because of the brutal way in which they operated – they frequently raided houses and beat up people while interrogating them – such soldiers were seen as a main source of the trouble. People suggesting this way out pointed out that the resistance against the Dutch, the Islamic rebellion in Aceh in the 1950s and

Demonstration demanding a fair referendum in Aceh (photo *Tempo*)

the DOM period had all shown that Aceh could not be subdued by military force. The plight of the Acehnese people was taken up by students outside Aceh, who staged meetings and demonstrations protesting army brutality in Aceh and calling for the withdrawal of troops. Other demands made by demonstrating students were a referendum in both Aceh and Irian Jaya, and independence for East Timor. In Aceh itself, voices calling for a referendum swelled. In the streets, banners and slogans chalked on walls propagated this demand, which was not only inspired by army brutality, but also by the feeling that Aceh, rich in oil and natural gas, was being economically exploited by the central government.

Such challenging ideas clashed with those of Habibie and Wiranto. In his Independence Day speech Habibie said he was afraid that the general population would become the victims if the Indonesian army withdraw unilaterally without the GAM guerillas laying down their arms. Wiranto adamantly refused to consider lenience towards separatists. He claimed that more troops were needed, not fewer (*The Jakarta Post*, 28-7-1999). Carrying through this claim, the army planned an offensive. Early in August 1999, the chief of police of Aceh, Colonel (Pol.) Drs Bachrumsyah, announced that a special operation was to be staged involving 7000 security troops. Their task would be to track down 200 armed civilians who, he said, were guilty of violations of human rights and other crimes.[9]

Civilian politicians adopted a more conciliatory standpoint. At the end of July, Jakarta, at the suggestion of a special team of presidential advisors for Aceh, established an independent committee of inquiry into violations of human rights in Aceh. The committee included people from Aceh, representatives from the government, and from the National Committee for Human Rights. This was a little too late, as faith in such committees seemed to have dwindled.

Another suggestion made at that time by the presidential advisors was that Aceh, known as one of the regions in Indonesia where Islam is adhered to most strictly, should be allowed to adopt Islamic law. In actual fact the proposal was merely a confirmation of the special status Aceh already had on paper within the Indonesian state. In May 1959 the province had been granted the freedom to manage its own affairs in the spheres of religion, customary law, and education, but these rights had never been implemented. The suggestion won the support of the Minister of Religion, Malik Fadjar, of Muladi, and of Syarwan Hamid. It was also endorsed by Achmad

---

9   Unless absolutely necessary, government spokesmen refused to soil their mouths with the words Free Aceh Movement; in the past such organizations had always been dismissed with the pejorative term Gerakan Pengacau Keamanan, Movement of Disturbers of the Peace, avoiding the use of the name by which such groups denoted themselves.

Tirtosudiro, Eggi Sudjana, and by a group styling itself Front Islam Bersatu Peduli Aceh, United Islamic Front of Those Concerned about the Situation in Aceh, which KISDI, GPI, Hammas and Front Islam Priok had joined. On another occasion Ahmad Soemargono dismissed the military operations as an attempt to thwart a further development of Islam in Aceh. There was also no lack of voices calling for negotiations with leaders of the Free Aceh Movement.

In Aceh itself, people demanding the withdrawal of troops that had been sent to the province organized a two-day general strike on 4 and 5 August, during which people all over Aceh stayed at home. In vain the provincial administration asked the population not to participate, threatening adminis-trative sanctions against civil servants who stayed home. August 4 and 5 were not a national holiday and people should come to work, they said. During the strike, according to newspaper reports, Aceh was completely paralysed (*Media Indonesia*, 5-8-1999; *Jawa Pos*, 5-8-1999). Streets were desert-ed and shops, food stalls, and markets remained closed. Government offices, banks, hospitals, and schools were open, but almost no civil servants, cus-tomers, patients, or schoolchildren turned up. Army and police vehicles drove through towns appealing to the people by megaphone to resume their normal daily activities.

After the strike, public life in Aceh continued to be unsettled. As they had already been before the strike, people were hesitant to take the main road from Banda Aceh to Medan. In the middle of the month, the days before and after Independence Day, traffic once more came to a complete standstill. Only military vehicles used the road, the soldiers holding their rifles at the ready. Civilians had been scared off by the fact that in the preceding days vehicles had been stopped and set on fire by masked men and by exchanges of fire between government troops and GAM members. Part of the road, a stretch along both sides of the border between Pidie and North Aceh, had become GAM territory. Trees had been felled to obstruct traffic. By this time, the first decapitated corpses were being found in roads in Aceh, making people fear that it was now the turn of Aceh to become the scene of Petrus murders.

By the middle of 1999 the situation had become so untenable that the gov-ernment seemed prepared to make every possible concession, except, Habibie was to underline at the end of August, granting a referendum. Even Wiranto backed down when he visited Banda Aceh on 18 August. During a three-hour-long meeting with local leaders and students, a meeting which was as tense as the one when Habibie had visited the city, he promised an end to army operations in the countryside within five days. The task of keep-ing the peace was to be left solely to the police. Soldiers would return to their barracks, where they would be held in reserve to act if necessary. Others were to be redeployed to guard strategic objects. Wiranto explained that he had reached his decision after considering the many victims who had already fallen. He made it clear that if GAM members did not lay down their arms, and, an act which he seemed to consider particularly offensive, continued to raise their own flag, severer military operations lay in store. If such a situation were to arise, a state of emergency would be declared. It was reported that after Wiranto had made his vow, thousands of refugees returned to their homes, and that the number of refugees dropped to 90,000. Wiranto also promised that the province would get its own separate provincial military command, headed by an officer from Aceh.[10] The announcement occasioned some debate. Wiranto said that he had decided to reconstitute the Aceh command on the basis of the discussions in Aceh. In Jakarta human rights activists attacked the step as yet another attempt by the army to find a military solution. Within days, students in Aceh followed suit, condemning his decision.

On the same day, using Hamzah Haz as his spokesperson, Habibie made it known that the government would comply with everything the people in Aceh asked for, including the adoption of Islamic law in Aceh. Two days later, back in Jakarta, Wiranto announced that a general amnesty in Aceh was being considered. Able-bodied GAM members who surrendered were promised a place in the army in Aceh. After having stressed that, for various reasons, the implementation of promises made during Habibie's March visit had been delayed – people in Aceh had not heard anything about Habibie's pledges for four months – at the end of August Jakarta earmarked Rp 1.7 trillion for social and economic projects in Aceh. Acehnese were not sure what to make of the gesture. Students rejected the offer. To them, an end to oppression and insecurity, and the trial of those guilty of violation of human rights, were more important than money. In the middle of September Habibie's gesture also failed to deter about five hundred leading *ulama* in Aceh from asking for a referendum to be held under international supervision. On hearing this, Abdurrahman Wahid, who was present at the meeting in Banda Aceh where the request was presented, wept. He and Amien Rais, also present, both agreed that a referendum should be planned with care to avoid disasters afterwards.

Jakarta had not consented to a referendum, but steps to give substance to what the special status of Aceh implied were being worked out. An act dealing with this was tabelled and accepted by parliament on 22 September. The discussion had only taken three weeks. The act stated that the provincial administration had the duty to foster compliance with Islamic law. To ensure

---

[10]   During an army reorganization in 1985 the provincial military command had been merged with that of North Sumatra. Since then Aceh had formed part of the Bukit Barisan Military Region commanded from Medan.

that religion was taken due account of by the provincial administration, an advisory council of *ulama* would be established. This would be endowed with powers equal to those of the provincial parliament. The concessions did not work. The mood in the province had become increasingly hostile, and GAM had succeeded in crippling the local administration, after its army had ordered village heads, *camat*, and other local administrators to lay down their work on 1 October. Nine hundred village mayors, about eight hundred of them in Pidie, had done so almost immediately. A later estimate spoke of eighty percent of all village mayors. The offices of the *camat* had also stopped working, as had the *kabupaten* offices in Pidie and North Aceh. The *kabupaten* office in West Aceh was to go up in flames in November (*D&R*, 18-10-1999:56-7; *Republika*, 11-11-1999).

CHAPTER XVI

Communal violence

Kala cobaan datang mendera
Mengguncang kharisma Nusantara
Jangan pernah menyerah
Jangan pernah lengah
Jangan biarkan sengketa
Cerai beraikan
Pembela bangsa sejati.[1]

In the closing months of 1998, at the time the *dukun santet* killings in East Java were still in the centre of public attention, other parts of the country were gripped by communal violence. One of the first places where this happened was on the island of Sumba. At the beginning of November at least 23 people, according to some counts 50, were killed during fights between two ethnic groups in the town of Waikabubak. The immediate cause had been the publication of the results of an entrance exam for the civil service and the fact that some persons who had not taken the test were offered a job.

On 22 November, on the Islamic holiday Isra Miraj, violence erupted in the Ketapang neighbourhood, near Jalan Gajah Mada in Jakarta. Churches, banks, a hotel, two schools, and a number of shops went up in flames or were damaged. Fourteen people, criminals from the Moluccas and East Timor, were killed. Some of them had been brutally slain and mutilated. Their eyes were gouged out and their stomachs split open. Like some of the scenes which had taken place during the *dukun santet* scare, the incident illustrated the gruesomeness of mob anger. Calls for moderation were not heeded. 'Let him die slowly,' people shouted. watching the slaying of one of the victims (*Krisis* 1998:36). The cause had been a quarrel between a local resident and a gangster, a Christian Moluccan, employed as a guard at a Mickey Mouse gambling establishment. The incident was to evolve into an act of retaliation

---

[1]   When ordeals come to try us/ Shaking the charisma of the Fatherland/ Do not ever surrender/Do not ever be indifferent/ Don't let the disputes divide us/ True defender of the nation. Fragment from *Tegarlah Indonesia*, 'Stand Firm Indonesia', by Ully Sigar Rusady.

taken against local Muslims by a group of criminals. When the window of an Islamic prayer house was broken, the rumour spread that the building had been torched. Thousands of residents set out to take revenge. They were reinforced by Furkon supporters and by members of Front Pembela Islam, Front of Defenders of Islam, a new militant organization founded in August 1998. Almost two hundred criminals had to seek police protection. To prevent a repeat of the incident, the governor of Jakarta decided to deport local criminals, sending them back to their place of birth. In the middle of December about two hundred of them – according to some reports a multiple of this – were shipped back to Ambon. Within a month the deportees would again be in the full glare of public attention.

Next to have a taste of violence was Kupang on Timor. On 30 November, people had flocked to churches in the city to mourn the victims of Ketapang and other violent incidents. They were provided with the information that 21 churches had been set alight in Ketapang, and that during the whole New Order period five hundred churches had been destroyed by Muslim mobs (*Ummat*, 14-12-1998:22). Afterwards the churchgoers marched through town in procession. After the rumour had spread that Muslims had set fire to the cathedral, the crowd ran wild. Three days of rioting followed, spreading to the neighbouring city of So'e, and to the island of Rote. Local Roman Catholic leaders put the blame on outsiders, suggesting that the trouble had been stirred up by a well-organized attempt to create havoc (*Tajuk*, 10-12-1998:75). They pointed out that trouble had started after truckloads of people from neighbouring cities and from Dili, armed with clubs, sharp weapons, and carrying jerrycans full of petrol, had come to Kupang to join the demonstration. Afterwards the National Committee for Human Rights also voiced its suspicions that agitators had been at work. Its members singled out youngsters, whom they suspected of being from East Timor, who were said to have incited the mob to riot. Another matter that fuelled their suspicions was that the telephone service and the electricity supply broke down, making it impossible for security forces to be alerted. The local Muhammadiyah University (at which most of the students were Protestants and Roman Catholics) was besieged. Nine mosques, a hajj dormitory, Islamic schools, and houses and shops of Muslims, many of them immigrants from South Sulawesi, were destroyed. Thousands of Muslims fled to the provincial police headquarters in the city, the naval base, a Protestant university, and other safe places. Others tried to escape the violence by boat.

In its issue of 24 December, the PBB tabloid *Abadi*, of which Ahmad Soemargono is the general manager, put part of the blame for the rioting on Theo Syafei, a Roman Catholic. He was accused of having delivered an anti-Islam speech, a tape of which had circulated in Kupang. Uppermost in people's minds were remarks allegedly made about a plot by members of the political élite to transform Indonesia into an Islamic republic by the year 2010. Commenting on such an undertaking, he is said to have pointed out that Indonesia's penal code and the ideals of human rights were based on Christian-inspired thought, and, giving a bird's-eye view of Indonesia's history, he allegedly had stressed that the idea that Roman Catholics did not know what it meant to make sacrifices for their religion should be dismissed immediately. In Jakarta, where a tape of the much disputed speech was widely circulated in the Islamic community, a three-hour mass meeting advertised as 'A Critical Study of the Theo Syafei Cassette' was organized by KISDI and held at Istiqlal Mosque. A variety of organizations and individuals demanded an apology from Syafei. Some asked that he be brought to trial. An Asosiasi Pembela Islam, Association of Defenders of Islam, representing HMI, ICMI, KAHMI, KISDI, and a number of other Islamic organizations, actually started legal proceedings. Megawati instructed PDI-P officials not to comment. Syafei himself stressed that he had not been anywhere near Kupang for a long time and that it had never been his intention to insult anybody. In turn, he filed a libel case against *Abadi*, which had carried the banner 'Theo Syafei and the Kupang Riots' on its front cover. Before the end of the month Syafei was interrogated by the police as a 'suspect', accused of having provoked religious hostility.[2]

The violence which seemed to grip Indonesia, of which Kupang and Ketapang were the most brutal manifestations, elicited renewed calls for a national dialogue.[3] Many feared that the situation might only worsen in 1999. Most articulate was Abdurrahman Wahid, who saw himself as a kind of patriarch of the country, a person to whom everyone turned for advice or support in troubled times. He was indeed called Bapak Bangsa, Father of the Nation, by some. In the eyes of others he was like a saint, who could do no wrong. Shocked by Semanggi and fearing the imminence of what he called a social revolution, which he defined as 'a situation where the people revolt against everything, resulting in a total chaos with nobody in control', Abdurrahman Wahid decided to act (*The Jakarta Post*, 7-12-1998). Early in December he announced that he intended to visit a number of key political leaders to

---

[2]   Syafei himself refused to say when and where he had given the disputed speech. According to the newspaper *Radar Bogor*, Syafei had done this in Anyer in September; according to *Media Indonesia* Syafei had given the speech even earlier, in June, before he had joined PDI-P.
[3]   According to data collected by the newspaper *Kompas* (18-1-1999) the number of disturbances in 1998 was 197; of which 134 happened after the May riots. Larger disturbances not already mentioned took place in Cirebon (19 October), Mataram (31 October), Lampung (4 November), Pinrang (25 November) Tarutung (26 November), Ciamis (1 December), Buleleng (10 December), Surakarta (13 December), Poso (25 December), Jeneponto (25 December), and Lampung (29 December). Communal violence in Poso continued in 1999 and 2000. In May and June over one hundred bodies were discovered in mass graves. The death toll was set at 246 in August 2000. At that time the number of refugees was estimated to be 69,000.

encourage them to discuss a solution to the problems the country was facing. From the outset, Habibie and his political friends were against such a step, reiterating the familiar argument in use before Soeharto's fall that the places for such a dialogue were parliament and the People's Congress. Habibie said any other alternative would only increase the number of problems, of which Indonesia already had plenty. People would start to quarrel about who should be invited and who represented which segment of society.

Undeterred, Abdurrahman Wahid conferred with Wiranto who, as he had done prior to May, stressed the importance of a dialogue. He also went to see Soeharto, which earned him the accusation that he had abandoned the reformation cause. Abdurrahman Wahid met Soeharto for the first time on 13 December at the home of Bambang Trihatmodjo. A second visit took place on 19 December, the morning of the same day he had visited Benny Moerdani at CSIS, an event which caused just as much of a stir.[4] Abdurrahman Wahid defended his resolve to involve Soeharto in a national dialogue by pointing out that Soeharto had remained a key factor in Indonesian politics and could not be left out of a national reconciliation. Abdurrahman Wahid tried to hammer home his conviction that many underestimated Soeharto's influence. He stressed that Soeharto had many followers, some of them in powerful positions. Abdurrahman Wahid did not accuse Soeharto directly of having a hand in the violence, though this was the way Soeharto, castigating Abdurrahman Wahid for such a charge during one of the latter's visits to him, and probably others as well, interpreted his words. In public he had merely suggested that it was members of Soeharto's inner circle, angry about the way Soeharto was being badly treated and scorned outright, who were behind what had happened in Banyuwangi, Kupang, and Ketapang. Such persons should no longer be given any excuse to express their discontent through violence. One of the implications of this was that students should restrain themselves and refrain from actions which would enrage Soeharto's supporters even more.[5] Privately he did talk about Soeharto as a Javanese and a ksatria, a warrior, striking back (Al-Zastrouw Ng 1999:212). In arranging the meeting, Abdurrahman Wahid was quite prepared to accept that Soeharto's presence meant that Amien Rais could not join in the talks. Were he to do so,

---

[4]   One of the aims of the visit had been to seek Benny Moerdani's advice about the persons Abdurrahman Wahid wanted to invite to sit on an Independent Committee for Truth Finding and Reconciliation, which would investigate what had happened in Aceh, Tanjung Priok, East Timor, West Irian and other places. In April the following year Abdurrahman Wahid joined CSIS.
[5]   See for instance the interview with Abdurrahman Wahid in Tajuk, 23-12-1998:29-33. In the same interview he suggests that a small group of students involved in the demonstrations were paid, some by persons afraid of losing out in the coming general election, some by a foreign company which wanted to finish off Indonesia as a commercial rival.

Soeharto would refuse to participate. Megawati was ignored. Abdurrahman Wahid, convinced that Soeharto was going to participate and praising the former president for his willingness to contribute to solving the nation's problems, envisaged a talk involving four persons: he himself (he had a lot of *rakyat*, or followers, he was to explain), Wiranto, Soeharto, and Habibie (*Republika*, 20-12-1998; Asmawi 1999:227).

Habibie, whom Abdurrahman Wahid had also visited, could not be persuaded. He refused a meeting with Soeharto. Abdurrahman Wahid's suggestion put Habibie in a no-win situation. Were he to refuse, he would be attacked for avoiding a dialogue; were he to accept, people would see it as an indication that he was still controlled by Soeharto. Achmad Tirtosudiro called Abdurrahman Wahid's suggestion 'the strangest, maddest and most risky political manoeuvre' (*Merdeka*, 24-12-1998). Disappointed, Abdurrahman Wahid warned that without a dialogue, the nation might well fall apart, and that if this were to happen, tens of thousands could die. Without a political solution – which in Abdurrahman Wahid's mind seems to have been a pardon in return for the transfer of much of Soeharto's fortune to the state, or at least postponing the discussion of a trial till the economic and political crisis had been overcome – people loyal to Soeharto would generate disturbances in the first quarter of 1999 all over the country.[6] They were everywhere. Kupang and Ketapang could happen all over Indonesia. Others argued exactly the opposite. If supporters of Soeharto were behind the unrest, an end might well come to the violence if Soeharto was brought to trial. That would put them off for good. The sooner a trial took place, the better. One of their number was Amien Rais, who said that the solution was not to embrace Soeharto, but to isolate him and bring him before a court. Such a course of action would sap his followers of their courage (Rais 1999:3).

When it became clear to Abdurrahman Wahid that the dialogue he had in

---

[6]   Abdurrahman Wahid, fearing unrest if Soeharto was tried, was among the few who had publicly supported Muladi's statement at the end of July about a political solution to the Soeharto investigation. This time he argued that Islamic law should be applied, suggesting an amnesty for Soeharto in return for the transfer of the part of his wealth that he had acquired in an improper way. A five-member team, including two representatives of the Soeharto family, should investigate Soeharto's wealth. Abdurrahman Wahid wanted Mar'ie Muhammad to head the team, but when Soeharto opposed this, he was prepared to settle for Fuad Bawazier. Abdurrahman Wahid claimed that because it was difficult to collect evidence, and also because of the attitude of those prosecuting and judging Soeharto, a court probably would find Soeharto not guilty. Legally not much could be done, though everybody knew that Soeharto's transgressions were many. Soeharto's lawyer, Juan Felix Tampubolon, rejected the suggestion. He said that Soeharto wanted to stick to the legal rules (*Panji Masyarakat*, 18-8-1999:69, 27-10-1999:41). According to the *Far Eastern Economic Review* (12-8-1999:24) at that same time Megawati's aides were working out an amnesty deal with Soeharto's lawyers in return for the transfer of part of Soeharto's wealth to the state.

mind would not materialize, he suggested a meeting between Soeharto and Habibie. This, he claimed, had been his original plan, but Soeharto had suggested the other two names. Habibie and Soeharto had to meet to prevent the latter being offended by the legal proceedings started against him. Were Habibie to refuse, Abdurrahman Wahid stated, this would simply confirm that he lacked a 'sense of politics'. He said that Soeharto and Moerdani were much more sensitive to the political situation in Indonesia and to what was needed to avert chaos (*Jawa Pos*, 26-12-1998; Asmawi 1999:170). Abdurrahman Wahid did not preclude the possibility of a civil war if such a talk could not be arranged. Soeharto, he continued to warn, was a powerful person with great influence. Abdurrahman Wahid saw additional proof of this in a new series of mutations in the army, as always presented as a routine matter, on 4 January. He, and many others as well, qualified it as a move by Wiranto to replace green generals by red and white ones, some of whom were suspected of still being on good terms with Soeharto.[7] Pessimists described the new appointments as a defeat for reformation.

Abdurrahman Wahid met Soeharto once more on 14 January. By this time it seemed that riots were erupting somewhere at least once a week. What made an additional impression was that the violence continued unabated during the fasting month. Communal violence, described in the Indonesian press as *amuk massa*, was to erupt in the first months of 1999 on an unprecedented scale. Some of the mob wrath was directed towards 'places of sin'. Other riots were the consequence of animosity between neighbourhoods, villages, or other clearly defined social groups. The more persistent and bloody affrays had an ethnic and religious component, and were in part the unanticipated consequence of the greater intra-Indonesian mobility which had got under way during the New Order.

In the first weeks of January there had already been a vicious battle between two neighbourhoods in East Jakarta, fights between villages in Luwu in South Sulawesi – where since early 1998 sporadic fighting between indigenous Toraja and Javanese migrants had intensified – costing the lives

---

[7]   Highlighted in particular were the appointment of the new Chief of Staff for General Affairs, Lieutenant-General Sugiono, a former adjutant of Soeharto, replacing the 'green' Lieutenant-General Fachrul Razi, and that of the new head of the Armed Forces Intelligence Body, Major-General Tyasno Sudarto. Both Sugiono and Tyasno were said to be New Order, Soeharto officers. When Soeharto had celebrated the end of the fasting month in Surakarta, Sugiono together with Wiranto, Moerdani, and Hartono – had been among the officers who had visited him there – an event which had led to renewed speculations about Soeharto's influence in the army. Johny Lumintang became Deputy Chief of Staff of the Army. Among those who were replaced was the head of BIA, Zacky Anwar Makarim. It was further rumoured that Habibie had prevented Wiranto from replacing Maulani as head of Bakin. According to the *Far Eastern Economic Review* (18-3-1999:28) the mutations indeed did not go down well with Habibie's Muslim inner circle.

of at least five people, an attack on a police station in Surabaya (caused by reports about the death of a prisoner, who in fact had died from wounds inflicted by a crowd who had caught him stealing), and rioting in Karawang and Rengasdengklok in West Java. The question seemed to have become not whether new fighting was going to erupt, but where. At the time of the Kupang riots it had been predicted that Ambon and Alor would be next. There had already been trouble in Ambon at the end of November, when a Muslim village was attacked. On walls people scrawled the text '*usir* BBM', chase away the BBM, an acronym standing for Butonese, Buginese, Makassarese, of whom most had settled in the Moluccas since the 1970s. On 14 January, this was followed by fighting in the small town of Dobo on Wamar, an island in the Aru Archipelago in the Southeast Moluccas, which cost the lives of eight people. Five days later, on Lebaran, the festive day after the end of the fasting month, Ambon city exploded, leading to months of carnage and ferocious battles between Muslims and Christians.

The bloodshed started with a fight between two neighbourhoods in the north of the town: Muslim Batumerah and Christian Mardika. Muslims and Christians could not even agree on the incident which set it all off. The first reports mentioned an attempt by a Buginese inhabitant of Batumerah Bawah to extort money from Yopie Saiya, a Christian minibus driver from Mardika, as the immediate cause. Saiya was beaten up and decided to go to Batumerah Bawah with some friends to settle the score. When they had failed to find the person they were looking for, they set on another inhabitant, incurring the wrath of the villagers. The intruders were chased away, and after they had escaped, houses in Mardika were set on fire. Muslims dismissed this version of the facts as a tissue of lies and slander. Their version of the story emerged six weeks later, after the leader of Al-Fatah Mosque in Ambon gave a press conference at Al-Azhar Mosque in Jakarta on 4 March. He stated that Saiya had refused to pay the rent for the minibus he had hired from a Buginese inhabitant of Batumerah Bawah. This had aroused the anger of the conductor of the minibus, who lived in the same neighbourhood and who had to collect the rent. A row was the result, and during this the conductor had been attacked by Saiya and Christian passengers on the minibus. He fled to Batumerah to call for help. When others wanted to come to his assistance, Christians armed with poisonous arrows and spears, plus machetes, had attacked Batumerah. It was argued that in view of this course of events, it seemed obvious that, far from being the spontaneous outcome of a quarrel, the attack on Batumerah Bawah had been planned in advance.

Whatever the cause, within a few hours rumours that churches and mosques had been destroyed had done their work and had set in motion disorder on a large scale, affecting all parts of the city of Ambon. By 24 January 52 people had died, 13 churches and mosques and almost 500 houses had gone up in flames. Muslims accused Christians of having transformed the meaning of BBM into *Bakar, Bunuh Muslim* (Burn, Kill Muslims). The number of refugees taking shelter in mosques, churches, military barracks, and government buildings had reached twenty thousand. The fact that assaults on Muslim property and life took place at different places around the same time provided yet another reason for Muslims to argue that Christians had planned the Ambon unrest well in advance.

Reaction from Armed Forces headquarters in Jakarta was swift. The first reinforcements, a Kostrad unit from South Sulawesi, arrived in Ambon at noon on 20 January. Three days later the local military commander announced that his troops were going to confiscate all weapons being carried around and that he had instructed his soldiers to shoot on the spot those who resisted (after, as it was stressed a few days later by the chief of police of the Moluccas, 'following correct procedures') (*Suara Pembaruan*, 3-2-1999). The outburst of the violence in Ambon forced Wiranto to call a meeting of senior officers and the Ciganjur group to discuss the situation on 24 January. In view of the political constellation of that moment, the by-passing of Habibie fanned speculations about Wiranto's motives. This time it was he on whom the suspicion of *makar* fell. Nurcholish Madjid was also present. Abdurrahman Wahid disclosed that at this so-called 'Ciganjur plus' meeting, Wiranto had acknowledged that he knew who the persons behind the disturbances were, but that it was difficult to collect proof and arrest the culprits. A few days later, on 6 February, Wiranto issued a nationwide order to shoot rioters on the spot. On 7 March Wiranto appointed a crisis team made up of 19 Christian and Muslim Moluccan officers, headed by Major-General Suaidy Marasabessy, to try to regain control in the Moluccas. The team failed to achieve anything.

As the weeks passed, stories began to circulate about acts of cruelty committed in the Moluccas: an inflammatory cocktail featuring decapitated corpses, children brutally killed, people chopped to bits or set alight, the wombs of pregnant women being ripped open, and even the eating of organs of victims. In his speech at Al-Azhar Mosque, the leader of Al-Fatah Mosque also spoke of injured Muslims who had been killed after they had been transported to a general hospital, and of a similar fate which had befallen pregnant women who had come to the hospital to give birth. The identity cards of the victims had been checked to verify their religion.[8]

Army and police were helpless to contain the fury. Part of the reason for this new example of the apparent failure of the Armed Forces to nip violence in the bud may well have been the lack of coordination between the army

---

8   *Republika*, 5-3-1999. According to another version of the story, the victims had been abducted from hospital (*Tragedi* 1999:152).

and police, not to mention the less than ideal relations between the two forces. Keeping law and order was the task of the police, which had overall command, but the army, its officers considering themselves superior to those of the police, at times seemed to have been hesitant to follow orders. For months, punctuated by weeks of uneasy quiet in between sudden eruptions of brutal fights, full-scale civil war was to rage. Christians donned a red headband, Muslims a white one. Red and white neighbourhoods were tightly guarded, roads were blocked. Traditional war dances were staged, and people turned to magic to make themselves invulnerable. Various Islamic journals, *Abadi* and *Tekad*, copied a story first published in *Sabili* recounting how Muslims besieged in a mosque were saved because the Christians who were attacking them were frightened off by the appearance of an army of hundreds of boys about ten years old, all decked out in white, and commanded by a bearded old man dressed in a white *jubbah*. Both sides armed themselves with whatever weapon they could lay their hands on or make: swords, machetes, bows and arrows, spears, *bambu runcing*, iron clubs, and homemade firearms and bombs were all the order of the day. Later, firearms of a more sophisticated make were also used. Attacks and defence were coordinated with 'handy talkies'. Appeals issued by local leaders to stop the violence and the peace pacts they concluded went completely unheeded.

Fighting spread all over the province: to other parts of Ambon; to other islands in the Central Moluccas such as Seram, Saparua, Haruku and the Banda Islands; to Dobo and the Kai Islands in the Southeast Moluccas; as well as other islands. The spreading of the unrest gave the crisis team constituted by Wiranto food for thought, leading them to conclude by the middle of March that the pattern of violence had changed. As agitators no longer succeeded in inciting massive clashes in the city of Ambon itself, they had moved their activities to the outskirts of the town and to other islands, where 'hidden provocateurs' tried to stir up emotions by committing brutal killings, leaving the mutilated bodies for everybody to see, and by torching empty houses.

By March 70,000 people had fled their homes. Many of them were Muslims from South Sulawesi, and to a lesser extent from Java and Sumatra. Most tried to flee the province. Desperate to leave, they boarded outgoing ships en masse, some even scrambling up the mooring cables. By the middle of March the official death toll had risen to 187. Later figures spoke of 350 people killed between January and March. A statement made by the local branch of Partai Keadilan mentioned over 1,300 victims. Whole residential quarters in and near Ambon city were destroyed.

The Armed Forces were caught in between. At times people turned against the security forces which were trying to put an end to the violence. Both sides, moreover, were sure that the army and police sided with the other side. Soldiers and policemen were denounced by Muslims and Christians alike for not acting or not acting promptly enough when attacks took place, for allegedly participating themselves in such assaults, for being partial in their efforts to disarm people, and for firing at their co-religionists when trying to restore order. Reports of soldiers or policemen participating in Christian attacks or firing at Muslim crowds fanned Islamic resentment. A major problem in this respect was that, as local residents, policemen and their families were as much a party in the conflict as were other inhabitants, and suffered equally from the fighting. Many were also Christians. Likewise, reports of security forces helping Muslims aroused Christian indignation and anger. Troops sent to the Moluccas from elsewhere consisted of Muslim soldiers and officers, which in such a fraught atmosphere raised the suspicions of Christians. Initially their distrust centred on a Kostrad unit from South Sulawesi, which was later replaced by army units from Java.

Outside Ambon, Muslims clearly considered their co-religionists in the Moluccas the beleaguered party. Muslim anger reached unprecedented heights when the news spread that Christians in Ambon had attacked Muslims who were praying in a local mosque in the early morning of 1 March. In Muslim circles the incident became known as the *Tragedi Subuh Berdarah*, Bloody Tragedy of the Early Morning Prayer. People began to speak of a full-blown war in Ambon. There were even reports that 'alumni from Afghanistan, Moro, and Lampung' had arrived to train local Muslims. Five hundred such former fighters from Afghanistan and the Philippines were said to have entered Ambon on tourist visas, while others were reported to be Indonesians who had trained Moro troops (*Tekad*, 8-3-1999:14-5, 19).

The news of the attack on the mosque served as a catalyst. All over Indonesia mass demonstrations were held, organized by groups like KISDI, KAMMI, HMI-MPO, and PII. On such occasions the appeal to launch a holy war could frequently be heard. Many young Muslims testified to their readiness to go to Ambon to fight, vowing they were prepared to die for the Muslim cause. In Ujungpandang, in the region from which most of the migrants came, volunteers could actually register. They could also do so in Jakarta at the secretariat of Bulan Bintang Youth, while it was reported that GPI had already sent soldiers for the holy war to Ambon. Yet, when leaders of organizations talked about such activities, they usually stressed that their sole intention was to provide humanitarian aid, not precluding that this might change at a later stage.

Probably out of fear of such a reaction, the government and a number of Islamic leaders, among them Said Aqil Siradj, argued that religious and ethnic animosities had not caused the Ambon violence or other similar conflicts. Others stressed that poverty lay at the root of the fighting. Part of the Muslim community refused to be convinced. As far as they were concerned, what was happening was religious war. Comparisons with Bosnia, Serbia, and Kosovo were made. What transpired in eastern Indonesia, in the Moluccas, Kupang, East Timor, Irian Jaya, all areas where Muslims were the victims of communal violence, was a 'Muslim-cleansing policy', a qualification vehemently denied by Christian church leaders (*Abadi*, 4-3-1999:10; *Suara Pembaruan*, 13-3-1999).

The familiar theme that NGOs remained silent when Muslims fell victim to violence was once again reiterated. Surprise was expressed at the fact that the Voice of Concerned Mothers remained silent, and demonstrations were staged at the offices of the National Committee for Human Rights and of Kontras. During some of these protests, small change was flung at NGO offices to express the supposition that these institutions only acted when it pleased their Western sponsors. In his reaction Marzuki Darusman was able to point out that his committee had sent representatives to Ambon early on, and that in cases like that of Ambon the government was better equipped to investigate what was going on. Munir denied the charge that Kontras treated Ambon any differently, adding that Kontras had not published its findings with respect to the riots in Kupang, afraid that if it did, this might lead to unrest elsewhere. How deep the suspicion in some Muslim circles ran came to the fore when the Human Rights Watch suggested that international humanitarian organizations should send medicines to the Moluccas. The reaction was that it was well known that under the guise of humanitarian motives such organizations often actively interfered by helping their own, Christian group (*Sabili*, 24-3-1999; *Tragedi* 1999:73).

Another major target was formed by the Armed Forces and their impotence when it came to protecting Muslim lives. Military leaders, according to one of the conclusions drawn by Muslims, were too preoccupied with the political strife in Jakarta and their own position. These officers forgot that one of their major tasks was to keep peace in the country. There were many calls for Wiranto, already under fire from certain Muslim quarters because of Habibie's revelations about the troop movements on 22 May, at least to account for what was going on, if not to resign. It seemed a perfect moment for the 'green faction' to try to get rid of Wiranto. Among the persons suggesting that Wiranto should leave was Baramuli. Others used the Ambon violence to plead for the separation of the functions of Minister of Defence and Commander of the Armed Forces, fielding the argument that this would lead to a more efficient leadership of the Armed Forces. The only positive side-effect for Wiranto was the plea, also advanced by Ahmad Soemargono of KISDI, that criticism of the Armed Forces for their violations of human rights should be temporarily halted. The Armed Forces should be given the opportunity to regain their self-confidence so as to be able to act resolutely again. The blasting of the Armed Forces, it was argued, was one of the reasons officers had grown hesitant to act when it was imperative they should (*Abadi*, 11-3-1999; *Tragedi* 1999:102). Such Muslim political leaders might have their objections to Wiranto, but the Armed Forces they wanted as part of Habibie's administration had to be strong.

While the first fights were still raging on Ambon, on 5 February demonstrators, protesting about the government-approved list of candidates for the election of the new regent, set fire to the parliament building of Pontianak regency at Mempawah in West Kalimantan. Two days earlier, three persons had died in a clash at a bus terminal in East Jakarta, when bus personnel joined by school pupils and onlookers had started a round-up of pickpockets after a passenger had been robbed. The police had to employ eleven armoured vehicles to end the disturbance.

In Kalimantan, where at the end of 1996 and the beginning of 1997 Dayak and Madurese had clashed, ethnic conflicts flared up again. The centre of the disturbances was *kabupaten* Sambas in the northern tip of West Kalimantan. In its early stages the fight was not between Dayak and Madurese, but between the Madurese and the Coastal Malay population. Dayak joined in later. Troubles had started there on the same day as in the Moluccas, 19 January, when Madurese attacked Parit Setia, a small village, and killed three people. During the raid the attackers shouted 'God is Great' and 'Madurese-Malay three-nil'. The assault on the village was an act of retaliation for the beating up of a thief by the villagers. (Thereupon the thief had been handed over to the police, who immediately set him free, fearing an attack on their police station by Madurese (Suparlan 1999b:14-5).) The atmosphere was further heated up by a row between a Madurese bus passenger – according to some sources a criminal – who refused to pay and the Malay driver's assistant on 21 February. The latter had been rude. Insulted, the passenger had got off the bus, gone home to fetch a sickle, and then proceeded to the bus station and slashed the driver's assistant. The victim of the attack had only been wounded, but the story spread that a Malay had been killed by a Madurese. Consequently, early the next morning angry Malays, mostly young men, went in search of Madurese, destroying and setting fire to houses and killing a number of them. The rampage went on for two days. Severed heads were displayed in the streets, bodies were mutilated, and hearts and livers of the victims were consumed.[9]

Leaders of the two communities succeeded in calming down emotions and agreed that nobody was to carry weapons in public. The accord held for a couple of weeks, but unrest erupted in full force in the middle of March, when on the 18th and 19th alone, 64 people were killed and more than a

[9]   Suparlan 1999b:16. From his report it appears that the first victims were Madurese criminals.

thousand houses were set on fire. Proudly, people again displayed the severed heads of their victims. Even a hospital in the town of Singkawang, where the injured were being treated, was attacked. During one particular incident security troops shot dead at least eleven people when a crowd tried to force its way into Singkawang, arriving by truck and by motorcycle, demanding the release of people arrested in connection with the violence. By the middle of April there were more than 30,000 refugees, mostly Madurese. Many of them were evacuated to Pontianak by sea and air. Some fled to nearby Sarawak, where they were denied entry by the authorities, who wanted them to go to Pontianak. Others, reportedly thousands of them, hid in the forest for days – even for weeks – without food. By the end of March the official death-toll had reached 165.

Besides troops, the government sent a team of anthropologists, sociologists, and psychologists to Sambas. The main finding of their investigation was that the troubles had been caused by cultural differences and the arrogant, rowdy behaviour of the Madurese immigrants, which gave Malay residents the impression that they were being robbed of their possessions (see Suparlan 1999a, 1999b). One of the recommendations was to strengthen the local police, who in the past had been able to prevent the behaviour of Madurese criminals becoming the role model for many of the other Madurese living in the region as well (Suparlan 1999b:17-9). One solution advocated by others was the evacuation of all Madurese from the region, at least till order had been restored. One of the persons who held this point of view was Libertus Ahie, a Dayak leader. He blamed the Madurese, who he said had not adjusted to local culture. Another was Raden Winata Kusuma, the traditional ruler of Sambas (*The Jakarta Post*, 23-3-1999, 24-3-1999).

The bloodshed in Aceh, the Moluccas, and Kalimantan meant that in June the Indonesian government had been forced to begin a programme to build houses for 200,000 refugees. Some of these were to be built in the violence-torn regions themselves, some in the region of origin of the refugees or in new places of settlement assigned to them: in Seram in the Moluccas and in Tembang Kakang in Kalimantan. In early August, after a new outburst of violence in Ambon, a spokesman for the Social Service Department of Southeast Sulawesi, mentioned that 56,830 refugees from Ambon had fled to this province. By that time the refugee camps in Southeast Sulawesi were jam-packed and could no longer cope. The new wave of violence in Ambon, which again was sparked off in Batumerah and Mardika, had begun in July. Various authorities commented that the fighting was more vicious than before. In November the official death toll had reached 693, including 11 members of the army and the police. PBHI spoke of 1,395 people killed.

During the violence on Ambon at the end of July and early August, Chinese shops also went up in flames. The result was that Chinese started to flee the province in great numbers. Up to that moment in the Moluccas (as in Sambas), Chinese residents had mostly escaped the violence. The Armed Forces had to send fresh reinforcements from Java to Ambon. Other units had to be sent to Batam, where people from Sumatra clashed with fellow-residents from Flores. There were at least 19 fatalities. Some of the victims had been hacked to pieces, one decapitated corpse had been left lying in the streets. By August 1999, Habibie and Wiranto must have been at their wits' end. Ambon had exploded again, the situation in Aceh had become untenable, and in East Timor the time for holding the plebiscite drew near.

As with the onset of the economic crisis, the scope and brutality of the violence was difficult to comprehend, the more so because Indonesians themselves had been taken in by the stereotype of Indonesians, with the possible exception of some ethnic groups such as the Madurese, as a friendly people. People were quick to point out that the Moluccas and Kupang had acquired a reputation for inter-religious harmony – though the same person could state in almost the same breath that these regions were prone to SARA provocations. It was observed that in Kupang, when brawls had happened in the past, these had mostly been fought between Roman Catholics and Protestants, not between Muslims and Christians (*Ummat*, 14-12-1998:24). A similar observation was made about Ketapang. Residents stated that in the neighbourhood it was tradition for Muslims to visit Christians at Christmas, while Christians would ask their Muslim neighbours for forgiveness on Lebaran (*Kompas*, 4-12-1998). The violence of the Malays in Kalimantan also did not fit the image of these people as being 'usually gentle of character' (Suparlan 1999a:8).

Consequently, conspiracy theories abounded. Immediately after Semanggi, Amien Rais advanced the theory that some group was applying a scorched earth tactic and, in trying to accomplish its aim, was playing for high stakes. He expressed the fear that Indonesia could well experience the same fate as Yugoslavia. Later, during the Ciganjur Plus meeting, he told Wiranto that he had the impression that agitators had been at work in Ambon. Had only ethnic and religious animosities lain at the heart of the matter, there would surely have been earlier incidents, which had not been the case in the Moluccas. It seemed to him that the rioting was organized and systematic, and he had the impression that the people involved were well financed. Ketapang gave rise to similar speculations. In a joint statement, Abdurrahman Wahid and Megawati expressed the opinion that this had been planned and executed by criminals on somebody's orders.

Ambon fortified Abdurrahman Wahid's resolve to draw Soeharto into the deliberations which it was hoped would put an end to the violence all over Indonesia. On 26 January he visited Soeharto for the fourth time. Soeharto, Abdurrahman Wahid stated afterwards, could assist in the arrest of the *dalang* behind the Ambon riots, thus giving reassurance that the unrest would not spread to other parts of the archipelago. Again Abdurrahman Wahid left no doubt that he believed Soeharto was the only person who could put a stop to the breakdown of order in Indonesia. Soeharto did not respond. He remained silent. Seemingly undeterred, on 2 February Abdurrahman Wahid visited Soeharto once more.

The Sambas killings convinced Abdurrahman Wahid, who was sure that agitators had been at work, to call a halt to his efforts. He exclaimed that he was *kapok*, that he had enough of visiting Soeharto. He had run out of patience. However, he did not cut off ties with the Soeharto family completely, regularly meeting Siti Hardijanti Rukmana in the months to come. On 20 March, he stated that he had visited Soeharto seven times since May 1998, each time asking the former president to keep his followers in check. He might as well have saved his breath; riot after riot had erupted. Again, he did not accuse Soeharto of personally having a hand in the wave of violence, but reiterated that Soeharto was the only person who could stop it. Two days later Abdurrahman Wahid predicted that violence would rage in five more strategically located regions, prone to SARA agitation. He listed Kupang, Ambon, and Sambas as belonging to the nine regions which from the outset had been targeted to become scenes of carnage. Out of fear that something would happen, Abdurrahman Wahid refused to disclose the other targets.

The government's inertia came in for a fair share of the blame. On 20 March, after a brief visit to the United States, Amien Rais disclosed that he had asked the Americans to issue a moral warning to the Habibie government, intimating that it should quickly put an end to the violence. Such a gesture might frighten Habibie and the generals into action. Three days later, demonstrating FKSMJ students presented Habibie with the Gorbachev Award. The reason was explained by the citation: 'Gorbachev: Mister Disintegration USSR by introducing the Perestroika concept. BJ Habibie: Mister Disintegration without any concept (unintentionally)' (*Merdeka*, 24-3-1999).

One of the institutions on which criticism focused was the army. People were convinced that the military was always involved when there were violent troubles. Such distrust of the army was particularly strong when reference was made to the troubles in Aceh and East Timor, but it was not absent elsewhere either. When no direct connection was made between the violence in Aceh, East Timor and other places and army scheming, the link perceived was the inability of army and police to prevent the unrest from spreading. People were quick to point out that under the New Order, the response of the Armed Forces to unrest had been resolute and swift. Agitators had been arrested without much ado, and demonstrations had been nipped in the bud. Quite apart from the current irresolution, the intelligence network seemed to have crumbled. Incidents had taken the Armed Forces by surprise, and with respect to Ambon, even the gangsters deported from Jakarta had not been closely watched on their return home. The response of army officers to such observations was to point out that with the fall of Soeharto times had changed. A spokesman for Feisal Tanjung explained that in contrast to the situation before May 1998, the Armed Forces were taking good care not to be accused of violations of human rights. The army and police could no longer arrest people arbitrarily, or – though he did not say so explicitly – torture people. The public should understand that collecting legal proof to make a convincing case which would stand up in court was a time-consuming process. Feisal Tanjung said much the same thing (*Republika*, 26-1-1999; see also interview with Feisal Tanjung in *Tajuk*, 18-2-1999:74-5). The same reason, the fear of being accused of intimidating people, was put forward to explain why the army had waited so long to act against the Free Aceh movement, which for months after Soeharto's fall had been allowed to spread its propaganda unhindered (*Far Eastern Economic Review*, 2-9-1999:17).

All the theories advanced in relation to the *dukun santet* killings were given another airing, although by now some people had become convinced that behind the widespread violence was a plot to have a state of emergency be declared, in which circumstances the Armed Forces would have the upper hand. With respect to the Moluccas some specific variants were put forward. Muslims specifically put the blame on Christians – some singled out Roman Catholics – who, disappointed that they had lost out in national politics in the 1990s and particularly after May 1998, were accused of steering things towards chaos and national disintegration.[10] Occasionally it was even ventured that 'fundamentalist Roman Catholics' in the army and the police who hated Protestants and Muslims deliberately fanned fights between members of the two latter communities in the Moluccas. People advancing this theory also blamed Roman Catholics who, according to them, were strategically placed in the security forces dispatched to Aceh for giving orders to Indonesian troops to kill Acehnese Muslims (*Suara Ambon on line*, 27-8-1999). Some Muslims also mentioned the United States, and to a lesser extent Australia, or in more general terms the West, with some frequency, averring in support of their thesis that the West was apprehensive of a strong, united Islamic Indonesia. In Malaysia it was Mahathir who, in an interview with a Japanese newspaper, linked the Western attitude towards East Timor with an effort to create a weak Indonesia fallen apart into several states (see *Panji Masyarakat*, 27-10-1999:27). Among those in Indonesia commenting that the United States would welcome the disintegration of Indonesia was Ahmad

---

[10]   An example of theories blaming Christians is the book published by Rustam Kastor (2000), a retired general, about the political conspiracy by RMS and Christians to destroy the Islamic community in the Moluccas.

Soemargono. Reports of the violence in the foreign press fortified Muslims in their opinion that the West, though it appears that it was mostly American newspaper reports which gave them that impression, was against them and wanted to portray the Islamic community in Indonesia in the worst possible light, equating it with the more radical fundamentalists (see, for instance, *Ummat*, 14-12-1998:22, 25). Other Muslims were sure that all was part of a plan by fellow countrymen fearful of the present advance of Islam to depict the Islamic community in Indonesia as radical and violent, just as they thought Benny Moerdani and his associates had tried to do in the 1970s and early 1980s. The unrest preceding the 1997 election campaign and the stories about the rape of Chinese women in May 1998 had prepared the climate for taking revenge on Muslims, and, where possible, for a campaign for chasing them away from the regions to which they had migrated (*Tragedi* 1999:183-4). Yet another scenario was put forward by M. Alfian, general chairman of Himpunan Mahasiswa Muslim Antarkampus (Hammas), Inter-Campus Association of Muslim Students. Linking the Ambon violence to the rivalry between Moerdani and Prabowo, he – along with others – saw it as part of a plot to champion PDI-P interests by Christians who viewed the steady advance of Islam in politics with apprehension. He singled out Theo Syafei's speech to substantiate his thesis (*Tekad*, 1-3-1999:19).

In more general terms, Christians as well as Muslims were convinced there was a conspiracy to create instability. Banyuwangi, Kupang, Ambon, all were part of one great plan. Communal violence instigated here would spread to other regions. Medan, Ujungpandang, East Java and Surabaya, North Sulawesi, Pontianak, Batam, Sorong in Irian Jaya, and Aceh were mentioned as second Ambons in the making. 'Provocateurs from Jakarta' had already been sighted in some of these places. Riots in Jakarta even worse than this city had experienced in May the previous year were also expected. The governors of West Java, East Java, and North Sulawesi took precautions to prevent their provinces from becoming a stage for communal violence.

The intention of those held responsible for creating the turbulence was thought to be to show that Habibie and Wiranto were unable to keep the domestic situation under control, and to pave the way for a state of emergency and the advent of a strongman. Others saw the violence as a ploy to turn attention away from Trisakti and Semanggi, as an attempt to make people forget the economic and political crimes committed by Soeharto and his family for the moment, or as an effort to postpone the coming election or make its results seem less valid in the eyes of the population. In short, the violence was being fanned by 'pro-status-quo' people desperate to prevent reform and intent on putting an end to the democratization process. Even revenge being taken by Soeharto was not precluded.

Abdurrahman Wahid had his own ideas. Part of his analysis made sense.

Within days of the outbreak of violence in Ambon, he put part of the blame on people who wanted to control the civil administration without taking the interests of other groups into account. The incident to which he alluded was the fact that in the autumn of 1998 the governor of the Moluccas, M. Saleh Latuconsina, had fired 38 senior civil servants, all Christians, and had replaced them with Muslims. Here Abdurrahman Wahid touched on the wider problem that Christians in Ambon, the favoured group in the past, were now getting the impression that they were losing out to recent Muslim immigrants and Muslims born in the Moluccas. Christians had the impression that they were being edged out of the administration and the trading sector. In their turn, Muslims pointed out other factors. Indigenous Moluccans were less prepared to work hard or preferred to become civil servants. In one letter to the editor, the contrast between Muslim migrants and Christians was captured fairly rudely: migrants from Sulawesi worked hard, and did not mind becoming *becak* drivers, peddlers, manual labourers, or taking up other menial occupations, while Ambonese, especially Christians, preferred to become singers, boxers, or gangsters in Jakarta or other cities (*Tekad*, 8-3-1999:2).

Rather more controversial was Abdurrahman Wahid's statement that a certain person, whom he described as having a full beard and living not far away from his own house in Ciganjur and who commanded an army of criminals, had had a hand in the troubles in Ambon. He claimed that on their return to Ambon, 160 of the man's subordinates – on another occasion he was to allude to Ambonese who had been trained in Situbondo to incite the Kupang riots – had become enraged over dismissals of Christians. Not able to take revenge on the administration, they had turned on the ordinary people (*Merdeka*, 22-1-1999; *D&R*, 8-3-1999:51). Abdurrahman Wahid's description, especially his mention of a full beard, left little doubt in people's minds. It fitted Yorrys Raweyai like a glove; he was a friend of some of Soeharto's children and executive chairman of Pemuda Pancasila, who to Abdurrahman Wahid's amazement had been present when he had met Soeharto on 19 December.[11] Within days Yorrys Raweyai was questioned by the police. Later, Abdurrahman Wahid was to accuse Brigadier-General K – within a few days, after Brigadier-General Rustam Kastor had angrily protested that he was not the one Abdurrahman Wahid meant, corrected by him to Major-General K – of the Armed Forces headquarters of being the *dalang* behind the violence in Ambon and other places in Indonesia. K, he dis-

---

11   On 19 May 1998 Yorrys Raweyai – a person of mixed Chinese and Papuan descent – had also played a major role in organizing the Pemuda Pancasila protest in favour of Soeharto at the parliamentary complex. On 26 February 1999, he was among a hundred people from Irian Jaya who visited Habibie and demanded independence for the region.

closed, cooperated with a number of civilians in a conspiracy by what Abdurrahman Wahid called 'hard-line Muslims' to bring down Wiranto.[12]

Abdurrahman Wahid considered K's actions such a serious threat that he had not only presented Wiranto with the information, but also called together a special press conference to make his accusation known. If K were to continue his activities, it could well mean the end of Indonesia as a nation (D&R, 8-3-1999:50-1). Again, it was not difficult to conclude whom Abdurrahman Wahid meant. Sniggering, he explained that, of the three 'K generals' who worked at Armed Forces headquarters, it was neither Rustam Kastor nor Kirbi he meant. The only general left was Major-General Kivlan Zein, by now coordinator of the specialist staff of the army. However, when Kivlan Zein and other officers visited Abdurrahman Wahid to ask him to explain, Abdurrahman Wahid denied that Kivlan Zein was the officer to whom he had alluded. He had meant *Mayjen Kunyuk*, Major-General Stupid Ass.

Yet another occasion presented itself to indulge in the developing conspiracy theories when a bomb exploded in Istiqlal Mosque in Jakarta on 19 April. The explosion damaged the walls of the ground floor and shattered the windows of the office of the Indonesian Council of Ulama. Five people were injured.[13] In Ujungpandang a demonstration organized by students to protest about the attempt and to demand a thorough investigation ran out of control, resulting in the burning down of a Catholic dormitory and elementary school and a PGI office on 20 March. Once more all kinds of speculations ran riot, given full reign as the authorities remained silent for weeks. Nurcholish Madjid, calling to mind Germany just before the rise to power of Hitler, blamed desperate, frustrated Muslim fundamentalists who were making a bid for power by creating chaos. He precluded the possibility that non-Muslims were behind the explosion. For them such an attempt would be tantamount to suicide. It would inexorably spell their end. Jimly Asshiddiqie did not go as far as Nurcholish Madjid. In his eyes, those who had placed the bomb feared that they were bound to fail in the general elections. Others expressed the fear that those responsible apparently would stop at nothing to reach their aims. They might well try to kill Megawati or Amien Rais. Consequently it was reported that the Satgas of PDI-P in Jakarta, headed by B.B. Janis, one of whose tasks was the protection of Megawati, was inundat-

---

[12]   At that moment a new offensive to curb Wiranto's power appeared to be taking place. It was the time of the controversy over Wiranto's role in alerting Habibie in May the previous year to the deployment of troops by Prabowo, while in the Islamic press the separation of Wiranto's functions as cabinet minister and Commander of the Armed Forces was once again a topic of discussion.

[13]   Based on information from the Jakarta municipality, *Merdeka* (19-4-1999) listed 19 instances of bomb threats and bomb explosions in Jakarta (including the Soekarno-Hatta airport) between April 1997 and April 1999.

ed with advice and requests from retired officers and soldiers of the Marines and the Mobile Brigade asking to join up. Retired Kopassus officers made no secret of their intention of forming a special team to protect her, working secretly and without Megawati knowing anything about their effort. A number of subjects were apprehended. Their leader was Surya Setiawan alias Wawan, a Muslim from Tangerang, who, it turned out, had planted the bomb with the help of six others. The motive remained a mystery. Surya Setiawan's defence was that he had been forced into the bombing attempt by five men who had approached him in front of the Gambir railway station and threatened to kill him and his family if he did not cooperate. In October Surya Setiawan was sentenced to 38 months in jail.

CHAPTER XVII

Struggling along

Bangun bangsa Indonesia
Ingat sumpahmu bersama
Ikrar sakti seluruh bangsa
Rakyat yang adil sejahtera
Jiwa raga kita korbankan
Kini saatnya cita kita menang.[1]

In the middle of December 1998 when registration for the hajj was closed, it turned out that for the first time in years, fewer Indonesian Muslims intended to go on pilgrimage than the quota of 200,000 which had been agreed upon with the Saudi Arabian government. In previous years the number of prospective pilgrims had always exceeded this figure. By mid-December a mere 64,000 Muslims had registered. In January the registration was reopened. The stated reason for this step was that the rupiah was strengthening. Inflation had also slowed down and the distribution of *sembako* products seemed to be under control. The result of the fall in the upward spiral of prices was an overall inflation rate for the whole of 1998 of 77.7 per cent. As a consequence, interest rates were brought down from 70 per cent in September to 38 per cent in December.

Economically seen, 1999 started on a promising note. In January, when the new national budget was presented, the premises were for zero economic growth, and an inflation rate of between 15 and 20 per cent. In March the monthly inflation rate dropped below zero for the first time. Deflation continued as the months passed. At the end of July, in yet another Memorandum of Economic and Financial Policies attached to a new letter of intent to IMF, the Indonesian government noted a markedly improving market buoyancy and a recovering consumer demand. A growth rate of between 1.5 and 2.5 per cent, coupled with an inflation rate of between four and five per cent, was

---

[1] Arise Indonesian people/ Remember your common oath/ The sacred pledge of the nation/ Justice and prosperity for the people/ Body and soul we sacrifice/ Now is the time for our ideals to be realized. Fragment from *Bangun bangsaku*.

expected between March 1999 and March 2000. Interest rates had fallen to between 13 and 20 per cent. At that moment the exchange rate of the rupiah had climbed to around Rp 6,500 and 7,000 to the dollar. At the end of December the exchange rate had still been between 7,800 and 8,000. The stock exchange was showing signs of recovery as well. The improved economic circumstances were one reason for Hamzah Haz to argue in April that the *dukun santet* murders in Ciamis were the work of communist-style terrorists. His reasoning was that, with a stabilizing exchange rate and the supply of basic commodities assured, it had become impossible to use the economic situation to incite people to create chaos in an attempt to thwart the general elections and discredit the government.

Progress was also made in the streamlining of the economy. In August 1998, parliament had approved a bankruptcy bill, put forward by the government in the same way it tried to get the act on the curbing of protests accepted (which came up for revision again the following year because it had been flawed). An act granting greater regional autonomy and an act regulating the financial relationship between Jakarta and the regions were both passed in April 1999. Both acts seemed to be drafted under the threat of regionalism and separatism. The regions' share in income from natural resources was put at 80 percent in forestry, mining and fishery, but at only 15 and 30 per cent respectively in the case of oil and natural gas. If implemented, the act could give a boost to the economy in export-earning provinces such as Aceh, Irian Jaya, Riau, and East Kalimantan, but would also cause extra financial problems in the poorer provinces. The central government, in dire need of money to restore the economy, would also suffer. IMF and the World Bank were not overjoyed.[2]

As a follow-up to the session of the People's Congress, an act about a clean government, one free of corruption, collusion, and nepotism, was promulgated in May 1999. Among its articles was one calling for an independent committee made up of representatives of government and of society to investigate the wealth of cabinet ministers, governors, judges, and senior civil servants. It also required such persons to publish their wealth before and after occupying their position. In the same month the much hated Subversion Act was abolished. To curtail some of the freedoms opened up by the abolition, yet another act, enlarging the Penal Codes' list of crimes against the state, became effective on the very same day. The new stipulations included in the

---

[2]   Regional autonomy would take effect on 1 January 2001. As this date drew nearer, criticism increased in Indonesia and abroad. It was said that legislators had grown overzealous in transferring authority to the regions. One of the problems foreseen was that regions might lack the necessary qualified manpower to execute the new tasks. The Consultative Group on Indonesia, Indonesia's donor countries and financial organizations, feared that regional autonomy might result in a decentralization of corruption (*Kompas*, 2-11-2000).

Penal Code mainly concerned a ban on the dissemination of Communism and Marxism-Leninism. In March a law called the Prohibition of Monopoly Practices and Unhealthy Competition was enacted. In July parliament endorsed an anti-corruption bill to replace the old act dating from 1971. Parliament also accepted a new Basic Forestry Law, replacing the old one dating from 1967. An act on the Bank Indonesia, confirming the central bank's independence from the government, had also been passed. As of 17 May the central bank became an independent body. The central bank act as approved by parliament on 16 April 1999 held a number of stipulations which would influence future political developments. One is that the governor and deputy governors are appointed by the president on his suggestion and with the approval of parliament. Another is that they cannot be dismissed during their five-year term of office except if it is proven that they have committed a crime or are incapacitated.

In general parliament was very productive, passing 67 acts in total between May 1998 and October 1999. Among these was a Human Rights Act submitted by the government in February 1999 and passed in September. One of its articles called for the establishment by law of a human rights tribunal. The suspicion was that the clause had the deliberate aim of protecting the Indonesian military from being tried before an international tribune for crimes committed in East Timor.

In spite of indications of a recovering economy and political reform, the banking sector remained a source of concern. The bad shape many of the banks were in had forced the Habibie government to push on along the road of reorganizing the banking sector, although it often wavered about the steps to be taken. One thing which was beyond doubt was that measures were urgently needed. Not only was there the spectre of the high percentage of non-performing loans, suspected by some to be as high as 50 to 70 per cent, and according to even gloomier predictions 80 to 90 per cent. Banks also suffered from a negative interest rate spread, the fact that the expenditure for interest on deposits was higher than the income generated from credit. According to figures provided by Bank Indonesia in the middle of June 1998, it had already pumped Rp 132 trillion into ailing banks as liquidity support. The Minister of Finance mentioned a sum of Rp 155 trillion (a difference neither side could explain), an amount that equalled half of the Indonesian state budget. By April 1999 the sum was said to have risen to Rp 200 trillion. As with many other financial data provided by government institutions or officials, the figures mentioned often varied wildly or appeared to be based on pure guesswork. In July 1999 the State Auditor's Office could only trace liquidity support to an amount of Rp 85 trillion (*Suara Pembaruan*, 29-7-1999). In December the same office put the total amount of liquidity credit provided up to 29 January 1999 at Rp 164.5 trillion.

Even before the end of the Soeharto era, BPPN had frozen seven banks and taken over their assets on 4 April 1998. Among these were Bank Surya and Bank Subentra of Sudwikatmono (rumours had circulated during the previous year that both banks would be among the banks to be liquidated in the first wave of closures in November 1997), and Bank Pelita and Bank Kredit Asia, in which Hashim Djojohadikusumo held a stake.[3] To say they were frozen did not go as far as meaning that their licences had been revoked, but that the banks were not allowed to operate. In this way the Indonesian government could keep its promise of November about not liquidating any more banks. At the same time, BPPN took over management of seven other banks which were considered to be poorly administered. These included Bob Hasan's Bank Umum Nasional (BUN), Bank Danamon, Bank Dagang Nasional Indonesia (BDNI), owned by the head of the Gajah Tunggal concern, Sjamsul Nursalim (a bank in which Sultan Hamengkubuwono had a stake), and the state bank, Bank Exim. The last had run at a loss estimated at US$ 800 million because of unhedged forward foreign exchange transactions when the rupiah had still been worth Rp 2,500 to the dollar, but apart from this lack of judgement was considered to be well managed. Bank Danamon and BDNI were the seventh and eight largest banks in Indonesia respectively. 199 owners and managers were prohibited from leaving the country. As usual, their names were not disclosed, but soon the complaint was heard that no such sanctions had been taken against the largest and most influential culprits.

The next step had come on 21 August 1998. BCA and three other banks – Bank Danamon, Bank PDFCI, and Bank Tiara – became semi-state banks, so-called BTOs, short for *Bank Take Over*. BUN, BDNI, and Bank Modern of Samadikun Hartono were 'frozen', bringing the total number of such banks to ten. They were now officially BBOs, short for *Bank Beku Operasi*. In December Glenn Muhamad Surya Yusuf, the new chairman of BPPN, revealed that the freezing of these ten banks in April and August and the honouring of their obligations had cost the government Rp 1.6 trillion (US$ 222 million) plus US$ 4 million.

Owners of BBOs and BTOs were told that within one month, that is before 21 September, they had to repay all the liquidity support, BLBI, they had

---

3   Sudwikatmono put the blame for the deplorable state of the Bank Surya on his former business partner, Bambang Sutrisno. He accused the latter of having withdrawn Rp 1.9 trillion through the founding over one hundred companies in the name of employees, all of whom had been given a loan by Bank Surya. Bambang Sutrisno denied the accusation, reporting Sudwikatmono to the police for slander. In September 1999 the court, being of the opinion that Sudwikatmono was in the wrong, ordered him to pay Bambang Sutrisno US$ 10 million, the amount of money he had promised the latter in September 1997 for his leaving Golden Truly, but had never paid.

received, both principal and interest. The office of the attorney-general was assigned, as it was described, the role of debt collector, calling in the bank owners for questioning and holding out the treat of criminal charges if the BLBI were not repaid in time. An additional reason for an investigation was that it had become known that some of the liquidity credits had been used for speculative purposes, for reinvestment in companies of the same concern, or had been transferred into high-interest deposits (Subandoro 1999:102).

Bankers moaned, but the government reminded them that the time limit was not as unfair as they complained. They had known for months that they would have to redeem the money they had received. To meet their obligations, bank owners in the course of time were to hand over land, cash, office buildings, houses and housing estates, shares, factories, companies, and even luxurious cars and hospitals. Among other property, Bob Hasan had to part with shares in Kiani Kertas and a score of other companies. The Salim concern transferred part of its shares in over one hundred of its companies, including Astra, Indocement, Indofood, Indomobil, First Pacific, and QAF. Such individual companies also had to sell shares to redeem their own debts. One of the consequences was that 52 per cent of the shares of Indofood were bought in the middle of 1999 by First Pacific, the Hong Kong-based company in which Liem holds the majority of shares.

One of the immediate problems the handing over of assets initially entailed was that of their value. Foreign accountancy firms (such expensive foreign auditing had been agreed upon in the IMF negotiations) had made an estimate. According to the outcome of these audits, the banks were in a worse state than the figures provided by their owners indicated. The assets of BUN, for instance, were estimated at Rp 11.25 trillion instead of Rp 15.6 trillion, while its obligations were calculated to amount to Rp 21.3 trillion instead of Rp 15.4 trillion. Based on the results of the audit, the governor of Bank Indonesia stated that bank owners had transferred assets and cash to a value of only Rp 93 trillion, not Rp 206 trillion, as they themselves claimed and which would have been more than the aggregate liquidity credit provided up to that moment, though even the Ministry of Finance was not sure about the actual amount of such support. The banks disputed the low valuation of their assets. They were furious that these had been made on the basis of the current value, whereas prices of land, shares, buildings, and factories had taken a dive because of the economic crisis.

The deadline of 21 September passed without any measures being taken. To the relief of the bankers, on 26 September the Minister of Finance, Bambang Subianto, announced that they were being given five years instead of one month to redeem the liquidity credit. The following day Ginandjar rectified the statement: the grace period was one year. Two days later, bankers went into a state of shock when Bambang Subianto announced that Habibie had decreed that the government wanted cash, not assets. The decision had been taken in view of the yawning difference in the estimated valuations and the government's urgent need of cash. Banks were given a year to effectuate the sale of the assets they had waived. Plans of how they were going to accomplish this had to be submitted before the end of the following month. In November, after IMF had put in a plea for a repayment period of five years, the government changed course again. The bankers were given four years to pay off the liquidity credit. As the bankers concerned did not have enough cash money to pay their debts, they concluded agreements with BPPN in which they promised to hand over cash and assets to BPPN.

Progress was also made with the reorganization of the state banks. A new state bank, Bank Mandiri, meaning something like the bank that can stand on its own feet, was established in October 1998. By some, the merger was seen as just a ploy to save the fortune of the Soeharto family and their associates, who were supposed to be the state banks' largest borrowers. For the time being, the four banks to be merged in it – Bank Exim, Bapindo, BDN, and BBD – were supposed to continue to function under their own names. In April the following year their uncollectable and problematic credit would be transferred to BPPN. A month later, debts amounting to less than Rp 25 billion – of a total amount of Rp 4 trillion – were returned to them. How huge the total amount of bad credit of the state banks was was difficult to ascertain. According to figures provided by a deputy governor of Bank Indonesia, as its directors were called after the acceptance of the new Act on Bank Indonesia, Subarjo Joyosumarto, the aggregate value of the uncollectable debts of all state banks in June was Rp 94.5 trillion, that of their problematic debts Rp 158.3 trillion, or half and three-quarters respectively of the total amount of such domestic bad loans tackled by BPPN.[4] On 30 July 1999, Bank Mandiri was officially inaugurated. According to its president, Robby Djohan, the new bank was sound. Nevertheless, its first steps were faltering. A much needed cash injection, which was estimated would have to amount to Rp 137.8 trillion in total, by the government was delayed till the middle of October, when the Indonesian government issued Rp 103 trillion worth of bonds. Because of this delay, the amount of money needed by Bank Mandiri had risen to Rp 178 trillion by the middle of December. At that time Bank Mandiri had a capital adequacy ratio (CAR) of minus ten per cent. The low CAR had prevented Bank Mandiri from granting any loans. In December Robby Djohan, by now its chief director, had to admit that since the found-

---

4   *D&R*, 7-6-1999:60. A month earlier the president of Bank Mandiri had disclosed that the aggregate non-performing loans of the four banks merged amounted to Rp 61 trillion. Five per cent of this sum was not restructurable as the debtors' businesses were no longer viable (*The Jakarta Post*, 14-5-1999).

ing of Bank Mandiri, its losses amounted to Rp 10 trillion. The recapitalization of BNI, initially estimated to require Rp 52.8 trillion, was also delayed.[5]
In March 2000, when a list was published of the 20 state companies with the
biggest losses in 1999, it was headed by Bank Mandiri (Rp 36.8 trillion) and
BNI (Rp 10.2 trillion).

Yet another step to promote the task of cleaning up the banking sector was
to decide which banks could continue to operate on a sound basis and which
had to be closed down. To this end, a programme for the recapitalization of
banks was started in September 1998. It was a gigantic undertaking. About a
thousand persons were set to work. Scores of expensive foreign consultants
were hired, which earned Glenn Yusuf the accusation of practising KKN and
of splashing money about. These people were employed by BPPN to evaluate which of the 166 banks still in operation could be saved and which could
not. They also had to launch a campaign to prepare the public for yet another set of closures to prevent a new bank scare. To assist BPPN in performing
its task, the World Bank provided a special loan of US$ 20 million.

The banks were divided into three categories: Class A, consisting of banks
with a capital adequacy ratio, the ratio between equity capital and risk-
weighted assets, of 4 per cent or more; Class B, banks with a CAR between
minus 25 percent and plus 4 per cent; and Class C banks, with a CAR of
lower than minus 25 per cent. Initially the stated intention was that all Class
B banks would take part in the recapitalization programme, which was
designed to raise their CAR first to four per cent, and after this to the international standard which requires that outstanding credit is covered by eight
per cent of the bank's own capital. Category C banks had to bring their CAR
to minus 25 per cent in order to be eligible for recapitalization support. If
they could not do this, they would face liquidation. The government was to
provide 80 per cent of the funds required. After a period of three years, the
government would withdraw from the private banking sector, selling its
shares to the former owners and others. Bank owners had to cover the
remaining 20 per cent, though it was not altogether clear how they were to
manage this. Bad loans could be transferred to BPPN, which would try to collect them.

The cost of the recapitalization scheme was initially estimated at around
Rp 300 trillion, an amount equalling the national budget. About half the
money, Rp 136 trillion, was thought to be needed for the recapitalization of

---

[5]   Robby Djohan stressed that the liquidation of Bank Mandiri would be even more expensive than its recapitalization. Were the bank to be liquidated, the government would have to take
over the bank's obligations, which amounted to Rp 170.5 trillion and US$ 8 billion. A second
round of capital was injected into Bank Mandiri at the end of December, when bonds worth Rp
75 trillion were issued. It was calculated that the other state banks, BRI and BTN, needed a capital injection of respectively Rp 31.5 trillion and Rp 11.2 trillion.

the state banks. It was a figure that would swell as the process got under way. In July 1999 Bambang Subianto mentioned a figure of Rp 550 trillion, that is, about half of Indonesia's gross domestic product. In his accountability speech in October, Habibie gave a more moderate figure, Rp 350 trillion, but this was a figure that was generally considered to be too low. In November Glenn M. Yusuf mentioned a figure of Rp 643.3 trillion. Needless to say, the government did not have such an amount of extra money. Government bonds had to be issued. The interest on these bonds would be partly paid by income generated by the sale of the assets handed over and the recovery of loans by BPPN, and would partly come from the national budget. Rp 15 trillion of the 1998-1999 budget was reserved for this, and of the 1999-2000 budget initially Rp 18 trillion. There was not much optimism, either about the success of the issuance, or about the capability of BPPN to come up with its share of the money.

There was also more fundamental criticism. The recapitalization programme was called an affront. Huge sums of money were to be given to rich bankers and directors of concerns whose irresponsible behaviour was considered to have lain at the root of Indonesia's financial and economic crisis, and who were still living in their luxurious houses and driving around in their expensive cars. Admittedly, bankers and debtors had handed over property belonging to their companies, but, though holding out this measure out as a threat, BPPN had not yet seized any of their personal property. The impression such people gave was that as far as they were concerned, it was business as usual. Some had even made new business acquisitions.

It took months before it was announced which banks were to be saved and which not. In such a fraught climate, rumours flew around about banks which were to be liquidated. Some of them, according to the victims of such stories, were spread by banking rivals to lure away customers. At last, on 11 February 1999, it seemed progress had been made. During a meeting of the Indonesian Chamber of Trade and Industry, Habibie announced that the names of banks to be liquidated (or as it was more elegantly phrased: clearing would be stopped) were to be made public on 27 February. It may well be that Habibie had dreamt up 27 February out of the clear blue sky, putting his economic advisors into an awkward position, and forcing them to work overtime to meet the date he had mentioned. On 26 February, after consulting Habibie, Ginandjar Kartasasmita in his capacity as Coordinating Minister of Economy, Finance and Industry completely unexpectedly announced that the deadline had been postponed till the middle of March. The reason stated was that owners of eight banks had received the outcome of their audit late, and that it would only be fair to give these bankers time to adjust their business plans and take the necessary financial steps to have their banks qualify for the recapitalization scheme.

Ginandjar's announcement created a furore. Once again the credibility of Habibie and his government was at stake. The decision to give a number of banks a respite seemed to have been cooked up by an inner circle of a few people. As in so many instances of government policy on sensitive issues, various sides chose to describe what was happening as a 'comedy'.[6] One of the reasons for suspecting foul play was that the Minister of Finance, Bambang Subianto, had apparently been overlooked. He heard the news of the postponement from journalists. Subarjo Joyosumarto, who often acted as spokesman for the government when measures had to be explained affecting the banking sector, had also not been informed in advance. Miffed, he refused to go into the background of the decision, confining his statement to the press to stressing that he was just the messenger.

A second reason for the commotion was that the postponement immediately raised the issue of pressure allegedly being exerted by people whose banks were in danger of liquidation. It was rumoured that they had threatened to unveil immense bank accounts held by cabinet ministers and other high officials abroad. Others spoke of intensive lobbying by politically well-connected bankers and business tycoons, backed up by senior officials and cabinet members. One of the names that came up was that of Aburizal Bakrie, owner of Bank Nusa Nasional (BNN), a close friend of Ginandjar, former employee of Tanri Abeng, and by now secretary-general of DPKEK, Council for the Stabilization of Monetary and Economic Resilience.[7]

The uncertainty gave bank owners, at least that was the suspicion voiced afterwards, more time to ensure their assets were safe and sound. There was a precedent. At the end of March, Subarjo Joyosumarto had to admit that the assets of the banks which had been liquidated in November 1997 had been 'eaten away' and that all that remained were the 'bare bones'. A mistake had been made. The former owners and managers had been left in charge till liquidation teams had been formed at shareholders' meetings. The oversight meant that what the bankers had done was, though morally wrong, legally unassailable (*Media Indonesia*, 31-3-1999). A similar story was spread about the banks which had been taken over. Not much money had been left in these banks. The shareholders, including Bob Hasan (not mentioned by name but described as a Chinese who had been a cabinet minister), it was insinuated, had transferred their money to foreign bank accounts (*D&R*, 8-3-1999:54).

Certainty came on 13 March, when the Minister of Finance announced that

---

[6]   In view of the avalanche of criticism it evoked, the announcement was also seen as an attempt to turn attention away from the investigation of Soeharto.
[7]   BNN was a recent merger of banks of the Bakrie concern. Among these banks was Bank Perniagaan, which was responsible for the low CAR of BNN of minus 110 per cent. Without taking Bank Perniagaan into account, the CAR was minus 24 per cent.

the government was to close 38 banks and to take over seven others. Immediately after the news was made public, clients began to empty their safe-deposit boxes. At some banks they came too late. The doors of the buildings were already sealed. The seven banks taken over included BNN, Bank Duta, and Bank Risjad Salim International.[8] All became the responsibility of BPPN.

Among the banks closed, many more than had been expected, this time captured under the acronym BBKU (Bank Beku Kegiatan Usaha, Banks Whose Business Activities Are Frozen), were 21 of the B-class, banks which had failed, as it was described in English, a *fit and proper* test, or whose owners had not been able to present a sound business plan. Bambang Subianto stated that the problematic credit of these banks was higher than their owners had reported. The 17,000 employees who lost their jobs were offered a redundancy scheme developed and paid for by BPPN, entitling them to between two and ten months' salary, double the amount mentioned in a regulation of the Ministry of Labour from 1996.[9] The arrangement did not satisfy them. At nearly all branches of the shut-down banks employees went on strike demanding a better redundancy pay agreement, especially as, because of the economic crisis, their job opportunities were slim. The employees' actions alarmed customers who needed certified proof that they held an account at the shut-down banks in order to be paid out by other banks which had been assigned this task. At some banks clerks threatened to disclose illegal practices and expose examples of mismanagement by owners and managers. All in all this would, they promised, be a long list. They would also provide the names of members of the cabinet who had played a role in providing non-performing loans. BPPN refused to give in to the demands. It took the position that the extra payment had to come from the owners, and that it was they to whom the bank employees should turn. BPPN simultaneously rejected the possibility that BPPN would provide the owners with yet more money to enable them to offer their employees a better deal.

Nine private banks were to be recapitalized, the cost of which was estimated at Rp 21.3 trillion, of which the government was to bear Rp 17 trillion. Among these *bank rekap*, as they were sometimes called, were Bank Lippo, Bank Niaga in which the Tirtamas concern had a ten per cent share, Bukopin, Bank Bali, and Bank Internasional Indonesia (BII).[10] Bank Lippo, in which Liem had a stake, was owned by the Riady family, one member of which,

---

8   The others were Bank Rama, Bank Tamara, Bank Pos Nusantara, and Jaya Bank International. Initially the cost of the takeovers was estimated at Rp 5.2 trillion; at the end of May, because of a rising interest rate and a falling rupiah, this figure had to be adjusted to Rp 12.1 trillion.
9   To this number of fired bank employees should be added another 18,000 who became redundant because of the merger of the four state banks in Bank Mandiri.
10   The others were Bank Universal, Bank Prima Express, Bank Artha Media, and Bank Patriot.

James Tjahja Riady (Li Bai), had caused some international commotion by contributing to the Clinton campaign coffers in 1996. According to Bambang Subianto, 73 banks had enough capital of their own and did not need recapitalization. Finally, in early May, the Minister of Finance announced that the government would also recapitalize twelve provincial development banks. As with the other banks, their owners, the provincial administration, had to come up with 20 per cent of the costs. It was not just the CAR which had been taken into consideration. State banks and regional development banks which would have had to be liquidated if strict rules were applied, were recapitalized because their liquidation would have required between two and three times as much money – an argument also to be put forward later to justify why some private banks were selected to be saved from ruin. The government had shrunk from closing banks in which there were a large number of account holders or which had many branches, fearing disruption of financial traffic if it were to take such a step.

Among the banks closed were Bank Yama and Bank Tata connected with Siti Hardijanti Rukmana, Bank Alfa linked with Bambang Trihatmodjo, and Bank Pesona Kriya Dana in which Sigit Harjojudanto and Hutomo Mandala Putra had a share. Other banks frozen were Bank Danahutama of Yusuf Wanandi and The Ning King, Bank Baja Internasional of The Ning King, Bank Ciputra, owned by Ciputra or Tjie Tjin Hoan, a large property developer, Bank Intan owned since July 1996 by Fadel Muhammad, Bank Arya Panduarta of Hashim Djojohadikusumo, and Bank Bahari of the Navy Cooperative Society. The freezing of these banks heralded the prospect of yet another new round of visits to the office of the attorney-general for Tommy. Following the same procedure as it had done in the case of the BBOs, BPPN announced that it would involve the public prosecution in recovering the state credit. Though not a new measure, when this announcement was made in July it still created a small furore. Bankers suddenly were afraid of having to pay the slush money employees of the attorney-general's office would demand, pointing out that the office had quite a reputation for extorting money.

One of the banks frozen in the latest round had been in the centre of public attention for more than two weeks: Bank Papan Sejahtera (BPS). Its hour in the limelight came after it had become public knowledge that the Harawi [Haji Abdurrahman Wahid] Sekawan Group of NU had acquired a 20 per cent share in BPS in November through a transaction effected with Hashim Djojohadikusumo. Another of Abdurrahman Wahid's companies, Adhikarya Sejati Abadi (ASA), had bought shares in Bank Ficorinvest, which was now also frozen. The takeovers surprised many, the more so because both banks had clearly been among the candidates ripe for closing down by the government. Abdurrahman Wahid averred he had acted as he did because there were many poor people among the clients of these banks. He pointed out that Bank Papan Sejahtera had provided soft loans to 500,000 clients to enable them to buy a 'very simple house'. He also explained that an international bank had been willing to inject money into BPS.

The acquisition of BPS was all the more dubious as one-third of the Harawi Sekawan shares were held by Edward Seky Soeryadjaya (Tjia Han Sek), the eldest son of William Soeryadjaya. Edward Soeryadjaya had made himself notorious in banking circles. In the early 1990s, as director of Bank Summa and of the affiliated Summa Group, he had been at the centre of one of the greatest banking scandals to rock Indonesia to date. Bank Summa, at the time Indonesia's tenth largest private bank, had been liquidated in November 1992 because it had been unable to honour its obligations. The bank had gone down in the same way as many of the banks closed or frozen after it, serving as a source of investment money for companies of the same concern. Its demise forced William Soeryadjaya to sell his Astra shares (see Barker n.d.). Edward Soeryadjaya was blacklisted by Bank Indonesia and was no longer allowed to own or manage a bank.

The downfall of Bank Summa had had consequences for NU. Two years earlier, Abdurrahman Wahid and Edward Soeryadjaya had signed an agreement to launch a programme to establish two thousand Bank Perkreditan Rakyat (BPR) Nusumma, or Nusumma People's Credit Banks, over a period of twenty years. These were designed to cater to the needs of farmers and small entrepreneurs. Forty percent of the BPR bank shares were to be held by Bank Summa, sixty by a company especially established by NU for this purpose, PT Duta Dunia Perintis. BPR Nusumma had managed to survive the scandal, but had not flourished. The acquisition of BPS and Bank Ficorinvest were supposed to turn the tide. Because of the 1992 scandal, Abdurrahman Wahid had to deny that Edward Soeryadjaya was the person who was to provide the money for the acquisitions. Edward, he joked, was a member of ICMI, Ikatan Cina Melarat Indonesia, Indonesian League of Poor Chinese (*Ummat*, 8-3-1999:31). Edward Soeryadjaya sold his Harawi Sekawan shares in February.

Another upshot of the purchase of BPS was a bitter row between Abdurrahman Wahid and Hashim Djojohadikusomo. Abdurrahman Wahid lodged a petition for bankruptcy against Semen Cibinong (one of the bank's bad debtors) and Tirtamas Majutama. He threatened that he would leave Hashim only his *celana kolor*, 'his underpants'. The crux of the matter was a promise made by Hashim Djojohadikusumo that he would redeem all his financial obligations regarding BPS if Harawi Sekawan bought the BPS shares. Moreover, as part of a recapitalization agreement signed in January, Tirtamas Majutama had pledged Hashim Djojohadikusumo's petrochemical plant in Tuban. Defending his actions, Abdurrahman Wahid insistently stressed that Hashim Djojohadikusumo had not honoured his part of the deal. Spokespeople for the latter argued that a transfer was only planned to take place after BPS had had an international auditor assess the debts accrued at the bank by Tirtamas (see for the transaction *Ummat*, 8-3-1999:31-2; *Media Indonesia*, 30-3-1999, 31-3-1999).

Bankers whose banks were closed were livid. Some announced that they would take the state to court. Aburizal Bakrie was one of them. Another was Fadel Muhammad of Bank Intan. In an initial reaction he blamed the government for having bowed to IMF pressure, and excoriated the former for the fact that many of the banks which had been closed were owned by indigenous Indonesians. He claimed that both Ginandjar Kartasasmita and Syahril Sabirin had agreed to a proposal he had submitted in which he had proposed that Bank Intan be turned into an Islamic bank under the new name Indo-Oman Islamic Bank, with the help of a bank from Oman. The new bank was to focus on assisting small businessmen. Its closure was proof that the government was totally unconcerned about the fate of such people. Confronted with the closure of the two banks he had just acquired, Abdurrahman Wahid also made this accusation.

After the bank closures, Muladi announced that a list of owners and managers of banks who would be forbidden to leave the country was being compiled. Initially he ventured an estimate that the ban might affect 700 persons. Within a fortnight he had adjusted his estimate to 200. Muladi was sure that Abdurrahman Wahid's name would not be on such a list. Only bankers about whom there were strong suspicions that they might try to flee were to be banned from leaving the country. Another person who might be affected by a ban was Hashim Djojohadikusumo. However, he was confident that he would escape such a fate. After all, he was Habibie's special economic envoy for economic relations with Europe. Indeed, little more than a week after the bank closures, in his capacity of Habibie's envoy, Hashim Djojohadikusumo left for a one-month trip to Europe. A list containing 172 names was handed over by the Ministry of Finance to the Ministry of Justice on 1 April. The government was not prepared to reveal whose names were on it. By that time it was widely reported that a number of bankers and bank managers had already fled the country.

Another list which seemed to be growing by the day was Bank Indonesia's blacklist of people banned from doing banking business, the so-called DOT – sometimes also referred to as DOR, onomatopoeia in Indonesian for the sound of shots being fired – short for Daftar Orang Tercela, List of Culpable Persons. It was a list on which the names of bankers of A-class banks could also be entered. In early August it was disclosed that 38 of the 700 directors, commissioners, and owners of the A-class banks had been ordered to withdraw from the banking sector. They had not passed the *fit and proper* test. They had violated banking regulations or had maimed the performance of their bank in other ways. They had to sell their shares to buyers who were unrelated to them. Almost 200 had passed only conditionally. They had to improve themselves. No names were made public by the government. The recapitalized banks had to come up with 20 per cent of the money needed before 21 April. Two days after this date it was announced that Bank Niaga, which had failed to do so, would be taken over by the government, which meant that it was the state which had to furnish the total cost of the bank's recapitalization. To justify this move, the governor of Bank Indonesia stated that the government had decided to take over Bank Niaga because in this instance it was a large bank with a good reputation. Its main problem in acquiring the money it needed was that it lacked the backing of a major shareholder. On 23 April, two joint-venture banks, both with joint Japanese-Indonesian ownership, were also closed: Bank Indovest and Bank LTCB Central Asia. In the middle of May the other eight banks were told that the original estimates of the initial calculation of their recapitalization had been too optimistic and that they had to come up with additional money before 30 June. The reason for this was that the negative spread was forcing up the cost of the recapitalizations. To prevent further closures, the maximum equity share of the government's participation was increased from 80 to 90 per cent.

To steer the cleaning up of the banking sector, two bodies were established in July. One was the Independent Review Committee. The IRC was chaired by Mar'ie Muhammad and had representatives from IMF, the World Bank, and the Asian Development Bank among its members. It was set up to advise the Minister of Finance on BPPN policy and programmes. Control of BPPN was put in the hands of the Financial Sector Action Committee. Among its members were Ginandjar Kartasasmita, Bambang Subianto, and Tanri Abeng. The FSAC had to report to the president. In November parliament called for the disbanding of both bodies. They were considered ineffective in overseeing BPPN. Mar'ie Muhammad agreed with this view.

When the recapitalization of the banks was finally settled, there still remained the matter of the bad debtors of the banks for which BPPN had taken over responsibility or which had been closed altogether. To find a solution was an equally complicated task, as the same powerful persons were involved. As *The Jakarta Post* described it: BPPN had 'to pass through political minefields set up by well-connected businessmen' (*The Jakarta Post*, 8-5-1999). These conglomerates, who also had to settle their foreign debts, had saddled the banks with a huge amount of uncollectable credit. In June, Subarjo Joyosumarto disclosed that the total value of uncollectable debts falling within the jurisdiction of BPPN was Rp 170.7 trillion, while problematic loans amounted to Rp 204.2 trillion. At that time BPPN feared that 20 per cent of the non-performing bank loans could not be restructured and redeemed.[11] A new estimate was revealed by Glenn Yusuf in November. Presenting a strategic plan for the management of the assets acquired by BPPN, he said that of the Rp 267 trillion problematic loans taken over from the state banks only four per cent could be recovered. The assets of the private banks taken over in 1999 he said amounted to Rp 21 trillion. Only three per cent was to be recouped. Not much later, the new Coordinating Minister of Economy, Finance and Industry, Kwik Kian Gie, speculated that the total amount of bad loans was as high as Rp 600 trillion, three times the size of the national budget and 60 per cent of Indonesia's gross domestic product.

Some of the indebted tycoons did not seem to have any intention of paying their debts or even bothering about the interest. They embraced the economic crisis as *force majeur*. They did not even seem to know how much they owed the banks. In June 1999, when BPPN announced it was to open on-line branches in eleven cities, one of the aims was to 'provide debtors with information on the exact amount of their debt' (*The Jakarta Post*, 15-6-1999).

In April Ginandjar had promised that the government would publish a list of the 20 worst debtors. It was not before June that the public got its first real inkling of the amounts owed. On 9 June, in an effort to 'shame' debtors into joining a debt-restructuring scheme and to show that the government was in earnest in its intention to have them redeem their loans, BPPN published a list of 1,689 bad debtors (listing companies, not persons, since the Minister of Finance had forbidden the latter) on the Internet. The information was immediately copied avidly in the press. Surprisingly, the list was headed by a lesser-known plantation company, Gerak Maju, of which even the ownership was something of a mystery. It was not clear whether the company did indeed belong to the Mantrust Group of Tegoeh Soetantyo (Tan Kiong Liep) of which it was said to form part.[12] Gerak Maju's debts amounted to Rp 4.2 trillion. Coming second, with Rp 3.3 trillion, was Timor Putra Nasional. Fifth was Chandra Asri Petrochemical Centre, a producer of ethylene and other basic materials for plastics, partly Japanese-owned, which has among its domestic shareholders Bambang Trihatmodjo and Prajogo Pangestu. Its stated debt was Rp 2.9 trillion. Featuring among the top thirty were Kiani

---

[11] *D&R*, 7-6-1999:62; *The Jakarta Post*, 25-6-1999. According to Subarjo Joyosumarto, the uncollectable and problematic loans of the A-banks amounted to Rp 3.55 and Rp 9.2 trillion respectively, those of foreign banks to Rp 5.9 and Rp 17.4 trillion.
[12] There were reports that Gerak Maju had become the property of Tommy Winata, head of the Artha Graha group, and a businessman well-connected in army circles. Tommy Winata denied having bought Gerak Maju. In March 2000 it was reported that Tommy Winata was suspected of being the man behind illegal gambling in the tourist resort of Cipanas in West Java. The following month Abdurrahman Wahid asked for Winata's arrest. The reason given was that Winata was the owner of a pleasure boat used for gambling. Marzuki Darusman denied that Winata was the owner.

Kertas (Rp 2.3 trillion), Tirtamas Majutama (Rp 1.1 trillion), IPTN (Rp 960 billion), Humpuss PT (Rp 929 billion), Humpuss Inc. (Rp 921 billion) and Bakrie Investindo (Rp 900 billion).

Persistently prodded by IMF, BPPN stepped up pressure. On 12 June, the two hundred largest debtors were invited to come to the Dharmawangsa Hotel to discuss the terms for instalments.[13] Among those who came were some of the mightiest tycoons of the New Order: Bob Hasan, Aburizal Bakrie, Ponco Sutowo, and Tommy Winata.[14] Bambang Trihatmodjo, Hutomo Mandala Putra, and Prajogo Pangestu did not turn up. The conglomerates were given to understand that they had to sign a letter of commitment within ten days, affirming that they agreed to a restructuring of their debts and that they were financially capable of doing so. The names of those who refused would be made public, their assets would be seized, and their companies nationalized. If necessary, bankruptcy proceedings would be started against them. Once again the tycoons moaned and protested. The time allowed was too short and the debt list was unfair. Some complained that they were already rescheduling their debts or were in the process of redeeming the loans they had contracted. Among those businessmen were spokesmen of Semen Cibinong, Astra International, and Bakrie and Brothers. Their complaints were not completely unfounded. The list published by BPPN was based on the situation as it had been in March.

By the end of June, most of the two hundred largest debtor firms, including those of the Humpuss, Bimantara, Bob Hasan, and Bakrie concerns, had signed a letter of commitment. The children of Soeharto did not pose many problems. The impression they made was that they wanted to cooperate. Twenty-six companies were declared 'non-cooperative' by BPPN. They had either not signed a letter of commitment or had made some demands. Among them were Gemala Industries of Sofyan Wanandi, two companies belonging to Sudwikatmono, and Semen Cibinong and two other companies which were part of the Tirtamas Concern of Hashim Djojohadikusumo.[15] Another company listed was Sempati. The airline had already begun procedures to get itself declared bankrupt by the commercial court of Jakarta. When the court consented a few days later, BPPN appealed, demanding that

---

13   In March 2000 the chairman of BPPN said that the number of debtors at banks falling within the jurisdiction of BPPN amounted to 144,500.
14   In February 2000 it was revealed that, besides James Riady, Tommy Winata had also contributed to the Clinton campaign coffers (*Tempo*, 20-2-2000:31).
15   A spokesman for the Tirtamas Group explained that the three companies of the concern were prepared to sign a letter of commitment, but wanted the additional stipulations that the restructuring would take place in accordance with Indonesian law and would take into account the special characteristics of the companies involved.

Sempati Air should settle its debts with Bank Exim and BCA first.[16] BPPN announced that by the end of August it would have made up its mind about whether to restructure these bad debts or begin litigation. It kept its promise. On 1 September BPPN revealed that it would take legal action against 17 debtors. Their combined debt was Rp 3.9 trillion and US$ 70 million. Among the firms were Sempati Air and Gemala Industries. The companies of Hashim Djojohadikusumo had agreed to a restructuring of their debts. An official memorandum of understanding on the restructuring of its debts was signed by the Humpuss Group of Tommy Soeharto on 19 October. The debts of this concern amounted to US$ 307 million, Rp 167 billion, and M$ 12 million.

Besides their banks being closed and the debts they had to repay, the tycoons had other worries as well. Various well-known businessmen were called in for questioning by the police or the office of the attorney-general on suspicion of embezzlement. One of the points they had to account for was overlending to companies of the concerns their banks belonged to. The investigation of such cases was handed over to the police. The police and the office of the attorney-general, which had to investigate the use of liquidity credit, found themselves questioning a number of mighty tycoons: Sudwikatmono, Bambang Trihatmodjo, Bob Hasan, Hashim Djojohadikusumo, Arifin Panigoro, and The Ning King. Some of them, and Bob Hasan is one example, were interrogated concerning several cases.[17] About 80 per cent of the credit advanced by his BUN had gone to companies belonging to the same concern, among them Kiani Kertas.[18] The Ning King, against whom prosecution had started in November 1998, was accused of corruption involving credit he had received from BRI. Among the projects for which he had received money was the building of 'simple houses' and 'very simple houses' for the poor in Tangerang. No houses had been built.[19] In December 1998 it was the turn of Hashim Djojohadikusumo. He was questioned in relation to credit of Rp 500

---

[16]   The Supreme Court upheld the bankruptcy verdict in August. According to a company spokesman, Sempati's debts in June 1999 amounted to Rp 646 billion and US$ 104 million. Its assets had a value of only Rp 83 billion (*The Jakarta Post*, 8-10-1999).
[17]   As early as July 1998, Bob Hasan had been summoned by the Public Prosecution Service to respond to accusations by members of Apkindo, united in Masyarakat Perhutanan Indonesia Reformasi, among them Agus Miftach, about levies the Indonesian Wood Panel Association collected between 1985 and 1997 destined as 'promotion funds', which had not been returned to them. Part of these funds had been returned, but in rupiahs while the levy had been in dollars, and had been interest-free. Bob Hasan claimed he had done nothing wrong. The money had been used to improve export performance, for reforestation, for transmigration, and for social purposes.
[18]   To circumvent the lending rules, in this case the credit had first been transferred to Bank International Indonesia (BII), which in turn transferred it to Kiani Kertas.
[19]   Because of lack of evidence the investigation was discontinued in September 1999.

billion provided in 1997 by one of the state banks which he had used to
finance the construction of a petrochemical factory in Tuban, on which work
had been discontinued because of the crisis in early 1998, but this was not the
purpose he had mentioned in his request for the money.

Initially, in the summer of 1998, Bambang Trihatmodjo had managed to
stay clear, but ten employees of his Andromeda Bank were among those suspected of foul play and of having misused liquidity credit. In early September 1998, when Bambang was interrogated for the first time with regard to
overlending by Bank Andromeda, Probosutedjo was indignant. He wondered what had become of the promise made by Wiranto that the Armed
Forces would protect Soeharto and his family.

One businessman the office of the attorney-general came down on was
Arifin Panigoro, suspected of having given financial support to demonstrat-
ing students. He found himself a suspect in a corruption case in early
November 1998. It concerned the issuing of promissory notes worth around
US\$ 200 million in 1997, before the onset of the crisis, by Medco Central Asia
(MCA). They had been bought by a subsidiary of the state company PT Jasa
Asuransi Indonesia (Jasindo), with among other securities all MCA shares as
guarantee. Overtaken by the financial crisis, Arifin Panigoro's side had not
been able to honour the obligation. Arifin Panigoro considered his prosecu-
tion to have been politically motivated, and denied all charges of financial
misconduct. What he had done was no more than normal business practice.
He also stressed that after the financial crisis had started, in conjunction with
Jasindo he had tried to find a solution to his financial problems. Medco had
also started to sell companies. Another point put forward in his defence by
Arifin Panigoro to support the idea that his prosecution had been politically
inspired was that if there was to be a case filed against him, it ought to be a
civil and not a criminal one. It did indeed seem that Arifin Panigoro had been
specially targeted by the government for his support to the student movement. Habibie took a special interest in the case. On 3 February 1999, during
a cabinet meeting, he instructed the attorney-general to start a prosecution.
In the middle of May Arifin Panigoro was given city arrest. He protested. His
lawyer suspected that the ban was meant to prevent him, as a member of
PDI-P since April, campaigning for this party. When the trial against him
began in June 1999, Arifin Panigoro was accompanied to the courtroom by
over one hundred members of the PDI-P Task Force and other party supporters. In July Arifin Panigoro was acquitted. The office of the attorney-general had blundered. According to the judge who presided over the case, the
subpoena should have been sent to the board of directors of the Medco concern, and not to Arifin Panigoro, the group's chief commissioner. Within days
Arifin Panigoro was being interrogated again by the office of the attorney-
general, this time as a witness in the same case – proof, he claimed, that

Habibie was out to get him.

Legal action was also taken against Sofyan Wanandi. On 29 January, while he was abroad, he was officially barred from leaving the country. The reason given for the ban was information unearthed after the Tanah Tinggi explosion (see Chapter V). He was also accused of having been found to have bad credit at three state banks worth a total value of Rp 550 billion. At the end of June, Sofyan Wanandi was formally declared a fugitive. The assistance of Interpol was enlisted. His lawyer, Mulya Lubis, denied that Sofyan Wanandi had fled. He was in the United States for medical treatment. Four months later Sofyan Wanandi returned to Indonesia.

In the middle of 1999 there were indications that the measures taken to cure the banking sector of its manifold ills had had some results. BCA had recovered from its debacle and public faith in it had begun to be restored. Both BCA and Bank Danamon had also made some progress in repaying the liquidity support they had received.[20] Another indication was that the price of shares in banks rose at the stock exchange, though this may have been occasioned mainly by the fact that as of the end of May foreign banks were allowed a 99 per cent stake in Indonesian banks. Whatever optimism there might have been about the economic performance of the Habibie government evaporated when the Bank Bali scandal erupted. Bank Bali, a large bank with about 280 branches, had been founded by Djaja Ramli. It had been listed among the banks to be recapitalized. In April it had been disclosed that the UK-based Standard Chartered Bank (SCB) would spend US$ 56 million to buy 20 per cent of its shares. An agreement was signed, but at the end of July SCB suggested that BPPN should take over Bank Bali and withdrew its initial offer. BPPN complied. It took over Bank Bali on 23 July and entered into a partnership with SCB, which was to take over management of Bank Bali. This made the Standard Chartered Bank the first foreign bank to do so, and for the time being also the only one. At a rights issue to raise capital for Bank Bali – announced to be imminent – SCB would take at least a 20 per cent stake in Bank Bali. BPPN would be the standby purchaser of any unsubscribed issues. The Standard Chartered Bank would be allowed to acquire one hundred per cent of the shares over a period of five years.

Among the conditions stipulated was that Bank Bali's chief president, Rudy Ramli, son of Djaja Ramli, had to go. At first the only explanation given was that the Standard Chartered Bank had postponed entering Bank Bali because an account had shown that if the bank were to be given a CAR of four per cent, Rp 4.3 trillion was needed, and not Rp 2.8 trillion which had

---

[20]   At the end of April 2000 BCA was declared healthy. Its CAR had reached four per cent. Consequently BCA was removed from the list of BTOs and became an ordinary bank again, no longer falling under the control of BPPN.

been the initial estimate. In the middle of August, by then a much plagued man, Rudy Ramli was to suggest unprofessional conduct by the auditing firm KPMG and the Standard Chartered Bank with the aim of taking over his bank.[21] The steady rise in the estimated amount of money needed to raise Bank Bali's CAR also made other people suspicious. At the very least, it increased doubts about whether enough money could be raised by the government to pay for the recapitalization scheme. The adjustment of the Bank Bali figures was yet another indication that the actual costs might be much higher than initially envisaged.

Within days it had emerged that there was still another reason for the Standard Chartered Bank to hesitate before taking a share in Bank Bali. At the critical moment, a money transaction was revealed which blemished the image of BPPN and had wide-ranging political ramifications, as it involved Golkar, cabinet ministers, and Habibie and his closest advisors.

On 30 July at a seminar on the Prospects of the National Banking World a banking expert, Pradjoto, disclosed that, as the Standard Chartered Bank had also uncovered, Bank Bali had paid the total sum of Rp 550 billion to a number of persons. Among the recipients were Golkar leaders, a 'celebrated conglomerate', and a BPPN official. Pradjoto suspected that 'money politics' was at play, venturing to suggest that the money might have been used to finance the Golkar election campaign which, it must be remembered, could no longer count on the stream of money generated by the Dakab Foundation. The crux of the matter was an attempt by Bank Bali to recoup its inter-bank loans to BDNI, BUN, Bank Tiara, all three frozen banks. In theory such obligations were guaranteed by BPPN, but there were exceptions.[22] In practice, moreover, verification of claims was a very time-consuming process. Release was also delayed by the fact that the government did not have the money required to pay all claims at once. Bonds had to be issued to raise the money

21 He found it suspicious that an audit by the accounting firm KPMG, undertaken at the request of Bank Indonesia, had estimated recapitalization costs as of December 1998 at Rp 1.4 trillion, a KPMG audit on behalf of BPPN had raised this figure to Rp 2.6 trillion as of March, and a third one by the same auditing firm spoke of Rp 4.3 trillion as of June.
22 Initially, one of the exceptions concerned forward transactions. This had, for instance, made the Bank Bali claim at BDNI fall outside the guarantee. It concerned an unhedged dollar loan to be repaid in rupiahs dating from 1997. The rules were adjusted to allow more lenience for honouring claims by a joint decision of Bank Indonesia and BPPN in May 1999. One of the reasons for changing the rules was that by releasing extra money the government was obliged to put less money into the recapitalization of the banks. Nevertheless, in December it was disclosed by BPPN that an audit had shown that of the 216 inter-bank claims to be processed by BPPN with a total value of Rp 6 trillion, only 11 were eligible. 48 claims did not meet the conditions, while 157 claims described as inconclusive and unverifiable were to be examined once more. In February 2000 45 claims had been found eligible to be honoured under the government's guarantee programme and 63 ineligible. Another 63 claims were removed from the lists because they were to be settled bilaterally between the creditor and debtor banks.

needed. Banks suffered from this delay. They needed the money for their recapitalization and in order to be able to provide credit to diminish their negative spread, which was draining their resources. Failing to have Bank Bali's money released, at his wits' end Rudy Ramli had accepted the offer of a cession agreement by two persons in January. Pradjoto described them as N, a member of the Golkar central board, and Dj, a conglomerate who owned the hotel chain M. To ensure that the money was cleared, they had contacted PL of BPPN. Later it became known that Rudy Ramli had entered the cession agreement without informing his board of commissioners, BPPN, or Bank Indonesia. He had committed himself to the agreement 'out of desperation and total frustration' after being repeatedly told that his credit could not be repaid, which drove him to begin to consider his claims worthless (*The Jakarta Post*, 16-8-1999). BPPN had transferred Rp 904 billion – money BDNI owed Bank Bali – to the Bank Bali account at Bank Indonesia in early June. Thereupon Bank Bali had debited from the same account Rp 546 billion (about US$ 80 million) as a commission fee for the successful mediation. Afterwards Pradjoto said that he had decided to reveal the scandal because he knew that at least twelve other banks were threatened with a similar fate (*The Jakarta Post*, 24-10-1999).

It did not take much imagination to conclude that N was Setya Novanto, a member of the People's Congress and a vice-treasurer of Golkar, who began his business career as a manager in some of Siti Hardijanti Rukmana and Sudwikatmono's companies. He is owner and chief director of Era Giat Prima (EGP), a trading and investment company founded in the middle of 1998, which had succeeded in recouping the money. PL was Pande Nasorahona Lubis, who had worked at Bapindo bank between 1973 and 1997. In this capacity he had been one of the witnesses at the Eddy Tansil trial. In 1999 he was vice-chairman of BPPN, heading its department for the management of the obligations of the closed banks, and as such was one of the persons who could set in motion the procedure for the honouring of financial claims. The hotel owner was Djoko Sugiarto Tjandra (or Tjan Kok Hui), a large property developer, who headed the Mulia Group and was managing director of EGP. He had allegedly spent Rp 252 billion to effectuate the clearing of the money. Djoko Tjandra was thought to be the brains behind the scheme, using Setya Novanto as a front man because of his own bad reputation in banking circles.[23] Other names were mentioned as well. One of these was that of Tanri Abeng, to whom Pande Lubis was supposed to be 'close' and whose son was a business partner of Setya Novanto. Tanri Abeng and Setya Novanto also

---

[23]   *Media Indonesia*, 11-8-1999. Djoko Tjandra was involved in a financial embezzlement case involving BRI. He had allegedly borrowed US$ 50 million from the bank for the construction of a shopping mall in Jakarta, but the mall had never been built (Samhuri and Setiono 1999:178).

had had a lion's share in the publication in 1996 of the book *Manajemen Presiden Soeharto: Penuturan 17 menteri* (The management qualities of President Soeharto: A narrative by 17 ministers). Another name mentioned was that of Baramuli, author of the book *BJ Habibie pemimpin kaliber dunia*, B.J. Habibie a leader of world stature. His name was frequently mentioned as a key member, if not the leader, of Habibie's 'success team', the team of whose task was to secure Habibie's re-election as president. People were sure the team needed money to buy votes from members of the People's Congress. Referring to such accusations, Baramuli, who himself was the owner of the Poleko concern, boasted that he was capable of collecting billions of rupiahs for such a campaign (*Pos Kota*, 13-8-1999). Earlier, in the run-up to the general election, he had already been accused of money politicking. On a tour through Sulawesi he had thrown money about. Baramuli denied there had been anything wrong in this. He had given the money to Golkar cadre members who would have voted for that party whether they had received money or not (Ismawan 1999:45). Arraigned for the Bank Bali affair, Baramuli also maintained his innocence, stating that he was prepared to swear a *sumpah pocong* to prove this.

Djoko Tjandra and Setya Novanto denied that they had done anything illegal. The cession agreement had been normal business practice. The money received by ECP was the company's fee for getting the money released. Setya Novanto denied that his firm was a debt collector. Unfortunately, when he said this (or, as he later claimed, journalists had quoted him as saying this) he had linked the term with Yapto Suryosumarno, president of Pemuda Pancasila. He was to pass a few terrible nights before he was able to convince Yapto that it was not his fault that the latter's name had been mentioned in the press as an example of a real debt collector. His houses became the target of Pemuda Pancasila demonstrations organized by Yorrys Raweyai. Pemuda Pancasila members also demonstrated outside the office of the attorney-general, demanding a thorough investigation into the scandal. Yorrys Raweyai even announced his intention of having half a million Pemuda Pancasila members march to the parliament building to underscore this demand (Samhuri and Setiono 1999:50).

BPPN admitted that it had transferred Rp 904 billion to the Bank Bali account, but persisted in claiming that the transaction had been all legal and above board. The legality of the claim had been verified, and thereupon the transfer had been approved, as was compulsory, by the Minister of Finance, Bambang Subianto, on the recommendation of BPPN and of the governor of Bank Indonesia, Syahril Sabirin. BPPN had refused to redeem the loan to BUN, as this was considered to be a loan to a concern. BPPN threatened – as it indeed was to do – to stop the recapitalization of Bank Bali (which was scheduled to begin in October) till the affair of the Rp 550 billion had been cleared up, but did not want to put it off indefinitely, because it considered Bank Bali a healthy bank. The money had to be returned. This was done in the middle of August by various persons in whose accounts money had ended up. Djoko Tjandra was adamant that the money still belonged to Era Giat Prima. He said that transferring the money had been a gesture to show that the money had not been used for political ends.[24]

Confronted with Pradjoto's revelation, leading Golkar politicians – Akbar Tanjung, Marzuki Darusman, and Fadel Muhammad – hastened to comment that Golkar was not involved and that the party had not received any of the money. They took great pains to stress that the cession deal was a private transaction by Setya Novanto and had nothing to do with Golkar. Two teams to investigate the affair were appointed, one headed by Marzuki Darusman and the other by Fadel Muhammad. The task of the first was to check the investigation of the second. Among Fadel Muhammad's first tasks was to trace Setya Novanto, whose whereabouts at that moment were unknown. At the end of August Setya Novanto resigned as deputy treasurer of Golkar.

Within days, the Public Prosecution Office launched an inquiry. Among those interrogated was Marimutu Manimaren, a deputy treasurer of Golkar, whose family controls the Texmaco Group, and who is considered to be 'close' to Habibie. His name was mentioned as one of the persons with whom part of the money had ended up. Another allegation was that he had used his influence to have the Bank Bali loan released. One of the immediate victims was Pande Lubis. He was suspended on 9 August. Five days later the police conferred on him the status of a suspect in its investigation into the Bank Bali case. The picture pieced together from the information gradually disclosed was that Pande Lubis was strongly backed by Baramuli, who wanted him to replace Glenn Yusuf, or at least maintain his position within BPPN, asking Glenn Yusuf not to dismiss him. The alleged reason for this was that Baramuli needed Pande Lubis's help to pull off similar financial deals.[25]

The affair and the way it was handled tainted the already impaired reputation of Indonesia's financial institutions even more. The rupiah fell from Rp 7,340 to Rp 8,400 to the dollar on the morning of 11 August. Government intervention forced it up to Rp 7,770 in the afternoon. It was still at a two-month low. Foreign investors were deterred. Iman Taufik, a member of the board of the Indonesian Chamber of Commerce and Habibie's special envoy to ASEAN countries, even ventured to say at the end of September that the

---

[24] Interview with Djoko Tjandra in *Gatra*, 28-8-1999 (Samhuri and Setiono 1999:187). In October Bank Indonesia demanded that Djoko Tjandra also hand over Rp 10 billion he had received as interest after they had put part of the fee money in a bank account.
[25] In the middle of September Muladi stated that Baramuli and Pande Lubis had come to his office with information about irregularities committed by Glenn Yusuf in an effort to get him fired.

international business world had completely lost faith in Indonesia and would make no long-term commitments till after a new government had been formed.

Confronted by such strong opinions, in the middle of August the State Auditor's Office invited accounting firm PricewaterhouseCoopers (PwC) to investigate the whole affair. An additional reason for taking such a step was that rumours had started to fly around that Habibie himself had received Rp 400 billion of the Bank Bali money. The audit by PwC was hampered by the fact that some of the people said to be involved in the scandal, among them Baramuli, his tennis partner and compatriot from South Sulawesi, Tanri Abeng, and Setya Novanto, refused to be interviewed, and by the fact that Bank Indonesia had denied PwC access to a number of bank accounts. Bank Indonesia argued that these accounts fell outside the scope of the audit and that allowing the auditors access to them would be a breach of bank secrecy. The audit was completed on 6 September. It revealed that the release of the Rp 904 billion by BPPN had been illegal. In the course of their investigation, the auditors had 'uncovered numerous indicators of fraud, noncompliance, irregularity, misappropriation, undue preferential treatment, concealment, bribery and corruption during the processing and payment of the Bank Bali claims' (*The Jakarta Post*, 21-9-1999). The PwC findings also indicated that at least twelve other banks had been contacted and that other persons besides Setya Novanto and Djoko Tjandra had also offered cession agreements to banks.

At the instigation of the head of the State Auditor's Office, Satrio Budi-hardjo Joedono, only an abridged version of the report was published. The full report, the so-called long form which named names, remained secret. The result was a barrage of speculations and accusations about persons to whom some of the cession fee had been transferred, which could only be proved or disproved after the full report had been made public. Billy Joe-dono, as he was usually called, took the position that the long form could only be handed over to the police and the office of the attorney-general and under no circumstances was it to be divulged to others, not even to parliament. He stressed that this course of action was in accordance with the rules of bank secrecy, the regulations governing the State Auditor's Office, and other regulations to boot. Acting otherwise might result in imprisonment for a long time and stiff fines for the staff of his office and for PwC employees.[26] He wanted to protect these people from such a fate. Another argument he fielded was that he wanted to protect the people who were mentioned in the

---

[26]   In the middle of September PwC asked the Indonesian parliament for immunity from the court to be able to publish the full report.

long form, but who were innocent.[27] Satrio B. Joedono accused PwC of having audited private bank accounts which had no connection with the Bank Bali case. He also tried to play down the importance of the report. He said that the data was inaccurate and ventured to state that 'while providing many interesting leads, the investigation undertaken by PwC personnel is proven to be inconclusive' (Satrio B. Joedono to Neiss 16-9-1999 cited in *The Jakarta Post*, 30-9-1999). Others joined him in his criticism of PwC. Syahril Sabirin described the report as speculative. The police also voiced their reservations, questioning the methodology of the investigation and labelling its conclusions illogical. Those directly involved used the many business links there were between members of the élite to explain why sums had been transferred from one bank account to another.

The decision not to publish the full report caused a storm of protests and accusations averring that the State Auditor's Office had assisted in a cover-up of the scandal, trying to protect Habibie. It implied that the PwC findings about the flow of money and the 'members of the House and senior public and political party officials who appear to have received funds' would not be made public (*The Jakarta Post*, 22-9-1999). Initially the State Auditor's Office withstood pressure from IMF, World Bank, IRC, and others to do otherwise. Parliament also formally asked to be presented with the full report. IMF and the World Bank were relentless. They suspended their loans in mid-September. Having threatened from the moment the scandal broke to withhold their aid if the Indonesian government did not make an adequate response, they made publication of the full report a prerequisite for the release of their loans. Their spokesmen made it clear that its contents, of which IMF and World Bank were also ignorant, would be one of the factors they would take into consideration in deciding whether or not they would resume their aid. The long form would be invaluable in assessing whether Jakarta had indeed taken appropriate steps to address the Bank Bali affair. The Asian Development Bank followed suit. IMF gave the Indonesian government until 10 October to publish the long form report. According to an estimate by the World Bank, the amount of aid withheld might well reach US$ 2.7 billion by the end of the year and US$ 4.7 billion by March 2000 (*The Jakarta Post*, 2-10-1999). As part of the aid was needed to close a budget deficit, the Indonesian government had to consider the possibility of being faced with acute cash problems, if foreign aid were withheld for a longer period. The World Bank threat especially touched a sensitive spot, as it concerned support for the

---

[27]   In a fax to the *Far Eastern Economic Review* (23-9-1999:11-2) he explained that by not publishing the whole report he wanted to protect the PwC auditors against people 'who just walked away with 70 million US dollars and who would not take kindly to any attempt to reveal their identity and take away their money. Even a fraction of US$ 70 million would buy all the guns,

national budget earmarked for the Social Safety Net, the government programme to help the poor.

Because of the Bank Bali affair, BPPN came in for fierce criticism. In the short span of its existence, BPPN had grown into an immensely rich institution, which was preyed upon by people who wanted to control at least part of its wealth. Usually it was stated that BPPN managed about Rp 600 trillion in bank assets, an amount which included the bad loans. In November 1999 Glenn Yusuf explained that this was the value on paper. The real value was about a third of this. Nevertheless, around the same time, Kwik ventured to say that, because of the assets handed over to BPPN, the Indonesian government controlled about 80 per cent of the production units. To repay debts, bankers had handed over shares in companies and valuable property. The result was that surely and not so slowly BPPN acquired an important stake in companies such as Astra, Indocement, and First Pacific and gained control of hundreds more companies. It tried to streamline some of these before putting them up for sale. Another consequence was that, having the right to seize and auction assets of bad debtors, BPPN found itself acting as an auctioneer of valuable cars and paintings. Because of the amount of money it controlled, one of its deputy chairmen, Arwin Rasyid, stated in early August that BPPN 'faced massive pressure' from outsiders who wanted to take advantage of the wealth it controlled.[28]

BPPN was already under attack from indebted tycoons for the slowness with which it tackled the rescheduling of their debts, and in the Bank Bali scandal it had to take a great deal of the flak. The Bank Bali case was seen as yet another indication of BPPN's inertia. It also saddled BPPN with the accusation of being tainted by corruption and collusion. BPPN staff blamed the government for BPPN's apparent inefficiency. After a new president had been elected, one of its deputy directors, Eko S. Budianto, asked the government not to interfere in BPPN, mentioning government intervention and its lack of commitment in the past as a major reason why BPPN had not functioned as it should have done. Among his complaints was that inertia on the part of the government had prevented BPPN from taking legal action against uncooperative debtors. A similar appeal was made at the time by Robby Djohan of Bank Mandiri. Mar'ie Muhammad concluded that because of lack of effective control, BPPN had been prone to political and bureaucratic interference.

The ensuing political storm was enormous. People began to speak about

---

28   *The Jakarta Post,* 7-8-1999. During a meeting with one of the parliamentary committees in the middle of September, Bambang Subianto complained about the pressure exerted through the launching of various plans to establish special bodies to which part of the money managed by BPPN was supposed to be transferred.

Baligate, implying by the use of this compound that they expected that the scandal could well lead to the downfall of Habibie. Students took up the affair demanding the resignation of the new attorney-general for passivity, and that of Habibie. Talk of death threats and powerful people skulking behind the scene added to the suspense. This had already become apparent right from the start. Unidentified people tried to intimidate Pradjoto and his wife and children in order to make him retract his revelation. He received threatening phone calls, hulking figures watched his house and dogged his footsteps. Harassed though he was, on 5 August he vowed that he would continue his crusade against irregularities in BPPN in spite of threats made against him and his family. Another banker disclosed that he had also been visited by persons who said they were able to speed up the recouping of their loans through their contacts with Pande Lubis. He did not dare to mention names, because the people concerned had the backing of mighty cabinet members.

Demands for a thorough-going investigation poured in from all sides. Amien Rais, acting as chairman of the Advisory Council of the Center of Banking Crisis (CBC), without going as far as to accuse Baramuli, beseeched journalists to unearth information about Baramuli's involvement and to find out whether the money had gone to Habibie's success team.[29] His fellow PAN politician Faisal Basri suggested that if all the stories were true, Habibie should go and Golkar should be disbanded. Others who came under fierce attack from politicians and demonstrating students were Bambang Subianto, Glenn Yusuf, and Syahril Sabirin. They were the persons who, in the last resort, were responsible for the release of the inter-bank loan, and consequently had to go.

In the Commission for the State Budget, Finance and Banking, a number of Golkar members of parliament who were no friends of Habibie threatened to bring a motion of no confidence, if the government did not act resolutely. The explanation provided during a twelve-hour marathon session before the commission on 19 August by Bambang Subianto, Glenn Yusuf, and Syahril Sabirin, who persisted in claiming that in paying the Bank Bali loan, procedure had been followed, did nothing to lift the cloud of suspicion. PPP and Golkar representations in parliament urged them to step down. The three were fiercely attacked, a spectacle which, like the other hearings of the parliament in the Bank Bali affair, could be watched on TV by the general public. Such a broadcast would have been impossible under the New Order. In October Habibie was to mention it in his accountability speech as an example

---

[29]   CBC had various meetings with Bank Indonesia, providing information on banking irregularities, including those concerning BII committed by the Eka Tjipta Widjaja family, the owners of the Sinar Mas groups. Director of CNC is Deni Daruri.

A country in despair

of the new, more open domestic climate he had made possible. At the time it actually happened he was less sanguine. The way in which the three were criticized aroused his anger. He summoned Akbar Tanjung and urged him to discipline the Golkar members of parliament who had not bothered to mince their words.

A new dimension was added when PDI-P politicians took up the scandal. This happened after Rudy Ramli had met a number of them on 12 August and, in return for legal help, had presented them with chronological notes which disclosed which ministers, Golkar leaders, and senior civil servants were involved. On behalf of PDI-P, Kwik Kian Gie issued a press statement on 19 August, stating that a number of cabinet ministers and one of Habibie's brothers were implicated. He declared the Bank Bali scandal an unvarnished case of economic subversion and suggested life imprisonment as the appropriate punishment for those involved. Again a 'death threat' was made, this time by Hariman Siregar (according to some sources a member of the Habibie success team), one of the leaders of the student protests in 1974 and a protegé of Fanny Habibie (see Aditjondro 1998a:22). Kwik Kian Gie disclosed that he had been informed by a fellow PDI-P leader that Hariman Siregar had threatened to shoot him. That this indeed was the case was denied by Fanny Habibie, who had been present at the breakfast at a hotel when Hariman Siregar was supposed to have uttered his threat. A few days later, Dimyati Hartono also said he had received a death threat. The document was made public in September, complete with names. Besides the names already circulating, it mentioned those of Timmy Habibie, Hariman Siregar, and Anthony Salim.[30]

Even before the end of August a counter issue had begun to circulate. This happened after Amien Rais hinted that another large party was involved in a case which resembled the Bank Bali scandal. PAN leaders mentioned no names. Fatwa only disclosed that PAN had proof to back up the accusation, and would release this at the appropriate moment. This did not prevent circulation of the story that Bank Lippo had donated Rp 1.3 trillion to PDI-P,

---

[30] Bambang Subianto's name was mentioned in relation to Rudy Ramli's efforts to cancel Bank Bali's contract with EGP. He had advised Rudy Ramli to contact Manimaren. The latter had informed Rudy Ramli that 'RI 1' [that is, Habibie] should be involved. Working with them would cost Rudy Ramli only Rp 300 billion. Later, both were to agree to the deal with EGP. In the notes, Tanri Abeng and Baramuli were identified as the force behind Djoko Tjandra. The diary also stated that about a month after the fee had been transferred to EGP, Rudy Ramli had received a phone call from Anthony Salim. He had called the transfer problematic, and had advised Rudy Ramli to contact Timmy Habibie. Rudy Ramli had not done so. Thereupon he had been asked to come to Anthony Salim's office. When he arrived, Timmy Habibie was already there. The two warned him to be careful. Djoko Tjandra was making no secret of the fact that he had bought 'Kuningan (Cendana)' [that is, Habibie's house] for Rp 300 billion, while they had only received Rp 200 billion via Tanri Abeng. Those mentioned denied this version of the facts.

which was much more than the new Act on Political Parties allowed. According to some, it was Indonesia's own 'Lippogate'. Judging from a statement by Teten Masduki of ICW about the alleged Lippo support for PDI-P, a feeling of deep disillusionment in the new political system was beginning to erase initial euphoria. He said that the political parties had all been founded by members of the élite, which made it very likely that these parties were financed by businessmen looking for political protection. Later, Amien Rais and others did become specific about business tycoons who allegedly had contributed money to PDI-P. Mentioned were among other conglomerates Liem, Muchtiar Riady, Prajogo Pangestu, The Ning King, Sofyan Wanandi, Arifin Panigoro, and some of Soeharto's children.[31]

At the same time as disenchantment set in, the meeting of 12 August had become an issue in itself. Out of the blue, Rudy Ramli suddenly denied all the information he had confided to PDI-P politicians. The chronological notes they had been given were not his. He had not written them. There was great relief in the Habibie camp. On the instructions of Habibie, the denial was read in full – complete with mention of the value of the seal attached to it – by Muladi during a press conference on 26 August. The offices of Muladi and Abdul Gafur faxed Rudy Ramli's statement to the press. It was an indication of how damaging the scandal was to the government that these persons took such pains.[32] It was even alleged that PDI-P leaders who had spoken to Rudy Ramli, among them the former chief of police of Riau, Police Major-General (Retired) Suhartoyo, and Police Major-General (Retired) Sidarto Danusubroto, had abducted him and forced Rudy Ramli – said to be in a very unstable state of mind because of the stress to which he had been subjected – to implicate government officials and Timmy Habibie. Feeling betrayed, PDI-P lodged a complaint against Rudy Ramli with the police.

The government was put in an even more embarrassing situation on 9 September. During a hearing that day before the financial commission of parliament, Rudy Ramli, who had come to parliament accompanied by four lawyers and six bodyguards, apparently feeling cornered by the questions of its members, denied that he had written the denial read by Muladi. He had only signed it. On the other hand, his chronological notes were real. He did so after the commission had promised to write a letter to Wiranto asking that Rudy Ramli be protected. When Rudy Ramli made his statement, members of the commission and people in the public gallery cheered and applauded. Muladi demanded that Rudy Ramli should repeat his testimony using a lie

---

[31]   See Ahmad Muflih Saefuddin, 'Momentum bagi bank syariah', *Republika*, 7-10-1999.
[32]   It was even speculated that Soeharto was behind Rudy Ramli in an effort to discredit the Habibie government.

detector.[33] The question which remained was who had written the denial. Within a day it emerged that it was Baramuli who had handed the letter over to Habibie. The upshot was a conflict between Habibie and Baramuli. Habibie was not pleased with Baramuli for providing him with false information. He gave permission to begin a police investigation into Baramuli's action. Baramuli himself, who was streets ahead in a contest to become one of Indonesia's least popular figures, said he had found the denial in his letter-box. Not much later, it turned out that an employee of Kim Johannes Mulia had delivered the letter to Baramuli's house.[34] Kim Johannes Mulia was said to be a business associate of Baramuli's, but the latter hastened to deny that they were 'close'. To substantiate his denial, Baramuli stated that no Chinese was allowed to set foot in his house.[35] It was Kim Johannes Mulia who, Rudy Ramli stated, had promised that the police investigation against him would be stopped if he signed the denial. Kim Johannes Mulia had another story. He explained that Rudy Ramli had come to his office with a draft of the letter composed at the office of Adnan Buyung Nasution (who had briefly been Rudy Ramli's lawyer) to ask his advice about whether he should send the denial to the press or not.[36] By now Rudy Ramli, who was called a drug addict and liar by Baramuli, who said that the former's disputed notes were a tissue of lies, was at the end of his tether. He turned to the National Committee for Human Rights for protection. He and his family were threatened by phone, being browbeaten to remain silent. Fearing for his own skin, he himself frequently changed residence, moving from hotel to hotel. The policemen of the Mobile Brigade who guarded his house had been withdrawn. The story which was put about was that the reason for this was that the police wanted to remain neutral in the Bank Bali case.

To the chagrin of some of its members, parliament decided not to summon Habibie, a move which some of the Golkar members had also favoured, but to institute a special committee of inquiry in early September. The committee was ordered to finish its task before the parliamentary term ended on

---

[33]   A few days later Baramuli stated he was prepared to be interrogated, but not to use a lie detector. This, he said, violated his human rights. He added that Rudy Ramli's case was different. A lie detector was used when there was some doubt about a statement.

[34]   Kim Johannes Mulia was the owner of a textile enterprise and had himself been accused in 1994 of being involved in a case of fictitious export credit to the detriment of Bapindo. He owned shares in companies of the Poleko concern. Baramuli and Kim Johannes Mulia also held shares in Indowood Rimba Pratama, one of the companies into whose bank account it was suspected Bank Bali money had been transferred.

[35]   Interview with Baramuli in *Tempo*, 30-8-1999 (Samhuri and Setiono 1999:217).

[36]   One of the lawyers at Adnan Buyung Nasution's office confirmed that Rudy Ramli had come to the office asking for a denial to be drafted because not everything mentioned in his notes was true. At the PDI-P meeting he is said to have been asked to give an account of what he remembered (Samhuri and Setiono 1999:118).

24 September. The special committee met behind closed doors. It was the first time since the end of parliamentary democracy in the late 1950s that parliament had taken such a step.

The committee concluded that the Bank Bali affair was indeed a piece of money politics. It identified Baramuli as the head of the Habibie success team, and mentioned the name of Tanri Abeng as its fundraiser. Pande Lubis was its 'factory'. Djoko Tjandra and Setya Novanto were its 'salesmen'. It was suspected that they had planned other coups similar to that carried out at Bank Bali. These dealings allegedly involved 13 people. Among them were Glenn Yusuf (accused of failing to exercise proper control), Farid Harianto (deputy chairman of BPPN, and interrogated by the police as a suspect at that time), Bambang Subianto (by now suspected of having had a role in speeding up the release of the Bank Bali money), Syahril Sabirin, and Kim Johannes Mulia. Marimutu Manimaren was not mentioned. The committee asked Habibie to fire Baramuli, a superfluous request as he resigned as head of the Supreme Advisory Council in order to be able to take up his seat in the People's Congress as one of the representatives from South Sulawesi. One of the Golkar members on the committee, Ichsanuddin Noorsy (most vocal in his attacks on the persons involved in the scandal), expressed his disappointment that the committee had not asked for the sacking of the head of the State Auditor's Office. The parliamentary committee of inquiry had come to its conclusions without having had the opportunity to study the PwC long form. Indeed, parliament only came into possession of it on 19 October. This happened after the State Auditor's Office had sought a ruling from the Supreme Court, which decided that it could be handed over to parliament. The date on which the report was handed over meant that its contents could not be made public till after the session of the People's Congress and therefore after the presidential election.

BPPN had clearly been frightened by the whole affair. The staff, Farid Harianto, one of its executives, admitted, had become demoralized (*The Jakarta Post*, 8-10-1999). Its secretary, Franklin Richard, disclosed on 29 September that BPPN had decided to stop the honouring of inter-bank claims until stricter procedures had been developed by the monetary authorities and IRC. Another condition they required was that an investigation into the validity of the inter-bank claims being conducted since 20 September by Ernst & Young be completed. It hoped that this would take only about one month. The decision would hurt the banks participating in the recapitalization scheme, but BPPN did not want a repeat of the Bank Bali affair and the avalanche of criticism it had poured on its head. BPPN was also very hesitant about selling the assets it had acquired. It was afraid of being accused of being guilty of collusion at some time in the future when the value of, for instance, shares it had sold at the current low market value had markedly

Bank Bali employees express their concern
over the arrest of their former director,
Rudy Ramli (photo C. van Dijk)

increased in price (*The Jakarta Post*, 1-12-1999).

Rudy Ramli and three other former directors of Bank Bali were arrested on 29 September. The reason given for their arrest was that they had violated the Banking Act by not reporting the cession agreement. A spokesman of the Jakarta Public Prosecution Office said that the PwC long form had no relevance in their case. Djoko S. Tjandra was also taken into custody. As the arrests happened on the eve of the general session of the People's Congress, some suspected it was a move by the police to support Habibie, allowing him to state in his accountability speech that action was being taken to solve the scandal. About 400 employees of Bank Bali went to the police station to testify to their support for their former director. They were able to catch a glimpse of Rudy Ramli in tears. As an additional token of their concern, banners expressing their apprehension about the arrests were set up in front of Bank Bali branch offices. They, and others as well, wondered why Baramuli (questioned by the police as a witness) and Setya Novanto (also declared a suspect in the case, but protected by his status as a member of the People's Congress) stayed free. It was argued that if the government was really serious in its attempt to tackle the case, the others mentioned in relation to the Bank Bali scandal also should be arrested. The police saw no compelling reason to arrest staff of Bank Indonesia and BPPN who were said to be involved. To make matters worse for Rudy Ramli and his colleagues, within a fortnight they were transferred from a cell in the police station to Cipinang prison, where to their horror they had to share the place with common prisoners. After Abdurrahman Wahid became president, the four were given city arrest in November.

CHAPTER XVIII

Between hope and despair

Maju tak gentar membela yang benar
Maju tak gentar hak kita diserang
Maju serentak mengusir penyerang
Maju serentak tentu kita menang[1]

Apart from the Bank Bali scandal, there were other developments that gave rise to pessimism. The most important of these was that a national consensus seemed difficult to reach, with Islam as the major stumbling block. In the months leading up to the general election there had been some fighting between supporters of different parties during pre-campaign rallies. In a number of cases there had been fatalities. Supporters of PDI-P and Golkar had clashed in the *kabupaten* of Singaraja in Bali on 10 October and 11 December 1998. Four people had died. On 21 March of the following year one person was killed during a fight between PDI-P and PPP supporters in Yogyakarta. Another serious incident took place on 2 April in Purbalingga in Central Java, when PDI-P supporters in their hundreds attacked and threw stones at the cars in which Akbar Tanjung and other Golkar politicians were travelling on their way to a Golkar mass rally. Having done this, the PDI-P crowd marched on to the venue of the meeting, where they destroyed the stage and forced those male and female Golkar supporters who had not already fled to take off their yellow Golkar shirts. Golkar politicians and Syarwan Hamid asked PDI-P to apologize. PDI-P refused. Its spokesmen maintained that PDI-P supporters had not been involved. They argued that the incident had been deliberately planned to damage the image of PDI-P. As Dimyati Hartono stated on behalf of Megawati at a mass meeting in Jakarta, PDI-P T-shirts could be bought everywhere. Abdurrahman Wahid supported the conclusion drawn by PDI-P leaders. He told journalists that a Golkar member had confided to him that Golkar had planned the whole incident.

---

[1] Advance without fear to defend the truth/ Advance without fear when our rights are attacked/ Advance all together to chase away the aggressor/ Advance all together, we certainly will be victorious. Text of the song *Maju tak gentar*.

General election 1999. The text on the banner reads: We want a general election
which is democratic, honest, fair, direct, general, free, and secret, as well
as peaceful (photo C. van Dijk)

The aim had been threefold: to discredit PDI-P, PKB, and himself. As was his
wont, Abdurrahman Wahid, who had to admit that his observation was not
supported by conclusive evidence, refused to disclose the name of his source.
    Because of these and other incidents coupled with the regular outbursts
of communal violence, the campaign period and the ballot were awaited
with a great deal of trepidation. The overriding fear was that this time the
campaigns might be even more violent than they had been in 1997. People
again left the country en masse. Schools extended the holidays so that they
covered the campaign period and the days immediately after polling day.
Most international schools followed suit. Precautions like barbed wire fences
became very visible obstacles in front of houses, hotels, shops, and office
buildings.
    In spite of the fear and trepidation the general elections were awaited
with high expectations. There was a feeling that, once successfully over, all
troubles which were now besetting Indonesia would disappear. A credible
government would take charge with the support of the majority of the population. Domestic harmony would reign. If the elections were postponed or
marred by irregularities, more domestic violence, even a social revolution,
might be in the offing. Students were less optimistic. They had stopped

demonstrating during the fasting month, but immediately afterwards they had resumed their actions, making the general elections one of the focal points of their protests. They doubted that free and fair elections could be organized under the Habibie government which, in their eyes, lacked popular legitimation and was in essence a pro-status quo regime. The new political parties which had emerged they also viewed with distrust, suspecting that their leaders only wanted power. This line of reasoning encouraged the students to stick to their call for a transitional government. Another of their demands was that Golkar be disbanded or at least be barred from participating in the elections.

The precautions taken in 1999 to limit the chance of clashes between supporters of the various parties were similar to those taken in 1997. Care was taken to arrange that the largest parties did not have public campaign events scheduled in the same place on the same day. To assure an uninterrupted flow of food and other essential commodities, campaigning was forbidden along the main route along the north coast of Java, the vital artery not only for the transport of food and commodities in Java, but also for traffic between Sumatra, Java, and Bali.

The campaign period, from 19 May to 4 June, was marred by the usual fights. At various places there were clashes between supporters of PDI-P and Golkar, between those of PDI-P and PPP, Golkar and PPP, PAN (which had chosen blue as its colour) and Golkar, Golkar and PUDI, and so on. More often than not, it was Golkar which was the target of such attacks. Its rallies and parades almost unerringly unleashed the anger of onlookers.

Fights between PPP and PKB supporters, two parties which both looked to the NU community for support, occurred frequently. A region particularly troubled by this was the north coast of Central Java. Clashes between the two camps had been frequent here since the beginning of April. On 30 April, one such incident in a village in the Jepara area had cost the lives of four people. Other reports spoke of a death toll of six. Feelings of animosity extended to relatives, who stopped talking to one another when they took opposite sides. It was even reported that *kiai* in these northern coastal regions had reached an agreement that those who decided to support any party other than PKB would be ostracized, a ban which was even extended to the administering of the death rites (*Tajuk*, 27-5-1999:22). Some put the blame for the intense animosity between supporters of PPP and PKB on religious orators who, here as well as elsewhere in NU strongholds, stirred up a brew of suspicions and discontent by reviling leaders and members of the opposite camp and by branding siding with the other an act of treason if not of apostasy. Occasionally it was even said that there need be no compunction about killing such people. The military commander of Central Java, Major-General Bibit Waluyo, suggested an additional reason for the violence. Invulnerability mantras had been handed out by *kiai* of both parties. When fighting broke out, according to Bibit Waluyo, people had wanted to put their newly acquired magical power to the test. The result had been that 'many hands were cut off by swords' (*The Jakarta Post*, 5-6-1999). Others detected provocations engineered by pro-status quo groups who did not want Muslims to form one united force, or were simply set on destroying the influence of NU as an important religious organization in the region.

One of the salient features of the campaign period was that PDI-P rallies drew immense crowds, turning cities, including Jakarta, into a sea of red.[2] In contrast, Golkar, which had always been able to mobilize large mass meetings and parades in previous elections, performed poorly in Jakarta and other places in Java. To avoid becoming the target of mob violence, its supporters were hesitant about wearing Golkar T-shirts or jackets in public. They put these on only after arriving at the venue of the Golkar campaign meetings. In a sense, Golkar fell victim to its own past habits. There were occasions in which urban poor turned on Golkar campaigners, furious because, contrary to their expectation, no money was handed out to them for attending Golkar campaign events (*D&R*, 31-5-1999:51). In spite of the incidents and with the exception of the troubled provinces of Aceh, the Moluccas, East Timor, and Irian Jaya, the atmosphere during the campaign period had been joyous rather than tense. Nevertheless, there had been a number of fatalities. Traffic accidents during parades cost the lives of 19 people. When traffic accidents happening before and after campaign rallies are included, the death toll was still high: according to one estimate 164 people. One hundred and fifty-two people had been seriously injured (*Kompas*, 5-6-1999; *Pemilihan* 1999:73).

The campaign period marked the political demise of Adi Sasono, up to then considered a very influential politician with a bright future. The signs that all was not well had emerged in January 1999, when Adi Sasono submitted his resignation as a Golkar chairman and refused to become a Golkar campaigner, to be able, as he said, to concentrate on his work as a cabinet minister. It took till the election campaign before the Golkar board reacted and dismissed him as one of its chairmen. The reason why it decided to do so was Adi Sasono's close association with a new party, Partai Dalaut Rakyat (PDR), People's Sovereignty Party. Though Adi Sasono initially had denied any link with PDR, it was a public secret that he was the man behind the scenes and that there were close ties between the department which he headed and PDR. After *Kompas* had carried a full-page advertisement of PDR mentioning him as presidential candidate and as Bapak Rakyat, Father of the

---

[2]   In April Dimyati Hartono had complained that in an effort to stymie PDI-P some group was buying up all the red cloth, and that almost none was any longer available in Jakarta.

Instruction poster on how to cast a vote,
pasted on the wall of a polling station,
Jakarta, 7 June 1999 (photo C. van Dijk)

People, Adi Sasono was dismissed from the Golkar board on 30 May, or, as he himself interpreted it, his request of January was finally granted.

48 parties met the criteria set for participation in the election (see for a description of these parties, Pompe 1999). Among these parties was PRD, of which the principal leaders were still in jail.[3] Among its candidates the party had three of the people who had disappeared and still had not resurfaced: Herman Hendrawan, Suyat, and Petrus Bimo Anugerah. Polling took place under the watchful eyes of scores of expensive foreign observers and thousands of much less expensive domestic observers, many of them students, who went to the polling booths to ensure that the casting and counting of votes proceeded in accordance with the rules.[4] Polling day, 7 June, was festive, but this atmosphere did not extend to troubled regions like Aceh, where Lhokseumawe was described as a dead city (*Panji Masyarakat*, 16-6-1999:80). Naturally not everything ran like clockwork. It turned out that some voters, particularly those who could not read, were confused by the proliferation of parties competing. The ballot paper, crammed with 48 symbols, made them, as it was described, *grogi*. By sheer force of habit, people pierced the symbol of list number one, two, or three, the numbers of the PPP, PDI, and Golkar lists respectively in previous elections. Others were dazed by the many parties which had taken as their

---

[3]   Budiman refused an amnesty offer by Habibie, demanding a full pardon. He, Petrus Hariyanto, Bartholomeus Garda Sembiring and some eighty other political prisoners, among them fifteen people detained because of the Lampung affair, were released on 10 December 1999, Human Rights Day. At the end of the year yet another 105 prisoners were released. The Minister of Law said that these releases meant that there were no longer any political prisoners in Indonesia. Earlier, after his release, Budiman had said that he had heard that many PRD members who were illegally imprisoned outside Jakarta had not been released.
[4]   No less than 119 Indonesian and 20 foreign institutions registered as observers. Among the observers were representatives from 13 embassies.

Counting votes at a polling station in Jakarta on 7 June 19999. Each individual
ballot paper is shown to the public and the name of the party to which
the vote went is read aloud. The announcement is received with
cheers and jeers by the people watching. (Photo C. van Dijk.)

party symbol one that resembled the symbol of NU, or the many parties
which had a buffalo head as their symbol. Afterwards, foreign observers,
Jimmy Carter perhaps the most prestigious, were satisfied with the way the
polling had proceeded. Indonesian observers and spokesmen of political parties were less pleased, pointing to a plethora of instances of 'money politics',
'dawn operations', and other irregularities. Some of these incidents had actually happened prior to the election. PDR and Golkar bore the brunt of the
blame. There were reports that members of the staff of regional offices of Adi
Sasono's department were instrumental in the drive to enlist PDR members
and voters. The main accusation directed at Golkar was that local cadre had
given the impression that the cheap or free food distributed to the poor under
the Social Safety Net programme came from Golkar. It was also suggested
that local PDR and Golkar members had tried to use the various low-interest
or non-interest credit schemes offered by the government to win members
and voters.[5] As has so often happened in Indonesia, the office of the bearer of

5   That such aid to the poor was used for political ends was admitted by the head of the
Indonesian National Planning Bureau in June. He mentioned no names of parties involved.

the news, in this case that of the Urban Poor Consortium (UPC), was stoned. Though official results were slow in coming in, within days it was clear that PDI-P had done extremely well, especially in Java. This was confirmed when the official results were finally published. PDI-P had received 35.7 million votes, Golkar 23.7 million, PKB 13.3 million, PPP 11.3 million, and PAN 7.5 million. The other parties had scored far less. It took until September for the composition of parliament (and thus a large part of the People's Congress) to be decided upon. The use of the remaining votes and the demand of the parties which had won no seats that they still had to be represented in parliament formed the main problems. In the end PDI-P was allotted 153 seats, Golkar 120, PPP 58, PKB 51, PAN 34, PBB 13, and Partai Keadilan 7. PDI still won two seats.

Besides the good performance of PDI-P, the poor result of PAN and the 'failure' of the purely Islamic parties attracted a flurry of debate. In some Muslim quarters, particularly among those who supported purely Islamic parties, the election result was received as a defeat for the Islamic community. One author even used the word tragedy (Suharsono 1999:43). Confronted with the uncomfortable fact that the PDI-P had done well, leaders of the Muslim community intensified their objections to Megawati. For a number of months some of them had been waging a campaign to disqualify Megawati as a presidential candidate, concentrating on the fact that she was a woman. The kickoff, as it were, had been given at the time of the PDI-P congress in Bali in the middle of October, when pictures of Megawati praying in a Balinese temple had appeared in Indonesian newspapers, pictures which resurfaced during the campaign period. Saefuddin, a PPP minister in Habibie's cabinet, seized the occasion to suggest that Megawati was a Hindu. As she was a woman and a Hindu, he stated, he could beat her hands down in the race for the presidency. Indonesian Muslims did not want a Hindu as president. Part of the Islamic community joined in the fray. The temple visit became the subject of Friday sermons. Koran verses and traditions about the life of Muhammad were cited to demonstrate that Megawati had sinned. The picture of Megawati in the temple appears to have had a much greater effect in certain Muslim quarters than the much more numerous ones showing Megawati with her hair covered attending Islamic events. Some Muslims even considered Megawati, whose grandmother was from Bali, to have converted to Hinduism, forcing a Hindu religious leader to make a public state-

---

Around the same time the Interfaith Committee postponed the distribution of American rice aid in Purbalingga, afraid that the aid would be used as propaganda for a particular party during the campaign period. The World Bank postponed the payment of the already mentioned US$ 600 million loan intended to be used for such purposes. It did so out of fear that the money would be thrown into the campaign. It only took this step after it had failed to reach agreement with Jakarta over supervision of the spending of the money.

ment stressing that she had not performed the rites required to become a Hindu.

Saefuddin's observation brought an avalanche of protests from Hindus who felt insulted. They demanded Saefuddin's resignation and that a charge of slander and inciting religious hatred be brought against him. Public indignation ran high particularly in Bali, where people threatened to occupy the airport if Saefuddin were not called to book for his remarks. Saefuddin's statement had done far more than trespass on religious feelings, it was also seen as an indication of the low regard in which Jakarta held the regions outside Java. The local KPNI branch went as far as to suggest that Habibie should sack Saefuddin. If he did not, Bali would declare independence. After an emergency meeting with Habibie, Saefuddin apologized. His gesture did nothing to alleviate the resentment his words had created. Nor did the announcement by the governor of Bali that Habibie had apologized to him 'off the record' assuage wounded feelings. At the end of the month a mass demonstration in which tens of thousands, including Muslims and Christians, participated, was staged in Denpasar demanding Saefuddin's resignation and prosecution. It was a chain reaction: in their turn such demonstrations caused ill feelings among some Muslims, members of ICMI and KISDI, for instance, who came out in support of Saefuddin, or wondered aloud why protests had shown no sign of abatement after he had apologized. Though the government could ill use a flaring up of regional sentiments, Habibie and ICMI refused to let Saefuddin down. Adi Sasono explained that it would be a bad precedent if a member of the cabinet were fired because of popular pressure.

More specifically the whole affair was being used to block Megawati's road to the presidency at a time that Islam did not allow a woman to be head of state. Among those who supported this opinion was the influential NU *ulama* KH Ilyas Ruchiyat. This subject shot into public prominence in November during the Kongres Umat Islam Indonesia, at which it emerged as a hot issue. The KUII committee that had been asked to formulate recommendations relevant to the fields of politics and defence spoke out against the idea of a female president or even a woman as vice-president. Debate among the delegates had been fairly acrimonious, and in the committee on religion as well, where no agreement had been reached on the point. No reference to the question about whether or not a female president was allowed was included in the KUII final recommendations. It was decided to await a ruling by MUI, the institution which, it was argued, had the authority to issue a binding legal interpretation, a power not accorded to KUII.[6] In his

---

6   Those arguing against a female president pointed to Chapter 4 Verse 34 of the Koran, which specifies that men are the leaders of women. Reference was also made to a Tradition about the

first comment on the situation Abdurrahman Wahid disqualified the religious reasoning for rejecting a female president, alleging it was weak. To
strengthen his opinion, he said that the presidency was a matter for the state
not for *ulama* (Megawati Soekarnoputri 1998b:12). The same position was
taken by Said Aqil Siradj. He stressed that neither the Koran nor the Traditions about Muhammad's life forbade women from becoming president.
Rather provocatively, he posed that in order for NU itself to make any
progress, it needed a woman as its leader (Hidayah 1998:82, 104). Amien Rais
agreed with the repudiation of the idea of a female president, but did point
out that Muslims should not forget that Islam recognized the principle of
istithna, exceptions, and emergency situations in which it was permitted to
depart from a prescript (*Tajuk*, 12-11-1998:17; Hidayah 1998:40). Such a situation could arise, various sides pointed out, if there was no proper male candidate for the post.

The argument that a woman could not become president was not meant
simply to deflate Megawati's chances of succeeding Habibie. Some used it to
take the wind out of Abdurrahman Wahid's sails. They stressed that the latter's support of Megawati was an indication of his capricious behaviour,
which clashed with the opinions held by a section of the NU community and
some PKB politicians who could not accept a women as head of state for religious reasons. Others pointed out that by cooperating with the secular PDI-
P, Abdurrahman Wahid was disregarding opinions of NU villagers, who
might even 'rebel' against him in consequence. Among NU leaders who left
no doubt that they decried Abdurrahman Wahid's stand was Yusuf Hasyim.
PKB support for Megawati was a 'sin' (Hassan et al. 1998:215). *Ulama* and
politicians who entertained such opinions disregarded the fact that at various meetings *ulama* spoke out in favour of Megawati as the future president
or publicly declared they had no objections to a woman becoming head of
state. Ordinary NU supporters at times voted with their clothes, as it were,
wearing a Megawati T-shirt or dressing in red at NU mass prayer gatherings.

Opposition to a female president made Abdurrahman Wahid waver.
What he decided might well turn the scales in deciding who the People's
Congress was to elect as president. Not only would his position probably
decide what way PKB members of the People's Congress would vote, he
might also influence NU politicians in other parties, including Golkar.
Abdurrahman Wahid began to state that he did support Megawati's nomination, at times going as far as to stress that it was obligatory to do so, but
that because a majority of Indonesian Muslims rejected a female president he
could give no assurance that the People's Congress indeed would elect her.

---

life of the Prophet according to which he had commented that no group would prosper under
female leadership.

The impression Abdurrahman Wahid created by such utterances was that he had abandoned Megawati. Indeed, as the months passed, it became increasingly clear that Abdurrahman Wahid considered himself, and no other, the most suitable person for the post. One of the first times he publicly stated this was in an interview with the *Far Eastern Economic Review* in March. He explained that the election of Megawati depended on the support of PKB voters, who rejected the idea a female president on religious grounds. The choice would be between himself and Amien Rais. Confident that he himself would be the next president, he rejected a coalition with Amien Rais. He averred he could not cooperate with Amien Rais because the latter changed his opinion every day (*Far Eastern Economic Review*, 11-3-1999:28). There were no holds barred when he paid a visit to Singapore at the end of the month. Observing that the democratic system should be upheld and that the wishes of the majority of the Indonesians should be followed, he suggested that Megawati should become vice-president, or, should she refuse what was in essence a ceremonial function, chairperson of parliament and of the People's Congress. Abdurrahman Wahid tried to make a humble impression. He deprecated the idea that he might become president, giving his failing eyesight as the reason, but would not refuse if he was nominated. His favourite at the moment was Sultan Hamengkubuwono.[7]

Other arguments were brought to bear as well in the attacks on Megawati's PDI-P. One was the supposedly large number of non-Muslim, that is Christian, candidates put forward by the PDI-P. Hartono Mardjono of PBB mentioned a figure as high as 60 per cent. Others even spoke of 80 per cent (Suharsono 1999:35). Later, at the time of the presidential election, Amien Rais, for whom this was one of the reasons to reject the idea of a Megawati presidency, was to speak of 40 per cent (*Tempo*, 17-10-1999:25). It was sheer guesswork. The lists of candidates did not mention the religion of the candidate. Muslim mass media, including the ICMI-related newspaper *Republika* and the tabloids *Tekad* and *Adil*, highlighted the point in the latter case, resulting in protests from its journalists of whom most favoured Megawati. The observation was easily transposed into the accusation that PDI-P candidates were the enemies of Islam. Hussein Umar, secretary-general of Dewan Dakwah Islamiyah Indonesia, pointing out the prominence of Christians in Megawati's inner circle, called PDI-P a hub of Islam-phobia and a bulwark of Christian politicians who felt cornered by the advance of Islam in Indonesia (*Siar*, 7-6-1999:4, 6). It was even claimed that the pupils of Father Beek (a Jesuit priest considered to have been the advisor of Ali Moertopo in

---

[7]   *Republika*, 25-3-1998. In June the *New Straits Times* (18-6-1999) reported Abdurrahman Wahid, who in Singapore had described his relationship with Megawati as one between a brother and a sister, as saying about her: 'Although she is stupid, she loves people'.

Members of Front Pemuda Islam Surakarta (photo *Tempo*)

laying down the fundamentals of the New Order), that is, Roman Catholic intellectuals who were held responsible for the anti-Islam policy of the first decades of the New Order, had changed their allegiance from Golkar to PDI-P (*Siar*, 7-6-1999:6).

Yet another accusation tailored to disqualify PDI-P in Muslim eyes was that PDI-P had been infiltrated by former members of the communist party (PKI). The only concrete example which could actually be presented was a candidate from West Sumatra who in actual fact had belonged to the leftist wing of the pre-1965 PNI (*Forum Keadilan*, 13-6-1999:67-8). Such allegations fell on fertile soil among Muslims who cherished a deep distrust of everything that was leftist. Others, who also considered that they themselves had been victims of PKI agitation during the Old Order, shared such misgivings. Among them was Goenawan Mohammad. He did not preclude the possibility that if Megawati were to become president, forces which had suppressed artists who had not bowed to the strictures of the PKI artists' organization, Lekra, before 1965 would make a comeback (*Siar*, 7-6-1999:6).

The growing tide of aversion to PDI-P in Muslim circles culminated in the week before polling day. MUI, Muhammadiyah, ICMI, NU (signed by KH Ilyas Ruchiyat), Perti, Friendship Forum of Ulama-Descendants of Muhammad and Islamic Public Figures, Front Pembela Islam (FPI), and a score of other Islamic organizations in Jakarta and elsewhere in the country issued appeals in joint or separate statements urging Muslims not to cast a vote for parties who did not really represent the interests of Islam or for any candidates who where not Muslim or whose religious affiliation was not explicit. In some of these, the names of the non-Muslim candidates fielded by PDI-P were listed. In its 'message', which was supported by 40 Islamic organizations, MUI inveighed against the re-emergence of communism, of authoritarianism, and of secularism through the instrumentality of a party (PDI-P often was not mentioned by name) which, when all was said and done, harboured hatred of Islam. FPI denounced as *haram*, forbidden by Islam, the act of voting for a party which fielded more than 15 per cent non-Muslim candidates. The warnings were widely circulated by distributing them as pamphlets at mosques and other places – in the case of the MUI statement also at the offices of the Ministry of Religion – and by placing them in newspapers as advertisements. In Jakarta the anti-PDI-P campaign culminated in a mass meeting at Al-Azhar Mosque on 6 June called Exposing the Conspiracy of the Secular and Radical Non-Muslim Movement. The speakers stressed that Islam forbade voting for a political party which did not explicitly present itself as an Islamic party. In the streets, banners were carried around warning of an anti-Islamic plot.

In reaction, on 6 June lawyers for PDI-P filed with the police a case against

Members of PDI Satgas (photo *Tempo*)

MUI alleging inciting hatred against their party. At that moment the police
had already summoned a number of people for questioning in relation to the
propagation of such anti-PDI-P pamphlets. Among them was Faisal Biki,
who did not deny that some of the disputed pamphlets were his doing. There
were also instances in which PDI-P Satgas members arrested Islamic religious teachers and other people who they claimed had turned the population
against PDI-P, for instance, by distributing the MUI appeal. Those apprehended were handed over to the police, a move local PDI-P leaders stated
was to protect them from the wrath of an angry crowd. Some of the victims
said afterwards that before being handed over to the police, Satgas members
– in some instances also referred to as gangsters – who interrogated them
about where they had received the pamphlets had beaten them up and tortured them with burning cigarettes. They claimed that their only crime was
that they had been in the possession of the MUI statement or a pamphlet
which simply said that it was wrong to vote PDI-P. Defending their stance,
Muslims who supported or had issued the appeals not to vote for a party
which fielded many non-Muslim candidates pointed out that there was nothing wrong with such appeals, and that it was only logical to ask Muslims not
to vote for a party if there were doubts about its willingness to take the interests of the Muslim community to heart.

The issue continued to be bandied about after polling day, which had
shown that Megawati's gender had not prevented part of the NU rank and
file from voting for PDI-P and that PDI-P had made inroads in what were traditional NU bulwarks. Posters attacking the many non-Muslim PDI-P candidates remained in circulation, and Muslim politicians and *ulama* refused to
hold their peace and continued to reject the idea of a female president. More
Islamic ardour was fuelled by reports about a statement made by a leading
PDI-P politician, Subagio Anam, who was cited in an Israeli newspaper of 8
June saying that if Megawati became president, PDI-P would take steps to
establish diplomatic relations with Israel.

Uncertainty about the support for Megawati among NU leaders and consequently also from PKB meant that Try Sutrisno's name surfaced briefly in
June as a presidential candidate. His contacts with *ulama* were excellent, PKP
had advanced him as the party's presidential candidate, and the relationship
between the retired generals and PDI-P and PKB was cordial. Try Sutrisno
could be ready to step in should PKB reject Megawati. One indication that
Try Sutrisno and PKP were betting on this scenario was the surprise statement made on 31 May by a number of Tanjung Priok victims who said that
Try Sutrisno could not be blamed personally for what had happened in
September 1984. Responsibility for the whole affair rested on the government
of the time. The statement, which was not allowed to pass unchallenged by
Syarifin Maloko and other victims, had been drawn up by Syarifudin Rambe,

who himself had been imprisoned for two and a half years for having spread the story about the soldier who had entered the prayer house without removing his boots and who is said to have started a fight with the soldier when the latter refused to apologize. Rambe, who stressed that he and the other signatories still wanted to bring the Tanjung Priok case to court, defended his action by pointing out that the Tanjung Priok massacre had been exploited by certain people in their efforts to reach specific political aims. He saw proof of this in the fact that Try Sutrisno had been attacked much more frequently for his role in the massacre than Moerdani had ever been. As a Muslim this made him feel uncomfortable. Equally illuminating was the fact that the list of PKP candidates held the names of two Tanjung Priok victims, a reward, it was suspected, for their role in trying to bring about a reconciliation between Try Sutrisno and the Tanjung Priok victims.[8]

Try Sutrisno did not stand a chance. At that point in time the race for the presidency appeared to be a contest between Megawati and Habibie, the candidates of the two largest parties in the People's Congress. PDI-P supporters claimed Megawati's right to become president because her party had won the election. Her opponents argued that the election had shown that 65 per cent did not want her as president. Political strife focused on the question of whether or not a woman could become president. The purely Islamic parties were vehemently opposed to the idea. In the middle of June, Hamzah Haz of PPP stressed that the president had to be the country's 'best Muslim son'. At best he was prepared to assign Megawati the job of Minister of Social Affairs. PBB, PNU and Partai Keadilan made their implacable position crystal clear during a mass meeting at Al-Azhar Mosque organized by KISDI on 4 July.

The PKB position was less unequivocal. It contained a strong faction in favour of Megawati, but opinions among its leading politicians differed. Matori Abdul Djalil indicated that PKB would support Megawati in the race for the presidency. Nevertheless his statement did not mean that Megawati could indeed count on PKB when it came to the vote in the People's Congress. One of the major stumbling blocks was Abdurrahman Wahid, sure that he had the backing of the overwhelming majority of the NU community, some of whom revered him almost as a saint. His position remained enigmatic. Abdurrahman Wahid saw himself as a strong candidate for the presidency, but refrained from stating so unequivocally. In an interview with *Asiaweek* of 18 June, he included himself among the candidates. If for reasons of health he could not run himself, he would support Megawati. He still

---

[8]   Hendropriyono had set the example for Try Sutrisno. He had succeeded in reconciling victims of the Lampung case by offering them jobs or a place in the transmigration programme run by his ministry and by pleading for the release of all political prisoners. It was suspected that one of his ulterior motives was that he wanted to succeed Wiranto.

refused to commit himself. Referring to the rejection of a female president by some Muslims, he again mentioned Sultan Hamengkubuwono as the best alternative should PKB opposition against Megawati prove too strong. Within days he presented yet another suggestion: the functions of head of state and head of the government should be separated. The speculations and the mental scramble about how to accommodate PDI-P without having Megawati gain the presidency had begun in earnest. The following month Habibie suggested a different solution: two vice-presidents, Megawati and Wiranto, instead of one.

Abdurrahman Wahid and Amien Rais began to look for an alternative presidential candidate to avoid an outright choice between Megawati and Habibie. For Abdurrahman Wahid the stated reason for taking this step was the possibility that a great many members of the Muslim community, including those of his own NU, would reject a female as Indonesia's next president. Without a third candidate, acceptable to both camps, a dangerous situation began to cast a long shadow over future stability. The chance was great that whatever the outcome of the presidential election, violent protests would be the result. *Berontak*, to rise in rebellion, was the verb used to describe what would happen if Megawati were elected president and, alternatively if she were not and Habibie remained in office. There might be a violent reaction from militant Muslims if Megawati was elected. In preceding months this

One of the banners displayed in October. It reads: Megawati or revolution
(photo C. van Dijk)

group had made no secret of their willingness for a confrontation with demonstrating students and others who were unhappy with Habibie's presidency. For their part, the millions of PDI-P voters, or, as they were now also called, *promeg*, and the demonstrating students might not take kindly to the idea of Habibie remaining in power. That Megawati's supporters were deadly serious in their resolve to ensure her election by every possible means was there for all to see as early as the end of June. Much to the horror of Abdurrahman Wahid and to the amazement of Amien Rais, they began to put a thumbprint in blood on large cloths. The practice, which had started in East Java, spread and was immediately copied elsewhere. An alternative way Megawati supporters found to express their resolve was to put their signatures on huge banners, some up to two hundred and fifty metres long, carrying texts such as 'Megawati or revolution'. They flocked to do so in the thousands.

In his efforts to gain support for an alternative candidate (that is, for himself) Abdurrahman Wahid won the endorsement of an unlikely ally: Amien Rais. In order to discuss the matter, Abdurrahman Wahid first met Amien Rais on 26 June. Afterwards, Abdurrahman Wahid disclosed that the latter had suggested that he, Abdurrahman Wahid, should become the 'compromise candidate'. He added that he had refused. Other reports gave a different impression. They claimed that Abdurrahman Wahid had indicated he was prepared to become president (*Jawa Pos*, 28-6-1999; *Rakyat Merdeka*, 28-6-1999). It was also reported that Abdurrahman Wahid had confided to Amien Rais that he considered himself 'second to nobody' and did not want to be 'the second person' (*Republika*, 21-7-1999). Before the day was out, Abdurrahman Wahid conferred with Hamzah Haz. The meeting created quite a stir. In many places throughout Indonesia, PKB and PPP members were engaged in wars of words and exchange of abuses, if not, as in north-central Java, in outright physical clashes. Other persons he met were Nur Mahmudi Ismail of Partai Keadilan and Akbar Tanjung. Habibie was not forgotten either. Abdurrahman Wahid visited him to report on 'his mission to unite the Indonesian nation' (*Suara Pembaruan*, 21-7-1999). The only person he seemed to ignore was Megawati.

The round of talks fell on fertile soil. Some of the leaders of the parties concerned were already considering joining forces in an Islamic coalition. What emerged from all this on the initiative of Amien Rais was Poros Tengah, Central Axis, a loose form of cooperation between leaders of PPP, PBB, PAN, and Partai Keadilan. Originally the name Poros Islam had been considered, but this sounded too 'sectarian'. Central Axis, if PKB joined, would have more members in the People's Congress than either PDI-P or Golkar, and was meant to increase the bargaining power of the parties cooperating in it. Habibie's camp understood this and immediately began putting out feelers. PDI-P remained aloof. This gave those who opposed Megawati an additional reason to argue that PDI-P politicians did not play the political game by the rules, refusing to indulge in the usual give and take. This blow came on top of their argument that it was impossible to back Megawati, because she always remained silent (mega-silent, as it was occasionally phrased), which made it impossible to have any inkling of her political programme (Suharsono 1999:93).

Amien Rais went further than other Central Axis leaders. Rating his own chances nihil because of PAN's poor performance in the general election and correctly interpreting the reservations built in by Abdurrahman Wahid in his statements in support of Megawati, he put forward the latter as presidential candidate on 7 August. Amien Rais gave a variety of reasons to explain his choice. One was that the people in Aceh might be encouraged to pursue their separatist ideas if Megawati were to become president. Other objections he raised were that a presidency of Habibie was unacceptable to the students and would set PDI-P supporters on the rampage. In Amien Rais's view Abdurrahman Wahid was a much better choice. He was trusted by the minorities and did not have a bad press abroad. What was more, the Armed Forces would react neutrally, and last but not least, Abdurrahman Wahid had given him assurances that a great many PDI-P followers would accept him as president (see for instance Basyaib and Abidin 1999:352-61). The announcement of this backing came as a shock. Amien Rais was considered one of the least likely persons to back Abdurrahman Wahid. Other Central Axis politicians hastened to state that Amien Rais had not spoken on behalf of Central Axis. Yusril Ihza Mahendra, for instance, preferred Hamzah Haz, whose party had done best of all the Islamic parties in the general election, as a candidate. Such politicians wanted to keep the options open, which in actual fact for some of them meant room to manoeuvre to gain concessions in the shape of ministerial posts, in return for support for Habibie. Still, Abdurrahman Wahid had what he wanted. He had not nominated himself. He considered any such direct action contrary to Oriental culture. To cement the new-found bond between Amien Rais and Abdurrahman Wahid, a rally joining Muhammadiyah and Nahdlatul Ulama leaders was held in Jakarta on 26 September. It was the first of its kind ever held. Central Axis and the cooperation between Muhammadiyah and NU were greeted as a new-found unity within the Islamic community. Some even hailed it as an indication that Indonesia had refound its strength. They argued that a united Islamic community could resist any foreign pressure. A tape of the meeting was published. By that time Abdurrahman Wahid and his uncle, Yusuf Hasyim, of PKU had already been reconciled on 2 September. When Yusuf Hasyim visited his nephew, Abdurrahman Wahid had kissed his hand.

Now all that remained to be done was to remove the impression that Abdurrahman Wahid had changed course. In an attempt to do so, Abdurrahman Wahid and others explained that in the past, journalists had misunderstood his words. What he supported was the act of nominating Megawati (just as, he added, Amien Rais supported his nomination). Whether or not she was indeed elected should be left to the members of the People's Congress.

To persuade NU and PKB circles to accept Abdurrahman Wahid's nomination, there was a great deal of convincing to be done. Some suspected that Amien Rais had ulterior motives in endorsing Abdurrahman Wahid. Those who had their reservations remained sceptical about Amien Rais's intentions right up to the general session of the People's Congress. One interpretation was that this was a deliberate attempt to drive a wedge between Abdurrahman Wahid and Megawati, easing the way to the presidency again for Habibie, another was that Amien Rais aimed at the vice-presidency. Said Aqil Siradj and Matori Abdul Djalil were opposed. In an initial reaction on TV, Matori confirmed that PKB would back Megawati as presidential candidate. In the middle of August a PKB leadership meeting still came out in favour of Megawati. Abdurrahman Wahid tried to overrule resistance against his candidacy. To silence those in NU (and thus also in PKB) in favour of siding with Megawati and still claiming that he had no ambition at all to become Indonesia's next president, Abdurrahman Wahid used his authority as NU general chairman to have its board forbid any discussion of the imminent presidential election in public. The stated reason for the imposed silence was not to upset relations between supporters of PDI-P and NU. To add conviction to his position, Abdurrahman Wahid underlined the fact that NU members were legally obliged to follow the decision of Central Axis. Another NU leader, KH Wahid Zaini SH, stressed that PKB was bound to obey the directions of the central board of NU and of the 'declarator' of PKB, Abdurrahman Wahid.

Habibie's chances were also threatened by Central Axis, maybe even more so than those of Megawati were. Though not all of the leaders of the parties involved had made up their minds, if indeed Central Axis was intent on opting for Abdurrahman Wahid this would rob him of much of the potential Islamic support he had probably hoped to enlist outside Golkar. Within Golkar, Habibie's position was not uncontested either. One of the objections raised against him was his association with Soeharto and the New Order. In an effort to free him from this stigma, during a meeting with ulama, a high official of the Ministry of Religion compared his relationship with the former president with that between Moses and the pharaoh (D&R, 28-6-1999:16).

The Bank Bali scandal posed a much more serious threat to his image. The alleged involvement of some of his closest political friends, like Tanri Abeng and Baramuli, put Habibie in a very precarious position.[9] Coupled with the

---

9   It aroused public ire that Baramuli, Bambang Subianto, Harmoko, and Tanri Abeng were all awarded a decoration on 14 August.

reluctance, as it was perceived, of the authorities to get to the bottom of the case, the scandal provided his political enemies with additional arguments to reject his re-election. Coming on top of the criticism about the way his government had handled the prosecution of Soeharto and his family and cronies, the scandal overshadowed the signs of economic recovery which Habibie could claim to his credit in the race for the presidency.

Another upshot was that the struggle for power within Golkar once again erupted into the open. To some Golkar members, the Bank Bali scandal was an additional reason to repudiate the nomination of Habibie. Even if he himself were not involved, his close advisors might well be. The conflict within Golkar had begun well before the general election. The chief bone of contention was Habibie's nomination as the sole presidential candidate of Golkar. Marzuki Darusman, who had publicly begun to question Habibie's nomination after the Ghalib tape furore, had been in favour of postponing a decision on Golkar's candidate for the presidency till after the general elections. Akbar Tanjung tended to share this view. They won the support of former KNPI members and of those Golkar politicians with an HMI background who could not forgive Habibie for not preventing the fall of Beddu Amang. They lost. Habibie was nominated as Golkar's presidential candidate. Money, it was whispered, had changed hands (*Far Eastern Economic Review*, 27-5-1999:20; *Jawa Pos*, 13-5-1999). At the time it was reported that the Akbar Tanjung camp had threatened to strike back during the general session of the People's Congress (*Jawa Pos*, 14-5-1999). Their opponents were to toy with the idea of summoning an extraordinary Golkar congress to get rid of Akbar Tanjung, whom they saw as a major obstacle to the chances Habibie had of gaining the presidency.

Marzuki Darusman and Akbar Tanjung continued to question the suitability of the candidacy of Habibie after 7 June, Akbar Tanjung on the grounds that in view of the election results it was Megawati's right to become Indonesia's next president. Marzuki Darusman blamed Habibie for the poor election result gained by Golkar. It was a reason for him to plead that Habibie's nomination be reconsidered.[10] Had he succeeded, it would have been easier for other parties to enter into a coalition with Golkar. In PAN there was a faction which, right from the moment the first election results were made known, spoke out in favour of cooperating with Golkar in pref-

---

[10] It was reported that this view was supported by the branches of West Java, Central Java, Yogyakarta, Bali, North Sumatra, and Lampung, but that only the first two persisted in their opposition to Habibie. The branches supporting Habibie cooperated in the so-called Iramasuka-Nusantara (Irian Jaya, Maluku, Sulawesi, Kalimantan) coalition, which had originally been founded to discuss the economic development of eastern Indonesia. Baramuli had played an important role in its founding. Among its leading members was also Fadel Muhammad. Habibie could also count on ICMI.

A country in despair

Members of Pemuda Pancasila protesting that the Bank Bali case has to be
examined down to the last detail (photo *Tempo*)

erence to joining in with Megawati. Gender played a role, but it was not the
only factor. In the eyes of Dawam Rahardjo, for instance, PDI-P (which had a
number of military and police officers on its central board) was too much a
'status quo' group, which he thought had set its sights on maintaining the
constitution, the dual function, and a strong central government.[11] A coalition of Golkar with PDI-P was also a possibility. Again Marzuki Darusman
failed. During a meeting between the party board and the provincial boards,
it was unanimously decided on 9 July to stick to Habibie's nomination. The
outcome failed to silence Marzuki Darusman. As a consequence, within days
of the Golkar meeting there were demands that he and his political friends be
sacked from the Golkar board for not abiding by the meeting's decision.
Supporters of Akbar Tanjung rallied to their support. Whereas Marzuki's critics called for the removal of people who displayed what they chose to call
'NGO behaviour', Akbar Tanjung's supporters stressed their right to dis-
agree. These developments caused Kwik Kian Gie of PDI-P to draw the conclusion that there was a 'white' Golkar, namely Marzuki Darusman, Akbar
Tanjung, and their supporters, by some dubbed the reform group, and a
'black' Golkar, composed of Baramuli and other loyal supporters of Habibie.

---

11   *DëTAK*, 15-6-1999:9. He also expressed his doubts about whether a Megawati government
would press for the trial of Soeharto.

The Bank Bali scandal goaded Baramuli into action. He and his political associates accused Marzuki Darusman of being one of the persons who had incorrectly linked the scandal to the government and of being behind a conspiracy to corner Golkar by mentioning this party in the same breath as the Bank Bali scandal. It must have been he who had provided Pradjoto with information about the cession agreement. One of Baramuli's allies was a Golkar chairperson, Mrs Marwah Daud Ibrahim, who also hailed from South Sulawesi and who was said to be one of the members of Habibie's success team. To rally support, she called together a meeting of a number of chairmen of provincial branches on 13 August. The following day a statement was issued asking Akbar Tanjung to take action against Marzuki Darusman, announcing that if he failed to do so, they would call together an extraordinary party congress to oust Marzuki Darusman from Golkar (and almost certainly also to replace Akbar Tanjung as the party's general chairman). Later Marwah Daud Ibrahim denied that the group had actually threatened to call an extraordinary congress. It was those who did not agree with their action who had circulated the report.

Marzuki Darusman countered Baramuli's attack by speaking of 'guerrilla politics' in Golkar and about moves made by amateurs, which in the Indonesian context seems to be considered a strong term of abuse. Other leading Golkar politicians asked for a special meeting to 'try' Baramuli and Marwah Daud Ibrahim. Akbar Tanjung defended Marzuki Darusman, who, he claimed, had done nothing more than give an analysis of the nomination of Habibie. Marzuki Darusman himself also denied that he rejected Habibie's candidacy. He had only wanted to do justice to all the opinions prevailing in Golkar.

The conflicts in Golkar were talked over during a five-hour meeting convened by Akbar Tanjung and Muladi in Habibie's house on 22 August. The meeting was fraught with tension. As one magazine put it, it was Marzuki being put on trial by the Habibie camp (*Panji Masyarakat*, 1-9-1999:32). The harsh criticism meted out by Golkar members of parliament in the discussion of the Bank Bali cession was also raised. It was reported that Habibie flew into a rage when Marzuki Darusman suggested that he could never hope to become president as long as the investigation into the corruption of Soeharto and a number of violations of human rights were not resolved in the way many among the public wanted them to be (*Tempo*, 30-8-1999; Samhuri and Setiono 1999:211). Marzuki was also reported to have rattled Habibie by criticizing the rash way the latter's nomination as Golkar's sole presidential candidate had been forced through. Afterwards the dust was said to have settled, but the rift had not been bridged. The Bank Bali scandal provided members of the Akbar Tanjung camp with ammunition to attack Baramuli. Or as one of them, the member of parliament, Ade Komaruddin, chose to

phrase it in the middle of September: Baramuli had not yet been found legally guilty, but the political conclusion could be drawn that he was not to be
trusted and that he had become a liability to Golkar. In and outside Golkar
the scandal was used to argue against the renomination of Habibie. It was
even adduced as a reason for his stepping down earlier. In the end a Golkar
leadership meeting decided to stick with the nomination of Habibie. Marzuki
Darusman explained this decision by pointing out that if this compromise
were not accepted, Golkar might split up.

On top of the Bank Bali scandal came the situation in East Timor. International indignation reached a peak with the killings and deportations in
East Timor following the announcement on 4 September that in the referendum of 30 August 78.5 per cent of the population had voted against autonomy and in favour of independence. Throughout Indonesia there was an
upsurge of nationalist sentiment in which many blamed Habibie for the loss
of the province and for allowing an international peacekeeping force.

The loss of international and domestic faith in the Habibie government
occasioned by the Bank Bali scandal and the developments in East Timor
were reasons to propose that the presidential election be brought forward. A
government which would be credible in the eyes of the world should be
established as soon as possible. Leaders of Golkar, PAN, PKB, PPP, PBB, and
Partai Keadilan met Abdurrahman Wahid's home on 18 September. A work-
ing-group was formed to decide on the rules, agenda, and a time schedule for
the general session of the People's Congress. The initiative had come from
Akbar Tanjung. When the initial response was no more than lukewarm, he
had asked Abdurrahman Wahid to step in and help. Megawati was not present but had sent a representative. To get her commitment to the decisions,
and probably also because Akbar Tanjung was determined to discuss the
political situation with her, Abdurrahman Wahid and Akbar Tanjung visited
Megawati on 20 September. PDI-P promised to participate in the deliberations, but its participation could not be described as more than halfhearted.
Contrary to the leaders of the other parties, Megawati never attended a meeting. Her party did not feel committed to what the others agreed upon.
Among the points difficult for PDI-P to stomach was the suggestion that the
presidential candidates should present their plans for the future to the general session of the People's Congress before the actual election took place.
When the People's Congress had to decide on this point, PDI-P spoke out
against, arguing that the task of a president was just to implement the Broad
Outlines of State Policy. Megawati's opponents interpreted this rejection as a
move to protect Megawati from making a bad impression.

Political deliberations about the procedures to be followed during the
general session were taking place as domestic unrest flared up once again at
the end of September. The reason for new massive demonstrations was the

passing by parliament of an emergency act (and to a lesser extent of a bill on Ratih), initially called Keselamatan dan Keamanan Negara (National Safety and Security) Bill, which resulted in the ironic abbreviation KKN, and later rechristened Penanggulangan Keadaan Bahaya (Overcoming a Dangerous Situation) Bill, with the equally problematic abbreviation PKB. The act, in every sense the last act of the parliament, was conveniently passed just prior to the general session of the People's Congress. It gave the Armed Forces far-ranging powers once a state of danger or of emergence had been proclaimed. Not only did the act tend to undo the adjustments to the Freedom of Expression Act passed by the parliament the previous year, among other measures it allowed the Armed Forces to prohibit people from entering or leaving a certain region, and to force residents of a particular place to move elsewhere. Its opponents argued that the act could usher in 'constitutional dictatorship' and militarism (Haryanto 1999:x). Moerdiono disclosed that the act had already been lying around in the State Secretariat for about ten years. By stating this so explicitly, he was dropping a heavy hint that the bill was a New Order product, which even at the time it was first introduced had been considered to be too repressive to be submitted to parliament.

Demonstrations to protest against the act, and clashes with the army and police which resembled those of November in intensity and fierceness, took place in Jakarta on 23 and 24 September. Fighting lasted for fourteen hours. *Gugur Bunga* had to be played again. Six people died during the *Tragedi Semanggi II*. Among them were an UI student, a twelve-year-old street singer, and a member of the Mobile Brigade. The next few days, students died during demonstrations against the act and against the Armed Forces in Bandarlampung and Palembang. In an effort to calm the situation down, the government decided that the ratification of the security bill by the president should be postponed. The reason given was that time was needed to inform the public at large about the content and purport of the act.

Comparisons with earlier tragedies were easy to draw. The army apologized. The police denied that the security troops had been equipped with live ammunition. According to the chief of police of Jakarta, the bullets that had killed one of the victims, the UI student, had been fired by unidentified persons from a car which had slipped behind a convoy of trucks carrying security troops leaving the Semanggi area when the worst of the fighting was over. At the end of the year, however, police sources allowed the information to leak out that the soldier who had fired the shot had been identified. According to this source, the student had been killed by a shot fired at random, after the bullet had ricocheted. The authorities also claimed to know who was behind the demonstrations, staged, in their view, to thwart the coming general session of the People's Congress and to bring down Habibie and Wiranto. Among the persons suspected of masterminding the unrest were

Subroto, Ratna Sarumpaet, and Faisol Reza, as well as a number of other PRD members. Some of them were alleged to have met in Hotel Sahid Jaya on 23 September. Aliansi Jurnalis Independen (AJI), SBSI, Kontras, Pijar, and Aldera were accused of being involved as well. Another person blamed with orchestrating the unrest was Arifin Panigoro. He was said to have financed the demonstrations. It was quite evident that his house had served as a centre for providing demonstrators with food and drinks. In reprisal, two Molotov cocktails were lobbed at his house on 28 September. Subroto, who was in Sydney for a medical check-up, decided to delay his return to Indonesia. Amien Rais and Abdurrahman Wahid were among those who agreed that the demonstrations had been masterminded and that they formed part of a wider plan to impede the general session of the People's Congress. Abdurrahman Wahid went as far as to warn that NU would mobilize thousands of Banser members to safeguard the general session.

As in November of the previous year, a religious confrontation threatened to engulf the general session of the People's Congress. There was also an additional factor involved. This time the smouldering antagonism between Java and the other parts of the country played a more prominent role. Habibie not only figured as a true exponent of Islam, he was also put forward as the person representing eastern Indonesia. Habibie, who had selected Yogyakarta-born Wiranto as his running mate, used his Sulawesi background as a trump card. In an attempt to gain Akbar Tanjung's support, he threateningly suggested that if he were not elected president, parts of eastern Indonesia might want to break away from the nation (*Kompas*, 20-9-1999). As far as he was concerned, a Habibie-Wiranto ticket was the ideal combination, uniting Java and the non-Javanese regions. Akbar Tanjung took up the argument, stating that the combination formed a balance between Java and the non-Javanese regions and between eastern and western Indonesia.

One of the points still to be resolved before Habibie could give his accountability speech before the People's Congress was that of the prosecution of Soeharto, by now suffering ill health and shielded by his children from any news that might upset him. The outcome was an anti-climax. First, one of Soeharto's lawyers, Juan Felix Tampubolon, asked for the investigation against Soeharto to be halted because there was no proof of any corruption committed by the former president. One of the reasons for Tampubolon to draw such a conclusion was the long silence on the part of the office of the attorney-general. Soeharto, who to the indignation of many Indonesians had never been formally declared a suspect, and his lawyers got what they wanted. On 11 October Ismudjoko announced that because of the lack of evidence his office had stopped the investigation into the case against the former president. The decision concerned Soeharto's role in charitable foundations. The investigation had concentrated on this particular aspect of the charges against Soeharto. Ismudjoko explained that a decision about KKN in relation to the Timor national car fell under the aegis of the Coordinating Minister of the Supervision of Development and the Reform of State Institutions. Supporters of the former president, calling themselves Forum Penegak Kebenaran dan Keadilan, the Forum of Upholders of Truth and Justice, presented the attorney-general's office with a hawk as a token of their appreciation of the courage the public prosecution had shown.

Three days later, on 14 October, Soeharto's son, Hutomo Mandala Putra, was acquitted. The court decided that there was no evidence that Bulog had suffered losses from the land-swap deal.[12] The court had also found no indication that Tommy had misused his position as Soeharto's son in concluding the deal. It was not the end of the matter. Beddu Amang, now no longer protected by his status as member of the People's Congress, was heard again as a subject in this case by the attorney-general's office on 19 October.

After a rehearsal of the swearing in of the members on 30 September, the general session of the People's Congress commenced its sitting on 1 October. When Habibie entered the assembly hall on 1 October he was greeted by the members. with boos as well as applause Most members remained seated. It had been agreed that nobody would stand up when Habibie entered or left the hall, to show that the People's Congress and not the president was the highest political authority in the country. As another token of the new era, Habibie was only allowed twenty minutes for his opening address. Some had wanted no speech from Habibie at all, considering such a speech a deplorable New Order custom.

Apart from deciding on who would become president and vice-president, the People's Congress had to decide on two other key positions in the Indonesian political structure: the chairpersons of the People's Congress and parliament. It was agreed that all had to be done by secret ballot, opening wide the possibility for dissension within the ranks of the parties and groups represented in the People's Congress. The second two positions were decided early on during the general session. Amien Rais, by now a professor at Gadjah Mada University, was elected chairman of the People's Congress on 3 October. He defeated Matori Abdul Djalil by the small margin of 26 votes. Amien Rais's nomination had been backed by Golkar, which presented itself as the Golkar Reform faction, and Abdurrahman Wahid; that of Matori Abdul Djalil by PDI-P. Akbar Tanjung was elected chairman of parliament in the early morning of 6 October. He received an overwhelming 411 of the 491 votes. PDI-P supported his nomination, but afterwards were made to under-

---

[12]   In his capacity as head of Bulog, the Minister of Trade and Industry had cancelled the landswap contract on 31 March. At that time he had also already stated that the state had not suffered financial damage because of the deal.

Security measures in Jakarta in October 1999 during the general session of the People's Congress which had to elect a president (photo C. van Dijk)

stand that they could expect nothing in return for this. The election of Amien Rais and Akbar Tanjung was the first indication that PDI-P politicians were not very deft in striking deals with other parties, and that in the People's Congress they might not be able to make the best use of the fact that their representation was the largest one. It was also intimated that Amien Rais might play a central role behind the scenes in the deliberations and that he might well succeed in his bid to have Abdurrahman Wahid elected president.

The general session of the People's Congress took place amidst the now familiar demonstrations in the major Indonesian cities, which at times, but not invariably, deteriorated into violence. The focal point was Jakarta. This time the demonstrating students cooperated in Gerakan Mahasiswa Jaringan Kota, Urban Network Student Movement, bringing together Forum Kota, FKSMJ, Famred, and a number of other student organizations. The authorities prepared for the worst. At all costs, Wiranto wanted to prevent that students from occupying the Congress Building and proclaiming a presidium. He vowed that if this happened, he would proclaim a military emergency and employ tanks to retake the building (Parmana 1999:17). As on previous occasions, there was a massive build-up of security forces to guard the Congress Building and the roads leading to it and the other places in town where demonstrations were likely to be staged. Sixty thousand soldiers and policemen were deployed for this purpose. Twelve thousand of them had been brought in from outside Jakarta. Participation of the various task forces of the political parties was also sought. Forewarned, the public also took precautions. Over time the barbed wire barriers and other constructions to keep demonstrators at bay had grown steadily more impressive. Shopkeepers in Glodok equipped themselves with clubs. Female office employees in the areas most likely to see violence who were required to dress in tight skirts and high-heeled shoes held trousers and sports shoes in reserve to change into in case they were to find themselves in a situation in which they had to run to safety. Their male colleagues also brought sports shoes to the office. Plans to evacuate employees were drawn up. Shops and offices remained closed and buses stopped running, especially on the day the presidential election took place.

The atmosphere turned even more tense as PDI-P supporters determined to see Megawati elected had thronged into Jakarta in great numbers from the villages and cities of Java and Sumatra. The authorities tried to prevent the influx of Megawati supporters into the city by putting a guard on the roads into Jakarta and the railway and bus stations. They did not succeed in their aim. Many Megawati fans slipped through the net, travelling in small groups and concealing their PDI-P 'attributes'. As the protesting students had done in the preceding days, they made the roundabout in front of Hotel Indonesia the centre of their demonstrations, a move which attracted food stalls and street vendors to the place. In an attempt to avoid clashes between supporters of different candidates, the municipality of Jakarta in vain issued a regulation forbidding demonstrations between the roundabout and the Semanggi area. If the letter of the text of the Act on the Freedom of Expression was complied with, this decision made the municipality itself liable to a punishment of one-year's imprisonment. A few days later, on the eve of the presidential election, the governor of Jakarta even considered declaring a state of civil emergency in the city.

Apart from the fear the outpouring of PDI-P supporters evoked, there was the additional worry that their presence could easily turn into a riot if Megawati did not become president. Therefore, politicians from other parties suspected that their presence was being used as a leverage to bring home to the members of the People's Congress that there was no other choice but to elect Megawati. Her supporters left no doubt about what might happen were Megawati not to become president. The phrase 'Megawati or revolution' again took centre stage. The pace of this hotting up of the campaign had been set by Pius Lustrilanang on 12 October. Addressing the crowd during one of the demonstrations at the Hotel Indonesia roundabout, he had stated that the only alternative to Megawati not being elected was a revolution. His words were greeted with shouts of 'revolution' from the crowd. Afterwards Pius Lustrilanang explained that what he had envisaged was not a revolution like those which had occurred in China or Cuba, but a peaceful one, 'people power' in action, as had happened in the Philippines (*Bidik suplemen Republika*, 20-10-1999:1-2). PDI-P leaders fuelled the fear that PDI-P crowds would run riot by stating that they could not answer for the consequences if Megawati's bid for the presidency failed. Addressing students and members of NGOs on 16 October, Theo Syafei predicted that in such a situation PDI-P crowds would revolt. To make his statement all the more threatening, he explicitly referred to the fact that his party's supporters were used to making bloody sacrifices. It would not matter if one or even two thousand of them were to fall. Above all else, the revolution would carry on. Asked to comment the following day, another PDI-P chairman, Jacob Tobing, was quoted by *Republika* as having spoken of millions of people who would be angry and demand a revolution if Megawati were not elected. He promised that PDI-P would try to prevent such an event, but added that when the crunch came, the party would probably be powerless to control the masses whose feelings about what was just and right had assailed (*Republika*, 17-10-1999, 18-10-1999, 20-10-1999).

Though PDI-P politicians stressed that the calls for revolution were nothing more than expressions of grassroots rhetoric and that they themselves

A hawker at the roundabout in front of Hotel Indonesia waits for Megawati supporters to assemble, Jakarta, October 1999 (photo C. van Dijk)

The text above the portrait of Megawati reads: The people are ready to die if
Megawati does not become president of Indonesia, Jakarta, October 1999
(photo C. van Dijk)

did not want a revolution to take place, such denials did not sound very convincing. The statements confirmed the suspicions of their Islamic adver-
saries, who feared that PDI-P leaders were prepared to use every means
within their power to have Megawati elected and that they wanted to force
their will on the People's Congress. *Republika* wrote that if PDI-P wanted a
revolution, their opponents were ready for the confrontation (*Bidik suplemen
Republika*, 20-10-1999:3).

The calls for revolution and the participation of PDI-P supporters in the demonstrations brought home once again that, as in the days before the fall of Soeharto, the demonstrations were not simply a student affair. Others, the city poor for instance, euphemistically referred to in the press as *massa* or *masyarakat* (society) had joined in. Well aware of this, security forces conducted 'razzias' to round up loafers and beggars, a group of people they considered to be particularly susceptible to what they called 'provocations'.

Counter-demonstrations were held in Jakarta and in Ujungpandang, renamed Makassar since 13 October. In Makassar students took to the streets to protest about the pro-Megawati rallies and the anti-Habibie protests orchestrated by students in Jakarta. In Jakarta counter-demonstrations were set in motion by people who had travelled especially from Sulawesi to Jakarta to show their support for Habibie, by organizations like GPI, Gerakan Pemuda Ka'bah (GPK), Movement of Ka'bah Youth, dressed in green striped army-like uniforms, and Lasykar Fisabilillah, dressed in white. Another active group was Forum Bersama Umat Islam (FBUI), made up of eighteen Islamic organizations. This Joint Forum of the Islamic Community was coordinated by Eggi Sudjana. He stated that a revolution would certainly be launched by Muslims if Megawati were elected (*Tempo*, 24-10-1999:29).

The counter-demonstrations in Jakarta added to growing fear of a confrontation between Habibie and Megawati supporters. This tense situation was exacerbated by the fact that the various contending parties had their own task forces at the ready and rearing. PDI-P Satgas members were a very visible presence during PDI-P demonstrations, and they guarded the Hotel Indonesia, where some members of Congress (among them PDI-P members) were staying.[13] Banser members also guarded access to the PKB representatives staying in the hotel and awaited further instructions from Abdurrahman Wahid. They and the *jinn*, the spirits, on their side were said to be ready to safeguard the Congress Building and the city. Habibie supporters also claimed that they had 'troops' standing by at various places in Jakarta. The rank and file had prepared as well. Some of the PDI-P supporters who had come to Jakarta had been trained in *pencak silat* and had received charms said to make them invulnerable to bullets.

Golkar formally reaffirmed Habibie's candidacy on 12 October. During a party leadership meeting, 25 provincial branches spoke out in his favour.

---

[13]   Members of PDI-P Satgas and of other task forces also guarded their party offices. In another respect they and some other organizations also took over tasks of the police. During the demonstrations on 23 and 24 September, for instance, members of Lasykar Pembela Islam (LPI), Army of the Defenders of Islam, the task force of Front Pembela Islam, took to the streets in an attempt to prevent destruction. Not all went according to plan. When what according to a LPI leader were outsiders shouted slogans in support of Habibie, onlookers pelted the LPI members with stones.

One important reservation was made. The Golkar central board was given the mandate to decide what to do if Habibie's accountability speech were to be rejected. Only the Yogyakarta branch had been against Habibie's nomination. The West Java branch had abstained.[14] Initially no agreement was reached on the name of the candidate for the vice-presidency. In the end, Habibie's choice of Wiranto was endorsed, when Golkar leaders left it to Habibie himself to decide on the matter.[15] Once more Habibie stressed the need for a Javanese-non-Javanese duo. He explained that he had selected Wiranto as his partner to counterbalance his own civilian and non-Javanese background.

Banser members in front of a poster depicting Abdurrahman Wahid (photo *Tempo*)

Habibie gave his accountability speech about, as he himself recalled, the 512 days or 12,021 hours he had been in office on 14 October. Massive demonstrations staged by students and Megawati supporters outside the People's Congress forced him to take an alternative route in order to reach the building. The demonstrations were the start of two days of savage, almost uninterrupted fighting between security forces and demonstrators denouncing Golkar's nomination of Habibie and Wiranto and inveighing against 'militarism'. The slogan 'revolution or death' was frequently heard. When some quiet had been restored, students and others erected roadblocks, in a spirit of revenge, stopping cars and buses in

---

[14]   At the end of September the Golkar branch of North Sumatra had also called for a re-evaluation of Habibie's candidacy.
[15]   Some Golkar leaders had wanted to keep their options open and to select four possible candidates: Wiranto, Ginandjar Kartasasmita, Sultan Hamengkubuwono, and Akbar Tanjung. Hartarto was also suggested as a possible candidate.

search of policemen and soldiers on 15 and 16 October. A spokesman for the Armed Forces said that 80 per cent of the people arrested on the suspicion of being agitators had admitted they had received either Rp 20,000 or Rp 30,000 from unidentified people. In an interview published on 15 October in the Singapore *The Straits Times* his boss, Wiranto, aired his conviction that many of the protesters who fought security forces were in the pay of rich people. He dismissed them as professional demonstrators. Among the suspected agitators placed under arrest was Ki Gendeng Pamungkas, beaten up by the police during a demonstration at Jalan Sudirman. He himself claimed that, anticipating violence was on the verge of breaking out, his only intention had been to burn incense at various sites where this was likely to happen.

Habibie's speech was rejected outright by PDI-P and PKB. To the horror of Abdurrahman Wahid, PDI-P's standpoint was read out by a Shi'ite; he saw this as another indication that PDI-P leaders did not understand Islam (*Tempo*, 24-10-1999:23). The central board of PAN also suggested rejecting Habibie's account. In the reactions to the speech, the Bank Bali scandal figured prominently. PDI-P representatives even stated there was no question that the long form had to be handed over to the People's Congress. They called it an indispensable tool for judging Habibie's performance as president. Habibie answered his critics on 17 October. He failed to convince them, but remained optimistic about the outcome of the vote on his accountability speech. His optimism was unfounded. Habibie's account was rejected by 355 to 322 in a vote on 19 October. The previous evening there had been another blow to Habibie when Wiranto, who had been formally advanced by Habibie five days earlier as his candidate for the vice-presidency, stated in a televised speech and surrounded by the top brass of the army that he was not prepared to run for the vice-presidency. Later, Wiranto himself said that, aware that his nomination might result in riots, he had withdrawn to avoid bloodshed. According to the *Far Eastern Economic Review*, there were two stories doing the rounds to explain why Wiranto had decided not to accept his candidacy. Western diplomats said he had heeded the advice of retired generals. Indonesian military sources pointed to pressure exerted by the United States, who would not accept a military officer as vice-president. Later it was surmised that a number of active officers had urged Wiranto to withdraw his nomination. Reportedly Wiranto had gone beserk. Among the officers was said to have been the head of BIA, Lieutenant-General Tyasno Sudarto. One of the reasons given was that the United States threatened to bring Wiranto before an international tribunal because of East Timor.[16] Yet another factor which caused Habibie's chances to ebb was the fact that, though Habibie

---

[16] *Far Eastern Economic Review*, 28-10-1999:13; *The Straits Times*, 8-2-2000; *Forum Keadilan*, 27-2-2000:18.

In anticipation of demonstrations (photo C. van Dijk)

could count on some support in the Central Axis, at least some of the PAN
and PKB members of the People's Congress had turned against him. Matori
Abdul Djalil and Faisal Basri had publicly given their blessing to a plan by
Masyarakat Profesional Indonesia (MPI), Indonesian Society of Profes-
sionals, to call for a one-day strike of the business community. They had done
so while attending a demonstration during the lunch hour at the Jakarta
Stock Exchange on 16 October to protest against any nomination of Habibie
and Wiranto. They repeated their appeal two days later at a second demonstration at the Jakarta Stock Exchange. Their actions were not well received
by everyone. In a pamphlet distributed by Front Pembela Islam, Matori

Abdul Djalil was accused of being a leftist allied with PRD and Forum Kota and of having received Rp 10 billion from PDI-P. Fellow PAN politicians apologized for Faisal Basri's behaviour.

Habibie withdrew his nomination in the early morning of 20 October. The race for the presidency was now between Megawati and Abdurrahman Wahid.[17] In the days leading up to 20 October, the latter had met a great variety of people, including Megawati and Siti Hardijanti Hastuti Rukmana. He had also visited the grave of his father, and a number of times had indicated that signs from Above had encouraged him to decide to continue to stand as candidate. In spite of all his efforts, he could not count on PKB for his nomination. Matori Abdul Djalil had continued to pledge the support of his PKB for Megawati. His obduracy meant that Abdurrahman Wahid had to be nominated by what was called the Reform coalition, made up of PAN and Partai Keadilan, on 6 October. They presented him as the one person who could bridge all the differences in society. Initially PDI-P politicians remained optimistic, clinging to the support Abdurrahman Wahid had expressed for Megawati in the past, hoping or expecting that he would withdraw at the last moment, giving his poor health as the reason for this decision. This feeling was shared by Muslim politicians. To prevent that Megawati in the end would be the only candidate, Yusril Ihza Mahendra was nominated. He withdrew when it had become clear that Abdurrahman Wahid was serious about his intention to become president.

Abdurrahman Wahid defeated Megawati in the vote for the presidency on 20 October. He received 373 votes, Megawati 313. Almost immediately riots broke out in Jakarta, Surakarta, Bali, and Batam. In Jakarta two bombs exploded. One destroyed a car which a government source told the *Far Eastern Economic Review* was the one Pius Lustrilanang had been driving around in for most of the day (*Far Eastern Economic Review*, 4-11-1999:8). In Surakarta, among the houses ravaged was that of Amien Rais.

On the eve of his election Abdurrahman Wahid had disclosed that he and Amien Rais had agreed that if he became president he should express his preference for Akbar Tanjung as his vice-president. Megawati could become chairperson of parliament, or, and this was what Abdurrahman Wahid preferred, the leader of the opposition in parliament. He believed that the parliament of Indonesia needed a strong opposition (*Tempo*, 24-10-1999:22-3).

---

[17]   Initially Akbar Tanjung had been nominated as the Golkar candidate for the presidency. According to some stories, pressure by Iramasuka Nusantara contributed to Akbar Tanjung's decision to withdraw his nomination. Golkar leaders of this group are said to have threatened to call an extraordinary party congress to bring him down as general chairman of Golkar had he persisted.

Another scenario was followed. Megawati was elected vice-president on 21 October. After her defeat in the race for the presidency, she and PDI-P had refused to run for the vice-presidency, not replying to Abdurrahman Wahid's request that Megawati should stand, and at first refusing a nomination by PKB. When Megawati agreed in the early morning of 21 October to a PKB nomination, she initially demanded that her election should be by acclamation. Akbar Tanjung, who had repeatedly stated that he nurtured no aspirations for the presidency or vice-presidency and who could not count on the support of the Habibie faction within Golkar, and Wiranto, who had also been nominated and whose election might well have led to renewed unrest, withdrew. Hamzah Haz refused to follow their example, an indication of the dislike of Megawati nurtured in some Islamic quarters. Another who tried to throw a spanner in the works was Mrs Marwah Daud Ibrahim. She called for a second vice-president representing eastern Indonesia and was immediately rebuffed by Marzuki Darusman, Golkar chairman in the People's Congress. Hamzah Haz did not succeed in defeating Megawati. Nevertheless, he received 284 votes. Megawati received 396 votes. Her election restored peace in Jakarta, where her supporters greeted her success as a victory of the people. In Bali disturbances continued. Habibie's failure to gain the presidency instantly acted as a spark causing the struggle within Golkar to flare up again. Between 30 and 40 Golkar members of the People's Congress were thought to have rejected Habibie's accountability speech. The Habibie camp in Golkar asked for sanctions against them. They blamed Akbar Tanjung, Marzuki Darusman, and Ginandjar Kartasasmita for the 'treason' of these members of the People's Congress. Another consequence of Habibie's defeat was that it unleashed unprecedented regional sentiments in South Sulawesi. In Jakarta members of Forum Pemuda dan Mahasiswa Indonesia Timur (FPMIT), Forum of Youths and Students from Eastern Indonesia, vilified Akbar Tanjung as a traitor who should be exterminated. They had already made their position more than clear when Habibie's speech was rejected. Furious, they had clashed with people from Akbar Tanjung's entourage at the Congress Building. They interpreted the rejection of Habibie's accountability speech as an unerring indication that Javanese were unwilling to accept people from eastern Indonesia assuming positions of leadership. To substantiate this accusation, they recalled the fate of Ghalib and Baramuli. The anger of such Habibie fans swelled to overwhelming proportions after Megawati's election. Bursting to voice their dismay, 50 members of FPMIT disturbed a Golkar meeting. They protested about the fact that nobody from eastern Indonesia had become president or vice-president and demanded the establishment of a federal state. Habibie was their obvious candidate for president of eastern Indonesia.

In erstwhile Ujungpandang, trouble had started after Habibie's accountability speech had been rejected. In frustration, students occupied a number of buildings and assaulted the local PDI-P office. It was the start of days of massive demonstrations. Students, mostly from IAIN, Universitas Muslim Indonesia, Universitas Negeri Makassar (UNM), and Muhammadiyah University, proclaimed their belief that the People's Congress had disregarded the aspirations of the inhabitants of eastern Indonesia and demanded an independent Sulawesi within a federal structure.[18] They carried around a flag of an independent Sulawesi: a green banner bearing a red map of Sulawesi against a white background in the middle. Indonesian flags were torn down. The students succeeded in forcing the local station of the state radio to broadcast their demands and also marched to the airport and harbour. At the airport they were allowed to hoist the Sulawesi flag. An East Indonesian state was actually proclaimed on 22 October. The ceremony was accompanied by the hoisting of the Sulawesi flag. Neither the students nor the Indonesian press were very bothered by the fact that there is a difference between Sulawesi and eastern Indonesia, or that in other parts of the island people might not agree to students in South Sulawesi speaking in their name. The governor of South Sulawesi tried to downplay the demonstrations by stating that the student actions should be taken with a grain of salt. They did not really want independence. They were simply angry and letting it be known. Outraged by his words, on 25 October, students marched to his office, lowered the Indonesian flag, and forced him to lead a ceremony during which the flag of a free Sulawesi was raised.

The People's Congress unanimously decided to revoke the 1978 decree regarding the integration of East Timor. A great deal of attention was spent on how to assist those people in East Timor who were in favour of continued integration. Among the other important decisions made were adjustments of the constitution. In the new Broad Outlines of State Policy the need for far-reaching regional autonomy was stressed. Aceh and Irian Jaya got special mention. The two provinces should remain part of the unitary republic. Acts were promised to regulate the special status of these two provinces. New was the decision to have the People's Congress convene once a year, and not once in five years, to hear an account by the president.

After talks between Abdurrahman Wahid and Megawati with Akbar Tanjung, Wiranto, and Amien Rais, the composition of the new cabinet was announced on 26 October. Initially it was stated that for the first time in decades the cabinet would not be given a specific name. This novelty seemed difficult to swallow. Within days it was being referred to as Kabinet Persatuan Nasional, Cabinet of National Union. The cabinet consisted of 35

---

[18]   Judging from the newspaper reports, students from Hasanuddin University did not join in the demands for an independent state.

members. No longer included were a Minister of Information or a Minister of Social Affairs. Both ministries were dissolved. Despite these steps, the cabinet still had more ministers than originally intended. Abdurrahman Wahid had to admit that his cabinet was a compromise. He had been called upon to do a balancing act, accommodating all the major political forces.

In composing the cabinet, Abdurrahman Wahid had also had to return favours to those who had made his own election possible. Though he himself denied that there was any truth in the allegation, an indication that this was exactly what he had done was the background of the party politicians in the new cabinet. The Central Axis was very well represented. Eight ministers or ministers without portfolio were drawn from the Central Axis parties: four from PAN, two from PPP (both taken by NU members), one from Partai Keadilan, and one from PBB. PDI-P was represented with a mere three posts. In contrast, Golkar politicians controlled four ministries (including the position of Marzuki Darusman as new attorney-general). Military officers headed five ministries (including one without portfolio). Among them were that of Internal Affairs, which went to Lieutenant-General (Ret.) Surjadi Soedirdja, and that of Mining and Energy, which was held by Susilo Bambang Yudhoyono. Surjadi Soedirdja's and Susilo Bambang Yudhoyono's image were tainted by the fact that at the time of the attack on the PDI office the former had been governor of Jakarta and the latter chief of staff of the military command of Jakarta. Wiranto was appointed Coordinating Minister of Political Affairs and Security. Among his first announcements was that the efforts to explain to society the purpose and content of the Overcoming a Situation of Danger Act were to be stepped up. As Commander of the Armed Forces he was succeeded by Admiral Widodo Adi Sutjipto from the navy.[19] Never before had a non-army officer held this post. For the first time in many years, a civilian was made Minister of Defence: Juwono Sudarsono. Security had been dropped from the task description of his ministry. Kwik Kian Gie became Coordinating Minister of Economy, Finance, and Industry. The third coordinating minister was Hamzah Haz. He headed the cabinet section for people's welfare and poverty eradiction. Nur Mahmudi Ismail of Partai Keadilan became Minister of Forestry and Plantations. Yusril Ihza Mahendra was appointed Minister of Law and Legislation. Hasballah M. Saad, a PAN politician born in Pidie, became Minister without Portfolio of Human Rights.

New (and Abdurrahman Wahid had alluded to this as soon as he was elected), was a Minister of Maritime Exploration – a post which went to Sarwono Kusumaatmadja. In two senses the creation of this ministry was a

---

[19]   Widodo in turn was replaced as deputy commander of the Armed Forces by Lieutenant-General Fachrul Razi, an Acehnese officer. Johny Lumintang was appointed governor of Lemhanas.

nationalist move. Abdurrahman Wahid argued that Indonesia had to become a strong maritime nation. Her seas were rich, but because of the lack of strength of the Indonesian navy its products were being plundered by others. Hence he put the strenghtening of the navy among his priorities. A second advantage Abdurrahman Wahid saw in stressing Indonesia's maritime nature was that the Indonesian culture would be enriched by inputs from its maritime cultures. In explaining the new policy, Abdurrahman Wahid recalled the days when the archipelago had been renowned for its great seafaring states, mentioning Aceh, Makassar, and Javanese Jepara as examples. He explained that with his new conception there would no longer be a Javanese 'Mataram' stamp on Indonesia.

FRONT PEMBELA ISLAM

- Mathori Abdul Jalil ternyata "Musang Berbulu Ayam" karena terbukti menerima *"money politics"* sejumlah Rp 10 milyar dari PDI Perjuangan.

- Mathori Abdul Jalil pada 11 Nopember 1998 di Tugu Proklamasi bersama PRD, KOMRAD, FORKOT, dan organisasi kiri lainnya melakukan orasi mendukung tuntutan kekuatan kiri.

WASPADAI
KEGIATAN TERSELUBUNG
PROVOKATOR
MATHORI ABDUL JALIL

A pamflet of Front Pembela Islam attacking Matori Abdul Djalil.

CHAPTER XIX

The first months of
the Abdurrahman Wahid administration

Referendum .... referendum
wajib kita tuntut Aceh ini harus kita ambil alih kuasa
Kita pertahan ... kita pertahan, bersama kita bertanggung jawab.[1]

By the time he was elected, national strength had become a key word in Abdurrahman Wahid's vocabulary, convinced as he appeared to be that the weak position of Indonesia had been seized upon abroad and exploited and that Indonesia had been badly treated. Even before the new cabinet was announced, he made it known that he did not agree with the picture of the country which he claimed was being spread abroad and seemed to have seized hold of IMF. This depicted Indonesia as an economically impoverished and worthless country. He promised that his government, unlike its predecessors, would not just meekly acquiesce in the orders of IMF, the World Bank, or anyone else.[2] Abdurrahman Wahid's views on this point tallied with those of some PDI-P politicians. Providing that international support could be found, Kwik Kian Gie had proposed a return to a managed float for the rupiah at an exchange rate of Rp 5,000 to the dollar as part of PDI-P's financial policy as early as April. Though he had backpedalled after meeting the executive deputy director of IMF, Stanley Fischer, PDI-P politicians in June had not completely discarded the idea of a fixed exchange rate. Early in October another PDI-P financial expert, Theo F. Teomeon, aired the possibility of introducing such a policy should the rupiah remain weak after

---

[1]   Referendum .... referendum/ It is our duty to demand that we take over power in Aceh/ We stand firm .... we stand firm, it is our joint responsibility. Indonesian translation of a song performed in Aceh (*Kompas*, 14-12-1999).
[2]   *Tempo*, 24-10-1999:23; *Panji Masyarakat*, 27-10-1999:41. In December, when his government was being subjected to fierce criticism, he accused the press and NGOs of being instruments used by foreign interests which wanted to debilitate Indonesia. Speaking on the anniversary of the news agency Antara, he accused NGOs of relying on foreign funds for publishing reports or staging activities which he called 'nonsense'.

the presidential election in spite of the improved domestic political climate. He said he believed that under such circumstances a weak rupiah could only be the result of what he vaguely described as a continuation of unfair treatment, which should elicit a fitting reaction on the part of Indonesia.

The new cabinet immediately broached a number of controversial topics. Among the most sensitive ones was the announcement by the new Minister of Foreign Affairs, Dr H. Alwi Shihab, a chairman of PKB and close confidant of Abdurrahman Wahid, that Jakarta intended to enter into commercial and cultural relations with Israel. Pointing to the strong international lobby by Israel, Alwi Shihab stressed that the investments this might generate would contribute to the restoration of the Indonesian economy. There was one major condition. This was that Indonesia, the largest Islamic nation in the world, would be involved in the peace process in the Middle East. The envoys from the Middle East, and indirectly also the Islamic community at home, were assured that Jakarta was not considering opening up diplomatic relations with Israel. In view of the strong anti-Jewish feelings prevailing in part of the Islamic community it was a brave step, one which was not allowed to pass without enormous protests (for an impression of the commotion stirred up by the proposal, see Husaini 1999 and Tim Pustaka Cidesindo 1999). Israeli flags were burnt and students from KAMMI, Hammas, UI and organizations like GPI and PII staged demonstrations. *Ulama* also joined in the chorus of disapprobation. KISDI held a large protest meeting at Al-Azhar Mosque. Among the politicians who maintained that matters should not be rushed was Amien Rais. Abdurrahman, who after visiting Israel in 1994 amid outcries of disapproval had already argued for opening up diplomatic relations, did not understand what all the fuss was about. After all, he said, as he had already done during a television interview in May 1999, Indonesia maintained diplomatic ties with the People's Republic of China and Russia, two atheistic countries. He asked Muslims not to generalize and not to consider all Jews their enemy. Made cautious by the mass protests, on 18 November Alwi Shihab announced that the opening of trade relations with Israel would be postponed. For some Muslims this did not go far enough. The plan had to be cancelled.[3] Despite the commotion, an Israeli trade delegation visited Indonesia at the end of December. Abdurrahman Wahid denied any involvement. He said he had learned about the visit from reports in the media.

Other problems the new government faced had been inherited from its predecessor: the tackling of the Bank Bali scandal, the prosecution of Soeharto and other persons suspected of being guilty of KKN, separatist movements, and communal violence. The unrest had resulted in an ever increas-

---

3   During a visit to Jordan at the end of November, Abdurrahman Wahid announced that an Indonesian Chamber of Commerce would be set up in the Gaza Strip.

ing number of refugees. By mid-November the number of people in refugee camps had reached 640,000. The figure included 260,000 people from East Timor who had fled or had been forced to leave their homes during the carnage following the referendum.[4]

High on Abdurrahman Wahid's agenda was to find a solution to regional unrest. Regionalism ran highest in Aceh, Irian Jaya, and Riau. In Aceh people still demanded a referendum, and even ventured to suggest the possibility of international supervision. Regionalist sentiments in oil-rich Riau prompted people in Jakarta to proclaim a Riau Merdeka (Free Riau) movement. Abdurrahman Wahid indicated that he knew who the persons responsible for the proclamation were. As was his wont, he mentioned no names, but Syarwan Hamid took the accusation personally. He said that the intelligence officers who had told Abdurrahman Wahid that he was involved in the movement were misinformed. Later in November Syarwan Hamid spoke out in favour of considering a federal state.

In Jayapura demonstrators demanded independence for Irian Jaya or, as they themselves called it, West Papua.[5] Conspicuously present at a number of such protests was Yorrys Raweyai, whose sudden, not undisputed role as champion of Papuan independence, had found its expression in his becoming a kind of representative outside Irian Jaya, heading a Lembaga Adat Papua Perantauan, or Adat League of Overseas Papuans. He was among the signatories to a statement drawn up in Jayapura on 12 November asking Indonesia to withdraw from Irian Jaya. Those present also asked Jakarta to allow the flying of the Morning Star flag and the singing of the national anthem *Hai Tanahku Papua* (Papua My Land). The role of Yorrys Raweyai caused such a person as the director of Papua Human Rights, Jimmy Damianus Ijie, to conclude that accomplices of the New Order regime were behind the freedom movement. Another explanation was advanced by Lieutenant-General (Ret.) Harsudiono Hartas. He was convinced that a superpower lurked behind it all. After having succeeded in separating East Timor from Indonesia, it had turned its attention to Irian Jaya. Agents of what he described as an international conspiracy worked via NGOs and used calls for greater democratization, respect for human rights, and environmental concerns to achieve their aim of controlling the rich natural resources of Irian Jaya. At the end of May and early June 2000, when the National West

---

[4]   These figures were presented by the Minister of Internal Affairs during a hearing in parliament on 14 December.
[5]   Abdurrahman Wahid celebrated New Year in Jayapura. After sunrise he announced that Irian Jaya was to be renamed Papua. The stated reason for this step was that in Arabic Irian means 'naked'. The regional administration started to use the new name immediately. In reaction Akbar Tanjung stated that parliament had to be consulted before there could be any such name change. A personal remark on the part of the president was not enough.

Papua Congress was convened in Jayapura, Yorrys Raweyai's inclusion in a
Papua Presidium Council met with opposition. The chairman of the Presidium Dewan Papua was Theys Hiyo Eluay, chairman of Lembaga Adat Masyarakat Irian Jaya, the Irian Jaya Adat Foundation. The congress unequivocally spoke out in favour of independence. This was much to the horror of
Abdurrahman Wahid and other Indonesian leaders, who promised, tough
actions if Independence were proclaimed.

Infected by the mood of the day, people elsewhere called for greater
autonomy for their province, for the upgrading of their region to a province,
or for transforming Indonesia into a federation. Among the last was the
provincial parliament of East Kalimantan. To show that his administration
was serious about addressing such sentiments, Abdurrahman Wahid created
a new post of Minister without Portfolio of Regional Autonomy in his cabinet. The person appointed was Ryaas Rasyid, a native of South Sulawesi.
Another gesture made to convince people that he was serious about solving
the problems of the country was Abdurrahman Wahid's announcement that
he and Megawati had agreed on a division of labour. He himself would deal
with the problems in Aceh, economic development, and food production.
Megawati would devote her attention to Ambon, Irian Jaya, and Riau.
Laughingly, he added that he had given her the difficult part of the job.

Among the first measures Abdurrahman Wahid took to tackle the problems in Aceh was to order Widodo to launch an investigation into the human
right abuses committed by the military in Aceh and to withdraw combat
troops brought in from outside the province as soon as possible. In secret, he
also met prominent GAM members and said he was prepared to speak to its
leader in exile, Hasan Tiro, as well. Such gestures failed to persuade people
in Aceh to accept Jakarta's authority. Responding to this obduracy, Abdurrahman Wahid, like Habibie, seemed prepared to make the largest possible
concessions.[6] He even said he would agree to a referendum, arguing that if a
plebiscite could be held in East Timor this could also be implemented in
Aceh. As usual, his early statements on this point made it difficult to pinpoint
what exactly Abdurrahman had in mind. He remained vague about the date
of a referendum, the choice which would be presented to the Acehnese (independence or greater autonomy), and whether he would accept independence
for Aceh. What Abdurrahman Wahid might have aspired to at that moment,
he could well have revealed on 24 October: a federal administrative structure, without actually calling it so. In fact, he was of the opinion that the new

---

[6]   In September 2000 Abdurrahman Wahid signed two government decrees to redeem a
promise he had made in January that the port of Sabang was to become a free port and bonded
zone. Sabang had lost this status in 1984 when the central government decided to develop the
island of Batam.

legislation granting greater regional autonomy had accomplished this, creating a federal structure within a unitary state.

The two other major civilian political players, the chairmen of the People's Congress and of parliament, Amien Rais and Akbar Tanjung, reacted with reservations to Abdurrahman Wahid's early referendum statements. At the outset it was also the vagueness of Abdurrahman Wahid's statements which irked them. They and others raised the same criticism which Habibie had had to face. The president could not decide on such a vital matter without involving parliament and the People's Congress. Amien Rais, whose PAN had continued to float the idea of federalism during the election campaigns, could agree to a referendum but only as a solution of the very last resort. Calling independence of Aceh a disaster, Amien Rais suggested trying other solutions first, for instance contemplating the establishment of a federal state. Akbar Tanjung considered it unfitting for a president to suggest holding a referendum.

His opposition was shared by the major political parties. On 17 November, the chairmen of parliament and the leaders of its factions spoke out against a suggestion made by Abdurrahman Wahid the day before in which he said that a referendum could be held within seven months. Parliament, they stated, was intent on maintaining the integrity of the unitary state. Assuming that one of the choices presented would be independence, a referendum was rejected. Somewhat piqued, and calling the spectre of East Timor to mind, Akbar Tanjung pointed out that what Abdurrahman Wahid had expressed was his personal opinion. Akbar Tanjung stressed that were a referendum to be held, it should be a nation-wide one, or be about the choice for a federal state or for regional autonomy. Abdurrahman Wahid addressed parliament about a referendum on 18 November. He remained vague.[7] Only later was he to become specific. At the end of the month he said that the option to be offered to Aceh was far-reaching autonomy with the right to implement Islamic law.

Strong opposition to a referendum and to changing the structure of the state came from the Armed Forces. The military made its position crystal clear. Wiranto indicated that as far as he was concerned the unitary state was final and was not negotiable. In the same vein the new spokesman for the Armed Forces, Major-General Sudrajat, in office since August, stressed that if a referendum were to take place it had to be within the framework of the uni-

---

[7]   The main reason for parliament to invite Abdurrahman Wahid was to give him the opportunity to explain the closure of the Ministries of Social Affairs and Information. On the occasion Abdurrahman Wahid rattled the members of parliament by accusing them of being swayed by their emotions instead of using their brains when criticizing his policy. He said that parliament resembled a kindergarten.

tary state. There were only two options open to Aceh: autonomy or having the status of a special region. Sudrajat announced that were the Acehnese to speak out in favour of independence in a referendum, the Armed Forces would strive to hold a referendum in the rest of the country to ask the Indonesian population whether they agreed to the secession of a part of their country's territory. To underline this position, he argued that Aceh was not just the property of the Acehnese, but of the whole nation. If the independence of Aceh was rejected in a nation-wide referendum, the Armed Forces would act to defend Indonesia's territorial integrity. To put an end to any doubts, 84 senior active and retired officers announced on 11 November that the calls for a referendum should be tackled within the framework of a unitary state. To avoid a repetition of what had happened in the case of East Timor, they urged Abdurrahman Wahid not to assume prematurely that the Acehnese would choose to remain part of Indonesia. They, too, suggested the possibility of a national referendum on Aceh.

In Aceh itself, the scope of the power of the central authority had dwindled still further. Government tasks had been taken over by an organization called Sentral Informasi Referendum Aceh (SIRA) and the local population, questioning strangers and arresting thieves, prostitutes, and others whom they suspected of having committed crimes. In Banda Aceh a group styling itself Gerakan Aksi Mahasiswa Anti Maksiat (GAMAM), Anti-Sin Student Action Movement, paraded such people, whose heads had been shaven, through the town on a pick-up truck in early December. Their victims had to carry texts like 'I am sorry I have stolen' and 'I am sorry I have committed adultery'.

Far from abating, anti-government sentiments only seemed to have proliferated in the province. People had begun to greet one another with the cry 'Merdeka', and demands for a referendum swelled. Among those who personally experienced what one Jakarta newspaper described as 'referendum euphoria' and 'referendum hysteria' were three ministers in Abdurrahman Wahid's cabinet (*Media Indonesia*, 8-11-1999, 9-11-1999). When they visited Banda Aceh in the middle of November they were forced to call out 'Long Live a Referendum' loudly three times during a discussion meeting with representatives of local NGOs. Their visit came at a moment when the campaign for a referendum had just been stepped up to a higher tempo. Large, *kabupaten*-wide demonstrations in which hundreds of thousands of people participated had been held in late October and early November. Most proceeded without major incidents, but West Aceh was an exception to this. The building of the *kabupaten* parliament in Meulaboh went up in flames when its chairman refused to sign a statement in favour of a referendum. The office of the *bupati* was set ablaze as well. Apart from this, 60 inmates were set free when a crowd marched on the prison. When demonstrators tried to force their way into the compound of the local military command in an attempt to lower the Indonesian flag, troops opened fire. At least 23 people were injured.

The *kabupaten* demonstrations had culminated in a mass rally in the provincial capital, Banda Aceh, on 8 November. The demonstration organized by SIRA was baptized Sidang Umum Masyarakat Pejuang Referendum Aceh, General Session of the Fighters for a Referendum in Aceh, abbreviated to SU MPR, the same acronym as the People's Congress in Jakarta is known by. Over one million people attended. As in August, shops, offices, and schools remained closed. Public transport came to a standstill. The doors of the two prisons in the town were also thrown open (a few days later, inmates also walked out of the prison in Lhokseumawe). Simultaneous demonstrations were organized by Acehnese in Medan and Jakarta.

A few days after the mass rally in Banda Aceh, the leader of Thaliban, Tengku Bulqaini, gave Jakarta till 4 December, the anniversary of the founding of GAM, to agree to a referendum. If not, protests would be resumed. The mention of the date sent a stream of refugees pouring out of Aceh. A figure of 15,000 persons was mentioned. The exodus swelled still more after the rumour spread that GAM had ordered Javanese to leave the province temporarily and pamphlets bearing this message began to circulate. Threats of physical violence against non-Acehnese were also reported. GAM and students in Banda Aceh dismissed such activities as the work of agitators who were set on blackening the name of GAM. Among the refugees were non-Acehnese policemen stationed in South Aceh and their families. The reason they fled was that scores of their colleagues had been kidnapped by armed men. Some had been killed. The fate of others was unknown.[8]

The immense manifestations of discontent in Aceh brought home the message that Jakarta had to act quickly. In early November the independent committee of inquiry constituted by Habibie three months earlier reported that it had listed seven thousand violations of human rights committed in Aceh between 1989 and 1999. To speed up proceedings, the committee suggested that a military court be constituted to try those suspected of having committed the crimes. Delay would only fan heated emotions and whip up anger in Aceh. Later in the month when its findings were made public, the committee designated the killings, rapes, including gang rapes and rapes in the presence of husbands and children, and torture of civilians war crimes. Most of these were said to have been committed by Kopassus members.

---

[8]   In December the chief of police of Aceh revealed that in the previous six months 72 members of the security forces, among them 33 policemen, had been killed in Aceh. The fate of 16 others, including ten policemen, who had been abducted was unknown. Figures provided by the police headquarters in Jakarta put the death toll for 1999 at 293, including 91 members of the security forces (*Suara Pembaruan*, 13-12-1999; *The Jakarta Post*, 19-2-2000). In the first six months of 2000 151 civilians and 28 members of the army and police were killed.

Among the persons mentioned as being responsible for the brutality displayed during military operations in Aceh were – as was mentioned in the report – generals TS, ES, FT, and Wrt. The committee emphasized that it decided to publish its findings because it was disappointed with the lack of response on the part of the government in the fortnight since it had handed in its report.

Others, who did not show much faith in military courts, were in favour of a trial before a special civil court or a tribunal made up of civilian and military judges. The suggestion was taken up by the independent committee. Politicians were also prepared to honour such calls. Marzuki Darusman promised that he would ask the president to draft a Government Regulation in Lieu of a Law to give his office the authority to prosecute members of the Armed Forces. He, Munir, Yusril Ihza Mahendra, and Amien Rais were among those who spoke out in favour of a civil court. In the middle of December Abdurrahman Wahid followed suit. The army was not left much choice. During a meeting between members of the independent committee and officers of the Armed Forces on 13 December it was agreed that at least some of the cases should be tried by a *pengadilan koneksitas*, a combined civilian military court. The first case, which was prepared in February 2000, was the one concerning the shooting in July 1999 of Tengku Bantaqiyah and those who had attended his Koran recitation meeting in Beutong Ateuh in West Aceh.

Parliament did not remain silent either. It formed a special committee to tackle the Aceh problem. One of its members announced that it was very likely that Soeharto and the senior officers who had been in charge of military operations in Aceh in the 1980s and 1990s at the national and local levels would be summoned. Names mentioned in this respect were Benny Moerdani, Try Sutrisno, Edi Sudradjat, Feisal Tanjung, Syarwan Hamid, and the commanders of the Bukit Barisan Command. The first to be heard were Wiranto and Widodo. They were questioned by the special committee of parliament on 25 November. On that occasion members of parliament gave free rein to their suspicions that the fresh trouble in Aceh had been engineered by the Armed Forces. Both Wiranto and Widodo defended the army, pointing out that in recent months it had adopted a defensive stance. They said that the pursuit of GAM members and house-to-house searches had been stopped because such operations had led to abuses and had frightened people into fleeing from their homes. Wiranto revealed that 151 cases of soldiers suspected of what was described as undisciplined behaviour had been brought to court.[9] Generals Moerdani, Try Sutrisno, Feisal Tanjung, Syarwan Hamid, Pramono Anam (a former commander of North Sumatra), and Zacky Anwar

---

9   Widodo said that at that moment only 814 soldiers, 600 marines, and a platoon of the special force of the air force were stationed in Aceh.

Makarim (in his capacity as former Kopassus commander) were heard, but the decision whether or not to summon Soeharto was postponed. Members of parliament did not look forward to the political implications which would arise should he refuse to appear pleading ill health.[10]

Belying Wiranto's statement about the defensive stance adopted by the security forces in Aceh, the army and the police waged a campaign for tougher military action. This was conducted so intensely that *The Jakarta Post* spoke of a media blitz (*The Jakarta Post*, 25-11-1999). Admitting that the police were powerless to maintain order and stressing that policemen had not been trained to deal with a guerilla war and were even unwilling to do so, Roesmanhadi called for a limited military state of emergency on 17 November. On the same day Juwono Sudarsono announced that his department was considering proclaiming a state of military emergency in parts of Aceh. One of the arguments he advanced for making such a move was the many policemen who had fallen victim to the violence in Aceh or had simply deserted. Others were cowed by the threats made by GAM and the burning of police and army posts. Describing Wiranto's reaction to the troubles in Aceh as passive, Juwono Sudarsono called for a more 'responsive' attitude. Three days later he seemed to do a bit of a double take, stating that the government would consider very carefully before proclaiming a state of emergency. Prudence was the order of the day, as a military action might well engender more violence. A third person who was in favour of a state of emergency was the Chief of Staff of the Army, Subagyo Hadisiswoyo. He, too, pointed out the manifest impotence of the police to maintain law and order. Shortly afterwards, on 20 November, Subagyo Hadisiswoyo was replaced by Lieutenant-General Tyasno Sudarto.[11]

The references to martial law were not well received by civilian politicians. Hasballah M. Saad accused the military of undermining the govern-

---

[10]   One of Soeharto's lawyers said at that time that the condition of the former president, especially his capacity to communicate, as a hearing would require, was doubtful. When Soeharto in November inaugurated a mosque at Taman Mini Indonesia Indah and travelled to Surakarta to visit his wife's grave, people began to doubt whether he was indeed so ill that he could not be questioned.

[11]   On the same day, Lieutenant-General Arie J. Kumaat took over from Z.A. Maulani as head of Bakin. People did not fail to notice that Wiranto and Bambang Yudhoyono were not present at their installation. Kumaat's appointment did not go down well in Aceh. He had been commander of the Bukit Barisan Military Command in 1994 and 1995. Roesmanhadi was suddenly replaced by Lieutenant-General (Pol.) Kanjeng Pangeran Haryo Rusdihardjo, a Solo aristocrat, in early January. Both, incidentally, had been involved in the investigation of the Marsinah murder. Roesmanhadi had been chief of police of East Java, while Rusdihardjo had headed a forensic team from police headquarters which had been ordered to reinvestigate the case. In March 2000 it was revealed that an audit team of the Ministry of Defence had accused Roesmanhadi of corruption.

ment's efforts to find a constructive solution to the problems in Aceh. The United States also indicated that it repudiated the proclamation of a military state of emergency. In spite of such negative reactions, the spokesman for the Armed Forces, Major-General Sudrajat, continued to call for a state of emergency. His main argument was that in parts of Pidie, North Aceh, West Aceh, and South Aceh the civil administration had ceased to function and economic life had come to a standstill. These were regions where disturbances of the peace were now rampant and where no Indonesian flags could any longer be seen flying.

The military could not persuade Abdurrahman Wahid. Speaking at a press conference in Amman on 24 November, he stressed that martial law was out of the question. The following day, speculating about what might happen on 4 December, Sudrajat became even more bellicose, threatening that were the Indonesian flag to be lowered and replaced by the GAM flag on that day, the Armed Forces would send troops to Aceh to set matters right. He said that in such a confrontation there were only two possible outcomes: either the Indonesian Armed Forces or GAM would go under, one or the other. The statement was softened somewhat by Sudrajat's assurance that the Armed Forces would bow to the political choice made about giving independence to Aceh or not, just as had been done in the case of East Timor. This was more in line with the formal position of the Indonesian government, also voiced by Wiranto, that a solution had to be found by means of a dialogue. Nevertheless, even Abdurrahman Wahid made it clear that if considered necessary, repressive force would be used against separatist movements. He said this on 3 December while in Beijing.

Centre stage in the speculations about imminent violence was the question what the reaction of the Indonesian security forces would be to the raising of the GAM flag and the lowering of the Indonesian one. The military were not the only body to look upon such acts with misgivings. Amien Rais said that deeds like these amounted to a de facto proclamation of independence, while Akbar Tanjung ventured the opinion that the security forces would certainly act against blatant anti-government activities such as the lowering of the Indonesian flag. Others, including the spokesmen for the PKB and PPP representations in parliament urged for decisive action to be taken if the latter were to happen. Related points on their agenda were the worry that security troops would not be able to restrain themselves and the suspicion that, at the instigation of those who wanted to immerse the country in chaos, agitators would use 4 December to incite unrest. Expecting trouble in the run-up to 4 December, two additional battalions of the Mobile Brigade were sent to Aceh. They were stationed in Banda Aceh and Lhokseumawe. Roesmanhadi stated that this brought the total number of policemen in Aceh to eleven thousand.

Jakarta had to make up its mind about how to react to the flying of the flag of a separatist movement at mass demonstrations, and not only in Aceh. It was facing the same problem in Irian Jaya, where the founding date of the independence movement preceded that of Aceh by a few days. 1 December was the anniversary of the declaration of an independent Papua state in 1961. After negotiations it was decided that during the planned commemoration the West Papua flag would be hoisted alongside the Indonesian flag. During the main ceremony, which took place in Jayapura and was attended by thousands of people, both flags were indeed raised. As a second compromise, the West Papua national anthem was allowed to be struck up after the Indonesian one had been played. Flag-hoisting ceremonies were also held in most of the other regency capitals in the province.[12]

In Aceh the same prudence was shown. Initially the prospects for 4 December had seemed gloomy. In Lhokseumawe people had left the city and shops had remained closed after the local GAM commander had ordered the flying of the GAM flag in front of houses and shops from 3 till 5 December. As the flag-raising ceremonies in Irian Jaya had shown, the Indonesian authorities were prepared to go some way towards a compromise. Beforehand, Juwono Sudarsono had indicated that GAM flags could be hoisted at private houses for a couple of hours, but not at Armed Forces or police barracks, or on government buildings. He called the flag the symbol of people who demanded justice. What was important was that the Indonesian flag was not lowered and continued to fly from government buildings. The chief of police of Aceh, Brigadier-General (Pol.) Bahrumsyah Kasman, made a similar statement. The raising of the GAM flag would be tolerated, but people should not try to lower its Indonesian counterpart. Equal restraint was shown by GAM leaders. The commander of its army, Teuku Abdullah Syafei, decreed that for the sake of public safety the GAM flag should only be raised at regional GAM commands, and not at private premises.[13] As a consequence, on 4 December there were only minor incidents in Aceh, during which security forces fired shots to disperse demonstrators. Afterwards Abdurrahman Wahid said that this unrest had been stirred up by agitators from 'society'. He acquiesced in the official army explanation that security forces had been shot at from the demonstrating crowds before they themselves had opened fire. Abdurrahman Wahid also ventured the opinion that the security forces were not responsible for the killings in Aceh. He blamed

---

[12] Even so, it was reported that on 2 December troops in Timika guarding the Freeport mine had opened fire on people who had raised the Morning Star (*Kabar dari Pijar,* 13-1-2000).
[13] The flag is composed of a white crescent and star on a red background with white and black stripes at the top and bottom. Because GAM does not yet have a national anthem, at least at one place the hoisting of the flag was accompanied by a call to prayer.

agitators from outside the province and did not preclude the idea that the activities of such people were being financed from Jakarta. Earlier he had attributed killings to persons not belonging to the Armed Forces who had donned army uniforms (*Republika*, 27-10-1999; *Suara Pembaruan*, 8-12-1999).

In Jakarta, meanwhile, the tug-of-war of the flags had sparked off some nationalist counter-demonstrations. A Forum Pembela Kedaulatan Bangsa, Forum of Defenders of the Sovereignty of the Nation, urged the Armed Forces and police to ensure that the Indonesian flag still flew all over Indonesia, irrespective of the risk such an endeavour might entail. Another group, Perjuangan Kedaulatan Rakyat dan Kesatuan Bangsa (Perkasa), Fighters for People's Sovereignty and Unity of the Nation, solemnly pledged to defend the Indonesian flag regardless of the perils which might be involved. The ceremony took place at the Proclamation Monument. A few days later, on 8 December, Abdurrahman Wahid also spoke out. Acehnese were allowed to fly the GAM flag, as part of the freedom of expression to which they were entitled. They should, however, not try to do so on government buildings. This was very similar to the sentiment he expressed on 1 January 2000, regarding Irian Jaya, when he tried to convince people that freedom of expression was guaranteed, which went as far as allowing local inhabitants to demand independence. Actual efforts to establish an independent state would not be tolerated.

If people rejected a state of emergency in Aceh, the situation with regard to the Moluccas was a very different story. At the end of November a delegation made up of Christian and Muslim members of its provincial parliament on a visit to Jakarta called for the declaration of a military emergency to halt the violence in the province. Others had lost faith in the army and the police. In early December Kontras and twelve other organizations asked for intervention by the United Nations to put an end to the bloodshed in the Moluccas. From various sides Abdurrahman Wahid and Megawati were criticized for the lack of interest they had shown. Finally, on 12 December, Abdurrahman Wahid and Megawati, accompanied by Widodo, Wiranto, and a number of other ministers, visited Ambon. Abdurrahman Wahid tried to impress upon the population that it was they themselves who had to find a way to end the unremitting violence. Perceived as yet another indication that he could not make up his mind about drastic action to be taken, the statement did not go unchallenged. Megawati travelled on to Irian Jaya. Advocates of independence used her visit for a show of force. In Biak a 'Papua Satgas' contingent – reportedly one thousand men strong – guarded the town and formed a 'human wall' around the airport where her plane was to land, seeing to it that nobody entered the airport without their permission. Bursting into tears during a speech, she implored her audience not to declare independence. She said that Indonesia would not be complete without Irian Jaya.

Supporters of independence were not impressed. [14]

A third wave of mob violence exploded in the Moluccas first on Buru on 22 December, then spreading to Ambon on 26 December. Violence spilled over to Halmahera and the surrounding islands. On Buru, at least 125 people died within a couple of days. According to figures released by the Armed Forces, the same fate befell at least 265 people on Halmahera and 63 people in Ambon during the first four days of the renewed fighting. *Republika*, on the authority of the *camat* of Galela in North Halmahera, mentioned a figure of 2,080 Muslims killed in that subdistrict between 28 December and 4 January; the Protestant newspaper *Suara Pembaruan*, citing a spokesman for Front Jihad Maluku, wrote of 3,000 Muslims killed. Such figures, a spokesman for the army in the Moluccas said, were a gross exaggeration. He put the number of casualties at 200. Later, the military commander in the Moluccas was to put the death toll on Halmahera and Seram between 26 December and 16 January at 771. At the end of January a local government official mentioned the figure 1,692 (*Republika*, 5-1-2000, 31-1-2000; *Suara Pembaruan*, 5-1-2000, 7-1-2000; *Kompas*, 17-1-2000).

The new violence heaped even greater criticism on the head of Megawati, already impugned for seemingly taking no action to stop the carnage. Condemnation swelled at the end of the year when, while fighting in the Moluccas continued unabated, she went to Hong Kong for a holiday. Giving open vent to such feelings, a headline on the front page of *Republika* proclaimed 'Ambon bleeds, the vice-president on vacation to Hong Kong' (*Republika*, 29-12-1999). Muslim demonstrators demanded her resignation. Abdurrahman Wahid defended her. He said that Megawati's visit to Hong Kong was not just a private affair. She went to try and stimulate investments from Hong Kong.

The renewed carnage prompted the Indonesian Communion of Churches to join those who called for international intervention. On 27 December, PGI called for the withdrawal of the Indonesian army and police from the Moluccas. An international peacekeeping force should take their place. This time, however, the military seemed to react with resolve. On 29 December, formally at the request of the governor of the Moluccas, Saleh Latuconsina, the military took over the responsibility for maintaining law and order from the police. Extra troops were drafted to the region.

The measures did not go far enough for Muslim quarters. As in March of the previous year, mass demonstrations were staged by Muslims protesting

[14] *Suara Pembaruan*, 13-12-1999. During the visit of Abdurrahman Wahid to Irian Jaya two weeks later, the authorities tried to downplay such taking over of tasks of the Republican security forces by calling it a joint effort of the police and Satgas Masyarakat Irja, or People of Irian Jaya Task Force, to protect the president during his visit (*Suara Pembaruan*, 31-12-1999).

Members of Lasykar Jihad (photo *Tempo*)

about genocide and calling for a *jihad*. Again, Islamic leaders hastened to explain that a *jihad* did not necessarily mean physical combat, but acting on reports that 400 people had left from Tanjung Priok bound for the Moluccas, the government instituted a naval blockade. This did not prevent radical Muslims from reaching Ambon. Similar to what happened in March 1999, when the news had spread that Christians on Ambon had attacked Muslims who were praying in a local mosque, Muslims took concrete steps. Much covered by the Indonesian and international press was the training since 6 April of a Lasykar Jihad Ahlus Sunnah Wal Jamaah in a special camp near Bogor. The Holy War Army, headed by Ja'far Umar Thalib, claimed to have 3,000 members, who as its name indicated had been recruited from the community of 'traditional' Muslims. Some were indeed later sent to Ambon by ordinary ferry, the government claiming it could do nothing to prevent this.

Doubts about the sincerity of some NGOs and the National Committee for Human Rights were also raked over once again. Muslim organizations like MUI and FPI demanded the dissolution of the committee or at least that some of its members be replaced. Resentment centred on a number of members: Munir, by now often accused by Muslims of being a foreign agent and a Jew, T. Mulya Lubis, Albert Hasibuan, and Asmara Nababan.[15] Amien Rais, who spoke of the ethnic cleansing of Muslims by Christians, joined in the chorus of condemnation. He wondered why the committee had reacted so vehemently to the crisis in East Timor during which one or two people had died, but remained silent about the hundreds of people who were being killed on Aceh and Halmahera (*Republika*, 7-1-2000). In January, Muslim protests triggered off anti-Christian riots on Lombok and disturbances in Makassar. Questioned on the suspicion of being one of the 'provocateurs' was Eggi Sudjana, who had been in Mataram at the time of the rioting.

As had happened a year earlier, after Ketapang and the outbreak of the fighting on Ambon, these new instances of violence reawakened the old fear that religious confrontations would spread to other parts of the country. Nervousness increased. Inter-religious conflicts seemed to be encroaching on Java from the east, from Lombok. Security was stepped up in such places as Bali, Surabaya, and Jakarta, special attention being paid to passengers on ships entering port. In Surabaya permits for mass meetings were refused, in Yogyakarta they were banned after a Muslim protest gathering had deteriorated into an attack on churches, and in Jakarta shops remained closed on 19 January after rumours of imminent rioting had spread. In Bali the head of police ordered the shooting of agitators on the spot, after a report that 600

---

[15] A few days later, in the middle of January, the members of the National Committee for Human Rights elected Djoko Soegianto as their new chairman to replace Marzuki Darusman. Asmara Nababan was elected secretary-general.

troublemakers behind the riots on Lombok had now turned their attention to this island. A similar nation-wide policy was announced in Jakarta by the chief of police.

The troubles in Aceh and the Moluccas were not the only problems Abdurrahman Wahid had to face. Equally sensitive was the question how to tackle the demands for the prosecution of Soeharto and the conglomerates who were accused of having brought about the economic downfall of the country by their malpractices. The president had to steer a middle course between being lenient toward the conglomerates, as he himself probably wanted to be, and the demands from society for stern, undiscriminating action. Initially, just after he had been appointed, Marzuki Darusman had promised to bring about the prosecution of all persons found guilty of KKN. He promised that old cases were to be re-opened and that priority was to be given to investigations into KKN in BPPC, Pertamina, and PLN. The Timor national car was also scheduled for special attention.

Abdurrahman Wahid was inclined to be more forgiving. On 10 December, receiving a delegation from the Indonesian Association of Indigenous Entrepreneurs, he said that the biggest culprits should be tried, but that other conglomerates who repented and who changed their ways should be exonerated. The dilemma the Indonesian government faced was put into words by Kwik Kian Gie, who pointed out that if legal action were taken against all guilty of KKN, a host of businessmen would end up in jail and this could well cripple the Indonesian economy.

The association of many businessmen and financial experts with the New Order and its economic abuses meant that Abdurrahman Wahid, as Habibie had also done, turned for advice on how to revitalize the economy to a number of highly controversial people. The signs of this were evident within days of his election when the establishment was announced of a Dewan Ekonomi Nasional (DEN), National Economic Council. Contested were the nominations of Subiakto Tjakrawerdaya, a former Minister of Cooperative Societies, and of Fuad Bawazier. In next to no time, people began to speculate that these two 'New Order figures' had been able to become members of the inner circle of Abdurrahman Wahid thanks to the efforts of Siti Hardijanti Hastuti Rukmana in her attempt to rescue the economic interests of the Soeharto family.[16] The following month, yet another advisory council was founded, Dewan Pengembangan Usaha Nasional (DPUN), National Council for Business Development. It raised at least some eyebrows when it was announced that DPUN was to be headed by Sofyan Wanandi, whose investigation by the office of the attorney-general had been dropped only a few days earlier, but

[16] *Jawa Pos*, 4-11-1999. Subiakto was a member of PKB, Fuad Bawazier of PAN. A month later, the composition of DEN was announced. It was to be chaired by Emil Salim, with Subiakto as deputy chairman. The name of Fuad Bawazier had been dropped.

was still on the list of bankers who were not allowed to leave the country.[17] Equally controversial were the appointments of Arifin Panigoro and Aburizal Bakrie to the council. Another wave of criticism broke out at the end of January when it was reported that among those to accompany Abdurrahman Wahid on a sixteen-day trip to Saudi Arabia, Europe, India, and South Korea were Setya Novanto and Marimutu Manimaren's brother, Marimutu Sinivasan, chief director of the Texmaco group. In December the latter had been declared a suspect in yet another financial scandal because he was among the businessmen who at the end of 1997 and early 1998, at the height of the economic crisis and on the recommendation of Soeharto, had received special credit from state banks to facilitate exports.[18] When Abdurrahman Wahid finally left the country, the two did not accompany him.

An immediate problem Abdurrahman Wahid had to face was the Bank Bali scandal. Shortly after the session of the People's Congress had drawn to its conclusion, the chairman of the financial committee of parliament announced that the long form would be made public after it had been discussed by parliament. He ventured a guess that this might well take till mid-December. Such a delay was too long for Kwik Kian Gie. The release of the audit had become almost an absolute necessity for the Indonesian government. Foreign aid was desperately needed to balance the next government budget, for which the drafting was to start in early November. Because of the suspension of loans at least until the long form was published, the 1999-2000 budget already showed a deficit. This, it was suggested, could make it impossible for the government to pay the civil service. Indonesia was 'broke, broke, broke because of its debts', the senior deputy governor of Bank Indonesia, Anwar Nasution, said at the end of the month to explain why the

---

[17]   Soon Kwik Kian Gie was to call DPUN the Dewan Pengemplangan Utang Nasional, National Council for the Non-Payment of Debts, because of its appeals for the remission of debts.

[18]   The providing of special credit to Texmaco had been revealed by the PDI-P minister, Laksamana Sukardi. Golkar members of parliament, Tunky Ariwibowo, and the former governor of Bank Indonesia, Soedradjad Djiwandono, maintained that nothing out of the ordinary had happened. They argued that the money had been needed at that time to keep export going and to obtain the desperately needed foreign currency. The affair led first, in early December, to a rush on the concern's bank, Bank Putera Multikarsa, and its being taken over by BPPN, and later, at the end of January, to its 'freezing'. At the height of the political row over the Texmaco case, Deni Daruri of the Centre of Banking Crisis (CBC) accused Laksamana Sukardi and Marzuki Darusman of acting as agents of another conglomerate by singling out Texmaco. In March 2000, when PDI-P held its national congress in Semarang, tens of Texmaco banners were placed near the hotel where the congress was held. Consequently it was rumoured that Marimutu Sinivasan was conducting a campaign to become the party's treasurer. In May 2000 the office of the attorney-general terminated its investigation into the Texmaco corruption case. No proof had been unearthed that the state had suffered from the provision of the special credit or that rules had been broken.

central bank did not intervene at that moment to stop the rupiah from sliding. In December Kwik Kian Gie confirmed that to all intents and purposes
Indonesia was bankrupt.

Highly aware of such financial considerations, Abdurrahman Wahid
issued a presidential instruction to Kwik Kian Gie ordering him to release the
long form on 2 November. Within hours, the document was handed over to
Hubert Neiss of IMF in the presence of dozens of journalists. To counter the
impression that the Indonesian government had yielded to foreign pressure,
on that occasion Kwik Kian Gie stressed that the report had been divulged
because of the commitment of the new government to ensuring its release,
and not because threats of IMF.

Among the information disclosed in the long form was that Manimaren
had transferred Rp 30 billion to the account of Arung Guak Jarre, a businessman and relative of Tanri Abeng, on 27 May. This money had come from a
loan from Bank Lippo to Manimaren's company, Ungaran Sari Garment.
Arung Guak Jarre had thereupon transferred half the amount to the general
election coffers of Golkar on 2 June. As such a contribution was much larger
than legally allowed, it was immediately suggested that Golkar might be
barred from the 2004 elections. Acting as spokesman for Golkar, Akbar
Tanjung said that what he described as a 'loan' of Rp 15 billion to finance
Golkar election activities had already been repaid. He went to great pains to
emphasize that the money had nothing to do with the Bank Bali cession fee
(which had been transmitted to Era Giat Prima on 3 June). What did raise
suspicions of illicit dealings, however, was that EGP had transferred Rp 30
billion to Ungaran Sari Garment on 9 June. Other Golkar leaders mentioned
in the long form as having received money (though it was not certain that
this came from the cession fee) were Arung Guak Jarre's business partner,
Setya Novanto, and Freddy Latumahina. Other sums were said to have gone
to companies in which Tanri Abeng and members of his family had a major
stake.

The publication of the long form did not clear the air. Initially there were
even doubts raised about its authenticity. Various names, which rumours
indicated were mentioned in it, were not. Mistrust was aggravated by the fact
that a number of pages were missing in the copy handed over to parliament.
Copying errors, it was explained, were the reason for this. An additional
cause for speculation arose when Amien Rais caused embarrassment to the
government by stating that a member of parliament had told him that two
cabinet ministers were among the recipients of Bank Bali money, but he did
not know who the persons concerned were. He had not read the account. In
the twinkling of an eye, the rumour that the two were Hamzah Haz and
Yusril Ihza Mahendra began to do the rounds.

After the long form had been published, criticism of Standard Chartered

Bank (SCB) and PwC swelled. Employees of Bank Bali protested about the management of their bank by SCB. They accused it of behaving arrogantly, in a style worthy of British colonialists. The term 'hostile takeover' was even mentioned. Another complaint concerned the high salaries of some fifty foreign managers imposed on Bank Bali by SCB. Their aggregate salary was said to almost equal the aggregate salary of the 6,300 Indonesian employees. The atmosphere at Bank Bali, where employees continued to support Rudy Ramli, became grim. The managers from abroad hired bodyguards; in one instance they were pelted with plastic bottles, and on 11 November, angry local staff forced them to vacate their offices. In view of the turmoil, BPPN decided to replace the SCB management team. Initially announced as a temporary measure, the replacement of the foreign staff signified the end of SCB's involvement in the management of Bank Bali. SCB withdrew from Bank Bali on 8 December. Its London office, stating that it remained committed to the recapitalization of Bank Bali, blamed 'continuing misinformation' (*The Jakarta Post*, 17-12-1999).

SCB was not alone in coming under assault. Demonstrations were staged to protest the way PwC, where early one morning employees entering their office had found bullet holes in the window, had handled matters. On 8 November a team of lawyers representing persons mentioned in the long form – Manimaren, Freddy Latumahina, Fadel Muhammad, Arung Guak Jarre, and Agus Sudono (a deputy chairman of the Supreme Advisory Council) – brought an action for libel and violation of bank secrecy against the firm. They also accused PwC of shoddy workmanship and asked for information about the fee it had received, which according to their information amounted to US$ 3 million. Tanri Abeng, who was added to the list of suspects at the end of January and subsequently was forbidden to leave the country, averring that what was mentioned about him in the long form was untrue, also threatened to bring a libel suit. Rudy Ramli did not remain idle either. In the middle of November he filed a lawsuit against the governor of Bank Indonesia for handing over the management of Bank Bali to Standard Chartered Bank, one of his most cogent arguments being that the decision had not been discussed with the management and shareholders of Bank Bali.[19] On 1 December the court dismissed the case against Rudy Ramli and

---

[19] Some maintained that SCB had had no right to bring in its own management team because the agreement signed stipulated that it would only take effect after Bank Bali's rights issue, which had been postponed because of the scandal. In return for the promise that Bank Bali would be recapitalized, Rudy Ramli dropped his lawsuit in April 2000. The formal decision to recapitalize the bank was taken in July. Bank Bali was to get a capital injection of Rp 5 billion. As part of an out-of-court settlement, BPPN gave Rudy Ramli a compensation of Rp 9 billion (to pay the fee of his lawyers and two months salary). The money was to be transferred after the recapitalization of Bank Bali.

the other directors of Bank Bali. The judge ruled that the indictment was unclear, inaccurate, and incomplete. Their city arrest was lifted, but a corruption case still loomed over the heads of Rudy Ramli, Pande Lubis, Setya Novanto, Djoko S. Tjandra, and Tanri Abeng. Djoko S. Tjandra was the first to be tried. His trial started at the end of February. As had been the case with almost all previous KKN cases in Jakarta, the court case ended in a fiasco for the public prosecution. Ruling that insufficient evidence had been presented, the court dismissed the case within days. At the end of March the government suffered a second defeat when the administrative court of Jakarta ruled that the takeover of Bank Bali by BPPN had been illegal and that the bank should be returned to Rudy Ramli. A new attempt to try Djoko S. Tjandra also failed. In August the court exonerated him of all charges. To the dismay of the public, only an eighteen-month jail term had been demanded. Pande Lubis was acquitted by the court of South Jakarta on 23 November.

The biggest question of all was probably how to deal with Soeharto. From the outset, both Abdurrahman Wahid and Marzuki Darusman indicated that the investigation into Soeharto was to be reopened. Abdurrahman Wahid explained that the primary aim of such a step was to find out whether Soeharto and his family had enriched themselves illegally, and if so, how much money they should hand over to the state. Marzuki Darusman took pains to stress that a legal basis needed to be constructed before the political decision about whether to show clemency or not could be taken. The person who eventually had to answer this question was Abdurrahman Wahid. Abdurrahman Wahid made no secret of his belief that a former president and vice-president deserved clemency. When he first talked about this, journalists asked him to explain who he meant by the latter. Laughingly, he replied that he might have had Habibie in mind. Family and cronies would not be pardoned. Abdurrahman Wahid at first chose to remain vague about whether amnesty should be granted after an investigation had established that Soeharto was guilty of KKN or only after a court had passed a sentence. Subsequently he expressed his preference for the first alternative, arguing that the prosecution of Marcos and the shah of Iran had shown that a court case could drag on for years. Later Amien Rais would speak out in favour of a pardon after a trial.

Such a discussion could not but elicit a response from the Soeharto camp. At the end of November both the spokesman for Soeharto's lawyer, Felix Tampubolon, and Probosutedjo said that the former president rejected an amnesty. He wanted a trial if the public prosecution thought it had enough proof to have him convicted. Soeharto and his lawyers got what they wanted. On 6 December the office of the attorney-general announced that the investigation into Soeharto had been reopened. In explanation of the decision, it was revealed that new evidence had been unearthed suggesting misuse of authority and power by issuing presidential decisions and decrees to raise funds for the foundations he chaired, from which members of his family and the business associates of Cendana had benefited. Soeharto was forthrightly called a suspect. On that same day 41 people died in renewed fighting in Ambon. Some people saw this as irrefutable proof that people close to Soeharto were behind the ongoing violence in Indonesia. Others blamed the military. As a next step Marzuki Darusman summoned Soeharto to his office. He insisted, even when Soeharto's lawyers argued that the former president was to weak to be questioned. Marzuki Darusman said that his office would decide whether the former president indeed was too ill. When the day came, 14 February, Soeharto did not appear. Only his lawyers visited the attorney-general's office to explain that Soeharto's physical condition did not allow questioning.

Some muscle was also shown in dealing with the bad debtors. At the end of November BPPN published a list of twenty business groups with the largest debts at banks falling under the jurisdiction of BPPN. These twenty concerns had an aggregate debt of Rp 72.14 trillion. The total amount of debts managed by BPPN was said to amount to Rp 207 trillion. At the top of the list was the Barito Group, with a debt of Rp 9.4 trillion. Coming in second and third were the Humpuss Group (Rp 7.5 trillion) and the Bob Hasan concern, and by extension the Soeharto foundations (Rp 5.4 trillion). The Bakrie Group (Rp 5 trillion) ranked fourth, Tirtamas (Rp 3.6 trillion) sixth, and Bimantara (Rp 2.9 trillion) tenth. The Danamon Group (Rp 2.5 trillion) was listed seventeenth.[20] The following month a publicity campaign successively disclosed the debts of the individual companies in these concerns, each revelation highlighting one of the conglomerates. In December land forming part of the assets of PT Sinar Slipi Sejahtera, a company headed by Siti Hardijanti Hastuti Rukmana and her husband, was confiscated by BPPN in its efforts to recoup some of the debts it managed. In the same month, two of Hashim Djojohadikusumo's companies, Tirtamas Comexindo and Sumi Asih, were formally designated non-cooperative debtors by BPPN. In January BPPN filed a bankruptcy lawsuit against Tirtamas Comexindo to recoup the bad loans of the company it managed.[21] Nevertheless, in the middle of the month the Indonesian government, which had categorically refused to consider a debt reduction for the companies indebted to BPPN, changed course. Kwik Kian Gie announced that debt reduction was possible under

[20]   Aburizal Bakrie put the debts of his concern at Rp 18.7 trillion, of which Rp 4.3 trillion fell under the jurisdiction of BPPN. After the Texmaco scandal broke, lists began to circulate on which the Texmaco Group (with a debt said to amount to Rp 19 trillion) had replaced the Barito Group as the concern with the largest debts at banks falling under the jurisdiction of BPPN.
[21]   In March the court refused to declare Tirtamas Comexindo bankrupt, and granted the company six months to settle its debts.

certain conditions, but there should be no evidence of crime or fraud, and the companies should have shown a cooperative attitude in attempting to settle their debts. In April BPPN announced that it was initiating legal procedures against one thousand bad debtors. One of the companies against which a petition in bankruptcy was to be filed was the ALatief Corporation, said to owe a debt of US$ 17 million at banks controlled by BPPN.

A new cloud appeared on the economic horizon at the end of 1999 when the Minister of Finance, Bambang Sudibyo, and others spoke openly about the possibility that Bank Indonesia would have to be recapitalized. They did so after the State Auditor's Office had audited Bank Indonesia on the basis of its balance sheet as of May 1999, when the bank became an independent institution and had issued a disclaimer. Billy Joedono described the decision of his office as an extraordinary step. Nowhere else in the world had the audit of a central bank ever resulted in a disclaimer. Among the reasons mentioned by the State Auditor's Office for its refusal to express an opinion about the balance sheet of Bank Indonesia were what was described as the chaos at the bank and the weakness of internal control. Another quandary was that part of the money injected into troubled banks as liquidity credit at the end of 1997 and in early 1998 when the public had lost confidence in the Indonesian banking world had not been supplied in accordance with the rules governing the channelling of such money.[22] Initially a figure of Rp 51.7 trillion was mentioned in this respect, an amount adjusted to Rp 80.25 trillion when the audit report leaked out in January.[23] The implication was that if it had indeed been provided in this irregular way, the government might not take responsibility for guaranteeing these loans. This would saddle Bank Indonesia with a substantial problem of how to regain these credits and with the prospect that it might have to book a substantial loss. It was even speculated that the bank might go bankrupt. Because there were strong suspicions that felonies had been committed, the attorney-general was asked to begin an investigation. The intention was there, but Bambang Sudibyo, who spoke of the biggest corruption case ever in Indonesia, doubted whether the attorney-

---

[22] A receiving bank should have a CAR of at least two per cent, should hand over promissory notes equivalent to the money received, and should have an additional asset collateral of 50 percent of the credit facility or more.

[23] According to figures provided by the State Auditor's Office, the banks with the largest liquidity credit obligations at the end of January 1999 were BDNI (Rp 37 trillion), BCA (Rp 26.59 trillion), Bank Danamon (Rp 23 trillion), and BUN (Rp 12 trillion). Other accounts give different figures, estimating the liquidity credit channelled to BCA as high as Rp 47.8 trillion. In March Bob Hasan said that he was only responsible for Rp 6.2 trillion of the Rp 14 trillion liquidity credit channelled to BUN. The rest was the responsibility of the Ongko Group of Kaharudin Ongko. Bob Hasan was confident that his share could be covered by the sale of 33 of his companies. Doubts about Aburizal Bakrie's role arose because of the fact that BNN had received liquidity support which amounted to Rp 3.02 trillion.

general was powerful enough to arrest the persons involved. Without becoming specific, he indicated that their power was vested in money, weapons, and experience.

The governor of Bank Indonesia, Syahril Sabirin, rejected the conclusions of the audit and dismissed the criticism as government intervention displayed to corner the central bank. He denied that Bank Indonesia had broken the rules, and said that people in the government were the only ones who had any quarrel with the way the credit had been provided. He shifted the responsibility to the government. One reason for him to pursue such an argument was that Bank Indonesia had provided the disputed liquidity credit on behalf of the government (which had to pay interest to Bank Indonesia on the outstanding liquidity credit).

A row between Syahril Sabirin and the government was the result. In its next step, Bank Indonesia threatened to recover the money from the banks which had received credit, including BCA and Bank Danamon. Syahril Sabirin warned that this would mean that the clearing of some twenty banks would be stopped. The economic cost of such closures would be higher for the government than taking over the Rp 51 trillion in debts. This time it was Kwik Kian Gie's and Bambang Sudibyo's turn to be angry. Bambang Sudibyo warned Bank Indonesia not to threaten the government. Pointing out that Bank Indonesia had received Rp 164.5 trillion (the new figure mentioned for the liquidity support) in government bonds to replace the liquidity credits provided, Kwik Kian Gie saw no reason why Bank Indonesia should debit the commercial banks involved. He wondered whether Bank Indonesia was not out to create chaos. In February Kwik Kian Gie enraged the management of Bank Indonesia even more by stating that audits had revealed strong indications that bankers had marked up the amount of liquidity credit they needed, and that the extra money provided had been divided up between the banks and the management of Bank Indonesia.

Bank Indonesia and the government initially also publicly differed in opinion about the financial state of the central bank. Bambang Sudibyo at first expressed the fear that even if the government did not take punitive action and did not (as it indeed would not) recall part of the Rp 164.5 trillion worth of government bonds, Bank Indonesia's equity would still be negative and a recapitalization would still be required. Syahril Sabirin denied that this would be so. It took till the end of January before Bambang Sudibyo publicly agreed that there was no need to recapitalize Bank Indonesia. The reason he gave was that the bank had made huge profits on foreign exchange transactions.[24]

---

[24]   By the end of 1999 the total value of government bonds issued to cover liquidity credit (which besides banks had also gone to Bulog), the settlement of inter-bank claims, and the recapitalization of banks amounted to about Rp 500 trillion.

Though the disputed liquidity credit had been provided under his predecessor, the controversy put Syahril Sabirin's position in jeopardy. Kwik Kian Gie said that Bank Indonesia had lost much of its credibility, making it difficult for the government to cooperate with its present management. Abdurrahman Wahid suggested that Syahril Sabirin should be replaced, a step which, as Bank Indonesia was an independent institution, only could be taken by parliament. Advanced as his desired successor was Laksamana Sukardi, treasurer of PDI-P, a former director of Bank Umum Asia and Lippo Bank. His chances diminished at the end of February when it had become clear that Syahril Sabirin refused to step down voluntary, as according to some reports Abdurrahman Wahid had already asked him to do a number of times in December, giving Syahril's inability to cooperate with the economic team in the cabinet as the main reason. Syahril's resolution formed one of the reasons for one of Laksamana's promoters, Megawati, to publicly withdraw her support of his candidacy as Syahril's successor.

Parliament saw the disputed credit as yet another reason for a hearing of Soeharto. As in so many other cases, it formed a special committee, which summoned Soeharto for 18 February (which was only four days after Soeharto had failed to come to the office of the attorney-general). Apart from being considered one of the key persons responsible for releasing the credits, he was accused of having seen to it that some of the money was channelled to Bank Utama, owned by his children. As the chairman of the committee had announced in advance, its members travelled by bus to Soeharto's house in Jalan Cendana when the former president did not appear. In their wake, reporters followed. They were refused access to Soeharto. It was explained that the former president had difficulty in verbal and non-verbal communication and that his memory was failing him. Whether or not Soeharto was indeed *pikun*, senile, the word with which the press summarized the verdict of Soeharto's medical team, remained for some time a matter of debate. When on 5 March, Abdurrahman Wahid suddenly visited Soeharto, the former president appeared healthy.

CHAPTER XX

Abdurrahman Wahid loses support

Apa artinya pembangunan
kalau timbul kesenjangan
Apa artinya kemakmuran
kalau tanpa keadilan

Negeri yang kaya raya
bisa jatuh sengsara
jika tak dikelola
dengan iman dan takwa[1]

The ongoing violence in the Moluccas, the upsurge of regional sentiments, and the obvious difficulty the Abdurrahman Wahid administration had in dealing with the economic scandals inherited from the past added to the criticism of Abdurrahman Wahid's performance. Protests and demonstrations broke out immediately after he had announced the composition of his cabinet – by the employees of the two departments which were disbanded, by NGOs, and by the students, whose demonstrations no longer had the massiveness and intensity they had had under Habibie's presidency.[2] Apart from their usual demands, the students called for a cabinet absolutely free of New Order figures and military officers. They argued that without this step and without a full investigation into the human rights abuses committed by the Armed Forces, reformation could never be complete. The NGOs protested about the appointment of Bomer Pasaribu, a Golkar politician and leader of

---

[1]   What is the meaning of development/ when the result is a gap between rich and poor./ What is the meaning of prosperity/ when there is no justice./ An immensely rich country can fall into misery/ if it is not governed/ with religious faith and devotion. From the song *Membela yang benar* (Defend what is true) written by Matori Abdul Djalil (PKB Audi Klip, *Gus Dur Indonesia menyanyi* (Gus Dur Indonesia sings)).

[2]   At the end of the year Abdurrahman Wahid accused Major-General (Ret.) Adang Ruchiatna, a former inspector-general of the Ministry of Social Affairs, of being behind the demonstration by the civil servants. Another name he mentioned in relation to financing demonstrations was that of Sri Roso Sudarmo.

the New Order labour union, SPSI, as Minister of Labour and of Sonny Keraf as Minister of the Environment.

Initially his critics singled out the fact that Abdurrahman Wahid spent much time abroad, seemingly neglecting the many domestic problems Indonesia was facing. By the beginning of December he had already visited the ASEAN countries, the Middle East, the United States, Japan, and China. On top of this came his visit to 13 countries during his 16-day tour at the end of January. It was an accomplishment for which the director of the Indonesian Museum of Records in Semarang wanted to present Abdurrahman Wahid with an award, while _The Straits Times_ in Singapore wrote that the Indonesian president had earned a place in record books (_The Straits Times_, 18-2-2000). The award was presented to Abdurrahman Wahid in April after he had visited 29 countries. The chairman of the museum disclosed that initially they had wanted to proclaim Abdurrachman Wahid 'the funniest president in the world', but had decided not to do so after protests from the Association of Indonesian Clowns, who feared a loss of their members' income. Abdurrahman Wahid himself said that it would have been more appropriate to award him the title 'most criticized president'. Others were annoyed by his frequent absence. They condemned the fact that at a moment when decisive action needed to be taken and a clear policy was called for to deal with the unrest in Aceh and the violence in the Moluccas, Abdurrahman Wahid was abroad and Megawati remained silent. By acting the way they did, Abdurrahman Wahid and Megawati gave the impression that they did not take the problems in Aceh and the Moluccas as seriously as they should have done, and that they lacked any clear concept of how to cope. Late in 1999 Akbar Tanjung even sent two formal letters to Abdurrahman Wahid urging him to take immediate and concrete steps to tackle the problems in the two provinces. A third was to follow in January. As a token of such criticism, Partai Keadilan presented Abdurrahman Wahid in May, after yet another trip abroad, with a 'travellers' award'. The secretary-general of Partai Keadilan said that the situation in Aceh and the Moluccas was still as bad as before. He also pointed out that, though Abdurrahman Wahid maintained that his foreign trips were intended to restore international faith in Indonesia, this could not yet be observed in the economic field. Leadership seemed to be lacking. Quietly, however, Abdurrahman Wahid set about mobilizing international support against allowing independence for Aceh and Irian Jaya. He also seemed to be convinced that time was on his side, and that if he allowed matters to take their course, people in Aceh would see reason and would no longer demand independence. In tackling other problems in the country Abdurrahman Wahid also refused to be hastened. 'Wait and see' became one of the characteristics of the way he intended to solve these. His attitude gave rise to a special term: _biarisme_, let things run their course.

Cracks in the government soon appeared. The national unity his compromise cabinet should have cemented failed to emerge in the day-to-day business of politics. One of the first conflicts was triggered off by a statement made by Abdurrahman Wahid in the middle of November. While visiting the United States, he said in Salt Lake City on 14 November that three members of his cabinet might be guilty of KKN, and that he was quietly preparing for their resignation. To whom he was alluding, even Marzuki Darusman was not sure initially. After a while he explained that the public prosecution had already launched an investigation into the three, as well as into other cabinet members about whom its was rumoured that their hands were not free of KKN. Speculations were rife as Marzuki Darusman, citing presumption of innocence as the reason, refused to become specific. Speculation had it that Abdurrahman Wahid had referred to Yusril Ihza Mahendra (said to have received campaign funds worth Rp 1.5 billion from Habibie) and Hamzah Haz (also alleged to have received campaign money from Habibie).[3] Two other ministers whose names were linked to Abdurrahman Wahid's accusation were Bomer Pasaribu, suspected of embezzlement of Jamsostek funds, and Yusuf M. Kalla (head of the Kalla businessconcern), also from Golkar, Minister of Trade and Industry and head of Bulog, about whom it was rumoured that he had taken over assets of Eddy Tansil's Golden Key Group illegally. In a press statement issued on 17 November, Abdurrahman Wahid denied that Yusril Ihza Mahendra was among the ministers under investigation. About other ministers whose names were mentioned he remained silent, a gesture seen as an indication that Abdurrahman Wahid refused to come to these people's rescue.[4] Abdurrahman Wahid complicated matters even further, when after returning to Indonesia he explained that in the United States he had asked a rhetorical question and had not stated positively that there were three cabinet ministers suspected of being guilty of KKN.

Abdurrahman Wahid announced the resignation of Hamzah Haz on 26 November. Hamzah Haz seemed baffled. Though for some time he had been making no secret of the fact that he intended to resign, the announcement came as a surprise to him. He had never tendered his resignation, nor had he

[3] At that moment people, including PPP members, were already asking for detailed information about the source of the roughly Rp 14 billion campaign money of PPP. After PBB had held its first congress in April 2000, some commotion was created by the fact that the party's financial report mentioned a gift of Rp 1 billion by Habibie to that party. Spokesmen for Habibie denied that he had ever given money to PBB. They said that in November 1998 Habibie had refused a request by Yusril Ihza Mahendra for money to finance a PBB national working conference.
[4] Marzuki Darusman asked the press to read the statement carefully. It said that 'at this moment' Yusril was not among the ministers under investigation. Marzuki also stressed that one should not speak of three, but of a number of ministers. In January Akbar Tanjung said that Marzuki Darusman had assured him that Kalla and Bomer were not involved in KKN cases.

received a formal letter of dismissal.[5] PPP considered the sacking of Hamzah Haz an affront. Hamzah Haz had asked Abdurrahman Wahid to state publicly that an investigation by the public prosecution had cleared him from the charges of corruption, but instead of having his name cleared, his resignation had been announced. In response to this treatment, Hamzah Haz announced his intention to turn PPP into an opposition party. In actual fact, he and other PPP politicians hesitated to use this term, preferring the Islamic phrase *amar makruf nahi mungkar*, to advocate what is reputable and to refrain from what is disreputable. To complicate matters further, on 4 December Abdurrahman Wahid indicated that three other ministers might be next to resign or be asked to resign. Rumours tossed about the names of Bomer Pasaribu, Yusuf Kalla, and State Secretary Ali Rahman, a former HMI leader, who was under suspicion of corruption committed when he was deputy chairman of the National Planning Bureau.

Such hints cast a cloud over the relationship between Abdurrahman Wahid and Golkar and the parties which made up the Central Axis. Abdurrahman Wahid, it was reported, was not happy with the ministers from PAN and Golkar, and was scheming to use accusations of KKN as a pretext to get rid of a number of cabinet ministers whom he had been forced to take on board in the wake of the negotiations in October about the composition of his cabinet. Golkar leaders were not pleased with the series of rumours, which each time bandied the names of Bomer and Kalla about. Some threatened that they thought Golkar should become an opposition party and should withdraw its ministers from the cabinet. Though Hamzah Haz's replacement, Basri Hasanuddin, a former rector of Hasanuddin University in Makassar, came from PAN and not from PPP, this choice did nothing to squash speculations that Abdurrahman Wahid had aired such unspecified predictions about ministers who might have to go to prepare the ground for decreasing the role of the Central Axis and of Golkar in his cabinet. Commenting on such views, Amien Rais stated that if there was indeed a secret agenda to undermine the interests of the Central Axis, the latter would hit back – yet another indication that positions were hardening. At the end of December, PBB joined

---

5   Why Hamzah Haz had wanted to resign was a source of much speculation. One reason mentioned was disagreement with Abdurrahman Wahid's Israel policy. Another was that Hamzah Haz was disappointed that his party had received fewer ministerial seats than PKB. According to yet another rumour, Hamzah Haz wanted to preserve unity in PPP, and might again take up his position as a deputy chairman of parliament which he had vacated after becoming a cabinet minister. To replace him as deputy chairman of parliament, there were two main PPP candidates, one, Ali Marwan Hanan, from Muslimin Indonesia and the other, Tosari Widjaja, from NU. In the end Hamzah Haz also resigned as deputy chairman of parliament. His seat was taken by Tosari Widjaja. It was also reported that Abdurrahman Wahid had asked Alwi Shihab to try to convince Hamzah Haz not to resign.

the critics. Its members of parliament accused the Abdurrahman Wahid administration of showing a tendency to deviate from the Broad Outlines of State Policy. The convening of an extraordinary session of the People's Congress was not ruled out.

Disappointment with the performance of the cabinet had set in. The cabinet was accused of not forming a unity, of being riddled with internal strife, and, according to some observers, of having too many unprofessional ministers who were incapable of performing their tasks properly and who lacked leadership qualities. Other critics warned that the administration was too much of a one-man-show by Abdurrahman Wahid, and that he tended to overshadow Megawati. Even ministers expressed their disappointment, complaining about the constraints they were experiencing. One of them was Hasballah Saad, who criticized the lack of resolve to end the violence in the Moluccas. Another was Ryaas Rasyid, who complained about the lack of co-operation by other cabinet members and had already threatened to resign in early December if no substance was given to the goal of regional autonomy.[6] Economic performance also came in for attack. Though some claimed to see beginnings of an economic recovery, others observed that other countries in Southeast Asia were doing much better, using this as an instrument to question Kwik Kian Gie's performance and his ability as coordinating minister to have the ministers in the economic and financial sectors work as a team. The latter's relationship with Sofyan Wanandi deteriorated over time. The animosity between the two men and the mutual accusations vented took such a form that in March parliament asked Abdurrahman Wahid to take measures. In March Kwik Kian Gie accused 'black entrepreneurs' of trying to topple him.

A point at issue within the cabinet was that of the definition of competence. One of the early victims was Ali Rahman, of whom it was reported that he was unhappy because the once powerful position of State Secretary had been eroded. Some of the former tasks of the State Secretary such as supervision of letters for and from the president and the drafting of presidential decrees, had been taken over by the Presidential Secretary, Ms Ratih Hardjono, appointed shortly after Abdurrahman Wahid's election, and by the Ministry of Law and Legislation. An additional factor at play was who were to hold the key posts. It was reported Ali Rahman wanted to fill the State Secretariat with former HMI members, which clashed with Abdurrah-

---

[6]   Ryaas Rasyid, the driving force behind the autonomy legislation tendered his resignation as Minister without Portfolio of State Administrative Reform in January 2001. Rumours that he would do so had been circulating for weeks. He was said to be dissatisfied with Abdurrahman Wahid's type of leadership and interference, which made it impossible to develop a sound policy. When Ryaas Rasyid made his intention to resign public, he drew especial attention to the delegation of authority to the regional administrations, which according to him had been implemented without proper preparations.

man Wahid's intention to have the inner circle made up of people 'close' to him, such as Ms Ratih Hardjono. That the latter indeed was Abdurrahman Wahid's wish became the more clear when in early January Marsilam Simanjuntak and Bondan Gunawan, both members of Forum Demokrasi, were appointed respectively as Cabinet Secretary and Secretary of Government Supervision.[7]

Another conflict was between the Minister without Portfolio of Capital Investment and Development of State Enterprises, Laksamana Sukardi, of PDI-P and Bambang Sudibyo of PAN, who were disputing with one another about control over the state-owned banks. Initially, on 22 December, Abdurrahman Wahid had assigned supervision to Laksamana Sukardi. Five days later he revoked this decree, and made decision making concerning the state-owned banks dependent on the agreement of the Minister of Finance. This was followed by yet another decree by which Sukardi's authority was limited to matters outside the financial sector. A similar transfer of control befell the Directorate General of Forestry. On 22 December, the directorate general was taken away from the Ministry of Forestry and Plantations, headed by Nur Mahmudi Ismail of Partai Keadilan, and placed under the Ministry of Agriculture of Mohammad Prakosa from PDI-P. Five days later the transfer was cancelled. Both cases were presented as examples that Abdurrahman Wahid and his inner core of secretaries were unable to outline a clear and persistent policy.

By extension, the appointment and replacement of managers of state companies and a number of the most senior civil servants was interpreted in terms of inter-party competition and a politicization of the bureaucracy. Reports about strife over positions and competence fuelled the suspicion that it was party politics that counted and that ministers tried to secure money-spinners to serve the interests of the parties to which they owed their allegiance and that this took preference over the national interest. Three ministers were especially prone to such suspicions: Bambang Sudibyo, Nur Mahmudi Ismail, and Laksamana Sukardi. In February Megawati sent them a letter questioning their appointment policy.

One of those who lost their job was Glenn Yusuf, who was replaced by

---

7   While in London, at the end of January Abdurrahman Wahid stated that Ali Rahman had resigned from the cabinet at his own request. Other stories claimed that Abdurrahman Wahid, who had made no secret of it that he wanted the State Secretariat to function only as a sort of archive, had asked him to go. In Jakarta Ali Rahman denied that he had tendered his resignation. In the middle of the following month Ali Rahman did resign. The stated reason was that he had completed his task of reorganizing the State Secretariat. He was said to have informed Abdurrahman Wahid of this at the end of January. Ali Rahman's function was taken over by Bondan Gunawan. In an interview with *Forum Keadilan* (27-2-2000:29) the latter maintained that Ali Rahman had tendered his resignation at the end of January.

Cacuk Sudarijanto (a chairman of Adi Sasono's Partai Daulat Rakyat) in January. His forced departure had been a subject of rumours since November, when it was reported that one of the persons who wanted him to go was Amien Rais. Apart from stating that the replacement had been planned long in advance and that neither he nor Amien Rais had proposed it, Bambang Sudibyo initially refused to go into the reasons for the decision. All he said was that Cacuk's appointment was a decision by the president. Nevertheless, when Cacuk Sudarijanto was installed Bambang Sudibyo said – and these words reaped a wave of protests – that the senior civil servants were political figures and that it was only natural that political considerations would influence their selection.

Accusations about the politicization of the bureaucracy were part of the renewed rivalry between political parties. By January mutual recriminations flew thick and fast. One major reason for this was the renewed carnage in the Moluccas. Abdurrahman Wahid did not take kindly to Muslim protests about the lack of resolve on the part of the government to end the killings and the calls for a holy war, protests in which people like KH Abdul Qadir Djaelani and Ahmad Soemargono played a prominent role. An early bone of contention was Aksi Sejuta Umat, Action of a Million Muslims, organized on 7 January, the last day of the fasting month, at the National Monument in Jakarta. The crowd had been addressed by Amien Rais, Hamzah Haz, and other Central Axis politicians. All called for quick decisive action by Abdurrahman Wahid. Hamzah Haz called for reconsideration of support for the government if Abdurrahman Wahid failed to end the violence in the Moluccas. Amien Rais urged Abdurrahman Wahid and the Armed Forces to solve the Moluccan crisis within the shortest possible span of time, in one or two weeks to be precise.

The meeting, and Amien Rais's words, were interpreted by Abdurrahman Wahid as a kind of ultimatum. He called the protest and the calls for a holy war a failed attempt to muster a show of force to bring his government down. Abdurrahman Wahid made matters still worse by belittling the demonstration, calling it small and insignificant because there had been fewer than twenty thousand people present and not the one million its organizers claimed. He dismissed such a number of demonstrators as a mere trifle, adding that PDI-P formed the real majority. For his critics, Abdurrahman Wahid's reaction formed one of the indications that the president had difficulty coping with criticism – much more, it was occasionally pointed out, than his predecessor Habibie, who had had to face much harsher and far more frequent attacks.

Central Axis politicians called Abdurrahman Wahid's reaction too emotional and denied that they had any intention of toppling him. Amien Rais reiterated his support for the government. Hamzah Haz pointed out that the meeting was no more that a warning to a good friend to remind him that the Ambon problem should be resolved as quickly as possible. Not all Muslim reactions were that moderate. *Media Dakwah*, with links to PBB and KISDI, accused Abdurrahman Wahid of siding with the Christians, mentioning his attending Christian celebrations as an example (*The Jakarta Post*, 15-2-2000). Hammas identified Abdurrahman Wahid as a source of conflict and called him a person under whose presidency Islam would never gain its rightful place in society. Threatening demonstrations by hard-line Muslims, Hammas called for Abdurrahman Wahid's resignation, a job as columnist or intellectual would be more fitting for him (*Bangkit*, 21-2-2000:8). The new general chairman of NU, KH Hasyim Muzadi, came to Abdurrahman Wahid's support, begging the Central Axis not to mobilize mass support. Matori Abdul Djalil was even sharper in his criticism of Amien Rais, calling him a 'sponsor' of mass mobilization, and arguing that, morally speaking, Amien Rais was a 'provocateur'. At the end of January the organizer of the meeting, Al Chaidar, was questioned by the police. At a speech during the protest meeting, he had suggested an Islamic state as the remedy for the violence in Indonesia.

An unnamed third party was blamed for the political excitement. Tosari Widjaja of PPP and Ahmad Soemargono, who had become chairman of PBB representatives in parliament, accused *pembisik*, whisperers, who had the ear of the president and who wanted to drive a wedge between Abdurrahman Wahid and politicians of the Central Axis and to create friction between Abdurrahman Wahid and Amien Rais by providing the president with wrong information about the intentions behind the mass meeting. People who acted in this way, tricking the president into making wrong moves, were political criminals, another PBB politician, Hartono Mardjono, said. After Abdurrahman Wahid had made a number of other controversial statements, the 'whisperers' providing the president with disinformation became a real political issue in February; the more so as Abdurrahman, with his failing eyesight, was dependent on oral information. His daughter, Zanuba Arifah (Yenny), who accompanied him and who was one of the persons who supported him when he had to walk, was accused of being one of the whisperers. Ratih, detested by some NU and PKB leaders for limiting access to the president, was supposed to be another one. Having lived in Australia as a *Kompas* correspondent for some years, she was even accused of being an Australian spy. Parliament took up the matter. One of its committees questioned persons like Bondan Gunawan, Marsilam Simanjuntak, Ratih Hardjono, and the president's military secretary, Air Force Major-General Budhy Santoso, about the whisperers and about the role of Zanuba Arifah.[8]

---

8   Ratih resigned at the end of March. Bondan Gunawan, who announced the news, said that Abdurrahman Wahid had accepted her resignation to enable her to concentrate on her wedding

The antagonisms and mutual suspicions prevalent before the presidential election had resurfaced. Abdurrahman Wahid saw the Action of a Million Muslims as an attempt to topple him; Harjanto Taslam of PDI-P argued that behind the criticism of Megawati was 'a certain party' which wanted to replace her with one of its own; and PDI-P supporters staged a demonstration at the congress building protesting about Amien Rais's alleged intention to bring the government down. Joining in, PAN filed a slander case against *Demokrat* and its general manager, Megawati's husband, Taufik Kiemas, for depicting Amien Rais on its cover as a political vampire.

Tension was also developing between Abdurrahman Wahid and the military. Apart from feelings of frustration about their changing role since Soeharto's fall and the limits set to their participation in politics and in the economy, army officers were weary of the bashing of the army and not overjoyed by the spectacle of their most senior members being charged with having committed crimes against humanity and, for the first time, also being forced to give a proper account of their actions. Past and present commanders were in for a rough time, much more so than during Habibie's presidency. In November and December they were summoned to hearings about the violations of human rights in Aceh and East Timor. On 6 December a deputy chairman of parliament also announced the intention of hearing Wiranto and others about the ongoing violence in Ambon.

The hearings related to East Timor were an immediate threat to the position of the top brass of the army. These did not take place before a commission of parliament but before Komisi Penyelidik Pelanggaran Hak Asasi Manusia Timtim (KPP HAM Timtim), Commission of Inquiry into Human Rights Violations in East Timor. Chairman of the commission, which had been constituted by the National Committee for Human Rights in September when Habibie was still president, was Albert Hasibuan. In an interim report published in early December, the committee revealed that it had come across indications that the army had been involved in the planning and committing of the violence following the referendum in East Timor. A similar conclusion had been reached by a United Nations Commission of Inquiry on East Timor, sent to East Timor by the UN High Commissioner for Human Rights, Mary Robinson.

The charges brought by KPP HAM Timtim enraged part of the military. Among the outraged officers was the commander of Kostrad, Lieutenant-General Djaja Suparman. He warned that the army might react angrily if its generals were put on trial. Wiranto himself claimed that the charges were not based on balanced research, and had been made public without hearing the version of military officers, senior civil servants, and advocates of integra-

---

plans. The marriage was scheduled for November.

tion. Other officers criticized the lack of objectivity, vituperating against a 'trial by the press'. Part of the Muslim press, including *Republika*, joined in the attack, wondering why only Muslim generals were being questioned. Support for the beleaguered army and police officers also came from former pro-integration people. Just before the Commission of Inquiry was to announce its verdict, one hundred of them, stressing their patriotic feelings by a prominent display of the colours red and white in their choice of costume, staged a protest in front of the office of the National Committee for Human Rights. They proclaimed that it was they who had killed and burned down buildings and that the army and police had not been involved.

Officers suspected of being responsible for the carnage in East Timor could count on legal advice provided by a team of lawyers, headed by Adnan Buyung Nasution and the former Minister of Justice, Muladi, called Tim Advokasi HAM Perwira TNI (TAHT), Human Rights Team of Lawyers of the Officers of the Armed Forces. These lawyers, too, criticized the accusations made by the Commission of Inquiry as premature and spoke of efforts to discredit the officers concerned and statements made for international consumption. To counter the charges of the Commission of Inquiry, Adnan Buyung Nasution in a statement to the press emphasized that the research carried out by his own team of lawyers had shown that the violence had been committed by local residents who had been outraged by the fact that the referendum had been organized in what they considered an unfair way. He stressed that what had happened in September formed the climax of internal strife which had started at the time of the integration of East Timor into Indonesia in 1975. Referring to the houses set on fire, Adnan Buyung Nasution said that this had been done by immigrants who had been residents in East Timor for years and had been loath to see their property taken over by others. Another conclusion he presented was that the refugees in West Timor had not been forced to flee. The team had come to these conclusions after a three-day visit to West Timor. Interfet, International Forces in East Timor, had refused its members entrance to East Timor. Later that month Adnan Buyung Nasution hinted at a conspiracy between KPP HAM Timtim, pro-independence groups, and UNTAET, the United Nations Transitional Administration in East Timor. Another of the lawyers attacked the UN report for its inherent weaknesses.

Sessions of the Commission of Inquiry were held behind closed doors, as the army officers had insisted that they should. The officers and civil servants called generally denied any knowledge about the activities of the militias. Instead, they talked about the Pam Swakarsa established by the local authorities to give the people a means to protect themselves. Later, in an interview with *The Straits Times*, Wiranto also stressed that what he referred to as 'the so-called militia' already existed long before he became Commander of the

Armed Forces. He said that such groups had been established not only in East Timor but all over the country since the late 1970s to 'protect remote villages against insurgencies' (*The Straits Times*, 8-2-2000).

In a sense, KPP HAM Timtim acted upon Adnan Buyung Nasution's words. One of its recommendations, made public at the end of January, was that the inquiry should be extended to the violations of human rights committed in East Timor since 1975. The implication was that if the suggestion was followed, an investigation should be launched into the actions of a host of other officers, including not only Prabowo, but also figures like Benny Moerdani and Theo Syafei; a fact which was welcomed in Islamic quarters.

The hearings by parliament and by the East Timor Commission and the plans to estabish a special tribunal to try crimes committed by the military in Aceh created the impression that Abdurrahman Wahid had abandoned the army top, or as a heading of *The Jakarta Post* read in December: 'Gus Dur refuses to aid Wiranto' (*The Jakarta Post*, 14-12-1999). Though initially Abdurrahman Wahid persisted in stating that the accusation that Wiranto was guilty of violation of human rights in East Timor was only the opinion of KPP HAM and not of a court and that he would not put Wiranto on the non-active list, he did little to protect Wiranto and the other generals, not even at the time the interim report was published. The only assurance Abdurrahman Wahid gave was that he would not allow Indonesian officers to be tried by an international court. This statement was as much inspired by nationalist feelings as by anything else. The president considered an international tribunal a violation of Indonesia's sovereignty. Though it was hoped that for their own domestic reasons Russia and China would never agree to an international East Timor tribunal, a diplomatic offensive was undertaken to prevent such an affront. In December, speaking before a committee of parliament, Alwi Shihab mentioned efforts to forestall any attempt to make Indonesian generals stand trial before an international tribunal for war crimes as an additional reason why Indonesia needed the 'Jewish lobby'. The lobby could help. A situation had to be avoided in which Indonesia was put into the same class as nations like Rwanda, Kosovo, and Bosnia. To underline his argument, Alwi Shihab pointed out that the American Congress was controlled by Jews and that Madeleine Albright had Jewish blood. More support for the generals than Abdurrahman Wahid was prepared to offer was seen to come from Habibie. The initial reason for reaching this conclusion was that the former president allowed his office in The Habibie Center to be used by Wiranto and Zacky Anwar Makarim (heard in his capacity as advisor for security to the Task Force to Implement the East Timor Referendum) to meet their legal advisors in the middle of December.[9]

[9]   The Habibie Center was presented as a 'think tank'. The head of its Institute for Democracy

One of the consequences of discontent in military circles generated by the hearings and by differences of opinion on how to deal with the violence in the country was that in the course of December persistent reports and speculations about a rift between Abdurrahman Wahid and Wiranto began to go the rounds. At the end of the year there was talk of plans for a military coup d'état for the first time, a rumour at once dismissed by Sudrajat as yet another attempt to corner the Armed Forces. Nevertheless, the rumours were so persistent that on 14 January the American ambassador to the United Nations, Richard Holbrooke, warned the Indonesian army not to attempt such a move. Alternative reports insisted that Abdurrahman Wahid contemplated getting rid of Wiranto through a cabinet reshuffle, using violations of human rights as an excuse. In these circumstances a brief visit to Jakarta by Prabowo, in itself already a striking event, in the first week of January to see his father, who was seriously ill, was loaded with additional significance. With the newspapers full of stories about the conflict between Abdurrahman Wahid and Wiranto and about a rift in the Armed Forces, speculations about the purpose of the visit had a field day. It was reported that Prabowo had met Tyasno Sudarto and the commander of Kostrad, Djaja Suparman, to discuss the problems in the Armed Forces. Sudrajat denied that such a meeting had taken place. It was even said that, while in Jakarta, Prabowo would discuss his imminent appointment as military advisor to the president.[10] Speculations about Abdurrahman Wahid turning to Prabowo continued when the president visited Kopassus on 21 January. Among the persons Prabowo met in Jakarta was Soeharto.

Speculations about a struggle for power between Wiranto and Abdurrahman Wahid grew in strength when, during a meeting with editors-in-chief on 13 January, Abdurrahman Wahid suddenly announced the replacement of Sudrajat as spokesman for the Armed Forces. The announcement came as a shock. Abdurrahman Wahid, who had taken the initiative to replace Sudrajat, had dealt an extra blow to the army's prestige by not leaving it to officers of the Armed Forces to make the news public. It was reported that more such 'interventions' were pending. By enforcing his will upon the army and reportedly asking the commander of the Armed Forces, Widodo, to effectuate still more changes, Abdurrahman Wahid had acted in

---

and Human Rights was Muladi. Among the board members of the center were Dewi Fortuna Anwar and Jimly Asshiddiqie. Another person involved in the centre was Marwah Daud Ibrahim.

10   Prabowo returned to Indonesia in May, announcing that he had returned for good. For the first time, he himself (and not his friends or relatives as in previous years) called a press conference. His main reason was to refute an accusation made by Abdurrahman Wahid that Prabowo had been involved in the killing of over one hundred people during military operations in Iran Jaya.

a way which at least came close to what a few months before, on the eve of the session of the People's Congress, Wiranto had censured as an extreme tendency which might lead to a permanent conflict between civilians and the military, constituting too great an interference in the internal management of the Armed Forces by civilians. It seems that Sudrajat had displeased the president with his statements that the Armed Forces were in favour of declaring a military emergency in Aceh and by a remark in which he stressed that Abdurrahman Wahid did not hold the formal rank of Supreme Commander of the Armed Forces, a title which had adorned both Soekarno and Soeharto.[11]

Although in voicing his opinions about Aceh Sudrajat may have gone further than Wiranto may have chosen to do, he was still considered a Wiranto officer. Consequently people began to speculate about a 'de-Wiranto-ization'.[12] Wiranto's position seemed to become even more precarious at the end of the month when rumours that Wiranto (who in April was to turn 53 and was still two years from retirement) and the other three active military officers in the cabinet would have to take early retirement from the military service as of 31 March were confirmed. It might not have been all Abdurrahman Wahid's doing. One of the ministers concerned, Susilo Bambang Yudhoyono, said that Widodo had told him that this had been his suggestion.

The East Timor investigation developed into a fully fledged confrontation between Abdurrahman Wahid and Wiranto when, a few days later, on 31 January, the Commission of Inquiry singled out Wiranto as one of the persons responsible for the carnage in East Timor, alleging he had taken no measures to prevent or suppress it.[13] In view of this, the commission asked the attorney-general to start an investigation into the role of Wiranto and 31 army and police officers, civilian administrators, and leaders of the militias. Among the other officers implicated by the Commission was Zacky Anwar

---

[11]   How to interpret the constitutional powers of the president over the Armed Forces and the term Supreme Commander remained a matter of debate. In February Widodo said these powers did not extend to the internal management of the Armed Forces.

[12]   Sudrajat was replaced by Air Force Major-General Graito Usodo. Abdurrahman Wahid also disclosed that Air Force Major-General Yan Santoso would become the new head of BAIS, a position which had been vacant since Tyasno Sudarto had been appointed Chief of Staff of the Army.

[13]   It was reported that at that moment a human rights tribunal bill was being drafted with a retroactive clause which made it possible to try people who by omission had allowed human rights violations to take place. It was to replace a special Government Regulation in Lieu of a Law for the establishment of a human rights court. The latter, dating from the Habibie period, had been issued especially with the aim of dealing with what had happened in East Timor after the referendum. In March parliament refused to turn the special government regulation into an Act. During the debate on the government regulation, Golkar members of parliament suggested the establishment of a 'Lembaga Amnesia', an Amnesia Body, which had the right to grant pardons (*Suara Pembaruan*, 13-3-2000).

Makarim. Not featuring was Syafrie Syamsuddin. After appearing before KPP HAM Timtim on 29 December, he said he was shocked by the suggestion that he had been in Dili on 6 September and had been spotted among the people who had attacked the house of Bishop Belo. He demanded a rectification, explaining that he had been in Jakarta on that day. He also said that there had been nothing sinister about his visit to East Timor on 27 August. He had gone to the province as a staff member of the Commander of the Armed Forces, assigned the task of supervising the officers stationed in East Timor.

The findings of the Commission of Inquiry were made public at a moment when Abdurrahman Wahid was on his tour of Europe, of which one of the aims was probably to prevent the establishment of an international tribunal. The conclusions of the committee and Abdurrahman Wahid's relationship with the army put a special stamp on the president's trip. Most of the comments made by Abdurrahman Wahid while abroad concerned Wiranto and how the army would react when he was forced to step down. In London Abdurrahman Wahid, who considered a domestic trial one of the best arguments to prevent the calling into being of an international tribunal, immediately called for Wiranto to resign. Wiranto refused to comply. He said he wanted to speak to Abdurrahman Wahid first, after the president had returned from abroad. Abdurrahman Wahid repeated a number of times that Wiranto had to go, on one occasion stating that he would pardon Wiranto if found guilty, and adding that otherwise he had no choice but to suspend Wiranto. He even phoned Juwono Sudarsono from Europe to have him convey the message to Wiranto. Juwono Sudarsono complied, but that was all he did. He and Wiranto agreed that it was best to await the return of the president before taking a decision. The stand-off between Abdurrahman Wahid and Wiranto was a reason for both Akbar Tanjung and Amien Rais to ask the president again to be more prudent in his public statements. It also intensified the speculations about a military coup d'état. On the eve of his departure to Europe, Abdurrahman Wahid had already tried to dismiss the rumours of a coup d'état by talking about officers who were cowards and would never dare try to bring him down. To underline that he was a loyal officer, Wiranto stressed that at two moments he could have committed a coup d'état and had not done so: in the days before Soeharto's resignation, and at the time of the extraordinary session of the People's Congress in November 1998 (*The Straits Times*, 8-2-2000). Nevertheless some Indonesians again concluded that it was safer to await developments abroad, though the number of people leaving Indonesia was far smaller than on previous occasions when tension had mounted.

One of the persons who supported Abdurrahman Wahid in urging that Wiranto step down was Tyasno Sudarto. Another who clearly came out on the side of Abdurrahman Wahid was Major-General Agus Wirahadikusumah, military commander of South Sulawesi. Agus Wirahadikusumah – or AWK, as people often called him –, a nephew of the former vice-president, Umar Wirahadikusumah, had presented himself at least since December as a staunch advocate of the *reformasi* ideals and the adjustments these demanded from the Armed Forces. He called for an end to the dual function of the Armed Forces and for the disbanding of the provincial and other territorial commands, which formed a vital instrument of the army in having its influence felt down to the village level. Maybe an even greater sin in the eyes of fellow officers was that Agus Wirahadikusumah supported the investigation by the National Committee for Human Rights, publicly disagreeing with those generals, often his superiors in rank, who called the investigations started into the abuses of human rights in East Timor and Aceh a humiliation of the Armed Forces. He also had made no secret of his opinion that Wiranto should resign, even stating that there was no need for Abdurrahman Wahid to be afraid of Wiranto because the latter's influence within the Armed Forces had waned.

Wiranto did not bend, and attended a meeting of the cabinet as if nothing out of the ordinary was happening. He refuted all charges, stressed the efforts he personally had made to maintain peace in East Timor just prior to the referendum, and argued that in Indonesia resigning was often seen as an admission of guilt. His lawyers disqualified the 4,000-page thick report and the mention in it of names as having been motivated by political considerations. They visited the chairman of the National Committee for Human Rights to protest, and accused Marzuki Darusman of siding with the National Committee for Human Rights.

Abdurrahman Wahid returned to Jakarta on Sunday 13 February at one o'clock in the morning.[14] Banser units were put on the alert to counter any demonstrations against him. No such demonstrations took place. At the airport the president got the customary welcome. Assembled to greet him were Megawati, Wiranto, and other ministers and dignitaries. After Abdurrahman Wahid had talked with Wiranto, Megawati, Marzuki Darusman, and others later in the morning it was announced around noon that Wiranto would remain in office. Whether or not he had to go at a later date would depend on the results of the investigation by the attorney-general. Twelve hours later in the evening of the same day it was announced that Wiranto had been put on non-active.[15] The Minister of Internal Affairs, Surjadi Soedirdja, mention-

---

[14]   In South Korea Abdurrahman Wahid had made arrangements for a new agreement with KIA Motors to produce an Indonesian national car. Abdurrahman Wahid said that the new car would not be called Timor. This project had failed. Nevertheless KIA's most likely partner was the ailing TPN, of which it was expected that the government was to become the major or only shareholder after the restructuring of the former Timor producer's debt.
[15]   In April it was reported by *The Straits Times* (19-4-2000) that Juwono Sudarsono had said

ed as early as December as the most likely candidate to replace Wiranto, was appointed Interim Coordinating Minister of Political Affairs and Security.

Wiranto was only notified by fax in the morning. After he had taken his decision, Abdurrahman Wahid had tried to contact him by phone to inform him personally of the decision, but Wiranto had been fast asleep and his adjutant had not dared to awake him. Abdurrahman Wahid said that he had planned to contact Wiranto again but that he had forgotten to do so, only remembering again shortly before he installed Wiranto's successor.[16] Ostensibly Abdurrahman Wahid had taken the decision to allow Wiranto 'to concentrate on the problems outside his ministerial post' (*Kompas*, 14-2-2000). A more important motive for him was that with Wiranto no longer holding his ministerial post, the investigation of the office of the attorney-general would proceed more smoothly and would be less open to allegations of bias. Abdurrahman Wahid said that Wiranto were found innocent, people could not say that this conclusion had been drawn because of his position as coordinating minister. What was at play here was also that in a sense Wiranto was Marzuki Darusman's superior. The office of the attorney-general fell within the domain of Coordinating Minister of Political and Security Affairs.

Apart from this, Wiranto was identified by Marzuki Darusman as the person in the cabinet who obstructed investigations by the public attorney's office. Specifically, he pointed at Wiranto's recent opposition to a decree to establish a national commission to investigate KKN by Soeharto and his family, a decree, he said, which was supported by Abdurrahman Wahid and Megawati (*Far Eastern Economic Review*, 30-3-2000:27). Indeed, with Wiranto out of the way, Marzuki Darusman seemed to take a tougher stance. Bob Hasan was arrested in connection with the financial losses suffered by the state due to the activities of the aerial photograph company, Mapindo

---

that Wiranto had been retired since 31 March. Abdurrahman Wahid had signed the notice of retirement. Juwono Sudarsono did not preclude the possibility that Wiranto had not received the notice. In the middle of May, after he had been interrogated as a witness about the East Timor massacre, Wiranto formally resigned from the government. When in September 2000 the office of the attorney-general finally published the names of the people suspected of having played a leading role in the violence in East Timor in 1999, Wiranto's name was not on the list. Neither was that of Zacky Anwar Makarim.

16   *Tajuk* (17-2-2000:73) and *Forum Keadilan* (27-2-2000) both mention the same reasons from Abdurrahman Wahid for changing his mind. One was that information had reached him that Wiranto had turned to Habibie and that the latter had urged him to stand firm, promising him his full support. A second reason mentioned in the two weeklies was information about *silat* fighters from Banten preparing for a demonstration in case Wiranto was sacked. This information came on top of untrue reports – disclosed by Abdurrahman Wahid in Holland on 2 February – about a meeting of a number of generals in Jalan Lautze in Jakarta. Other reasons mentioned were that Marzuki Darusman had threatened to resign, pressure exerted by the United States, and the fact that acting upon the army was one of the ways to improve Indonesia's image abroad in an effort to secure foreign aid.

Parama, at the end of March. It was, he confessed to journalists, not a nice experience. The public had to get used to such new circumstances as well. In May the Minister of Forestry and Plantations, Nur Mahmudi Ismail, asked his fellow countrymen to check the whereabouts of Bob Hasan and to ensure that he was still in prison. He said that experience had shown (and had been brought home by Eddy Tansil's escape) that important persons could leave prinson, in particular at night. Soon Bob Hasan was also to be questioned about the money he had received from Soeharto's foundations, said to amount to Rp 450 billion.

Abdurrahman Wahid had killed two birds with one stone. He had secured his hold over the army and had – at least for the moment – averted an international tribunal. His action reaped the praise of Kofi Annan, who a few days later visited Indonesia. Kofi Annan indicated that with a credible trial in Indonesia there would be no need to form an international tribunal. He warned that the Security Council was to monitor how matters developed.

After being suspended, Wiranto started what was considered to be a rather belated public relations campaign. He appeared on radio talk shows and was interviewed on TV. For the first time, Wiranto publicly displayed his dislike of Agus Wirahadikusumah. He referred to a regional military commander who should concentrate on the many problems he faced in his region but raised matters of national politics which were the preserve of the Commander of the Armed Forces and the Chief of Staff of the Army. Wiranto stressed that a two-star general should not make comments about a four-star general. Such behaviour did not suit an army officer. Agus Wirahadikusumah was called to account by his superiors but did get his reward. He had earned himself the support of Abdurrahman Wahid, who, it was said, had been much impressed by the volume *Indonesia baru dan tantangan TNI* (The new Indonesia and the challenges of the Armed Forces) edited by him. Before the month was over, during a major reshuffle of the Armed Forces Agus Wirahadikusumah was appointed to the prestigious and important position of Commander of Kostrad. He got his new command on the recommendation of Abdurrahman Wahid, who wanted him to be stationed in Jakarta. His predecessor, Djaja Suparman, was far from happy with the way the transfer was effected. He had learned about it from the press and complained that proper procedures had not been followed. In March one of the ordinary committees of parliament and Juwono Sudarsono agreed that the president had a say in the appointments of the Commander of the Armed Forces, the chiefs of staff, and the chief of police.

Wiranto was not the only one who lost his job. Within days, Abdurrahman in one large move got rid of presidential advisors who had been appointed by Habibie. Businessmen like Marimutu Sinivasan, James Tjahja Riady, and Hashim Djojohadikusumo who had served as special envoys also had to go, while Parni Hadi was sacked as editor-in-chief and general manager of the press agency Antara.[17] Also dissolved were a number of institutions through which the government and the army in the past had monitored political life, using these when deemed necessary to intervene. One was DPKSH, Council for Maintaining Security and the Legal System, whose establishment had created such an uproar in December 1998. Another was the Badan Koordinasi Bantuan Pemantapan Stabilitas Nasional (Bakorstanas), Coordination Body for National Stability, the successor of Kopkamtib. The department of social and political affairs of the Ministry of Internal Affairs was also abolished, as was the 'litsus', the special screening, of civil servants.

One of the consequences of the East Timor investigation by the National Committee for Human Rights was that once again the military violence committed during the New Order was brought into the limelight of public attention. In February various other investigations were demanded or proposed. A number of organizations called for a KPP, a Commission of Inquiry, to be established by the National Committee for Human Rights, to investigate Tanjung Priok. As in the past, they vented their disappointment over the fact that the committee appeared slow in responding. Others asked for a Commission of Inquiry into the May 1998 riots and the Semanggi I and II incidents. People who had been abducted wanted Abdurrahman Wahid to allow Prabowo to return to Indonesia to have him reveal what he knew about the affair. Venturing that Prabowo might have been the victim of a political plot, they suggested that he should be given special protection. On 7 March, the National Committee for Human Rights finally decided to constitute a Commission of Inquiry into Tanjung Priok.

In a number of other cases the government did act. On the instruction of Abdurrahman Wahid, the Minister of Labour, Bomer Pasaribu, promised a new investigation into the murder of Marsinah. It seems that a factor in the decision to start a fresh inquiry was the continuous pressure by ILO to bring the murderers to justice and a planned trip by Abdurrahman Wahid to Geneva where he would address an ILO convention. The police reopened its investigation into the attack on the PDI-P office in July 1996. Among the persons declared suspects were Soerjadi and Buttu R. Hutapea. Buttu Hutapea was arrested on 7 March, Soerjadi on 11 April. A third person arrested was Yorrys Raweyai. He was suspected of having ordered members of Pemuda Pancasila to take part in the attack on the PDI-P building. The three were released again at the end of May. Perceiving a connection with the dismissal of Wiranto, the new investigation into the assault on the PDI building was linked by some to a scheme by Abdurrahman Wahid to get at a number of

17   Parni Hadi had been editor-in-chief of Antara since 1992. In June 1999 he was also appointed its general manager.

powerful New Order generals.[18] The first in line was supposed to be Feisal Tanjung, whose name was now frequently mentioned in the press as being one of the main plotters of the assault on the PDI office. That this suspicion arose was also occasioned by yet another disputed remark by Abdurrahman Wahid. During his visit to the Vatican, he said that Wiranto had saved his life by informing him that Feisal Tanjung had ordered him and Megawati to be eliminated (in the Indonesian media the word *menghabisi* 'finish off', was frequently used) a word which some pointed out need not necessarily be interpreted in the physical sense.[19] A few days later, in India, Abdurrahman Wahid added that it was Feisal Tanjung (with others, on Soeharto's instructions) who had ordered the attack on the PDI office, and that his men also had played a role in the efforts in 1994 to prevent his re-election as general chairman of the NU. It was one of the many speculations of those days which disappeared as quickly as they came up. Nevertheless, all these new investigations implied that in the weeks to come, important New Order generals had to account for their deeds. Syarwan Hamid, Susilo Bambang Yudhoyono, Hartono, and Sutiyoso were questioned by the police in relation to the attack on the PDI office. Moerdani and Try Sutrisno had to appear before the committee investigating the Tanjung Priok massacre.[20]

At the time of Wiranto's dismissal at the end of February, public quiet had apparently returned to the streets of Jakarta. Barbed wire roadblocks had disappeared from sight at the major roads and near business and shopping centres, and the anti-riot troops patrolling the city in great numbers in the previous months had been withdrawn. What remained were persistent rumours – encouraged by remarks by Abdurrahman Wahid to this effect – about effort to topple the government, complete with forecasts of mass demonstrations and unrest in the streets of Jakarta and other cities. Islamic groups supporting Habibie and loyal followers of Wiranto were mentioned. Feisal Tanjung's name also came up in this respect.

In April a case before a combined military civilian court was started in Banda Aceh against 25 soldiers accused of having played a role in the killing of Tengku Bantaqiyah and his community in Beutong Ateuh in West Aceh in July 1999. Not tried was an intelligence officer, Lieutenant-Colonel Sudjono,

---

[18] Megawati opened the Hendropriyono Law Office (Helo) on 29 October 2000. Hendropriyono, now also one of the army officers who had become a member of PDI-P, said that Helo was meant especially to defend members of the army and police.

[19] To Prabowo's friends this was yet another example of a 'false whisper' by Wiranto, just as he had convinced Habibie in May 1998 that Prabowo tried to commit a coup d'état.

[20] The team which investigated the 27 July attack on the PDI office branded eighteen army and police officers as 'suspects'. Among them were Syarwan Hamid, Sutiyoso, Zacky Anwar Makarim, and Hamami Nata. Not among the suspects was Feisal Tanjung, who when he was questioned by the team had hit a journalist who tried to take a picture of him in the stomach.

the person responsible for the raid. He had disappeared. In view of all the new investigations, this time it was the turn of people in Irian Jaya to complain that their cause was being neglected. They said that Jakarta did nothing to investigate human rights abuses in Irian Jaya or to put a halt to these.

Action was also taken against Soeharto and his family. After a third refusal by Soeharto's lawyers to have the former president be investigated at the attorney-general's office, Marzuki Darusman sent a team of five attorneys to Soeharto's house on 3 April. The visit took place after a team of doctors, on the attorney-general's order, had examined Soeharto at Cipto Mangunkusumo General Hospital. One of the team's conclusions was that Soeharto's memory was failing him; another was that he was still able to understand simple questions, but that in discussing complex matters he needed assistance, and the quality of his answers was not guaranteed. After 90 minutes, the interrogation had to be cut short on the advice of Soeharto's own doctors and doctors of Cipto Mangunkusumo General Hospital. The reason given was Soeharto's rising blood pressure and irregular heartbeat.

Two questions, posed as simply as possible, had been asked. A week later, a team of prosecutors again went to Soeharto's house. This time an ambulance stood ready. No questions could be asked at all. For medical reasons, members of the team were not allowed to speak with Soeharto. As one indication of how bad the former president's condition was, it was said that Soeharto had not been able to repeat the number 4578. He had only repeated the word eight a number of times. Soeharto was put under city arrest on 12 April, but for reasons of health did not have to report regularly to the office of the attorney-general. On the advice of his medical team, Soeharto's lawyers did not inform the former president of the decision. According to one story, too good to be true, published on 15 April in *Jawa Pos*, Soeharto had been told, and to the discomfort of his children had since remained silent. Soeharto was interrogated once more in his own home on 15 May. This time part of the questions were phrased in Javanese, or more precisely, in its most polite form, Kromo Inggil. An interpreter was needed, as four of the five prosecutors who had come to Jalan Cendana did not speak Javanese. Around the same time, and almost exactly two years after Soeharto's resignation, demonstrations staged around Jalan Cendana demanding legal action against him intensified. In response, the Indonesian government contemplated moving Soeharto to a place where demonstrations would be impossible, or at least would be less disruptive. Suggestions were a house in North Jakarta or on one of the islands north of Jakarta. In the end, it was decided to place the former president under house arrest on 29 May. According to a spokesman for the office of the attorney-general, Soeharto himself signed the notification of his new status. The public prosecution was not deterred by the obstruction of Soeharto's lawyers. A court case was prepared. On 8 August

2000 his 3,500-page dossier was presented to the court of South Jakarta. Soeharto's house arrest was changed into city arrest. A date for the trial was set. The charge was that through misuse of the funds of the foundations chaired by him, Soeharto had caused damage to the state of Rp 1.4 trillion. By that time one of the witnesses, the treasurer of the Dharmais Foundation, had already died. On the first day of the trial – 31 August – Soeharto did not turn up.

A team of Soeharto family doctors and a medical team for the public prosecution continued to argue over the question whether the former president was fit enough to appear in court. The court decided that a third, independent team of doctors should examine Soeharto. The medical examination took place on 23 September at the 'Very Very Important Person' section of Pertamina Hospital. The most obvious choice, Cipto Mangunkusumo General Hospital, where Soeharto had been examined in March by a medical team for the public prosecution, was rejected out of fear of demonstrations. It was too close to Salemba campus. The examination lasted nine hours. The team that examined Soeharto was so large that journalists lost count, reporting a medical team consisting variously of twenty-three, twenty-four, or twenty-six members. In view of its findings the judges decided that Soeharto's physical and mental health made it impossible for him to appear. The case was dismissed on 28 September. Soeharto's city arrest was lifted. The appellate court overruled the decision of the South Jakarta court and demanded that the case against the former president be reopened on 8 November. The reason it gave for this decision was that Soeharto had never been present in court. The appellate court said that in such a situation the South Jakarta court should not have taken a decision. The accused should have been present. Soeharto's lawyers filed an appeal on 17 November.

The initial decision to dismiss the case against Soeharto had come only a few days after the recently overhauled Supreme Court on 22 September had overruled the decision of the court of South Jakarta to acquit Tommy Soeharto of the charge of corruption in the Bulog land transfer case.[21] The Supreme Court concluded that the transaction had caused financial damage to the state. Tommy Soeharto was sentenced to eighteen months of imprisonment and a Rp 10 billion fine. He also had to pay a compensation of Rp 30 billion.

The only option left for Tommy, who was now described in the newspapers as 'the criminal', was to stall. Tommy turned to Abdurrahman Wahid and asked for a pardon on 3 October, thus forcing a delay in the execution of the sentence. He also secretly met Abdurrahman Wahid at least once, in Hotel Borobudur in Jakarta on 5 October. As an additional move to keep him

---

[21] Sixteen new judges had been appointed in the Supreme Court earlier in September. One of them was Muladi.

out of jail, his lawyers challenged the ruling of the Supreme Court and asked for a judicial review of its decision on 30 October.[22] Abdurrahman Wahid turned down the plea for a pardon early in November. Tommy, who had been banned from leaving the country on 7 October, was scheduled to start his term in prison that very day, 2 November. He was summoned to begin his sentence, but did not come. The first attempt having failed, the head of the public prosecution of South Jakarta, Antasari Azhar, stated that Hutomo Mandala Putra had to enter jail on 3 November after the Friday prayer. This was not to be. When he did not show up, public prosecutors accompanied by policemen of the Mobile Brigade went to Tommy's residence at Jalan Yusuf Adiwinata in the early evening. They did not find him. Tommy had left one hour before the deadline expired. It appears that no orders had been issued at that time to arrest him.

Tommy was declared a fugitive and placed on the list of wanted people. Antasari Azhar issued a new deadline: Hutomo Mandala Putra had to report at Cipinang prison on 6 November, where a cell of four by two metres in a special block in the prison awaited him. For Anton Medan this was a reason to protest. He and about a hundred former prisoners staged a demonstration at Cipinang prison, singing songs such as *Tembok Derita*, The Wall of Sorrow, and *Hidup di Bui*, Life in Prison. Tommy should not be housed in a block reserved for special cases such as 'rapists, transvestites, informants, and members of the civil defence', they said (*Media Indonesia*, 5-11-2000). He should be placed in an ordinary cell. On that Monday, hundreds of people went to Cipinang prison to watch Tommy enter it. Tommy failed to appear. Public prosecutors went to his house. His lawyers prevented an arrest by claiming that they wanted to stick to the correct legal procedure and stating that they had not yet received a notarized copy of the presidential decision refusing him a pardon. It was the moment for the newspapers to start writing about a farce (*The Jakarta Post*, 7-11-2000). Negotiations were started in Soeharto's residence about Hutomo Mandala Putra's safety while in prison. His laywer claimed that Tommy had intended to report, but that he had become too scared to do so after receiving a death threat on the morning of 6 November. The person who had threatened him was said to have been Anton Medan (*Far Eastern Economic Review*, 23-11-2000:32). Tommy feared that he might be killed in prison. He asked for special security measures and a 'special prison house' (*The Jakarta Post*, 8-11-2000). While these negotiations were being conducted, Muslims held a special prayer session in support of Tommy at the residence of Tutut.

22 On 7 November the judge of the court of South Jakarta ruled that new evidence submitted by Tommy's lawyers met the criteria and that the plea for a review could be advanced to the Supreme Court.

A new attempt to arrest Tommy was made on 8 November. Again it was to no avail. Failing to find Tommy in his own residence, the nearby houses of Soeharto, Tutut, Bambang Trihatmodjo, and Siti Hutami Endang Adiningsih were searched. Tommy had fled. Later in the month the houses of other relatives, friends, and his former lady friend, the singer Maya Olivia Rumantir, were also searched. Among these were the houses of Sudwikatmono, Probosutedjo, Bustanil Arifin, and Setiawan Djody. Naturally Tommy's escape was headline news for weeks. One newspaper, the *Jawa Pos*, each day put a small picture of Tommy on the front page with the text *pemburuan*, the hunt, also mentioning how many days the chase was already on. *Jawa Pos* stopped doing so after day 14.

Soeharto's residence was searched again on 14 November. When the search took place the former president was confined to his bed. He had fallen into a relapse and needed a resuscitator. Rumours that Soeharto was soon to die made the exchange rate drop to Rp 9,400 to the dollar.[23] Tommy's siblings and his wife, Ardhia Pramesti Regita Cahyania (more familiarly known as Jeng Tata or Tata), were quizzed by the police. Even Tommy's favourite sate seller was questioned. The interrogation of Tutut lasted for nine hours, that of Tata eleven hours. Siti Hutami Endang Adiningsih was questioned by police for two different cases. She was quizzed about her brother's disappearance, and, separately, for nine hours, about the possession of two handguns for which she had failed to renew the permit, and for which she would be sentenced to ten days' imprisonment. Siti Hediati Harijadi Prabowo caused some commotion by referring to the meeting in Hotel Borobudur, and suggesting that people should ask Abdurrahman Wahid about the whereabouts of Tommy. The word Borobudurgate was born. Members of parliament indicated that they intended to invite the president to parliament to explain. At the end of November the public prosecution threatened to declare members of the Soeharto family and Tommy's lawyers 'suspects' for obstructing the execution of Tommy's sentence. The first to become a suspect was Tata's father, Raden Mas Bambang Sucahyo Aji Suryo Bandoro.

The public prosecution made an attempt to seize property belonging to Tommy – sixteen houses – to be used as collateral for the fine he was sentenced to pay. The public prosecution experienced some problems in getting this done. Most of the property had been signed over to others. Three houses had been pledged as security with BPPN, ownership of one house had been transferred to Olivia Maya Rumantir. Tommy's houses at Jalan Yusuf Adiwinata and Jalan Cendana were confiscated. Here too there were complications. Both houses were said not to be owned individually by Tommy, but

---

[23] One of the persons who visited Soeharto's residence on hearing that the health of the former president had deteriorated was Susilo Bambang Yudhoyono.

jointly by him and his wife.

Economically there were signs of recovery. At the end of 1999 there was praise from Hubert Neiss, who said that the Indonesian financial situation had stabilized and that its foreign exchange reserves had been replenished. In January, when the new national budget was presented to parliament, it was based on an exchange rate of Rp 7,000 (much lower than it had been, but for some businessmen still too high to repay their dollar debts), a growth rate of 3.8 per cent, and an inflation rate of 4.8 per cent. The release of the long form had paved the way for a new round of negotiations with IMF. Though in some circles Kwik Kian Gie had acquired the reputation of being 'anti-IMF', or at least of being rather critical of IMF, negotiations were said to have been conducted in a cordial atmosphere. Still, pressed afterwards in February by questions from one of the deputy chairmen of parliament, Kwik Kian Gie had to admit that at times he had had to disregard his own opinions when confronted with pressure exerted by IMF. After all, IMF was the strongest of the two. Still needing foreign aid for its routine budget including the Social Safety Net, Indonesia had to bow to some of its demands and those of the World Bank. Otherwise, suspension of aid threatened, with all its consequences for the lives of ordinary people.

Nevertheless, the Indonesian delegation scored some successes. IMF allowed Jakarta to levy an import tariff on rice and sugar in order to protect domestic producers. The tariffs only provided minor relief. They did not prevent a drop in domestic rice prices and farmers getting into trouble, nor could they help sugarcane growers and factories to meet the competition of cheap imports. For its part, the Indonesian government committed itself to a gradual and selective abolition of subsidies on fuel oils and electricity. It was agreed in December that the prices of fuel oils and the basic electricity tariff would rise on average by 20 and 35 per cent respectively in April 2000. Abdurrahman Wahid admitted that the Indonesian government had had to bow to IMF pressure. The Minister of Mining and Energy promised that the measure would not affect economically weak consumers. Fuel prices would remain low for public transport, and electricity subsidies would remain in force for small consumers. The agreement needed the fiat of parliament. Aware of the precarious financial situation of the state, members of parliament did not object to a price rise in fuel oils and electricity. They indicated that they did not want to go higher than 10 per cent for fuel oils (in the end settling for twelve per cent) and 20 per cent for the basic electricity tariff. As compensation, they demanded a thorough investigation into Pertamina KKN cases and a satisfactory solution to the disputes with private electricity companies and their foreign investors, which the Abdurrahman Wahid administration, amidst an outcry of protests, had decided to settle out of court in December. It was announced that seventeen million families were to be given special coupons to allow them to buy petroleum at the old price. Public transport and PLN were also to receive a special subsidy through the issuing of coupons. Though government spokesmen maintained that a coupon system was safe from misuse, the government concluded that the project was not feasible and that cash money had to be provided to the poor and to public transport companies. The fuel price hike was delayed on 31 March amid threats of mass demonstrations. Kwik Kian Gie said that a delay of more than three months would be fatal. If a price rise had not gone into effect by that time, the government would have to cut other expenditures. People recalled what had happened in May 1998. From various sides it was pointed out that time was needed to convince society of the need of the price rises. Organizing a distribution system for the subsidies also played a role in the delay.[24]

Negotiations between Jakarta and IMF resulted in a new agreement signed on 20 January (which noted that 'the Bank Bali investigation is being credibly advanced'). This opened the way for the resumption of financial aid by IMF, which is to total US$ 5 billion in loans up to February 2002. Early in February, the Consultative Group on Indonesia promised Indonesia US$ 4.7 billion, including a grant of US$ 520 million for the coming budget year (which in 2000 only runs from April to December 2000). Part of the amount was carried over from the 1999/2000 US$ 5.9 commitment, which had partially been suspended because of East Timor and the Bank Bali scandal. The Paris Club decided on a rescheduling of US$ 2.2 billion of debt.

Optimism was tempered at the end of March when the IMF representative in Jakarta, John R. Dodsworth, announced that IMF had delayed the disbursement of US$ 400 million. Disappointment over Indonesia's failure to meet targets of reform measures agreed on in January lay at the root of the decision. Dodsworth stressed that the Indonesian government should make haste in formulating a corporate restructuring strategy, recapitalization of state banks, and reform of the tax system. Other points which he said had priority, were good procedures for debt restructuring by BPPN, including the taking of clear sanctions against uncooperative debtors, and a more effective bankruptcy court. Also, the initially much praised Jakarta Initiative came in for criticism because of lack of results. In April the Paris Club did agree to a rescheduling of US$ 5.8 billion in foreign debt. IMF made it clear that the agreement would only become effective after a new review of Indonesia's performance and if its board of directors was satisfied with the progress Indonesia had made in carrying out the reforms agreed upon. The decision would fall in early June.

As difficulty in scheduling a meeting of cabinet ministers to decide on the

---

[24] A rise in fuel prices became effective on 1 October. There were demonstrations protesting the increase, but not on the scale some had feared.

reforms was singled out as one of the reasons why Indonesia had made slow progress, Abdurrahman Wahid forbade them to make trips abroad. They were '*dicekal*', the *Jawa Pos* concluded (*Jawa Pos*, 31-3-2000). Publicly Abdurrahman Wahid blamed the ministers. He said that they put their personal interests before national ones. At once rumours started to fly around that the ministers involved, Yusuf Kalla, Laksamana Sukardi, Bomer Pasaribu, Kwik Kian Gie, and Bambang Sudibyo were to be replaced. At the end of April, the first two were fired by Abdurrahman Wahid. Laksamana (a few weeks earlier still mentioned as the person most suited to head Bank Indonesia) also lost his position as chairman of the Jakarta Initiative. The decision created much displeasure in PDI-P and Golkar circles. Later, in August, when political opposition against Abdurrahman Wahid had intensified, Bambang Sudibyo claimed that the realization that they might be dismissed had negatively influenced the performance of the ministers in the economic sector, thus putting at least part of the blame on Abdurrahman Wahid. On that occasion he also disclosed that Abdurrahman Wahid had told them in February that his foreign advisors, which included Lee Kuan Yew and Henry Kissinger, had advised him to change the economic team. Initially Abdurrahman Wahid mentioned disunity among the economic ministers as the reason for his decision. A few days later it leaked out that during a closed meeting with parliament, Abdurrahman Wahid had said that alleged involvement in KKN had made him decide to replace Kalla and Laksamana Sukardi. Disputed were the replacement of a number of directors of state enterprises – imitating Abdurrahman Wahid, newspapers used the word 'thieves' to denote the new directors – by Laksamana and the acceptance of tenders by brothers of Kalla. Both denied the accusation and demanded that Abdurrahman Wahid should publicly apologize for his words. Laksamana blamed 'whisperers' who were motivated by private interests or those of their 'group'. Kalla spoke of a Chinese businessman and persons who were handed out bribes.

The delay in the disbursement of the IMF money, the sacking of Laksamana and Kalla, and the political implications of this step had made for a downcast atmosphere in May. There were even voices demanding that at the coming session of the People's Congress its members should decide on Abdurrahman Wahid's political future. Some of them strongly objected to the president's suggestion to lift the ban on communism. Others argued that Abdurrahman Wahid's own appointment policy was not free of KKN. People accusing Abdurrahman Wahid of nepotism pointed at the appointment (still by Glenn Yusuf) of the president's brother, Hasyim Wahid, to a top position within BPPN. The news broke in early May.[25] Before the end of the month

---

[25]   One PKB member of parliament, KH Nur Iskandar SQ, gave as his opinion that Hasyim Wahid had been appointed at BPPN to be able to employ *jinn* in the effort to have bad debtors

'Gus Im' resigned. The appointment of Rozy Munir, a chairman of Nahdlatul Ulama, as Minister without Portfolio of Capital Investment and Development of State Enterprises to fill the vacancy left by the sacking of Laksamana was equally disputed. Laksamana accused Abdurrahman Wahid of initially having dropped his confidant Rozy Munir as secretary to the minister at his ministry. He added that he and Rozy Munir had not been able to work together well; this was denied by Rozy Munir. Speculation about 'KKN' in the circle around Abdurrahman Wahid involved the illegal transfer of Rp 35 billion from the Welfare Foundation of Bulog Employees by the deputy head of Bulog, Sapuan, who was said to have been urged to do so by Abdurrahman Wahid's masseur, or as some other reports had it, spiritual advisor of the president, Suwondo. Some reports said that Suwondo held out Sapuan's promotion to Bulog chairman. After 'Baligate' and 'Lippogate', it seemed that a 'Buloggate', as the affair indeed was to be dubbed, was in the making. Buloggate could be traced back to a meeting of Sapuan with Abdurrahman Wahid in early January, during which the president had inquired about the possibility of using non-budgetary Bulog funds to provide humanitarian aid in Aceh. Sapuan had discussed the request with his boss, Kalla. When the latter refused to release the money because, as he was to explain later, there was no written request, Sapuan had done so on his own account. For Abdurrahman Wahid and his supporters the case was yet another indication of an offensive launched by his political enemies, including 'Soeharto's cronies', to bring him down. The Bulog financial scandal led to the resignation of Bondan Gunawan at the end of May.[26] He said that he had decided to do so because he had become an intermediate target to strike at the president. Among the other persons mentioned as being implicated was Alwi Shihab. Jusuf Kalla disclosed that Alwi Shihab had phoned him in early April to inquire about the Bulog money. Though Kalla stressed that Alwi Shihab had inquired after the money and had not, as some newspapers reported, asked for it, Alwi Shihab's alleged involvement became headline news. Alwi Shihab, who had recommended Sapuan for the position of deputy head of Bulog, himself said that he had phoned Kalla to verify rumours he had heard about the release of the Bulog money. Abdurrahman Wahid stated that the money used for humanitarian aid for Aceh had not been paid out of Bulog money, but had come from a donation of US$ 2 million by the Sultan of

---

pay their debts now that more earthly methods did not seem to work. Laksamana claimed this appointment had been at the instigation of Abdurrahman Wahid.
[26]   Bondan Gunawan was said to have arranged the meeting of Sapuan with Abdurrahman Wahid and to have discussed with Sapuan the use of Bulog money for the State Secretariat. He denied both accusations. Bondan Gunawan was succeeded by Djohan Effendi, a well-known Muslim intellectual.

Brunei.[27] Accepting the money made Abdurrahman Wahid subject to accusations that he had broken the law and might even be sentenced to six years' imprisonment. This case came to be known as Bruneigate.

On top of the political turmoil, the Central Bureau of Statistics predicted an economic growth of 1.5 per cent instead of the initial forecast of 4 per cent, while the exchange rate of the rupiah slid to below Rp 8,500 to the dollar. Some blamed the performance of the government, and especially Abdurrahman Wahid's unpredictable actions and statements, for the latter. He himself singled out student demonstrations held to commemorate the Trisakti shooting of May 1998, announced to last for two or three days, as the reason why the exchange rate did not improve. He said that dollar purchases by businessmen who wanted to be out of the country while these demonstratons lasted had pushed the price up. He was confident that once the demonstrations were over the exchange rate would drop. Others were less optimistic. Kwik Kian Gie ventured that without an increase in exports the rupiah might drop still further to an exchange rate of Rp 12,000 to the dollar. The drop in the exchange rate even led the *Asian Wall Street Journal* to suggest the introduction of a currency board system, the solution advanced in 1998 by Soeharto and Hanke (*Merdeka*, 17-5-2000). In Indonesia the new Minister of Industry and Trade, Luhut Pandjaitan, revealed in early June that the Indonesian government was contemplating capital control to halt a rupiah plunge. Around the same time the successor of Camdessus, Horst Koehler, said that an exchange control was not completely out of the question, but that it should be considered a last resort and that, if applied by a country with a weak economy, it would not suffice to withstand an attack on its currency.

When Horst Koehler made his statement, IMF had finally decided to resume its financial support. It had taken until 17 May till a new agreement with IMF was signed. IMF announced the release of US$ 372 million on 2 June.

And, as if the Indonesian government did not already have enough problems to face, further misfortune had already struck in March. Forest fires in Sumatra and Kalimantan were declared a national disaster by the Indonesian government.

---

[27]   During a hearing by a parliamentary committee, Sapuan stated that Abdurrahman Wahid had asked for half of Bulog's Rp 370 billion non-budgetary funds, but that the president had refused to issue a special decree to that effect. With respect to the release of the Rp 35 billion, Sapuan said that Suwondo had promised him that the money would soon be returned and that the government was waiting for money from abroad to finance humanitarian aid in Aceh.

Epilogue

Abdurrahman Wahid's position and political skills were seriously tested in August 2000 during the annual session of the People's Congress, the first ever held. By that time he had only been in office for ten months, but had already forfeited much of the support he had received from politicians of PAN, Golkar, PPP, and PDI-P in October 1999 when he was elected president. Indicative of the bad publicity he was receiving and of the intensified political strife of the previous months was that newspapers began to write about 'palace cronies'. A few weeks before the annual session, indignity among politicians dissatisfied with his performance reached a high when Abdurrahman scolded parliament. This happened after members of parliament, using the right of interpellation, asked him to explain the sacking of Laksamana Sukardi and Yusuf Kalla. Abdurrahman Wahid came to parliament on 20 July, but refused to explain why he had taken this step. He claimed that the composition of the cabinet was a presidential prerogative and that he did not have to account for replacing ministers.

The president's position had apparently become very weak; some onlookers saw evidence of this in his agreement to the removal of Agus Wirahadikusumah from command of Kostrad in early August, a move which seems to have had the explicit endorsement of Megawati, whose relations with senior army officers had become increasingly cordial. Apart from his political clash with Wiranto, Agus Wirahadikusumah had created still more animosity among fellow officers by revealing misuse of money by the Kostrad Dharma Putra Foundation, implicating his predecessor Djaja Suparman. He was also accused of scheming to take control of the army. Agus Wirahadikusumah was, as it was phrased, 'parked' at army headquarters. How unpopular Agus Wirahadikusumah was among his fellow officers became evident in October. Forty-six officers, including most provincial commanders (those not present were reported to agree) proposed that he be tried by an Officers' Honour Council after a meeting in Bandung on 2 October. They accused him of having violated the military code of ethics. Among the examples given were the statements which he had made without consulting his superiors first, and a recent trip he had made to the United States, also without inform-

A banner displayed in Jakarta during the annual session of the People's Congress in August 2000. The text reads: Gus Dur and Megawati, the saviours of the Indonesian nation. (Photo C. van Dijk.)

ing his superiors. His enemies alleged that he had gone to the United States to meet Abdurrahman Wahid, who was in New York to attend the UN Millennium Summit and get the president's support, and maybe also that of Washington, in his bid to become Chief of Staff of the Army. Agus Wirahadikusumah said that he had gone to the United States to attend his son's graduation from Ohio State University and that his superiors knew of his trip.

Before and during the annual session of the People's Congress many points were held out against Abdurrahman Wahid by his critics. One was that he and his cabinet had not been able to make significant headway in restoring Indonesia's economy. Apart from the troubles experienced in settling liquidity credits and bad debts, another indication put forward to illustrate this was that in the middle of July the rupiah stood at Rp 9,500 to the dollar. Though the exchange rate improved somewhat to Rp 8,300 to the dollar when the annual session drew near, there were politicians who pointed out that no significant improvement had taken place since the presidency of Habibie. Further, there was much criticism of the way the domestic security problem was being tackled. Points criticized were the lenience Abdurrahman Wahid had shown towards the independence movement in Irian Jaya and the

A banner displayed in one of the streets of Jakarta during the annual session of the People's Congress in August 2000. The text reads: Reject an alliance/coalition of whatever party with Golkar intended to topple the duo Gus Dur-Mega.
(Photo C. van Dijk.)

fact that he had allowed the use of the word Papua and the flying of the Morning Star.

With respect to one of the other trouble spots, Aceh, some progress had been made during Abdurrahman Wahid's months in office. A memorandum of understanding about a three-month humanitarian pause in the fighting had been agreed upon with GAM representatives in Geneva on 12 May, to become effective 2 June. Nevertheless, fighting had continued. *The Jakarta Post* (12-8-2000) wrote that between 2 June and early August at least 47 people had been killed.[1] As had become typical since the fall of Soeharto the approach of 17 August led to much anxiety in Aceh. Busses stopped operating, and ordinary people feared trouble whatever flag they hoisted or did not hoist.[2]

[1]   The acting governor of Aceh said in September that material damage in the previous year amounted to Rp 42 billion. The number of people who had been killed in that period was 444, while 96 persons were still missing.

[2]   Local Republican authorities in a local newspaper and in flyers dropped from helicopters appealed to the Acehnese to hoist the Indonesian flag. They threatened to punish anyone who tried to prevent its hoisting. The acting governor of Aceh allowed for the not flying of the

The problems in Aceh, the continued fighting in the Moluccas, and the explosions of communal violence in other parts of the country meant that the number of refugees had swelled. In August 2000 the total number of refugees was estimated to have surpassed 800,000. In view of this figure the Indonesian government decided that it had become too costly to have the refugees settle elsewhere as transmigrants. The only – and cheaper – way out was to have them stay in refugee camps till calm had been restored in their place of origin and it was safe enough for the refugees to return home.

At the annual session of the People's Congress, which took place from 7 to 18 August, old customs were restored. The members stood up when Abdurrahman Wahid and Megawati entered and left the meeting hall. A more serious repetition of past practices was that four students who staged a hunger strike during the annual session disappeared on 14 August. They resurfaced two weeks later, still too confused to reveal what they had experienced.

At the start of the annual session, rumours were rife that Abdurrahman Wahid's political enemies were preparing for an impeachment of the president. How much goodwill Abdurrahman Wahid had lost became evident almost immediately. PDI-P, Golkar, and the Central Axis parties all seemed to oppose Abdurrahman Wahid and to support Megawati. Newspapers were full of speculation about deterioriating relations between him and Megawati. PDI-P 'sources' put the blame on Abdurrahman Wahid's wilfulness and his disregard of Megawati's suggestions in the past months. Proof of the strained relations was seen in Megawati's refusal to read out Abdurrahman Wahid's speech during the first day of the annual session about his performance as president. The speech – Abdurrahman Wahid called it a progress report and refused to call it an account, as others did – did not make a great impression. Spokesmen for PDI-P, Golkar, PPP, PAN, and PBB asked Abdurrahman Wahid to delegate the daily tasks of government to Megawati and accept a position which resembled a ceremonial head of state. Some even asked him to resign.

Confronted with the opposition, Abdurrahman Wahid announced in his reply to the criticism brought forward by spokesmen for the various parties that he would transfer the day-to-day running of the government to Megawati. Such a way out had been suggested in advance by the PDI-P faction in the People's Congress and was supported by politicians from PBB, Golkar, PPP, and PAN. A PDI-P spokesman had even hinted that if Abdurrahman

---

Indonesian flag when circumstances forced people to do so. Police officials in Jakarta and in Aceh also announced measures against people hoisting other flags. SIRA proposed flying the United Nations flag. Authorities confiscated tens of these flags. GAM leaders stressed that they did not forbid the people the raising of the Indonesian flag.

Wahid refused, the annual session of the People's Congress could well turn into an extraordinary session, implying impeachment. Abdurrahman Wahid saved his position by announcing a more important role for Megawati. The solution found was probably a compromise worked out by Golkar, PDI-P, and PKB. In any case it removed much of the venom that had characterized the first days, when spokesmen for almost all the parties had strongly attacked Abdurrahman Wahid. Nevertheless, within days Abdurrahman Wahid played down the implications of his announcement somewhat by saying that he had given Megawati additional tasks, not additional powers. Megawati's extra 'tasks' were specified in a presidential decision issued before the end of the month. Indeed, these concerned the day-to-day running of the government. She was to chair the meetings of the cabinet, had to formulate the cabinet's working agenda and program, and evaluate the performance of the cabinet. In future she would also be allowed to sign certain decrees. She was authorized to sign decrees to appoint and promote senior civil servants and military officers and change the structure of departments. This new authority gave her only limited freedom of action. She could only issue decrees if the content was in accordance with the policies approved by the president. As an additional constraint, the presidential decision instructed her, in the execution of her new tasks, to involve first and foremost the State Secretariat and not her own vice-presidential staff.

Abdurrahman Wahid was also forced to accept a decree of the People's Congress stating that the appointment and replacement of the Commander of the Armed Forces and of the Chief of the National Police had to be done with the consent of parliament. Within a month he would disregard the decree, when in the middle of September he sacked the chief of police for making no progress in the search for who was behind a number of recent bombing attempts in Jakarta.

In a final concession to his critics, Abdurrahman Wahid announced shortly after the annual session had ended that the National Economic Council (DEN) and the Council for Business Development (DPUN) were dissolved.

Abdurrahman Wahid's statement about Megawati's future political role did much to cool down the atmosphere of the annual session. There was no further attempt to start the procedure for an impeachment. Outside the People's Congress the atmosphere remained calm, too. In advance the chief of police, Rusdihardjo, had revealed that almost 30,000 soldiers, policemen, and members of the civil defence were to be deployed to maintain order in Jakarta. An additional 30,000 people were held in reserve to be deployed if needed. No additional security forces had to be mobilized. Violent confrontations did not occur. There were various demonstrations by students and other groups, but not on a scale that had characterized the previous sessions of the People's Congress. With some exceptions, supporters of political parties and members of groups like Satgas PDI-P and Banser remained invisible. This in spite of the many reports prior to and during the annual session that they were going to come to Jakarta in their thousands as they had done at previous sessions of the People's Congress. This time most of the rumours concerned Banser. It was reported with some frequency that Banser members had already assembled in Jakarta and were ready to come out in support of Abdurrahman Wahid if his position was threatened. One of the reasons massive demonstrations failed to take place was that the leaders of the main political parties had agreed not to mobilize their supporters.

Even two disputed decisions taken by the People's Congress did not spark off mass demonstrations. One was that the presence of the Armed Forces and the police in the People's Council was to be maintained till 2009. Those who did not agree pointed out that the prolonged stay of the military and the police in the People's Council was in violation of one of the basic aims of political reform, and was contrary to what the Ciganjur meeting had agreed upon. On 15 August 2000 *The Jakarta Post* devoted an editorial to the decision entitled 'A betrayal'. Even the Minister of Defence, Juwono Sudarsono, said he did not agree.

The second disputed decision was an amendment to the Constitution of 1945 which makes retroactive application of laws impossible. As a human rights tribunal bill was still being debated, one of the implications was that the nonretroactive principle might obstruct the prosecution of human rights offences of the past, including those which were allegedly committed in East Timor. The clause passed almost unnoticed. Protest came only at the last moment, when the People's Congress had already reached a consensus. Alwi Shihab said that the decision would blemish Indonesia's image abroad. He admitted that it would be difficult for him to explain the amendment abroad in the context of Indonesia's efforts to avoid an international tribunal on East Timor. The chairman of the People's Congress, Amien Rais, claimed ignorance of the decision. He maintained that people had pointed out what the implications could be only after it was too late and the clause could no longer be dropped. As an additional point to explain why the amendment had been phrased in the way it was, he admitted that he and the members of the committee responsible for the drafting of the clause were not legal experts.[3]

After the annual session had ended, attention focused on the composition of a new cabinet. Yet another concession Abdurrahman Wahid had made was

---

[3]   Parliament accepted an Act on Human Rights Tribunals on 6 November 2000. The act stipulates that past human rights abuses can be tried by an ad hoc tribunal. The establishment of such an ad hoc tribunal must be approved by parliament and by the president. The act also makes it possible to hold high ranking officers and civilians responsible for crimes committed by their subordinates. The maximum sentence provided for in the act is a prison term of 25 years.

that he promised to change his cabinet. He said that what he had in mind was a restructuring, a reduction of the number of departments and ministers, and not a mere reshuffle. For a time it was said that part of this restructuring would be the creation of a new function, that of *menteri utama*, chief minister. The stated candidate for this post was Susilo Bambang Yudhoyono, who had become a confidant of Abdurrahman Wahid. Susilo Bambang Yudhoyono, or simply SBY, since June 2000 had conducted secret negotiations with the Soeharto family represented by Siti Hardijanti Rukmana – some said that he had been a speech writer for Tutut – over the return to the state of money which the former president allegedly had amassed through KKN in exchange for amnesty. He had also been coordinator of the team that had drafted Abdurrahman Wahid's report to the People's Congress, became a member of the team which had drafted the answers given by Abdurrahman Wahid to questions posed by the members of the People's Congress, and was to play a role in deciding on the composition of the new cabinet. The idea that there was to be a chief minister, and especially that Susilo Bambang Yudhoyono would be its first office holder, did not go down well with PDI-P politicians. One reason for this was that such a configuration would put restrictions on any new role Megawati would get. Another reason was that Susilo Bambang Yudhoyono had been Chief of Staff of the Military Command of Jakarta at the time of the attack on the PDI office in July 1996.

There was to be no chief minister, but the composition of the cabinet indicates that Abdurrahman Wahid had no intention at all to relinquish any of his powers to Megawati. In advance Golkar and PDI-P had been in favour of assigning Megawati the task of composing the cabinet. At that time Abdurrahman Wahid and Matori Abdul Djalil of PKB had already vehemently rejected such a possibility. After his announcement of the new 'tasks' to be given to the vice-president, Abdurrahman Wahid made it clear that he would remain the person who decided on the composition of the new cabinet. He stressed that he had not delegated any of his constitutional powers.

How the new cabinet was to be composed gave rise to many rumours and conflicts. One was that Abdurrahman Wahid had distanced himself from Akbar Tanjung and was to include Marwah Daud Ibrahim of the Iramasuka group in his cabinet. Even the names of Laksamana Sukardi and Yusuf Kalla were mentioned as candidates for a ministerial post. Much speculation was heard about who was to hold the position of Coordinating Minister of Economic, Industrial and Financial Affairs. During the annual session of the People's Congress the incumbent, Kwik Kian Gie, had to the surprise of almost everybody announced his resignation on 10 August. As Kwik Kian Gie said he was prepared to sit on the new cabinet, his name continued to circulate as the new coordinating minister. Another name mentioned was Dorodjatun Kuntjorojakti. He refused. Initially mentioned as one of the reasons he refused was his rejection of Sofyan Wanandi, the chairman of DPUN, as a close advisor to Abdurrahman Wahid.

The new cabinet was announced on 23 August. It had 26 members. The previous cabinet had had 35 ministers. Susilo Bambang Yudhoyono became Coordinating Minister of Politics, Social Affairs and Security. Rizal Ramli, the head of Bulog, became Coordinating Minister of Economic Affairs. A few days later Kwik Kian Gie used the transfer of his coordinating ministership to Rizal Ramli to reveal that during a meeting of the cabinet Abdurrahman Wahid, praising their contribution to the recovery of Indonesia's economy, had insisted that three conglomerates – Marimutu Sinivasan, Sjamsul Nursalim, and Prajogo Pangestu – should be allowed to continue undisturbed as entrepreneurs.[4] Publicly Abdurrahman Wahid repeated his appeal to go easy on the three in October when he was in Seoul and said that their prosecution should be postponed till 2002. The reason he gave for his plea was the contribution of the concerns of the three businessmen to Indonesia's exports. Marzuki Darusman was forced to explain that what the president had meant was not that the prosecution of the three should be postponed, but the payment of the debts their companies had accumulated. Sjamsul Nursalim was declared a suspect accused of misuse of liquidity credit to the amount of Rp 7.2 trillion on 23 October. For a similar offence Bob Hasan (Rp 12 billion) and Samadikun Hartono (Rp 766 billion) were also declared suspects.

The position of Minister of Finance and Development of State Companies went to Prijadi Prapto Suhardjo. Immediately his selection was disputed. Critics pointed out that Prijadi PS was an old friend of Abdurrahman Wahid, who had failed a fit and proper test by the central bank for the function of chief director of BRI. Teten Masduki of ICW went as far as to write a letter to Abdurrahman Wahid protesting the appointment. He aired his suspicion that Prijadi PS had, at the time when he had been one of the directors of BRI, been involved in providing disputed loans to The Ning King and Djoko Sugiarto Tjandra. Prijadi PS denied the accusation. Surjadi Soedirdja was made Minister of Internal Affairs and Regional Autonomy. Alwi Shihab remained Minister of Foreign Affairs. Minister of Defence was Prof. Dr Mahfud, rector of the Indonesian Islamic University in Yogyakarta. Rizal Ramli described his colleagues as problem-solvers and men of action (*Far Eastern Economic Review*, 7-9-2000:26).

Reactions were mixed or negative. The cabinet was completely Abdurrahman Wahid's doing. Akbar Tanjung of Golkar had not been consulted.

---

4   On information provided by the economist Sri Mulyani Indrawati, Michael Vatikiotis in the *Far Eastern Economic Review* (19-10-2000:76) also mentions the Salim group as a business concern of which Abdurrahman Wahid had stressed that it was vital to the Indonesian economy and thus needed to be saved.

PPP politicians also stated that their opinion had not been asked. Megawati had had no real say either. Amien Rais disclosed that she had been informed about the composition of the cabinet just a few hours before it had been announced, and that she had questioned the appointments of Mahfud and Prijadi PS. Megawati refused to be present when the composition of the new cabinet was made public. The explanation Abdurrahman Wahid gave for her absence was that she had returned home to take her afternoon bath. Megawati denied speculations that she intended to resign. Though some suggested that she also should not be present at the installation of the cabinet on 26 August, she was. She administered the oath of office to the new ministers. Those dissatisfied included two ministers of the new cabinet. Ryaas Rasyid, Minister Without Portfolio of State Administrative Reforms, and Yusril Ihza Mahendra, Minister of Justice and Human Rights, publicly vented their disappointment. The first said that Megawati had urged them not to resign on 24 August. The second indicated that the structure of the cabinet was different from what had been agreed upon and at that time had the blessing of Abdurrahman Wahid and Megawati.

A major cause of discontent among the politicians of the largest parties was that they felt that their party was left out. PDI-P supplied one minister, Sonny Keraf, Minister Without Portfolio of Environment, but he was not considered a PDI-P core politician. A similar reaction came from PPP. Zarkasih Nur, Minister Without Portfolio of Cooperatives and the Development of Small Enterprises, was a PPP member, but not all PPP leaders thought that he represented the party. Golkar held no seats at all. Marzuki Darusman remained attorney-general but the attorney-generalship was no longer considered to be part of the cabinet. In reaction, Golkar spokesmen said that their party was preparing for the opposition. PAN had two cabinet members (Al Hilal Hamdi and Yahya Muhaimin), but its leading politicians were very critical of the new cabinet. Confronted with such criticism, Abdurrahman Wahid claimed the opposite. He said that various members had the explicit support of Golkar, PDI-P, PAN, and PPP. His denial did not make a great impression.

Amien Rais and Hartono Mardjono of PBB called the new cabinet worse than the old one. Amien Rais expressed shock, especially so in view of the ministers appointed in the economic and financial sector. He said that the new cabinet did not serve the interests of the country, composed as it was to serve the interests of Abdurrahman Wahid. He ventured that many of its members had been selected because it was expected they would become 'yes men' and 'yes women'. Amien Rais gave the cabinet three months to prove itself.

Although Abdurrahman Wahid escaped impeachment by giving Megawati extra tasks, Buloggate and Bruneigate remained a weak spot for him. During the annual session of the People's Congress, Abdurrahman Wahid had stated that the money received from the sultan of Brunei was a private gift and could not be considered public money. The answer did not deter his opponents. Some members of the People's Congress booed when Abdurrahman Wahid made his statement. At the end of the month 307 members of parliament, including most of the PKB representatives, voted in favour of a parliamentary inquiry into Buloggate and Bruneigate. Only three members, all from PKB, voted against. Members of parliament representing the military and the police abstained. The public prosecution also announced that it would hear Abdurrahman Wahid at the Buloggate court trial. To make matters worse for Abdurrahman Wahid, at the end of August the press began to report about an extramarital affair he had had with a married woman.

In the financial sphere control over Bank Indonesia developed into a hot political issue. The position of Syahril Sabirin had become even more precarious when he was declared a suspect in the Bank Bali case in June. The news triggered off a new round of discussions about whether he should be replaced or not. Some accused Abdurrahman Wahid of being behind the decision to declare Syahril a suspect. The deputy governor of Bank Indonesia, Achjar Iljas, said that Abdurrahman Wahid and Marzuki Darusman had presented Syahril a number of times with the choice of either resigning or becoming a suspect in the Bank Bali case. Abdurrahman Wahid said that he had offered Syahril an ambassadorship or a membership of the Supreme Advisory Council to save Syahril's face.

Syahril Sabirin was arrested on 20 June 2000. Appointed acting governor of the central bank was Anwar Nasution, who himself, when he had been appointed senior deputy governor of Bank Indonesia in July 1999, had described Bank Indonesia as a robbers' nest. In August the State Audit Office put the blame for misuse of liquidity support squarely on the disfunctioning of Bank Indonesia. New figures were released in a report to parliament which were even more alarming than the previous estimates. Rp 84.8 trillion in liquidity credit to 48 commercial banks of the total credit, now estimated to amount to Rp 144.5 trillion had been misused. Once again it was stressed that the money had not been used to pay customers during the runs on the banks but for foreign exchange speculation, buying fixed assets, lending to affiliated companies, and other such illegal activities. A further Rp 53.6 trillion in loans had been extended in violation of banking rules. A few days later it was announced that the public prosecution would start an investigation into misuse of liquidity credit. Besides the bankers concerned, about eighty employees, among them deputy governors, of Bank Indonesia were to be questioned. The task was so enormous that Marzuki Darusman announced that he would have to call in the help of public prosecutors from outside Jakarta. The information about failure of Bank Indonesia to exercise proper control made Fuad Bawazier and other politicians suggest disbanding the central bank and replacing it by a new one or by another monetary authority. Abdurrahman Wahid, in a letter to parliament, asked for the replacement of all members of its board of governors. Akbar Tanjung refused his request.

The misuse of liquidity credits also brought up again the question who had to bear the cost of the liquidity credit extended: Bank Indonesia, which had failed to exercise proper control, but which claimed that the then government had ordered the bank in September 1997 to provide the money, or the government. If the bank was held to account, it most probably would have to be recapitalized to prevent it from bankruptcy. The government threatened to withdraw the treasury bonds worth Rp 144.5 trillion which it had issued to reimburse the central bank. A deal between the government and the bank took till November to be finalized, and it was agreed that Bank Indonesia would be responsible for Rp 24.5 trillion of the Rp 144.5 liquidity credit given. There was to be no recapitalization of the bank. Among those held responsible for the debacle as listed by the Coordinating Minister for Economic Affairs of that moment were former presidents Soeharto and Habibie, former ministers Moerdiono, Fuad Bawazier, and Mar'ie Muhammad, former heads of BPPN Glenn Yusuf and Bambang Subianto, former governor of Bank Indonesia J. Soedradjad Djiwandono, its present governor Syahril Sabirin, and members of DPKEK, among them Widjojo Nitisastro, Ali Wardhana, Saadilah Mursjid, Bob Hasan, Aburizal Bakrie, and Anthony Salim.

Anwar Nasution and four other deputy governors of Bank Indonesia tendered their resignation on 17 November 2000.[5] The following day Abdurrahman Wahid suggested to parliament that Anwar Nasution and two other persons would be convenient candidates for the offices of governor and deputy governor of Bank Indonesia. After this drew much criticism, Abdurrahman Wahid rectified the nomination at the end of November. It was now said that the three were suitable candidates to become senior deputy governor.

Syahril Sabirin refused to resign. According to existing law he could only be forced to leave if he had been found guilty of committing a crime or was permanently incapacitated. To be able to remove him as governor, the government proposed to parliament to amend the Central Bank Act, and allow for the replacement of members of the board of governors, if they had not been in their office and had not performed their tasks for three consecutive months. The government's amendment to the Central Bank Act stipulated that governors of the central bank could also be fired if parliament considered their performance unsatisfactory. As a final blow, the amendment stated

[5] A few days later another deputy governor wrote a letter to parliament stating that he left it to parliament to decide on his remaining in office or not.

that the moment the act came into force, all governors of Bank Indonesia were discharged from office. An additional complication arose in December. Syahril Sabirin had been released at the end of September, and put under house arrest. The house arrest was lifted on 5 December 2000, after the legally allowed time of his detention had expired. The following day Syahril Sabirin went to his office at Bank Indonesia to resume work. Almost immediately reports started to circulate that Syahril Sabirin was involved in other crimes, including the counterfeiting of banknotes.

BPPN also suffered from the way it tackled the liquidity credit problem. In August 2000 much commotion was created by the nature of the so-called Master of Settlement and Acquisition Agreements (MSAA) concluded by BPPN in September and November 1998 to settle the liquidity debts of BCA, BDNI of which Sjamsul Nursalim had been the owner, Surya and Subentra Banks of Sudwikatmono, and BUN of Bob Hasan. In an MSAA agreement, the bankers handed over assets to the total value of their debt to BPPN. Contrary to Master of Refinancing Agreements concluded with other bankers and except in the case of misrepresentation at the time of the concluding of the agreement, the MSAAs had no stipulation forcing bank owners to hand over additional assets when the assets were sold for less than they had been valued. As had been feared in 1998, the assets pledged to repay the debt in full had been greatly overvalued. According to the lowest estimate, the real value would only cover between thirty and forty per cent of the liquidity credit. The matter came to light when Anthony indicated that his group was to buy the assets BCA had handed over to BPPN for Rp 20 trillion, while BCA's liquidity debt amounted to Rp 53 trillion. It was concluded that collusion must have been at play. Some even suggested that business tycoons had been able to place somebody in BPPN or the relevant government agency to have the MSAAs drafted as they were. The public debate on the MSAAs had started after Kwik Kian Gie had refused to approve the sale. If the deal were approved, the state would have to make up the remaining Rp 33 trillion. Worried by such financial damage to the state, Kwik Kian Gie reported the matter to parliament. Parliament formed a special committee to. investigate the MSAAs. In an initial reaction the attorney-general, Marzuki Darusman, did not preclude an investigation of former and present BPPN employees and the government officials involved in the drafting and signing of the MSAAs.[6] There were also calls that the MSAAs should be reviewed, but some legal experts warned that it would be a bad precedent were the government

---

6   An investigation was announced by an Oversight Committee for BPPN formed in July by the government. The committee was chaired by Mar'ie Muhammad. In August Cacuk Sudarijanto said that the former owners of BCA were the only ones who had fulfilled the MSAA. That he had not met his obligations was denied by a spokesman of Sjamsul Nursalim.

to nullify the agreements unilaterally. It was disclosed by Marzuki Darusman that Sjamsul Nursalim, Anthony Salim, and Bob Hasan had agreed to hand over additional assets to BPPN and had given a personal guarantee that they were responsible for the debts of their banks in mid-November.

By the end of 2000 Abdurrahman Wahid's political position had not improved. Amien Rais had withdrawn his support, publicly stating that he regretted his role in getting Abdurrahman Wahid elected. Others continued to suggest a special session of the People's Congress to impeach the president. In reaction, representatives of Banser and PKB Satgas Garda Bangsa said they were prepared to mobilize their followers, and tension between traditional and modernist Muslims mounted. Amien Rais was advised not to visit East Java. Civil war continued in the Moluccas, where in the two provinces that had been created in 1999 – the Moluccas and the North Moluccas – civil emergency had been imposed on 3 July 2000. The civil emergency status allowed for tough security measures such as control over the media, the banning of gatherings, and house-to-house searches, but did not go so far as to put the military in charge of the administration. In Aceh and Irian Jaya positions hardened. Anticipating massive protests in November and December in Aceh and Irian Jaya, the Indonesian government made it clear that it would not accept independence of the two provinces and would not tolerate blatant separatist acts. Susilo Bambang Yudhoyono also said that the government did not want to repeat the mistake made by holding the referendum in East Timor. The Chief of Staff of the Army added that the army was prepared to send troops to Aceh and Irian Jaya. At the end of November Abdurrahman Wahid joined in. Appearing on television he said that any attempt to proclaim independence would be dealt with accordingly. He gave his speech after two Papuan leaders, Theys Hiyo Eluay and Thaha al-Hamid, had been arrested. Early the following month Abdurrahman asked for the release of Theys Hiyo Eluay, but his plea was ignored. He also appealed to the chief of the national police to carefully consider more arrests of pro-independence leaders in view of the domestic and international consequences.

In Banda Aceh a mass demonstration to mark the anniversary of the massive protest demonstration of the previous year took place on 11 November. It was called Sidang Raya Rakyat Aceh untuk Kedamaian dan Kedaulatan (SIRA RAKAN), Mass Gathering of the Acehnese People for Peace and Sovereignty. In the days leading up to the SIRA RAKAN tens of thousands of people from all over the province travelled to Banda Aceh to participate. Police tried to prevent them from entering the city by setting up road blocks. Government spokesmen said that in the ensuing violence 14 people had been killed between 8 and 10 November. SIRA spokesmen mentioned much higher figures ranging from 32 to 200. Protesting the escalating violence by Indonesian security forces in Aceh, GAM withdrew on 13 November from the negotations with Jakarta to extend the humanitarian pause reached in May and which had been extended for three months in September. In Jakarta the spokesman for the police urged the government to reconsider the truce in view of the many members of the security forces killed by GAM. The gathering itself took place peacefully, but violence in Aceh remained rampant. Shots and grenades were fired from a passing car at the house of the governor of Aceh on 9 December. The attack took place when the governor and a number of guests, among them the Minister of Forestry, Nur Mahmudi Ismail, broke the fast. Such armed incidents coupled with dissatisfaction over the negotiations with GAM about the humanitarian pause again made for harsh words on the side of the Indonesian government. The Minister of Defence, Mahfud MD, warned on 11 December that a military operation might have to be launched if the talks with GAM in Geneva failed to produce results before the middle of January. Conciliatory gestures were also made. In an attempt to placate the Acehnese, Abdurrahman Wahid travelled to Aceh to add lustre to the commemoration of the day of Koran's Descent. In advance the Minister of Foreign Affairs, Alwi Shihab, had announced that Abdurrahman Wahid would be accompanied by 34 ambassadors and other diplomats from Islamic countries. He said that the reason for this was to show solidarity with the people of Aceh. When he addressed a crowd in Baiturrahman Mosque in Banda Aceh on 19 December, wearing a bulletproof vest, Abdurrahman Wahid spoke out in favour of a peaceful solution on 19 December.

In Irian Jaya Papuans and police clashed over the raising of the Morning Star flag. During one such incident, in Sorong on 22 August, three people died. In Wamena on 6 October around thirty people were killed. Some reports said forty people. Fighting between immigrants and Papuans also occurred. More violence erupted after 1 December, when the declaration of independence of 1961 was celebrated. The following day at least ten people were killed when police tried to lower the Morning Star flag. Six of them fell in Merauke, two in Fakfak. Elsewhere in Indonesia at least 15 people were killed when bombs exploded in or outside churches in Jakarta, Sukabumi, Mojokerto, Bandung, Pekanbaru, and Mataram on Christmas Eve. Bombs also exploded in Batam.

Main parties and organizations

Partai Demokrasi Indonesia (PDI)
One of the only two political parties which were allowed during the New
Order. PDI was founded in 1973. Four parties were forced to merge into PDI
at that time. By far the most important one was Partai Nasional Indonesia
(PNI), which was generally considered to be the party of Indonesia's first
president, Soekarno. PNI drew much of its strength from Java, in particular
from the religiously less strict Islamic community. In 1955, during the only
pre-New Order general election, PNI was the largest party with 22.3 per cent
of the votes. The other three parties which merged in PDI were the Roman
Catholic Partai Katolik, the Protestant Parkindo (Partai Kristen Indonesia),
and the army-linked IPKI (Ikatan Pendukung Kemerdekaan Indonesia).
Throughout its existence, PDI has been plagued by internal party conflicts, in
which the main players came from different groups within PNI. During one
of these conflicts Megawati declared herself chairperson when the participants in an extraordinary party congress in December 1993 had overwhelmingly supported her but party machinations had prevented a definite decision. In May 1996 her opponents organized an extraordinary party congress.
They turned to Megawati's predecessor Soerjadi to replace her as general
chairperson. A party split was the result. Megawati and many other members
and supporters of PDI did not recognize her replacement. The government in
turn did not recognize the PDI headed by Megawati. The conflict took a violent turn when on 27 July 1996 party headquarters, which had become the
physical centre of opposition against Soerjadi and by extension against the
government, was attacked. Megawati's party, first unofficially and later officially called PDI-Perjuangan, was only formally recognized after the fall of
Soeharto. Soerjadi's PDI continued to exist as a minor party.

Partai Persatuan Pembangunan (PPP)
One of the only two political parties which were allowed during the New
Order. PPP was founded in 1973. Of the four Islamic parties which were
forced to merge into it, the two most important ones were: Nahdlatul Ulama
and Parmusi (Partai Muslimin Indonesia). Parmusi, founded earlier in the

New Order period, had been intended as the political party of those who would have voted for Masjumi had not this party been banned in 1960. Because of government restrictions and interventions in party affairs, Parmusi was in no way comparable to Masjumi, a party for 'modernist' Muslims. In 1955 Masjumi had been Indonesia's second largest political party with 20.9 per cent of the votes. Masjumi drew much of its support from non-Javanese regions (including West Java), and, with respect to Java, especially from modernist Muslim city dwellers. During the New Order there were repeatedly conflicts in PPP between politicians originating from Parmusi and Nahdlatul Ulama. Difference in religious outlook lay at the root of such conflicts but especially the fact that due to government support, Parmusi leaders had a disproportionate share in determining PPP policy, while Parmusi's vote-attracting capacity was far less important than that of Nahdlatul Ulama. This was one of the reasons why, on the initiative of Abdurrahman Wahid, Nahdlatul Ulama distanced itself from PPP in December 1984 and no longer urged its members to vote PPP. After May 1998 most of the Nahdlatul Ulama people who had remained loyal to PPP left the party to support PKB. PPP came to present itself as an exclusively Islamic party, championing a much more prominent political and social role for Islam.

Golkar
The name is an abbreviation of Golongan Karya, or Functional Groups. What is meant by this term is in fact organizations of youth, labourers, women, students, and other social groups. Golkar was founded in 1964 under the auspices of the army to protect a number of such organizations against leftist agitation. Between 1965 and 1998 the authorities refused to call Golkar a political party. Consequently, political legislation always spoke of political parties and functional groups. Nevertheless during the New Order Golkar functioned as the government party. Due to the support of the local civil servants and military during general elections, it always won an overwhelming victory. Party policy was determined by Soeharto in his capacity as chairman of Golkar's advisory board. It took till after the end of the New Order till Golkar formally became a political party. In the closing years of the New Order, Golkar was led by Harmoko. After May 1998 he was succeeded as Golkar's general chairman by Akbar Tanjung.

Partai Amanat Nasional (PAN)
The political party of Amien Rais, PAN was founded in August 1998. Formally PAN is not exclusively an Islamic party. Its board brings together some non-Muslim intellectuals and Muslims who are well known for their opposition to New Order Islamic policy. Nevertheless, and also due to Amien

Rais's background, PAN is associated with the modernist Islamic community and especially with Muhammadiyah.

Partai Bulan Bintang (PBB)
PBB was established in July 1998. Its founders envisaged PBB as the heir to Masjumi. PBB belongs to the parties which represent political Islam. Among its leaders are some of the more radical champions of the drive to have the constitution acknowledge the special position of Islam in Indonesian state and society. General chairman of PBB is Yusril Ihza Mahendra.

Partai Kebangkitan Bangsa (PKB)
PKB was founded on the initiative of Abdurrahman Wahid in July 1998. In theory it is a 'national' party open to all Indonesians irrespective of their religion. In practice PKB draws heavily on the Nahdlatul Ulama network, thus getting its main support from 'traditional' devout Muslims and having its main base in Central and especially East Java. Initially Abdurrahman Wahid in his capacity as 'deklarator' of PKB gave the appearance of staying in the background, without having any formal function in the party. In July 2000 he became chairman of its religious advisory council and as such the most powerful person in PKB. In view of this, critics started to call PKB the 'second Golkar'. General chairman of PKB is Matori Abdul Djalil.

Ikatan Cendekiawan Muslim Indonesia (ICMI)
The Association of Muslim Intellectuals was founded in 1990. From its inception it was chaired by Habibie. ICMI functioned as a pressure group to give Muslims a greater say in Golkar and thus also in Indonesian politics. Its opponents accused ICMI of being a sectarian organization. One of the persons who consistently opposed ICMI was Abdurrahman Wahid. On various occasions he made no secret of deploring ICMI's use of Islam as an exclusive group marker and symbol to gain political aims.

Muhammadiyah
Muhammadiyah was founded in 1912 as an organization for Muslims who wanted to purify and modernize Islam as it was practised at that time in Indonesia. Hence it is often referred to as an organization of Indonesian modernist Muslims. In the course of time Muhammadiyah became a mass organization with millions of members and supporters. Contrary to Nahdlatul Ulama, Muhammadiyah never turned into a political party. From the time of its founding, part of Muhammadiyah's activities were devoted to the establishment of schools, hospitals, orphanages, and similar institutions. Amien Rais became chairman in 1990.

Nahdlatul Ulama
Nahdlatul Ulama was founded in 1926 as a socio-religious organization. One of its founders was Abdurrahman Wahid's grandfather, KH Moehammad Hasjin bin Asj'ari. Nahdlatul Ulama is the organization for those Muslims who reject the Islamic reform movement which reached Indonesia in the beginning of the twentieth century. As opposed to such 'modernist Muslims', followers of Nahdlatul Ulama are described as 'traditional' Muslims. Nahdlatul Ulama is based on a network of *ulama* (religious leaders) and *pesantren* (Islamic boarding schools). Abdurrahman Wahid became general chairman of Nahdlatul Ulama in 1984.

Indonesian cabinets between 1993 and 2000

Sixth Development Cabinet – 1993-1998

President
   General (Ret.) Soeharto
Vice-President
   General (Ret.) Try Sutrisno

Coordinating Minister of Politics and Security
   Lieutenant-General (Ret.) Soesilo Soedarman
Coordinating Minister of Economy, Finance, and Development Supervision
   Prof. Dr Saleh Afiff
Coordinating Minister of Industry and Trade[1]
   Ir Hartarto Sastrosoenarto
Coordinating Minister of People's Welfare
   Major-General (Ret.) Ir H. Azwar Anas
Minister of Internal Affairs
   General (Ret) M. Yogie Suardi Memet
Minister of Foreign Affairs
   Ali Alatas SH
Minister of Defence and Security
   General (Ret.) Edi Sudradjat
Minister of Justice
   Oetojo Oesman SH
Minister of Information
   Harmoko
   General (Ret.) R. Hartono (June 1997)
Minister of Finance
   Drs Mar'ie Muhammad

---

[1] In December 1995 the function was renamed Coordinating Minister of Production and Distribution.

Cabinet members and their wives

Minister of Trade
Prof. Dr Satrio Budihardjo Joedono[2]
Minister of Industry
Ir Tunky Ariwibowo
Minister of Agriculture
Prof. Ir Sjarifuddin Baharsjah
Minister of Mining and Energy
Lieutenant-General Ida Bagus Sudjana
Minister of Forestry
Ir Djamaloedin Soeryohadikoesoemo
Minister of Public Works
Ir Radinal Mochtar
Minister of Communications
Dr Haryanto Dhanutirto
Minister of Tourism, Post, and Telecommunications
Joop Ave
Minister of Cooperative Societies and Development of Small Entrepreneurs
Drs Subiakto Tjakrawerdaya
Minister of Labour
Drs Abdul Latief
Minister of Transmigration and Resettlement of Shifting Forest Cultivators
Ir Siswono Yudohusodo

[2]   In December 1995 the ministries of trade and industry were merged. The new minister was Tunky Ariwibowo.

Minister of Education and Culture
    Prof. Dr Ing. Wardiman Djojonegoro
Minister of Health
    Prof. Dr Sujudi
Minister of Religion
    Dr H. Tarmizi Taher
Minister of Social Affairs
    Mrs Drs Endang Kusuma Inten Soeweno
Minister without Portfolio of Research and Technology
    Prof. Dr Ing. B.J. Habibie
Minister without Portfolio/Secretary of State
    Drs Moerdiono
Minister without Portfolio/Secretary of the Cabinet
    Drs Saadillah Mursjid
Minister without Portfolio of National Development Planning/Head of the
    National Planning Bureau
    Prof. Ir Drs Ginandjar Kartasasmita
Minister without Portfolio of Food/Head of Bulog
    Prof. Dr Ibrahim Hasan
Minister without Portfolio of Population
    Prof. Dr Haryono Suyono
Minister without Portfolio of Investments/Head of the Investment
    Coordination Board
    Ir Sanyoto Sastrowardoyo
Minister without Portfolio of Agrarian Affairs
    Ir Sony Harsono
Minister without Portfolio of Public Housing
    Ir Akbar Tanjung
Minister without Portfolio of Environment
    Ir Sarwono Kusumaatmadja
Minister without Portfolio of Women's Role in Society
    Mrs H.J. Mien Sugandhi
Minister without Portfolio of Youth and Sport
    Hayono Isman
Minister without Portfolio of Efficiency of State Companies
    Major-General (Ret.) Tiopan Bernhard Silalahi

Attorney-General
    Singgih SH
Governor of the Central Bank
    Dr J. Soedradjad Djiwandono
    Dr Syahril Sabirin (February 1998)

Seventh Development Cabinet – March-May 1998

President
  General (Ret.) Soeharto
Vice-President
  Prof. Dr Ing. B.J. Habibie

Coordinating Minister of Politics and Security
  General (Ret.) Feisal Tanjung
Coordinating Minister of Economy, Finance, and Industry
  Prof. Dr Ir Ginandjar Kartasasmita
Coordinating Minister of Development Supervision and State Administrative Reform
  Ir Hartarto Sastrosoenarto
Coordinating Minister of People's Welfare and Combating Poverty
  Prof. Dr Haryono Suyono
Minister of Internal Affairs
  General (Ret.) R. Hartono
Minister of Foreign Affairs
  Ali Alatas SH
Minister of Defence and Security
  General Wiranto
Minister of Justice
  Prof. Dr H. Muladi SH
Minister of Information
  Prof. Dr Alwi Dahlan
Minister of Finance
  Dr Fuad Bawazier
Minister of Industry and Trade
  Mohamad Hasan
Minister of Agriculture
  Prof. Dr Ir Justika Sjarifuddin Baharsjah
Minister of Mining and Energy
  Dr Ir Kuntoro Mangkusubroto
Minister of Forestry and Estates
  Ir Sumahadi
Minister of Public Works
  Ir Rachmadi Bambang Sumadhijo
Minister of Communications
  Ir Giri Suseno Hadihardjono
Minister of Tourism, Art, and Culture
  Drs Abdul Latief

Minister of Cooperative Societies and Development of Small Entrepreneurs
 Subiakto Tjakrawerdaya
Minister of Labour
 Drs Theo L. Sambuaga
Minister of Transmigration and Resettlement of Shifting Forest Cultivators
 Lieutenant-General A.M. Hendropriyono[3]
Minister of Education and Culture
 Prof. Dr Ir Wiranto Arismunandar
Minister of Health
 Prof. Dr H. Farid Anfasa Moeloek
Minister of Religion
 Prof. Dr M. Quraish Shihab
Minister of Social Affairs
 Siti Hardijanti Hastuti Rukmana
Minister without Portfolio/Secretary of State
 Drs Saadillah Mursjid
Minister without Portfolio of Research and Technology
 Prof. Dr Ir Rahardi Ramelan
Minister without Portfolio of Investment/Head of the Investment
 Coordination Board
 Ir Sanyoto Sastrowardoyo
Minister without Portfolio of Agrarian Affairs
 Ary Mardjono

---

[3]   In September 2000 he became a member of PDI-P.

Minister without Portfolio of Public Housing
    Ir Akbar Tanjung
Minister without Portfolio of Environment
    Prof. Dr Juwono Sudarsono
Minister without Portfolio of Food, Horticulture, and Medicine
    Dr Haryanto Dhanutirto
Minister without Portfolio of Efficiency of State Companies
    Tanri Abeng
Minister without Portfolio of Women's Role in Society
    Mrs Drs Tutty Alawiyah
Minister without Portfolio of Youth and Sport
    H.R. Agung Laksono

Attorney-General
    Soedjono Chanafiah Atmonegoro SH
Governor of the Central Bank
    Dr Syahril Sabirin

Development Reformation Cabinet – May 1998 - October 1999

President Prof. Dr Ing. B.J. Habibie
Coordinating Minister of Politics and Security
    General (Ret.) Feisal Tanjung
Coordinating Minister of Economy, Finance, and Industry
    Prof. Dr Ir Ginandjar Kartasasmita
Coordinating Minister of Development Supervision and State Adminis-
    trative Reform
    Dr Ir Hartarto Sastrosoenarto
Coordinating Minister of People's Welfare and Combating Poverty
    Prof. Dr Haryono Suyono
Minister of Internal Affairs
    Lieutenant-General Syarwan Hamid
Minister of Foreign Affairs
    Ali Alatas SH
Minister of Defence and Security
    General Wiranto
Minister of Justice
    Prof. Dr Muladi SH
Minister of Information
    Lieutenant-General Yunus Yosfiah

Cabinet members and their wives

Minister of Finance
  Dr Bambang Subianto
Minister of Industry and Trade
  Prof. Dr Ing. Rahardi Ramelan
Minister of Agriculture
  Prof. Dr Ir Soleh Salahudin
Minister of Mining and Energy
  Dr Ir Kuntoro Mangkusubroto
Minister of Forestry and Estates
  Dr Ir Muslimin Nasution
Minister of Public Works
  Ir Rachmadi Bambang Sumadhijo
Minister of Communications
  Ir Giri Suseno Hadihardjono
Minister of Tourism, Art and Culture
  Drs Marzuki Usman
Minister of Cooperative Societies and Small and Medium Entrepreneurs
  Adi Sasono
Minister of Labour
  Drs Fahmi Idris
Minister of Transmigration and Resettlement of Shifting Forest Cultivators
  Lieutenant-General A.M. Hendropriyono SH
Minister of Health
  Prof. Dr Farid Anfasa Moeloek

Minister of Education and Culture
  Prof. Dr Juwono Sudarsono
Minister of Religion
  Prof. Drs Malik Fadjar
Minister of Social Affairs
  Prof. Dr Ir Justika Sjarifuddin Baharsjah
Minister without Portfolio/Secretary of State
  Ir Akbar Tanjung
Minister without Portfolio of National Development Planning
  Dr Boediono
Minister without Portfolio of Research and Technology
  Prof. Dr Ir Zuhal
Minister without Portfolio of Efficiency of State Companies
  Tanri Abeng
Minister without Portfolio of Food and Horticulture
  Dr Ir A.M. Saefuddin
Minister without Portfolio of Population
  Prof. Dr Ida Bagus Oka
Minister without Portfolio of Investment/Head of the Investment
  Coordination Board
  Hamzah Haz
Minister without Portfolio of Agrarian Affairs
  Drs Hasan Basri Durin
Minister without Portfolio of Public Housing
  Drs Theo L. Sambuaga
Minister without Portfolio of Environment
  Dr Panangian Siregar
Minister without Portfolio of Women's Role in Society
  Dr H. Tutty Alawiyah
Minister without Portfolio of Youth and Sport
  H.R. Agung Laksono

Attorney-General
  Soedjono Chanafiah Atmonegoro SH
  Andi Muhammad Ghalib (June 1998)
  Ismudjoko (June 1999)
Governor of the Central Bank
  Dr Syahril Sabirin

Cabinet of National Union – October 1999 - August 2000

President
  KH Abdurrahman Wahid

Vice-President
  Megawati Soekarnoputri
Coordinating Minister of Politics and Security
  General Wiranto
  Lieutenant-General (Ret.) Surjadi Soedirdja (February 2000)
Coordinating Minister of Economy, Finance and Industry
  Drs Kwik Kian Gie (resigned 10 August 2000)
Coordinating Minister of Health and Combating Poverty
  Dr Hamzah Haz
  Haryono Suyono (November 1999)
Minister of Internal Affairs
  Lieutenant-General (Ret.) Surjadi Soedirdja
Minister of Foreign Affairs
  Dr Alwi Shihab
Minister of Defence
  Prof. Dr Juwono Sudarsono
Minister of Justice and Legislation
  Prof. Dr Yusril Ihza Mahendra
Minister of Finance
  Dr Bambang Sudibyo
Minister of Industry and Trade
  Drs Yusuf Kalla
  Lieutenant-General Luhut Binsar Panjaitan (April 2000)
Minister of Agriculture
  Dr M. Prakosa
Minister of Mining and Energy
  Lieutenant-General Susilo Bambang Yudhoyono
Minister of Forestry and Estates
  Dr Nur Mahmudi Ismail
Minister of Communications
  Lieutenant-General Agum Gumelar
Minister of Exploration of the Sea
  Ir Sarwono Kusumaatmadja
Minister of Labour
  Dr Bomer Pasaribu SH
Minister of Education
  Dr Yahya Muhaimin

Minister of Health
  Dr Ahmad Suyudi
Minister of Religion
  Drs KH Tolchah Hasan
Minister of Housing and Regional Development
  Mrs Ir Erna Witoelar
Minister without Portfolio of Research and Technology
  Dr Muh. A.S. Hikam
Minister without Portfolio of Cooperatives and the Development of Small
  and Medium Enterpreneurs
  Drs Zarkasih Nur
Minister without Portfolio of Environment
  Dr Soni Kraff
Minister without Portfolio of Regional Autonomy
  Dr Ryaas Rasyid
Minister without Portfolio of Tourism and Art
  Drs H. Hidayat Jaelani
Minister without Portfolio of Investments and Development of State
  Enterprises
  Ir Laksamana Sukardi
  Rozy Munir (April 2000)
Minister without Portfolio of Youth and Sport
  Drs Mahadi Sinambela

Minister without Portfolio of Public Works
    Dr Ir Rafik Boediro Soetjipto
Minister without Portfolio of Women's Affairs
    Mrs Drs Khofifah Indar Parawansa
Minister without Portfolio of Human Rights
    Dr Hasballah M. Saad
Minister without Portfolio of Transmigration and Population
    Ir Al Hilal Hamdi
Minister without Portfolio of State Administrative Reform
    Rear Admiral Freddy Numberi
Minister without Portfolio of Social Problems
    Dr Anak Agung Gde Agung

Secretary of State
    Dr Ali Rahman
    Bondan Gunawan (January 2000)
Attorney-General
    Marzuki Darusman SH
Governor of the Central Bank
    Dr Syahril Sabirin
    Anwar Nasution (June 2000, acting governor)

Second Abdurrahman Wahid Cabinet (August 2000)

Coordinating Minister of Politics, Social Affairs and Security
    Lieutenant-General Susilo Bambang Yudhoyono[4]
Coordinating Minister of Economic Affairs
    Rizal Ramli
Minister of Internal Affairs and Regional Autonomy
    Lieutenant-General (Ret.) Surjadi Soedirdja
Minister of Foreign Affairs
    Alwi Shihab
Minister of Defence
    Prof. Dr Mahfud
Minister of Finance and Development of State Companies
    Prijadi Prapto Suhardjo
Minister of Religion
    Drs KH Tolchah Hasan

---

[4]   Susilo Bambang Yudhoyono was promoted to general at the end of September 2000. He retired from the army in November.

Minister of Agriculture and Forestry
   Prof. Dr Bungaran Saragih[5]
Minister of Education
   Dr A. Yahya Muhaimin
Minister of Health and Social Welfare
   Dr Ahmad Sujudi
Minister of Communication and Telecommunication
   Lieutenant-General (Ret.) Agum Gumelar
Minister of Manpower and Transmigration
   Al Hilal Hamdi
Minister of Industry and Trade
   Lieutenant-General (Ret.) Luhut Binsar Panjaitan
Minister of Energy and Mineral Resources
   Purnomo Yusgiantoro

[5]   As of 6 November 2000, that is after only two-and-a-half months, the Ministry of Agriculture and Forestry was split again. Bungaran Saragih was appointed Minister of Agriculture, Nur Mahmudi Ismail became Minister of Forestry.

Minister of Justice and Human Rights
    Prof. Dr Yusril Ihza Mahendra
Minister of Settlement and Regional Infrastructure
    Mrs Erna Witoelar
Minister of Culture and Tourism
    I Gde Ardika
Minister of Maritime Affairs and Fisheries
    Ir Sarwono Kusumaatmadja
Minister without Portfolio of Women's Affairs/Chairperson of the National
    Family Planning Board
    Mrs Khofifah Indar Parawansa
Minister without Portfolio of State Administrative Reform
    Prof. Dr Ryaas Rasyid
Minister without Portfolio of Cooperatives and the Development of Small
    and Medium Enterprises
    Drs Zarkasih Nur
Minister without Portfolio of Environment
    Sonny Keraf
Minister without Portfolio of Research and Technology
    Dr Muh. A.S. Hikam
Junior Minister of Forestry
    Dr Nur Mahmudi Ismail
Junior Minister of the Acceleration of Development in Eastern Indonesia
    Manuel Kaisiepo
Junior Minister of the Restructuring of the National Economy
    Cacuk Sudarijanto[6]

---

[6]   On 3 November 2000 Edwin Gerungan was appointed head of BPPN. Gerungan had been vice president of Citibank and executive vice-president of Bank Mandiri.

Military officers holding key positions in the cabinet since the 1980s

Coordinating Ministers of Politics and Security
General M. Panggabean (1978-1983)
General (Ret.) Surono (1983-1988)
Admiral (Ret.) Sudomo (1988-1993)
Lieutenant-General (Ret.) Soesilo Soedarman (1993-1998)
General (Ret.) Feisal Tanjung (1998-1999)
General Wiranto (1999)
Lieutenant-General (Ret.) Surjadi Soedirdja (February 2000)
Lieutenant-General Susilo Bambang Yudhoyono (August 2000)

Ministers of Defence and Security
General Andi Mohammad Jusuf (1978-1983)
General S. Poniman (1983-1988)
General (Ret.) L.B. Moerdani (1988-1993)
General (Ret.) Edi Sudradjat (1993-1998)
General Wiranto (1998-1999, succeeded by Prof. Dr Juwono Sudarsono)

Ministers of Internal Affairs
General Amir Machmud (1978-1983)
Lieutenant-General Soepardjo Roestam (1983-1988)
General (Ret.) Rudini (1988-1993)
General (Ret.) M. Yogie Suardi Memet (1993-1998)
General (Ret.) R. Hartono (March-May 1998)
Lieutenant-General Syarwan Hamid (1998-1999)
Lieutenant-General (Ret.) Surjadi Soedirdja (1999-)

Some key military functions since the 1980s[7]

Commanders of the Armed Forces
General Andi Mohammad Jusuf (April 1978)
General L.B. Moerdani (March 1983)
General Try Sutrisno (February 1988)
General Edi Sudradjat (February 1993)
General Feisal Tanjung (May 1993)
General Wiranto (February 1998)
Admiral Widodo Adi Sutjipto (October 1999)

Deputy Commanders of the Armed Forces
Admiral Widodo Adi Sutjipto (July 1999, new function)
General Fachrul Razi (November 1999 till September 2000)[8]
No new appointment

Commanders of Kopkamtib
Admiral R. Sudomo (April 1978)
General L.B. Moerdani (April 1983 till June 1988)
In September 1988 Kopkamtib was abolished and replaced by the less powerful Bakorstanas, which in turn was abolished in March 2000.

Chiefs of Staff/Deputy Commanders of Kopkamtib
General Yoga Soegama (May 1978)
General Wijoyo Suyono (December 1980 till December 1982)
No new appointment

Assistants for Security/Intelligence of the Ministry of Defence and Security
Major-General L.B. Moerdani (August 1974)

---

7   The rank mentioned is that at the time of appointment.
8   Since January 1999 Fachrul Razi had been secretary-general of the Department of Defence and Security. Before that he had been Chief of the General Staff of Armed Forces Headquarters.

Major-General M.I. Sutaryo (?)
Major-General Soedibyo (?)
Major-General I Gde Awet Sara (September 1987)
Major-General M.I. Sutaryo (October 1988)
Major-General Asmono Arismunandar (August 1990)
Major-General Bantu Hardjijo (August 1992)
Major-General Arie Sudewo (January 1994)
Major-General Syamsir Siregar (September 1994)
Major-General Yusuf Kartanegara (November 1995)
Rear Admiral Yuswadji (August 1997)
Rear Admiral Berty Ekel (March 1998)
Rear Admiral Yos Mengko (?)

Chiefs of Staff for Social and Political Affairs of Armed Forces Headquarters
Lieutenant-General M. Kharis Suhud (September 1978)
Lieutenant-General Gunawan Wibisono (February 1984)
Lieutenant-General Triantoro (August 1985)
Lieutenant-General Soegiarto (January 1987)
Lieutenant-General Harsudiono Hartas (March 1988)
Lieutenant-General Hariyoto Pringgo Sudirjo (May 1993)
Lieutenant-General R. Hartono (January 1994)
Lieutenant-General Moch. Ma'ruf (February 1995)
Lieutenant-General Syarwan Hamid (February 1996)
Lieutenant-General Yunus Yosfiah (September 1997)
Lieutenant-General Susilo Bambang Yudhoyono (March 1998)
Function abolished at the end of 1998

Heads of the Information Centre of the Armed Forces
Major-General Syarwan Hamid (March 1993)
Brigadier-General Suwarno Adiwijoyo (February 1995)
Brigadier-General Amir Syarifudin (February 1996)
Brigadier-General Slamet Supriadi (March 1997)
Brigadier-General Abdul Wahab Mokodongan (August 1997)
Major-General Syamsul Ma'arif (June 1998)
Major-General Sudrajat (August 1999)
Junior Marshal Graito Usodo (January 2000)

Chiefs of Staff of the Army
Lieutenant-General Widodo (January 1978)
General Poniman (April 1980)
Lieutenant-General Rudini (March 1983)
General Try Sutrisno (June 1986)

General Edi Sudradjat (February 1988)
General Wismoyo Arismunandar (April 1993)
General R. Hartono (February 1995)
General Wiranto (June 1997)
General Subagyo Hadisiswoyo (February 1998)[9]
Lieutenant-General Tyasno Sudarto (December 1999)[10]
Lieutenant-General Endriartono Sutarto (October 2000)

Deputy Chiefs of Staff of the Army
Lieutenant-General Poniman (October 1977)
vacant (April 1980)
Lieutenant-General Triantoro (May 1983)
Major-General Try Sutrisno (August 1985)
Lieutenant-General Edi Sudradjat (June 1986)
Lieutenant-General Wismoyo Arismunandar (August 1992)
Major-General Soerjadi (May 1993)
Lieutenant-General F.X. Sudjasmin (February 1995)
Lieutenant-General Subagyo Hadisiswoyo (June 1997)
Lieutenant-General Soegiono (March 1998)
Lieutenant-General Johny Lumintang (January 1999)
Lieutenant-General Djamari Chaniago (November 1999)
Lieutenant-General Endriartono Sutarto (March 2000)
Lieutenant-General Kiki Syahnakri (November 2000)

Chiefs of the National Police
Police Lieutenant-General Dr Awaluddin Djamin (September 1978)
Police Lieutenant-General Anton Sudjarwo (December 1982)
Police General Drs Moch. Sanoesi (July 1986)
Police Lieutenant-General Drs Kunarto (February 1991)
Police Major-General Drs Banurusman (April 1993)
Police General Drs Dibyo Widodo (March 1996)
Police General Roesmanhadi (June 1998)
Police Lieutenant-General KPH Rusdihardjo (January 2000)[11]

---

[9]   In September 1999 Subagyo Hadisiswoyo became military advisor of Abdurrahman Wahid. In November 1999 he was appointed chairman of the Supreme Advisory Council.
[10]   In June 2000 newspapers reported on the alleged involvement of Tyasno Sudarto in the printing and distribution of counterfeit money.
[11]   Abdurrahman Wahid gave as the reason for the replacement of Rusdihardjo that the latter had disregarded his order to arrest Tommy Soeharto in relation to a bombing attempt at the Jakarta Stock Exchange. Tommy Soeharto had been questioned by police, but had been released because of lack of evidence.

Police General Suryantoko Bimantoro (September 2000, acting Chief of Police)[12]

Commanders of the Marine Corps
Lieutenant-General (Marines) Kahpi Suriadiredja (July 1977)
Brigadier-General (Marines) Muntaram (May 1983)
Brigadier-General (Marines) Aminullah Ibrahim (January 1987)
Major-General (Marines) Baroto Sardadi (August 1990)
Brigadier-General (Marines) Gafur Chaliq (December 1992)
Major-General (Marines) Djoko Pramono (April 1994)
Brigadier-General (Marines) Suharto (February 1996)
Brigadier-General (Marines) Harry Triono (November 1999)

Commanders of Kostrad
Major-General Wiyogo Atmodarminto (January 1978)
Brigadier-General Ismail (March 1980)
Major-General Rudini (January 1981)
Major-General Soeweno (May 1983)
Major-General Suripto (January 1986)
Major-General Adolf Sahala Rajagukguk (August 1987)
Major-General Soegito (March 1988)
Major-General Wismoyo Arismunandar (August 1990)
Major-General Kuntara (July 1992)
Major-General Tarub (September 1994)
Lieutenant-General Wiranto (April 1996)
Lieutenant-General Sugiono (June 1997)
Lieutenant-General Prabowo Subianto (March 1998)
Major-General Johny Lumintang (22 May 1998)
Lieutenant-General Djamari Chaniago (May 1998)
Lieutenant-General Djaja Suparman (November 1999)[13]
Major-General Agus Wirahadikusumah (March 2000)
Major-General Ryamizard Ryacudu (August 2000)[14]

Commanders of RPKAD/Kopassandha/Kopassus
Major-General M. Yogie Suardi Memet (May 1975)
Brigadier-General Wismoyo Arismunandar (April 1983)
Brigadier-General Sintong Panjaitan (May 1985)
Brigadier-General Kuntara (August 1987)

12   Bimantoro is deputy chief of the national police.
13   Djaja Suparman became Commander of the Staff and Command School.
14   Ryamizard is a son-in-law of Try Sutrisno.

Brigadier-General Tarub (July 1992)
Brigadier-General Agum Gumelar (July 1993)
Brigadier-General Subagyo Hari Siswoyo (September 1994)
Major-General Prabowo Subianto (December 1995)
Major-General H. Muchdi Purwo Pranyoto (March 1998)
Major-General Syahrir M.S. (May 1998)
Brigadier-General Amirul Isnaini (June 2000)

Heads of Bakin
General Yoga Soegama (January 1974)
Major-General Soedibyo (April 1989)
Lieutenant-General Moetojib (April 1996)
Lieutenant-General Zaini Azhar Maulani (September 1998)
Lieutenant-General Arie J. Kumaat (November 1999)

Heads of BIA (the continuation of BAIS after January 1994)
Major-General Arie Sudewo[15]
Major-General Syamsir Siregar (November 1994)
Major-General Farid Zainuddin (September 1996)
Major-General Zacky Anwar Makarim (August 1997)[16]
Major-General Tyasno Sudarto (January 1999)
(November 1999)
Junior Marshal Ian Santoso Perdanakusuma (January 2000)

Military Commanders of Aceh (the command was disbanded in April 1985)
Brigadier-General R.A. Saleh (January 1978)
Brigadier-General Djoni Abdurachman (January 1982)
Cavalry Brigadier-General Nana Narundana (May 1983)

Military Commanders of North Sumatra (after Aceh was included in the command in April 1985)
Major-General Suripto (April 1985)
Major-General Djarot Supadmo (January 1986)
Major-General Ali Geno (April 1986)
Major-General Asmono Arismunandar (June 1987)
Major-General Djoko Pramono (August 1988)
Major-General H.R. Pramono (July 1990)
Brigadier-General A. Pranowo (April 1993)

---

[15] Arie Sudewo had been deputy head of BAIS.
[16] Zacky Anwar Makarim was transferred to Armed Forces Headquarters.

Brigadier-General Arie Kumaat (September 1994)
Major-General Sedarjanto (August 1995)
Major-General Tengku Rizal Nurdin (August 1997)
Major-General Ismed Yuzairi (April 1998)
Major-General Abdul Rahman Gaffar (January 1999)
Major-General Affandi (November 1999)
Major-General I Gede Purnawa (June 2000)

Military Commanders of Jakarta
Brigadier-General Norman Sasono (October 1977)
Major-General Try Sutrisno (December 1982)
Major-General Soegito (April 1985)
Major-General Surjadi Soedirdja (March 1988)
Major-General Kentot Harseno (August 1990)
Brigadier-General A.M. Hendropriyono (April 1993)
Major-General Wiranto (December 1994, his previous position was Chief of
   Staff of the Military Command of Jakarta)
Major-General Sutiyoso (March 1996)
Major-General Syafrie Syamsuddin (September 1997)
Major-General Djaja Suparman (July 1998)
Major-General Ryamizard Ryacudu (November 1999)
Major-General Slamet Kirbiantoro (August 2000)
Major-General Bibit Waluyo (January 2001)

Military Commanders of the Lesser Sunda Islands
Brigadier-General Dading Kalbuadi (October 1978)
Brigadier-General R.P.D. Sutarto (April 1985)
Major-General Adolf Sahala Rajagukguk (March 1986)
Brigadier-General Djoko Pramono (August 1987)
Major-General Sintong Panjaitan (August 1988)
Major-General Herman Bernard Leopold Mantiri (January 1992)
Major-General Soewardi (August 1992)
Brigadier-General Theo Syafei (March 1993)[17]
Major-General R. Adang Ruchiatna Purwadirdja (February 1994)
Major-General H. Abdul Rivai (September 1995)
Major-General Syahrir M.S. (July 1997)
Major-General Yudomo Sastrosuhardjo (May 1998)

[17] His previous function had been Commander for Operations in East Timor. In January 1992 he had succeeded Brigadier-General R.S. Warouw in this post.

Major-General Adam Damiri (June 1998)
Major-General Kiki Syahnakri (November 1999)[18]

Military Commanders of West Irian (after May 1985 of West Irian and the Moluccas)
Brigadier-General Chalimi Imam Santoso (July 1978)
Brigadier-General Raja Kami Sembiring (June 1982)
Major-General Hasudungan Simandjuntak (May 1985)
Brigadier-General Setiyana (March 1986)
Major-General Wismoyo Arismunandar (January 1987)
Major-General Abinowo (February 1989)
Major-General E.E. Mangindaan (August 1992)
Major-General Tarub (June 1993)
Brigadier-General I. Ketut Wirdhana (September 1994)
Brigadier-General Dunidja D. (September 1995)
Major-General Johny Lumintang (August 1996)
Major-General Amir Sembiring (April 1998)
Brigadier-General A. Inkiriwang (November 1999)

Military Commanders of the Moluccas (formed in May 1999)
Brigadier-General Max Markus Tamaela
Colonel (Infantry) I Made Yassa (June 2000)

Main source: *Indonesia* no. 26 (October 1978), pp. 159-177; no. 29 (April 1980), pp. 155-175; no. 33 (April 1982), pp. 129-148; no. 36 (October 1983), pp. 99-134), no. 37 (April 1984), pp. 145-169; no. 40 (October 1985), pp. 131-164; no. 45 (April 1988), pp. 137-162); no. 48 (October 1989), pp. 64-96; no. 53 (April 1992), pp. 93-137; no. 55 (April 1993), pp. 177-198; no. 56 (October 1993), pp. 119-53; no. 58 (October 1994), pp. 83-103; no. 60 (October 1995), pp. 101-147; no. 65 (April 1998), pp. 179-195; no. 67 (April 1999), pp. 133-163.

[18] Adam Damiri became Assistant for Operations of the Chief of Staff for General Affairs at Armed Forces Headquarters.

Governors, military commanders and chiefs of police of Jakarta 1996-2000

Governors of Jakarta
Major-General (Ret.) Surjadi Soedirdja (1992)
Major-General (Ret.) Sutiyoso (1997)[19]

Military Commanders of Jakarta
Major-General Sutiyoso (March 1996)
Major-General Syafrie Syamsuddin (September 1997)
Major-General Djaja Suparman (July 1998)
Major-General Ryamizard Ryacudu (November 1999)
Major-General Slamet Kirbiantoro (August 2000)

Chiefs of Police of Jakarta
Police Major-General Hamami Nata[20]
Police Major-General Drs Nugroho Djajusman (May 1998)
Police Major-General Nurfaizi (February 2000)
Police Brigadier-General Drs Mulyono Sulaiman (October 2000)[21]

19 He had to enter 'real retirement' in November 1999.
20 He was first placed at the national police headquarters, became governor of the Police Academy in May 1999, and coordinator of the specialist staff of the chief of national police in May 2000.
21 Mulyono Sulaiman's appointment was not undisputed. As chief of police of Yogyakarta he had been responsible for the investigation into the Udin murder.

List of suspects in the violence in East Timor in 1999 named by the office of the attorney-general

Abilio Soares (former governor of East Timor)

Major-General Adam Damiri (former commander of Irian Jaya and the Moluccas)

Brigadier-General (Pol.) Timbul Silaen (former chief of police of East Timor)

Brigadier-General FX Tono Suratman (former military commander of East Timor)

Colonel M. Nur Muis (former military commander of East Timor)

Lieutenant-Colonel (Pol.) Drs Hulman Gultom (former chief of police of Dili)

Lieutenant-Colonel Sujarwo (former military commander of Dili)

Lieutenant-Colonel Asep Kuswandi (former military commander of Liquica)

Leonito Martins (former regent of Liquica)

Lieutenant-Colonel (Pol.) Drs Adios Salova (former chief of police of Liquica)

Colonel Herman Sediono (former regent of Covalima)

Lieutenant-Colonel Lilik Kushardiyanto (former military commander of Suai)

Lieutenant-Colonel (Pol.) Gatot Subiaktoro (former chief of police of Suai)

Captain Ahmad Samsudin (former army chief of staff of Suai)

Lieutenant Sugito (former subdistrict commander in Suai)

Lieutenant-Colonel Yayat Sudradjat (former commander of the Tribuana Satgas, a Kopassus unit)

Izidio Manek (militia leader)

Olivio Mendosa Moruk (militia leader)[22]

Martinus Bere (militia leader)

In October four more suspects were added to the list. One of them was Eurico

---

[22] He was murdered on 5 September. His death was the immediate motivation for the attack the following day on the office of the United Nations High Commissioner for Refugees in the West Timor town of Atambua, during which three employees were killed.

Guterres, perhaps the most notorious of all the militia leaders. The other three were Vasco da Cruz (militia leader), Motornus (militia leader), and Lieutenant-Colonel Endar Priyatno (former Dili military district commander). Guterres was arrested in Jakarta on 4 October.[23]

---

23   The arrest was said to be unrelated to an appeal by Abdurrachman Wahid, who had called for Guterres's arrest in relation to the attack on the UNHCR office in Atambua. The reason for the arrest was said to be an inflammatory speech held by Guterres on 24 September in Atambua in which he urged militia members to retake the weapons which had been handed over to the police.

Glossary

aliran kepercayaan	(Javanese) mystical groups
alun-alun	town square
amuk massa	communal violence
anak mas	protégé
asas Pancasila	principle that on the penalty of disbandment social, religious, and political organizations have to pledge that Pancasila is their only ideological base, and not, for instance, a religion
asas tunggal	'sole base', = asas Pancasila
bambu runcing	bamboo spears
bank rekap	recapitalized bank
banteng	wild ox
becak	pedicab
bedug	mosque drum
bintang	star
bupati	regent
camat	subdistrict head
dakwah	Islamic missionary activities
dalang	puppeteer (in wayang)
dangdut	Indian and Arabic influenced pop music
daulat	(here) mass action to force a civil servant to lay down his function
dukun	traditional healer
dukun santet	dukun practicing black magic
dukun teluh	dukun practicing black magic
Gerakan Pengacau Keamanan	Movement of Disturbers of Peace (euphemism used to denote armed resistance groups)
halal bi-halal	giving and asking forgiveness at the end of the fasting month
Idul Fitri	feast at the end of the fasting month

ilmu kebal	(knowledge of) invulnerability
intel	intelligence
ishlah	(Ar) reform
istighotsah	mass prayer gatherings of Nahdlatul Ulama
jilbab	veil
jubbah	long flowing robe
kabupaten	regency
kapok	have enough of something, learn one's lesson
kauman	religious quarter of a town or city
kebablasan	blunt remarks
ketoprak	(Javanese) theater
kiai	title of an Islamic religious teacher or leader
koloran	cotton loincloth
kraton	palace
kredit macet	uncollectable credits
kretek	clove cigarettes
krismon	krisis moneter 'monetary crisis'
kuningisasi	'yellowing'; the practice of painting public buildings and objects yellow (the colour of the ruling party Golkar)
lagu wajib	compulsory songs (sung at school)
Lebaran	feast at the end of the fasting month
makar	subversion
melati	jasmine
merdeka	freedom
milik Muslim	Muslim property
milik pribumi	indigenous property
ngamandhito	(Jv) concentrate on spiritual affairs
non pribumi	'not indigenous'
Pancasila	Five Pillars, the Indonesian state principles
pandhito	(Jv) wise man
pantun	quatrain
pembekalan	to inform (literally 'to supply with, to provision')
pencak silat	kind of self-defence
peranakan	Chinese whose family has lived in Indonesia for many generations
pesantren	religious boarding school
petrus	penembakan misterius 'mysterious shootings' (of criminals whose bodies were left lying on the street)

pikun	senile
preman	hoodlum
pribumi	indigenous (as opposed to Chinese)
reformasi	reform(ation)
ruilslag	financial deal in which land is swapped
santri	strict Muslim
sembako	sembilan bahan pokok 'nine basic commodities'
semut merah	red ants (used for Megawati supporters)
sepi	quiet, deserted
suksesi	succession
sumpah pocong	a strong oath
susuhunan	traditional ruler of Surakarta
tahu	tofu, soybean curd
tempe	fermented soyabean cake
ulama	Muslim religious teacher or leader
warung	food stall
wayang	(Javanese) shadow theatre

Abbreviations and acronyms

AJI	Aliansi Jurnalis Independen - Alliance of Independent Journalists
ABRI	Angkatan Bersenjata Republik Indonesia - Indonesian Armed Forces
AKRAB	Aksi Rakyat Bersatu - United People's Action
Aldera	Aliansi Demokrasi Rakyat - People's Democracy Alliance
AMP (Yayasan)	Yayasan Amalbhakti Muslim Pancasila - Pancasila Muslim Charity Foundation
AMPERA	Amanat Penderitaan Rakyat - Suffering of the People
AMPI	Angkatan Muda Pembaharuan Indonesia - Indonesian Younger Generation for Reform
AMPII	anak, menantu, ponakan, istri, ipar - children, children-in-law, nephews, nieces, wives, in-laws (of powerful people who become a member of the People's Congress)
AMUK	'go beserk'; Aliansi Mahasiswa Untag untuk Keadilan - Seventeenth of August University Students' Alliance for Justice
APHI	Asosiasi Pengusaha Hutan Indonesia - Association of Indonesian Forest Entrepreneurs
Apkindo	Asosiasi Panel Kayu Indonesia - Indonesian Wood Panel Association
ASA	Adhikarya Sejati Abadi
ASEAN	Association of South-East Asian Nations
Asmindo	Asosiasi Mebel Kayu Indonesia - Indonesian Wood Furniture Association
ASOI	'fun'; Akal Sehat Orang Indonesia - Sound Common Sense of Indonesians
AWAM	Abdurrahman Wahid and Megawati (Soekarnoputri)

ATM	Automated Teller Machine
BAIS	Badan Intelijen Strategis - Strategic Intelligence Service
Bakin	Badan Koordinasi Intelijen Negara - State Co-ordinating Intelligence Service
Bakom PKB	Badan Komunikasi Penghayatan Kesatuan Bangsa - Communication Forum for the Internalization of the Unity of the Nation
Bakorstanas	Badan Koordinasi Bantuan Pemantapan Stabilitas Nasional - Coordination Body to Assist in the Consolidation of National Stability
balon	bakal calon - future candidate
Bank Exim	Bank Expor Impor
Banser	Barisan Serba Guna - Multi-Purpose Front
Bapindo	Bank Pembangunan Indonesia - Indonesian Development Bank
Barnas	Barisan Nasional - National Front
BBD	Bank Bumi Daya
BBKU	Bank Beku Kegiatan Usaha - Banks Whose Business Activities Are Frozen
BBM	1. Buton, Bugis, Makassar; 2. Bakar, Bunuh Muslim - Burn and Kill Muslims
BBO	Bank Beku Operasi - Frozen Operations Bank
BCA	Bank Central Asia
BDN	Bank Dagang Negara
BDNI	Bank Dagang Nasional Indonesia
BIA	Badan Intelijen ABRI - Armed Forces Intelligence Service
BKSPP	Badan Kerja Sama Pondok Pesantren - Cooperative Body of Pesantren
BKUI	Badan Koordinasi Umat Islam - Coordination Body of the Islamic Community
BLBI	Bantuan Likuiditas Bank Indonesia - Liquidity Credit from Bank Indonesia
BNN	Bank Nusa Nasional
BPIS	Badan Pengelola Industri Strategis - Body for the Management of Strategic Industries
BPPC	Badan Penyangga dan Pemasaran Cengkeh - Body for the Buffer Stock and Marketing of Cloves
BPPN	Badan Penyehatan Perbankan Nasional. Its official English name is IBRA, Indonesian Bank Restructuring Agency

BPPT	Badan Pengkajian dan Penerapan Teknologi - Body for the Study and Application of Technology
BPR Nusumma	Bank Perkreditan Rakyat Nahdlatul Ulama-Summa - Nahdlatul Ulama-Summa People's Credit Banks
BTN	Bank Tabungan Negara
BTO	Bank Take Over
Bulog	Badan Urusan Logistik - Body for Logistic Affairs
BUN	Bank Umum Nasional
CAR	Capital Adequacy Ratio
CBC	Center for Banking Crisis
CBS	Currency Board System
CCN	Corruption, Collusion, and Nepotism
CGI	Consultive Group on Indonesia
CIDES	Centre for Information and Development Studies
CLG	Citra Lamtoro Gung Persada
CMNP	Citra Marga Nusaphala Persada
CSIS	Centre for Strategic and International Studies
Dakab (Yayasan)	Yayasan Dana Karya Abadi - Eternal Work Fund Foundation
Damandiri	Yayasan Dana Sejahtera Mandiri - Autonomous Welfare Fund Foundation
DDII	Dewan Dakwah Islamiyah Indonesia - Indonesian Council for Islamic Mission
DEN	Dewan Ekonomi Nasional - National Economic Council
Dharmais (Yayasan)	Yayasan Dharma Bhakti Sosial - Social Voluntary Work Foundation
DOM	Daerah Operasi Militer - Military Operations Area
DOR	= DOT
DOT	Daftar Orang Tercela - List of Culpable Persons
DPKEK	Dewan Pemantapan Ketahanan Ekonomi dan Keuangan - Council for the Stabilization of Monetary and Economic Resilience
DPKSH	Dewan Penegakan Keamanan dan Sistem Hukum - Council for Maintaining Security and the Legal System
DPR	Dewan Perwakilan Rakyat - Parliament
DPRD	Dewan Perwakilan Rakyat Daerah - Regional parliament
DPUN	Dewan Pengembangan Usaha Nasional - National

	Council for Business Development (also ironically called Dewan Pengemplangan Utang Nasional - National Council for the Non-Payment of Debts)
DRN	Dewan Riset Nasional - National Research Council
DSTP	PT Dua Satu Tiga Puluh - Two One Thirty Inc.
EGP	Era Giat Prima
Famred	Front Aksi Mahasiswa untuk Reformasi dan Demokrasi - Student Action Front for Reform and Democracy
FAO	Food and Agriculture Organization
FBSI	Federasi Buruh Seluruh Indonesia - All Indonesia Workers' Federation
FBUI	Forum Bersama Umat Islam - Joint Forum of the Islamic Community
FKOI	Forum Komunikasi Ormas Islam - Communication Forum of Islamic Mass Organizations
FKPBT 1984	Front Keadilan Peristiwa Berdarah Tanjung Priok 1984 - Front for Justice for the 1984 Bloody Event of Tanjung Priok
FKPI	Forum Kebangsaan Pemuda Indonesia - National Forum of Young People of Indonesia
FKPPI	Forum Komunikasi Putra Putri Purnawirawan ABRI - Communication Forum of Sons and Daughters of Retired Armed Forces Officers
FKSMJ	Forum Komunikasi Senat Mahasiswa Jakarta - Communication Forum of Jakarta Student Senates
Forbes	Forum Bersama - Joint Forum
Forkot	Forum Kota - City Forum
Formasi	Forum Mahasiswa Riau untuk Reformasi - Riau Student Forum for Reformation
FPB	Front Penyelamat Bangsa - Front of Saviours of the Nation
FPI	Front Pembela Islam - Front of Defenders of Islam
FPKR	Forum Pemurnian Kedaulatan Rakyat - Forum for Full People's Sovereignty
FPMIT	Forum Pemuda dan Mahasiswa Indonesia Timur - Forum of Youths and Students from Eastern Indonesia
Fretilin	Frente Revolutionaria de Timor Leste Indepen-

	dente - Revolutionary Front for the Independence of East Timor
FSAC	Financial Sector Action Committee
FSPI	Federasi Serikat Petani Indonesia - Federation of Indonesian Farmers' Unions
Fungsi	Forum Ummat Pendukung Konstitusi - Forum of the Islamic Community Supporting the Constitution
Furkon	Forum Umat Islam Penegak Keadilan dan Konsitusi - Muslim Forum of the Upholders of Justice and the Constitution
G 15	Group of 15
GAM	Gerakan Aceh Merdeka - Free Aceh Movement
GAMAM	Gerakan Aksi Mahasiswa Anti Maksiat - Anti-Sin Student Action Movement
Ganti	Gerakan Anti-Kiai - Anti-Kiai Movement
Gantung	Gerakan Anti Tenung - Anti-Sorcery Movement
GATT	General Agreement on Tariffs and Trade
GCR	Gerakan Cinta Rupiah - Love the Rupiah Movement
Gempita	Gerakan Masyarakat Peduli Harta Negara - Movement of the People Concerned about the State's Finances
Getar	'shake', Gerakan Cinta Rupiah - Love the Rupiah Movement
GINSI	Gabungan Importir Nasional Seluruh Indonesia – All-Indonesia Association of National Importers
GKPB	Gerakan Keadilan dan Persatuan Bangsa - Movement for Justice and Union of the Nation
GMKI	Gerakan Mahasiswa Kristen Indonesia - Indonesian Protestant Student Movement
GMNI	Gerakan Mahasiswa Nasional Indonesia - Indonesian National Student Movement
Golkar	Golongan Karya
Golput	Golongan Putih - White Group
GPI	Gerakan Pemuda Islam - Islamic Youth Movement
GPK	Gerakan Pemuda Ka'bah -Movement of Ka'bah Youth
GRN	(Forum) Gerakan Reformasi Nasional - (Forum of) the National Reformation Movement
GRUP	Gerakan Rakyat untuk Perubahan - People's Movement for Change

GUPPI	Gabungan Usaha Perbaikan Pendidikan Islam - Federation for the Improvement of Islamic Education
HAM	Hak Asasi Manusia - Human Rights
Hammas	Himpunan Mahasiswa Muslim Antarkampus - Inter Campus Association of Muslim Students
Harawi Sekawan	Haji Abdurrahman Wahid Sekawan - Haji Abdurrahman Wahid and Friends
Helo	Hendropriyono Law Office
HKTI	Himpunan Kerukunan Tani Indonesia - Indonesian Farmers' Association
HMI	Himpunan Mahasiswa Islam - Islamic Student Union
HMI-MPO	HMI Majelis Penyelamat Organisasi - HMI Council of Saviours of the Organization
Humpuss	Hutomo Mandala Putra Soeharto Sumahardjuno
IAIN	Institut Agama Islam Negeri - State Islamic Institute
IBRA	Indonesian Bank Restructuring Agency (= BPPN)
ICMI	Ikatan Cendekiawan Muslim se-Indonesia -All-Indonesia League of Muslim Intellectuals
ICW	Indonesian Corruption Watch
Ikadin	Ikatan Advokat Indonesia - Indonesian League of Lawyers
IKIP	Institut Keguruan dan Ilmu Pendidikan - Teachers' Training College
Iluni	Ikatan Alumni - Alumni Federation
IMF	International Monetary Fund
IMPETTU	Ikatan Mahasiswa dan Pemuda Timor Timur - League of Students and Young People from East Timor
INDRA	Indonesian Debt Restructuring Agency
INFID	International Forum on Indonesian Development
Interfet	International Forces in East Timor
IPB	Institut Pertanian Bogor - Bogor Institute of Agriculture
IPKI	Ikatan Pendukung Kemerdekaan Indonesia - League of Supporters of Indonesian Independence
IPS	Institute for Policy Studies
iptek	ilmu pengetahuan dan teknologi - science and technology

IPTN	Industri Pesawat Terbang Nusantara - National Aircraft Industry
Iramasuka	Irian Jaya, Maluku, Sulawesi, Kalimantan
IRC	Independent Review Committee
ITB	Institut Teknologi Bandung - Bandung Institute of Technology
IUD	Intra-uterine device
Jabotabek	Jakarta, Bogor, Tangerang, Bekasi
Jakker	= JKR
Jamsostek	Jaminan Sosial Tenaga Kerja - Workers' Social Security
Jasindo	Jasa Asuransi Indonesia - Indonesian Insurance Services
JKR	Jaringan Kesenian Rakyat - People's Art Network
KAHMI	Keluarga Alumni Himpunan Mahasiswa Islam - Alumni of the Islamic Student Union
KAMMI	Kesatuan Aksi Mahasiswa Muslim Indonesia - Action Front of Indonesian Muslim Students
Kamra	Keamanan Rakyat - People's Security
KARMA	Komite Aksi Reformasi Mahasiswa Aceh - Reformation Action Committee of Acehnese Students
KBUI	Keluarga Besar Universitas Indonesia - Greater Universitas Indonesia Community
KIPP	Komite Independen Pemantau Pemilu - Independent Election Monitoring Committee
KIPP HAM	Komite Indonesia untuk Pencegahan Pelanggaran Hak Asasi Manusia - the Indonesian Committee for the Prevention of Violations of Human Rights
KISDI	Komite Indonesia untuk Solidaritas Dunia Islam - Indonesian Committee for Islamic World Solidarity
KKN	Korupsi, Kolusi, dan Nepotisme - Corruption, Collusion, and Nepotism
KKNF	Korupsi, Kolusi, Nepotisme, dan Feodalisme - Corruption, Collusion, Nepotism, and Feudalism
KKO	Korps Komando (former name of the Marines)
KMPRK	Kelompok Mahasiswa Pendukung Reformasi Konstitusional - Students Supporting Constitutional Reform

KNI	Komite Nasional Indonesia - Indonesian National Committee
KNI-Reformasi	Komite Nasional Indonesia untuk Reformasi-Indonesian National Committee for Reformation
KNIPP	Komite Nasional Indonesia untuk Perubahan dan Penyaluran Aspirasi Rakyat -Indonesian National Committee for Change and Conveying of the Aspirations of the People
KNPD	1. Komite Nasional Perjuangan Demokrat - National Committee for the Democratic Struggle; 2. Komite Nasional Pro Demokrasi - National Pro-Democracy Committee
KNPI	Komite Nasional Pemuda Indonesia - National Committee of Indonesian Youth
KNUD	Koalisi Nasional untuk Demokrasi - National Coalition for Democracy
Kobar	Komite Buruh untuk Aksi Reformasi - Workers' Committee for Reformation Action
KOKAM	Korps Kesiapsiagaan Angkatan Muda Muhammadiyah - Vigilance Command of Muhammadiyah Youths
kolap	koordinator lapangan - field coordinator
Komnas HAM	Komisi Nasional Hak Asasi Manusia - National Committee for Human Rights
Komrad	Komite Mahasiswa dan Rakyat untuk Demokrasi - Students' and People's Committee for Democracy
Kontras	Komisi untuk Orang Hilang dan Korban Kekerasan - Committee for People who Disappeared and for Victims of Violence
Kopassus	Komando Pasukan Khusus - Special Forces Command
Kopkamtib	Komando Operasi Pemulihan Keamanan dan Ketertiban - Command for the Restoration of Security and Order
Korpri	Korps Pegawai Republik Indonesia - Corps of Indonesian Civil Servants
Kosgoro	Kesatuan Organisasi Serbaguna Gotong Royong - Multi-Purpose Cooperation Organization
Kostrad	Komando Cadangan Strategis Angkatan Darat - Strategic Reserve Command of the Army

KPEHR	Komite Penyelamat Ekonomi dan Hak Rakyat - Committee of Saviours of the Economy and the Rights of the People
KPKD	Koalisi Perempuan Indonesia untuk Keadilan dan Demokrasi - Coalition of Indonesian Women for Justice and Democracy
KPM	Komite Pendukung Mega - Committtee of Mega Supporters
KPNI	Kesatuan Pemuda Nasional Indonesia - Indonesian National Youth Union
KPP	Komisi Penyelidik Pelanggaran - Commission of Inquiry
KPP HAM Timtim	Komisi Penyelidik Pelanggaran Hak Asasi Manusia Timor Timur - Commission of Inquiry into Human Rights Violations in East Timor
KPTAPOS	Komite Penyelidik Kejahatan Politik Soeharto - Committee of Investigators of the Political Crimes of Soeharto
KPU	Komisi Pemilihan Umum - General Election Commission
KRI	Komite Rakyat Indonesia - Indonesian People's Committee
krisek	krisis ekonomi - economic crisis
krismon	krisis moneter – monetary crisis
krismor	krisis moral - moral crisis
krisper	krisis kepercayaaan - crisis of confidence
kristal	krisis total - total crisis
KSR	Komite Suara Rakyat - Committee of the Voice of the People
KUII	Kongres Umat Islam Indonesia - Congress of the Indonesian Islamic Community
KUIRK	Komite Umat Islam untuk Reformasi Konstitusional - Committee of the Islamic Community for Constitutional Reform
LBH	Lembaga Bantuan Hukum - Legal Aid Foundation
LBHN	Lembaga Bantuan Hukum Nusantara - Nusantara Legal Aid Foundation
Lemhanas	Lembaga Pertahanan Nasional - National Defence Institute
Lekra	Lembaga Kebudajaan Rakjat - People's Cultural Association
LIPI	Lembaga Ilmu Pengetahuan Indonesia - Indo-

	nesian Institute of Science
litsus	Penelitian Khusus - Special Screening
LPI	Lasykar Pembela Islam - Army of the Defenders of Islam
Malari	Malapetaka Limabelas Januari - 15 January Disaster
MAR, MARA	Majelis Amanat Rakyat - Council of the Message of the People
MARI	Majelis Rakyat Indonesia - Indonesian People's Council
Masjumi	Madjelis Sjuro Muslimin Indonesia - Advisory Council of Indonesian Muslims
Masyumi Baru	New Masyumi (Masyarakat Umat Muslimin Indonesia - Indonesian Muslim Community)
MCA	Medco Central Asia
MKGR	Musyawarah Kekeluargaan dan Gotong Royong - Conference of Brotherhood and Mutual Assistance
MMI	Majelis Muslimin Indonesia - Council of Indonesian Muslims
Mobnas	Mobil Nasional - National Car
MPI	1. Masyarakat Perhutanan Indonesia - Indonesian Forestry Society; 2. Masyarakat Profesional Indonesia - Indonesian Society of Professionals
MSAA	Master of Settlement and Acquisition Agreement
MUI	Majelis Ulama Indonesia - Indonesian Council of Ulama
muntaber	'cholera', munafik tapi beruntung/berhasil - hypocritic but profitable/bringing results
Murba	Musyawarah Rakyat Banyak - People's Conference
NU	Nahdlatul Ulama
Nusamba	Nusantara Ampera Bhakti
OIC	Organization of the Islamic Conference
ONH	Operasi Naga Hijau - Green Dragon Operation
OPEC	Organization of Petroleum Exporting Countries
OPM	Organisasi Papua Merdeka - Free Papua Organization
Ortilos	Orang tidak mencoblos - People who do not perforate (the ballot paper)
PAB	Partai Amanat Bangsa - Party of the Message of the Nation

Appendix H

PADI	Persatuan Rakyat Demokratik Indonesia - Indonesian Democratic People's Union
pahe	paket hemat - thrifty package
PAL	Perindustrian Angkatan Laut – Naval Industry
PAM	Perusahaan Air Minum - Drinking Water Company
Pam Swakarsa	Pasukan Pengamanan Swakarsa - Voluntary Security Guards
Pamsung	Pasukan Pengamanan Langsung - Direct Security Troops
Pamtaksung	Pasukan Pengamanan Tidak Langsung - Indirect Security Troops
PAN	Partai Amanat Nasional - Party of the National Message
Parkindo	Partai Kristen Indonesia - Indonesian (Protestant) Christian Party
Parmi	Parlemen Mahasiswa Indonesia - Parliament of Indonesian Students
PBB	Partai Bulan Bintang - Crescent and Star Party
PBHI	Perhimpunan Bantuan Hukum dan Hak Asasi Manusia Indonesia - Indonesian Association for Legal Aid and Human Rights
PDBI	Pusat Data Bisnis Indonesia - Centre for Indonesian Business Data
PDI	Partai Demokrasi Indonesia - Indonesian Democratic Party
PDI-P	Partai Demokrasi Indonesia Perjuangan - Struggle Indonesian Democratic Party
PDR	Partai Dalaut Rakyat - People's Sovereignty Party
Perbanas	Perhimpunan Bank-Bank Nasional Swasta - Association of Private National Banks
Perkasa	Perjuangan Kedaulatan Rakyat dan Kesatuan Bangsa - Fighters for People's Sovereignty and Unity of the Nation
Persis	Persatuan Islam - Muslim Union
Pertamina	Perusahaan Pertambangan Minyak dan Gas Bumi Negara - State Oil and Natural Gas Company
Perti	Pergerakan Tarbiyah Islamiyah - Movement of Islamic Education
petrus	penembakan misterius – mysterious shootings
PGI	Persatuan Gereja-Gereja Indonesia - Indonesian Communion of Churches

PII	Pelajar Islam Indonesia - Indonesian Islamic Pupils
Pijar	Pusat Informasi dan Jaringan Aksi untuk Reformasi - Centre of Information and Action Network for Democratic Reform
Pindad	Perindustrian Angkatan Darat - Army Industries
PK	Partai Keadilan - Justice Party
PKB	Partai Kebangkitan Bangsa -Party of the Awakening of the Nation
PKP	Partai Keadilan dan Persatuan - Justice and Union Party
PKU	Partai Kebangkitan Umat - Party of the Awakening of the Religious Community
PLN	Perusahaan Listrik Negara - State Electricity Company
PMKRI	Perhimpunan Mahasiswa Katolik Republik Indonesia - Roman Catholic Students Association of the Indonesian Republic
PNI	Partai Nasional Indonesia - Indonesian National Party
PNI Baru	Partai Nasional Indonesia Baru - New Indonesian National Party
PNU	Partai Nahdlatul Ummat - Party of the Awakening of the Muslim Community
PPBI	Pusat Perjuangan Buruh Indonesia - Indonesian Centre for Labour Struggle
PPP	1. Partai Persatuan Pembangunan - Unity and Development Party; 2. putra putri presiden - sons and daughters of the president
PPRI	Persatuan Pengacara Reformasi Indonesia - Union of Indonesian Reformation Lawyers
PPSK	Pusat Pengkajian Strategi dan Kebijakan - Strategy and Policy Research Centre
promeg	pro-Megawati
PRD	Persatuan Rakyat Demokratik - People's Democratic Union; later Partai Rakyat Demokratik - People's Democratic Party
PSII	Partai Sarekat Islam Indonesia – Indonesian Islamic League Party
PT	Perseroan Terbatas - Limited/incorporated (company)

PTUN	Pengadilan Tata Usaha Negara - State Administrative Court
PUDI	Partai Uni Demokrasi Indonesia - Indonesian Democracy Union Party
Puspitek	Pusat Penelitian Ilmu Pengetahuan dan Teknologi - Centre for Scientific and Technological Research
PwC	PricewaterhouseCoopers
PWI	Persatuan Wartawan Indonesia - Indonesian Union of Journalists
QAF	Quality Asian Food Ltd
Ratih	Pasukan Rakyat Terlatih - Trained People's Troops
RCTI	Rajawali Citra Televisi Indonesia
RPKAD	Resimen Pasukan Komando Angkatan Darat – Commando Regiment of the Army
RRI	Radio Republik Indonesia – Indonesian Radio Broadcasting
SARA	Suku, Agama, Ras, dan Antargolongan - Ethnicity, Religion, Race, and Inter-Group Relations
Satgas	Satuan Tugas - Task Force
Satgas Masyarakat Irja	Satuan Tugas Masyarakat Irian Jaya - People of Irian Jaya Task Force
SBSI	Serikat Buruh Sejahtera Indonesia - Indonesian Prosperous Worker's Union
SCB	Standard Chartered Bank
SCTV	Surya Citra Televisi
SDM	Semua dari Makassar - All from Makassar
SDSB	Sumbangan Dana Sosial Berhadiah – Social Fund with Prizes
Semar	Sembilan Bahan Pokok Manunggal ABRI-Rakyat - Nine Basic Commodities Unite the Armed Forces and the People
sembako	sembilan bahan pokok - the nine basic commodities
SIAGA	Solidaritas Indonesia untuk Amien dan Mega - Indonesian Solidarity for Amien and Mega
sikon	situasi dan kondisi - the situation and condition
SIRA	Sentral Informasi Referendum Aceh – Information Centre for the Acehnese Referendum
SIRA RAKAN	Sidang Raya Rakyat Aceh untuk Kedamaian dan Kedaulatan - Mass Gathering of the Acehnese People for Peace and Sovereignty

Smalam	Komite Solidaritas Mahasiswa Lampung - Lampung Students'Solidarity Committee
SMID	Solidaritas Mahasiswa Indonesia untuk Demokrasi - Indonesian Student Solidarity for Democracy
SOKSI	Sentral Organisasi Karyawan Swadiri Indonesia - Indonesian Central Organization for Independent Employees
Sontak	Solidaritas Nasional Peristiwa Tanjung Priok - National Solidarity for the Tanjung Priok Event
SOS	Semua Orang Sulawesi - All People from Sulawesi
SPI	Serikat Pengamen Indonesia – Indonesian Street Singers'Association
SPSI	Serikat Pekerja Seluruh Indonesia – All-Indonesia Workers'Association
SRI	Serikat Rakyat Indonesia - Indonesian People's Union
STN	Serikat Tani Nasional - National Farmers'Union
SU MPR	1. Sidang Umum Majelis Permusywaratan Rakyat - General Session of the People's Congress 2. Sidang Umum Masyarakat Pejuang Referendum Aceh - General Session of the Fighters for a Referendum in Aceh
Suni, Partai	(Partai) Solidaritas Uni Nasional Indonesia –Indonesian National Solidarity Union Party
Supersemar	Surat Perintah Sebelas Maret - Order of 11 March
TAHT	Tim Advokasi Hak Azasi Manusia Perwira Tentara Nasional Indonesia - Human Rights Team of Lawyers of the Officers of the Armed Forces
TGPF	Tim Gabungan Pencari Fakta - Joint Fact-Finding Team
Timor	Teknologi Industri Mobil Rakyat - People's Car Industrial Technology
TNI	Tentara Nasional Indonesia - Indonesian National Armed Forces
TOPP	tua, ompong, peot, pikun - old, toothless, wrinkled, and senile
TPDI	Tim Pembela Demokrasi Indonesia - Team of Defenders of Indonesian Democracy
TPI	1. Televisi Pendidikan Indonesia; 2. Tugu Pratama Indonesia

TPN	Timor Putra Nasional
TPULNS	Tim Penanggulangan Utang Luar Negeri Swasta - Private Foreign Debt Settlement Team
Trikora	Tri Komando Rakyat - Three Commands of the People
Tritura	Tri Tuntutan Rakyat - Three Demands of the People
UI	Universitas Indonesia
UNDP	United Nations Development Program
UNHCR	United Nations High Commissioner for Refugees
UNTAET	United Nations Transitional Administration in East Timor
Wanhamkamnas	Dewan Pertahanan Keamanan Nasional -National Security and Defence Council
Wanra	Perlawanan Rakyat - People's Resistance
YDSM	Yayasan Dana Sejahtera Mandiri - Autonomous Welfare Fund Foundation
YKPK	Yayasan Kerukunan Persaudaraan Kebangsaan - National Brotherhood Foundation
YLBHI	Yayasan Lembaga Bantuan Hukum Indonesia - Indonesian Legal Aid Foundation

Bibliography

Journals, newspapers, periodicals, Internet sites

Abadi
Adil
Aksi
Asiaweek
Bangkit
Bidik suplemen Republika
Business Week
D&R
DëTAK
Far Eastern Economic Review
Forum Keadilan
Gatra
Indonesia Times, The
Indonesian Observer, The
Ishlah
Jakarta Post, The
Jawa Pos
Kabar dari Pijar
Kompas
Media Indonesia
Merdeka
Merdeka Minggu
New Straits Times
Opini
Panji Masyarakat
Perspektif
Pos Kota
Prospek
Radar Bogor
Rakyat Merdeka
Republika
Sabili
Siar
Straits Times, The
Suara Ambon on line

Suara Pembaruan
Tajuk
Tekad
Tempo
Tempo Interaktif
Ummat
Visi

Books and articles

1996
1997   *1996: Tahun kekerasan; Potret pelanggaran HAM di Indonesia.* Jakarta:
               Yayasan Lembaga Bantuan Hukum Indonesia.
Abdullah
1998   '"Kesadaran" menuju reformasi total', in: Alfiah Hamzah et al., *Suara*
               Mahasiswa, suara rakyat; Wacana intelektual di balik gerakan moral maha-
               siswa, pp. 41-52. Bandung: Remaja Rosdakarya.
ABRI
1998   *ABRI dan reformasi: Pokok-pokok pikiran ABRI tentang reformasi menuju*
               pencapaian cita-cita nasional. Jakarta: n.p.
Adirsyah, H.A, Boyke Soekapdjo, Dana K. Anwari, and Riyanto DW (eds)
1997   *Pemilu 1997; Antara fenomena kampanye dialogis & Mega Bintang.* Jakarta:
               Penakencana Nusadwipa.
Aditjondro, George Junus
1998a   *Harta Habibie.* N.p.: Manakutahu.
1998b   *Harta jarahan Harto.* N.p.: Manakutahu.
1998c   *Dari Soeharto ke Habibie: Guru kencing berdiri, murid kencing berlari;*
               Kedua puncak korupsi, kolusi, dan nepotisme rezim Orde Baru. Jakarta:
               Masyarakat Indonesia untuk Kemanusiaan (MIK) / PIJAR Indonesia.
Adnan, R.S. and Arvan Pradiansyah
1999   'Gerakan mahasiswa untuk reformasi', in: Soemardjan (ed.), *Kisah per-*
               juangan reformasi, pp. 133-97. Jakarta: Pustaka Sinar Harapan.
Al-Zastrouw Ng
1999   *Gus Dur siapa sih sampeyan; Tafsir teoritik atas tindakan dan pernyataan*
               Gus Dur. Jakarta: Erlangga.
Aminudin
1999   *Kekuatan Islam dan pergulatan kekuasaan di Indonesia sebelum dan sesudah*
               runtuhnya rezim Soeharto. Yogyakarta: Pustaka Pelajar.
Anderson, Benedict R. O'G.
1972   *Java in a time of revolution; Occupation and resistance, 1944-1946.*
               Ithaca/London: Cornell University Press.
Anwari SB, Dana K.
1998a   *Melacak dana revolusi Sukarno & dana yayasan Soeharto.* Jakarta: GMN
               Orayta.
1998b   *Pelacakan dana revolusi & harta Sukarno di era Orde Baru; Dana yayasan &*
               harta KKN Soeharto versi internet SiaR George J. Aditjondro, versi
               Christianto Wibisono, dan pendapat Amien Rais. Jakarta: Orayta Book.

Ardie, Tonny
1984   *Dakwah terpidana; Sebuah pleidoi.* Jakarta: Yayasan Bina Mandiri.
Arryman, Arif
1998   'Kondisi ekonomi menjelang Pemilu tahun 1999', in: Trimedja Pan-
            djaitan and Budiman Tanuredjo, *Dari Trisakti ke Semanggi; Perjalanan
            menuju Indonesia baru*, pp. 117-27. Jakarta: Serikat Pengacara Indonesia.
Asmawi
1999   *PKB; Jendela politik Gus Dur.* Yogyakarta: Titian Ilahi Press.
Aubrey, Jim (ed.)
1998   *Free East Timor; Australia's culpability in East Timor's genocide.* Milson's
            Point, NWW: Random House.
Barker, J.
1998   'State of fear; Controlling the criminal contagion in Suharto's New
            Order', *Indonesia* 66:7-42.
Barker, T.
n.d.   *Bank SUMMA; The 'sacred promise' shadow play (or the story of a father
            and his family).* Clayton: Monash Asia Institute. [Working Paper 106.]
Basri, Faisal H,
1997   'Mobil Nasional; Nasionalisme yang keruh', in: *Evaluasi Pemilu Orde
            Baru; Mengapa 1996-1997 terjadi pelbagai kerusuhan? Menyimak gaya poli-
            tik M. Natsir*, pp. 54-72. Bandung: Mizan. [Seri Penerbitan Studi Politik.]
Basri, Faisal H. et al
1999   *Mahasiswa pelopor dan penggerak people power; Kumpulan tulisan terpilih
            dari Kampus Perjuangan Rakyat.* Jakarta: Gramedia Widiasarana Indo-
            nesia.
Basyaib, Hamid
1998   *Agar Indonesia tetap bernyanyi.* Jakarta: Lentera.
Basyaib, Hamid and Hamid Abidin
1999   *Mengapa partai Islam kalah? Perjalanan politik Islam dari pra-pemilu '99
            sampai pemilihan presiden.* Jakarta: Alvabet.
Bhakti, Ikrar Nusa et al.
1999   *Tentara yang gelisah; Hasil penelitian YIPIKA tentang posisi ABRI dalam
            gerakan reformasi.* Bandung: Mizan.
Cahyono, Heru
1998   *Pangkopkamtib Jenderal Soemitro dan Peristiwa 15 Januari '74; Sebagai-
            mana dituturkepada Heru Cahyono.* Jakarta: Pustaka Sinar Harapan.
Djajadi, M. Iqbal
1999   'Kerusuhan dan reformasi', in: Selo Soemardjan (ed.), *Kisah perjuangan
            reformasi*, pp. 1-77. Jakarta: Pustaka Sinar Harapan.
DOM
1998   *DOM di Aceh; Laporan Amnesty International.* Jakarta: Institut Studi
            Arus Informasi.
DPR
1998   *DPR RI dalam menyikapi proses reformasi dan berhentinya Presiden
            Soeharto.* Jakarta: Sekretariat Jenderal Dewan Perwakilan Rakyat
            Republik Indonesia.

Dwipayana, G. and Ramadhan K.H.
1989   *Soeharto; Pikiran, ucapan, dan tindakan saya; Otobiografi seperti dipaparkan*
            kepada G. Dwipayana dan Ramadhan K.H. Jakarta: Citra Lamtoro Gung
            Persada.
Dijk, C. van
1997   'Recent developments in Indonesian politics; The Partai Demokrasi
            Indonesia', *Bijdragen tot de Taal-, Land- en Volkenkunde* 153:311-44.
Edwin, D., Hartono, Sri Budi Eko Wardani, and Ucu Aditya Gana
1997   '1996-1997: Tahun gejolak politik', in: *Evaluasi Pemilu Orde Baru;*
            Mengapa 1996-1997 terjadi pelbagai kerusuhan? Menyimak gaya politik M.
            Natsir, pp. 113-35. Bandung: Mizan. [Seri Penerbitan Studi Politik.]
Ghazali, Abd. Rohim (ed.)
1998   *Suara-suara perih masyarakat Indonesia setelah Orde Baru tumbang; What*
            is to be done. Bandung: Mizan.
Gill, Ranjit
1997   *Black September; Nationalistic ego, indifference and greed throw Southeast*
            Asia's equity and financial markets into turmoil. Singapore: Epic
            Management Services.
Golkar
1999   *Golkar retak?* Jakarta: Institut Studi Arus Informasi.
Habeahan, B.P., Ruduan L. Tobing and Edonard Sipahutar
1999   *Sidang Istimewa MPR dan Semanggi Berdarah.* Depok: Permata AD.
Habibie
1999   *Habibie status quo?* Jakarta: Tifa Demokrasi.
Hamzah, Alfian et al.
1998   *Suara Mahasiswa, suara rakyat; Wacana intelektual di balik gerakan moral*
            mahasiswa. Bandung: Remaja Rosdakarya.
Hanafi, A.M.
1998   *A.M. Hanafi menggugat; Kudeta Jend. Soeharto dari Gestapu ke Supersemar;*
            Catatan pengalaman pribadi seorang eksponen Angkatan 45. Lille: Edition
            Montblanc.
Hariyanto, I. (ed.)
1998   *Melangkah dari reruntuhan tragedi Situbondo.* Jakarta: Gramedia
            Widiasarana Indonesia.
Harta Soeharto
n.d.   *Harta Soeharto.* N.p.: n.n.
Haryanto, Ignatius
1999   *Kejahatan negara; Telaah tentang penerapan delik keamanan negara.* Jakarta:
            Lembaga Studi dan Advokasi Masyarakat.
Hassan, Sahar L., Kuat Sukardiyono and Dadi M.H. Basri
1998   *Memilih partai Islam; Visi, misi, dan persepsi PKB–PBB–PUI–PKU–*
            Keadilan–PPP–dll. Jakarta: Gema Insani.
Hendratmoko, Heru (ed.)
1997   *Terbunuhnya Udin.* N.p.: Aliansi Jurnalis Independen/Institut Studi
            Arus Informasi.

Hidayah, Nur
1998   *Kontroversi presiden wanita*. Jakarta: Pabelan Jayakarta.
Husaini, Adian (ed.)
1999   *Zionis Israel PREK; Pergolakan umat Islam Indonesia melawan zionis Israel.*
              Jakarta: KISDI/Global Cita Press.
Ismawan, Indra
1998   *Pengusutan harta Soeharto; Trik pencucian uang haram.* Edisi revisi.
              Yogyakarta: Media Pressindo.
1999   *Money Politics; Pengaruh uang dalam pemilu.* Yogyakarta: Media
              Pressindo.
Iswandi
1998   *Bisnis militer Orde Baru; Keterlibatan ABRI dalam bidang ekonomi dan pen-*
              garuhnya terhadap pembentukan rezim otoriter. Bandung: Remaja
              Rosdakarya.
Jaiz, Hartono Ahmad
1998   *Polemik presiden wanita dalam tinjauan Islam.* Jakarta: Pustaka al-
              Kautsar.
1999   *Bahaya pemikiran Gus Dur.* Jakarta: Pustaka al-Kautsar.
2000   *Bahaya pemikiran Gus Dur II; Menyakiti hati umat.* Jakarta: Pustaka al-
              Kautsar.
Jasin, M.
1998   *'Saya tidak pernah minta ampun kepada Soeharto'; Sebuah memoar.* Edited
              by Nurinwa Ki S. Hendrowinoto et al. Jakarta: Pustaka Sinar Harapan.
Jay, R.R.
1963   *Religion and politics in rural central Java.* New Haven, Conn.: Yale Uni-
              versity Southeast Asia Studies. [Cultural Report Series 12.]
Jenkins, D.
1984   *Suharto and his generals; Indonesian military politics 1975-1983.* Ithaca,
              N.Y.: Cornell Modern Indonesia Project.
Kastor, Rustam
2000   *Fakta, data dan analisa konspirasi politik RMS dan Kristen menghancurkan*
              ummat Islam di Ambon-Maluku; Mengungkap konflik berdarah antara
              ummat beragama dan suara hati warga Muslim yang teraniaya. Yogyakarta:
              Wihdah Press.
Katoppo, Aristides et al. (eds)
1999   *Menyingkap kabut Halim 1965.* Jakarta: Pustaka Sinar Harapan.
Kontroversi
1998   *Kontroversi Supersemar dalam transisi kekuasaan Soekarno-Soeharto.* Yog-
              yakarta: Center of Information Analysis Publications/Media Press-
              indo.
Krishna, Anand
1998   *Reformasi: gugatan seorang 'Ibu'.* Jakarta: Grasindo.
Krisis
1998   *Krisis ekonomi IV: Dari krisi moril ke ancaman chaos.* Jakarta: Kepus-
              takaan Populer Gramedia. [Illustration Database, Vol. 2, No. 1.]

Kristiadi, J., T.A. Legowo and Nt. Budi Harjanto (eds)
1997   Pemilihan Umum 1997; Perkiraan, harapan dan evaluasi. Jakarta: Centre
            for Strategic and International Studies.

Kunio, Yoshihara
1988   The rise of ersatz capitalism in South-East Asia. Singapore: Oxford Uni-
            versity Press.

Kwik Kian Gie and Nurcholish Madjid
1998   Masalah pri dan nonpri dewasa ini. Jakarta: Pustaka Sinar Harapan.

Lampito, Octo et al.
1998   Lengser keprabon. Yogyakarta: Grafika Wangsa Bakti.

Liotohe, Wimanjaya K.
1993   Prima dosa; Wimanjaya dan rakyat Indonesia menggugat imperium Suharto.
            Jakarta: Yayasan Eka Fakta Kata.
1997a   Prima duka; Pembantaian manusia terbesar abad ini. Jakarta: Yayasan Eka
            Fakta Kata.
1997b   Prima dusta; Dusta terbesar abad ini; Dokumen negara terpending raib.
            Jakarta: Yayasan Eka Fakta Kata.
1998   10 dosa besar Soeharto. Ciputat: Upaya Warga Negara.

Loebis, A.R.
1999   Kemelut berdarah Indonesia. Jakarta: Pabelan Jayakarta.

Mahathir bin Mohamad
1998   Currency turmoil. Kuala Lumpur: Limkokwing.

Mahendra, Yusril Ihza
1999   'Lengser keprabon', in: Selo Soemardjan (ed.) Kisah perjuangan refor-
            masi, pp. 197-211. Jakarta: Pustaka Sinar Harapan.

Majidi, Nasyith (ed.)
1994   Megaskandal; Drama pembobolan dan kolusi Bapindo; Catatan harian war-
            tawan. Bandung: Mizan.

Malik, Dedy Djamaluddin (ed.)
1998   Gejolak reformasi menolak anarki; Kontroversi seputar aksi mahasiswa
            menuntut reformasi politik Orde Baru. Bandung: Zaman Wacana Mulia.

Manggut, Wenseslaus
1998   Kami menolak Soeharto: kumpulan jajak pendapat. Jakarta: Institut Studi
            Arus Informasi.

Mangoenprawiro, Djoko Moelyo
1999   Kiat Andi Mohammad Ghalib memeriksa KKN Soeharto, keluarga dan kro-
            ninya; Mengulas langkah dan kebijaksanaan Jaksa Agung R.I. dalam mem-
            bongkar Korupsi, Kolusi dan Nepotisme, yang dilakukan oleh mantan Presi-
            den Soeharto, keluarga dan kroninya serta penyadapan telepon Presiden-
            Jaksa Agung. Jakarta: Raga Mukti Makmur.

Mann, R.
1998   Economic crisis in Indonesia; The full story. Singapore: Gateway Books.

Mardjono, Hartono
1997   Politik Indonesia (1996-2003). Jakarta: Gema Insani.
1998   Reformasi politik suatu keharusan. Jakarta: Gema Insani.

Marsinah
1994   *Preliminary report on the murder on Marsinah.* N.p.: Indonesian Legal
            Aid Foundation.
Massardi, Noorca M. (ed.)
1997   *Udin darah wartawan; Liputan menjelang kematian.* Bandung: Mizan.
Muhammad, Munib Huda
1998   *Pro-kontra Partai Kebangkitan Bangsa.* Jakarta: Fatma Press.
Mustaib AR and G. Yudarson Basumin (eds)
1999   *Profil dan visi 100 partai di era reformasi.* Jakarta: Kipas Putih Aksara.
Nadjib, Emha Ainun
1998   *Menyibak kabut saat-saat terakhir bersama Soeharto; 2,5 jam di istana
            (Kesaksian seorang rakyat kecil).* Yogyakarta: Zaituna, Jakarta: Hamas,
            Jombang: Padhang Bulan.
Najib, Muhammad
1998   *Membunuh Amien Rais.* Jakarta: Gema Insani.
Nasution, A.H.
1985   *Memenuhi panggilan tugas; Jilid 5: Kenangan masa Orde Lama.* Jakarta:
            Gunung Agung.
Pandjaitan, Trimedya and Budiman Tanuredjo
1998   *Dari Trisakti ke Semanggi; Perjalanan menuju Indonesia baru.* Jakarta:
            Serikat Pengacara Indonesia.
Parianom, Bambang and Dondy Ariesdianto
1999   *Megawati & Islam; Polemik gender dalam persaingan politik.* Surabaya:
            Antar Surya Jaya.
Parmana, Wahyu A. (ed.)
1999   *Melangkah di tengan badai; Pokok-pokok pikiran Jenderal TNI Wiranto.*
            Jakarta: Yayasan Kebangsaan Bersatu.
Patty, Servas Mario
1999   *Pak Harto; Pemimpin bangsa yang besar pasca Bung Karno.* Jakarta:
            Sahabat.
Pemilu
1997   *Pemilu 1997; Jajak pendapat dan analisa.* Jakarta: Institut Studi Arus
            Informasi.
Pemilihan
1999   *Pemilihan Umum 1999; Demokrasi atau rebutan kursi?* Jakarta: Lembaga
            Studi Pers dan Pembangunan.
Peristiwa
1997   *Peristiwa 27 Juli.* Jakarta: Institut Studi Arus Informasi/Aliansi Jurnalis
            Independen.
Pidato
1999   *Pidato pertanggungjawaban Presiden/Mandataris Majelis Permusyawa-
            ratan Rakyat Republik Indonesia di depan Sidang Umum Majelis Permus-
            yawaratan Rakyat Republik Indonesia 14 Oktober 1999.* Jakarta: PNRI.
Pompe, S.
1999   *De Indonesische algemene verkiezingen 1999.* Leiden: KITLV Uitgeverij.

Pour, Julius
1998   *Jakarta semasa lengser keprabon (100 hari menjelang peralihan kekuasaan).*
              Jakarta: Elex Media Komputindo.

Prasetyohadi
1998   *Media keserempet Timor.* Jakarta: Institut Studi Arus Informasi.

Profil
1999   *Profil partai politik peserta pemilu 1999.* Jakarta: Pabelan Jayakarta.

Pusat Studi dan Pengembangan Informasi
1998   *Tanjung Priok berdarah; Tanggung jawab siapa? Kumpulan fakta dan data.*
              Jakarta: Gema Insani.

Rahim, S. Saiful
1998   *Merah darah santet di Banyuwangi.* Jakarta: Metro Pos.

Rais, Amien
1998   *Mengatasi krisis dari serambi mesjid.* Yogyakarta: Pustaka Pelajar.
1999   'Nasib reformasi', in: Sunaryo Purwo Sumitro (ed.), *Merenda hari esok,*
              pp. 1-7. Yogyakarta: Bigraf Publishing.

Ramadhan K.H.
1994   *Soemitro; Dari Pangdam Mulawarman sampai Pangkopkamtib.* Jakarta:
              Pustaka Sinar Harapan.

Rekaman
1993   *Rekaman peristiwa 1992.* Jakarta: Pustaka Sinar Harapan/Media
              Interaksi Utama.

Ryter, L.
1998   'Pemuda Pancasila; The last loyalist freemen of Suharto's order?'
              Indonesia 66:45-73.

Saidi, Zaim
1998   *Soeharto menjaring matahari; Tarik-ulur reformasi ekonomi Orde Baru
              pasca-1980.* Bandung: Mizan.

Samego, Indria et al.
1998a   *Bila ABRI berbisnis; Buku pertama yang menyingkap data dan kasus peny-
              impangan dalam praktik bisnis kalangan militer.* Bandung: Mizan.
1998b   *Menata negara; Usulan LIPI tentang RUU Politik.* Bandung: Mizan.

Samhuri, Ana and Andi Setiono
1999   *Skandal Bank Bali; Tumbangkan Habibie?* Yogyakarta: Tarawang Press.

Santoso
1996   *Sri Bintang Pamungkas; Saya musuh politik Soeharto.* Jakarta: Pijar
              Indonesia.

Sarumpaet, Ratna
1997   *Nyanyian dari bawah tanah.* Yogyakarta: Yayasan Bentang Budaya.

Sasongko, HD Haryo (ed.)
1998a   *Dusta dan rekayasa Orde Baru.* Jakarta: Yayasan Pustaka Grafiksi.
1998b   *Pak Habibie mau ke mana?* Jakarta: Pustaka Grafiksi.
1998c   *Rezim Suharto menumpuk harta menuai bencana.* Jakarta: Yayasan
              Pustaka Grafiksi.
1998d   *Bapak Pembangunan atau Bapak Penjarah Nasional.* Jakarta: Yayasan Pus-
              taka Grafiksi.

Sastrosatomo, Soebadio
1997   *Era baru pemimpin baru; Badio menolak rekayasa rezim Orde Baru*. Jakarta:
            Pusat Dokumentasi Politik Guntur 49.
1998   *Manifes kedaulatan rakyat*. Jakarta: Pusat Dokumentasi Politik Guntur
            49.
Schwarz, A.
1994   *A nation in waiting; Indonesia in the 1990s*. St Leonards, NSW: Allen and
            Unwin.
Sembiring, Ita
1998   *Catatan dan refleksi tragedi Jakarta, 13 & 14 mei 1998*. Jakarta: Elex Media
            Komputindo.
Sinansari ecip, S.
1998   *Kronologi situasi penggulingan Soeharto; Reportase jurnalistik 72 jam yang
            menegangkan*. Bandung: Mizan.
Siswoyo, P. Bambang
1989   *Peristiwa Lampung dan gerakan sempalan Islam*. Solo: Mayasari.
Soekarnoputri, Megawati
1998b   *Saya siap jadi Presiden*. Edited by Indra et al. Yogyakarta: Media
            Pressindo.
Soemardjan, Selo (ed.)
1999   *Kisah perjuangan reformasi*. Jakarta: Pustaka Sinar Harapan.
Soesilo
1998   *Monopoli bisnis keluarga Cendana; Asal usul - kiprah akhir kejatuhannya*.
            Depok: Permata AD.
Sonata, Thamrin
1998   *Tragedi Semanggi 13 November 1998*. Jakarta: Yayasan Pariba.
Sophiaan, Manai
1994   *Kehormatan bagi yang berhak; Bung Karno tidak terlibat G30S/PKI*. Jakarta:
            Yayasan Mencerdaskan Kehidupan Bangsa.
Subandoro, Ali Winoto
1999   'Dari krisis nilai tukar ke krisis ekonomi', in: Selo Soemardjan (ed.),
            Kisah perjuangan reformasi, pp. 77-133. Jakarta: Pustaka Sinar Harapan.
Suharsono
1999   *Cemerlangnya Poros Tengah*. Jakarta: Perenial Press.
Suhartono and Nurartha Situmorang (eds)
1999   *Dicari: orang hilang*. Jakarta: Institut Studi Arus Informasi.
Suparlan, Parsudi
1999a   Kerusuhan Sambas. [Unpublished paper.]
1999b   Kerusuhan Sambas dan rekomendasi penanganannya. [Unpublished
            report.]
Suryadinata, L.
1997   *The culture of the Chinese minority in Indonesia*. Selangor: Times Subang.
Suryakusuma, J.I. et al.
1999   *Almanak parpol Indonesia; Pemilu '99*. Jakarta: API.
Tanjung, Feisal
1997   *ABRI-Islam mitra sejati*. Jakarta: Pustaka Sinar Harapan.

Tanuredjo, Budiman
1999   *Pasung kebebasan; Menelisik kelahiran UU unjuk rasa.* Jakarta: Elsam.
Tim Pemburu Fakta
1998a   *Tragedi Megawati; Pengkhianatan 27 Juli & daftar para pembelot.* Jakarta:
              Yayasan Karyawan Matra.
1998b   *Partai Amanat Nasional; Amien Rais tantang Habibie.* Jakarta: Yayasan
              Karyawan Matra.
Tim Pustaka Cidesindo
1999   *Yahudi & jurus maut Gus Dur.* Jakarta: Pustaka Cidesindo.
Trimansyah, Bambang
1998   *Para tokoh di balik reformasi; Episode sang oposan; Lokomotif itu bernama
              Amien Rais.* Bandung: Zaman Wacana Mulia.
Urbaningrum, Anas
1999   *Ranjau-ranjau reformasi; Portret konflik politik pasca kejatuhan Soeharto.*
              Jakarta: Raja Grafindo Persada.
Wangge, Mike and Fr. Wenyx Wangge (eds)
1999   *Adili Soeharto; Jerat dengan kasus pembunuhan massal.* Jakarta: Permata
              Media Komunika.
Wangge, Vincent
1999   *Direktori partai politik Indonesia.* Jakarta: Permata Media Komunika.
Winarno, Bondan
1997   *Bre-X; Sebungkah emas di kaki pelangi.* Jakarta: Penerbit Inspirasi Indo-
              nesia.
Wirahadikusumah, Agus et al.
1999   *Indonesia baru dan tantangan TNI; Pemikiran masa depan.* Jakarta:
              Pustaka Sinar Harapan.

General index

Ciawi document 334
Ciganjur Agreement 345-6, 345, 386, 526
Citra Flour Mills Nusantara 79
Citra Lamtoro Gung Persada 79
Citra Marga Nusaphala Persada 79, 260,
    276, 290
Citra Mobil Nusantara 81
Citra Permatasakti Persada 260
Citra Transport Nusantara 79
civil servants 276; and elections 8-9,
    monoloyalty 145; after May 1998 306,
    319, 510
cloves 91, 108-9, 157
communists, warnings against 333-5,
    342, 442; *see also* Partai Komunis
    Indonesia, September 1965
Consultative Group on Indonesia 297,
    400, 517
Cuba 458
currency board system 154-5, 520

Daerah Operasi Militer 228-9, 372
Daftar Orang Tercela 411
Danamon concern 87, 489
dangdut 15, 29, 38, 48
debt restructuring 297, 413-5, 424
Demokrat 501
Dëtak 231
Dëtik 146
Dewan Dakwah Islamiyah Indonesia
    131, 186, 440
Dewan Ekonomi Nasional 484, 525
Dewan Pemantapan Ketahanan Ekono-
    mi dan Keuangan 106, 154, 407, 531
Dewan Penegak Keamanan dan Sistem
    Hukum 356, 510
Dewan Pengembangan Usaha Nasional
    484-5, 525, 528
Dewan Pertahanan Keamanan Nasional
    144
Dewan Riset Nasional 61
Dharma Wanita 177
Dua Satu Tiga Puluh 107
dukun santet killings 361-9, 394, 400
Duta Dunia Perintis 410

Editor 146

Elang Realty Concern 86
election 1997 campaign 2, 4-9, 23-4;
    polling 44-7; result 1, 48-9
election 1999 campaign 431-4; polling
    435-6; result 437
electricity prices 106, 182, 216, 516
Era Giat Prima 419-21, 426, 486
Ernst & Young 429
European Union 80, 173
export credit 485
extraordinary presidential powers 147,
    195, 207, 236, 249, 354

Federasi Buruh Seluruh Indonesia 113
Federasi Serikat Petani Indonesia 332
Financial Sector Action Committee 412
First Pacific Holding 75, 403, 424
floating mass 4, 6, 145
Food and Agriculture Organization 113
food supply/prices 96, 114, 124, 153,
    291-4, 296, 330
Ford Foundation 297
forest fires 114, 520
Forestry Law 401
Forum Bersama 343
Forum Bersama Umat Islam 460
Forum Demokrasi 23, 498
Forum Kaum Muda Muhammadiyah
    Yogyakarta 58
Forum Kebangsaan Pemuda Indonesia
    171
Forum Kerja Indonesia 316
Forum Komunikasi Mahasiswa Islam
    Jakarta 125
Forum Komunikasi Mahasiswa se-Jabo-
    tabek *see* Forum Kota
Forum Komunikasi Ormas Islam 32,
    340
Forum Komunikasi Pemuda dan Maha-
    siswa Jakarta 125
Forum Komunikasi Putra Putri Purna-
    wirawan 205, 328-9
Forum Komunikasi Senat Mahasiswa
    Jakarta 125, 162, 212, 302, 330, 336,
    338, 343, 345, 393, 456
Forum Kota 162, 212, 302-3, 329-34, 336,
    340, 343, 355, 456, 464

Solidaritas Nasional Peristiwa Tanjung Priok 224
South Korea 79, 156, 273, 296, 507
Southeast Asia Games 256
Soviet Union 147, 164
Standard Chartered Bank 417-8, 486-7
State Auditor's Office 423, 429, 490, 530
state companies 106, 149, 498
state of emergency Jakarta 456-7; Aceh 477-8, 505; Moluccas 480-1, 533; see also Undang-Undang Penanggulangan Keadaan Bahaya
State Secretary 497-8
student demonstrations 125, 137-9, 146-7, 161-7, 175-7, 520; and 1999 general election 432-3; and 1999 presidential election 446-7, 460-2, 465-6; and 1999 session of People's Congress 456, 460-1; and 2000 People's Congress session 525; against Abdurrahman Wahid 493; and Bank Bali 425; and emergency act 453-4; Habibie era 212-3, 243, 268, 302-4, 319; May 1998 179-83, 199-200, 204-7; and November 1998 People's Congress session 329-31, 334-6, 338-9, 344, 346-51, 355; and prosecution of Soeharto 281, 284, 382, 512-3; Ambon 170; Bali 170, 350; Bandung 125, 163, 170, 183, 206; Bengkulu 165; Bogor 139, 183; Jakarta 137-40, 147, 152, 163, 166, 175, 180-1, 183, 187-8, 329-30, 334, 336, 346-51, 355, 453-4, 456, 460-2, 520; Jember 139, 183; Lampung 165, 170, 206, 453; Manado 330; Medan 126, 180-1, 350, 361; Padang 188, 350; Palu 126; Palembang 453; Pontianak 170; Purwokerto 170; Samarinda 183; Semarang 170, 188; Surabaya 126, 139, 163, 170, 188; Surakarta 163, 166, 170, 183; Ujungpandang (Makassar) 139, 183, 350, 397, 460, 465-6; Yogyakarta 126, 139, 163, 170-1, 177, 183, 188, 206
student links with farmers and labourers 332
Suara Rakyat Surabaya 126
Subentra Group 80
Subversion Act 166-7, 186, 214, 300, 400-1
Sumi Asih 489
Summa group 410
Supreme Advisory Council 305, 429, 487, 530
Surat Perintah Sebelas Maret 140, 166, 217-8, 235, 285
Surya Citra Televisi 81, 258
Switzerland 285-6
Syarikat Islam 131

Taman Mini Indonesia Indah 258, 283, 477
Tapos Ranch 82, 271-2, 283
Team of Five 238
Team of Golkar's Saviours 306
Team of Volunteers to Help the Victims of the Jakarta 27 July 1996 Incident 236
Team to Defend Indonesian Democracy see Tim Pembela Demokrasi Indonesia
Tekad 440
Televisi Pendidikan Indonesia 81, 258
Tempo 146, 193, 216
Texmaco concern 421, 485, 489
Thailand 71, 296
Thaliban 373, 475
Thames Water International 260
theft of agricultural produce 294-5, 303, 333
Tim Advokasi Hak Asasi Manusia Perwira Tentara Nasional Indonesia 502
Tim Gabungan Pencari Fakta 238, 241-2, 249-51
Tim Mawar 245, 247-8
Tim Pembela Demokrasi Indonesia 230-3, 301
Tim Penanggulan Utang Luar Negeri Swasta 73
Tim Relawan untuk Kemanusiaan see Humanitarian Team of Volunteers
Time 285-6
Timor Putra Nasional 44, 48, 79-81, 93, 106-8, 120, 157, 237, 262-4, 283-4, 290, 413, 455, 484, 507
Timsco concern 266
Tirtamas Comexindo 81, 489

Index of Indonesian geographical names[*]

---

[*] Non-Indonesian geographical names are listed in the General index.

Index of personal names*

---

* All names, including Indonesian names, are arranged according to their last component.

618 *Index of personal names*

Suaidy, Achmad Sjukry 26
Subianto, Bambang 214, 403, 406-7, 408, 412, 420, 424-6, 429, 448, 531
Subianto, Prabowo 59, 120, 131-2, 141-2, 177, 191-3, 195, 236, 367-8, 504, 510; and army brutality 222, 245-49, 503-4; and May 1998 riots 238, 249-52; and Soeharto's fall 196, 204-6, 209-13, 238, 395, 511
Subrata, Suryatna 9
Subroto 143, 152, 198, 301-2, 328-9, 335-6, 344, 454
Subroto, Djoko 366, 368
Sudarijanto, Cacuk 499, 532
Sudarmo, Sri Roso 220, 269, 493
Sudarsono, Juwono 115, 139, 149, 214, 344, 351-2; as minister of defence 467, 477, 479, 506-8, 526
Sudarto, Tyasno 183, 384, 462, 477, 504-6, 555
Sudibyo, Bambang 490-1, 498, 499, 518
Sudjana, Eggi 213, 340, 343, 367, 375, 460, 483
Sudjana, Ohan 310
Sudjatmiko, Budiman 17, 22
Sudjono 511
Sudomo 68, 84, 99, 134
Sudono, Agus 140, 487
Sudradjat, Edi 69, 116, 120, 134, 196, 284, 302, 309, 311, 356; and army brutality 229, 476; and leadership contest Golkar 1998 326-9, 335, 338
Sudrajat 473-4, 478, 504-5
Sudwikatmono 38, 72, 80-1, 87, 126, 256, 258, 261, 402, 414-5, 419, 514, 532
Sugandhi, Mien 306, 328
Sugiono 384
Suhardiman 68
Suhardjo, Prijadi Prapto 528-9
Suhartoyo 427
Suhud, Muh. Kharis 197, 301, 328
Sukardi 197
Sukardi, Laksamana 485, 492, 498, 518-9, 521, 527
Sumardi, Sandyawan 173, 236, 238, 249
Sumarlin, J.B. 84
Summers, L.H. 97

Sunaryo, Irawan 310
Sunaryo, R. 232
Suparman, Djaja 211, 353, 501, 504, 521
Supeli, Karlina Leksono 139, 173, 188
Supeni 117, 185, 188, 197, 301, 310
Suryohadiproyo, Sayidiman 197
Suryosumarno, Yapto 205, 420
Suseno, Frans Magnis 311
Sutanto, Djuhar 80
Sutiman 227
Sutiyoso 34, 35, 42, 232, 260, 511
Sutjipto, Widodo Adi 467, 476, 480, 505
Sutowo, Ibnu 81, 85
Sutowo, Ponco 260, 414
Sutrisno, Bambang 402
Sutrisno, Try 55, 61, 63, 69, 88, 116, 119, 121-3, 133-4, 138, 203, 207, 302, 311, 443-4, 511; and army brutality 221, 226, 229, 443-4, 476; and leadership contest Golkar 1998 324-7
Suwandi, Rini Mariani 90
Suwito, Noto 220
Suwondo 519-20
Suwondo, Meliono 352
Suyat 174, 435
Suyono, Haryono 121, 153
Swasono, Sri Edi 117, 138-9, 301, 327, 329, 336, 352-3
Syafei, Abdullah 479
Syafei, Theo 309, 328, 353, 380-1, 395, 458, 503
Syafi'ei, Abdul Rasyid Abdullah 347
Syafrie *see* Syamsuddin, Syafrie
Syafruddin, Fuad Muhammad *see* Udin
Syamsu *see* Djalal, Syamsu
Syamsuddin, Syafrie 90, 127, 132, 140, 179, 191, 205, 211-2, 222, 244, 248-9, 506

Taher, Tarmizi 130
Tambunan, R.O. 230
Tampubolon, Juan Felix 383, 454, 488
Tan Kion Liep *see* Soetantyo, Tegoeh
Tan Tjioe Hin *see* Rahardja, Hendra
Tan Tjoe Hong *see* Tansil, Eddy
Tanjung, Akbar 56, 67, 99, 149, 208, 214, 251, 282, 319-21, 329, 356-7, 421, 426,